UNDERSTANDING
THE POLITICAL WORLD

Understanding the Political World

A Comparative Introduction to Political Science

FIFTH EDITION

James N. Danziger
University of California, Irvine

New York San Francisco Boston
London Toronto Sydney Tokyo Singapore Madrid
Mexico City Munich Paris Cape Town Hong Kong Montreal

To Lesley, Nick, and Vanessa

Publisher: Priscilla McGeehon
Senior Acquisitions Editor: Eric Stano
Associate Editor: Anita Castro
Marketing Manager: Megan Galvin
Supplements Editor: Kristinn Muller
Production Manager: Ellen MacElree
Project Coordination, Text Design, and Electronic Page Makeup: Electronic Publishing Services Inc., NYC
Cover Designer/Manager: Nancy Danahy
Cover Photo: © AP / Wide World Photos
Photo Researcher: Mira Schachne
Manufacturing Buyer: Roy Pickering
Printer and Binder: The Maple-Vail Book Manufacturing Group
Cover Printer: The Lehigh Press, Inc.

For permission to use copyrighted material, grateful acknowledgment is made to the copyright holders on page 482, which is hereby made part of this copyright page.

Library of Congress Cataloging-in-Publication Data

Danziger, James N.
     Understanding the political world: a comparative introduction to political science /
   James N. Danziger.--5th ed.
          p. cm.
     Includes bibliographical references and index.
     ISBN 0-8013-3296-6
     1. Political science.   I. Title.
JA66.D36 2001
320-dc21   00-041209

Please visit our website at http://www.awl.com

ISBN 0-8013-3296-6

12345678910-MA-03020100

Contents

Boxed Features

Preface

It is always exciting to introduce students to political science. The subject of political science is the political world. And this political world, in the early years of the twenty-first century, seems especially laden with complexity, possibility, and even danger. The "new world order" that was supposed to emerge rather effortlessly at the end of the cold war is not particularly orderly. Whether the changes occurring in the political world are desirable or threatening is somewhat a matter of one's own attitudes.

At this time, there are a variety of "more than ever" situations that intersect with politics in many ways. There are more electoral democracies than at any time in history. The power of transnational/multinational actors, whether the European Union or a large corporation, is at its highest point ever. The political world has never been characterized by as many countries or as many ethnic groups attempting to establish new states which correspond to their identity group. Potent technologies, ranging from those manipulating information to those capable of mass destruction, are more prevalent and pervasive than ever. The political economies of individual countries have never been as interdependent. At no time have larger numbers of people lived in such material abundance and/or so many suffered from relative deprivation in the distribution of resources.

These circumstances are indicative of a period that is extraordinary and that poses fascinating challenges to those of us who attempt to use information and concepts in order to understand better the real world of politics.

Objectives

Addressing such challenges is at the heart of this book. The central objective is, as the book's title indicates, to help the reader better understand the political world. It attempts to link the central analytic concepts of political science that have emerged over decades of research to the realities of the political world in the early twenty-first century. These recent changes influence the examples and content of many topics in this book. The emphasis is on concepts and empirical research that illuminate the processes and structures of politics. The level of analysis ranges from the individual's political beliefs and actions through the politics of groups, states, and the dynamics of the international system.

This book asks the reader to assess whether it is possible and useful to develop generalizations about political phenomena. It combines attention to systematic descriptive analysis—the *what* questions—with efforts to explain underlying patterns—the *why* and *how* questions. And readers are continually reminded that they must consider the important normative questions that are embedded in most issues about politics. Many topics are also presented in a manner that encourages the reader to think as a political scientist, structuring questions and assessing evidence in order to make inferences.

Features

This fifth edition has retained most key features of the earlier editions:

- A strong, comparative framework
- Coverage of micropolitics, macropolitics, and international relations
- Focus on political economy, including a complete chapter on this important topic
- Thorough analyses of key political processes
- An engaging, readable style
- The instructive use of political cartoons and photographs throughout the book

In addition, the book features sixty-two boxed discussions that offer rich, memorable examples of key concepts and issues, such as the different paths of political activism taken by Gandhi and Abu Nidal, the rational choice perspective on why a person should not vote, Russia's struggles to establish democratic politics and a market economy, the political impacts of television, the effects of colonialism and neo-colonialism on Congo, the different policies for dealing with population growth in developing countries, the extensive social control exercised by the state in Singapore, and the American imposition of a constitution on Japan.

New to This Edition

Given the extraordinary rate of change in the political world, there are updated examples throughout this edition. In addition, there are significant changes:

- The recent evidence is applied in order to analyze both the challenges associated with the efforts to consolidate democratic processes and also the countertrends toward authoritarianism in many countries.
- There is an attempt to identify more fully the conditions that seem most conducive to the effective pursuit of the dual goals of economic development and deepening democracy.
- The powerful impacts of nation-based identity and ethnonationalism are detailed in numerous settings.
- The recent economic, political, and social changes in the post-communist developed countries, both positive and negative, are analyzed.
- The resource inequalities between countries and within countries are explored.
- The chapter on the developing countries focuses more explicitly on the challenges generated by the globalization of political and economic institutions.
- The assessment of the NICs (newly industrializing countries) has been enriched by extending the analysis to the key emerging NICs of Latin America as well as those in Asia.

- Many discussions have been tightened to increase clarity and shorten the chapters.
- A glossary of more than one hundred twenty key concepts has been added.
- A list of URLs to particularly useful internet sites is included.

Organization

The fifth edition retains the conceptual framework of the fourth edition, focusing on micropolitics and macropolitics.

- Chapter 1 and the Appendix introduce students to the logic of political science and the methods of political analysis.
- Chapters 2 through 4 examine political behavior at the individual and group levels, describing and explaining the causes of individual political beliefs and actions.
- Chapters 5 through 8 emphasize the structural and institutional elements of political systems, offering analytic frameworks for characterizing the different ways in which people organize themselves politically.
- Chapters 9 through 11 analyze interesting and important political processes, such as decision making, political and economic development, and political violence.
- Chapter 12 examines the patterns of cooperation, competition, and conflict among countries in the international environment.
- Chapters 13 through 15 explain in detail how certain groups of countries try to achieve their broad goals of prosperity, stability, and security within the complex international environment. Specific analysis is provided for the more developed countries, the developing countries, and the sets of transitional countries, grouped as the post-communist developed countries and the newly industrializing countries.
- Chapter 16 concludes with a prospective assessment of the major political challenges in the early twenty-first century.

Audience

This book is written for any person who wants to enrich his or her basic understanding of the political world and to learn how political scientists attempt to describe and explain politics. Such a person might be in an introductory course in political science or comparative politics, but could also be in a "capstone" course that integrates one's political science studies. Such a person might also be any individual who wants to think about the fascinating and confusing world of politics in a more informed and systematic way.

Supplements for Instructors

Instructor's Manual to Accompany *Understanding the Political World, Fifth Edition*   Written by James N. Danziger himself, the *Instructor's Manual* includes up-to-date chapter summaries, key terms, multiple-choice questions, essay questions, and discussion questions.

Supplements for Students

Microsoft® Encarta® Interactive World Atlas CD-ROM   Deeply discounted when ordered packaged with the text! This state-of-the-art CD-ROM provides over 1.2 million place names, 192 country home pages, 7,000 articles, a map gallery with 21 styles of interactive maps; a statistics center with current information about any country, measured by more than 350 statistical indicators; and much more!

Discounted Subscription to <u>Newsweek</u> Magazine.   Students can receive 12 issues of <u>Newsweek</u> at an 80% savings off the regular subscription price! An outstanding way to engage students and get them involved in the most current events and issues in politics today. Contact your local Addison Wesley Longman rep for ordering information.

Acknowledgments

Many sources of ideas and information constitute the basis of *my* understanding about politics. Broadly, you should know that I was born and have primarily been educated in the United States. I have studied, lived, and/or spent significant periods in North America, Western and Eastern Europe, Asia, the Middle East, and Africa. The people I met and the events I experienced in these places have certainly influenced my perceptions about politics.

More direct contributions to this book have come from my colleagues in political science and from the many students with whom I have interacted. I have drawn deeply and often from the ideas of these two important groups.

By the publication of a fifth edition, the layers of contributions and ideas to the construction of this book are deep, rich, and rather indescribable. Explicit guidance and advice regarding the writing of this particular edition have come from several valuable sources: the cadre at Addison Wesley Longman, including the senior acquisitions editor, Eric Stano, and the associate editor, Anita Castro; scholarly colleagues who have offered useful suggestions, including Russ Dalton, Vincent Pollard, Rein Taagepera, and Marty Wattenberg; and several students who have provided specific material for the book, especially Kim de Fronzo, Mei Mei Peng, and Zach Zwald. The reviewers, who offered very thoughtful and constructive commentaries for this edition, are: Nancy Singleton Brown, San Diego State University; Barbara L. Brown, Southern Illinois University; Orlando J. Perez, Central Michigan University; and Kathryn Wilson Breeden, Eastern Kentucky University.

I am grateful for the help provided by all these sources. Regarding the roads not taken and the missteps in this book, the responsibility is mine.

James N. Danziger

To the Reader

The aim of this book is revealed by its title: It is meant to help you understand the political world. It assumes that you are interested in politics. It does not assume that you have substantial knowledge about politics or political science. It does not assume you know the difference between politics and political science. I hope that when you complete the book (especially in conjunction with instruction about politics from a teacher), you will feel that you have increased your knowledge about the contemporary political world.

The study of politics is full of fascinating questions. First are the questions about *what is:* Who exercises political power and what values and purposes guide them? Why do people accept political authority? How do people organize themselves politically? What causes individuals and groups to take political action? A second set of questions concerns *what ought to be:* Who should exercise political power and what values should they pursue? Why should people accept political authority? How should political structures be organized? Why should individuals and groups act politically? People disagree sharply about answers to both these descriptive (what is) and normative (what ought to be) questions. In addition, the study of politics provokes a third set of questions regarding *what we can actually know* about the political world. Here also there are major disagreements about the appropriate methods for describing and understanding politics.

Although this book cannot resolve the underlying disputes, it offers you the basis for making sense out of politics at all three levels. As author, I make some basic assumptions: that you can think systematically about politics and make general statements about how politics works; that you will learn more about politics by considering the politics of many different places; that every observer of politics (certainly including you and me) has biases, only some of which can be understood; that you need a variety of sources of ideas and information before you can make informed and sensible decisions about the value disagreements pervading politics; and that this book is one such source that can be helpful to you. My efforts will be successful to the extent that *you* ultimately judge my assumptions to be correct (especially the last one...).

It is inevitable that you will be frustrated with the treatment of politics at some (many?) points in this book. I would say: Reader, be merciful! The study of politics is incredibly complex. Gather bits of understanding where you can find them.

About the Author

James N. Danziger is a professor and former chair of the Department of Political Science at the University of California, Irvine, where he also served as campuswide Dean of Undergraduate Education from 1995-1999. He is recipient of many honors and awards, including a Marshall Scholarship (to Great Britain) and a Foreign Area Fellowship. He received the first UC Irvine Distinguished Faculty Lectureship Award for Teaching in 1987 and the UC Irvine Distinguished Service Award in 1997. His research has received awards from the American Political Science Association and the American Society for Public Administration. He has published extensively, particularly on information technology and politics and he is on the editorial board of *Local Government Studies.* He has been an active participant in local politics and especially enjoys sports, travel, and cinema.

PART ONE

On Knowing the Political World

CHAPTER 1

Politics and Knowledge

ON POLITICS

Fang Zheng is one of China's outstanding disabled athletes. Yet the Chinese government refused to allow Fang to compete for China in the international games for the disabled in September 1994. This denial is deeply embedded in politics. Can you think of a political reason why the government would prevent him from participating?

> Stop for a moment. I encourage you to reflect on this question for twenty to thirty seconds, rather than rushing ahead in order to complete your reading. Questions like this appear throughout this book. Your responses to these brief "reflections" should help you to clarify your own thinking on the subject being discussed. As novelist E. M. Forster said: "How do I know what I think until I see what I say?" So, can you think of a political reason for stopping Fang?

Fang had been a senior at Beijing Physical Education College in 1989. He was among the many students who, despite their state-provided education, rejected the political leadership and political institutions in China. In a series of dramatic protest demonstrations, the students and other citizens demanded that China establish a democratic government. In turn, the Chinese political authorities rejected these demands and used the military to suppress the demonstrations. In the violent confrontation between demonstrators and the military in Beijing's Tiananmen Square, Fang's legs were crushed by a tank. It is for this reason that the government now judges Fang to be an unfit representative of China in international sports competition. It is not prepared to allow attention to focus on Fang.

This incident captures some of the crucial themes that relate to politics. **Politics** is defined in a variety of ways. Some of the most widely used definitions of politics are:

Politics is the exercise of power.

Politics is the public allocation of things that are valued.

Politics is the resolution of conflict.

Politics is the competition among individuals and groups pursuing their own interests.

Politics is the determination of who gets what, when, and how.

All of these definitions share the central idea that *politics is the process through which power and influence are used in the promotion of certain values and interests.* Politics operates at many levels in the Fang example. When Fang decides that his government is undemocratic and that he should publicly protest against his leaders and their programs, he is engaging in politics at the individual level. There is group-level politics when Fang joins with other students and workers to demonstrate against the government in Tiananmen Square. At the societal level, the government uses its political power to allocate benefits to Fang when it provides him with a free university education. But the government also uses its powers to withhold benefits when it prevents him from participating in the international games for the disabled. And the government has exercised its political powers even more dramatically when it sends troops to stop the protests by force, a government action resulting in Fang's loss of his legs.

As individuals, groups, and governmental actors make decisions about what is good or bad for society, and as they try to implement their decisions, politics is at work. For our purposes, politics is associated with those aspects of life that have *public* significance. Other aspects of life, in contrast, are understood to be private, and thus beyond the domain of politics. However, we shall see that what is considered "public" in one country may be considered "private" in another. Even your choice about the job you take, the religion you practice, or the music you listen to can be either a private choice or one within the public domain. Can you see why a government might conclude that these choices have public significance? Within each country there is a constant debate about the appropriate areas for governmental action and the domains of life that should remain private and unrestrained by political action. Sometimes the term "politics" is used even more broadly than in this book, to refer to competition over values in domains that are not truly public, as when you hear of the "politics of the family" or "office politics."

In almost every contemporary society, the area that is subject to politics is very large. Politics, usually via government, determines how much education you must have and what its content will be. Politics establishes the words you cannot utter in a public place, how much of your hard-earned income you must give to government, and how that money is spent to provide different groups with a vast range of benefits (e.g., education, roads, fire protection, subsidized food, health care, and so on). Politics determines whether you are allowed to use a certain drug, the amount of pollutants that your car can emit, how secure you feel against violence by others within your neighborhood and within the global system, and whether you receive unequal treatment in the allocation of benefits, based on your ethnicity, gender, ideology, or some other factor.

TYPES OF POLITICAL KNOWLEDGE

Clearly, politics can have many impacts on our lives. Yet people differ greatly in their understandings about the nature of politics, the uses of political power, and the distribution of political benefits and burdens. If you have discussed politics with your friends, you probably have noticed that they differ in how much they know about politics and in their opinions about good and bad political actions. Your understandings about politics and your decisions about whether to undertake specific political actions are grounded in your knowledge of politics. But what are the sources of your political knowledge? How do you make sense out of the many conflicting issues and statements about the political world that confront you each day?

Here, for example, are three political statements:

A "single-payer" system is the most effective means of providing good health care to all citizens.

In a democracy, men are more likely to vote than women.

The United States is the most peaceful, least warlike nation in modern history.

When you hear or read a statement like one of these, you might

Ignore it

Accept that it is correct

Reject it

Try to assess it

If you decide to assess it, you would probably ask questions like these: Is it based on accurate information? Is it consistent with other things that I know about politics? Are its assertions persuasive? Does it influence any political actions I might take?

When you begin to ask assessment questions, and especially when you try to answer them, you are doing **political analysis**. At its core, political analysis is *the attempt to describe (i.e., to answer the* what *questions) and then to explain (to answer the* why *and* how *questions regarding) politics.* This book attempts to enhance your ability to do political analysis, to answer the *what, why,* and *how* questions about politics.

Suppose a group of people is instructed to give each of the three preceding statements a "truth score," ranging from 100 percent (absolutely true) to 0 percent (absolutely false). Do you think anyone would give all three statements a score of 100 percent? 0 percent? What truth score would you give these statements? Did you give every statement a score of either 100 percent or 0 percent? Do you expect that most other people will report scores close to your own? Why?

It is reasonable to assume that few people, if any, believe that all the things they hear about politics are absolutely accurate and true. One reason to be suspicious of statements about politics is that they usually reflect the values and interests of the source of the statement.

The first statement is by the American Association of Retired Persons (AARP), an interest group representing those more than fifty years of age. The second statement was made by political scientists Lester Milbrath and M. L. Goel (1982: 116) in a book summarizing the research on political participation. And the third was made by Ronald Reagan, president of the United States from 1981 to 1989, during his nomination acceptance speech to the Republican Party in 1984. Unless you view all these sources as equally reliable, your knowledge of who made the statements might alter your truth score in some cases. If it does, can you explain why?

There are many sources of statements about politics—family, friends, television, books, newspapers, teachers, politicians. Such sources can provide information about politics, but the information can be unclear, contradictory, or wrong. You are surrounded by competing claims regarding the political world. How are you to determine what you do know about politics?

Political science is one way of attempting to establish such knowledge. As you will discover in reading this book, **political science** is a *set of techniques, concepts, and approaches whose objective is to increase the clarity and accuracy of our understandings about the political world.* You will learn how some political scientists try to think systematically about political phenomena in order to describe "political reality" and explain how politics works. You will also be introduced to some of the findings about politics that have emerged from the work of political scientists and other social scientists.

It was noted earlier that people have very different views about politics. If you have discussed politics with your friends, you probably noticed that they differ in how much they know, for example, about the names of the leaders of various countries, that they do not agree on such questions as how easy it is for a president to get a law passed, and that they have significant differences of opinion on political issues such as whether there should be a system of "free" health care for all citizens. An individual's understanding of politics is composed of three general types of political knowledge: (1) descriptions of political facts, (2) explanations of how and why politics occurs as it does, and (3) prescriptions of what should happen in the political world.

Description

Many bits of political knowledge focus on *what* questions, which require a descriptive response based on one or more "facts." In your study of politics, you will encounter these kinds of questions, which can be answered with relatively straightforward political facts. Here are some examples:

The Soviet Union ceased to exist: on December 25, 1991, with the resignation of Mikhail Gorbachev

The number of states in Nigeria: 30

The country with the highest gross national product (GNP) per capita in the world in 2000: Switzerland

But on many questions about the political world, knowledge is subject to dispute. On some questions, it is difficult to get precise information. Suppose you want to know the number of countries with operational nuclear weapons. Seven countries acknowledge having operational nuclear devices (China, France, India, Pakistan, Russia, the United Kingdom, and the United States). Experts believe that at least one other country (Israel) has nuclear weapons, and three additional countries (Iran, Iraq, and North Korea) are suspected of building nuclear weapons. Several others (Argentina, Belarus, Brazil, Kazakhstan, South Africa, Taiwan, and Ukraine) had or were close to having nuclear weapons but are now assumed to have backed away from nuclear ambitions (U.S. Congressional Research Service 1994). Even the experts cannot reach consensus on the straightforward issue of which countries belong to the "nuclear club." Box 1.1 asks you an important question about these countries. Is your answer yes?

On some other questions about politics, description requires assessments that raise complicated issues about power, interests, and values. In such cases it can be difficult to reach agreement about the facts. Here are a few examples:

Do nonwhites and whites in the United States enjoy equal treatment before the law?

Can a country legally invade another country that has not used military force against it?

Explanation

Many questions about politics are even more difficult to answer because they ask *why* something happens and require political knowledge in the form of explanation.

BOX 1.1

Where in the World?

The section on "Description" briefly refers to twenty countries (and one country that no longer exists) on five continents. Do you have a clear sense of where they are?

There will be detailed discussions of many countries in this book. Knowing the location of a country and its geographic relation to certain other countries is sometimes extremely important for an understanding of its political choices and actions. When such discussions occur, you are strongly encouraged to locate the country on a map. For this purpose, there is a world map on the front inside cover of this book.

Several recent studies have shown that American students are more ignorant of world geography than are students in most other countries. If that characterization applies to you, help change the situation, by referring frequently to the map.

Why is one in eight families "poor" in the wealthy United States? What causes a country (e.g., Congo) to have inflation of more than 1,000 percent in a single year? Why does revolutionary violence overthrow the government in one country (e.g., Nicaragua) but not in another (e.g., El Salvador)? These are examples of the many questions about politics that require explanation, not mere descriptive facts. Such questions can be among the most fascinating in politics, but adequate explanation is often difficult because patterns of cause and effect can be extraordinarily complex.

Prescription

Statements about politics often include claims or assumptions that certain choices and actions are more desirable than others. These represent a third form of political knowledge, prescriptions. A prescription is a value judgment that indicates what *should* occur and *should* be done. Thus a prescription deals with "normative" political knowledge—answers to questions about what ought to be, not merely description and explanation of what is.

For example, there are many possible prescriptive responses to the question: What should be the government's role in the provision of health care? Answers vary from the viewpoint that government should take absolutely no action that interferes with the private provision of health care to a view that the full range of health care needs should be met by government employees at no direct cost to the patient. You can probably think of many positions between these two extremes.

The position you select is an element of your **normative political knowledge**— your value judgments. Notice that normative political knowledge combines three levels of understanding: (1) your descriptive knowledge of certain facts (e.g., the alternative forms of health care that are available in a particular society); (2) your explanatory knowledge about why certain outcomes occur (e.g., the causes of unequal health); and most importantly, (3) your priorities among competing values (e.g., equality, individual rights, lower taxes).

SOURCES OF POLITICAL KNOWLEDGE

Each individual's political knowledge is a unique combination of descriptive facts, explanations, and prescriptions about politics. This section describes three important sources of such knowledge about the political world: (1) authority, (2) personal thought, and (3) science.

Authority

The method of **authority** involves *the appeal to any document, tradition, or person that is believed to possess the controlling explanation regarding a particular issue.* Knowledge about politics can be based on three kinds of authority sources: (1) a specific authority, (2) a general authority, or (3) "everyone."

Specific authority sources.   A particular individual (but few others) might place great confidence in the knowledge about politics derived from a specific authority source, such as a parent, teacher, friend, or famous person. Those who are young and those who are minimally interested in politics are especially likely to rely on specific authorities for much of their political knowledge. Chapter 4 will argue that specific authority sources powerfully influence some important political beliefs of most individuals. Can you think of a significant piece of your own political knowledge that is derived primarily from a parent, an influential teacher, or a public figure you admire?

General authority sources.   A general authority source is one that has substantial influence on a large proportion of people in a society. Examples are constitutions, revered leaders, widely respected media or books, and religious teachings. General authorities are especially evident as a basis for normative political knowledge. (See Box 1.2 on the role of women in politics.)

"Everyone" as authority.   Sometimes we are convinced that something is true because it is a strongly held belief of many other people. If virtually "everyone" (i.e., the reference group to which you look for information and knowledge) seems

---

BOX 1.2

General Authorities and Normative Knowledge: The Role of Women in Politics

General authorities are particularly powerful in providing normative knowledge. It can be extremely difficult to decide how to judge political issues, and in such cases it can be helpful to find a widely accepted authority for guidance. For example, consider the question, "What is the role of women in a country's politics?" While some people see this as a straightforward question of fact, others view it as a normative question about what the role of women should be. In some societies there is disagreement about this question, and many look to an authority source to provide the answer.

In the United States, the crucial source of authority for such questions is the Constitution. The U.S. Constitution does not mention women. For nearly 150 years this omission was interpreted to mean that women should be excluded from any political role, even from voting. Finally, political pressure resulted in a formal change within the source of authority, with the Nineteenth Amendment in 1920, which added language to the Constitution granting women voting rights (and, implicitly, all political rights exercised by men).

In Iran, as in the United States, the key source of authority on women's political rights is a document; but it is a religious document, the Koran. During the political regime of Shah Reza Pahlavi (1941–1979), women were encouraged to participate more fully in politics than a strict interpretation of the Koran might suggest. However, when the Ayatollah Khomeini (in power 1979–1989) replaced the Shah, he insisted on such an interpretation, and the political roles of women were significantly limited. Since Khomeini's death, more moderate leaders have again extended the political rights and activities of Iranian women, and there are numerous female participants in the political process, including female members of the national government. However, there is continuing disagreement and debate in Iran about the appropriate political behavior of women, and some of the most "modern" Iranian women continue to be frustrated by constraints on that behavior.

(continued)

BOX 1.2 *(Continued)*

In contemporary China, it has been the authoritative pronouncements of a person, Mao Zedong (who ruled from 1949 to 1976), that established the contemporary political rights of women. Prior to the revolution of 1949, the role of women in China was defined by the religious traditions of Confucianism. Most women were essentially the property of men, and they had few political rights. As part of Chairman Mao's efforts to transform Confucian tradition, he granted women full equality under the law, and women were encouraged to participate actively in all aspects of political life.

Tens of thousands march in Washington, D.C., in support of an amendment to the United States Constitution that would guarantee equal rights for women.

to agree on a "fact" about politics, there is little reason for you to disagree or challenge that fact. One reason to place confidence in the strongly held beliefs of many people is the assumption that it is unlikely so many people will be incorrect. Such knowledge has stood the test of time, since it could have been challenged and repudiated in the marketplace of ideas. For example, you will probably find that virtually everyone agrees that political terrorism is bad.

However, there are fundamental problems with the method of authority as a way of knowing. This should be most obvious with specific authorities. You might think that your parent or best teacher or favorite celebrity has the correct view on an important political issue, but few of the other 6 billion people in the world have any confidence in this source of your political knowledge.

And, although "everyone knows that X is true," there is no guarantee that everyone is correct. First, as "Honest Abe" Lincoln observed, you can fool all of the people some of the time. Indeed, a political belief that is widely held might be particularly immune to careful assessment. Experiments in psychology have revealed the extent to which an individual's beliefs can be altered by the beliefs of others. For example, if several respondents (collaborating with the experimenter) all give identical wrong answers, the subject can thereby be persuaded to change his mind about what he knows, even when he is correct. Second, "everyone" often consists mainly of people whose cultural background we share. Using the preceding example, it is unlikely that virtually everyone living under an oppressive political regime believes that political terrorism is bad.

It is common for citizens in most political systems to believe that the citizens of rival political systems have been brainwashed and that they have beliefs *we* know are incorrect. Is it not likely that beliefs strongly held by most of us are equally suspect to them?

There are even problems with general authorities. Sometimes, as when listing the countries with nuclear weapons or explaining the Iran–Iraq War, even the most competent general authorities might not have access to crucial information or might disagree about how to interpret the available data. And sometimes, even when a people accepts a single authority, there can be ambiguities and problems of interpretation. Consider again the normative issue of the political role of women discussed earlier in Box 1.2:

> In the United States, all branches of government continually interpret and apply the rather limited framework outlined in the Constitution. The strong political agitation for an "equal rights" amendment indicates that many people feel that the Constitution, even with the Nineteenth Amendment, still fails to ensure women of political rights equivalent to those enjoyed by men.

> Women's political and civil rights in Iran have been extended somewhat since Khomeini's death, and especially after the election of a reformist President (Khatami in 1998) and legislature (in 2000). Women have become more active in Iranian politics and a female vice president was selected in 1998. However, powerful positions of authority in Iranian society, such as the judiciary and the Council of Guardians, continue to be dominated by those who share Khomeini's views regarding women's political rights. Consequently, the appropriate role of women in Iran's politics remains a highly contested issue. Indeed, there is considerable difference of opinion within the Muslim world regarding how to interpret the Koran's authoritative prescriptions regarding women's roles in political life. Their roles are sharply limited in some Muslim countries, such as Afghanistan and Sudan. Yet Bangladesh, the "Islamic Republic of Pakistan," and Turkey are Muslim-majority countries that have recently selected female heads of government (Prime Ministers).

> In China, some people in rural areas never accepted the changes Mao introduced regarding women's roles in political and social life, preferring to follow the traditional Confucian norms. The Chinese leadership since Mao's death has continued to support his view on the equality of women in politics, though the leadership has rejected Mao's views on many other subjects, especially on economic matters.

In short, it is common, and perhaps inevitable, for authority sources to offer inconsistent or conflicting knowledge claims about the political world. The overall problem with an appeal to authority as a source of knowledge is that it is extremely difficult to differentiate between alternative authorities or even to establish widespread agreement on precisely what political knowledge a particular authority source provides.

Personal Thought

Have you ever insisted that some fact is correct because it seemed so "obvious" to you? It is possible to feel confident that you know something on the basis of your own reason, feelings, or experiences. This second source of knowledge does not rely on outside authorities; rather, it assumes that the individual can use his own powers of thought to determine what he knows about the political world. Such knowledge can be based on rationality or intuition, or grounded in personal experience.

Rationality.   First, an individual can rely on his own rational thought as a means for deciding that something is correct. On occasion, you have probably decided that a certain fact is true because it is logical or obvious—when you think about it, it just "makes sense." The underlying assumption is that such a knowledge claim is verified because it will seem self-evident to all reasonable people and needs no further justification. For example, the Preamble to the American Declaration of Independence claims that there are "self-evident" truths—that all men are created equal and that they have inalienable rights to life, liberty, and the pursuit of happiness.

Intuition.   A second form of personal thought is intuition. Here, one's knowledge is based on feeling, on a sense of understanding or empathy, rather than on reason. You have probably had the experience of being convinced that something is correct because it *feels* right. For example, the key slogan of Barry Goldwater, the Republican presidential candidate in 1964, was an explicit appeal to intuition: "In your heart, you know he's right!"

Personal experience.   Third, you can be convinced that something is true because of your own personal experiences. For example, you might be convinced that government bureaucracies are inefficient because a specific agency handled your inquiries so ineptly. Or you might believe that different ethnic groups can live together in harmony based on your own positive experience in a multiethnic setting. Personal involvement in a dramatic event, such as witnessing a handgun murder or being physically harassed by the police, can have a particularly powerful impact on one's political beliefs.

A major problem with all three forms of personal thought as a source of knowledge is that there is no method for resolving "thoughtful" differences of opinion among individuals. This is most obvious with personal experience—because people have quite different personal experiences, they are unlikely to reach the same conclusions about what is true. Similarly, there is no reason to assume that different people will share the same intuitive feelings regarding what is true. Goldwater's poor electoral showing (he received 39 percent of the vote) suggests that many people concluded (intuitively?) that he was not right, or perhaps they decided (rationally?) that he was too far right, ideologically.

Even rational thought will not necessarily enable people to agree on political facts. We do not all employ the same logic. Consider again the key knowledge claim cited earlier: "We hold these truths to be self-evident—that all men are created equal." This seems a clear appeal to rationality, a political fact that is self-evident to all thinking individuals. But what exactly does this claim mean? Do all men have equal physical or mental traits at birth? Do they grow up with equal opportunities? Are they equal before the law, regardless of the quality of legal help they can purchase? Are all women created equal too? Many legal and political struggles in the United States during the two centuries since this "self-evident" truth was proclaimed have concerned precisely what equal rights *are* assured to every person in the American political system, with particular regard to race, gender, and age.

Science

In contrast to the two other sources of knowledge, science uses explicit methods that attempt to enable different people to agree about what they know. The goal of any science is to describe and explain—to answer *what, why,* and *how* questions. There are four essential characteristics of the scientific method:

1. Science entails a *search for regularities* in the relationships among phenomena.
2. Science is *empirical* in the sense that it is concerned with phenomena that can be observed, or at least measured.
3. Science is *cumulative,* because it tentatively accepts previously established knowledge on a subject as the foundation for development of further knowledge. One can challenge existing knowledge, but it is not necessary to reestablish the knowledge base every time.
4. The method of science is *testable.* Its practitioners, "scientists," specify the assumptions, data, analytic techniques, and inference patterns that support their knowledge claim. They look for some analysis or evidence that would invalidate ("falsify") the claim. Other scientists can evaluate all aspects of the claim and can repeat the analysis to ensure that everyone reaches the same conclusion.

POLITICAL SCIENCE

Most contemporary political scientists attempt to use the scientific method to establish shared knowledge about the political world. Box 1.3 provides a brief example of the key steps in applying the scientific method, focusing on one of the knowledge claims listed near the beginning of the chapter: that in a democracy, men are more likely to vote than women. This example reveals how the search for regularities is structured and the methods that are used. This book will offer many examples of generalizations and empirical findings about politics that are based on the scientific method.

Within the framework of the scientific method, there are different ways of undertaking political analysis. Some of the most important modes of political analysis are explained in detail in the Appendix. Each mode of analysis is distinct in terms of its assumptions, methods, use of data, and inference structures. However, all modes share a fundamental commitment: to discover regularities among political phenomena using approaches that are empirical, cumulative, and testable.

BOX 1.3

Gender and Voting: Applying the Scientific Method to Politics

Using the Appendix

Our analysis of gender and voting is typical of one form of political analysis employed by political scientists. As you read through it, ask yourself whether you understand how to interpret Table 1.1, whether you know the kinds of data that would strengthen the analysis, and whether you think this is a functional or relational analysis (see p. XXX). If you understand these terms and feel confident in answering such questions, you have a strong analytic basis for discussions later in the book. If you feel that you could use a bit more background on such issues, you should read the Appendix before you continue. The Appendix explains some of the major analytic approaches that are used in applying the scientific method to the study of politics, the types of empirical data that are employed, and the means of reaching conclusions through use of such data. Even those readers with some analytic background will find the Appendix helpful as a review and as a means of checking their understanding.

Is it true that men are more likely than women to vote in a democracy? Let us briefly consider how you might analyze this claim by means of the scientific method. Remember that applying the scientific method entails formulating a question with precision, gathering and analyzing empirical evidence that is relevant to the question, and then proposing a generalization or conclusion.

1. Your first step is to *examine existing evidence* that is relevant to the issue you are analyzing. In this example, it would be sensible to look in books and journals for studies of voting by political scientists or other social scientists (e.g., *Political Behavior of the American Electorate* by Flanigan and Zingale [1998], *Gender and Party Politics,* edited by Lovenduski and Norris [1994], and "Explaining the Gender Gap in Voting" by Studlar, McAllister and Hayes [1998]).

2. With this background, you *state the issue* you are examining in a precise manner. This particular issue is already stated in the form of a hypothesis (i.e., a proposition about a political fact): In a democracy, men are more likely to vote than women.

TABLE 1.1
Participation of Eligible Voters in the U.S. Presidential Election, by Gender

| | 1976 | | 1996 | |
	Men	Women	Men	Women
Voted	77%	67%	53%	56%
Did not vote	23%	33%	47%	44%

BOX 1.3 *(Continued)*

3. Next you *"operationalize" key concepts.* This means that you specify exactly what each concept means and how it might be measured. Defining political concepts such as democracy can be extremely difficult (as you will see in Chapter 7). In this example, let us tentatively propose that a political democracy is "a state with periodic elections in which most adult citizens are allowed to vote in order to select among genuine alternative candidates for public office." The probability of voting is operationalized as "the percentage of those eligible to vote who actually do vote on a major political office."

4. Fourth, you *gather appropriate data.* You need a strategy for collecting evidence that is *valid* (i.e., it measures what it is supposed to measure) and *reliable* (i.e., it is accurate). You also decide what specific cases you are going to analyze. In this example, you must choose one or more democracies and certain specific elections for which you are going to gather data. You might gather the relevant data from books or reports, or you might need to go "into the field" to measure the phenomena yourself. For this example, suppose you select the United States as the democracy, the presidential election as the vote on a major public office, and 1976 and 1996 as the elections for which you actually gather data. Do you think these are reasonable choices with which to assess the question? The survey data are displayed in Table 1.1. (Regarding the data in Table 1.1: These data are individuals' own reports, after the election, on whether or not they voted. The data were gathered for a carefully selected national sample of voters in a survey designed by academic researchers. Can you think of any problems with the validity of such data? How might more valid data be gathered?)

5. Then you *analyze the evidence.* According to the 1976 data in Table 1.1, men do vote at a substantially higher rate than women (77 percent versus 67 percent). In 1996, however, the voting rate for women (56 percent) is slightly higher than that for men (53 percent).

6. Now you need to *decide what, if any, inferences can be made* about the issue on the basis of your evidence. This is where your analytic skills must be especially rich. The Appendix illustrates a statistical technique that can help you judge whether the difference in the data for women and men is greater than might be expected by chance. In the absence of such statistics, what do you think?

   Is the evidence sufficient? Can you have confidence in a generalization about gender and voting in the United States based on only two elections? Table 1.1 probably would lead you to observe that you cannot generalize with any confidence until you have more data. In fact, if you did get comparable data for other presidential elections, you would discover that women have voted at a higher rate than men in every U.S. presidential election since 1980, and at a lower rate in every election prior to 1980. What is your inference now?

   Among the reasons that the study of politics is so fascinating are that things are rarely straightforward and can change (sometimes quite rapidly). For the political analyst, this means that generalizations must be made with care and

(continued)

BOX 1.3 *(Continued)*

with attention to longitudinal patterns (i.e., patterns over time). If you wanted to establish a broad generalization about gender and voting, you would need voting data from several democracies, not just the United States.

Even with data from more elections, you still must assess whether you have analyzed the evidence correctly. Have you overlooked some other important variable that might affect the relationship between gender and voting? To deal with this possibility, you need to identify the factors that might affect voting rates among men and women. Many other explanatory factors might seem relevant: age, ethnicity, education, party identification, attitudes on key policy issues, and so on. By analyzing the relationships among various factors, you can gain a clearer understanding about the importance of gender in explaining varying rates of voter turnout. As an example of the kinds of subtle relationships that exist among different explanatory factors, the Appendix reconsiders the 1976 data. The analysis reveals that the apparent relation between gender and voting in the 1976 data is virtually eliminated when the voter's education level is considered.

7. Ideally, the final stage of your analysis is to *offer a tentative conclusion* regarding the issue. Defensible conclusions in analyses of politics often require extensive data, thorough analysis, and consideration of several alternative explanations. Sometimes the phenomena are so complicated or the evidence is so mixed that no generalization is possible. In our example, the data seem too contradictory to support any clear generalization about gender and voting. Rather, more data and more thoughtful analysis are required. If anything, this brief analysis seems to support the conclusion that, in recent U.S. elections at least, men are not more likely to vote than women.

In the example of political analysis in Box 1.3, as in any scientific study, one's conclusions, as well as one's concepts, data, and methods, are subject to scrutiny and challenge by others. An analyst's conclusion is presumed to be correct until there is compelling criticism or contrary evidence that undermines it. Because many knowledge claims about politics concern complex phenomena, it is often difficult to establish with precision what we do know, even when the scientific method is used. Nonetheless, the scientific method does help people to identify more clearly the points on which they agree or disagree and, ultimately, to develop generalizations about politics.

Political science is composed of certain subfields that are usually defined by their specific subject matter, rather than by their mode of analysis. While there are different ways to categorize the subfields, four are prominent.

1. **Comparative politics** focuses on similarities and differences in political processes and structures. Comparison might be cross-national (e.g., comparing the legal systems of Iran and Taiwan or comparing the voting patterns in forty countries) or it might compare actors within a single country (e.g., comparing

the welfare policies of the fifty American states). (While U.S. politics is sometimes treated as a separate subfield, it is best classified as a part of the subject matter of comparative politics.) Comparative politics covers a huge domain within political analysis and it has many sub-subfields (e.g., public administration, political parties, development, individual political behavior, and public policy, among many others).

2. **International relations** examines the political relations between countries and the dynamics within the worldwide system of states. Subjects within international relations include war, interstate conflict resolution, international law, regional alliances, colonialism, and international organizations. The study of foreign policy is also within this subfield.

3. **Political theory** (or, more precisely, political philosophy) focuses on the ideas and debates dealing with important political questions. Some of this work attempts to characterize and interpret the writings of major political theorists (e.g., Plato, John Locke, Karl Marx, John Rawls), whereas other works are original explorations of the political questions themselves (e.g., What is political justice? Why is there conflict between groups?). Political theory is the source of many of the normative knowledge claims produced by political scientists. Much of the work in political theory is based on the methods of rationality or authority or on an appeal to moral truths, rather than on the scientific method.

4. *Boundary-spanning subfields.* Political science is an eclectic field that often links with other fields of inquiry or, at least, that borrows and adapts ideas from other disciplines. Some work actually spans the boundary between political science and another discipline. While the subject matter of much of this work fits within one of the preceding three major subfields, we could list these hybrids as components of a fourth subfield, which would include political anthropology, political economy, political psychology, political sociology, and biopolitics.

POLITICAL "SCIENCE"?
Criticisms of Political Science as a "Science"

Not everyone agrees that it is appropriate and desirable to apply the scientific method to politics. Four different kinds of criticism have been aimed at political science.

It is not a "real" science.   The first criticism is that political science is not "scientific" in comparison to "real" natural and applied sciences (e.g., chemistry, physics, engineering). Stimulated by Thomas Kuhn's (1970) book, *The Structure of Scientific Revolutions,* this view posits that there is general agreement on the four key elements that provide organization and direction within a fully developed science: (1) central *concepts,* which identify and name key phenomena (specifically, like "Persian Gulf War," or generally, like "war"); (2) *theories,* which are sets of systematically related generalizations that provide explanations and predictions about the linkages between certain concepts (in the form, "If A, then B under conditions C, D".); (3) *rules of interpretation,* which indicate the methods that will establish whether the explanations and predictions posited by the theory are right or wrong; and (4) a list of questions or *issues* that are worth solving within the area of inquiry.

These four key elements are well developed and widely shared within the research communities of every natural and applied science. In contrast, researchers in political science (and other social sciences) have not agreed upon a coherent set of concepts, theories, and rules of interpretation. As you will discover throughout this book, there are many different methods used in political science. There is disagreement regarding the key issues that ought to be solved, little consensus on what theories or generalizations have been proven, and even great difficulty in operationalizing key concepts, such as "power" and "democracy."

Its subject matter defies generalization.   The second criticism is the assertion that it is impossible to develop a science of politics because of the subject matter. In this view, the political world is far too complex and unpredictable for systematic generalizations. Politics is based on the actions and interactions of many individuals, groups, and even countries. Politics occurs in the midst of many changing conditions that can influence those actions. The range of variation in what people might do and in the conditions that might exist is so vast that clear "if A, then B" statements about politics are impossible. Thus it is not surprising that political analysts cannot precisely explain the causes of war, or why women vote differently from men, or what effect a law banning private handguns will have on crime rates.

Its "scientists" cannot be objective.   The third criticism is that the analysis of politics cannot be objective in the way assumed by the scientific method. The issues chosen for study and the manner in which variables are defined, measured, and analyzed are all powerfully influenced by the analyst's social reality (i.e., by his culture, ideas, life experiences, and so on). In this view, no individual (whether Sunni Muslim or agnostic, rural Nigerian or cosmopolitan Parisian, international lawyer or migrant farm worker) can be totally objective and unbiased in the way he tries to analyze political phenomena. (See Box 1.4.)

Its practice diverts attention from normative questions.   Finally, the fourth criticism faults the scientific method itself for not helping to answer the crucial normative questions of politics. Since the time of Aristotle (384–322 B.C.E.), classical political theorists have insisted that the ultimate aim of political analysis is to discover "the highest good attainable by action." In this view, political analysis is a noble endeavor because it helps determine what government and individuals *should* do so that valued goals (e.g., democratic politics, a good life, a just society) can be achieved.

However, even many of those who use the scientific method to study politics do not assume that it can achieve such goals. Max Weber (1864–1920), the influential German social scientist, argued that the scientific method is useful for describing and categorizing political and social reality. But, Weber added, it cannot provide answers to fundamental normative questions about goals and appropriate means. Weber (1958a: 152–153) approvingly quoted Russian novelist Leo Tolstoi's assertion that science can provide no answer to the essential question, "What shall we do, and how shall we arrange our lives?" According to this fourth critique, then, political science becomes an arid enterprise if its reliance on the scientific method discourages attempts to address essential questions about political values and political good (Strauss 1959; Wolin 1960).

BOX 1.4

How's Your Bias?

In its idealized form, the method of science might be value free. But in the analysis of politics, it is impossible for the analyst to describe and explain without being influenced by his own values. You should remember this fact as you consider the arguments and information in this book. It is likely that most readers (including the author) have lived primarily in Western democratic countries. As you will see in Chapter 4 and as you should recognize when you react to the claims throughout the book, your attitudes and judgments are biased by your experiences and your political socialization.

As I wrote this book, I attempted to be sensitive to my own political biases (I recognize some of them, but others are subconscious) and to be fair in describing, analyzing, and generalizing about different political systems. But throughout the book, value judgments are embedded in every choice about what content is included and how it is presented. There is likely to be material that is at variance with your own views.

It is most appropriate for you to assess whether the basis of the claims in this book seems sound and to consider what biases affect the discussion. The chapters are based on my study of social science research (mainly in the English language) and on my personal experiences, which have occurred in many parts of the world. I am aware that my writing includes many explicit or implicit evaluations and that it might reflect my biases (as an American) or political reality. It is important that you assess issues of bias whenever you encounter claims about politics, from any source.

It will take far more than this book to help you make your own judgments regarding political reality. As you read, try to become more conscious of *your* biases, which will undoubtedly influence your ultimate assessments of politics and even your openness to any claims made about the political world.

Political Science as a Means of Understanding the Political World

These four main criticisms of a science of politics are important; you should assess them throughout this book. In general, this book will make the case that, despite the complexity of politics, generalizations are possible—each political phenomenon is not *sui generis,* a unique thing. If political "science" means the attempt to apply the scientific method in order to understand the political world better, it is desirable to use such systematic and analytic thinking. And if we are to share *any* knowledge about the political world, we need methods to reach some interpersonal agreement about political facts. Although political science lacks precise concepts and theories, it does enable us to develop better concepts, improved methods, and sound generalizations, and thereby it makes the study of the political world an exciting intellectual challenge.

This book assumes that understanding politics is extremely important. As Austrian philosopher of science Karl Popper (1963: 227) suggests, "We must not expect too much from reason; argument rarely settles a [political] question, although it is the only means for learning—not to see clearly, but to see more clearly than before." In the face of fundamental value conflicts and the potential for massive political violence among individuals, groups, and nations, political knowledge might reduce our misunderstandings and misconceptions. Thus it can be the grounds for greater tolerance and wiser value judgments about normative political issues. Moreover, enhancing *what* we know about politics should make us more effective in knowing *how* to behave politically—as voters, political activists, and political decision makers. Thus the study of the political world is of crucial importance to the creation of humane social life. Ultimately it is up to you, as you read this book, to decide what can be known about politics and whether you think political "science" is feasible.

WHERE IS THIS BOOK GOING?

Just as there are different approaches to political science, there are different ways to introduce you to the political world. This book is organized to lead you along one route to understanding. But there are other routes, including a reading of the book in an order other than from Chapter 1 to Chapter 16. (For example, I think it would be helpful for you to read the Appendix now; it has also been suggested that Part Two could be read after Parts Three and Four.)

"Man is the measure of all things," observed the ancient Greek philosopher Protagoras (c. 490–421 B.C.E.). In that spirit, this book begins its exploration of the political world at the most personal and individual level. It initially examines what individual men and women think about politics and how they act politically (Part Two). It then focuses primarily on the politics of large collectivities of people that we call states and that are organized politically as governments. Thus Parts Three, Four, and Five offer perspectives and explanations from political science regarding how states and governments are organized for political action, how political processes occur, and how countries are attempting to fulfill their political goals in the challenging conditions of the post–cold war world.

Part Two, "Political Behavior," begins (Chapter 2) with an assessment of the kinds of *political beliefs* that people hold and the way in which those beliefs fit (or don't fit) into a more general framework of ideas. It continues (Chapter 3) with a consideration of the *political actions* that people and groups undertake. Chapter 4 moves from description to explanation: Can we explain *why* individuals seem to think and act in certain ways?

Part Three, "Political Systems," is about the politics of large numbers of people—about how the political world is organized and about *the structures of government.* Chapters 5 through 8 address such issues as: What is a state? How are the political system and the economic system linked? What features distinguish democracies or dictatorships? What are the responsibilities of such political structures as the bureaucracy or the legislature?

Part Four, "Political Processes," emphasizes *key dynamics of politics.* Chapter 9 details three major explanations for how political power is distributed and how political decisions are made. Chapter 10 explores the important processes of political change and development. The various forms and causes of political violence are analyzed in Chapter 11.

Part Five, "Politics among States," focuses on the actions and challenges facing *countries in the contemporary political world.* Chapter 12 explores the key issues of international relations—the manner in which states cooperate, compete, and fight. Chapters 13 through 15 then consider the major challenges facing countries at different stages of development as they pursue the general goals of prosperity, security, and stability in the complicated context of the post–cold war world. Finally, Chapter 16 summarizes the key themes of the book. The Appendix explains major concepts in political science, including four important frameworks for engaging in political analysis.

Whatever the order in which you read the sections of this book, I hope it will enhance *your* understanding of the political world.

FOR FURTHER CONSIDERATION

1. What do you think is the most serious obstacle to a "science" of politics?
2. Which authority have you relied on most extensively as a source of your knowledge about politics? What is the biggest shortcoming of this source?
3. What is the most important question that political science should attempt to answer? What might prevent political scientists from answering this question adequately?
4. Many people insist that most of their political knowledge is based on their own rational thought processes. What might be wrong with this claim?
5. Do you think political scientists can play an important role in government or are they just intellectuals who can only stand on the sidelines and analyze politics?
6. Which statement about the political world proposed within this chapter do you think would receive the greatest variations in "truth scores" among citizens in your society? Which statement would receive the greatest score variations between your society and another one that you identify? Why do you expect variation on the assessment of these statements?

FOR FURTHER READING

Almond, Gabriel. (1989). *A Discipline Divided: Schools and Sects in Political Science.* Newbury Park, CA: Sage. One of the major scholars of comparative politics assesses the diversity of approaches to political science and the possibility of a science of politics.

Goodin, Robert, and Hans-Dieter Klingemann, Eds. (1996). *A New Handbook of Political Science.* New York: Oxford University Press. Articles by well-known political scientists discuss the central concepts, institutional issues, and recent empirical research in many important subfields.

Kuhn, Thomas. (1970). *The Structure of Scientific Revolutions.* 2d ed. Chicago: University of Chicago Press. A short, understandable, and enormously influential discussion of how sciences develop and overturn paradigms.

Manheim, Jarol B. (1998). *Empirical Political Analysis: Research Methods in Political Science.* 5th ed. New York: Addison Wesley Longman. A very effective and understandable presentation of the primary methods that political scientists utilize in the attempt to understand politics and develop defensible generalizations.

Popper, Karl R. (1968). *The Logic of Scientific Discovery.* London: Hutchinson. A major and widely respected statement of the philosophy and application of the scientific method.

White, Louise G. (1994). *Political Analysis: Technique and Practice.* 3d ed. Belmont, CA: Wadsworth. A readable introduction to the methods of doing research and of gathering and analyzing data in empirical political science, emphasizing engaging, do-it-yourself examples.

PART TWO

Political Behavior

CHAPTER 2

Political Beliefs

It is 8:15 on a lovely morning. You take a quiet walk in a local park. As you pass some trees, you are surprised to see someone else. A young woman is sitting by herself, burning a red, white, and blue piece of cloth with a familiar pattern of stars and stripes. What would you do in this situation?

Assuming that you are an American, many reactions are possible. You are likely to recognize that the cloth is an American flag. You might feel anxiety, confusion, curiosity, or even anger. You might turn away abruptly and walk on as if you had noticed nothing. You might cast a disapproving look as you walk by, or you might stop and ask the person what she is doing. Your conversation might lead to a thoughtful political discussion, an angry confrontation, or even violence. You might feel sympathy with her action and offer verbal or actual support. Or you might decide to report the incident to law enforcement authorities.

Your responses to this incident offer interesting evidence about your reactions to the political world. Some of your responses might involve beliefs and others might involve actions. This combination of your political beliefs and actions is the essence of the domain of political science called *political behavior* or **micropolitics**. It is called *micro*politics because the key object of study is the smallest political unit—the individual as a thinker and actor in the political world. Micropolitics can also include study of the political beliefs and actions of small groups, such as families, committees, and juries.

Part Two of this book explores themes in the study of micropolitics. This chapter focuses on *political beliefs*. Initially, it develops a taxonomy of an individual's orientations toward the political world. It then describes configurations of beliefs held by individuals, a cluster called a *political belief system*. Third, it attempts to characterize the dominant patterns of political behavior for an entire society—its *political culture*. Finally, it characterizes some fundamental systems of beliefs, called *political ideologies*. Chapter 3 will then undertake a similar examination of individual political action and of the activities of groups in the political world. Chapter 4 assesses alternative explanations of the sources of individuals' political beliefs and actions.

INDIVIDUAL POLITICAL BELIEFS

Some of your reactions to the incident described at the beginning of this chapter might involve your factual *knowledge* about the political world: for example, what the piece of colored cloth is and the legality of burning it. Other reactions might involve your *feelings:* for example, embarrassment or indifference. And some reactions might engage your powers of *assessment:* for example, an attempt to determine the reasons for the action you have observed. These different reactions typify the three types of orientations that constitute our political beliefs. The following paragraphs describe these cognitive, affective, and evaluative political orientations.

A person's *cognitive orientations* include what she believes are political "facts." Such facts might be correct and accurate or they might be totally wrong. (Recall our discussion of "truth scores" in Chapter 1.) A person might know many things about the politics of her locality, region, and country as well as some things about the broader political world. This knowledge might include such facts as the names of political leaders; the policies supported by particular politicians, political groups, or nations; events in political history; the features of constitutions; or the procedures and actions of a governmental agency.

Affective orientations include any feelings or emotions evoked in a person by political phenomena. For example, what (if any) feelings are stimulated in you when

> You see your national flag?
>
> You hear statements critical of your country's political system?
>
> You learn of "aggressive" actions by your country's political opponents?
>
> You are faced with the option of voting in an election and you don't like the candidates?
>
> You are present at a political demonstration supporting a policy of which you disapprove?

The nature and intensity of your feelings in these kinds of situations are instances of your affective orientations.

Finally, an *evaluative orientation* involves your synthesis of facts and feelings into a judgment about some political phenomenon. If you become aware that your government has proposed a policy that restricts the right of a woman to have an abortion, many different thoughts might be stimulated—your knowledge about the constitutional rights of an individual to freedom of action and of the state to limit those rights; your religious, moral, or scientific beliefs about the status of a fetus; your personal knowledge of the experiences of people who have been involved in decisions about abortions; your gut-level responses to spokespersons for and against the proposed policy. In short, your judgment about a political issue, such as the state's policy on abortion, can be grounded in many different kinds of cognitive and affective orientations that are combined into an evaluation. Ultimately, many of the political attitudes that you would identify as your "fundamental beliefs" are likely to be evaluative orientations.

There are several stages in building our conceptual understanding of political beliefs. If we want to understand one individual's political orientations, we might begin by identifying one or a few specific beliefs held by that person. Does the person know the name of the country's chief executive? How does the person react to news that her state's governor has just prevented the execution of a convicted murderer? What is the person's opinion on a proposal to reduce the number of nuclear weapons stockpiled by her country? (Note that some political analysts distinguish among opinions, attitudes, beliefs, and orientations, with each successive category being more stable, general, and deeply held. In our discussion, this distinction will not be made, although the emphasis is on those understandings about politics that are more general and stable.)

A similar analytic strategy can be used to determine what many people think about a specific issue. When the attitudes of many people are gathered, aggregated, and summarized, they constitute the most widely available data about people's political orientations: *public opinion polls.* Virtually every day, the media and other sources provide data on the percentage of people who hold a certain opinion regarding a political issue. For example, a public opinion poll might gather data to answer the question, "Do Germans oppose further immigration of non-Europeans into Germany?" On the basis of the information reported from the poll, you might decide you know what Germans think about the issue. This information seems a stronger basis for a knowledge claim than a discussion with a few German friends or even a statement by a German political leader.

However, public opinion polls should be interpreted with care. In assessing the information, you should consider such questions as these: Did those who conducted the poll have a bias toward a particular result? Were the questions or the possible responses worded in a way that might distort people's opinions? Were those asked for an opinion a representative sample of the group to whom the opinion is attributed? Are different interpretations of the data possible? Even when the pollsters are unbiased, there are numerous instances in which their estimates are inaccurate (e.g., their predictions of how the population will vote in an election or a referendum).

BELIEF SYSTEMS

Beyond the identification of specific beliefs of individuals, other interesting analyses can focus on the array of political beliefs held by an individual. The term **political belief system** is often used to refer to *the configuration of an individual's political orientations.* A related concept used by political psychologists is an individual's "opinion schema." This is a network of cognitive, affective, and evaluative orientations that serves as a basic framework, guiding a person as she organizes her existing political knowledge and processes new information in order to establish an opinion on a particular subject (Hastie 1986; Lau 1986; Niemi and Weissberg 1993).

To examine any component of an individual's belief system, you can ask a series of questions:

1. What is the *content* of the belief(s)—that is, the subject and the nature of the belief(s)?
2. What is the *salience* of the belief(s)—that is, the importance or significance attached to the belief(s) by the individual?
3. What is the level of *complexity* of the belief(s)?
4. What is the *consistency* of the belief(s) with other beliefs held by the individual?
5. How *stable* is (are) the belief(s) over time?
6. Do(es) the belief(s) *motivate* the individual to undertake any political action?

Some empirical research on the nature of belief systems has been done, with a particular emphasis on the belief systems of the political elite and those of the "mass public"—that is, of ordinary people in the society. The most intensive, analytical research has focused on belief systems in the United States, and this work has been particularly influenced by the analyses of Philip Converse (1964). In general, Converse argues that a belief system has two levels of information. One level includes relatively straightforward *facts or opinions,* such as the opinion that American public schools should not allow Christian prayers during class time. The second level is *constraint knowledge,* in which more abstract and overarching concepts (such as liberalism and conservatism) operate to shape and link ideas. In the school prayer example, an individual might base her opinion on constraint knowledge about the constitutional separation of church and state or about free speech issues.

Belief Systems among Mass Publics

On the basis of his empirical analyses of (American) individuals' belief systems, Converse (1964) concludes that there are important and predictable differences between the elite and the mass publics in the nature and structure of their belief systems. As you might expect, the belief systems of individuals in the mass public are simpler and narrower, and they are organized far less by constraint knowledge, than those of members of the elite. Within the mass public, Converse distinguishes five gradations in the level of conceptualization in people's belief systems. Only about 15 percent of members of the mass public have substantial constraint knowledge in their belief system. And almost half of the U.S. public is characterized by the two lowest levels—extremely simplistic political beliefs and "political ignorance."

While there has been continuing debate regarding the precise nature of political belief systems among mass publics (Rosenberg 1988; Sniderman 1993), most researchers agree on certain generalizations about the citizens of Western democracies (e.g., the United States, Canada, and the Western European and Scandinavian countries). Like nearly every other generalization about politics, the following six generalizations are broadly accurate for "most people" but are subject to many qualifications and some exceptions.

1. Political issues have low salience in relation to other concerns in people's lives. Although Aristotle termed the citizen *homo politicus,* or "political man," most people do not locate political issues in the center of their interest and attention space.

2. People tend to focus attention on concrete issues and have minimal grasp of the abstract political concepts that serve as constraint knowledge.

3. Interest and knowledge are greater on immediate, short-term issues than on longer-term ones.

4. While people's fundamental beliefs are relatively stable, there can be considerable volatility in their short-term political opinions, which tend to shift when subjected to modest changes in political information. This volatility might be due to limited interest or to the sheer difficulty of trying to understand complicated political questions.

5. Significant inconsistencies can exist across political beliefs, in the sense that an individual can hold contradictory positions. (For example, an American might express support for the First Amendment right to free speech but deny the right of a Communist to speak at a public meeting or the right of the Ku Klux Klan to hold a public rally.)

6. The content of beliefs is often inaccurate. (In a survey, e.g., half the Americans questioned did not know how many U.S. senators serve their state and less than one in six knew who William Rehnquist is. You know the correct answers…don't you?)

The basic ideas of Converse (1964) and others have been challenged by those who acknowledge that the mass public might have a minimal grasp of political information and ideas, but argue that people *are* able to fashion reasonable political opinions. In this view, members of the mass public use simple rules of thumb to make sense of issues; focus most of their attention on some issue areas (e.g., foreign policy, race relations, and economic concerns) and have little knowledge of other issue areas; and receive considerable guidance from information provided by the elite and the media (Sniderman 1993; see also Chapter 4). Another challenge to the view that most people have simplistic belief systems is the viewpoint that individuals develop different structured ways of thinking about the world. Thus it is argued that the analyst must first study and understand how people think, not merely ask questions about their specific beliefs and then look for a pattern in their responses. When the analyst specifies an individual's structure of thinking, the person's political attitudes might be generally consistent and coherent within this structure (Rosenberg 1988). This is an intriguing, alternative way to analyze the political beliefs of the mass public that could change our unflattering picture of most people's belief systems, but there is not much empirical support for it. Moreover, even

with these refinements, most research continues to reveal a mass public whose political belief systems are neither rich nor sophisticated.

Belief Systems among Elites

The **political elite** is a term for *those who have relatively high levels of interest and involvement in political life*. Some actually hold positions of political responsibility and most communicate their knowledge and beliefs about politics to others. The belief systems of the elite are regarded as particularly important because the elites are presumed to have a major role in politics and because they can strongly influence the beliefs of the mass public.

Overall, Converse (1964) and others conclude that generalizations regarding the belief systems of the elites are the opposite of those for the mass public on each of the six points listed in the previous section. For the most part, their belief systems are characterized by relatively high levels of abstraction, accuracy, complexity, stability, and breadth. Constraint knowledge is well developed and influences most specific opinions. Despite the emphasis on consistency among beliefs, individuals in the elite can support core values that are in conflict. In contrast to those in the mass, those with an elite belief system are able to reconcile differences within their constraint knowledge in a manner that enables them to integrate their thinking as they generate political opinions (Tetlock 1984).

All individuals with sophisticated belief systems do not necessarily share the same core beliefs. For example, some individuals might have a coherent system of beliefs that support the protection of individuals' civil liberties, while others' constraint knowledge and specific opinions consistently support the right of the government to limit individual liberties substantially in the protection of social order (Sniderman et al. 1991). Several important systems of beliefs, termed "ideologies," are characterized later in this chapter; others are explored in Chapter 5.

Research has attempted to specify the central elements of belief systems among elites. For example, some studies of the belief systems of the elite responsible for U.S. foreign policy during the 1980s identified three distinctive perspectives held by many, but not all, members of that elite (Rosenau and Holsti 1986). Each was based on different assumptions about the nature of the international political environment, the source of the major threats to national security, and the most appropriate policy responses.

1. For the "cold war internationalist" belief system, the dominant fact was the fundamental conflict between the United States and the Soviet Union. In this global competition, expansion by the opponent had to be stopped anywhere in the world. Since war was most likely if military power was not greater than the rivals, continuous growth and development of the military should be the critical imperative.

2. From the "post–cold war internationalist" perspective, the most dangerous problems in the international system emerged from the huge inequalities between these relatively wealthy states and the many poor states among the less-developed countries. The primary danger of war was the irrational arms race and overly hostile relations between the major military powers. U.S. foreign policy should emphasize stable and noncombative relations with the Soviet bloc and greater sensitivity to defusing conflicts in the developing countries.

3. For those in the elite holding the "semi-isolationist" view, the most serious problems facing the United States and other major countries were domestic problems, such as inflation, unemployment, and crime, which threatened the pursuit of prosperity and stability. Thus the crucial policy objectives should be to limit military expenditure and to focus resources on domestic issues.

Empirical research concluded that most members of the American foreign policy elite held the cold war internationalist belief system in the early 1980s (Rosenau and Holsti 1986). However, at the beginning of the twenty-first century, the global system has changed in ways that none of these three perspectives anticipated. The U.S. foreign policy elite must adapt its belief systems to a world where the Soviet Union has disappeared, where economic power has become as important as military power, where regional cooperation is increasingly significant, and where ethnic groups and small countries are the primary sources of international instability. The evolving belief systems of the U.S. foreign policy elite and the translation of those beliefs into action will be important in shaping the responses of the United States to events in the international system.

POLITICAL CULTURE

Some analysts attempt to identify broadly shared patterns of political orientations that characterize a large group of individuals. The objective is to develop generalizations about the political culture of the group. **Political culture** is normally defined as *the configuration of a particular people's political orientations*—that is, as the generalized belief system of many individuals. For this reason, political culture is not precisely a topic in micropolitics, but it is examined here because it is embedded in individual-level analyses.

Most commonly, it is the political culture of a country or of a major (ethnic or religious) community within a country that has been studied. The composition of the group that is studied depends on the interests of the researcher. It might be the people of a geographic community (e.g., Londoners, English, British, or Europeans) or of a community of shared identity (e.g., Sikhs in the Indian state of Punjab, Sikhs in the Indian subcontinent, or all Sikhs in the world) or of a community of shared meaning (e.g., French Canadians or all French-speaking peoples).

National Character Studies

A traditional approach that attempts to capture the essence of a people's political culture involves "national character" studies (Inkeles 1996). When the Beach Boys sing about "California girls," their lyrics are meant to conjure up the image of a tanned, athletic, easygoing young woman who is not too cerebral. And when someone is described as being "so French," you might think of her as being sophisticated, romantic, and volatile.

At one level, we recognize immediately that such characterizations are stereotypes that do not fit the majority of individual subjects. Yet most of us, including people in the political world, use these kinds of labels (at least occasionally) as a shorthand method of describing groups or nations. Indeed, Franklin Delano Roosevelt (U.S. president from 1933 to 1945) revealed some belief in the notion when he observed that "the all-important factor in national greatness is national character."

Some political analysts have tried to specify the national character of certain countries and then to predict or explain their political behavior on the basis of such characteristics. Typically, these studies do not claim that everyone fits the national character profile, but they maintain that the profile is accurate for the politically relevant strata. Thus, the top ruling group in Britain has been defined in terms of English national character—control of emotions, a sense of propriety, a belief in class and national superiority, and reliance on "old boy" connections. This national character has supposedly been nurtured by a shared upper/upper-middle class background and training at a public school (in Britain, this actually means an elite private school) followed by Oxford or Cambridge. Interestingly, this class and early educational background is not so accurate for the three key Prime Ministers of the past two decades (Margaret Thatcher, John Major and Tony Blair), although the description of the English national character does fit Margaret Thatcher quite well, despite her differences in background and gender. While the backgrounds of those in the British political elite in Parliament and the higher civil service are becoming more varied, the national character profile is still evident in the orientations and behavior of many in this leadership elite.

In another example, Ervand Abrahamian (1993) analyzes what he terms the "paranoid style of Iranian politics." He describes the constant tendency of the political leaders and the mass public to fear foreign plots and conspiracies meant to subvert the culture and create societal chaos. He traces this political belief system to a "national culture" characterized by pessimism, subservience, egotism, dishonesty, and distrust of others. While he acknowledges that colonial dealings with the British and Americans provide Iranians with ample grounds for distrust of foreigners, Abrahamian argues that the character of the population is excessively paranoid. He details how this has resulted in disastrous consequences, undermining the Iranians' capacity to develop cooperative internal politics based on coalition building, the ability to compromise, and tolerance for domestic opposition.

National character studies such as that by Abrahamian (1993) and the one on Burmese political culture described in Box 4.5 can provide some fascinating insights into both the political culture and the political actions taken in a society. However, these studies are criticized by many analysts as impressionistic and loaded with gross generalizations that greatly oversimplify political reality. Consequently, most scholars dismiss national character studies as caricatures with little capacity to account for the complex actual political behaviors within a country.

Survey Research

There is a more systematic and scientifically acceptable method for establishing the nature of a political culture—the use of survey research. This involves taking a carefully selected sample of the population and then asking each person a series of questions that aims to tap individual political beliefs and actions. The researcher then aggregates the individuals' responses, searching for patterns or configurations that profile the political culture of the sample and, by inference, that characterize the political culture of the population from which the sample is taken.

The first major study of this type is still the most famous one: *The Civic Culture,* by Gabriel Almond and Sidney Verba (1963). Lengthy interviews were conducted with a large sample of citizens in each of five countries. The data were then aggregated and analyzed in a diversity of ways to provide rich descriptions of each country's political culture. Numerous comparisons between the five political cultures were also presented. Because *The Civic Culture* is a landmark in survey research on political culture, revealing both virtues and shortcomings in such analyses, it is detailed in Box 2.1

Most survey research on political culture has attempted to improve our understanding of the political orientations of citizens in "democratic" societies. One major study found widespread similarities in the social and political concerns among citizens in many countries. Personal desires for a happy family life, a decent standard of living, and good health were most important, and political concerns centered on fears about war and political instability (Cantril 1965). In research on Western societies, Ron Inglehart (1989, 1997; see also Dalton 2000) suggests that the central sociopolitical values held by citizens have recently changed for many, especially the younger generations. Inglehart concludes that older adults emphasize "materialist" values for strong defense, order maintenance, and economic growth; in contrast, many young adults stress "postmaterialist" values for a more esthetically satisfying environment, for freedom of expression, and for more personal power in social and political life. Another study found that between 1973 and 1990, the proportion of citizens with postmaterialist values was steady in the United Kingdom and United States (at about 20 percent) but nearly tripled in West Germany to 36 percent of the population. The range among Western democracies is from 39 percent (Netherlands) to 17 percent (Norway) (Dalton 2000: Table 5.2).

The extensive empirical research on political culture, as it has become more precise in its methods and more cautious about cultural biases, has revealed the considerable variability within political cultures across individuals, between groups, and over time. Chapter 4 will examine some of the factors that might account for differences in the political beliefs of individuals within a society. But it is also evident from the survey research that many societies do have a political culture—a general configuration of political beliefs that distinguishes them from certain other societies.

POLITICAL IDEOLOGY

You have probably heard certain political perspectives classified as "liberalism" or "conservatism" or "socialism." Such a general belief system can be termed a political ideology. A **political ideology** is *a comprehensive set of beliefs about the political world—about desirable political goals and the best ways to achieve those goals.*

Three points can help to clarify the different ways in which the term political ideology is used. First, a political ideology can be composed of the political beliefs of a single individual or of a group of any size—from a small set of friends to millions of people around the world. In this sense, "ideology" is used synonymously with "belief system," as discussed previously. Second, it is usually assumed that a political ideology displays high coherence, complexity, and salience, but it could be low on any of these dimensions. Third, the label "political ideology" is typically applied to one of a few comprehensive and widely held sets of beliefs. Most of these are "isms," like those cited in the preceding paragraph. However, any relatively complete bundle of political beliefs could be termed a political ideology.

The objective in this section is to introduce you to the basic tenets of some of the Western world's most general ideologies: conservatism, liberalism, and several variations of socialism, including communism. Elements of these sets of ideas influence the political thinking of large numbers of people.

BOX 2.1

Using Survey Research to Characterize Political Culture: The Civic Culture

Political scientists Gabriel Almond and Sidney Verba selected Italy, Mexico, the United Kingdom, the United States, and West Germany for the first large-scale empirical and comparative study of political culture. Based on survey research techniques, their analyses were reported in *The Civic Culture* (1963).

In each country, a sample of about 1,000 respondents was asked many questions about their individual political beliefs and actions, such as:

Can you identify the national leaders of the principal political parties (in your country)?

Suppose a regulation was being considered by your local government that you considered very unjust or harmful. What do you think you could do?

How would you feel if your son or daughter married a supporter of the (opposition) political party? Would you be pleased, would you be displeased, or would it make no difference?

How often do you talk about public affairs to other people?

Thinking about the national government, how much effect do you think its activities, the laws passed, and so on have on your day-to-day life?

Almond and Verba postulated a taxonomy of three "ideal-type" political cultures, as represented in Table 2.1. Each successive ideal-type entails more extensive involvement between individuals and the political order. In fact, after analyzing all the empirical data, only one of the five countries in *The Civic Culture* was actually classified as one of the three ideal types: the United States was termed a "participant" political culture. Italy was "alienated," Mexico was "alienated but aspiring," West Germany had "political detachment and subject competence," and the United Kingdom was a "deferential civic culture."

TABLE 2.1
Ideal-Type Political Cultures

Political Culture Type	Orientations Toward			
	Political System	Political Outputs	Political Inputs	Self as Political Participant
Parochial	0	0	0	0
Subject	+	+	0	0
Participant	+	+	+	+

Note: 0 means little or no explicit orientation; + means positive orientation.

Source: Adapted from Almond and Verba 1963.

BOX 2.1 *(Continued)*

Important criticisms were raised about the methodology of *The Civic Culture* (Verba 1980). For example, in Mexico only urban citizens were interviewed, a clearly inadequate basis for generalizing about the political culture of what was a predominantly rural society. In addition, the findings were very time-specific, with many responses contingent upon the country's political context at the point the survey was completed.

Perhaps the most serious fault with *The Civic Culture* was the ideological biases revealed by Almond and Verba. They praised the British political culture because its citizens had very positive attitudes toward the outputs they received from the government but they were not highly active participants in political processes. Almond and Verba worried that a highly participant political culture, like the United States, might not remain stable and democratic under the constant pressure of extensive citizen involvement and demands (Pateman 1980). Yet despite its shortcomings, *The Civic Culture* is a pathbreaking attempt to undertake a systematic, empirical, and comparative study of political cultures, and as such it has influenced virtually all subsequent work on the subject.

Key Issues

Ideologies can include a description of political reality, but they are primarily a normative expression of what ought to be. Each major ideology has its own internal logic, and each is based on assumptions and value judgments about the individual and her human nature, about the proper relationship between the individual and society, and about the desirability of establishing certain kinds of equality among individuals.

Individual human nature. The "nature versus nurture" debate centers on disagreements about whether an individual's fundamental beliefs and behaviors are determined primarily by innate needs and values with which she is born, or whether those beliefs and values are mainly a product of her environment and experiences. The implications of nature and nurture for political beliefs and actions will be assessed in Chapter 4. In this section our focus is on the key assumptions that political ideologies make about an individual's innate nature (e.g., the extent to which individuals are selfish or sharing, violent or nonviolent, emotional or rational) and about the adaptability of individuals (the extent to which they can be taught or induced to act and think in a way that is against their innate nature).

Individual and society. What is the proper relationship between the individual and society? One view is that the highest value in social arrangements is individual freedom of action. Alternatively, the collective good is seen as paramount, and individual freedom must be constrained to achieve that collective good.

Equality. To what extent should there be equality in terms of what individuals do and the benefits they acquire? One position is that there should be legal equality—that every individual should be equal before the law, have equal political rights, and enjoy equality of opportunity. A contrasting position is that there should be material equality—that every individual deserves a comparable level of benefits and goods. This second position places high value on equality of conditions, adding social and economic equality to legal equality. A third position posits that people and situations are intrinsically unequal and that it is neither possible nor desirable to attempt to legislate any kind of equality.

While there is broad agreement regarding the general perspective of each major ideology, you should be aware that each ideology is subject to varying interpretations across groups and especially across cultures. This variation is particularly evident for the term "liberalism," which has both a traditional meaning (described later in this section) and a very different meaning in the late twentieth century. Similarly, the ideology of socialism in its Marxist-Leninist form is quite distinct from its democratic socialist form.

Conservatism

Conservatism *attempts to prevent or slow the transition away from a society based on traditional values and social hierarchy.* As the word suggests, the essence of conservative ideology is to conserve the many valued elements of the system that already exists. What the conservative wishes to preserve varies with the time and place, but certain underlying elements are highly valued. Particular importance is placed on stability, tradition, and loyalty to God and country. The relation of the individual to society and an antipathy to egalitarianism (i.e., equality of conditions) are at the core of conservatism.

The individual. Conservatism makes few assumptions about human nature. It does posit that individuals are inherently unequal in intelligence, in skills, and in status. Some individuals and groups are viewed as superior to others, and it is clearly preferable that the superior groups be in positions of power in society and in government. Individual rationality is not usually regarded as a sound basis for decisions about appropriate social or political behavior.

Individual and society. Society is composed of many different groups, which are unequal in power, status, and material possessions. Members of these groups, which are linked together in an organic whole, work cooperatively to maintain the social order. Individual liberty is valued, but only within a framework of mutual responsibility. No majority or government should have sufficient power to abridge the rights of others. In particular, there should be no constraints on the rights of the superior groups to enjoy the benefits or exercise the responsibilities associated with their greater power, status, and wealth. One of these responsibilities is to protect the weak from severe hardships, a responsibility that the French term *noblesse oblige*—"the obligations of the nobility."

Existing values and social organization have evolved slowly and have survived the test of time. Tradition and religion, rather than reason, are viewed as the most reliable sources for guiding society, since they support stability and temper change. In the words of one British conservative, "The accumulated wisdom and experience of countless generations gone is more likely to be right than the passing fashion of the moment" (Hearnshaw 1933: 22).

Equality.   Since inequality is viewed as a natural aspect of society, it is considered foolish and even dangerous to seek egalitarianism. Forced equality is unwise because it disrupts the natural, cooperative hierarchy among groups and causes social conflict and unnatural change. Attempts to force equality are also unacceptable because they directly undermine individual liberty, a value of far greater importance.

Edmund Burke (1729–1797), a British member of Parliament, is perhaps the most articulate spokesperson for conservatism. Other important advocates of conservatism were British Prime Ministers Benjamin Disraeli and Winston Churchill and, to a lesser extent, American Founding Fathers James Madison and Alexander Hamilton. Many who are now called conservatives or neoconservatives are really more closely aligned to the philosophy of classical liberalism (discussed in the next section).

In those contemporary situations where government has become strong, and especially where government uses its power to equalize wealth and status, conservativism argues for a return to traditional values, for a contraction of government, and for individual freedom to be unequal. Many of the contemporary political actors who come closest to the spirit of conservatism are in certain countries in Asia and the Middle East (e.g., Brunei, Kuwait, Nepal, and Saudi Arabia) where social hierarchy, order, and traditional values are celebrated. Most contemporary conservatives are pragmatic and recognize that a return to eighteenth-century society is impossible. They accept some of the government policies implemented in their societies to equalize status and income. But even here the rationale is to change in order to preserve, as the British Conservative Party has put it. The conservative perspective is sympathetic to government intervention if the goal is to maintain or return to traditional values, such as patriotism, family, morality, and piety. Thus a conservative government might actively expand its military power to influence other countries, support a state religion, or make abortion illegal.

Classical Liberalism

The ideology of **classical liberalism** *places the highest value on individual freedom and posits that the role of government should be quite limited.*

The individual.   Each person enjoys natural rights to life, liberty, and property. In contrast to conservatism, there is no higher value in classical liberalism than these rights and the freedom of the individual to pursue these rights as an independent actor. Liberalism assumes that each person is a rational and responsible individual who is the best judge of what is in her self-interest. Thus an individual ought to be allowed to exercise freedom of action, guided by her own rationality and pursuing her own interests.

Individual and society.   A person's full capabilities can be realized only if the person is not limited by a social order in which tradition and hierarchy are dominant or by a government that restricts individual freedom. The ideology of classical liberalism emerged as a reaction to the conservatism of European feudal society, which was viewed as hierarchical and static, stifling individual freedom. It also repudiated mercantilism, government interventions in the economy that were viewed as benefiting only a few and severely limiting the opportunities of most.

According to liberalism, no principle justifies the limitation of individual freedom. In economic behavior, classical liberals celebrate a laissez-faire economy (i.e., one unconstrained by government regulations) guided by enlightened self-interest and the "invisible hand" of the market (this vision of the economy will be explained in detail in Chapter 8). Each individual should be free to pursue her self-interest by any legal activity and to amass as much property and wealth as possible. In political life, government authority, which rests on the consent of each individual to be governed, is explicitly limited so that government does not infringe on personal liberty (see Box 2.2 if you are wondering why this doesn't sound "liberal.")

BOX 2.2

Whither Liberalism? Is That Liberal or Conservative?

If you are an American, you probably have noticed that the description of classical liberalism given in this chapter, emphasizing limited government, is quite different from the political beliefs currently termed "liberal" in the United States. In the political language of today, a "liberal" in America is understood as someone who supports substantial government intervention and policies that increase equality of condition, not merely equality of opportunity.

This confusion of terminology is partly due to developments during Franklin Delano Roosevelt's tenure as U.S. president (from 1933 to 1945). Faced with a devastating economic depression, Roosevelt argued for a "New Deal" in which the central government had a clear duty and responsibility to assist actively in economic recovery and in social action. While not proposing the expansive government role in the economy and the egalitarianism of socialism, he did insist that government must be very active in solving economic and social problems. Among other things, government must actively regulate business, create jobs, and distribute extensive welfare services to the citizens, including cash payments and increased public provision of education, housing, health care, and so on.

To avoid the politically negative label of socialism, Roosevelt termed himself and his policies "liberal," contrasting them with the "conservative" policies of others (mainly Republicans, such as the previous president, Herbert Hoover) who emphasized limited government, laissez-faire economics, and individual freedom. Notice that in the general language of political ideology, what Roosevelt was terming conservatism was really classical liberalism, and what he was proposing himself was a very modest version of democratic socialism.

Eventually, Roosevelt's terminology was widely adopted in the United States, and thus political discourse in the United States is characterized as a debate between liberals and conservatives, even though the ideologies of both groups combine, in different amounts, elements of classical liberalism and democratic socialism. In this book, the traditional ideology of liberalism will be termed "classical liberalism" to distinguish it from the current understanding of liberalism as an ideology of big government and egalitarianism.

Equality.   While equality before the law (equality of opportunity) is regarded as important, government should not attempt to create material equality. Even in situations of hardship, government action is undesirable because it can undermine individual initiative and independence. Thus government has only a very limited role, with no responsibility for addressing inequalities.

Among the many political thinkers associated with classical liberalism were John Locke (1632–1704), Adam Smith (1723–1790), Jeremy Bentham (1748–1831), and John Stuart Mill (1806–1873). More contemporary advocates of classical liberalism (some of whom are labeled "neoconservatives") include economists F. A. Hayek and Milton Friedman, and political commentator William F. Buckley. Part Five of this book will reveal that many contemporary political regimes are powerfully influenced by classical liberalism. Its emphases on limited government, individual liberty, and laissez-faire economics are among the central themes in many debates about policy and government action.

Socialism

For **socialism**, *the most important goal is to provide high quality, relatively equal conditions of life for everyone, with an active state assisting in the achievement of this goal.*

The individual.   In the socialist perspective, individuals are not innately selfish and aggressive. If anything, humans are social and caring by nature. To a large extent, individuals' attitudes and behaviors are determined by the environment in which they live and learn, not by invariant features of human nature. Consequently, it is considered crucial to create an environment that encourages individuals to place the highest value on cooperation and sharing and to believe that the most important goal for each individual is to increase the collective good of all.

Individual and society.   While individual rights and freedom are valued, the most important value is identified as the good of the society as a whole. Thus the individual's interests must be subordinated to, or at least coordinated with, the overall interests and needs of everyone in the society. All groups, from national organizations (e.g., trade unions) to local organizations (e.g., social clubs) to the family, must encourage these attitudes of cooperation and service to the common good.

The government has a crucial role, both through education and civic training and through policies that provide every citizen with good material living conditions and security. Thus government must take an expansive role, ensuring that every citizen has access to quality education, shelter, health care, jobs, and financial security against economic uncertainty.

Equality.   Both the organic, hierarchical world of conservatism and the individualistic, self-serving world of classical liberalism result in societies in which there exist huge disparities of material conditions, status, and power. From the socialist perspective, these disparities cause misery, deep alienation, and pervasive conflict in the society.

Thus the ideology of socialism centers in a deep commitment to use the power and policies of the state to increase the material as well as the social and political equality of all its members. Such equality is believed to transform people into ful-filled, happy citizens who willingly contribute to the common good.

There are significantly different variations within the ideology of socialism. Among these, two major variations should be distinguished: Marxist-Leninist socialism and democratic socialism.

Marxist-Leninist socialism.   The Marxist-Leninist variant of socialist ideol-ogy begins with three assumptions regarding the changes necessary to produce equality and social justice. First, the old socioeconomic order will resist change by every means available, and thus change will require violent overthrow of the old order. Second, the transformation to socialism will be complex and difficult. To achieve the desired equality of conditions, a powerful government must be installed. Among the government's most important tasks is the restructuring of the economic system, with public ownership of all the major resources in the society and the pro-duction and distribution of goods and services for human need (see Chapter 8 on the command political economy for a fuller discussion of this point). And third, a small, dictatorial leadership group must be empowered to manage the government and to effect the complex changes in the economy and society. When relative equal-ity is achieved, both the small leadership group and the powerful government sup-porting it can be eliminated. They will be replaced by a decentralized, citizen-run politics and an efficient administration.

The core elements of this version of socialism are the theories of Karl Marx, and its modified practical applications by V. I. Lenin in the Soviet Union and Mao Zedong in China. These variations of socialism are often termed communism, Marx-ism, or revolutionary socialism, as well as Marxist-Leninist socialism. In the last fifty years this version of socialism has been attempted in more than sixty countries, ranging from A (Albania, Angola, Algeria) to Z (Zimbabwe). Most of the major regimes that implemented Marxist-Leninist socialism have now abandoned it (see, especially, Chapter 15 on the post-communist countries).

Democratic socialism.   The other major variation within socialist ideology is democratic socialism. This variant also treats egalitarianism as its primary goal, but it assumes that the changes can be affected by a government that comes to power and rules by democratic means, not by violence and repression. This government's author-ity is derived from consent of the governed in elections. In democratic socialism, the state's policies emphasize the substantial reduction of inequalities in material condi-tions, power, and status, but they do not attempt to achieve complete equality of mate-rial conditions. The approach to change is gradual, placing continued importance on the protection of individual rights and freedoms, even as it transforms the socioeco-nomic order. The government might own some of the major economic resources in the society and it strongly regulates much of the economic system, but it does not attempt to plan and control all aspects of the economic system (Przeworski 1985, 1993).

The ideology of democratic socialism is rooted in such Utopian socialists as Thomas More (1478–1535), Robert Owen (1771–1856), and Claude-Henri St. Simon (1760–1825); in Fabian socialists such as George Bernard Shaw (1856–1950) and Sydney (1859–1947) and Beatrice (1858–1943) Webb; and in revisionist Marxists such as Karl Kautsky (1854–1938). The ideology has been partially implemented in the contemporary "social market systems" present in such countries as Denmark, Germany, Great Britain, and Sweden (see Box 13.2 in Chapter 13). It is also advocated by some of the political elites in the post-communist countries of Central and Eastern Europe (see Chapter 15).

One vision of the welfare state as a set of specific government policies was articulated by the British economist Sir William Beveridge in a major policy statement to the British government in 1941. Beveridge argued that the state had clear responsibility to employ public policy actively in order to overcome five tragic effects on some individuals in a society operating according to the tenets of classical liberalism:

1. *Disease:* to be combatted by public provision of subsidized or free health care services, including doctors, treatment, hospitals, and medicines.
2. *Want:* to be eliminated by public provision of sufficient money and other services to raise people above poverty.
3. *Squalor:* to be reduced by publicly owned and subsidized housing affordable to all.
4. *Ignorance:* to be eliminated by universal, free public education.
5. *Idleness:* to be overcome by government policies that ensure meaningful work for all individuals.

Some Further Points about "Isms"

This section has identified the major political ideologies that are used to characterize the political belief systems of many citizens in Western countries. There are many other significant political ideologies in the contemporary political world, at least some of which are "isms." Examples include authoritarianism, corporatism, environmentalism, fascism (see Box 2.3), feminism, libertarianism, nationalism, and totalitarianism. There are also broader systems of religious-social beliefs that have great political importance, including Islamic fundamentalism, Confucianism, and Hinduism. Many of these other "isms" will be detailed at some point in this book, where they are particularly relevant to a topic. To advance your understanding of these kinds of belief systems, you might take a course in political theory, political ideology, or world religions, or pursue the "ism" of interest at the library or via the Internet.

In the contemporary political world, few individuals adhere absolutely to any one of these political ideologies. Almost no one has a complete grasp of the details and subtleties of any ideology, and even fewer are prepared to accept without reservation every element of an ideology. Some "true believers" do adhere almost totally to a particular ideology, and these people are the genuine ideologues. There is a larger set of people who are substantially influenced by one or more ideologies. They have developed their own system of political beliefs, which is a combination of basic principles of particular ideologies with ideas from other sources. And, as was noted earlier in our discussion of the beliefs of mass publics, in most societies many individuals have only rudimentary and inconsistent political beliefs, which are shaped by perceptions of underlying principles of one or more political ideologies.

BOX 2.3

From the "Ism" File I: Fascism

Fascism is one of the other political ideologies that has had a major impact on twentieth-century history. Nazism, its variant in Germany, was the pivot of the most devastating war in the century (World War II). **Fascism** *places fundamental importance on the unity and harmony of government and society and is defined particularly by its opposition to forces that might weaken that collective unity.* In particular, fascism is: (1) antisocialist—it opposes the egalitarian ethic, the idea that there might be persistent violence and struggle among groups in society, and the seizure of private property by the state; and (2) antidemocratic—it views competitive, multiparty politics as divisive and destabilizing.

Fascism shares with conservatism the idea that the society and the government should be unified into a single, organic whole. All groups should enthusiastically coordinate their social and economic activities to achieve the good of the entire nation. Fascism further assumes that the top leader is the embodiment of the national will and that all individuals and groups must obey the will of the leader. The ideology also usually distinguishes between a superior racial or ethnic group who form the nation and other, inferior groups who are reviled and persecuted (on the "nation," see Chapter 5).

While several twentieth-century regimes have included strong elements of fascism, this political ideology is most closely associated with the regimes of Adolf Hitler in Germany (1932–1945) and Benito Mussolini in Italy (1922–1943). Hitler's particular version of fascism, emphasizing nationalistic fervor and virulent racism, effectively mobilized the German people to support a war that spread across three continents, causing more than 51 million deaths (17 million military and 34 million civilian) and being particularly marked by the brutal extermination of more than 6 million Jews and other "undesirables" in the concentration camps of Europe.

In the 1990s, variations of fascism reemerged as a strong political force in Europe. While some "neo-Nazi" groups, such as skinheads and the American Ku Klux Klan, have continued to have small followings, there has been significant electoral support for neo-fascist parties such as Jean-Marie Le Pen's National Front in France, Georg Haider's Freedom Party in Austria, and Vladimir Zhrinovsky's Liberal Democratic Party in Russia. There were strong protests in Austria and by Austria's European Union partners when the Freedom Party became a key participant in a coalition government in 2000. As in earlier periods, these neo-Nazi groups appeal

BOX 2.3 *(Continued)*

to strong antiforeigner sentiment, particularly against immigrant groups, whose ethnicity and culture are dramatically distinctive from the dominant groups in the society. They also promise to use government power aggressively to eliminate crime and disorder in the society. Some predict that a severe crisis, such as a prolonged economic or health crisis, could spawn a dramatic increase in support because "the fascist ideology appeals to our deepest longings for community, for solidarity, for safety in the face of a seething world" (Segre 1993: 296).

Fascism in Germany under Adolf Hitler was among the most effective and destructive mass-mobilization ideologies in modern history.

LOOKING AHEAD

Chapter 2 has begun our exploration of micropolitics. It has introduced you to issues about political beliefs—what individuals know and think about politics. Analysis can focus on a single individual or on a group, and it can assess a single belief or an array of beliefs across many issues. While examining specific beliefs can be quite interesting, political analysis contributes most when it attempts to generalize about the belief system of an individual or a group. A belief or belief system can be analyzed in terms of its cognitive, affective, and evaluative components. The balance between these emphases and the composition of the group sharing a belief system, as well as the content of the beliefs, vary considerably when one is examining political ideologies, political cultures, mass belief systems, or elite belief systems.

The next step in micropolitical analysis is to move beyond description and develop explanations of political behavior (Chapter 4). However, we must first look at the second general form of political behavior, political actions. Thus the focus of Chapter 3 is the array of political actions in which an individual or group can engage.

FOR FURTHER CONSIDERATION

1. What are your general beliefs about human nature? Are these beliefs consistent with your most important beliefs about how people ought to behave and do behave politically?
2. What do you think is the most sensible assumption and the most questionable assumption of conservatism? Of classical liberalism? Of socialism?
3. Can you characterize your own political belief system? For example, what are your three to five most salient political beliefs? Do they deal with the same general content area?
4. If you were to analyze the political belief system of another person on the basis of five questions, what questions would you ask?

FOR FURTHER READING

Almond, Gabriel, and Sidney Verba. (1963). *The Civic Culture.* Princeton, NJ: Princeton University Press. As described in the chapter, this is the landmark empirical, comparative study of the political cultures of different countries.

Ebenstein, William, and Alan Ebenstein. (1991). *Great Political Thinkers: Plato to the Present.* 5th ed. Fort Worth, TX: Harcourt Brace. Includes extensive excerpts from many major political theorists, supplemented by very helpful editors' introductions.

Einhorn, Eric S., and John Logue. (1989). *Modern Welfare States: Politics and Policy in Social Democratic Scandinavia.* New York: Praeger. Describes the goals, policies, and problems associated with the important social welfare states.

Fromm, Erich, Ed. (1965). *Socialist Humanism.* New York: Doubleday. Prominent social scientists and political philosophers expound the virtues of socialism.

Griffin, Roger, Ed. (1998). *International Fascism: Theories, Causes and the New Consensus.* New York: Oxford University Press. A diverse and thorough selection of writings on fascism, by both fascists and anti-fascists, exploring the strong appeal of this ideology to many individuals and groups at mid-century and also in the 1990s.

Inglehart, Ronald. (1997). *Modernization and Postmodernization: Cultural, Economic and Political Change in 43 Nations.* Princeton, NJ: Princeton University Press. Building on his important earlier work (Inglehart 1990), the author further elaborates his thesis about the conditions under which there is a shift in political culture toward less materialistic values, especially in the more prosperous countries.

Love, Nancy S., Ed. (1998). *Dogmas and Dreams: A Reader in Modern Political Ideologies.* 2d ed. New York: Seven Bridges Press. A solid reader that includes important writings by many key theorists of the three major "isms" plus anarchism, fascism, and feminism.

Mayer, Lawrence, and Erol Kaymak. (1998). *The Crisis of Conservatism and the Rise of the New Right in Western Democracies: Populist Revolt in the Late Twentieth Century.* Armonk, NY: M.E. Sharpe. An interesting exploration of the activities of ideologically-driven and rather alienated populist groups who have their roots in traditional conservatism but have diverged substantially from it in both their attitudes and their political styles.

Murray, Charles. (1997). *What It Means to be a Libertarian.* New York: Broadway Books. A short, readable application of libertarian ideology to many contemporary issues (e.g., abortion, education, drugs, economic regulation, free speech), written by one of America's most controversial social critics.

Nisbet, Robert. (1986). *Conservatism: Dream and Reality.* Milton Keynes, England: Open University Press. A short, illuminating discussion which traces the development of conservative thought and its significance in contemporary politics.

Putnam, Robert D. (1993). *Making Democracy Work: Civic Tradition in Modern Italy.* Princeton, NJ: Princeton University Press. Using communities in northern and southern Italy as his cases, the author develops a significant, and widely cited, argument about the role of political culture in sustaining democracy, and especially about the crucial importance of "social capital"—the citizens' willingness to engage and interact with each other.

Pye, Lucian W. (1985). *Asian Power and Politics: The Cultural Dimensions of Authority.* Cambridge, MA: Belknap Press. Extending the interests of his study of Burma/Myanmar, (Box 4.5), the author presents an intriguing account of the varying political cultures in East Asia. See also Pye's *The Mandarins and the Cadre: China's Political Cultures* (Ann Arbor: University of Michigan Press, 1988).

Sniderman, Paul M., Richard Brody, and Philip E. Tetlock (1991). *Reasoning and Choice: Explorations in Political Psychology.* New York: Cambridge University Press. A careful assessment of the extent to which Americans in the mass public actually do reason about political choices, focusing on such issues as racial attitudes, poverty, civil liberties, and AIDS.

Spencer, William. (1995) *Islamic Fundamentalism in the Modern World.* Brookfield, CT: Millbrook Press. A sensitive and informative discussion of the diverse ideologies and approaches associated with those generally termed Islamic fundamentalists.

Tucker, Robert, Ed. (1978). *The Marx-Engels Reader.* New York: Norton. An extensive selection of the important writings, with commentaries, from the major theorists of revolutionary socialism, Karl Marx and Friedrich Engels.

CHAPTER 3

Political Actions

Help us get drunk drivers off the road so you and I can drive without fear. Please don't leave it up to the "other guy." We need you....My husband was nearly killed because of a drunk driver. The driver of a pickup truck crossed the center line and struck us head-on. My husband suffered a broken arm and severe head injuries. As a result of a concussion he contracted spinal meningitis and almost died. I had broken bones myself.

After the crash, I was angry and hurt. But rather than sitting back and feeling sorry for myself, I turned my energies toward working against this problem of drinking and driving. I joined the Mothers Against Drunk Driving crusade because MADD fights to make our roads safe...for you, me and our loved ones.

Since our founding in 1980, we've made a great deal of progress—Congress passed a national Minimum Drinking Age Act...judges nationwide now impose stiffer drunk driving sentences...and government is taking drunk driving more seriously. Yes, we've made progress. But there's so much more to be done....Please help us continue our fight.

—MICKY SADOFF, MADD solicitation letter

Chapter 2 considered the nature of people's political beliefs. Ultimately, the more important issues regarding the individual in politics might be questions about what people *do* politically, not merely what they think. For instance, in the flag-burning incident described at the beginning of Chapter 2, the most relevant question from the perspective of the political world would be, "What did you *do* when you saw the woman?" In this chapter, we examine the prominent modes of actual political behavior of individuals. Moreover, many individuals, like Micky Sadoff, decide that they can be more effective politically if they act with others rather than alone. Thus, instead of engaging in a lonely act of protest, a person could join a huge demonstration; instead of writing a letter requesting a change in public policy, a person could join an organization that speaks for thousands of people.

Broadly, **political participation** is the term that is applied to *all of the political actions by individuals and groups*. The explicit objective of most political participation is *to influence the actions or selection of political rulers* (Nelson 1993: 720). What is the range of behaviors that a person might undertake in the political world? At one extreme are people who are obsessed with politics, see political implications in most of life's actions, are constantly involved in political discussion and action, and want to make political decisions for others. At the other extreme are people who have absolutely no interest in politics, pay no attention to political phenomena, and engage in no politically relevant actions. (In some instances, such as not voting in an election, not doing something can also be a type of political participation.) The first half of this chapter focuses on individual political action, considering the range of actions between the two extremes.

An individual can engage in virtually the same political actions as a member of a group. The actions of groups can be analyzed on some additional dimensions because of their size and structure. Thus the second half of this chapter considers the activities and types of the two major forms of political groups—interest groups and political parties.

INDIVIDUAL POLITICAL ACTIONS
Modes of Political Activity

Table 3.1 lists various modes of individual political action, with specific examples of action given for each mode. Broadly, the modes are ranked on the basis of the effort or costs required to perform that type of political action, and the examples within each mode are ranked according to the frequency with which Americans tend to perform them (see Milbrath and Goel 1982: 17–20). Some of the most extensive empirical and cross-national analyses of political participation, by Sidney Verba and his colleagues (Verba and Nie 1972, 1975; Verba, Nie, and Kim 1978), have emphasized four broad categories of political participation: (1) voting (see Table 3.2 on p. 52), (2) campaign activities, (3) personalized contacts, and (4) communal activities.

There have been two important changes in the recent empirical studies of political participation. First, it has become clear that political action should not be treated as a single dimension. Most early studies of political participation assumed that political actions were hierarchical—that is, that a person who performs a more difficult act, such as communal contacting, will also perform all less difficult acts, such as voting. The richer empirical studies, however, have indicated that there are different dimensions of political participation. Thus a person high (or low) on one mode of political action is not necessarily high (or low) on another. While there is some overlap, the campaign activists, communal activists, and those making personalized contacts are not necessarily the same people, and many people specialize in one or another mode. Also, protestors might not engage in any of the other activities, or they might engage in all of them (Dalton 1996: ch. 3, 4; Rueschemeyer, Rueschemeyer, and Wittrock 1998; Verba, Schlozman, and Brady 1995: ch. 3).

Second, there has been an increasing recognition of the significant level of unconventional political action, such as demonstrations, protests, and rioting, in both democratic and nondemocratic countries. Whereas Verba and his colleagues gathered data only on conventional forms of political action, analysts today often include unconventional modes of political action in their research (Dalton 1996: ch. 4). This trend is reflected in Table 3.1 in the "Revolutionaries"/ "Protestors" category, as well as in Table 3.3. Indeed, some analysts conclude that group protest activities have become so widespread that they are now an accepted and institutionalized form of participation in many democratic countries (Meyer and Tarrow 1997).

TABLE 3.1
Modes of Political Action

Actor Type	Characteristic Actions
Revolutionaries/Protestors	Undertake political violence against the political order
	Riot
	Engage in civil disobedience
	Join in public protest demonstrations
	Attend protest meetings
	Refuse to obey unjust laws
	Protest verbally if government does something unacceptable
Government activists	Candidate for/hold public office
Partisan activists	Contribute money to party, candidate, issue
	Attend meetings, rallies
	Actively work for party, candidate, issue
	Persuade others how to vote
	Join and support party
Community activists	Active in community organization
	Form group to work on local problems
	Contact officials on social issues
	Work with others on local problems
Communicators	Write letters to media
	Send support or protest messages to political leaders
	Engage in political discussions
	Keep informed about politics
Contact specialists	Contact local, state, or national officials on particular problems
Voters	Vote regularly in elections
Supporters and patriots	Show patriotism by flying flag, attending public parades, etc.
	Express love of country
	Pay all taxes
Inactives	No voting, no other political activity
	No patriotic inputs

Source: Most categories adapted from Milbrath and Goel 1982, figure 1.1.

Political Activists

Although the more routine modes of political action (listed in the middle and bottom of Table 3.1) constitute the vast majority of actual political behavior, most of us are particularly interested in the extraordinary actions of the few political activists who seem to "live politics." They might hold government office, spend many hours furthering a political idea or leader, or even risk their freedom and life in the pursuit of a dramatic change in the political order. At least three different types of political activists can be identified: foot soldiers, extremist-activists, and political leaders.

Foot soldiers. *Foot soldiers* are those activists who do the basic work of politics. They link the government and the top political leadership to the masses by performing such tasks as raising money for candidates or political issues, working in the local offices of political leaders, communicating the views of top leaders to citizens, and regularly voicing their opinions to political leaders. In most countries foot soldiers are members of political parties or groups with a political mission, although such membership is not necessarily synonymous with political activism.

Extremist-activists. *Extremist-activists* are outsiders who are willing to engage in extensive political action in pursuit of their vision of an ideal political world which would require a dramatic shift in the nature of the existing system. "Extremism" is a subjective and relative concept; a person is politically extreme only in comparison to some standard position, typically the broad center of the existing political order. Like foot soldiers, extremist-activists might engage in some conventional political activities inside the system. However, they more often engage in intensive modes of political action, ranging from organizing grassroots movements to guerrilla warfare, that are on the edge of or outside the system.

Political analysts have focused considerable attention on individual extremist-activists, especially revolutionary leaders. (Two examples are featured in Chapter 4, Box 4.4.) A *revolutionary* is a person who desires to overthrow the existing political order and to replace it with a quite different one, using political violence if necessary (see Chapter 12). Some revolutionaries, such as Mao Zedong (China), Fidel Castro (Cuba), and Nelson Mandela (South Africa), eventually achieved leadership roles in their political system, after years or even decades of struggle. Others, including Che Guevara (Cuba, then Bolivia) and Steve Biko (South Africa), have died in the struggle and become martyrs to those committed to revolutionary change. The largest number of revolutionary leaders have acted in relative obscurity, eventually burning out, being captured by the state, or dying as a result of political violence.

There is also increasing attention being paid to extremist-activist groups. Contemporary examples range from such organized groups as the Zapatista National Liberation Army (EZLN) in the Chiapas area of Mexico to the looser groupings of anti-foreigner nationalists in Germany. The label "political extremist" can also be applied to other "radicals" whose beliefs locate them on the margins of the existing system, even when they either have no explicit goal to transform the entire political system or do not emphasize the use of violence. Examples of such extremist-activists are found in many countries, such as neo-Nazis in the United States, Islamic fundamentalists in Algeria, and Greenpeace environmental activists in Brazil.

Political Leaders.   Many of us are fascinated with such ultimate political activists as Fidel Castro, Winston Churchill, Adolf Hitler, Saddam Hussein, and Richard Nixon. These top political leaders are distinctive because they succeed in capturing supreme political power within a government and using it with extraordinary energy and effect (whether good or bad). Their titles vary by country and level of government and include chairman, chancellor, dictator, governor, king, mayor, president, prime minister, and supreme leader, among others. A top political leader might put his substantial political power and position to admirable purposes, might implement reprehensible policies, or might accomplish virtually nothing. These political leaders have been the subject of more descriptions, analyses, and evaluations than any other type of actors in the political world. They will frequently be a subject in this book.

Political Participation Studies

Once categories of political action are established, a basic research question is: How many people participate in each category, both within and across various national political contexts? In studying participation, Milbrath and Goel (1972) argue that only a small proportion of the population can be termed "gladiators"—those people who are active in the most demanding forms of political action, such as protest and extensive partisan political work. They concluded that only about 5 percent of the adults in the United States were gladiators and more than half of the adults were either "observers" or "apathetics." More recent empirical research reports that about one in five adults in the United States engages in no political activity and another one-fifth do little more than vote. This research also suggests that only about 5 percent of the population engage in a significant level of political activism (Verba, Schlozman, and Brady 1995: 50–54, 72–74).

Some empirical data compare levels of participation across many countries. The most reliable of these comparative data measure voting in national elections. Table 3.2 provides these data for selected countries. The most striking observation about these figures is the huge variation in voting level, ranging from a reported 98 percent in Vietnam to only 28 percent in Haiti. Notice the very high voter turnout in countries such as Cuba and North Korea (which reports voting participation at about 99 percent). In such countries, voting is primarily a symbolic act that is supposed to express support for the existing political leadership, not an action in which citizens select their leaders. Unlike Vietnam and Cuba, nearly every country in Table 3.2 does now offer the voters a choice among candidates. However, there is considerable variation in the extent to which the choice is genuine and the votes really do determine the top leadership. There are some countries (e.g., Kenya, Singapore, Zimbabwe) where one group is virtually assured of victory and other countries (e.g., Algeria, Myanmar) where the top leadership or the military has repudiated the elections if they do not approve of the electoral results. These variations regarding the act of voting alert us to a general problem in cross-national analyses of micropolitical data—the same action or belief might have a quite different meaning and significance in different settings.

It is even more difficult to do empirical, cross-national comparisons between other modes of individual political participation. Even more than with voting, the same act can vary in meaning in different political and cultural environments. For example, the significance and potential personal risk of a public political protest is far greater for a person in North Korea than in South Korea, and greater in both those countries than for someone in Sweden.

The most consistent finding in virtually all recent comparative research on participation in democracies is clear: Most people do not regularly engage in high levels of political activity (Dalton 1996; Rueschemeyer, Rueschemeyer, and Wittrock 1998; *World Values Survey* 1994; see also the earlier studies, such as Verba, Nie, and Kim 1978). Apart from voting, which *is* a political act completed by many/most citizens (Table 3.2), high levels of persistent political activity tend to be uncommon in most political systems. For example, Dalton (1996: Tables 3.3 and 3.5) finds that fewer than one in ten citizens engages in active, partisan activities in the four Western democracies in his study.

TABLE 3.2
Voting Participation in Selected Countries: Percentage of Adults Voting in National Election

Country	Percentage	Election Year	Country	Percentage	Election Year
Vietnam	98%	1998	Czech Republic	74%	1998
Cuba	97	1997	Bangladesh	73	1996
Singapore	96	1996	Netherlands	73	1998
Australia	92	1998	United Kingdom	71	1997
Mongolia	92	1993	Costa Rica	70	1998
Cambodia	90	1997	Russia	69	1996
Indonesia	87	1999	Poland	68	1995
Denmark	85	1998	Kenya	66	1993
Uruguay	85	1994	Portugal	66	1996
South Africa	85	1999	South Korea	64	1996
Italy	83	1996	Canada	62	1997
Greece	82	1993	India	62	1998
Turkey	85	1995	Algeria	60	1999
Slovak Republic	84	1998	Japan	60	1996
Iran	81	2000	Colombia	59	1998
France	80	1995	Ukraine	59	1999
Palestine (territory)	80	1996	Hungary	56	1998
Sweden	80	1998	United States	49	1996
Israel	79	1996	Ireland	48	1997
Mexico	78	1994	Guatemala	39	1996
Norway	78	1997	Pakistan	37	1997
Spain	77	1996	Nigeria	31	1993
Taiwan	76	1996	Haiti	28	1995
Sri Lanka	75	1994			

Sources: *Facts on File* (various, biweekly); *Electoral Studies Journal* (various, quarterly).

A second broad finding is that some citizens are willing to engage occasionally in more activist modes of political participation. While very few citizens participate in violent protests against people or property, Table 3.3 indicates that a significant number of people perform certain less-conventional political acts, including some actions that require considerable effort or risk. In the majority of countries listed in the table, 30 percent or more of the citizens have engaged in at least one "challenging act" (e.g., a lawful demonstration, boycott, or building occupation). The photograph that opens this chapter depicts citizens engaged in a demonstration against government policy, while other citizens protest against their protest. Skinheads and Ku Klux Klan members march in opposition to the celebration of Martin Luther King's birthday in Tennessee, flanked by African-Americans who mock them with fascist salutes.

These cross-national differences underscore the third broad observation based on these empirical participation studies. There is substantial variation, from country to country, in the proportion of citizens who undertake various forms of conventional and unconventional political action. In the data in Table 3.3, the difference in rates of activity (from highest to lowest) between countries is often a ratio of 3:1

"I'M HAVING SECOND THOUGHTS ABOUT THE ELECTION... I'M NOT SURE I VOTED AGAINST THE RIGHT PERSON."

or higher (except for voting). For example, nearly four out of five Canadians have signed a petition whereas fewer than one in ten Nigerians has done so. And more than one in three Italians and Russians have participated in a lawful demonstration, compared to about one in twenty Turks or Hungarians. In some countries, there can be an explosion of protest behavior and political violence against the regime during periods of unsatisfactory political or economic conditions. Such political behavior can manifest itself in strikes, violent demonstrations, insurrections, and revolutionary action.

In democratic countries, about which we have the most systematic empirical data, the evidence generally supports the conclusion that most individuals employ the conventional modes of voting and contacting public (elected or appointed) officials as the key means of achieving political objectives. But data like those in Table 3.3, which reveal a notable level of unconventional participatory modes involving protest or political violence, have increased recognition among analysts that individuals' choices of political action might not conform to the democratic model. It is also clear that many individuals continue to rely on nongovernmental channels to achieve objectives that could be pursued by contacting public officials (Nelson 1987: 117).

Although systematic, comparative data on less democratic and nondemocratic countries are limited, it seems that the reliance on nongovernmental channels and the incidence of unconventional political behavior are greater (and vary more substantially) there than in democratic systems. In some less democratic countries, state repression deters the great majority of citizens from participation. And there are

TABLE 3.3
**Level of Less-Conventional Political Actions in
Selected Countries**

| Country | Mode of Political Action | | | |
	Sign Petition	Boycott	Lawful Demonstration	Occupy Building
Belarus	27%	5%	18%	1%
Brazil	50	10	19	2
Bulgaria	22	4	15	2
Canada	77	23	22	3
Chile	23	4	30	4
Denmark	51	11	27	2
France	54	12	33	8
Great Britain	75	14	14	10
Hungary	18	2	4	0.1
India	25	17	17	1
Italy	48	11	36	8
Mexico	35	7	22	5
Nigeria	7	13	20	2
Japan	62	4	13	0.4
Poland	14	6	12	4
Russia	30	5	33	1
South Africa	34	15	15	2
South Korea	42	11	20	11
Sweden	72	17	23	0.2
Turkey	14	6	6	2
United States	72	18	16	2

Note: About one thousand respondents in each country indicated whether they had engaged in the action.

Source: *World Values Survey, 1990–1991* 1994.

countries characterized by "de-participation" in recent decades, as the political leadership has weakened or even eliminated the mechanisms that enable citizens to engage in political actions (Nelson 1987: 116–120).

GROUP POLITICAL ACTIONS

Recall the letter from Micky Sadoff of MADD at the beginning of this chapter. Rather than suffer privately, Sadoff decided to take political action. She became a leader, and ultimately the president, of MADD. This group has developed into an effective, nationwide organization in the United States. MADD recruits members and solicits contributions and then uses its resources to lobby politicians to pass more aggressive policies for punishing drunk drivers.

Sadoff's story is quite dramatic, but it illustrates the most common reason why people join political groups. A person might want to influence the actions of his government but might believe that his individual actions will not make any difference. People tend to feel that they are relatively powerless in politics when acting alone—but there might be strength in numbers. If a person joins with many others in a political group, it is possible that the group can exercise influence in the political world because of the group's numbers, organization, and capabilities.

Although a few political activists can have a major impact on politics, most individuals, most of the time, have a minimal effect on political decisions and actions. Even in democracies, casting a vote is their primary political act. But if huge numbers of votes are cast (more than 100 million votes are cast in a U.S. presidential contest), one individual's vote is politically insignificant.

To have a greater impact, an individual's best strategy is to combine his political actions with those of others through a political group. Groups are extremely important in politics because they are often the major mechanism through which individuals are linked to the political system; hence their label as "linkage institutions." Some political groups, such as a major political party, can have wide-ranging goals and a huge membership. Other groups, such as MADD, are more narrowly focused in their objectives and have limited membership. The rest of this chapter describes the nature and activities of various kinds of political groups and political parties.

As an analytic concept, a **group** can be defined as *an aggregation of individuals who interact in order to pursue a common interest*. It is the pursuit of a common interest that is most crucial to this definition, since the individuals do not necessarily interact directly with one another. The factor that distinguishes a **political group** from other groups is that the common interest which the group pursues is a political objective—an interest in a particular policy or action that might be taken.

A distinction is usually made between political interest groups and political parties, although both types fit under our general definition of political group. A political group enters the special category of *political party* when the group seeks not merely to influence political decisions but also to place its members in the actual roles of government, such as chief executives and legislators. Although this distinction can become rather fuzzy among the most politically active groups, we shall treat political parties as a category different from other types of political interest groups.

POLITICAL INTEREST GROUPS
Activities of Political Interest Groups

All political interest groups share the common objective of attempting to influence the allocation of public values. But such groups can employ a variety of strategies to achieve this purpose.

Political action.   The most direct methods to achieve political objectives involve some form of political action. Such action might be taken by all group members or by some members who formally or informally represent the entire group. Depending on the political system, this might entail voting and campaign activities to influence the selection and action of political authorities. Or the group might attempt to articulate its interest to political actors by such communication techniques as letter writing, personal contact, petitions, rallies, or political violence.

Provision of material resources.   Political interest groups also can provide goods or services to political actors. Such a strategy assumes that provision of goods and services will influence decision makers to be more favorably disposed toward the interests of a group. Each political system develops its own rules about the methods and amounts of money or goods that can be given legitimately to political actors. The line between legal and illegal provision of money and goods varies dramatically across political cultures. In some political systems, all it takes to shock people is the revelation that an interest group has given a political actor a small gift, but in many political systems it requires a multimillion-dollar kickback to a politician to shock the citizens and provoke action.

The United States is one of the countries where extraordinary amounts of money are now contributed to political actors by interest groups. In the 1996 elections, for example, political action committees (PACs) contributed $207 million to political parties and $214 million to congressional candidates, nearly ten times the PAC money contributed in 1976 (U.S. Federal Election Commission). Most of these contributions are legal, although some are not (e.g., in 1997 the Democratic Party returned more than one million dollars to questionable donors and President Clinton was widely criticized for "renting the Lincoln bedroom" for overnight visits in the White House by big contributors).

The ethics of a system in which political interest groups can make huge contributions is increasingly questioned. It is obvious that money is given in the expectations of influencing the making of public policies. Although cause-and-effect relationships are hard to establish, PACs for the utility companies contributed $10.3 million to 1988 campaigns for U.S. Congress members, who, in turn, supported an obscure provision within federal law. This law delayed the repayment of improperly collected funds from ratepayers for up to thirty years, netting the utility companies a savings of $19 billion (a handsome 1,845:1 return on investment) (Birnbaum 1993). No one knows the amount of illegal resources that are distributed, although scandals regarding bribes and kickbacks seem to be reported more frequently in most countries. In 1992, for example, the kingpin of Japan's dominant Liberal Democratic Party, Shin Kanemaru, was imprisoned for accepting more than $50 million in illegal contributions from construction companies. In a wry comment on American politics, humorist Will Rogers once observed that "our Congress is the best that money can buy."

Exchange of information.   Another activity of some interest groups is the provision of data and information to those within the political system. The interest group may have specialized information that the political system would find difficult or impossible to attain from other sources. These private groups have a vested interest in the public policies that emerge, and so most actively provide data that support their own interests. For example, in the early 1980s, the U.S. Congress began consideration of a law requiring mandatory air bags as a safety restraint in automobiles. In attempting to determine whether to pass such a law, legislators were particularly influenced by information provided by automobile manufacturers (whose data indicated that air bags were costly, would reduce fuel economy, and would not substantially reduce overall injury levels in automobile collisions). This critical information, from a highly interested party to the decision, was an important rationale behind the refusal of Congress to require air bags (Reppy 1984). Later in the decade, a barrage of counter-information from another interest group, the insurance industry, persuaded Congress and the public that air bags could save lives and lower insurance premiums, resulting in laws requiring air bags.

Political action can have an impact. Two Greenpeace activists chain themselves to a dump ship while other supporters demonstrate on a nearby boat. The group prevents the dump ship from loading industrial waste along the English coast, forcing it to return to port.

In many countries, as the scale of government and the reach of public policy have expanded, many organizations in society need detailed, insider information about what the government is doing or intends to do that might affect their organization. Thus Salisbury (1990; Salisbury et al. 1991) has concluded that American interest groups in Washington, D.C., now spend more time gathering information *from* the government that is relevant to their organizations' interests (e.g., changes in rules or laws) than they do providing information *to* the government that might influence its policies.

Cooperation.   Major interest groups can also exert influence through their compliance or noncompliance with the government policy process. In many countries, government actors understand that successful policy implementation is enhanced when they develop policies that are acceptable to the affected interest groups. There are many countries (especially industrial democracies such as France, Japan, South Korea, and Sweden) in which government cultivates a special relationship with the interest group representatives of major economic organizations, such as business, labor, and farmers. When such interest groups can help the government implement policy, they enjoy a privileged position. Governance based on close cooperation with major sectoral interest groups is termed "corporatism" (see Box 8.3). For example, the British ministry responsible for agriculture and food works closely with the interest group representing the food manufacturers, so that the manufacturers, rather than the government bureaucracy, take most responsibility for inspecting and monitoring food hygiene (Wilson 1991). Obviously, an organization benefits greatly when its interest group persuades the government to allow the organization to regulate itself.

Constraints on a Group's Behavior

Each interest group must decide what mix of activities is most likely to serve its political agenda. This mix is dependent upon many things. Among the most important constraints on the interest group's behavior are the nature of the group's political resources, the objectives it pursues, and the political environment in which it operates.

Political resources.   A group's **political resources** are *those elements, controlled by the group, that can influence the decisions and actions of political actors.* The political resources that are most effective can differ according to the situation and the political system. The previous section emphasized the impact of financial resources and information, but certain other political resources can also be influential: control of factors of production, social status, legality, special knowledge or skills, ability to mobilize large numbers of people (who are the source of demands or supports), capacity for social disruption, and access to decision makers. Various groups will usually have dramatically different levels of such resources. An interest group's behavior will depend on the kinds of resources it has available and its calculation of the costs and benefits associated with using a particular mix of resources.

Objectives.   The *objectives* that interest groups pursue in the political world are as diverse as the different policy issues upon which the government might act. One group might want one specific thing, such as a subsidy for growing wheat, while another group might have very broad objectives, such as a set of policies to eliminate poverty. The groups' strategies and the probability that they will be successful are each related to the nature of the groups' political objectives. In general, an interest group is advantaged to the extent that its objective (1) is quite similar to existing policy, and (2) is a value allocation that the political system has the capacity to make. For example, the Greenpeace groups in France and Germany are more likely to influence government policies on safer disposal of nuclear wastes than to stop the development of new nuclear power stations, and these groups have little capacity to achieve worldwide nuclear disarmament.

Political environment.   At the most basic level, the demands that groups can make and the actions in which they can engage depend on the boundaries of acceptable political action within the particular *political environment.* Every example of interest group action given thus far in this chapter has focused on a group operating in a democratic political system. An essential feature of democratic systems is that interest groups have quite extensive rights to make political demands and engage in political actions.

In democracies such as Great Britain, Italy, and Japan, professional representatives of interest groups (lobbyists) are as much a part of the accepted set of governmental actors as elected legislators and their staffs. In Japan it is common for senior government officials to "descend from heaven" (*amakudari*) to a high-paying lobbyist's job for a major corporate interest. In the United States, more than 23,000 registered, full-time professional lobbyists work in Washington, D.C. (Petracca 1992: 13), and one analyst contends that the total number of people engaged primarily in lobbying activities is more than 80,000 (that is, more than 140 professional lobbyists per member of Congress) (Birnbaum 1993).

In contrast, repressive political systems tolerate only a very narrow range of interest group activities that are in opposition to the leadership. Such groups, especially their leaders, usually face extensive harassment and punishment from the authorities. Nonetheless, groups periodically emerge to articulate demands for political, social, and economic changes. Occasionally, the state responds positively to these demands. Some interest groups are eventually granted a major role in the political process, as happened in Poland to Solidarity, which during the 1980s evolved from an illegal trade union to a legal trade union to a government opposition movement to an important political party whose leader (Lech Walesa) was elected president of the country. Other groups have successfully engaged in a combination of political violence and mass mobilization to overthrow the existing regime, as did the Sandinistas in Nicaragua in 1979.

In general however, one of the key features of a repressive political system is its capacity to stifle or crush opposition interest groups. Such groups therefore operate on the margins of the political system, ranging from small revolutionary cells such as the Sendero Luminoso in Peru to mass movements such as the democracy demonstrations in China in 1989.

Types of Interest Groups

A relatively simple and widely accepted taxonomy of political groups, proposed by Gabriel Almond (Almond and Powell 2000), can help us distinguish among political interest groups. Four types of political interest groups are identified: (1) associational, (2) institutional, (3) nonassociational, and (4) anomic.

Associational interest groups. The first type, the **associational interest group**, is organized specifically to further the political objectives of its members. One example is the British Medical Association (see Box 3.1). Another example is Common Cause, an American interest group whose citizen-members pay a membership fee to support the lobbying activities of a central staff. The leadership of Common Cause identifies political issues of significance to the group's members and then attempts to mobilize political action (such as letter-writing campaigns and press releases) in support of a particular position on the issue. The group also provides decision makers with information and data and contributes funds to some political candidates.

Institutional interest groups. Almond's second type, the *institutional interest group*, is an organization that has been formed to achieve goals other than affecting the political system but that also acts to seek political objectives. Most occupational and organizational groups recognize that the decisions of the political system sometimes have major impacts on their own interests. Thus they have a formal or informal subunit whose primary purpose is to represent the group's interests to the political system. For example, the University of California is a large institution of higher education, but its interests are strongly affected by local, state, and national policies on educational funding, research funding, regulation of research, discrimination in admissions and hiring, tax law, patent law, collective bargaining, and many other policies. Consequently, the university has full-time professional and student lobbyists on each campus, in Sacramento (the state capital), and in Washington, D.C.

BOX 3.1

The British Medical Association: An Effective Associational Interest Group

The British Medical Association (BMA), a professional organization for doctors in Great Britain, exists primarily to provide technical and professional information to member doctors and to protect the standards and practices of the medical profession on matters of education, training, qualifications to practice, and discipline in instances of malpractice.

The BMA is a good example of an effective associational interest group because, in protecting the professional and financial interest of its members, its professional staff and members take many actions to influence the policies of the British government regarding the health care system. Some of the policies of obvious interest to the member doctors are those concerning training of doctors, pay issues, client choice of doctors and hospitals, and the quality and quantity of medical facilities. The BMA also is concerned about public policies regarding such issues as advertising by professionals, judicial rulings on liability, personal and business taxation policies, certification of health care paraprofessionals (e.g., chiropractors), support for medical research, and so on.

Given the wealth of its members, the BMA can contribute substantial amounts of money to influence policy makers directly or to finance public information campaigns. Its members command respect from political actors because of the doctors' high status and social standing. The BMA is also a source of vast information and expertise about health care issues for those public officials who must formulate and implement health care policy. But the BMA's greatest leverage on political actors is its capacity to cooperate or withhold cooperation, since it can powerfully influence the extent to which most doctors support the nationalized health care system in Britain. Thus the British Ministry of Health works extremely closely with the BMA, as the interest group representing most doctors, in all public policy decisions relevant to health care.

Nonassociational interest groups.   In Almond's classification, *nonassociational interest groups* are fluid aggregates of individuals who are not explicitly associated with a permanent organizational entity but who share some common interest over certain issues and may become politically active on an issue. A loosely structured organization might temporarily emerge to plan and coordinate political activities, but the group will be temporary and relatively informal and, once the issue has lost its immediate salience, the group will disappear. If an interest group emerges in your community to stop a building development, or to recall a public official, or to promote a particular law, it can be categorized as a nonassociational interest group.

Anomic interest groups.   Short-lived, spontaneous aggregations of people who share a political concern are termed *anomic interest groups.* For Almond, a riot is the clearest example of this type of interest group—the participants tend to share a common set of political interests or grievances, which they express through a generally disorganized outpouring of emotion, energy, and violence. A political demonstration is a somewhat more organized version of anomic interest group activity. What defines an anomic interest group is a group political action that emerges with little or no planning and then quickly stops.

POLITICAL PARTIES

An interest group is transformed into a **political party** when *the group attempts to capture political power directly by placing its members in governmental office.* The political party is the broadest linkage institution in most political systems, because most parties are overarching organizations that incorporate many different interests and groups. While countries can have thousands of political interest groups, most have only a handful of political parties.

Activities of Political Parties

There are six broad activities, or functions, fulfilled by political parties in most countries: They (1) serve as brokers of ideas, (2) serve as agents of political socialization, (3) link individuals to the system, (4) mobilize and recruit activists, (5) coordinate governmental activities, and (6) serve as organized sources of opposition to the governing group.

Serving as brokers of ideas.   The first, most central activity of political parties is to serve as major brokers of political ideas. Many individuals and political groups have interests and demands regarding the policies of government. A crucial function of political parties is to aggregate and simplify these many demands into a few packages of clear alternatives. To the extent that political parties are effective in this activity, they dramatically reduce the complexity and scale of the political process for the decision maker, who must perceive and respond to the individual and group demands, and for the voter, who must select political leaders whose overall policy preferences are closest to his own.

While all political parties are brokers of ideas, parties can be differentiated into two broad categories—ideological and pragmatic—on the basis of their intensity of commitment toward those ideas. *Ideological parties* hold major programmatic goals (e.g., egalitarianism, ethnic solidarity, Islamic fundamentalism) and are deeply committed to the implementation of these goals to achieve comprehensive changes in the sociopolitical order. Ideological parties are usually extreme, within the context of their particular political culture. The Islamic Salvation Front in Algeria, the North Korean Communist Party, Sínn Fein in Northern Ireland, the American Libertarian Party, and the German Green Party (see Box 3.2) are examples of ideological parties.

In contrast, *pragmatic parties* hold more flexible goals and are oriented to moderate or incremental policy change. To achieve electoral success, pragmatic parties might shift their position or expand the range of viewpoints they encompass. Parties of the center are characteristically pragmatic parties. Examples include the Christian Democrats in Germany, the Congress-I Party in India, the Institutional Revolutionary Party (PRI) in Mexico, and the Democratic Party in the United States.

Facilitating political socialization.   A related activity of political parties is their socialization of individuals into the political culture (see Chapter 4). In many political systems, individuals develop a clear "party identification." This means that a person trusts one political party to represent his political interests. The person's political beliefs and actions are influenced by information that a political party provides or by the person's perceptions of what the party supports. Even if an individual does not have strong party identification, political parties can be an important source of political knowledge.

Linking individual and system.   In its role as a linkage institution, a political party connects individuals and the political system. Most individuals rely on political groups to represent their interests within the political system. More than other groups, political parties function in a general manner to formulate, aggregate, and communicate a coherent package of demands and supports. And, if the party gains political power, it can attempt to implement those demands on behalf of the individuals whose interests it serves. Thus political parties greatly facilitate the individual's sense of integration into the political process.

Mobilizing and recruiting political activists.   The political party offers a well-organized and obvious structure within which an individual can direct his political interests. It is a source of political information, of contact with other politically relevant individuals and groups, and of effective access to the political system. In many political systems, involvement with a political party is the primary mechanism through which individuals are drawn into roles as political foot soldiers and, ultimately, as political gladiators. Often it is political parties that select the candidates for political positions or have the power to place individuals directly in positions within the political system. Whether one is considering a highly democratic polity such as Great Britain or an extremely nondemocratic one such as China, most or all individuals in key executive and legislative positions have achieved these positions through recruitment and selection by a political party.

BOX 3.2

Let's Party! The Rise of the Green Party in Germany

Few political interest groups transform into successful political parties. The Green Party in Germany emerged from an interest group in 1980, won twenty-seven seats in the national legislature in the 1983 election, and then forty-two seats in the 1986 election. The party won no seats in 1990, but regained forty-nine seats in 1994 and held forty-seven seats after the 1998 election.

Where did the Green Party come from? Like all political groups, it began with people who wanted to influence politics. There were people in West Germany who were displeased by their government's policies in the late 1960s, especially the West German government's support of U.S. actions in Vietnam and Southeast Asia.

But some West Germans were also concerned about other political issues. For these people, their government, and the entire "establishment" in their society, had been corrupted in its quest for ever-expanding power and wealth. Some were angered by the huge inequalities in wealth and welfare within their society and between countries. Some disliked the discrimination against certain groups, such as women and ethnic minorities. Some were fearful that the huge buildup of nuclear weapons by the superpowers would result in war in Europe. And some felt that the quest for material well-being and the thoughtless use of new technologies were taking a huge toll on the quality of the environment.

In the late 1960s these antiestablishment sentiments appeared in most industrial democracies. Often, as in Germany, "leftists" and students were most visible and active in expressing these political views. They demonstrated, they marched, they formed protest groups, they tried all forms of political action that might reduce the political failures they saw. In contrast to most other countries, however, the politically disaffected West Germans did not disappear from politics with the end of the Vietnam War period. Energized mainly by young, countercultural Germans, thousands of small citizen groups emerged in many German towns.

These citizen groups continued to press policy makers at all levels to respond to the major political issues noted above, and they criticized the existing political parties for their failure to deal effectively with the problems. By the late 1970s these groups moved from protest politics to electoral politics and began to elect some of their members to local office, especially in larger cities. Some of the most dynamic individuals in these local groups developed a national network. They decided that the objectives shared by the local groups could be best promoted by the formation of a single, national political organization. After several conventions, representatives of more than one thousand of the local groups agreed in 1980 to form a national political party, Die Grünen (the Greens). (This discussion is based on Mewes 1987.)

The common concern that holds the many individuals in the Green Party together is a commitment to preserving the environment. Thus most Germans initially viewed the new party as an environmental party, and it drew support from the

(continued)

BOX 3.2 *(Continued)*

right, center, and left of the traditional German political spectrum. Its electoral support in the national elections of 1982 and 1986 came particularly from younger voters and from the more educated, middle classes. In Europe the Greens are viewed as the first important party representing the "postmaterialist values" discussed in Chapter 2 (Kolinsky 1993).

The Green Party is an ideological party, but it is composed of individuals with quite diverse ideological concerns. The core activists in both the local groups and the national party tend to be radical in their politics. Thus the platform of the Green Party includes strong antiestablishment elements. The party ideology emphasizes the transformation of Germany from capitalism to a system in which workers own and control industry; from a militaristic, NATO-based country to one that becomes neutral, eliminates nuclear weapons, and stops preparing for war; and from a leading postindustrial society to one that uses only those technologies that do not damage the environment.

The Green Party had substantial impact on German politics in the 1980s, struggled in the early 1990s, and became a somewhat uneasy partner in the governing coalition after 1998. Despite its resurgence, the future of the Green Party at the national level remains uncertain. Will major parties, especially the Social Democratic Party, capture the Green's electoral base by effectively promoting moderate environmental protection policies? Can it avoid self-destruction caused by the strong ideological differences among its moderate and its more radical factions? Many people believe that this party is too wild to last much longer.

Coordinating governmental operations.   The fifth major activity of political parties is to coordinate the actions of the government. The political party can encourage or require its members to work together to achieve shared policy goals. It can establish an internal hierarchy, with party leaders (e.g., in the U.S. Senate, majority and minority leaders, whips, committee chairs) controlling the actions of the party members in the conduct of government. The parties can also provide mechanisms for facilitating cooperation and regulating conflict among different parties. Leaders of several parties might form a coalition in order to secure majority support for certain policies. Such coalitions are especially important in legislatures where no single party commands a majority. Political parties can also establish forms of power sharing in the conduct of government business. For example, the parties can agree to formulate executive or legislative committees in a manner that reflects the political strength of the various parties.

Serving as sources of opposition.   Finally, where the political system has more than one party, the parties not participating in the governing group can serve as an explicit and organized source of opposition. The function is most fully institutionalized in Great Britain, where the major out-of-power party in Parliament is explicitly designated as "Her Majesty's Loyal Opposition." The party should oppose, but never obstruct, the actions of the governing party, since the opposition party remains loyal to crown and country. In Britain, the opposition party is guaranteed control of a specified amount of time during legislative sessions. The opposition leaders receive salaries to serve as a "shadow government," with a member of the opposition serving as the alternative, and potential future replacement, for each top official in the government. Hence there is a "shadow prime minister," a "shadow minister of defence," and so on, who articulate what they would do if they held ministerial positions as the governing party.

DOING POLITICS

Politics comes alive when people engage in political action. The participation in a protest march, the attempt to persuade a friend to share your political perspective, even the act of voting can be a moment of heightened experience. Acting alone or with others, the individual who takes political action can seek to serve his most crass self-interest or the altruistic goal of global prosperity.

This analysis has indicated the diverse modes of political action as well as the rather modest levels of such actions reported by most people. Some people are shocked that so many citizens do not even bother to vote in a country such as the United States. Others are surprised that anyone really thinks that one person's involvement in politics, whatever the level of commitment, will make any difference in the grander scheme of things. Political participation is a crucial topic for analysis because people's actions are at the heart of the political process.

In this chapter, you have been introduced to the methods and findings of micropolitical analysis. Could you undertake such an analysis yourself? Yes! Before you conclude this chapter, Box 3.3 shows you how you might do it by studying your own peers.

To this point in the book, our treatment of micropolitics has focused mainly on description and taxonomy—on what people believe about politics and on what political actions people are prepared to undertake. For a richer analysis, however, we must at least attempt to answer the *why* questions: Why do people engage in a particular political action? Can we explain the apparent differences in people's political beliefs and political actions? This is the essential issue in Chapter 4.

FOR FURTHER CONSIDERATION

1. Why and how might the failure to act politically be viewed as an act of political participation?
2. Apart from voting, what political action do you think is most important?
3. Imagine that you could engage in a conversation with the political activist, contemporary or historical, who most fascinates you. Whom would you choose? Why? What would you ask him or her?
4. Should there be any limits on people's rights to join political groups and to influence political decision makers? What principles can you offer to justify any such limitations?
5. What is the most extensive political action in which you have engaged? If the same circumstances arose now, would you behave any differently? Why?

BOX 3.3

Measuring Students' Political Behavior: An Example of Micropolitical Analysis

Let's consider how you might study the political participation of American college students. Do you consider yourself an active participant in the political world? How many of the actions listed in Table 3.1 have you engaged in during the last three years? How might you assess whether most college students are politically active? Using the methods of survey research, you might begin to analyze your own or others' political activity level. Here are the key steps.

1. *Conceptualizing variables.* Our objective is to describe and explain college students' political participation. The first task of such an analysis is conceptualization. This entails developing a set of concepts that clarify and elaborate on the basic idea(s) that you wish to analyze. Table 3.1 provides one useful framework for conceptualizing various modes of political participation (e.g., voting, rioting, contacting officials).

2. *Operationalizing variables.* Once you have decided which modes of participation you will study, you need to specify them more carefully so that you will be able to delimit those instances where the activities have actually occurred. This process is called the operationalization of variables. You indicate in detail how key concepts are identified and measured in actual research settings. Operationalization of variables must be done with care and often is more complicated than it initially seems. For example, in operationalizing the concept of voting, do you want to distinguish between voting in national elections and in local elections, as Verba and Nie (1975) did? Do you want to determine the proportion of elections in which the individual voted? Do you want to distinguish between those who are and are not registered to vote? Notice that many such questions merit consideration when you attempt to operationalize a major political variable. You must make these decisions before you gather data, or you will not get all the information necessary for your analysis.

3. *Data collection.* Once you have defined your operational indicators, the next activity is to collect data. This step entails identifying the population (the set of subjects) you wish to study and developing a strategy to gather empirical data that measure your key variables for all or some sample of this population. Assume that the population for your study is the students at your college (notice that this is an extremely limited sample for generalizations about all college students).

   Typically, it is not feasible to gather data for everyone in the group about whom the analyst wishes to generalize, and so a procedure is developed to sample a subset of the group. This can be done by gathering data for anyone who is willing to respond, by selecting people at random, or by devising a more sophisticated sampling strategy that ensures adequate representation of certain key characteristics among those studied (e.g., age, gender, ethnicity, socioeconomic class, region). This last strategy for sampling is normally

BOX 3.3 *(Continued)*

used by professional public opinion pollsters and by political scientists. The idea is to gather data from a subset that reflects the most interesting characteristics of the larger population.

In your study, you might not have time to gather data for all the students at your college (and certainly not all college students in America), so you might randomly select one out of every fifty students in the student directory to serve as your sample. It would be simpler to study the students in your political science class, but consider why a study of your political science class is likely to be more biased than a study from the sample from the student directory.

The next problem is deciding how to collect data about each student's actual political behavior. Since you cannot observe the behavior of all students, you would probably have to settle for asking them to report their own political activity, through some form of personal interview or questionnaire. To elicit accurate responses about the political actions you are interested in studying, you need an approach that encourages the respondent to answer honestly, with careful wording of the questions and precise recording of the responses.

4. *Data analysis: creating variables.* Once you have gathered the data, you must organize them in the forms that enable you to manipulate the data in various ways to answer your analytic questions. You can merely do analysis based on each student's response to each question. Often, however, the analyst wants to categorize or summarize the specific responses into broader variables.

For example, you might create a taxonomy of types of participants, based on the student's set of political activities or frequency of activities. For example, you could use ten modes of action based on the ten actor types listed in Table 3.1, counting the number of different modes in which a person had done something (during a specified time period). By this technique, each student would have a "political action score" ranging from 0 to 10. But you might decide that such a scoring system provides too little differentiation, because it gives equal value to types of political activity that are quite different in effort and political importance. A more sensitive measure might give a different *weight* to each political action, on the basis of its relative significance—for example, 10 points for protest behavior, 3 for partisan activity, 2 for voting, and so on. By summing such weighted scores for each subject of study, you could create an *index* that measures each subject's overall political activity more precisely.

Even more refinements could be added by the inclusion of additional data, such as the frequency with which each activity is undertaken. Most contemporary political analyses attempt to develop these more complex variables, because such measures allow for rich findings and generalizations.

Notice that virtually all of the decisions in the analysis, and especially those about measurement and variable creation, are made by you—the individual political analyst. There are no fixed rules regarding these decisions, although they are not arbitrary. The analyst must attempt to make decisions that are reasonable in terms

(continued)

BOX 3.3 *(Continued)*

of the analytic issues being considered and that are defensible, since others might question these decisions, in the spirit of the scientific method.

5. *Data analysis: description and explanation.* With your data and variables, you can now *describe* the political behavior of college students in your study. Some of the questions you might examine include the following:

What are the most frequent political behaviors that the students undertake?
How frequently do the students discuss politics?
What percentage are politically apathetic?
What percentage have participated in political rallies?

As you will find in Chapter 4, political analysts are rarely satisfied with answers to these kinds of descriptive questions. Whenever possible, they also attempt to generate more *explanatory* (correlational or causal) statements that search for general patterns among the behaviors or indicate the conditions that seem to cause certain types of political behavior to occur. To do this in your study, you might gather such additional data about your respondents as their personal traits, background experiences, and political beliefs. Then you might be able to offer tentative answers to such questions as these:

Do students who discuss politics more also have higher grade point averages?
Are older students more politically active than younger students?
Is political protest more common among social science majors than
    among science majors?
Is partisan activism correlated with parents' income level?
Is ethnicity associated with interest in politics?

As you can see, there are many fascinating questions that you can examine as you become a more insightful political analyst. For example, are college students different politically from young people who do not attend college? It would be even more interesting to examine these questions across different cultures: for example, what are the similarities and differences in the political behavior of students in China, France, Mexico, Kenya, Poland, and the United States? As political scientists gather more extensive databases and use more refined analytic techniques, they can begin to develop stronger generalizations about the nature and causes of political beliefs and actions.

FOR FURTHER READING

Brown, Michael, and John May. (1989). *The Greenpeace Story.* Scarborough, Ontario: Prentice-Hall. The fascinating history of an international group committed to fighting governments and huge corporations in order to protect the environment, but even more, a revealing study of its activist leaders.

Genovese, Michael A., Ed. (1993). *Women as National Leaders.* Newbury Park, CA: Sage. Detailed and interesting case studies of recent female political leaders, such as Corazon Aquino, Benazir Bhutto, Violeta Chamorro, Indira Gandhi, and Margaret Thatcher, assessing their leadership styles and whether they seem to govern differently than men.

Hoffman, Abbie. (1989). *The Best of Abbie Hoffman.* New York: Four Walls, Eight Windows. A selection of the funny, eschatological writings on radicalism and revolution by one of the key leaders (now deceased) of the student radical movement of the late 1960s and a member of the "Chicago 7," tried for conspiracy after the riots at the 1968 Democratic Party convention in Chicago.

Lowi, Theodore. (1979). *The End of Liberalism: The Second Republic in the United States.* 2d ed. New York: Norton. An incisive critique of the shortcomings of politics dominated by interest groups.

Ma Bo. (1995) *Blood Red Sunset: A Memoir of the Chinese Cultural Revolution.* New York: Viking. A harsh, gripping autobiography of a young person drawn into the fervor of Mao Zedong's Cultural Revolution. A Red Guard working on a hopeless program to create farmland in Mongolia, Ma Bo is transformed from a true believer into an embittered man fighting to clear himself from charges that he is a reactionary.

Meyer, David S., and Sidney Tarrow, Eds. (1997). *The Social Movement Society: Contentious Politics for a New Century.* Lanham, MD: Rowan & Littlefield. A stimulating set of essays examining the increasing acceptance of "social movements"—organized group social protest activities that are typically focused on a single issue area. Based on analyses in Western and Eastern Europe, Latin America, and the United States, there is an assessment of whether such protest is becoming a routine part of political participation and whether it has implications for democratic society.

Petracca, Mark P., Ed. (1992). *The Politics of Interests.* Boulder, CO: Westview Press. Diverse readings on the study of contemporary interest groups, with a primary focus on politics in the United States.

Randall, Vicky, Ed. (1988). *Political Parties in the Third World.* Ithaca, NY: Russell Sage; Newbury Park, CA: Sage. A useful collection of essays on political parties in Third World countries, ranging from democratic to dictatorial systems (e.g., Brazil, Cuba, Ghana, India, and Iraq).

Rueschemeyer, Dietrich, Marilyn Rueschemeyer, and Bjorn Wittrock. (1998). *Participation and Democracy East and West: Comparisons and Interpretations.* Armonk, NY: M.E. Sharpe. The current patterns of participation and activism are compared and analyzed, grounded in studies of the Czech Republic, Germany, Hungary, Norway, Poland, Sweden, and the United States.

Wilson, Graham K. (1990). *Interest Groups.* Oxford, England: Basil Blackwell. An introduction to the comparative study of interest groups.

The schools are a powerful setting in which political and cultural values are taught, as to these Young Pioneers in a Cuban school.

Influences on Beliefs and Actions

A friend who is skeptical about political science confronts you with a challenge. She brings three adults into the room and announces that one is an elected public official, one has never voted in a single election, and one has participated in many violent political protests. You must decide who has done what. You can ask each person one question that makes neither a direct nor an indirect reference to the three kinds of political behavior. How would you try to solve the problem? What questions would you ask?

In Chapters 2 and 3 we *described* people's political beliefs and political actions. Some of the most interesting questions in political analysis concern the *why* questions: Why do individuals hold particular political beliefs and engage in certain political actions? Figure 4.1 indicates four broad types of explanatory factors that might account for individual political behavior: (1) the person's environment, (2) agents of political socialization, (3) personal traits, and (4) personality. This chapter considers these four types of influences on the political beliefs and actions of individuals, from the apathetics to the activists. Thus it provides ideas about the kinds of clues that might help you respond to your friend's challenge.

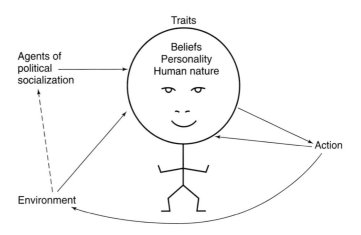

Figure 4.1 A framework for explaining individual political behavior

THE ENVIRONMENT

In a major election in Cuba in 1997, it was reported that 97 percent of the adults voted, whereas only about 49 percent of the citizens voted in a 1996 election in the United States. What best accounts for this difference? In Cuba, voting is an obligatory act, a required gesture of support for the current political leadership, rather than a genuine selection among candidates—indeed, there is no choice. Virtually everyone votes because a comrade who does not vote risks unwanted scrutiny by Communist Party authorities. In the United States, voting has always been a voluntary act; there are no sanctions for nonvoting. Thus the citizen decides whether her sense of civic responsibility or her desire to affect the outcome on ballot choices merits the effort of going to vote. Box 4.1 suggests why, from the perspective of rational choice theory, citizens might choose not to vote.

The example of voting in Cuba and the United States is suggestive of how a person's *environment*—the broad context in which an individual lives—can powerfully influence her political behavior. In its most comprehensive form, the environment includes literally everything outside the individual. It obviously includes political elements (e.g., governmental procedures, public policies, specific political events and actors), but it also includes elements of the social and cultural system (e.g., religious foundations, attitudes toward differences in such traits as ethnicity, gender, class), elements of the economic order (e.g., level of economic prosperity and development), and the physical features of the environment (e.g., topography, natural resources). For some analytic questions, it might also be important to distinguish between the environment as measured "objectively" by the analyst, and the environment perceived "subjectively" by the individual who is attempting to understand and act in the political world.

For any particular political belief or action, there are various possible effects from an environmental stimulus. An element of the environment might activate, repress, transform, or amplify an individual's political behavior. Since most elements of the environment are likely to have little or no effect at any given moment, the task of the political analyst is to identify those few environmental elements that do have especially significant effects on political belief or action, and to explain how these effects occur.

Since the environmental context is, at least in theory, of enormous scope, here are a few specific examples of how an aspect of the environment might affect political behavior. First, let us take two examples regarding the *political environment*:

1. *Effects on information about politics.* In Bolivia, information about politics is so limited that a villager might not be sure whether the most recent government coup has been successful and who the current political leaders are. In the United States, the politically interested citizen has access each day to hundreds of hours of television, radio, and reading materials regarding worldwide political events.

2. *Effects on individuals' political party involvement.* From the late 1940s to the late 1980s, Poland had only one legal political party, the Communist Party. Party membership, open to only about 10 percent of the population, was essential for citizens who wanted to hold political office or gain many other advantages in the society, such as preferential housing (see Chapter 15). During the 1990s, there were more than 200 active political parties in Poland. This opened

BOX 4.1

Are You Too Smart to Vote?

You know that you ought to vote in a democracy, so that you can help determine policies and political leaders. However, a logical argument can be made that if you are truly rational, you won't vote.

Many formal theories in political science are grounded in the approach called "rational choice theory" or "public choice theory" (see the Appendix). This theory assumes that political actors are rational and calculating. They can establish the costs and benefits to themselves of each outcome and they can select the most rational strategy to maximize the benefits relative to the costs. If you have studied microeconomics, you might recognize that this description is rather like the "economic man," another version of this rational actor.

From a rational choice perspective, you would be rather foolish to vote in a presidential election. The costs associated with voting are, at least, the time and energy you expend to register, to get to the polling place, to cast your ballot, and to get to the next place you are going. You could also consider the time and energy spent trying to understand which candidates will establish certain policies and to calculate the benefits to you of each likely policy. Even if you cannot think of things you would rather do with all that time and energy, the benefits side of the calculation is more daunting. Assume that you are smart enough to decide which candidate will actually enact policies that benefit you. As a rational actor, you still must ask: What is the chance that my vote will make a difference? In U.S. national elections, about 100 million votes are cast for the presidency. The probability that there will be a tie so that one vote (yours or anybody else's) will determine the outcome is infinitesimally small—certainly less than one in a trillion. So what's the point?

Since their theory assumes rational behavior, they need to explain why about 100 million folks are behaving irrationally. This is what rational choice theorists call the "paradox of participation" (Riker and Ordeshook 1973). (Of course, they could point to the 100 million people who do not vote and suggest that about half of the population *is* rational.) Why do people vote?

One argument is that your vote matters as part of the set of votes from a larger group that shares your interests. If all of your group acted rationally, the loss of the total set of votes might be large enough to affect the outcome of the election.

Secondly, the rationality of voting does increase somewhat in an election in which few votes are cast or in which you think the outcome will be close. This is occasionally true in local elections, where the margin between candidates can be rather small. Recent national elections in the United States have also been characterized by some very close races. In 1998, for example, Harry Reid, the victor for the Nevada Senate seat, received only 459 votes more than John Ensign, out of more than 415,000 votes cast. In 1994, a Connecticut seat in the House of Representatives was determined by less than 10 votes out of more than 158,000!

(continued)

BOX 4.1 *(Continued)*

A third kind of argument is that most people are not rational calculators. They make many decisions in their lives (e.g., whether to marry, whether to enroll in a class, whether to drive very fast) without any clear idea of the precise costs and benefits to them.

And a fourth explanation is that voting is primarily an expression of citizenship, social solidarity, and political communication. In this view, you might vote because you love your country and its democratic tradition, or because you want to be a small part of a large voice saying yes or no to political leaders, or because you want approval from your peers.

In short, the decision to vote can be based on some elements of self-interest or civic commitment. But if you are very rational and very selfish, voting should probably be rather low on your agenda.

party membership and opportunities to run for public office to virtually all citizens. However, party membership no longer affords the various advantages that existed during the Communist period, and thus the proportion of Polish adults who are active party members of *any* party is actually lower now under democracy than it was during communism.

Second, the broader *social, cultural, economic, and physical environment* can have more indirect but no less powerful influences on an individual's political behavior than the political environment. If the dominant religion in the cultural environment has traditionally relegated women to a secondary role, as in Afghanistan's adherence to the Shari'a laws of Islam, it is likely that most women's involvement in politics will be quite low. If the social environment has an undercurrent of racism, as in the United Kingdom, this will affect many aspects of the political behavior of both the majority and minority racial groups.

The impact of the environment on political behavior is sometimes quite hard to predict. If poverty is widespread in an economic system, will this influence the probability of political rebellion? On the one hand, such poverty might produce a frustrated population who will be responsive to a revolutionary movement promising future prosperity, and it might provoke a particular individual to become the leader of such a movement. On the other hand, the people might be too concerned about basic survival to have the time or energy to engage in political action.

It should be evident from these examples that there are many aspects of the environment that might influence political beliefs and actions. The analyst must be sensitive to possible environmental effects when attempting to provide an adequate explanation for a particular political behavior.

AGENTS OF POLITICAL SOCIALIZATION

Each person has a complex blend of political beliefs—of cognitive, affective, and evaluative orientations regarding political phenomena. (These three kinds of orientations were defined in Chapter 2.) Even individuals who exist in the same environment can hold very different political beliefs. Political socialization research attempts to explain how such differences in political beliefs can occur.

Political socialization can be defined as *the processes through which individuals acquire their orientations toward the political world.* An interest in how this process works is of obvious importance not only to political analysts but also to those, especially political leaders, who wish to influence people's political beliefs and actions. Plato (c. 428–347 B.C.E.) observed that society's most important function is civic training, the instruction of citizens regarding the nature of their social and political world and of their proper roles in that world. The appropriate content and style of such political socialization is subject to debate, since one person's vision of proper civic training might be viewed by another person as indoctrination and brainwashing.

Among political scientists, the emphasis in political socialization research has been on analysis of the *agents of political socialization*—the major sources of political training and indoctrination. The key concerns have been to identify these agents and to explain the processes through which they affect individuals' political orientations. There has been considerably less attention, and very limited empirical success, in linking the activities of specific agents of socialization to individuals' actual political actions. In this section we discuss some of the most important agents of political socialization: the family, the schools, peer groups, the media and culture, and events.

The Family

The family is the first, and often the most powerful and lasting, agent of political socialization. The political orientations of most individuals are deeply influenced by behaviors and beliefs experienced in the family environment. Before individuals are capable of making judgments for themselves, they have absorbed perceptions about the political world from conversations overheard within the family. For example, most 7-year-old children in the United States already identify with one political party and have affective orientations toward both major parties (Niemi 1974).

Even the pattern of interactions between parents and children can have political implications. If the family is very hierarchical, with the father or mother ruling with an iron hand, preventing discussion and using strong sanctions for disobedience, the child might assume that this is the appropriate pattern of authority relations in the society. If the family tends to discuss issues before it determines rules or decisions, the child might feel more strongly that she has the right to participate actively in decisions, even in the political world.

The family has been viewed as a major obstacle to the political agendas of some leaders. For example, Mao Zedong deeply opposed the traditional loyalties taught by Confucianism, which stressed obedience to the kinship group, to elders, and to males. When he came to power in China (1949–1976), he wanted every Chinese person to accept the equality of all individuals, regardless of age or gender. He also insisted that individuals should work cooperatively for the good of everyone in the society (the key

"I GOT RICH, DAD. WHERE DID I GO WRONG?"

NATIONAL REVIEW

slogan was "serve the people"). Mao identified the family as the major obstacle to these goals, called the family the "citadel of oppression" in society, and experimented with attempts to eliminate the nuclear family. When these attempts failed, Communist Party members put enormous pressure on families to "revolutionize" themselves by shedding their Confucian thinking and traditional behaviors. However, because Mao was pessimistic about the extent to which families would be able to change themselves, he relied heavily on other agents of political socialization, especially the schools and peer groups, to counter the influence of the family.

The Schools

From the perspective of the political authorities, the schools can be the state's most valuable agent for political socialization. Schools offer the opportunity for sustained and highly controlled contact with youth while they are at a highly impressionable age, when many political beliefs can still be molded. Apart from the family, the classroom is the most evident microcosm of society that most young people experience. The teacher is the authority figure, who rewards thinking and behavior that conform to what is deemed desirable by the society and who withholds rewards from or sanctions those who fail to conform. In most societies, students are taught to accept the authority of the teacher, to suppress their own desires, to value the symbolic rewards offered by the education system, and to interact with their peers in the manner approved by the school system. Moreover, in every school system there are rituals that support the political system. These might include songs, chants, or activities that express allegiance to political leaders or symbols.

Also important in shaping the student's understanding of the political world is the school curriculum. Educational authorities can control what subjects are taught, what textbooks contain, and even what teachers say and do. An extreme form of this central control over education was achieved during the French Fourth Republic (1946–1958). It was said that the minister of education in Paris could look at her watch and specify exactly what chapter in what textbook the children of a certain age were studying at that moment all over France.

Every textbook and every lesson in school is selective and thus contains biases regarding what is emphasized, what is ignored, and how meaning and value are established. Sometimes the level of indoctrination seems extreme, especially to those unsympathetic with the message. Here are three examples. As you read them, try to guess what subject is being taught and the country from which each example is taken.

> 1. Men are superior to women because God has made one superior to the other, and men spend their wealth to maintain the women.
>
> 2. Our forefathers believed, and we still believe today, that God himself made the diversity of peoples on earth....Interracial residence and intermarriage are not only a disgrace but also forbidden by law. It is, however, not only the skin of the Betas that differs from the Alphas. The Beta stands on a much higher plane of civilization and is more developed. Betas must so live, learn, and work that we shall not sink to the cultural level of the Alphas. Only thus can the government of our country remain in the hands of the Betas.
>
> 3. Imperialism knows no other type of relations between States except domination and subjugation, the oppression of the weak by the strong. It bases international relations on abuse and threat, on violence and arbitrariness. Between January 3 and June 10, 1961, Gamma military airplanes violated Delta airspace 3 times in the months of January, 15 in February, 17 in March, 9 in April, 8 in May, and 10 in June. What was the average monthly number of violations of Delta airspace by Gamma military airplanes?

Were you able to identify likely settings for these educational offerings? The first one is a chant by Moroccan 7-year-olds (substitute "Allah" for "God") (personal observation by the author, in Marrakesh). The second one is an excerpt from a South African textbook on race relations during the era of apartheid (1948–1988, substitute "whites" for "Betas" and "nonwhites" for "Alphas") (Thompson 1966: 100). The third one is mathematics as it is framed for Cuban children (substitute "Cuban" for "Delta" and "North American" for "Gamma") (Fagen 1964: 68).

These somewhat extreme examples reflect the manner in which the political authorities can influence the content of educational materials in order to buttress the view of the political world most aligned with their own interests. While subject matter in the schools of most nations is less openly political than these examples, the school system of every nation presents materials that are supportive of that nation's politics and dominant cultural norms.

Have you noticed anything odd about the use of pronouns *he* and *she* in this book? To counter the male dominance in the language of many American textbooks, I have alternated masculine and feminine pronouns in odd and even chapters. If you were conscious of the "strange" use of gender references in Chapter 2 and this chapter, your reaction may be indicative of the subtle way in which your cultural norms are reinforced by language and education.

Peer Groups

Although most people absorb a large proportion of their political socialization by the time they leave the educational system, learning never stops entirely. (See Box 4.2.) As the importance of parents diminishes and after formal schooling ends, peer groups become an increasingly significant influence on many individuals' political socialization. *Peer group* is a general term that includes friends, neighbors, and colleagues, at the workplace or in clubs and organizations.

The section on "'Everyone' as Authority" in Chapter 1 suggests the attraction of bringing one's views into closer conformity with relevant peer groups. In general, a person is more likely to be accepted by her peers if her beliefs and actions are consistent with those in the peer group. Also, it is possible that there is a subtle tendency for a person to be influenced by what "people like me" think. There is evidence that a person's social context (i.e., her peer groups) does modify political behavior (Agnew 1987; for contrary evidence, see Dunleavy and Husbands 1985).

In many cases, peers and others influence a person's political views via a *"two-step" communication flow* (Bennett 1996; Zaller 1992). People with greater interest and knowledge of politics absorb new information from various sources (step one). Then they relay what they have learned to others (step two), especially those in the mass public whose political beliefs are less salient and developed (recall Chapter 2). In general, direct communications from peers allow for a rich exchange of political information, since such political messages have the immediacy, credibility, and power of face-to-face interaction.

As noted earlier, China used the peer group as a major mechanism for political socialization under Mao Zedong. Small groups on collective farms, in factories, and in other workplaces not only were required to discuss their political beliefs and actions, but also were supposed to monitor the political behavior of everyone in the group. If an individual's views or actions strayed from the "mass line," the group applied various types of pressure to help the individual recognize and rectify her errors and return to the proper political position. If this pressure failed, more aggressive forms of peer pressure, including public ridicule (and ultimately, imprisonment), were employed to force the individual to conform. In China, peer pressure reached an extreme form during the Cultural Revolution in the late 1960s. Groups of true believers in the views of Chairman Mao Zedong organized themselves as the "Red Guard" and engaged in widespread peer pressure, repression, and violence against any Chinese who did not conform to Mao's ideology (Wen 1995).

The Media and Culture

Very few of us directly experience the great majority of political phenomena about which we claim knowledge. For most adults, the media, especially television, radio, and the press, become the major source of political information. Dan Nimmo and

BOX 4.2

Persistence versus Change in Political Socialization

The initial political socialization research emphasized the overwhelming importance of early socialization, from the family and from early educational experiences. According to this *lifelong persistence* interpretation, there is considerable stability in the political behavior of most people after adolescence. However, this view was challenged by evidence that political learning and attitude change do continue throughout adult life. This second interpretation emphasizes *lifelong openness* to further socialization, asserting that there is continual response to agents of socialization and only minimal lasting effects of early socialization. The idea that a person's political views can continue to change even during adult life is captured in the European saying that anyone who is not a communist at 20 has no heart and anyone who is still a communist at 40 has no head.

The current interpretation is essentially a compromise between these two extremes, the *life cycle* interpretation. In this view, persistence is the rule for political attitudes and behaviors that are learned early. However, political orientations can change as the result of the agents of political socialization, especially peer groups, and as the result of the individual's personal and social changes, especially at certain key points of development such as young adulthood (Jennings and Niemi 1981).

It is rare for people to undergo a dramatic transformation in their political thinking, but it does happen. The following story recounts such a change.

Do You Know Me?

A widely publicized instance of several political transformations in one person involved a 19-year-old American college student. She had been raised in an extremely wealthy family, enjoying all the privileges of the upper class, and was a quiet, even dull, young woman. She had no apparent political views other than those of her conservative, Republican background. Suddenly, one evening in February 1974, she was kidnapped by a radical group, locked in a closet for fifty-five days, and subjected to extensive physical and mental abuse and indoctrination.

In her next public appearance—robbing a bank—she had become Tania, revolutionary sister in the Symbionese Liberation Army. Tape recordings were circulated in which she denounced the "fascist ruling class" and "capitalist pigs," including her own parents, and called for a people's revolution. After a lengthy effort, law enforcement officials captured her, jailed her again, and subjected her to another round of political indoctrination. Finally, she appeared in court in 1976, subdued and generally apolitical. She was convicted of bank robbery and served twenty-three months (of a seven-year sentence) in federal prison. President Carter commuted her sentence in February 1979. By this time, she had (again?) fallen in love with one of her jailors. She married him and now lives an apolitical life in suburbia, complete with service to social causes such as children with acquired immune deficiency syndrome (AIDS) and Alzheimer's disease, and she published a mystery novel in 1996.

(continued)

BOX 4.2 *(Continued)*

That young woman is Patty Hearst. Her story received enormous media coverage, perhaps because many people were fascinated with this incredible tale of political transformations. Many argued about the "true story" and about which, if any, of Patty Hearst's beliefs were authentic. (She tells her own story in *Every Secret Thing* [1982] and a movie based on her experiences was released in 1988.) Yet, we can never fully know what another person really thinks, and in many instances it is hard for us to be sure even of what we think ourselves. Most of us suspect what George Orwell (1949/1967) emphasized in his ominous novel *1984*—that under certain conditions of physical or psychological torture we can be made to think we believe anything, even that we love Big Brother.

Patty Hearst as Tania

James Combs (1990: xiii) argue: "Few people learn about politics through direct experience. For most persons, political realities are mediated through mass and group communication, a process that results as much in the creation, transmission, and adoption of political fantasies as it results in independently validated views of what happens." They claim that each of us creates a personal vision (a "fantasy") of political reality, based mainly on what is communicated to us by such information sources as other people, the mass media, and popular culture. Regardless of how fantastic our political visions are, it is important to understand that the media can be a crucial agent of political socialization for either stability or change.

These information sources really do *mediate* between the individual and most political reality. While most media content is not explicitly political, much of it does contain subtle information that influences how one thinks about politics and society. Exposure to television and radio is extensive in most countries. Thus the individual is bombarded with messages about values, lifestyles, and so on. While sweeping generalizations about the impacts of the media on individuals' political beliefs and actions are not possible, two broad observations can be offered.

First, the research generally concludes that few people absorb media information in a way that significantly changes most of their political attitudes or actions. Rather, people interpret and retain media information selectively to reinforce their existing attitudes. And many people, especially those with less sophisticated political belief systems and minimal political knowledge (Chapter 2), do not even pay much attention to the media that provide political information. The media-based information for such people often comes from a politically knowledgeable peer who, as described previously, seeks information from the media and then transmits such information to others.

Second, however, there is considerable evidence that the media are of growing importance in shaping many people's understanding of specific political phenomena. The mass media are especially significant in drawing people's attention to some political phenomena rather than others—a situation termed *agenda setting.* Also, the overall tone and key themes in the media coverage of the issue can be absorbed by the individual, influencing her reactions to it (Iyengar 1994).

For most people, the media have their greatest impact during situations of political drama (e.g., war, major political crises, elections). Newspapers are still credited with the greatest impact on knowledge about politicians and issues among more educated individuals (Davis 1997; Graber 1996; Korzenny and Ting-Toomey 1992). However, for the reasons suggested in Box 4.3, television is increasingly the mass medium with the most substantial political impacts on the largest number of people.

Consistent with Box 4.3, much of what you know about the political world from the media is contingent on what topics the media choose to expose you to and what content the media select to report. Like textbooks, the media are not neutral; someone has made selections regarding subjects and content. Of course, you are not completely passive in the process. In most countries, the individual can choose among alternative media sources and can attempt to evaluate the truth of what she reads, hears, and sees in the media.

However, it is often the case that the major media are owned and controlled by the government or by members of the wealthy, dominant class in the society. The print and broadcast media are free of substantial government censorship in about one-third (36 percent) of the countries, which include only 20 percent of the world's population (Freedom House 1999). Through its ability to control the media in the past, the government had a significant resource for affecting people's political socialization, exposing them to "news" and information that reinforced its views of the political

BOX 4.3

What You See Is What You Get

You probably have a hunch that television has become *the* most powerful form of communication now shaping peoples' political orientations. While the empirical evidence on this point is not conclusive, there are some very significant reasons why television might increasingly be such a significant force in political life.

1. *High exposure.* Citizens in both industrial countries and developing countries watch greater amounts of television each year. In the United States, for example, most adults spend as many hours with the mass media (predominantly television) as they do at work, and their children spend more hours watching television than attending school. These levels are also being reached in many other societies (Skidmore 1993). There is growing evidence that such a high level of exposure has an impact on an individual's social and political values, even if little of the programming is explicitly political (Savage and Nimmo 1990).

2. *The power of the visual.* The biochemistry of the human brain affects the impact of television. Generally, the brain responds very strongly to visual cues, less to complex patterns of sound and imagery, and even less to sound or written text. Moreover, visual input produces direct emotional arousal, which is the most potent neurochemical condition for learning and attitudinal change. Because the images on television are generally simple and can evoke strong emotional response, they generate visual information that is both easy to process and has an extremely high impact on learning and attitudes (Masters 1992).

3. *Agenda setting.* People's immediate views on politics are greatly influenced by what they believe to be important. Television, and especially television news, focus on certain political issues, people, and events, and not others. Most people tend to identify as significant those political topics that are "in the news," and topics that receive little or no media coverage usually have minimal salience for the public. Thus television increasingly sets the political agenda by establishing what issues are worthy of attention and public concern (Iyengar 1994).

4. *Priming and framing effects.* Television "primes" a viewer about a political topic by providing her with information about how she should understand the topic, the kinds of information that are relevant, and the criteria that she should employ to evaluate it. Television "frames" the topic by providing the viewer with a broader structure and context within which to consider it. Television generally simplifies complex issues by using specific and dramatic examples to explain a topic. For example, television news will typically examine an issue (e.g., poverty) by concentrating on a visually engaging story about specific individuals, not by emphasizing the basic societal dynamics that generate the problem. Thus television's treatment leads the viewer to attribute responsibility for a political issue to the

BOX 4.3 *(Continued)*

personal shortcomings of individual actors. It discourages the viewer from recognizing underlying social, political, or economic forces that have created the problem and are appropriate targets for solutions (Iyengar 1994).

Most people rely increasingly on television to provide them with information about the political world. As television directs our attention to the simple, the visual, the individual, and the evocative on only selected political topics, our ability to understand and evaluate politics in complex and subtle ways atrophies. Many researchers argue that these factors account for some of the most undesirable features of contemporary politics: the prevalence of simplistic political discourse based on sound bites, the decline of political parties, single-issue politics, negative political campaigns, and spin doctors who further distort the media's presentation of politics (Graber 1996; Kellner 1990; Neuman 1999).

world. The recent explosion of telecommunications technologies (such as satellite television transmissions and the Internet) has made it increasingly difficult for a government to control the sources of information reaching its citizens. Consequently, most governments are becoming less effective in shaping people's political beliefs through the media, even as the media are an ever more important source of people's political "reality."

Culture offers an interesting alternative to the media and to other agents of political socialization. Culture, like the media, can be extensively controlled by the dominant political order in a society and can be used to reinforce the state's view of the political world. Cuba, like many of the communist states in the past, has generally insisted that culture meet the standards of "socialist realism," which means that no art, theater, or cinema is to be produced that is abstract or, most importantly, that fails to celebrate the virtues of socialism.

Culture need not reinforce the dominant order, however. It can inform and criticize subtly, by means of metaphor and symbol, in ways less likely to be interpreted as a direct challenge to the established authorities. This is especially true in societies where there is considerable censorship of the media and state control of most sources of public information. During the 1980s in still-communist countries such as East Germany and Poland, for example, an extensive body of fiction, cinema, poetry, theater, art, and music emerged with political content critical of the state's views (Larkey 1990). Culture can also be openly subversive, directly attacking mainstream values or advocating opposing values. For example, Jamaican reggae music offers a revolutionary vision of an alternative social and political world for its people. While most contemporary Anglo-American music has little explicit political content, this kind of expression can be found in songs by such performers as Sting, U2, and Bruce Springsteen, as well as in some rap music (Hemphill and Smith 1990).

Events

The general effects of the environment on political beliefs and action have already been discussed. While the context of everyday life has slow, evolutionary effects on a person's political behavior, a particular event can act as a sudden and powerful agent of political socialization. For example, Sarah Brady shifted from "politician's wife" into a tireless activist on behalf of gun control legislation after her husband, James Brady, who was President Reagan's press secretary, was shot in an assassination attempt on the president. Another example of mobilization due to a dramatic event is the transformation of Micky Sadoff into a MADD activist (recall the example at the beginning of Chapter 3).

While an extraordinary event can transform an individual's political behavior, it is also possible that the general flow of events during an entire period can influence political orientations, especially of individuals who "come of political age" during the period. For example, the combined impacts of such events as American military involvement in Vietnam and Southeast Asia, the hippie culture, and the Nixon presidency seem to have had strong effects on the political understanding of many Americans who were reaching adulthood during the late 1960s. In Europe, many of those who experienced the rise of fascism in the 1930s developed intense feelings about Germany and Germans, about fascism, and about the dangers of attempting to compromise with an aggressive country or its leaders.

PERSONAL TRAITS

As one part of your strategy for solving the challenge at the beginning of the chapter (to link the three people to specific political behavior), you might consider their physical appearance or *personal traits*. The research suggests that you can make some broad inferences about political behavior on the basis of certain "objective" personal traits of the individual. These *personal traits*, sometimes called demographic characteristics, include age, education, gender, ethnicity, income, social class, and occupation. What underlying dynamic might link personal traits with political behavior?

Personal traits can be thought of as filters that influence the manner in which the environment and the agents of political socialization affect an individual's political behavior. For example, the relevance of the environmental factor of Islamic fundamentalism will have very different effects on the political beliefs and behaviors of Afghan men and women. Similarly, the current impact of parents as agents of political socialization is likely to be greater for a person of 14 than for one of 64.

Much of the empirical research on political behavior attempts to establish and clarify the relationships between personal traits and specific political beliefs or actions. No single personal trait is a certain predictor of political behavior, but empirical research (based on relational analysis) in many countries indicates that some personal traits are associated with certain political beliefs and actions. And when key personal traits seem to reinforce each other, you might have greater confidence in a correct prediction about political behavior. Of particular interest to researchers (and to politicians) have been studies indicating who is more likely to vote and identifying factors that seem to explain the particular voting choice.

For example, can you think of any personal traits that might inform your prediction of whether a particular person voted for Clinton, Dole, or Perot in the 1996 U.S. presidential election? Table 4.1 (like the example of correlational analysis in the Appendix) provides actual data for exploring those linkages. Do any personal traits seem associated with a tendency to vote for a candidate? In addition to comparing a particular category across candidates, another reasonable technique for assessing this question is to determine whether there are instances where the candidate's percentage for a category (e.g., high school graduates) is noticeably different from the candidate's percentage of the total vote.

While most of the differences are not dramatic, some demographic traits do seem to correlate with support for particular candidates. Notice, for example, that the probability of voting for Bill Clinton was substantially higher if a person had a certain trait: African-American, Latino, female, less than 30 years old, non-Protestant, a high school graduate or less, a post-graduate education. The probability of voting for Bob Dole was especially high among Protestants and among those at the highest levels of family income. It appears that Ross Perot voters were distributed more equally across demographic categories than were those of Clinton and Dole, although Perot had somewhat more support among high school graduates and those who did not identify with any religion. With which group did each candidate have the least success?

While there are clear associations between variables, we cannot conclude that any personal trait actually *caused* a person to vote for one of the three candidates (see the discussion of correlational and causal analysis in the Appendix). And when several personal traits are associated with voting choice, we also cannot determine which of them are the most powerful predictors of candidate choice without statistical

TABLE 4.1
Voting Choices in the 1996 American Presidential Election, by Personal Traits

Total	All	Clinton (49%)	Dole (41%)	Perot (8%)
Gender				
Male	48	43	44	10
Female	52	54	38	7
Ethnicity				
African-American	10	84	12	4
Asian-American	1	43	44	8
Caucasian	83	43	46	9
Chicano-Latino	5	72	21	6
Age				
18–29	17	53	34	10
30–44	33	48	41	9
45–59	26	48	41	9
60 and older	24	48	44	7
Education				
Not a high school graduate	6	59	28	11
High school graduate	24	51	35	13
Some college	27	48	40	10
College graduate	26	44	46	8
Postgraduate education	17	52	40	5
Religion				
Catholic	29	53	37	9
Protestant	38	41	50	8
Other religion	6	60	23	11
Jewish	4	78	16	3
No religion	7	56	26	14
Family Income				
Under $15,000	11	59	28	11
$15,000–29,999	23	53	36	9
$30,000–49,999	27	48	40	10
$50,000–74,999	21	47	45	7
$75,000–99,999	9	44	48	7
$100,000 and over	9	38	54	6

Source: CNN/TIME exit poll
Some rows do not total 100% due to rounding.

analysis (such as regression analysis, a statistical technique that identifies how much variance in the dependent variable—vote choice, in this case—can be attributed to each subject's level on various independent variables). Nonetheless, Table 4.1 does provide reasonable support for our assumption that personal traits are sometimes associated with political behavior.

While generalizations are always difficult, there is, for example, some consistency in the empirical research on the personal traits of those who do vote (in political systems where there are genuine voting choices). In general, a higher probability of voting is correlated with such traits as membership in organizations with interests in politics (e.g., political parties, unions), higher education, higher income, higher social class, greater age, and gender (male). Incidence of voting is also associated with the individual's political beliefs, especially a strong identification with a party, a greater sense of personal capacity to influence the political world ("political efficacy"), and better understanding of the available political choices.

Research findings on other modes of political behavior are less extensive and less consistent. As in the taxonomies of participation, the cross-national work by Verba and his colleagues (Verba and Nie 1972; Verba, Nie, and Kim 1978) remains among the most influential in identifying the individual traits correlated with each mode of political action. Participation in campaign activities is especially linked with higher education, higher income, and gender (male). Socioeconomic traits are also most strongly correlated with the likelihood that an individual engages in communal activities, and identification with a particular social group (religious, ethnic, or linguistic) can be extremely important if there are political cleavages associated with these group differences. Contacting government officials personally is least clearly related to personal traits, and some research suggests that the decision to engage in personal contacting depends more on whether the individual has an effective private means to gain her objective. Contacting might be the domain of political action that has increased most during the last several decades (Verba, Schlotzman, and Brady 1995).

In studying extremist-activists, many analyses attempt to specify the personal characteristics that typify a particular type of activist, relative to the general population. For example, most rural extremist-activists, who are usually engaged in a struggle for control over land, tend to be male, poor, and of limited education. The urban activists who promote leftist ideologies (e.g., Marxism, environmentalism) are generally characterized as being well educated, middle class, mainly young, and only slightly more likely to be male than female. The right-wing urban activists are more varied. Those promoting an ethnic or racist position (e.g., neo-Nazism) tend to be young, male, working or lower class, and somewhat lower in education. But those promoting causes such as the antiabortion movement are more middle-aged, female, middle class, and relatively well educated (Dalton 1996: ch. 4; Fendrich 1993; Meyer and Tarrow 1997).

Overall, what would you expect about the personal traits of top political leaders in a given society? Perhaps the broadest generalization is that leaders' personal traits tend to be quite consistent with the socially dominant traits within their society. Why do you think this occurs? Among the most common traits, across many societies, are high education, upper middle-class or upper-class background, adherence to the society's dominant religion, and male gender.

Given our general fascination with extraordinary political actors such as presidents, charismatic leaders, and revolutionaries, it is interesting to assess whether particular environments, socialization experiences, and/or personal traits seem to account for the political behavior of these individuals. Box 4.4 briefly describes the environment, socialization, and personal traits of two remarkable political activists. Do these factors seem relatively comparable for the two men? Do these factors seem to produce similar political behavior?

POLITICAL "PERSONALITY"

The three types of explanatory factors discussed to this point either are outside the individual (the environment and agents of political socialization) or are surface traits (e.g., age, ethnicity). However, some political analysts insist that an adequate

BOX 4.4

YOU GO YOUR WAY, I'LL GO MINE

The two young men have some common roots. Both are born into colonial societies ordered by traditional social systems of hierarchy and male domination and by strong, fundamentalist religion. Both are sons of prosperous professional fathers, who are devout and emphasize the importance of orthodox religion in the home. Each young man displays high intelligence and receives an excellent education in colonial schools.

As young adults, each trains successfully for a professional career and enters that career. At this time, each is shocked by his exposure to ethnic or racial discrimination and by his realization of the severe deprivation that characterizes the lives of the great majority of people in his society. Family background, training, and experiences cause each to develop a deep commitment to the independence of his people from their colonial masters, who each believes are the source of oppression and injustice. Each decides to devote his life to political activism and to employ extreme political acts, as necessary, to achieve his vision of social justice. But each man follows a very different path.

The first man is driven from his home when his father's extensive land holdings in Palestine are seized by another ethnic-religious group. This group proclaims sole political rights over the entire region, declaring it a sovereign country, Israel. Angered by what he perceives to be widespread victimization of his own ethnic group, he flees to Saudi Arabia, a country that shares his religion and ethnicity. Unable to get a job as an engineer, he is soon arrested, tortured, and deported because of his political activities on behalf of his former homeland. Further disillusioned, he concludes that his cause can be advanced only by more extreme acts.

In a rare interview, he observes: "There doesn't seem to be a peaceful way to solve a problem in this world. When you look at the Arab story throughout centuries, you see that peaceful solutions never work and it won't solve our problem.... My enemy is the Zionists in my homeland, Palestine. My enemy is also the imperialist government in any form. My dream is for a united Arab nation, freedom, righteousness and equality....The imperialists have united themselves and combat us everywhere. So have we also united under the motto: Repressed, unite yourselves!... Fair struggle means the right of a people to fight against the usurpation of their land by all available means. Terrorism is the liquidation of innocent people without reason..." (*Der Spiegel* 1985).

He goes underground, changes his name to "Father of the Struggle," and organizes a terrorist group, el-Fatah. He was not seen publicly or even photographed for more than twenty five years. His group has claimed credit for more than 250 terrorist acts, including killings at the Rome airport in 1986, seizure of the cruise ship *Achille Lauro* in 1985, and the bombing of a Pan American jetliner over Lockerbie, Scotland, in 1988. The CIA deemed his organization "the most dangerous terrorist organization in the world." He has been on the most-wanted list of the Israelis and Americans, as well as being on the death list of Yasser Arafat's

BOX 4.4 *(Continued)*

Palestine Liberation Organization. In 1999, some claim he was spotted in Egypt, taking treatment for cancer. Meanwhile, members of his group continue to function in support of the Palestinian cause.

The second man witnesses racism against blacks while serving as a lawyer in South Africa. To resist such injustice, he develops a strategy of political activism. This strategy, inspired by an American, Henry David Thoreau, as well as by his own religious principles, emphasizes civil disobedience. His fundamental principle is *ahimsa*—nonviolence in thought as well as in action. He advises his followers: "Not to submit; to suffer." He is repeatedly jailed for his nonviolent resistance to laws that he believes are unjust. He assumes that the opposition will discredit itself by its repressive responses to nonviolent protest.

Returning to his native India, he begins to organize protests demanding independence from the British imperialists. His protest techniques continue to be based on nonviolence and *satyagraha*—soul force. In contrast to brute force, soul force provokes constructive change through positive action and reconciliation, not through harming and angering the enemy. He observes, "My experience has shown me that we win justice quickest by rendering justice to the other party." He becomes an extraordinarily powerful and inspirational leader through his theatrical acts of civil disobedience and through his personal sacrifices, including extended fasts, lengthy marches, and sexual abstinence. His nonviolent activism captures world attention and his Indian followers expand into the tens of thousands. His supporters call him "*Mahatma*"—great soul. His tireless political activism, in deed and in word, contributes substantially to the developments that lead, three decades later, to the granting of independence to India by the British. His life of struggle is not a complete success. He fails to prevent the division of India into separate countries dominated by Hindus and Muslims, a struggle bloodied by 500,000 deaths. He fails to persuade Hindus to repudiate the divisive and unjust social caste system. And he is assassinated by a Hindu extremist within months of India's independence. (Discussion based on Broomfield 1982.)

Abu Nidal (1937–) and Mohandas K. Gandhi (1869–1948), despite their similarities, diverged onto nearly opposite pathways of political activism in the pursuit of their personal visions of social justice and human liberation.

explanation of political behavior requires explication of the *political personality*—the psychological dynamics inside the individual.

Personality

Personality can be broadly defined as *the propensities within an individual to act a certain way, given a particular context.* If someone is usually cheerful or aggressive or thoughtful under a variety of circumstances, this style of behaving could be termed a personality trait of the individual. The cluster of basic personality traits that dominates an individual's attitudes and behavior is what most people mean when they talk about someone's personality "type." It seems plausible that political personality could influence the political beliefs and actions of any individual. However, most of the empirical research examining political personality has focused on political activists. It is assumed that analyzing the political activists' personalities will promote a better understanding of their actions (past, current, and future). Political personality analyses are found in biographies, in opinion pieces in the media, in our conversations about top political leaders, and even in leaders' own speeches and writings.

Normative approaches.   People have always had strong opinions about the kind of personality that a political leader *ought* to have. What personality characteristics do you think are desirable in a political leader? Perhaps no one is better known for advice about the kind of personality a political leader needs than Niccolò Machiavelli (1469–1527), author of *The Prince* (1517/1977). Machiavelli believed that society tends toward disorder, in part because events are substantially dependent on "*fortuna*"—an amalgamation of chance, fate, luck, and unpredictable circumstances. The political leader must act decisively to overcome *fortuna*. She must think strategically, suppress moral judgments, and act with fierce resolve.

"Everyone sees what you seem to be," Machiavelli (1517/1977: ch. 18) observed, "few know what you really are." Thus the leader must combine the qualities of the lion (aggression, bravery) and the fox (cleverness) and must make the citizens completely dependent on her every decision and action. In the pursuit of the good society, the leader must be single-minded and, if necessary, ruthless, in order to achieve desirable ends. Machiavelli insisted that the effective political leader will face many situations where the ends justify the political means, even if ethics must be sacrificed: "To preserve the state, he often has to do things against his word, against charity, against humanity, against religion….[H]e should not depart from the good if he can hold to it, but he should be ready to enter on evil if he has to" (Machiavelli 1517/1977: ch. 18).

Empirical approaches.   While some studies offer normative perspectives on political personality, most contemporary studies are empirical and aim to explain the behavior of top political leaders and activists. These studies attempt to identify their key personality traits (such as idealism, aggressiveness, and decisiveness) and then to link those traits to specific political beliefs and actions. Some political personality approaches delve quite deeply, explaining the psychological needs, drives, or experiences embedded in the individual's psyche that are the underlying forces resulting in her political behavior.

In this perspective, activist political behavior is seen as a response to an individual's psychological life history. For example, Harold Lasswell (1960), one of the intellectual founders of behavioral political science, argues that the activist political personality is motivated primarily by the drive to overcome failure in the fulfillment of private needs. In his symbolic notation, $p > d > r = P$. This notation means that a person's private needs (p) are displaced onto public objects (d) and rationalized in terms of the public interest (r). The result is "political man or woman" (P). In Lasswell's formulation, the activist's political behavior is rather pathological, since the strong drive for power is essentially a substitution for a low sense of self-esteem.

A related example of political personality research is the classic study *The Authoritarian Personality*, by T. W. Adorno and his colleagues (1950). In the aftermath of the horrors of German Nazism and anti-Semitism during World War II, these scholars attempted to analyze people who become supporters of rigid, ideological political movements or who are deeply prejudiced. On the basis of many types of psychological testing of individuals, the researchers characterized a personality syndrome they termed **authoritarianism**. Initially, they defined the personality traits of those with this syndrome:

Authoritarians are extremely conventional in their attitudes and morality.

They are particularly hostile toward minorities or those with unorthodox lifestyles.

Their world is organized on the principle of hierarchy—they offer obedience to those of high status and they attempt to dominate those perceived to be below them in the sociopolitical order.

Adorno and his colleagues were particularly interested in moving beyond description to answer a crucial *why* question: Why does someone develop an authoritarian personality? While their answers are complex, their basic explanation, rather like Lasswell's, emphasizes "externalization." Like most of us, Adorno et al. argue, the people who become authoritarians experience aggressive impulses and strong sexual drives during childhood; but these people had iron-handed parents who suppressed their children's opportunities to express these impulses and drives. As teenagers and adults, they project (externalize) this pent-up hostility onto groups that they judge to be inferior to themselves, such as ethnic minorities and gays. At the same time, their love and fear of the authoritarian parent lead them to venerate those who exercise great power in the society.

There have been many criticisms of the methods and findings of Adorno et al. (1950). Some research (McClosky and Chong 1985; Rokeach 1960) has suggested that authoritarianism can be found among people who support extremist politics of either the right or the left. Adolf Hitler seems to have believed this. He instructed Nazi Party officials to accept immediately into membership anyone who had previously been a Communist, the archenemies of the Nazis. Presumably, Hitler assumed that these people, who were called "Beefsteak Nazis" (brown on the outside, red on the inside), would redirect their vigorous political support from one ideological extreme to the other. But most studies have reinforced the basic notion in *The Authoritarian Personality* that the syndrome is fundamentally associated with a psychological and political conservatism.

Empirical, personality-based approaches have also been used to account for the behavior of other types of political activists, such as student radicals. As someone who has experience with other students, what do you hypothesize about the student radicals? Are student extremists different from other students in their intelligence or idealism or independence? Are student radicals of the left different from student radicals of the right?

In terms of personality, most research concludes that student radicals tend to be more intelligent, creative, idealistic, and independent than the nonradicals (Fendrich 1993). In studies of British and French students, the radical (leftist) activists exhibit "highly principled moral reasoning," in which their political behavior is justified in terms of a logical and consistent belief system and abstract notions about social justice (O'Connor 1978). Although these admirable characteristics are often attributed only to leftist radicals, there is evidence that they apply to all political radicals, whether their political orientation is left or right (Kerpelman 1972). While a few empirical studies identify some student radicals with substantial personality disorders of the type hypothesized by Lasswell (1960), the research generally suggests that student radicals are different from their nonradical peers in positive ways. Similarly, the most systematic empirical evidence about top political leaders suggests that the majority are actually higher on self-esteem and psychological well-being than the average adult (Sniderman 1975).

At a general level, it has been posited (Woshinsky 1995: ch. 11) that the behavior of political leaders can be explained by their responsiveness to some combination of seven "incentives" that they connect powerfully with political action: (1) the urge to solve public problems; (2) the need to be accepted by others; (3) the search for fame and glory; (4) the desire to follow their conscience in serving society; (5) the pleasure derived from competition and manipulation of others; (6) the satisfaction from commitment to a transcendental mission; and (7) the desire for praise and adulation.

Some of the most detailed analytic work using the political personality approach develops an extensive *"psychobiography"* of the individual political activist. In essence, such analyses attempt to provide information about the political activists' personalities and to explain how such information helps us make better sense of how and especially why they act as they do. Erik Erikson (1958, 1969), among the most influential scholars in this tradition, adopts a Freudian framework to identify the crucial importance of child rearing and early socialization through adolescence in determining the activist's later political behavior. (See Erikson's psychobiographies of Martin Luther [1958] and Mohandas Gandhi [1969].) Lucian Pye

(1962) follows Erikson's approach in analyzing an entire class of political leaders in postcolonial Burma/Myanmar (Box 4.5).

BOX 4.5

Psychoanalyzing Burmese Political Leaders

Lucian Pye (1962) has provided an interesting application of the psychohistorical approach to explain the behavior of the top political leaders of a nation and, indirectly, to account for an entire political culture. Few studies are such ambitious efforts to explain the entire set of leaders in a political society. Pye, a political scientist influenced by the work of Freud and especially by its applications to cultural analysis by Erik Erikson, undertook a major study of Burma (now called Myanmar), one of the largest countries in Southeast Asia (about the size of Texas), with a population of about 47 million. Pye attempts to answer an important question: Why do transitional societies have such difficulties creating an effective modern state system?

Given Pye's theoretical orientation, he assumes that political culture can be understood as political personality writ large—that is, that Burmese political culture has been shaped by the political personalities of the set of individuals in key political roles. In turn, the political personalities of these individuals can be explained in terms of two factors: (1) their understanding of the political history of their society, and (2) their individual life histories, especially their childhood development of a sense of personal identity.

Regarding the political history of their society, Pye argues that the development of an identity as a modern nation-state in Burma has been profoundly affected by its political leaders' colonial experiences under the British. Pye observes that the Burmese leaders found themselves captivated by the British, whose political style and institutions they attempted to copy. But this capture by a foreign culture has left the Burmese uncertain about the authenticity and value of the hybrid culture that emerged after independence in 1948.

Pye's Freudian analysis of the childhood development of Burmese political leaders leads him to argue that the Burmese adult has no confidence about the world of social relationships. For Pye, these sets of understandings can be traced primarily to the patterns of child rearing practiced by Burmese mothers, who tease, love, reward, and ignore in a way that baffles the child. Thus the individual comes to believe that the behavior of others is unpredictable and is not based on trust and cooperation, and that there is no linkage between one's own behavior and rewards. One must appear cooperative, but only to lull others so that one can destroy them before one is destroyed by them.

From the perspective of building a modern political order, these understandings are devastating. There is no sense of a coherent national culture and identity that deserves the support and loyalty of the citizenry, or even of the leaders. In Pye's view, such a national identity must be an anchor point for a stable, modern nation-state. Furthermore, the political leaders' own political personalities make it virtually

(continued)

BOX 4.5 *(Continued)*

impossible for them to create and sustain the kinds of stable, interpersonal relationships necessary for effective bureaucratic organization and for political cooperation among opposing factions.

The failure in Burma to create a strong, modern state and tolerate different groups and political opposition is clear. When Aung San, a charismatic young army officer, united most of the ethnic groups in Burma shortly before independence, he was assassinated. Different ethnic groups within the country have been engaged in a civil war for more than forty-five years. After a series of short-lived democratic governments, the military overthrew the government in 1962 and established an isolationalist regime called the "Burmese Way to Socialism."

The military leaders (who later resigned to become "civilian" rulers) have been in power continuously since that point. Burma is a repressive, one-party state, and the few attempts to promote a more democratic politics have been brutally suppressed. When civil unrest boiled over in 1988, the military leadership again seized power directly, calling themselves the "State Law and Order Restoration Council (SLORC)." The attempt to create a shared national identity and to escape the shadow of colonial influence was again evident in 1989. The military leadership announced that the name of the country would be changed to the "Union of Myanmar," the Burmese word for their own country, replacing the British colonial word "Burma," which connotes one particular ethnic group.

When legislative elections were held in 1990 under domestic and international pressure, the opposition party won 392 of 485 contested seats. The military simply ignored the election. The opposition party leader, Aung San Suu Kyi (daughter of Aung San), who has been under house arrest since 1989, was awarded the Nobel Peace Prize in 1991 but was not allowed to leave the country to accept the Nobel Prize or, in 1998, to attend the funeral of her husband. In recent years, the country has experienced significant economic problems. Inflation has averaged about 50 percent per year, exports are less than half of imports, and Myanmar's overdue debt payments have jumped from $400 million to $1.5 billion. In 1998, SLORC reinvented itself, changing its name to the State Peace and Development Council. Despite this cynical manipulation of its name, the leadership group still rules repressively, harassing, imprisoning, or eliminating its opponents, especially the leaders of Ms. Suu Kyi's National League for Democracy. Political life in Myanmar continues to reflect the violent conflicts, incapacity to govern effectively, and absence of shared identity among leaders that was explained by Pye.

Human Nature

Some of those who offer a psychological explanation for political behavior do not focus on individual personality or even on a particular culture; rather, they emphasize a more generalized conception grounded in human nature—in innate motivation and invariant drives shared by all people. At some time, most of us have engaged in a discussion about the possibility of a utopian society. Typically, someone takes the position that a benign utopia is not possible because humans are imperfect—men and women are intrinsically greedy or individualist or violent. The person making such an argument is linking the political behavior of individuals and groups with notions about innate (and possibly universal) human nature.

Certain political psychologists address this issue, asking whether there are innate human motivations that affect political behavior. Some assume that such human nature is prior to nurture (i.e., prior to the learned behavior emerging from socialization) and is only marginally altered by personal traits. Given the obvious difficulty of studying political behavior independent of socialization and personal traits, the applications of this perspective to political behavior have been modest and quite derivative. In most cases, general psychological theories have been loosely related to politically relevant behavior.

The links between human nature and political behavior raise fascinating issues. Are there fundamental elements of human nature that cannot be significantly altered by socialization and institutions? On one side, some theorists claim that nearly all human behavior is based on essential biological/genetic foundations (see, e.g., the sociobiology approach of Edward Wilson [1978]). In dramatic contrast, a fundamental tenet of Marxist theory is that nothing is intrinsic about human nature (although this is not the view in some of Marx's own early writings, which do suggest basic human needs and patterns of development). From this second perspective, it is assumed that people's social values and behavior, if not their basic nature, can be shaped via proper socialization and enlightened institutions. Such shaping into a cooperative society is the theme of *Walden Two,* a novel by behavioral psychologist B. F. Skinner (1948). However, the power and danger of such pervasive socialization are a central theme in Aldous Huxley's (1932) classic novel *Brave New World.*

In general, one claim underpinning the human nature approach seems reasonable—we are not merely the product of our environment. But the crucial issue relevant to understanding politics concerns the extent to which individual personality and human nature *cause* political behavior. In the late-night debates in college dormitories about the possibility of a utopian society or the inevitability of conflict and war, the issues often boil down to one's view of the malleability of human nature. Are there innate characteristics of human nature which are so invariant that they are subject to only minor modifications from particular patterns of political socialization and from specific political environments? Empirical social science has yet to provide decisive answers to these questions about nature versus nurture in relation to politics.

CONCLUDING OBSERVATIONS

Our exploration of micropolitical analysis has continued with a consideration of primary explanations for individuals' political beliefs and political actions. The research and theories that attempt to answer the *why* questions regarding political behavior emphasize four types of explanatory factors: the environmental context, the agents of political socialization, personal traits, and political personality. The basic assumption is that some combination of these factors influences the kinds of political stimuli to which individuals are exposed, the manner in which they interpret these stimuli, and their responses to the stimuli.

The *environment* presents the individual with stimuli and opportunities as well as with obstacles to certain political beliefs and actions. While an individual can ignore or misperceive these broad environmental constraints, they do constitute a framework that guides, and to some extent determines, political behavior. In most micropolitical research, the analyst can (and should) identify the major features of the environment that might affect the probability that an individual will manifest certain political beliefs or actions.

In a similar manner, an individual's *personal traits,* such as age, gender, social class, and education, can have a powerful cumulative influence in several ways. First, they can influence the kinds of political phenomena to which the individual is exposed. Second, they can influence the expectations that others have regarding how the individual ought to think and act politically. The empirical evidence is sometimes quite clear (as are the data on voting in the 1996 U.S. presidential election) that certain personal traits (in a given environmental context) are correlated significantly with particular political beliefs and actions. Thus personal traits, like the environment, can be understood as a set of forces that influence the nature and intensity of, but do not determine, individual political behavior.

The inadequacy of either the environment or personal traits as a complete explanation for most individual political behavior is reflected in the fact that individuals with comparable personal traits or who operate in a similar environment do not necessarily manifest identical political beliefs or actions. For example, of two intelligent 19-year-old Chicanas at the same university, one might become an activist deeply involved in Democratic Party politics while the other might be politically inactive. Similarly, consider the quite divergent paths of political activism pursued by Mohandas Gandhi and Abu Nidal, despite some notable similarities in their traits and environments. While the environment and personal traits might not provide a total explanation, a strong case can be made that these factors do tend to set the boundaries within which much political behavior occurs.

The attempt to build an empirically validated causal theory of the effects of *political socialization* on political behavior is intriguing. However, a major analytic shortcoming in most of the empirical political socialization research has been the difficulty in demonstrating empirically that there is a clear causal linkage among a specific agent of socialization, a particular belief, and then a politically relevant action. In most instances, researchers lack the methodologies and the data-gathering instruments to measure how the messages of various agents of political socialization are absorbed, interpreted, and responded to by individuals. Rather, the researchers must attempt to infer what socialization agents have been important by asking individuals to recall the major sources of their own political beliefs.

Despite these empirical difficulties, the study of political socialization has been quite useful in increasing our understanding of the major forces that influence how individuals learn about the political world and evaluate political phenomena. In their attempt to use the agents of political socialization, political regimes affirm their own belief that these socialization processes can either create and preserve popular support for the existing political order or create a new political consciousness. Research suggests that where the agents of political socialization are ineffective or provide contradictory messages, a person's political behavior will tend toward apathy or, in a few cases, toward total activism (producing the politically committed gladiator). While the precise linkages among agents of political socialization, political beliefs, and political behavior have yet to be empirically verified, this area of inquiry remains an important one for political scientists.

The explanation of micropolitical behavior by reference to *political personality* is perhaps the most intriguing of the four sets of factors. The political behavior of ordinary men and women is seldom analyzed using explicit, personality-based approaches. The studies that have been done have tended to be broad and overly simplified characterizations of "national character" or "modal personality," like those described in Chapter 2. Most of the personality-based work has examined activists, such as the authoritarian personalities, revolutionaries, and top leaders.

Personality-based approaches are the explanatory framework for political behavior that has been least fully explored by means of social scientific inquiry. These approaches use some of the same evidence as the other approaches. For example, this approach might explain political personality in terms of the relation of the child to the parents, as would an explanation based on the family as an agent of political socialization. Thus personality is difficult to isolate from other forces—the environment, personal traits, and political socialization and learning—that intervene between human nature and political behavior and that shape personality. To a large extent, the psychological perspective differs from the other approaches less in the evidence it examines than in the more subjective, psychoanalytic framework within which the evidence is interpreted.

We began this chapter by asking whether it is possible to explain political beliefs and actions. In general, analyses can rarely prove that any of the four types of explanatory factors we examined is almost always *the* basic causal factor accounting for a particular micropolitical behavior. Nonetheless, the evidence summarized in this chapter suggests that appropriate knowledge about each of these four sets of explanatory factors can provide significant insights regarding political behavior.

FOR FURTHER CONSIDERATION

1. Which agent of political socialization has been most potent in influencing your key political beliefs? Which of your beliefs have been least influenced by this agent? What accounts for the agent's minimal influence on these beliefs?
2. Under what conditions are personal traits likely to have particularly powerful effects on an individual's political beliefs or actions?
3. To what extent are people either a blank page upon which political beliefs can be written ("nurture") or genetically determined actors ("nature")? Do you think that this overall assessment is valid for you?
4. In a contemporary society, what are the conditions under which the schools or the media are likely to be the more powerful source of individuals' political orientations?
5. What is your assessment of Machiavelli's advice to the leader that ethics, the leader's word, and even "the good" must sometimes be sacrificed to achieve desirable ends?

FOR FURTHER READING

Bao, Ruo-Wang (Jean Pasqualini). (1976). *Prisoner of Mao.* New York: Penguin Books. A French citizen of Chinese origin recounts his imprisonment in China and his rigorous indoctrination into the communist (Maoist) vision of class thinking and personal behavior.

Erikson, Erik. (1969). *Gandhi's Truth.* New York: Norton. Applying his rich psychobiographical approach, Erikson explains the crucial points of development shaping the personality and political style of Mohandas Gandhi.

Esposito, John, and John Voll. (1996). *Islam and Democracy: Religion, Identity and Conflict Resolution in the Muslim World.* New York: Oxford University Press. By means of a sensitive analysis of both Arab and non-Arab Islamic countries, the authors conclude that the core elements of Islam, as a system of beliefs, can be compatible with certain forms of participatory government.

Hayhoe, Ruth. (1992). *Education and Modernization: The Chinese Experience.* New York: Pergamon Press. An insightful analysis of the impacts of education on the political socialization process and on culture and modernization in China, from Confucianism to Marxism.

Huxley, Aldous. (1932). *Brave New World.* London: Chatto & Windus. A chilling vision of a society in which the state effectively uses socialization and material conditions to control the citizens.

Mandela, Nelson. (1995). *Long Walk to Freedom.* Boston: Little, Brown. In his autobiography, Nelson Mandela provides a compelling narrative of his extraordinary life of political activism against racial injustice and apartheid, culminating in his election as president of South Africa.

Masters, Roger. (1989). *The Nature of Politics.* New Haven, CT: Yale University Press. A fascinating exploration of the biological bases of people's political beliefs and actions.

Nixon, Richard M. (1962). *Six Crises.* New York: Doubleday. Nixon provides a revealing self-assessment of his reactions to six critical points in his early political career.

Sigel, Roberta, Ed. (1989). *Political Learning in Adulthood: A Sourcebook of Theory and Research.* Chicago: University of Chicago Press. Scholars of political socialization assess what we know about this phenomenon, particularly as it continues to occur for adults.

Skinner, B. F. (1948). *Walden Two.* New York: Macmillan. A renowned behavioral psychologist presents his conception of a setting in which socialization is used to create a benign and cooperative community. An intriguing counterpoint to Huxley's *Brave New World.*

Wills, Gary. (1970). *Nixon Agonistes: The Crises of a Self-Made Man.* Boston: Houghton Mifflin. A scathing psychobiography of Richard Nixon, which is an interesting complement to Nixon's *Six Crises.*

Wolfenstein, E. Victor. (1967). *The Revolutionary Personality: Lenin, Trotsky, Gandhi.* Princeton, NJ: Princeton University Press. A classic study of three great revolutionary leaders from a psychoanalytic perspective.

PART THREE

Political Systems

This land is *my* land! The Palestinian and the Israeli soldier each believes deeply that he is seated in a place (Hebron, in the West Bank of Israel) that belongs to his nation.

CHAPTER 5

States and Nations

"O, Canada! Our home and native land! True patriot love in all thy sons command...." *Voices fill Toronto's Skydome as the Blue Jays baseball game is preceded by the singing of the national anthem. But then as the vocalist intones "O Canada! Terre de nos aieux, ton front est ceint de fleurons glorieux!" there are boos and catcalls. The national anthem continues to glorify the same native land of brave forefathers and heroic exploits. What has happened?*

The lyrics are now a symbol of the conflict and disagreement within Canada. Canada is a single territorial space with one government that is attempting to rule a population in which "all thy sons" (and daughters) are deeply split into two groups that share neither culture nor identity. The English-speaking Canadians and the French-speaking Canadians are unable to establish peaceful coexistence within the same state. Many argue that the only solution is separation of Canada into two distinct countries.

The disjunction between state boundaries and peoples with shared identities, a central theme of this chapter, is a fundamental problem in many countries. It is arguably the greatest source of violence and death in the contemporary political world. While Chapters 2 through 4 primarily examined the political beliefs and actions of individuals, this chapter increases the scale of our subject unit considerably, focusing on large collectivities of individuals. Initially, this chapter examines and distinguishes two crucial concepts, *state* and *nation*. This is followed by discussion of the *political system*, a third major concept used to analyze these collectivities.

THE STATE

Anthropological evidence suggests that early social organization among humans was probably based on small living groups of family or kin. As suggested by humanistic psychologist Abraham Maslow (1954), human groupings formed to increase the capacity with which the physiological, safety, love, and belonging needs of people could be met. As groupings became larger, tribes or bands were formed on the basis of more extensive kinship ties. It might be argued that the first "state" emerged when a multiplicity of such tribes combined under some leadership structure and some pattern of organization. By this definition, there have been states since ancient times, in the sense that a state exists when there are distinctive leadership roles, rules for social interaction, and a set of organizational arrangements to identify and serve collective needs (See Box 5.1).

A Legal Definition

The social scientific concept of the state, however, is a relatively modern one, based on the legal notion that the **state** is *"a territorially bound sovereign entity."* The idea of sovereignty emerged in the sixteenth and seventeenth centuries. In current interpretations, **sovereignty** is *the premise that each state has complete authority and is the ultimate source of law within its own boundaries.* Sovereignty is the key element in the legal concept of the state. It is a basic assumption of international politics and is reflected in a fundamental principle of the United Nations, the sovereign equality of all member states. This means that, before the law, Chad is equal to China, Jamaica is equal to Japan. While sovereignty has legal standing and moral force in international law, the reality of international politics is that a state's sovereign rights depend ultimately on sufficient power to enforce the state's position. Thus it is not likely that, when major national interests are at stake, China will yield to Chad merely on the basis of Chad's sovereign rights.

Associated with the idea of sovereignty is the doctrine of **territorial integrity**. This holds that *a state has the right to resist and reject any aggression, invasion, or intervention within its territorial boundaries.* As with the more general notion of

BOX 5.1

The States of the "State"

"State" is among the most extensively used concepts in political science, and it has various meanings. A source of confusion for American students is that they are accustomed to thinking of a state as one of the fifty units of subnational government in the United States, such as Illinois or Alabama. This is one appropriate meaning of the concept. However, in the general language of political science, *state* usually refers to the set of organizational units and individuals that performs the political functions for a national territorial entity, such as France, Indonesia, or Nigeria. In this chapter, and in this book, the term "state" will usually denote this full array of governmental units and individuals within the society.

You should also be aware that the language of political science often treats the state as though it were a single actor. For example, consider the statement (above) in the discussion of sovereignty that "a state has the right to resist...any aggression...." In reality, the state is composed of many individuals who behave as individuals but whose combined behaviors are characterized as if they were performed by a single actor. In this book, there are other collectivities (e.g., the group, the political party, the army, and the bureaucracy) which are complex aggregates of individuals that are discussed as though they operate as a single actor.

sovereignty, a state's protection of its territorial integrity depends on the state's capacity and political power.

It might seem there are many relatively clear examples of a state's territorial integrity being violated, such as the invasion of France by the German army in 1940, but there is often considerable disagreement over claimed violations of territorial integrity. First, territorial integrity is a fuzzy concept when there is a *dispute over boundaries*. For example, both Canada and the United States claim that certain fishing waters are within their territorial boundaries and each state attempts to exclude the other's commercial fishing fleets from its territorial waters. In this case, the dispute has been settled by adjudication. But border disputes can also become a cause of violence between states, as when Iran and Iraq each claimed certain land along their mutual border, precipitating a war in 1980 (see Box 14.4).

Secondly, attempts to exercise sovereignty can be disputed when there is *disagreement about whom the legitimate rulers are*. Box 5.2 describes some of the puzzles about sovereignty that have remained during the devastating civil war that has absorbed Angola for almost thirty years. Similar problems have arisen recently in Afghanistan, Cambodia (see Box 5.5), Congo, and Somalia. And third, the international community has become less sensitive to protection of sovereignty when there is strong evidence that the government is committing *serious human rights violations* against its own citizens. A recent example of the aggressive intervention of outside powers is the actions of N.A.T.O., the United Nations and the United States in Kosovo, a region inside of Yugoslavia (Serbia). The stated justification for violation of Yogoslavia's sovereign rights to deal with "internal" affairs has been concerns about the government's support for "ethnic cleansing" targeting non-Serbs (mainly Albanians). Some are concerned about the increased use of such justifications (which occasionally have been used in the past), since they undermine a weaker state's legal protections via sovereignty from military intervention by outside powers (Sassen 1996).

A Structural-Functional Definition

As an alternative to defining the state in terms of its legal standing, the state can also be defined by the key organizational structures that operate as "the government" and the key functions that the state performs. In this structural-functional perspective, the **state** might be defined as *the organized institutional machinery for making and carrying out political decisions and for enforcing the laws and rules of the government.*

For Max Weber (1864–1920), the great political sociologist, the one function that distinguishes the state from all other organizations is its monopoly on the legitimate use of force and coercion in the society. That is, only the state has the right to use violence to enforce the laws and decisions of the society.

The "state-centered" definitions of the state offer a more expansive conception of the state's functions. In this view, the essential functions of the state are to maintain order and to compete with other actual or potential states (Skocpol 1979: 30). The state is an autonomous actor, composed of public officials making decisions. The state has goals, broadly understood as the "national interest," that it attempts to achieve against resistance from both domestic and international actors (Morgenthau 1985; Waltz 1995). The particular way in which a state's structures are configured has crucial effects—on the content of the public officials' policy preferences,

BOX 5.2

Don't Tread on My Sovereignty!: Angola

Despite its centrality in international law, sovereignty does not ensure that the international community will support a country's claim that its territorial integrity has been violated. In Angola, the period since independence in 1975 has been one of constant turmoil between competing leadership groups claiming to be the country's rulers and of serious issues about sovereignty. At independence, the three major nationalist groups were unable to agree on who should have government power in this resource-rich country of 10.5 million people in southern Africa. When one group (MPLA) took control of the capital city, the other two groups (UNITA and FNLA) began a military campaign from the regions where they were strong. Two years later, the United Nations recognized MPLA as the country's legitimate government.

However, some countries, especially South Africa and the United States, preferred to see the UNITA-FNLA groups in power. Thus South Africa provided military troops to fight MPLA, and both South Africa and the United States provided aid to UNITA and engaged in extensive covert activities within Angola to undermine MPLA. MPLA's leaders protested that such actions violated Angola's territorial integrity, and hence its sovereignty. The United Nations did not actively support Angola's rights. MPLA then requested and received military aid from the Soviet Union and more than 20,000 troops from Cuba. The arrival of Cuban troops drew protests from the United States and South Africa, which increased their involvement.

With all this outside "assistance," Angola became mired in a lengthy civil war. With the end of the cold war and the dismantling of apartheid in South Africa in the early 1990s, major outside powers lost interest in Angola. The rival groups in Angola finally agreed to a national election in 1992 and foreign troops withdrew. The MPLA won a relatively fair election, but the leader of UNITA, Jonas Savimbi, refused to accept the results of the election and asserted that his group would continue the fight until it controlled the country. Since that point, several cease-fires have collapsed and sporadic fighting continues.

This protracted struggle has resulted in social and economic disarray in Angola. The proportion of land under cultivation in this fertile agricultural country has declined to only 2 percent. More than 30 percent of GNP is spent on the military, and the country has among the lowest life expectancy levels and the highest infant mortality rates in the world. More than half a million Angolans have already died in this conflict and tens of thousands have lost limbs to landmines (Central Intelligence Agency 1996; Ramsey 1999: 143–144).

Given this history, consider the following questions:

Before the 1992 election, was the MPLA leadership correct in protesting that Angola's sovereignty had been repeatedly violated by South Africa and the United States?

BOX 5.2 *(Continued)*

Was it valid for states such as the United States to claim that the presence of Cuban troops violated Angola's sovereignty?

Should the United Nations have done something to protect Angola's sovereignty? What?

When there is a dispute over legitimate rulers, how should it be determined who can exercise sovereignty?

Clearly, answers to such questions depend on one's interpretation of how sovereign power is established and maintained. Similar claims regarding violation of sovereignty are made by almost every state experiencing substantial political violence generated by internal or external forces.

on determining whose preferences will be adopted as those of the state, and on the state's effectiveness in implementing those policy preferences in the society.

A widely used approach emphasizing the structures and functions of the state is based on the work of Gabriel Almond and his colleagues (see, e.g., Almond and Powell 2000). Their conceptual framework is based on two central questions:

1. What functions must be performed if the state is to persist?

2. What structures perform these necessary functions within a given state?

Chapter 12 provides a recent elaboration of this basic structural-functional approach, called "capabilities analysis." In the classic version of this approach, Almond identifies eight *requisite functions*—that is, functions that must be performed by every state (Almond and Powell 2000: 8–13):

1. *Political socialization* is the processes through which individuals acquire their cognitive, affective, and evaluative orientations toward the political world.

2. *Political recruitment* is the processes through which people are drawn into roles as political activists.

3. *Political communication* is the mechanisms by which political information is transmitted.

4. *Interest articulation* is the low-level communication, by individuals and groups, of what they need or want from the state.

5. *Interest aggregation* is the transformation of all these political needs and wants into a smaller number of coherent alternatives.

6. *Policy making* is the process by which the state establishes laws, policy decisions, and value allocations.

7. *Policy implementation* is the actual application by the state of such laws and policy decisions.

8. *Policy adjudication* is the interpretation and resolution of disagreements regarding what the policies mean and how they should be implemented.

Given these functions, analyses using Almond's approach have primarily attempted to identify the particular structures within a state that are most significant in the performance of each function and to describe how the structures contribute to performing each function. While it might seem obvious at first glance that a certain structure always performs a particular function, more reflection (and later chapters) will suggest that the actual situation can be quite complex. For example, it is not simply the case that Congress performs the policy-making function in the United States. Many policy decisions are made by the president, by the Cabinet departments, by the bureaucracy, by the courts as they both interpret and reshape laws, by structures at the local levels of government, and by the citizens through electoral initiatives.

In most contemporary states, virtually every political function is performed by a variety of political structures. Thus the central questions in structural-functional research address the characteristic processes of each structure and the subtle interrelationships among structures as they contribute to a given function. These questions are especially germane in comparative research, where the analyst attempts to specify how the structure-function patterns vary between states.

The Domain of State Action

One other way of characterizing the state is to define its appropriate domain of action. When we examine "appropriate" rather than "actual" state action, the central question is normative rather than descriptive or analytic. A normative question asks how something should be rather than how it is (recall Chapter 1). Many of the most fascinating and fundamental issues in the political world have normative components. Political scientists attempt to distinguish the normative elements of their discussion from the descriptive-analytic elements, but, as Chapter 1 observed, there are always subtle normative judgments organizing the manner in which every political question is examined.

A fundamental, unresolved debate in everyday political discussion, as well as in political theory, concerns how extensive the state's role in society should be. Everyone agrees that the boundaries of state activity should be limited to *res publica,* a Latin phrase meaning "things of the people." But what "things" should be included? And how expansive should the state's involvement with these things be?

In contemporary political thought, certain broad views regarding the appropriate boundaries of *res publica* are associated with the three political ideologies (the major "isms") outlined in Chapter 2. In the *conservative* view of the state, one important domain of state action is military power, which functions to defend against intervention by other states and to protect and promote the country's interests abroad. Internally, the expectation is that the state will use its monopoly of force to maintain social order and to protect private property rights. State policy will also be used to preserve traditional values, especially regarding family life, religion, and culture.

As suggested in Chapter 2, a view of *res publica* based on *classical liberalism* would be more limited. Similar to the conservative view, the state must defend the country's sovereignty against external aggression or influence. However, there is great confidence in the dynamics of the free market to motivate and coordinate human behavior. Thus the state should be mainly a night watchman, a low-profile policeman who ensures the basic safety of every individual. Otherwise, the role of government is quite limited. Jefferson's slogan captures this perspective on *res publica:* "That state governs best which governs least." In its extreme form, the domain of appropriate state action is reduced to almost nothing, a perspective usually termed *libertarianism.*

There are several different interpretations of the domain of state action across the major variants of *socialism* described in Chapter 2. Democratic socialists believe that the state must constrain many powerful and self-interested groups whose behavior will harm the collective good of the society. Also, the state must intervene to provide assistance to the many groups in the society who are deeply disadvantaged by the workings of the system and must enact policies that ensure greater equality of condition. Marxist socialists believe that most non-Marxist states are expansive and repressive, serving mainly to preserve the interests of the dominant class in the society. In the words of V. I. Lenin (1870–1924), the Soviet revolutionary leader and theorist, such a state is "a body of armed men, weapons, and prisons." After a successful revolution, however, a more benign and positive state can be installed. Its domain of action is to implement any policies necessary to serve the fundamental goal of equality of political, economic, and social resources in the society. Some Marxist socialists assume the state will ultimately be eliminated (in Marx's words, the state will "wither away"), but even in this view, organizational structures would remain to administer policy. The extreme form of this view, in which there is no role for the state, is labeled *anarchism.* This does not mean a situation of chaos and disorder; rather it is a stateless society where individuals and groups organize spontaneously to create a society in which all people participate and all benefit from the goods and services that are produced.

While these three views of *res publica* are dominant in Western political thought, there are other conceptions that do not emphasize a unique, political "state." For example, in some societies dominated by all-encompassing religions, there is no political state that is independent of the religious order. In fundamentalist Islamic regimes, Shari'a law, the law of Islam, establishes a religious state that defines all aspects of social life, including such issues as the content of *res publica.* And in historical terms, many societies have no conception of a distinct political order. For instance, no specifically political structures existed in most precolonial African societies. Rather, the rules governing the society were based on tradition, as interpreted by community leaders (such as tribal elders or religious authorities).

THE NATION

The concept of the nation has a psychological and emotional basis rather than a legal or functional basis (like the state). A **nation** is defined by *a deeply shared fundamental identification among a set of people.* Different factors might constitute the basis of such identification: shared descent (belief in a common kinship or history), shared culture, shared geographic space, shared religion, shared language, or shared economic order. The nation is a community of understanding, of communication, of trust (Connor 1994).

Most people feel some identity with a variety of different reference groups or communities. For example, you might identify with a religion, local community, ethnic group, social club, and sports team. In the usage here, what distinguishes a nation from other reference groups is that the nation is a major group, beyond the family group, with whom the individual identifies very powerfully. It is an essential division between "us" and "them." The strength of a person's primary national identity depends on the relative importance he places on various identities and the extent to which the most important identities reinforce this basic conception of "us" versus "them."

The ideal for effective governance is a *nation-state,* which has a citizenry whose primary national identity is coterminous with the territorial boundaries of the state. In only a few modern states have common culture, history, ethnicity, religion, and language all combined to result in a strong sense of shared nationality among nearly all the citizens governed by the state. Japan is an example of a relatively homogeneous nation-state.

Occasionally one nation is split into two states, such as North and South Korea. In such cases the citizens often dream of reunification, even when their governments and ideologies differ fundamentally. This occurred in Germany, which was split into communist East Germany and capitalist West Germany after World War II. In 1990, citizens of the single German nation were finally reunited in a single country, after nearly half a century of antagonistic separation in two very different states.

The reality of the post–cold war world, however, is that most countries are *multinational states.* Such countries include groups whose fundamental identities are associated with different nations. **Ethnonationalism**, a *powerful attitude of identity with and support for others perceived as sharing a crucial, nationality-based trait,* has become a major problem within (and between) states in the contemporary political world (Connor 1994). It is particularly dangerous where it produces intense animosity and violence between groups with different ethnic identities. The example of the Indian subcontinent in Box 5.3 illustrates the kinds of differences that exist between states and nations and how these can generate instability and political violence.

The problems of ethnonationalism and of multiple nations within a single state are endemic in the contemporary world. For many of the states that gained independence after 1945, territorial boundaries were based on the arbitrary administrative decisions of colonial powers. Thus in most of Africa and Asia, states were formed with boundaries that were not sensitive to nationality differences in the area. Many of these states have experienced traumatic nationality conflicts, and few of these conflicts have been permanently resolved. There are reports every day of such struggles as those of the Armenians in Azerbaijan; the peoples of East Timor and Aceh in Indonesia; and the Kurds in Turkey, Iran, and Iraq.

Even in some of the more established states, nation-based cleavages frequently explode (sometimes literally). When the Soviet Union, the world's most multinational state, collapsed in 1991, it was replaced by fifteen states that were generally organized on nationality grounds. However, the large nationality minorities in many of them (e.g., Chechnya in Russia) have produced extensive nation-based struggles. The bloodiest nationality violence in Central and Eastern Europe has been the devastating ethnic battles among the Bosnians, Croatians, Kosovars, Serbs, and others in the former Yugoslavia (See Box 15.). Yet this carnage is overshadowed by the devastating ethnic conflict in Rwanda and Burundi between the Hutus and the Tutsis, resulting in more than one million deaths since 1994.

BOX 5.3

State and Nations: The Indian Subcontinent

The problem of discontinuities between nations and states is often most severe in states that have gained independence within the last fifty years. The Indian subcontinent reflects the problems that these postcolonial areas have experienced. The vast Indian subcontinent was a feudal society divided into many small kingdoms ruled by kings (*maharajahs*). From the sixteenth century, the riches of India were pursued, and often exploited, by many traders, including the British, Dutch, French, and Arabs. The states from which these traders came began to struggle for dominance over the Indian trade, and the British finally gained hegemony in the eighteenth century after defeating the French. From that time until 1947 the Indian subcontinent was the major jewel in the British imperial crown, treated as a single territory under colonial rule.

After a lengthy and often violent campaign of political and social action by Indian nationalists, the British relented and granted the subcontinent independence in 1947. However, despite the desires of the British and the efforts of some Indian leaders such as Mohandas Gandhi (recall Box 4.4), the subcontinent was deeply split, on the basis of religion, between Hindus and Muslims. Since it seemed impossible to fashion a single state out of these two nations, two states were formed: India, which was predominantly (82 percent) Hindu; and Pakistan, which was predominantly (90 percent) Muslim.

The situation was further complicated by the concentration of Muslims in two geographically distinct areas in the northeast and northwest regions of the subcontinent. As a consequence, Pakistan was composed of two parts, separated by more than 1,500 miles of rival India's territory. Many Hindus in Pakistan and Muslims in India were forced to leave their homelands and migrate to the new state based on their own religion. The hostility and bloodshed associated with the partition resulted in one million deaths. There have been periodic violent boundary conflicts ever since.

While the major religious difference on the Indian subcontinent was generally resolved by this partition, many other nationality problems remained. For example, there has been continual disagreement between India and Pakistan since 1947 regarding which country should control the region of Kashmir and Jammu. Although the majority of the population is Muslim, India controls most of the territory. Even persistent United Nations' involvement has failed to resolve the dispute, leading to a half-century of military conflicts and intermittent guerrilla war.

Within Pakistan, an even more substantial nationality dispute emerged between two major ethnic groups, the Punjabis and the Bengalis, after independence. When the Bengalis, dominant in East Pakistan, were victorious in a national election, the Punjabi-dominated West Pakistan attempted to reassert political power through its control of the military. When the Bengalis attempted to form their own independent nation-state (with some support from India), a terrible civil war resulted. After hundreds of thousands of deaths due to war and starvation, the Bengalis of East Pakistan were successful in the civil war and created a new sovereign state, Bangladesh, in 1971.

(continued)

BOX 5.3 *(Continued)*

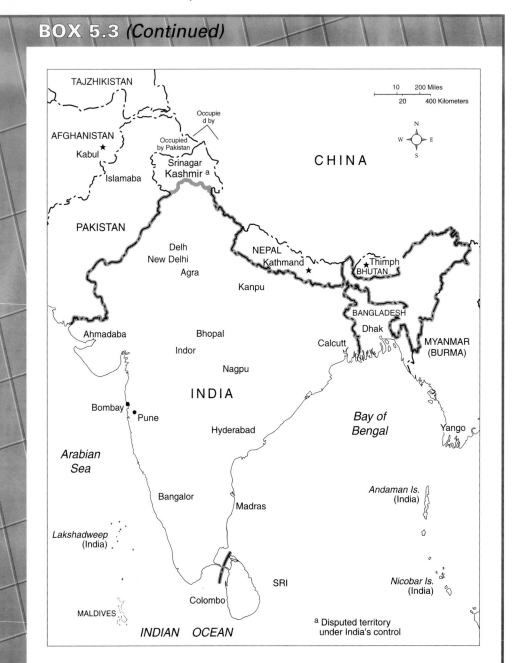

And while India is dominated by Hindus, major nation-based cleavages continue to plague the country, creating tremendous barriers to forging a single identity as a nation-state among the peoples of India. There are 17 official languages in addition to the two "national" languages, Hindi and English, which are each under

BOX 5.3 *(Continued)*

stood by only about one-third of the population. In all, there are about 1,650 different dialects in India, most of which are mutually unintelligible.

Moreover, there are at least five major religious groupings in India: Hindu, Muslim, Sikh, Christian, and Buddhist. Hindu nationalism has increasingly been expressed through a political movement, resulting in the growing power at the regional and national levels of Hindu parties, particularly the Bharatiya Janata Party (BJP). The BJP was the dominant party in the national legislature for several years in the late 1990s, constituting the most serious threat to a secular Indian government since independence. With this increase in Hindu nationalism, the levels of violence against Christians and Muslims have risen significantly.

Most of the non-Hindu groups are regionally concentrated, enhancing their identity as religion-based nations. One major source of political unrest in India since 1980 has been the Sikhs, who are concentrated in the northwest part of India, called the Punjab. The Sikhs have a very strong identity as a religious community and an ethnic group. Their sense of nationality is heightened by their belief that they are discriminated against politically by the Hindus. The Sikhs have been increasingly militant in demanding greater political autonomy, and since the early 1980s some have insisted on full independence, to create the state of Khalistan. The best-known of a continuing series of violent confrontations between the Sikhs and the Hindu majority in India began when the Indian army stormed the Golden Temple, the Sikhs' holiest shrine, to drive out Sikh militants who had taken refuge there. In retaliation, Indian Prime Minister Indira Gandhi was assassinated in 1984 by two Sikhs among her private guard.

Rajiv Gandhi succeeded his mother as prime minister, only to be the victim of another nation-based dispute. The Indian army had also intervened on the neighboring island-country of Sri Lanka in an attempt to limit the extremely violent civil war between the Tamil and the Sinhalese ethnic groups. Southern India has a substantial Tamil population who do not support the return of the Tamils from Sri Lanka. Sri Lankan Tamils have been angered by the lack of support from India and from the treatment they received from the Indian army. In 1991, Rajiv Gandhi was assassinated by a Tamil woman who had strapped a bomb to her body. In sum, the many deep cleavages in India, based on religion, ethnicity, culture, and region, have exposed the state to persistent instability, conflict, and nation-based carnage.

Meanwhile, the agitation of the Quebequois in Canada, the Basques in Spain, and the Irish Catholics in Northern Ireland are testimony to the possibility that even centuries-old states might split apart. Some scholars predict that the current reorganization of states based on nationality identities will produce more than fifty new states by 2010. In the interim, nation-based conflicts might remain the major cause of violence and instability in the post–cold war period (Barber 1995; Huntington 1996; but also see Sadowski 1998).

THE POLITICAL SYSTEM

While concepts such as state and nation are extremely useful, political scientists have sought an additional, more general and analytic concept to describe the structures and dynamics of organized politics at all levels. Many political scientists use some version of the concept of the political system, developed in the work of David Easton (1953, 1965). Easton was searching for an analytic concept that would facilitate the development of a general theory of politics. He found the basis for such a concept in the notion of general systems theory from biology.

Systems in General

The essential concept is the idea of a *system,* which is a group of components that exist in a characteristic relationship to each other and that interact on the basis of regular patterns. Because the components are interdependent, change in one component will have some effect on other components. Such change can cause minor or even major alterations in the manner in which the total system functions. In a mechanical analogy, an automobile engine can be viewed as a system, as a set of components interacting in a regular way. If one spark plug is dirty, the performance of the automobile-as-system will be substantially altered; if the spark plug is removed, the system might not work at all.

The same interdependency of components is evident in human systems, such as families, sports teams, factories, or bureaucracies. The components of human systems—people in roles—are more likely to vary in the range of their actions than are the components of most mechanical systems. This means that the performance of human systems tends to be far more variable and less predictable than that of mechanical systems. Human systems function relatively smoothly as long as most of the components (the people) interact within a tolerable range of expected action. For high performance, some human systems, such as a symphony orchestra or a drill team, require far more rigid adherence to predictable roles than others, such as a jazz combo or a basketball team. Because of people's capacity to adapt and improvise, human systems can sometimes adapt effectively to unexpected circumstances. But human variability can also result in system performance that is disorganized, with negative or even disastrous effects.

The Political System Defined

For Easton (1953, 1965), the **political system** is a system of behavior, and it is defined by its distinctive activities, the *authoritative allocation of values for a society.* This definition is central to the idea of a political system as it is used in this book and in many political analyses. Thus it is appropriate to examine each aspect of the definition in greater detail.

"Values."   *Values* are those things that have significance and importance to people. We can discuss values in terms of the idealized abstractions that inspire or justify much political action: liberty, equality, freedom, justice. Or values can be defined more specifically: They can be material goods, such as a decent house or road system; they can be services, such as quality health care or protection from crime; they can be conditions, such as security from national enemies or clean air; they can be symbolic goods, such as status. In addition to positive values, there are negative values, such as coercion or imprisonment, polluted water, epidemic disease, and so on. (Notice that this social scientific concept of values is broader than the notion of values as moral judgments that people use to guide their actions.)

By definition, values tend to be scarce resources—either there is an insufficient amount of a given value to satisfy everyone, or the enjoyment of one value by some requires a loss of value to others. To use an example from the previous paragraph, in no political system do all citizens have housing they would consider adequate. Some would view their housing as too small, or too expensive, or in the wrong location, or lacking in sufficient luxuries. Even if a state could provide everyone with identical housing, some would be dissatisfied because they want better housing or because they object to the use of their taxes or work to subsidize the housing of others. A vast arsenal of nuclear weapons in one's state may make one individual feel quite secure while making another individual extremely insecure. One person might favor large expenditures on missile systems while another would prefer to spend the resources on housing, and a third might prefer lower taxes to expenditure on either weapons or housing. Every value distribution entails trade-offs between different values as well as some inequality in the distribution of benefits and burdens. Thus there are always disagreements, competition, and even violent conflict over whose values will be served and whose will not. What are *your* top two values for a society?

"Allocation."   Pierre Mendes-France, a distinguished French premier, observed that "to govern is to make choices." *Allocation* refers to this choice making—to the process by which decisions and actions are taken to grant values to some and deny values to others. One useful definition of politics is that it is the processes through which competition and conflict over values are resolved by choice making. Value allocations occur at each moment when decisions are made to alter or even to sustain the existing distribution of values.

"Authoritative."   Value allocations are taken as *authoritative* when the decisions are accepted as binding by people affected by the decisions. One of the most fascinating questions in political analysis is: Why do people accept the authority of the political system to allocate values in a manner that is not to their direct advantage? Why do people accept the imposition of taxes, policies, and laws that they judge to be undesirable to themselves? The discussion in Box 5.4 suggests some of the reasons why the authority of the state is accepted.

"For a society."   The final element in Easton's definition of the political system is meant to solve the difficult analytic problem of defining the boundaries of the political world. Easton limits the domain of the political system to those areas where values are being allocated "for a society"—that is, to those values where the state must act to protect and serve the public's interests. Recall the notion of *res publica,* or "things of the people." The political system, in establishing the range of value allocations included in *res publica,* also sets the boundaries of its own domain of action.

Every political system defines its boundaries of legitimate action differently. This crucial point is reflected in the contrasting views of the role of the state discussed earlier in this chapter. We shall see throughout this book, and especially in Part Five, that some political systems allocate values in virtually every aspect of their

BOX 5.4

Why Do People Accept Authority?

There are many answers to the question of why people accept the authority of the state. In the classic definitions, authority is voluntaristic. **Authority** is based on a subjective belief in the *legitimacy* of the state: *A person willingly accepts the decisions of the state to be binding because it is "the right thing to do."* The individual's judgment that the state's authority is legitimate might be grounded in one or more of the following phenomena (see Weber 1958a: 295–301):

1. *Law.* The individual believes that the laws of the state are rationally established, purposeful, and enacted with formal correctness by appropriate public actors, and thus compliance with those laws is proper behavior.

2. *Tradition.* The individual is influenced by a long-standing habit among most people in the society to accept patterns of authoritative action.

3. *Charisma.* The individual is persuaded by a dynamic leader whose personal qualities are so extraordinary that the leader wins the individual's trust and unquestioning support. (Among the examples of twentieth-century charismatic political leaders are Adolf Hitler, Mao Zedong, and Nelson Mandela.)

4. *Social contract.* Most broadly, classical political theorists such as Thomas Hobbes (1588–1679) and John Locke (1632–1704) suggest that acceptance of the state's authority is due to a "social contract" in which each individual sacrifices certain personal values to a state whose actions ensure that social order will replace the violent state of nature.

5. *Socialization.* The effective efforts of the agents of political socialization might convince (indoctrinate?) the individual that the state has authority to make decisions and that obedience is proper, without relying specifically on any of these other sources of authority.

In many contemporary states, explanations of the acceptance of the state's authority by most citizens are often based on a more explicit assessment of material incentives or sanctions, as described by types 6 and 7.

6. *Individual utility.* The individual is satisfied with the array of values that the state provides specifically to him, or with the broad values provided to all citizens, such as economic growth or social stability, to which he attaches great importance.

7. *Fear of sanction.* The individual might fear the negative values, such as deprivation of valued benefits, coercion, imprisonment, or even death, that the state can inflict on him if he openly challenges the state's authority. With sanctions, the line between authority and power exercise might have been crossed.

The debate over the legitimacy of the state's authority is a perpetual one. A fascinating literary expression of the authority debate is Greek dramatist Sophocles's (496–406 B.C., 1967: 144) classic play *Antigone*. Antigone violates a rule promulgated by Creon, who is not only her uncle (and potential father-in-law), but also the king. In defense of social order, Creon argues, "He whom the State appoints

BOX 5.4

must be obeyed to the smallest matter, be it right or wrong....There is no more deadly peril than disobedience." In a similar way, contemporary political analyst Samuel Huntington (1968: 7–8) observes: "The primary problem is not liberty but the creation of legitimate public order. Men may, of course have order without liberty, but they cannot have liberty without order."

Ultimately, Antigone decides to do what seems morally correct to her, and she breaks the law. Thus Antigone represents the other side of the debate, which is characterized by eloquent defenders of the individual's right and even the obligation to resist his state's authority, when he believes the state to be wrong. In "Civil Disobedience," American philosopher Henry David Thoreau (1817–1862) writes: "If [the law of the state] is of such a nature that it requires you to be the agent of injustice to another, then, I say, break the law. Let your life be a counter friction to stop the machine. What I have to do is to see, at any rate, that I do not lend myself to the wrong which I condemn" (Thoreau 1849/1981: 92).

In some cases, the objective of resistance to authority is social change. Mohandas Gandhi's essential strategy in resisting British rule in India was repeated episodes of (generally) nonviolent resistance to a system of laws and authority that Gandhi judged to be immoral. Civil disobedience also was used by Dr. Martin Luther King, Jr. and others in the civil rights movement in the United States during the 1960s, to protest laws that failed to prevent discrimination on the basis of race. In other cases, the resistance to established authority is more aggressive, and the objective is establishment of a new political order. Marx and Engels, in the famous *Communist Manifesto* (1848/1978: 500), conclude: "In short, the Communists everywhere support every revolutionary movement against the existing social and political order of things....They openly declare that their ends can be attained only by the forcible overthrow of all existing social conditions. Let the ruling classes tremble at a Communist revolution. The proletarians have nothing to lose but their chains. They have a world to win. Working men of all countries, unite!"

Despite such stirring calls to question authority, most people do usually obey the commands of others who seem to be in authoritative positions. In a famous series of disturbing social psychology experiments, subjects were told by a researcher to administer increasingly high levels of electrical shock to another individual (who was collaborating with the researcher to fool the subject). Despite the shrieks of pain and suffering from the person being shocked, most subjects continued to increase and administer the electrical shocks when told to do so (Milgram 1974). At some point, almost everyone justifies the unjustifiable by relying on the "I was only following orders" defense most associated with Nazi war criminal Adolf Eichmann.

citizen's lives while other systems intervene minimally. One political system might provide a total health care delivery system to all citizens, with no direct charges for doctors, hospitals, or treatment, whereas another system might subsidize only hospitalization for the very poor. One political system might require daily religious instruction in school while another system might forbid even the general discussion of religious philosophies in the schools.

It should be noted that Easton's definition seems to cover only national political systems. The idea of a political system for an entire society serves the purposes of this book well, since the book focuses primarily on countries. But analytically, a political system could exist at any level, even one that does not have ultimate authority. This concept could certainly apply to subnational political systems (including such American examples as states, counties, and municipalities). It could also apply to a supranational system that encompasses more than one state (e.g., the European Union). Perhaps a more generalized definition of the political system might describe it in terms of "the authoritative allocation of values *for a collectivity*."

Conceptualization of the Political System

Easton's (1965) conceptualization of the political system, characterized in Figure 5.1, is based on the idea of an *input-output system* within a broader environment. This means that, within an environment, the system receives certain phenomena as inputs, does some processing of those inputs, and then generates outputs back into the environment. Each of the elements in Figure 5.1 can be specified more fully.

Environment.   The *environment* is the name given to all those activities that are not included within the state's activity domain of *res publica.* Thus it encompasses all those physical and social domains where the authoritative allocation of values for the society is *not* the dominant activity. Do not think of the environment as a separate physical area; the political system often operates in the same physical environment as other subsystems such as the economic environment and the social environment. The activities in the "intrasocietal" environment are occurring in the same

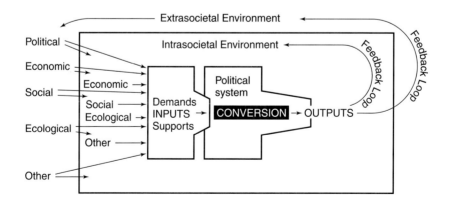

Figure 5.1   Conceptualization of the political system
SOURCE: Based on Easton 1965: 31.

spatial area as are the activities being performed by the political system. The environment is vast, because it includes not only all the activities within the society, but also an "extrasocietal" environment, which includes virtually every activity in the world that is external to the territory of the state.

Clearly, only a few aspects of this enormous environment are considered in any particular analysis of a political system. What is important about the concept of the environment is the idea that any aspect of it might affect the political system. That is, the environment provides opportunities and obstacles, resources and constraints, that are relevant to the functioning of the political system.

For example, there might be a shortage of fossil fuels within the state (i.e., in the intrasocietal ecological system). This "input" might provoke the political system to take some action (policy decision) to ensure more fuel for its citizens and its economy. Among the various policies the political system might adopt are these:

1. Stimulate additional fuel production within the society through subsidies for exploration
2. Reduce fuel consumption through a very high fuel-use tax
3. Encourage innovative alternatives by supporting research and development of synfuels
4. Obtain fuel resources from outside the state by using military force to capture some other state's fuel resources

Can you think of other feasible policy responses to this problem in the political system's environment?

Demands and supports.   Among the inputs from the environment, the most direct inputs to the political system are demands and supports. *Demands* are wants or desires for particular value allocations. Demands might come from individuals, groups, or systems either within or outside the society. When a citizen prefers lower taxes, or more expenditure on health care, or greater regulation of corporations, or a freeze on nuclear weapons construction, these preferences become demands to the political system when they are communicated directly by the citizen or by other actors such as spokespersons, interest groups, or political parties. (This process corresponds, in functional language, to interest articulation and political communication.)

Supports are actions by individuals or groups that indicate either favorable or unfavorable orientations toward the political system. These actions can be directed toward individual *actors* in the political system (e.g., Britain's Tony Blair, Cuba's Fidel Castro), toward elements of the *regime* (e.g., the prime minister, the supreme court, the municipal council), or toward a broad *political community* (e.g., the Sikhs, Francophones [all peoples speaking French], the Third World, dar al Islam [the World of Islam]). Support can be positive, as when an individual pays taxes, serves in the state's military, salutes the flag, or votes. There can also be negative support, in the sense of actions that criticize or oppose the political system, such as refusing to pay taxes, avoiding military service, burning the flag, or defacing the ballot.

Conversion.   At the heart of the political system framework is the *conversion process*—the process by which political actors assess demands and supports within the context of the relevant environmental forces and then determine what values will be allocated to whom. In Easton's own discussions, the conversion process is treated a bit like a black box, in the sense that little detail is provided about how decisions are made.

Many analysts, however, have been especially interested in studying how the political system actually does make policy decisions and allocate resources, whether or not they use Easton's systems model. The most widely proposed general explanations of the decision process are the *class approach,* the *elite approach,* and the *group approach.* In each, certain groups in society (the dominant class, the small ruling elite, or a diversity of private groups) exercise their power and influence. The state's decision makers respond to these societal forces, implementing public policy decisions that are responsive to the interests of the most powerful groups. Each of these three approaches will be explained in detail in Chapter 9.

There are other analytic descriptions of the dynamics of the political decision-making system in addition to the class, group, and elite approaches. Here are brief sketches of several of these alternatives:

> In the *state-centered approach,* the major public decision makers act autonomously from the diversity of groups in the society. They define a national interest and then formulate and implement policies to achieve this national interest, regardless of contrary views from subunits in the government or from groups in the society (Krasner 1978).

> In the *rational choice approach,* decision makers calculate the expected utility (the net benefits minus the net costs) for each alternative decision and then select the action with the most favorable benefit-cost calculus (Mueller 1993).

> In the *incremental approach,* policy decisions are typically marginal changes from existing policies. In this view, decision makers lack the cognitive capacity and the comprehensive information that would enable them to calculate expected utilities with precision. Moreover, the existing policy is usually a reasonable compromise—the result of a balance of political forces that has emerged over time. For these reasons, it is more sensible and more politically prudent to make periodic small changes that readjust policy toward the decision makers' current goals (Lindblom 1977).

> The *bureaucratic politics approach* emphasizes that a decision maker's particular role in the organization greatly influences the way he structures the issue, the information he receives, and the choices he makes. Decision makers are loyal to their own subunit and its perspective rather than to the organization as a whole. Decisions are compromises based on bargains blending the agendas and values of the different subunits involved in the process (Allison 1971).

> The *organizational process approach* assumes that an organization develops certain routinized, standard operating procedures that determine the flows of information, the formulation of alternatives, the patterns of interaction, and the criteria for choice. Thus the established routines for making decisions are more important than the views of particular actors (Cyert and March 1963).

Outputs.   Once political decisions have been made, they become outputs of the political system. Some analysts find it useful to distinguish *outputs,* which are the decisions and the implementation process, from the *outcomes,* which are the impacts of those decisions. Some outputs are visible and obvious, as when the political system authorizes the development of a new missile system, spends the money to build the missiles, and points them toward its enemies. But it is sometimes quite difficult to identify decisions (outputs), since they might involve subtle actions, secret policies, or even "nondecisions" that perpetuate the existing value distribution or bury issues. For example, if some people demand government subsidies for small farmers and the government does nothing, there has been an allocation decision even though no visible policy action can be identified. A policy might also be implemented in a multiplicity of ways for different people, making it difficult to specify exactly what the policy output is. For example, the state might have a law that an individual cannot kill another person, yet the state does not mete out identical punishment to all those who do kill.

Policy outcomes are another interesting subject for inquiry. Ultimately, it is the impacts of the political system's policy choices that really affect people's lives. The essential questions are: What difference did that policy choice (that value allocation) make? How does the implemented policy affect people's health, welfare, security, knowledge, self-worth? How does it influence their life, liberty, and pursuit of happiness? Even more than in the analysis of outputs, it can be extremely difficult to identify with precision the overall effects of a policy and its effects on particular individuals and groups.

Feedback. The final component in the systems approach is the "feedback loop." It is assumed that outputs might have impact on aspects of the environment and thus will affect the next round of demands and supports reaching the political system. *Feedback* is the term applied to the dynamics through which information about the changing nature of the political system and its environment are monitored by the system. Political actors are supposed to monitor this information, because changes in the environment, inputs, and the political system might require the political actors to revise the value allocations they have previously made. In Figure 5.1, feedback is characterized as a loop to emphasize that there is continuous, evolving interdependency among components in the system.

System Persistence

For Easton (1965), the underlying question is: How does a political system persist in a world of change? The political system is embedded within a complex and changing environment. The political decision makers must maintain a delicate balance of forces: The environments must be prevented from constraining or overwhelming the political system and must be exploited for the resources and opportunities that they present; political actors must be sensitive and accurate in their perceptions of the effects of all other components in the system; demands must be managed so that they are not irreconcilable and so they do not overload the resources available; positive support must be nurtured and negative support discouraged or suppressed through some mix of value allocations that maintain the loyalty or acquiescence of the citizens. In short, the conversion process must operate with political skill and political will.

What happens if there is insufficient political skill or political will? The pressures on the decision makers might overwhelm their capacity to respond effectively. If the political system's performance is poor, there is likely to be a reduction in the quality of the citizens' lives, more problems from the internal and external environment, loss of support for the political system, and a rise in disorder.

At any point, it is possible that there will be changes in the political system: (1) The *authorities* who hold political positions might be replaced, by election, by political pressure, or by violence; or (2) the *regime* might change, through the implementation of new governing structures or procedures, or through significant alterations in the pattern of value allocations. If these changes in the regime are massive and fundamental, it is even possible for a political system to "die." While Easton and others have never fully specified the necessary conditions for the death of a political system, they would involve sudden and major transformations in the nature of the conversion process or the configuration of value allocations. The discussion of Cambodia in Box 5.5 describes a rapid series of major changes, some of which might be considered deaths of the political system.

For political systems, the 1990s was the most deadly decade in history. The obituary list is headed by the Soviet Union and most of the regimes of Central and Eastern Europe, including Czechoslovakia, East Germany, Poland, Hungary, and Yugoslavia (all between 1989 and 1991; see Chapter 15). In Africa, political systems such as Congo (1997), Rwanda (1994), Sierra Leone (1996), and Somalia (1991) collapsed, and others, including South Africa (1994) and Uganda (1996), have undergone substantial political system transformations. One party, authoritarian regimes were replaced by multiparty democracies in such countries as Nicaragua, Nigeria, and Taiwan. Many political systems, while not "dying," have made substantial transformations away from command political economies (see Chapter 8) and toward greater political democracy (see Chapter 7). Whether a particular political system actually dies can be a matter of debate, but the recent period has provided ample evidence that rapid and dramatic changes do sometimes occur within political systems.

The Utility of the Political Systems Approach

Political scientists disagree about the utility of the political systems approach. Some political scientists think it is a flawed conceptual framework for political analysis. Crucial concepts are defined in several different ways, and clear operational measures have never been developed for these concepts. Moreover, the theory linking the concepts is not specified with much greater precision than is indicated in Figure 5.1. And the approach has provided few predictions or hypotheses that are subject to rigorous empirical measurement and testing. Given these shortcomings, critics dismiss the political systems approach as a nontheoretical and nonempirical abstraction that does little to advance a science of politics.

Few political scientists expect that the political systems approach will fulfill the early hope that it might become the basis of a "real science" of politics (recall pages 13-20 in Chapter 1). Still, the approach has been quite influential as a *metaphor*—as a conceptual framework that describes how the political system operates and that suggests key variables and their linkages. It encourages the analyst to think of politics in terms of political actors, structures, and processes which constitute a system that is dynamic and adaptive as it constantly interacts with its environment(s). The political system is open, in the sense that the environment and inputs generate forces that affect the system and to which it must respond. And the political system is itself an active force, since its decisions and actions are aimed at modifying and shaping its environment and inputs by means of a constant flow of outputs. Many political scientists use this conceptualization of the political system, either consciously or subconsciously, when they attempt to explain the dynamic processes of politics.

BOX 5.5

"Death" of a Political System: Cambodia

The idea that a political system might die can be best grasped by examining Cambodia, a state that has undergone several major transformations in a short time span.

The Cambodia of 1962 (*Cambodia I*) was a small, beautiful state in Indochina that had been granted its independence by France in 1953. It has been said that the most important activities in the lives of the Cambodians were to dance, make love, and watch the grass grow. They were ruled under a rather authoritarian political system by Prince Norodom Sihanouk, a hereditary leader who attempted to balance the forces of the left and the right within Cambodia and to maintain Cambodia on a course as a neutral state.

However, in the late 1960s Norodom Sihanouk was unable to prevent Cambodia from being drawn into the increasingly widespread and intense war in neighboring Vietnam, especially because of the underlying power struggle in the area between the Soviet Union, the United States, and China. Some Vietcong (the guerrillas attempting to overthrow the South Vietnamese state) took sanctuary in Cambodia; but Sihanouk insisted that Cambodian sovereignty prevented the United States and South Vietnamese armies from invading Cambodia to attack these Vietcong. Sihanouk also attempted to direct international attention to the "secret bombing" raids in Cambodia conducted by the American military but denied by the American political leadership.

Because of Sihanouk's resistance to their military objectives, the Americans supported (and perhaps directed) a March 1970 coup in which the leaders in the Cambodian army overthrew Sihanouk and replaced him with General Lon Nol, a rightist dictator who was generally viewed as a puppet of the United States. Under the Lon Nol government (*Cambodia II*), there were dramatic changes in the political structure and foreign policy of the country, and there were considerable changes in domestic policy. This political system was maintained by the United States from 1970 to 1975. In turn, the Cambodian government and military assisted the U.S. military in fighting the communist insurgents. There was escalation of the guerrilla war by Cambodian communists (the Khmer Rouge) against the Lon Nol government and extensive fighting in Cambodia by the military forces of the United States, South Vietnam, the Vietcong, Cambodia, and the Khmer Rouge.

With the collapse of the U.S. military effort in Southeast Asia, Lon Nol's government was among the casualties. Thus the Khmer Rouge came to power in April 1975 and created yet another political system, renaming the state Kampuchea. Under the communist regime of Pol Pot, Kampuchea (*Cambodia III*) experienced one of the most dramatic shifts in a political system during the twentieth century. The new government immediately relocated everyone from urban areas into the countryside, organized the entire population into collective farms that were really forced labor camps, and implemented a massive reeducation (indoctrination) program. In a brutal reign of terror, about one-third of the population of 7 million was either killed or died during a total restructuring of the society.

(continued)

BOX 5.5 *(Continued)*

The Vietnamese exploited this time of disruption, invading and conquering the Cambodians, their centuries-old enemies. The Vietnamese army installed a puppet government under Prime Minister Hun Sen (a dissident Khmer Rouge) in January 1979. Thus *Cambodia IV* replaced Pol Pot's barbaric regime with a new political system that operated as a satellite to the Vietnamese communist government.

After years of guerrilla warfare by groups loyal to the Khmer Rouge and Norodom Sihanouk, a treaty in Paris led to United Nations-supervised elections for a national legislature in 1993. The election and subsequent constitution created *Cambodia V,* an odd combination bringing together many of the old adversaries. Norodom Sihanouk became king, a constitutional monarch with mainly symbolic power. His anticommunist son, Prince Ranariddh, as "First" Prime Minister, shared political power with communist Hun Sen, the "Second" Prime Minister. The Khmer Rouge, who refused to participate in the election, continued a punishing guerrilla war and controlled large parts of the countryside.

This memorial to the victims of the Pol Pot regime is close to the capital city of Phnom Penh. The sign indicates that 129 mass graves were found and 86 of them were opened, yielding the remains of more than 8,985 Cambodians executed in "reeducation camps."

BOX 5.5

This unstable system collapsed in 1997. After a brief civil war, Hun Sen's forces were victorious in a coup that deposed Prince Ranariddh, who was exiled. Key supporters of the Prince's political party either fled the country or were executed. Meanwhile, rival forces within the Khmer Rouge captured Pol Pot, who was interned and soon died. Hun Sen's party now controlled the military and the national administration, although most of the country still seemed beyond the control of the central government. At the beginning of the century, it remains uncertain whether any group can govern Cambodia effectively.

In summary, the political system of Cambodia has undergone numerous dramatic changes during a twenty-five-year period. Minimally, four regimes failed to persist. And it seems reasonable to argue that there was at least one clearcut "death" of a political system, with the replacement of Lon Nol by Pol Pot. The elimination of the Pol Pot government by the Vietnamese might also be classified as a death and rebirth of the political system, since much of the coercive, massive restructuring of Cambodian society was undone (although not the commitment to collectivism). A phrase in the Cambodian national anthem aptly describes the country's recent history: "The bright red blood...spilled over the towns and over the plain." The life expectancy of Cambodia V is quite uncertain.

THREE MAJOR CONCEPTS: A REPRISE

This chapter has focused on three major concepts that characterize large political entities. *State* is a concept that emphasizes the legal standing of these governmental entities, the necessary functions that they perform, and the organizational structures through which they take action. The discussion of three alternative views of the appropriate domain of state activities reveals the considerable range of differences in defining *res publica*, "things of the people."

Nation is a concept indicating a mental state characterized by a sense of shared identity among a set of people, distinguishing "us" from "them" in the sociopolitical world. The widespread problem of disjunction between state and nation was revealed by the example of the Indian subcontinent.

Finally, the notion of the *political system* attempts to provide political scientists with the basic analytic concept for building a general theory of political entities. It specifies the crucial components in a dynamic and adaptive system whose essential function is the authoritative allocation of values for its society. The concept of political system is one abstraction that facilitates discussion and analysis of the major political units in the world. In Chapters 6 and 7, our discussion of these political units becomes more concrete, as we examine the actual political institutions and structures prevalent in contemporary political systems.

FOR FURTHER CONSIDERATION

1. Do you think there are circumstances under which a country's sovereignty should be violated? What is the most serious problem with your position on this question?
2. Do you identify with more than one "nation"? Is there any conflict between these identities? Under what types of circumstances might an individual's multiple nationality identities produce serious internal conflicts?
3. To what extent is it possible to align states and nations in the contemporary world? Would doing this be desirable?
4. Develop a dialogue between person A, who believes that the authority of the state must be obeyed under virtually all conditions, and person B, who believes that the authority of the state can be disputed in any situation in which B substantially disagrees with the state's decision.
5. Describe several situations in which the decision-making capacity of the most powerful actors in the political system is almost completely constrained by factors in the extrasocietal or intrasocietal environment.

FOR FURTHER READING

Barber, Benjamin R. (1995). *Jihad versus McWorld.* New York: Random House. An incisive analysis of the current world trends, in which there is a simultaneous globalization of culture and economics on the one hand, and the breakdown of peoples into distinct and hostile nationality groups on the other.

Barnett, Michael N. (1998). *Dialogues in Arab Politics: Negotiations in Regional Order.* New York: Columbia University Press. Focusing especially on the views of key leaders of Arab states of the Middle East and their attempts to create effective interstate relations, this study also offers insights about the struggle to define nation and state, given the complex identities based on Arabism, Islam, tribes, and countries.

Becker, Elizabeth. (1986). *When the War Was Over: The Voices of Cambodia's Revolution and Its People.* New York: Simon & Schuster. A gut-wrenching description of Kampuchea under the Pol Pot regime.

Connor, Walker. (1994). *Ethnonationalism: The Quest for Understanding.* Princeton, NJ: Princeton University Press. A detailed analysis of the nature of and the imperatives driving the strong identity with nation as opposed to state, enriched by many illuminating examples.

Deutsch, Karl W. (1981). *Nationalism and Social Communication.* 3d ed. Cambridge: Harvard University Press. A conceptual and empirical approach to defining the nation in terms of the intensity of patterns of human communication.

Evans, Peter B., D. Rueschmayer, and Theda Skocpol, Eds. (1985). *Bringing the State Back In.* Cambridge: Cambridge University Press. Significant essays arguing that the state is a major institutional actor whose role was being ignored in many analyses that emphasized individuals and groups.

Huntington, Samuel P. (1996). *Clash of Civilizations and the Remaking of the World Order.* New York: Simon & Schuster. The author elaborates his controversial thesis that very broad, nation-based conflicts have reshaped the patterns of world politics in the post–cold war era, with particularly powerful conflicts emerging between the cultural systems ("Civilizations") that the author characterizes as "Western," Chinese, Islamic, Japanese, and Orthodox Russian.

Kesey, Ken. (1962). *One Flew Over the Cuckoo's Nest.* New York: New American Library. A funny, gripping novel that, at its core, considers the virtues and costs of defying institutional authority.

Thoreau, Henry David. (1849/1981). *Walden and Other Writings.* Ed. J. W. Krutch. New York: Bantam. These essays, especially "On Disobedience," constitute one of the most influential arguments in English for resisting authority.

Vincent, Andres. (1987). *Theories of the State.* New York: Basil Blackwell. A thorough treatment of different conceptualizations of the state.

Government Bureau by George Tooker
(Metropolitan Museum of Art)

CHAPTER 6

Political Institutions I: Structures

In framing a government which is to be administered by men over men, the great difficulty is this: you must first enable the government to control the governed; and in the next place oblige it to control itself.
—JAMES MADISON

Along with the other American Founding Fathers, James Madison grappled with many questions regarding the design of a set of political structures and institutional arrangements that would result in an effective government. What responsibilities should be reserved for the political executive? How large should the legislature be and how should its members be selected? How powerful should the administration be? What should be the relation between the courts and the other branches of the government? Should subnational governments be under the control of the national government? Like the Founding Fathers, leaders in every country establish and later modify these structures and arrangements in the attempt to create a government that can achieve valued goals.

These issues are the central topics of Chapters 6, 7, and 8. Chapter 7 will examine forms of institutional arrangements regarding such matters as executive–legislative relations, party system, and citizen democracy. Chapter 8 will analyze the alternative frameworks through which the political system and the economic system are linked. We begin our consideration of these issues in Chapter 6 with an analysis of the four major structures that are basic components of most contemporary political systems. The generic names of these political structures are familiar: *legislatures, executives, administrative systems,* and *judiciaries.*

Chapter 5 made the analytic distinction between certain *functions* of governance, such as policy making and policy adjudication, and the institutional *structures* that might be involved in the performance of those functions. This distinction between functions and structures can be confusing, because there is a tendency to identify a certain function with a certain structure. For example, one might assume that the national legislature is the structure that dominates the policy-making function. However, the distinction between function and structure is useful because, minimally, there might be structures other than the legislature that are significantly involved in policy making; for instance, in the United States there are major policy-making activities not only in the Congress, but also from the chief executive (the president), the upper levels of the administration (the Cabinet departments), and the judiciary (particularly the Supreme Court). In China the national legislature has almost no real power over the policy-making function, which is carried out by the Communist Party and the political executive.

This chapter emphasizes the primary functions that are typically performed by each of the four major institutional structures, the basic building blocks of most contemporary political systems. As you read this chapter, remember that each major structure can perform a variety of functions in a particular political system and can be composed of many different substructures. For these reasons, the discussions emphasize broad patterns and generalizations, although there are always exceptions and variations across the many national political systems.

THE LEGISLATURE

Most states (about 89 percent) have a **legislature** as a part of their basic structures of governance (Derbyshire 1996). Among the names of legislatures (which can have one or two "houses") are the Senate and the House of Representatives (United States), the Senate and the Chamber of Deputies (Chile, Mexico, and Venezuela, among others), the Legislative Assembly (Costa Rica), the National People's Congress (China), the Majlis (Iran), the National Assembly (Egypt and Tanzania, among others), the Lok Sabha and the Rajya Sabha (India), the Knesset (Israel), the House of Representatives and the House of Councillors (Japan), and the House of Commons and House of Lords (United Kingdom).

Roles of the Legislature

Legislatures have always been structures in which policy issues are discussed and assessed. Indeed, the roots of the name of the first modern legislature, the British Parliament, suggest this crucial function—the French word *parler* means "to talk." Most early legislatures were initially created to provide advice to the political executive, typically a monarch, and to represent politically relevant groups. Many legislatures have also been responsible for a second major function—enacting public policies. The roots of the word *legislature* itself are the Latin words *legis,* meaning "law," and *latio,* "bringing or proposing." Some of the earliest legislatures, such as the Roman Senate (c. 500 B.C.E.–100 A.D.), had great power to discuss and enact laws.

Although a particular legislature might not exercise these powers, most legislatures are supposed to have three broad roles: (1) enacting legislation, (2) representing the citizenry, and (3) overseeing the executive. In the following discussion of these roles, be aware that it is difficult to generalize about the actual functions of the legislatures in all contemporary political systems. First, these functions are often quite different from those specified in the state's normative rules, such as those in constitutions. Second, the functions of legislatures vary considerably from state to state. Third, they vary through time within a state. Fourth, even in one time period, the role of the legislature within a state can vary by issue and by the personalities of those involved.

Enactment of legislation.   It might seem obvious that legislatures draft, modify, and then ratify public policy in the form of legislation. In fact, however, most contemporary legislatures do not have the dominant role in the policy-making function. As is suggested later in the chapter, dominance in policy making has passed to the executive in most political systems.

Nonetheless, many legislatures continue to have an active and significant role in policy making. The essence of the legislature's power in the policy-making process is, in most political systems, a constitutional provision that a majority vote of the members of the legislature is required to authorize the passage of any law ("legislative enactment"). The power to enact laws that raise revenue and to authorize its expenditure on public policies ("the power of the purse") has been a central responsibility of the legislative majority. In some systems, legislatures have a system of special committees that thoroughly assess and can amend all proposed legislation under the committees' jurisdiction. And in some political systems, many laws are initiated and drafted by members of the legislature.

Representation of the citizenry.   A second major role of the legislature is to represent, within the governing process, the opinions and interests of the citizenry. Most legislators are elected by some set of the eligible voters, and it is assumed that a key responsibility of a legislator is both to reflect and to serve the interests of those voters.

However, the concept of representation is not straightforward, because there are at least four different conceptions of the "interests" that a legislator might attempt to represent: (1) the group that is most dominant in the legislator's constituency, possibly a social class, religious group, or ethnic group; (2) the political party to which the legislator owes loyalty; (3) the country as a whole, whose broad interests might transcend those of any group or party; or (4) the legislator's own conscience, which provides moral and intellectual judgment about appropriate political behavior (a position made famous in a brilliant justification in 1774 by British parliamentarian Edmund Burke in his "Address to the Electors of Bristol" [1790/1955: 219–222]).

Is it possible for a legislator to represent all four voices simultaneously? In reality, the legislators in most contemporary legislatures do not experience deep conflict in dealing with the problem of representation.

> For some legislators there is no choice, because they hold office in undemocratic systems, where their actions are dictated by the political leadership, and thus they act as little more than "rubber stamps." This position would characterize the behavior of a legislator in Cuba or Libya, for example.
>
> Other legislators, in both nondemocratic and democratic political systems, are deeply committed to adhere to their political party's line or must obey the party to survive politically. This is usually the situation for most members of the British House of Commons, for instance.
>
> Still other legislators feel such deep loyalty to particular group or societal norms that they seldom experience seriously conflicting pressures.

There are only a few political systems where most national legislators are *not* significantly constrained by these forces. The U.S. Congress is an example. Legislators can experience underlying tensions as they attempt to balance legitimate but competing interests that would lead them to support different decisions or actions. Even in such systems, there is predictability in most legislators' choices (on the basis of such dimensions as conservative-radical ideology or party-political loyalty). But there can be considerable variation as the legislator attempts to balance competing interests and to trade votes, compromising on some issues to ensure greater support for the issues about which she cares most deeply.

Oversight of the executive.   The third major role of legislators concerns their interactions with the executive. In general, the legislature is responsible for overseeing the actions of the political executive. The legislators in some systems have substantial capacity to influence what the executive does. The legislature might have the constitutional right to select the executive, to authorize major policy decisions by the executive, and to approve the chief executive's selection of key appointments. In some systems, such as in India, the president is actually chosen by the legislature (although it is the prime minister, not the president, who is the most powerful executive officer).

Many legislatures have the right to approve the executive's selection of major appointments. The Israeli legislature must approve the cabinet as a whole. The U.S. Senate has the right to "advise and consent" on such presidential appointments as Cabinet members or Supreme Court justices. The Senate's 1987 rejection of Judge Robert Bork, President Reagan's nominee for the Supreme Court, is an example of a legislature asserting its power over appointments. In parliamentary systems, the cabinet and prime minister hold office only if they have the confidence of the majority of the members of the legislature, and the cabinet's policies are enacted only if they are approved by the legislative majority (see Chapter 7).

A second area of legislative oversight involves the right of the legislature to scrutinize executive performance. In many political systems there are regular procedures by which the legislature can question and even investigate whether the executive has acted properly in its implementation of public policies. At minimum, the legislature serves as a discussion and debating chamber. Subjecting the political executive's plans and actions to public debate serves as a modest check on executive power. Many legislatures have a regular opportunity, during their legislative sessions, to question the specific plans and actions of particular members of the executive. In Britain, Italy, and Germany, for example, ministers in the executive cabinet must appear before the legislature and respond to legislator's questions or criticisms about any actions taken by their department.

Most legislatures also have formal investigatory powers on a continuing or a case-by-case basis. The investigation of President Bill Clinton (regarding accusations associated with "Whitewater," sexual harassment, and perjury) in the late 1990s by Congress is a dramatic American example of such oversight. In addition, some legislatures have followed the innovative idea of Sweden, setting up an *ombudsman*—an independent agency that investigates complaints regarding the actions of the executive branch and its administrative units. If legislative questioning, committees, or the ombudsman discover inappropriate behavior by the executive, significant political pressure is placed on the executive to correct it. Of course, if the executive resists such pressure, the ultimate resolution of the dispute entails either legal adjudication or, in most cases, a power struggle between the executive and the legislature.

The most fundamental power of oversight held by some legislatures is their capacity to overturn the government. In a parliamentary system, the legislature can oblige or pressure the executive to resign from office by a vote of censure or of no confidence, or by defeating a major bill put forth by the executive (see Chapter 7). In Italy, for example, the legislature has forced the executive to resign about one time per year (on average, since the early 1950s). Even in presidential systems, the legislature has the power to overturn the executive by means of the extraordinary process of impeachment. Impeachment is quite rare in presidential systems. In the United States, no president has left office because of impeachment, although in 1868 Andrew Johnson was acquitted on the House of Representatives' impeachment charge by only one vote in the Senate, in 1974 Richard Nixon avoided an impeachment trial only by resignation, and in 1998, Bill Clinton was acquitted by the Senate on three articles of impeachment brought by the House.

Structural Arrangements

Number of houses.   There is one very visible difference in the structural arrangements of different legislatures—the number of houses (often called *chambers*). There are *unicameral* (one-chamber) *legislatures* in 71 percent of the countries with legislatures (Derbyshire 1996). The presumed advantages of a unicameral system are that political responsibility is clearly located in one body and that risks of duplication or stalemate between parallel legislative bodies are eliminated. Nearly four-fifths of the countries with a strong central government (see Chapter 7 on these "unitary states") have unicameral legislatures. Among the states with unicameral legislatures are Algeria, Bulgaria, China, Costa Rica, Denmark, Finland, Greece, Hungary, Israel, Kenya, New Zealand, South Korea, Sweden, and Tanzania. (See also Box 6.1.)

In contrast, 80 percent of the countries that have two legislative chambers— *bicameral legislatures*—are federations (states that share power between a central government and regional governments). These federal states include Australia, Canada, Germany, India, Mexico, the United States, and Venezuela. There are bicameral systems in 22 percent of the unitary states, including France, Great Britain, Italy, and Japan (Derbyshire 1996).

Given the apparent advantages of a unicameral system, what is the justification for a second chamber? The first argument is that two legislative houses ensure more careful deliberation on issues and laws. Second, the two houses can be based on two different and desirable principles of representation. In about two-fifths of the bicameral legislatures (e.g., Germany and the United States), one house represents the regional governments and the other house more directly represents the numerical and geographic distribution of citizens. Some upper houses also represent functional groups in the society, as in the Republic of Ireland, where members are appointed as representatives of such groups as agriculture, labor, industry, culture, and public services. Third, in a few bicameral systems, some members are selected

BOX 6.1

A Peripheral Puzzle: Nebraska

Nebraska is the only American state government with a unicameral legislature. Can you suggest why Nebraska's decision was a good one or a bad one?

on more individualistic criteria, as in the British House of Lords and the Canadian Senate (where all members are appointed for life).

Over time, some bicameral systems have evolved toward unicameral systems. This has occurred where the need for extensive checks and balances within the legislative branch has not seemed compelling, where representation in the "people's" chamber has seemed adequate, and where the problems of overlap and stalemate between the two chambers have increased. Some political systems, such as those of Sweden and Costa Rica, have constitutionally abolished one chamber. In other systems, such as Norway and Britain, the powers of one chamber have been so reduced that it can delay, but cannot veto, the decisions of the more powerful chamber. In fact, the United States is now the only bicameral political system in which the regional upper chamber (the Senate) is more powerful than the popularly based lower chamber (the House of Representatives) (Derbyshire 1989: table 27).

Size of legislatures.   The number of members within legislatures varies enormously, with some houses having fewer than ten members and others having thousands of members (e.g., the National People's Congress in China has 2,978 members). The single house or the lower house typically represents "the people," with legislators elected proportionate to the population. In general, there is a positive correlation between a country's population and its number of legislators (a ratio defined mathematically as a "cube root law" by Taagepera and Shugart 1989: 174–179). However, among the more populous countries, there is no obvious principle for determining the optimal numbers of legislators. In the U.S. House of Representatives, 435 members are elected, a ratio of one member per 554,000 people. Of the 165 countries with a legislature, only India has a higher ratio of population to members than does the United States. The United Kingdom, with less than one-third the U.S. population, has 650 elected members in its House of Commons, a ratio of one member per 87,000 citizens. More than half of all countries have a ratio of fewer than 50,000 people per representative (Derbyshire 1996).

Can you think of an appropriate criterion for deciding the number of members in a country's legislature? Similarly, are there persuasive reasons why, for example, the upper house in the United States (the Senate) has two rather than three—or four or more—representatives for each state?

The Decline of Legislatures

Many observers claim that in the twentieth century there has been a general decline in the power of legislatures, relative to executives and bureaucracies. Has the power of the legislature declined, and if so, why? Actually, it is very difficult to provide a definitive answer to these questions about relative power, using the techniques of cross-national empirical analysis. In large part, this is so because the precise measurement of power continues to be a puzzle for which political science has no clear solution. (See Box 6.2.)

Given the difficulty of assessing political power with precision, can *any* answer be provided to the question of measuring the decline of legislative power? An empirical test of the relative decline of legislative power is especially difficult. It requires measurement and comparison of the power not only of the legislature, but also of the executive and the bureaucracy, at several points in time and across several (many?) different countries. Since no studies have provided a rigorous analysis

BOX 6.2

The Problem of Defining Power

Few discussions about politics can occur without direct or indirect reference to power. There is general agreement that **power** *is exercised when A (one actor) induces B (another actor) to behave in a manner in which B would not otherwise behave.* This emphasizes a causal relation between what A wants and what B does. The two actors could be two individuals or groups, or even countries.

The key question, of course, is: How does A exercise this power over B? Many political scientists and other social scientists have grappled with this question. (For different views, see Bachrach and Baratz 1962; Boulding 1989; Dahl 1991; Lukes 1974; and Wrong 1980.) Kenneth Boulding (1993) suggests that there are three major varieties of power:

1. *Force* (coercive power). Here, A indicates to B that unless B does what A wants, A will cause something to occur that B does not want. The concept of "power politics" is usually understood as a situation involving force—typically based on coercion or at least the threat of coercion by A. The instruments of force available to A might involve direct bodily harm to B (e.g., guns, bombs, torture) or the imposition on B of undesirable conditions (e.g., imprisonment, discriminatory treatment). Of course, B might not yield to A's threat of force, responding, for example, with a counterthreat. Also, B might resist A's actual use of force with counterforce, resulting in a fight.

2. *Exchange* (economic power). Secondly, A can have economic resources that alter B's behavior. This exercise of economic power could be coercive, in the sense that A might prevent B from enjoying certain economic benefits. For example, A might refuse to sell or give to B an important resource that B needs (e.g., oil, economic aid) unless A's demands are met. Alternatively, A and B might engage in a more cooperative arrangement, where A promises a resource to B (e.g., a trade agreement, a bribe) in exchange for behavior from B that A desires.

3. *Mutuality* (integrative power). Power can also be exercised if B perceives a shared commonality with A. In this case, B conforms to A's demand because B feels a bond of affection or loyalty to A. For example, B might decide that A has legitimacy—that A should be obeyed because A is worthy of exercising authority (recall Box 5.3). Thus B feels a moral or social obligation to yield to A. Integrative power is the least coercive and most subtle form of power exercise; it is probably most widespread in the world of political relationships. It is a power relationship because it causes B to do something that A wants but that B would not otherwise do.

Notice that the three forms of power described cover an enormous range of processes. Many situations involve a complex mix of these dynamic processes, and it becomes very difficult to specify which particular type of power has actually caused observed behavior. These kinds of conceptual and empirical problems have

(continued)

BOX 6.2 *(Continued)*

led most political scientists to admit, often with embarrassment, that operational-ization and measurement of one of the central concepts in political science remains elusive. Because most people share a broad common understanding of the idea of power, it is reasonable to continue to refer to it. However, it remains difficult if not impossible to undertake a precise empirical test of a question such as: Has the power of legislatures declined in relation to the power of executives?

of this issue, we might begin with a more modest question: Is there evidence that contemporary legislatures display significant political weaknesses? Despite the absence of precise measures, there are a few types of circumstantial evidence that suggest legislative weakness.

To begin with, the weakness of the legislature seems undeniable in about one in twenty contemporary political systems, which have no working legislature whose power we might assess.

Moreover, in some states the legislature is essentially a rubber stamp for the actions of a powerful political executive. This lack of significant power applies to about one-fifth of the remaining states. Thus in about one in four contemporary political systems, the legislature need not be considered a major power structure.

Among the political systems in which there do seem to be real legislatures, there are indirect indicators of the relative weakness of most national legislatures. First, most legislatures do not provide a coherent structure within which power can be concentrated and exercised effectively. Many legislatures have relatively slow and cumbersome procedures for the lawmaking function, especially where there are regular legislative committees that amend legislation. This complexity in the legislative process is even more evident in bicameral systems, since there is often disagreement between the two chambers.

Second, most legislatures react to policy initiatives from the executive more than they create policy. The legislatures almost never have the level of support services that are available to the executive. Their budgets, facilities, staff sizes, and even the legislators' own salaries are significantly lower than those of top members of the executive and administrative structures. Similarly, the technical expertise and knowledge resources available to legislatures are far less than those of the executive and administrative structures, a major liability when legislators attempt to deal with the complex subjects facing governments in modern societies.

Some analysts have argued that a third, more social-psychological weakness of legislatures exists, although little empirical data support this point. The claim is that most citizens desire clear, dynamic, and singular political leadership, but legislatures are typically composed of many people who, for most citizens, are either indistinguishable or offer too many different identities. In the United States, for example, it is usually possible to answer this question: What does the president think about issue *Y*? But how does one answer the corresponding question: What does the legislature think about issue *Y*? In this case, there are not only two chambers and two parties, but also a great diversity of different opinions among the individuals and factions within the legislature. In a sense, even though legislatures usually have spokespersons and leaders, no one can truly speak for the legislature. One might even conclude that the legislature in a domestic society tends to fulfill one of its roles *too* well—its members too accurately represent the diversity of political beliefs among the society's population, and thus they speak with many voices.

While the empirical evidence is sketchy rather than systematic, the reasons cited in the preceding discussion suggest why the power of legislatures might not have kept pace with that of other institutions, especially the executive and the administration. Clearly, not all legislatures are impotent or dying institutions. Certain national legislatures remain extremely powerful political structures, such as those in Italy, Japan, Sweden, and the United States. In most other relatively democratic political systems, legislatures have significant impacts on the authoritative allocation of values through their roles in enacting legislation, in representation, and in oversight. And in virtually all societies that have a legislature, its members can exercise political power in many subtle ways. At the least, legislative members have dramatically more political power than most other citizens.

EXECUTIVES

The historical evidence indicates that as long as there have been political systems, there have been individuals or small groups who assume top leadership roles. Such a leader or leaders, who are responsible for formulating and especially for implementing public policy, can be broadly called the *executive structure*. The word executive comes from the Latin *ex sequi,* meaning "to follow out" or "to carry out." Thus the particular role of the **executive** is *to carry out the political system's policies, laws, or directives.*

One might be tempted to generalize that a few individuals emerge as the leadership cadre in *every* political order. But there are some historical counterexamples, especially from Africa and Asia, of societies that are "acephalous;" that is, "without a head." In such systems, many people in the community share power relatively equally, as a collective leadership. Nonetheless, in most sociopolitical systems a few people do assume the positions of executive power.

At the apex of the executive structure there is usually an actor who can be termed the chief executive. In a national political system this might be a single individual with a title such as president, prime minister, chief, premier, supreme leader, or queen. Or the top executive leader can be a role fulfilled by two or more individuals. In this case, there might be a president and a prime minister (as in the French example described in Chapter 7, Box 7.3) or a group exercising shared executive leadership (e.g., a junta).

A broader definition of the executive includes not only the chief executive, but also the entire administrative system. Such a definition derives from the notion that the policy implementation function (the "execution" of policy) is shared by the chief executive and the administration. The top executive group cannot survive without the continuing support of an extensive system of people who interpret, administer, and enforce the policy directives of the executive. However, in order for us to differentiate analytically among the major structures in most political systems, the chief executive and the administration are examined in separate sections of this chapter.

Roles of Executives

Leadership roles. In modern political systems, the crucial role of the chief executive is to lead. The leadership role entails taking the initiative in formulating, articulating, and implementing goals for the political system. In the contemporary political world, political leadership is virtually always identified with chief executives. The effective chief executive becomes the spokesperson for the aspirations of the people, can galvanize the people's support for these goals, and develops strategies that facilitate their accomplishment. The crucial skill of the "great" chief executive is this capacity to lead—to mobilize people and objects in the accomplishment of desirable goals.

To a large extent, initiative in policy formation is centered in the chief executive. Executive policy leadership is especially crucial during times of crisis because the executive structure has the potential for coherence and unanimity of action that are often lacking in the legislature. Moreover, in most political systems the chief executive has the capacity to veto, either directly or indirectly, the legislation that is initiated by the legislature. Increasingly, even the drafting of legislation is a function dominated by the executive, since many major bills require the expertise and policy direction of the chief executive and its staff.

Symbolic and ceremonial roles.   The actors in the executive role usually function as the unifying symbol of the entire society, becoming the ultimate mother/father figures for the people. This is especially true if the chief executive has a strong image, as do such leaders as Cuba's Fidel Castro, Libya's Muammar Qaddafi, and King Mswati III in Swaziland. The executive's presence becomes central to many rituals and ceremonies in the society, whether it be the Japanese emperor's wedding, the Kenyan president's official send-off of the national team to the Olympic games, or the British queen's Christmas Day televised message to her subjects.

Supervision of the administration.   In virtually all contemporary political systems, the executive has primary responsibility for the implementation of the policies and laws of the political order. At the apex of this administrative hierarchy, which might include millions of public employees in the state's departments, bureaus, and agencies, is the top group of the executive structure. Most systems have an executive cabinet, with each member directly and personally responsible for some major area of administration. Given the scale and complexity of the activities being supervised, these top executive actors can neither know nor control all of the actions that occur within their domain. Nonetheless, they are supposed to set the broad guidelines for policy implementation, and in many political systems they are accountable for any major failures that occur. In parliamentary systems, for example, the minister of a department will usually resign if there is a serious shortcoming or blunder in the area under her responsibility.

Supervision of the military and foreign affairs.   Given the state's monopoly of the legitimate use of force, the military (including internal security forces) is an area over which the top political executive usually has direct control. In such cases, the top executive is the commander in chief of the entire military system of the state, including personnel and other resources (aircraft, nuclear weapons, military intelligence, and so on). The chief executive must set policy and supervise the organization and utilization of the state's military capabilities, a task that can carry the most serious consequences for the security and well-being of the society.

Associated with control of the military is the executive's responsibility for foreign affairs—the state's relations with other states. As Chapter 12 will describe more fully, the relations between states involve complex patterns of cooperation and conflict, as each state attempts to accomplish its own goals in the international environment. The chief executive (or the chief executive's delegates) represents the state in its dealings with other countries. Particular significance is often attached to situations where the chief executives of different states meet directly, as in a state visit or a "summit conference." In fact, such meetings among heads of state typically are symbolic gestures of cooperation or occasions for ratifying agreements that have been reached by the chief executives' representatives. But the concentration of the states' political power in the chief executives is so great that such meetings can provide opportunities for major breakthroughs in the relations between the states.

Structural Arrangements

Fused versus dual executive.   Many political systems have a **dual executive**. One actor, the head of state, performs the more ceremonial aspects of top leadership while another actor, the head of government, is responsible for the more political aspects of the executive role. The essential virtue of the dual executive is that individual citizens can be angry or hostile toward the head of government while still remaining loyal to the nation and to the political system through their affection and support for the more ceremonial head of state.

Constitutional monarchies are obvious examples of political systems with a dual executive. In these systems there is a ruling king or queen (e.g. Queen Elizabeth II

Come together, right now, over me. The British Parliament opens yearly with Queen Elizabeth II, the head of state, delivering a speech written by the prime minister, the head of government. The speech outlined the legislation that the prime minister's government will introduce. The queen comes to the House of Lords, whose members surround the Law Lords (the highest judiciary group). By tradition, the prime minister and the members of the now-powerful House of Commons "force" their way into the chamber and stand in the back of the House (not shown).

in Britain, Queen Margrethe II in Denmark, or Emperor Akihito in Japan) as well as a prime minister or other head of government. The monarch has little or no power to make authoritative value allocations; rather the monarch serves mainly symbolic or ceremonial functions as an embodiment of the nation and the people. Some countries have attempted to create a dual executive in the absence of a monarch. They have established a second executive office as head of state (such as the presidency in Germany, India, and Ireland) that is typically insulated from the daily struggles of politics and thus can be a symbol of national unity. There are also countries where the culture is deeply grounded in a religious belief system and where the head of the religion can function like a head of state, as in Iran, where the president and legislature lead the political system, but the religious leader, Ayatollah Khameinehi, also has formidable power over aspects of political life.

Most political systems have a *fused executive.* Here a single actor fulfills both the ceremonial roles associated with the head of state and the political functions associated with the head of the government. In such cases, it can be difficult or impossible to distinguish (dis)loyalty to a partisan political leader from (dis)loyalty to the nation. Clever chief executives use this fusion of roles to their advantage, "wrapping themselves in the flag." Such executives criticize or even punish their opponents by claiming that the opponents are traitors to the political order (even though the opponents are usually only criticizing the political actions of the leader).

Some political systems have two actors who perform parts of the chief executive role but are not really dual executives in the sense described in the preceding paragraphs. For example, there are countries (e.g., France and Russia) where both a prime minister and a president perform essentially political functions, although one does usually have a stronger claim to the head-of-state role. In certain political systems, there is a political executive and a monarch who, in addition to serving as head of state, is also a powerful political actor. Bhutan, Kuwait, Morocco, and Swaziland are other examples where the monarch is the head of state but also has greater political power than the prime minister.

"The executive."   While the term *chief executive* refers to the one individual or small group at the apex of the executive structure, *the executive* is a broader term, including all the people and organizational machinery that are below the chief executive in the executive structure. Thus it encompasses upper- and middle-level decision makers in all the departments, agencies, or other administrative units that are in the chief executive's chain of command. As was noted earlier, a definition of the executive far broader than the one in this book might also include the entire administrative system.

In theory, and usually in practice, this is a hierarchical system of political control, in the sense that the actors in the executive structure are supposed to follow the directives of the chief executive. But the chief executive's power over the rest of the executive is rarely absolute. Among the reasons why the chief executive's directives might not be carried out are these:

1. Units within the executive might be too disorganized to act effectively.
2. The executive might lack the resources to carry out policies in the manner desired by the chief executive.
3. Some units might be more involved in competing against other units than in coordinating their actions to meet the chief executive's policies.

4. Units might misunderstand or resist or defy the chief executive.

Can you think of other reasons?

The Age of the Executive?

Although chief executives have nearly always been evident, and usually ascendent, in political systems, some analysts call the twentieth century the "age of the executive." This label reflects the apparent concentration of power in executives and the relative decline of legislatures' powers. Why do analysts claim that this has occurred? To some extent, this is a chicken-and-egg issue: The reduced capacity of the legislature for coherent and decisive state action is linked to the emergence of coherent and decisive executives.

In comparison to legislatures, the executive structure tends to be more streamlined and less prone to stalemate and inaction. Also the executive, centered in a single individual or small group, can offer a unified focus for a mass public that desires simplicity and clarity in an age of great complexity. If a contemporary mass public wants some form of heroic leadership, it is most likely to be sought from the chief executive. The chief executive typically speaks with one voice and, when effective, can assure the people that political power will be exercised with certainty and efficiency to respond to the pressures and demands in the society and in the international environment.

Even if a chief executive cannot deliver, she can at least promise decisive leadership in a manner that no other political structure can. Since most political systems have always had a significant or even a dominant executive structure, the twentieth century might merely be more executive dominated than many other historical periods. Can you specify conditions under which a state would be likely to be dominated by a structure *other* than the political executive?

THE ADMINISTRATION

While the chief executive can be understood as the top manager of the policy-implementation function, the administration consists of the thousands or even millions of public employees who do the ongoing business of interpreting and implementing the policies enacted by the state. These employees are divided into organizational units called by such names as departments, ministries, agencies, or bureaus. The state's military and police forces are often a particularly crucial component of the administration.

The administration is the machinery of government without which the political system could barely function. The units perform such important activities as maintaining order, collecting revenues, keeping records, providing public goods and services (e.g., roads, education, solid-waste disposal, health care, monetary aid for the needy), and regulating or controlling the factors of production (e.g., production of steel, provision of transportation, growth and distribution of food).

Bureaucracy as One Form of Administration

In most discussions, administration and bureaucracy are synonymous concepts; but in the attempt to clarify our language of political analysis, it might be helpful to distinguish them. In this view, **administration** is the general term used to describe *the machinery and the processes through which rules and policies are applied and imple-*

mented. **Bureaucracy** is a particular structure and style through which the administration can operate. Bureaucratic structure and style have received their definitive description from Max Weber, the great German sociologist we first encountered in Chapter 1. Structurally, bureaucracy is characterized by hierarchical organization and specialization by means of an elaborate division of labor. Weber also defined the concept of bureaucracy by several key characteristics of its style of operation: Its members apply (1) specific rules of action to each case so that the resulting treatment of each case is (2) rational, (3) nondiscretionary, (4) predictable, (5) and impersonal (Weber 1958a: 196–244).

Some readers might have regularly experienced treatment by public administrators that is consistent with these features. This is quite possible, since some countries have deeply incorporated this bureaucratic style. But there are also many contemporary political systems, and even more examples historically, with frequent instances of unpredictable and personal treatment by administrators. In these systems, the treatment that you receive can depend on the attitude of the administrator with whom you interact, as well as who you are and whom you know. Or it can depend on the favors or benefits you offer to the administrative actor who deals with your case. (See Box 6.3.)

Among contemporary political systems, situations like that in the imaginary system of Delta in Box 6.3 are widespread. Personal contacts and bribes (in various societies, called *chai, baksheesh, mordida,* or *dash*) are often an essential element of success in dealing with the administration. Indeed, in some societies a style such as that in Delta is viewed as normal and even appropriate because individual treatment and personal favors are assumed to be preferable to rigid application of the rules.

Is there a reasonable argument against a Weberian-style bureaucracy? In complex societies, terming an organization "bureaucratic" is not usually intended to be a compliment. Some criticisms of bureaucracy are really directed at all large administrative structures that exercise increasing control over people's lives and that expand their organizational domain (i.e., their turf) to a level where they are seen as too large and powerful. But at its heart, the negative use of the bureaucracy label has come to connote a system that is too inflexible and impersonal. The application of rules is so rigid that extenuating circumstances tend to be overlooked, and every individual is treated merely as a number. Bureaucrats themselves are seen to be relatively free of political accountability because they are protected by professional norms and hiring and firing rules, which give them quasi-permanent tenure and insulate them from political pressure.

Despite criticisms of its occasional excesses in practice, many people conclude that the Weberian bureaucracy is the best administrative form for most contemporary political systems. In the abstract, most people would prefer an administrative system that is overly rigid and impersonal to one that is based on corruption and personal favoritism. Many countries claim to be operating in terms of the ideals of Weberian bureaucracy, but there are enormous differences in the extent to which such ideals are consistently applied, especially in environments where the ideals are contrary to traditional practice.

Administrative Functions and Power

The scale of activity of a state's administrative structure depends on that political system's definition of *res publica.* As the political system penetrates a larger sphere of the society and economy, there is a corresponding need for a more extensive

BOX 6.3

"Dealing" with the Administration in Gamma and Delta

An imaginary example might help illustrate the contrast between a classic bureaucracy and an administrative system that does not fulfill Max Weber's criteria. Two citizens, A and B, each intend to undertake an identical activity: to open and operate a small shop selling tea and pastries in the market district.

In the country of Gamma, both A and B apply to the Ministry of Business, where an employee requires each to complete a standard form and to pay a fixed application fee. An inspector from the Ministry of Health examines the premises to ensure that all health and sanitation regulations are met. When rat droppings are found in both premises, both A and B are obliged to hire an extermination service. Each receives the health certificate only after pest eradication and a second inspection. Both A and B open their shops.

In the country of Delta, citizens A and B make the same application. However, A is a member of the dominant ethnic group and B is not. When A applies to the Ministry of Business, she is given a form to complete by the clerk, also a member of her ethnic group, and the form is approved. When B applies, she is told that the maximum number of permits for the market district has already been issued. After lengthy discussion, B telephones her cousin, who is an important politician in the local government. The cousin contacts the undersecretary in the Ministry, on behalf of B, and the application form is now provided and permission is granted. When the inspector from the Ministry of Health examines A's shop, she finds rat droppings. She threatens to refuse the certificate, and so A offers her a substantial amount of money if she will ignore the problem. The inspector takes the money and then completes a report in which the shop passes the inspection. When the same inspector goes to B's shop, she again claims to find evidence of rats. When she can show B no evidence, B demands her certificate. The inspector shrugs, provides the name of the only extermination service she "guarantees," refuses the certificate to open the shop, and leaves.

The contrast between the two imaginary cases is clear. The administrators in Gamma behave in accordance with the bureaucratic ideal. Both A and B receive fair and identical treatment and all rules of procedure are scrupulously followed. In Delta, however, the treatment of A and B is very different. Citizen A manages to succeed because she is a member of the favored ethnic group and because she is willing to bribe an inspector. Citizen B overcomes the hurdle of her unfavored ethnicity because she has an influential contact, but she fails to open her shop because she is not willing to accede to the extortion attempt by the inspector.

administrative structure, since the administration serves as the basic apparatus through which the state interprets, implements, and monitors its value allocation decisions. Thus the administrative system tends to be larger, in relation to the society, as the political system becomes more totalitarian. Given the very substantial variations in the definition of *res publica*, there are at least five broad functions that are performed, more or less extensively, by the administrative structures in contemporary political systems.

1. *Information management.* Administrators are responsible for the collection, storage, and analysis of huge amounts of information about the individuals and processes in the society. This information provides a crucial database—for recording activities and conditions in the society, for measuring the nature and impact of public policies, and for informing many ongoing decisions and actions related to the allocation of public values.

2. *Provision of knowledge.* Many administrators develop great expertise within their specialized areas. This knowledge can be of enormous utility for virtually every decision and action undertaken by the political system.

3. *Provision of public goods and services.* The essential work of the administrative structure is the implementation of policy. Administrators must constantly interpret and apply public policies that provide public goods and services to individuals and groups.

4. *Regulation and enforcement of public policies.* The administrators are also responsible for interpreting and applying many public policies that set guidelines for the behavior of individuals or groups. These can vary greatly, from monitoring collusion among corporations to enforcing traffic laws to protecting the civil rights of ethnic minorities.

5. *Extraction of resources.* In roles such as collector of revenues from citizens and businesses or operator of state-owned companies producing goods and services, the administrative structure is in charge of many tasks that generate resources for the political system.

This brief and general list of functions suggests the enormous breadth and depth of the administrative structure and its activities. Some observers argue that in the complex, extensive, and knowledge-based political systems of the late twentieth century, the power of the bureaucracy is supreme. Although the administrators are, in theory, "servants" of their political masters and clients, it might be that in reality these roles are reversed. Bureaucrats have such unmatched knowledge and experience in their specialized domains that generalist politicians rarely have sufficient expertise to question the bureaucrats' information, recommendations, or actions (Weber 1958). Also, their power to grant or withhold benefits provides them with considerable leverage over clients. Career administrators have quasi-permanent tenure while politicians and clients come and go. The modern bureaucracy has such wide-ranging power and competence that it is typically credited with maintaining political systems when executives and legislatures are ineffective, as in the Third and Fourth Republics in France and in many modernizing states in Africa and Asia. Max Weber himself might have had the last word when he observed that, "in the modern state, the actual ruler is necessarily and unavoidably the bureaucracy" (1958a: 211).

THE JUDICIARY

In a Hobbesian state of nature, disputes among individuals would normally be resolved by force or the threat of force. In such a setting, "might makes right." Thus a primary reason for the social contract is to authorize the state to intervene in the potential and actual disputes among individuals and groups by creating and enforcing rules regarding proper forms of interaction. Every society holds that those who violate its rules and laws (i.e., its policies) must be sanctioned. Because the rules in each society are deeply influenced by its unique culture, history, and politics, there are usually ambiguities regarding the rules:

What does the rule mean?

Has a rule been violated?

Who are the "guilty" actors?

How serious is the offense?

What sanctions are appropriate?

These kinds of ambiguities are resolved through the adjudication function in every political system. Many political systems have established judicial structures whose primary role is, or at least appears to be, adjudication.

Aspects of Adjudication

The **adjudication** function attempts to *interpret and apply the relevant rules or laws to a given situation.* When the issue involves civil law—the rules regarding the relations between private actors (individuals or groups)—the main objective of adjudication is to *settle the dispute.* Examples of such rules include divorce, contracts, and personal liability litigation.

When an individual or group behaves in a manner interpreted as an offense against the social order, adjudication can be an important mechanism of *social control.* Much of this is the area of criminal law, and examples of offenses are murder, substance abuse, theft, bribery, extortion, and environmental pollution. The state represents the public interest and protects the social contract, ensuring that the relations among actors are within the boundaries of "acceptable social behavior." In the same manner that the definition and scope of *res publica* differs greatly across political systems, the definition of acceptable social behavior varies dramatically. In some political systems, social control entails little more than regulation of the conditions under which people can do physical and economic violence to one another. In contrast, there are other political systems where mere public criticism of the political order or its leaders is viewed as a violation of acceptable social behavior, punishable by imprisonment or death.

In some instances, adjudication can center in *arbitration regarding the behavior of the political system itself.* This is especially evident in cases involving constitutional, administrative, or statutory law—the rules concerning the rights and actions of the political system. The main issues for adjudication involve questions about the legitimate domain of action by a governmental actor in its relations with other governmental units or private actors. Such a dispute might concern a highly technical disagreement over the implementation of a specific policy (e.g., is a person with vision correctable to 20/400 qualified to receive state-subsidized services for the "visually impaired"?) or it might raise fundamental constitutional questions about the distribution of political power (e.g., can the chief executive order the military into a violent confrontation with another country if the majority of the legislature opposes the action?).

Judicial Structures

Most, but not all, political systems have specialized **judicial structures**—the *system of courts and personnel that determine whether the rules of the society have been transgressed and, if so, whether sanctions ought to be imposed on the transgressor.* (Some broad definitions of judicial structures even include agencies of law enforcement, such as police and security forces, as well as agencies that apply sanctions against rule breakers, such as jails and prisons, although I have included these among the administrative structures.)

In the United States, the adjudication function is closely linked with explicit judicial structures. The United States has one of the world's most complex systems of judicial structures, with its Supreme Court and extensive system of federal, state, and local courts, including judges, prosecuting attorneys, defense attorneys for the indigent, court clerks, and so on.

While there are significant cross-national variations, most political systems do have a hierarchical system of judicial structures, with appeal processes possible from lower- to higher-level courts. Most judicial systems also have subsystems that are responsible for different aspects of adjudication. For example, the French judicial structure separates the criminal and civil law system from a second system that handles administrative law. In Ukraine, one major system handles criminal and civil law, while a second major system is composed of special prosecutors who monitor actions in all types of cases and who can challenge, retry, or even withdraw cases from the regular courts. In Great Britain, one major judicial system is responsible for criminal law and a second handles civil law.

Among the contemporary countries that do not have judicial structures as part of the government are the Islamic countries that adhere to Shari'a law. Shari'a is the divine law, detailed in the Koran and further elaborated in the *hadith*, the teachings of Mohammad. It is Shari'a, not the laws of humans, that is the judicial framework in such countries as Afghanistan, Saudi Arabia, and Sudan. The Koran prescribes all aspects of social, spiritual, and moral life. As part of that prescription, the sections on law provide the details of what, in Western jurisprudence, includes criminal law, civil law, and administrative law. Shari'a is strictly applied by religious courts, and even the punishments for violations of the law are specified in the Koran.

The constitutions of many states, especially those that have been written in the last three decades, include provisions meant to create an "independent" judiciary. The notion that a judicial system can be independent is an interesting one. The legal system and the set of judicial structures in *every* political system are political. By its very nature, adjudication entails crucial decisions about the allocation of values and meanings for a society. Thus the only sense in which it is reasonable to speak of an independent judiciary is in assessing the extent to which the judicial structures make decisions and take actions that are at variance with other powerful political structures in the society, particularly the executive, legislative, and administrative structures. While there is no systematic research to clarify this question, the judicial structures in most states consistently support and rarely challenge the power and authority of the top leadership groups in their society. In general, the judicial structures are *dependent* on political power for their own power and survival.

However, there are some political systems where the judiciary is relatively independent. By exercising the power of **judicial review**, such *judicial structures can reinterpret or even revoke the policy decisions of the other political structures.* About one in ten states has a very strong system of judicial review. These include Canada, Colombia, Germany, India, Israel, Italy, Mexico, Norway, Switzerland, and the United States. Even in states where the judiciary is relatively independent, it is ultimately dependent upon other political structures, especially the executive and the administration, to enforce its decisions.

Even when the judicial structure does strive to maintain some political independence, it still might respond to political pressure. The conflict between President Franklin Roosevelt and the Supreme Court in the 1930s (see Box 6.4) is a rather visible example of a process that occurs continually in a subtler manner—the impact of external political power on judicial processes and decisions. In most systems the individuals in top judicial positions are likely to share the values of the ruling groups, since they are appointed by chief executive leaders. And when judicial offi-

BOX 6.4

Packing the Supreme Court: FDR versus the Judicial Branch

There is a constant interplay of power between the judiciary and other structures. A classic example of this interplay occurred in the United States during President Franklin Roosevelt's New Deal (1933–1940). Roosevelt drafted and pushed through Congress a series of sweeping laws meant to use national government policies to pull the country out of the Depression. However, the Supreme Court consistently ruled these laws unconstitutional, since the New Deal legislation gave the central government a role far exceeding its constitutional powers, as the court interpreted them. After considerable grumbling and frustration, Roosevelt devised a different strategy for influencing the court. Since there was nothing in the Constitution that limited the court to nine justices, Roosevelt announced that he would significantly increase the number of members on the court.

Congress blocked President Roosevelt's initiative to expand the court. But his appointment of two replacement justices and his threat to "pack" the court were followed shortly by a change of heart on the court regarding the constitutionality of New Deal legislation. By 1937 the court majority no longer objected to the central government's expanded activities. While it cannot be proven empirically that Roosevelt's threat changed the judicial reasoning of the justices, it was punned at the time that "a switch in time saved nine."

cials displease the dominant power group, they can be ignored, replaced, or even eliminated. In Argentina during the 1970s, for example, more than 150 high-level judges disappeared, and it is speculated that the Argentinian government ordered their execution.

Actually, the most common pattern among contemporary states is for the judiciary to be little more than a loyal administrative arm of executive power. While the rituals of the judicial structures offer the appearance of protecting "justice," the reality is that the judicial structures serve the political elite. In short, while most judiciaries exercise some discretion in adjudication, the existence of a truly independent judiciary is a rarity.

CONCLUDING OBSERVATIONS

Traditional political science assumed that a description of political structures is the best means to explain how politics works. But empirical research reveals considerable diversity in the roles of particular political structures. There is no straightforward and necessary correspondence between a political structure and the political functions that seem logically associated with the structure. Thus precise, behaviorally-oriented and process-based analyses of politics now treat political structures more richly.

For a while, political structures seemed so fluid that they were treated as secondary elements, merely forming a context with which various political, economic, and social groups must deal as the groups' actions result in the allocation of values for the society. Recently, many scholars have reemphasized the importance of institutional arrangements. For these "new institutionalists," the particular configuration of political structures can powerfully shape political actions and outcomes (March and Olsen 1989). For the "neostatists," the structures of the state—its institutional arrangements, the actors who have major roles in its institutions, and its policy activities—are autonomous and have fundamental impacts on political, economic, and social life (Evans, Rueschemeyer, and Skocpol 1985; Nordlinger 1987).

A full understanding of the political world requires a clear grasp of the essential features of executive, legislative, administrative, and judicial structures. Institutional structures are the skeleton and organs of the body politic. As one could explain certain biological functions and processes of the body without explicit reference to skeleton and organs, so one could explain certain functions and processes of the political system without reference to structures. But such an abstract description of a biological organism would be incomplete without one's indicating the way in which the structures constrain and shape the functions. Similarly, attempts to describe or explain politics, especially in actual settings, are much richer and more complete if they include a characterization of how political institutions constrain and shape the political process. The next chapter will extend further the explanation of how the structures interact to produce different forms of the body politic.

FOR FURTHER CONSIDERATION

1. Who should a legislator represent on policy decisions? Develop an argument justifying your rank ordering of importance in representing the following: those

groups who voted for the legislator, the constituency, the legislative coalition, the political party, the party leader, the nationality group, the country, and the legislator's own best judgment.

2. Evaluate whether, on balance, it would be desirable to have an administrative system that is relatively flexible and is sensitive to unique, individual circumstances in the handling of each case.

3. The discussion of the judiciary asserts that every set of judicial structures is political. Is the notion of an independent judiciary a sham?

4. What are the benefits and shortcomings of a political system that has a weak chief executive? A fused chief executive?

FOR FURTHER READING

Abraham, Henry J. (1998). *The Judicial Process: An Introductory Analysis of the Courts of the United States, England and France.* 7th ed. New York: Oxford University Press. A clear introduction to the theory and practice of judicial decision making in the three countries, as well as reflections on the judicial process in other countries.

Cappelletti, Mauro. (1989). *The Judicial Process in a Comparative Perspective.* New York: Oxford University Press. A summary of different approaches to jurisprudence and judicial decision making among developed countries.

Derbyshire, Denis. (1996). *Political Systems of the World.* 2d. ed. New York: St. Martin's. A thorough inventory and discussion of the forms and processes of contemporary political institutions.

Fenno, Richard. (1978). *Home Style.* Boston: Little, Brown. A revealing, descriptive study of how members of the U.S. House of Representatives actually behave, with particular emphasis on their efforts to serve constituents in order to enhance their electoral support.

Hess, Stephen. (1996). *Presidents and the Presidency.* Washington, D.C.: Brookings. A series of thoughtful essays on executive leadership and power, spanning two decades, by a leading scholar of the modern American presidency.

Morris, Norval. (1992). *The Brothel Boy and Other Parables of the Law.* A distinguished legal theorist presents an intriguing set of fictional short stories, set in Burma/Myanmar, as a mechanism to explore some of the most controversial issues of the law and justice.

Osborne, David, and Ted Gaebler. (1993) *Reinventing Government.* New York: Penguin. An influential critique of large, bureaucratic government and a framework (using examples from the United States) of how to make government more responsive and entrepreneurial.

Peters, B. Guy. (1995). *The Politics of Bureaucracy: A Comparative Perspective.* 4th ed. New York: Longman. A rich, analytic comparison of the behavior and power of bureaucracies in many countries.

Pitkin, Hannah F. (1972). *The Concept of Representation.* Berkeley: University of California Press. A thorough descriptive and normative exploration of political representation.

Wilson, James Q. (1990). *Bureaucracy: What Government Agencies Do and Why They Do It.* New York: Basic Books. An interesting analysis of the performance of American national administration, identifying both the value and the flaws of the system.

It is an exceptional moment in the presidential system of government: The ledislature exercises its ultimate oversight of the executive, as U.S. Senator Strom Thurmond (far left) swears in Supreme Court Chief Justice William Rehnquist, who will preside over the Senate's impeachment trial of President Bill Clinton.

CHAPTER 7

Political Institutions II: Institutional Arrangements

Democracy is:

(a) *...an agreeable, lawless...commonwealth, dealing with all alike on a footing of equality, whether they be really equal or not.—Plato, c. 427–347 B.C.E., Greek philosopher*

(b) *...the theory that the common people know what they want, and deserve to get it good and hard.—H. L. Mencken, 1880–1956, U.S. journalist*

(c) *...a system where no man is good enough to govern another man without that other's consent.—Abraham Lincoln, 1809–1865, U.S. President*

(d) *...the substitution of election by the incompetent many for appointment by the corrupt few.—George Bernard Shaw, 1856–1950, Anglo-Irish playwright*

(e) *all of the above.*

(f) *none of the above.*

We know that all political systems are not democracies. But what constitutes a democracy? We know that all political systems are not identical. But are they all different? A basic task in political analysis is to determine whether there are some criteria by which political systems can be classified. This chapter considers various ways in which the structural elements of a political system can be arranged.

Consider the twenty-two countries listed here. Do you make any distinctions among these political systems? Does your distinction enable you to establish two or more categories and then place each of the twenty-two countries into one but no other categories? Would other people agree with your classification?

Some countries

United States	Iraq	El Salvador
Libya	Kenya	South Africa
Kuwait	Poland	Saudi Arabia
Japan	Italy	Laos
Cuba	Thailand	United Kingdom
Nigeria	Venezuela	Philippines
Singapore	Russia	
China	Egypt	

BROAD TAXONOMIES

As indicated in Chapter 6, the great majority of countries, including most of those in the preceding list, have executive, legislative, administrative, and judicial structures. You might attempt to classify countries based on similarities in the way these political structures relate to each other. Or you might emphasize other political institutions, such as the type of party system or the division of power among different levels of government. You might distinguish democracies from nondemocracies. Or you might use a nonpolitical criterion to categorize countries, such as their levels of economic development, or their regional location, or their predominant religious culture.

When you attempt to classify countries by some criteria, you are engaged in taxonomic analysis (as discussed in the Appendix). Developing a taxonomy is often the first stage in political analysis because it groups cases for comparative analysis and the effort to develop generalizations.

Are you satisfied with your initial attempt to classify the political systems in the preceding list? What criterion did you use? To the extent that you have distinguished the political systems by means of criteria that are *inclusive* (include all cases), *mutually exclusive* (each case fits in only one category), and *consistent* (others could apply the same criteria and make the same classifications), you have developed an adequate taxonomic scheme. Whether your classificatory system is useful is another matter, and this depends on whether it provides a meaningful ordering of the cases.

This chapter will suggest various ways in which political systems might be classified on the basis of their key *institutional arrangements*—that is, the way in which certain key political structures are organized. The discussion should be useful both in the sense that it provides *analytic information* about the taxonomies used in the study of political systems and, in the broader sense, that it provides *descriptive information* about the basic differences among actual political systems. No taxonomy is used in all political analyses, because each taxonomy emphasizes different aspects of the political world. The choice of a taxonomy depends on the interests of the political analyst. The discussion begins by considering the classification of political systems using the venerable concept of "democracy."

DEMOCRACIES AND NONDEMOCRACIES

One of the most common methods by which political systems are classified is to distinguish democracies from nondemocracies. From our education, as well as our other socialization and experiences, most of us have an intuitive sense about which countries are democracies and which are not. However, the concept can become slippery when we try to apply it. North Korea calls itself the *Democratic* People's Republic. Is it? Sri Lanka calls itself the *Democratic* Socialist Republic. Is it? Argentina, France, Kenya, and Poland also consider themselves democracies. Are they? "Democracy" is such a highly valued label that most states, except a few systems ruled by a hereditary monarch, claim that they are democratic. Is virtually every contemporary political system to be termed a democracy? If not, what general label do you give to countries that are not democratic? "Dictatorships?" "Communist systems?" "Totalitarian regimes?" "Authoritarian systems?"

While we work toward acceptable definitions and labels, let's use "dictatorship" as the opposite of democracy. To begin to clarify your thinking, use your current understanding of democracy and dictatorship to classify the eight political systems in the first column of the list of countries on page 151. If you have been raised in the United States or Western Europe, you probably view Japan, the United States, and possibly Kuwait and Singapore as democracies, and Cuba, Libya, and Nigeria as dictatorships.

The qualification in the previous sentence regarding the site of your upbringing is a crucial one—it alerts us to a fundamental problem with any such discussion. Chapter 4 attempted to persuade you that the understanding and use of political labels is deeply dependent on one's own political socialization and political environment. Thus you should not assume that individuals from other cultures will necessarily agree with your labels.

It might be argued that this problem regarding interpersonal differences in assessments underscores the virtue of the scientific method. The scientific method requires the analyst to specify what a particular concept means, with great precision and in an empirically measurable manner. This method might be the only way in which individuals with fundamentally different ideological views could agree on which of the states are democracies and which are dictatorships. Our discussion will proceed in the spirit of the scientific method, although the author acknowledges his own lifetime socialization, which is grounded in the political conceptions of the American and Western world.

How might individuals with dramatically different political worldviews attempt to establish whether they can agree on the accuracy of the classifications suggested earlier? For example, consider these issues:

> Assume that we are able to establish empirically that the majority of the Libyan population supports the government of Muammar Qaddafi (this is arguably the case, although we do not know it empirically, because there are no genuine elections or reliable public opinion surveys). Under such an assumption, is Libya a dictatorship?

> The same issue might be raised regarding Cuba under Fidel Castro. By what criteria is Cuba a dictatorship when a far greater proportion of people vote in Cuban elections and the government provides far more extensive social benefits to all its citizens than in either the U.S. or Japanese democracies?

> By what criteria is Nigeria not a democracy when there is a high level of electoral and governmental competition between different parties?

> By what criteria is Singapore a democracy when virtually all of the members of the national legislature have, since independence, been members of a single political party?

In asking and responding to such questions, you begin to establish the explicit or implicit standards that must be applied when you attempt to distinguish between democracy and dictatorship. These kinds of questions also underscore the importance of defining with precision the concepts that we use in political analysis.

Defining Democracy

What are the necessary and sufficient conditions for democracy? In its classic sense, true **participatory democracy** is government of and by the people—there is *active, direct participation by all citizens in the authoritative allocation of values*. Realistically, there is no such political system; indeed, Jean-Jacques Rousseau (1712–1778) claimed that only a society of gods could be a true democracy. If our definition is less stringent, democracy might entail the relatively equal capacity of all citizens to influence the allocation of values. It would be difficult to make a persuasive case that this condition holds in *any* political system, including Japan or the United States. In *every* political system, some are more equal than others. In every political system, some make value allocation decisions and others observe.

You might use a notion of **representative democracy**, wherein the *citizens elect people to represent them in the political process and to allocate values on their behalf* for the society. Another general term used to describe representative democracy is a *republic.* In fact, the majority of the countries in the world, in their formal title, call themselves republics (examples, from the *A*s: Republic of Afghanistan, Republic of Albania, Democratic and Popular Republic of Algeria, People's Republic of Angola, Argentine Republic, Republic of Armenia, Republic of Austria, Republic of Azerbaijan. You might think that some of these A "republics" are not particularly democratic).

Kuwait seems to meet this criterion for representative democracy, although few would classify it as a democracy since a substantial proportion of its resident adult population, even many who were born in Kuwait, are not allowed to vote in legislative elections.

Thus the definition needs to be refined to specify that the elections for representatives must be held under conditions of universal (adult) suffrage. Cuba meets this condition, but few would consider it a democracy, because, among other reasons, there are very limited choices for governmental office—all candidates are members of the single (Communist) party.

Is the definition of democracy adequate if it further stipulates that the elections provide voters with alternative choices among representatives? Since Cuba actually does present alternative candidates (from the single party) for the legislature, it seems the definition must also specify that there must be genuine choices. Even with this clarification, there are cases such as Singapore where more than 95 percent of legislators are elected from one party. Thus even the notion of genuine choices among alternative candidates can be ambiguous.

It also is important to establish the recurrent right of the people to select political leaders who do take office. This condition, called the *limited mandate*, means that the electorate grants the authority to govern (the mandate) for only a short, fixed (limited) period of time and that the electorate then has the opportunity to select representatives again. These are the key conditions of an *"electoral democracy,"* in which citizens periodically select political leaders from among alternative contenders who accept this limited mandate. In Nigeria, military leaders supervised a multiparty election in 1993 but then refused to allow the person elected president with broad support (Moshood Abiola) to take office. However, in 1999, a former military dictator (Olusegun Obasanjo) was selected as president in a generally free election. This latter election meets the minimal criteria for an electoral democracy. A key question: will Obasanjo (unlike his recent predecessors) support a legitimate electoral process and surrender power at the end of his term?

More broadly, should a complete definition of democracy have more than electoral components? Perhaps a democracy must ensure not only voting rights and a limited mandate but also must allow the citizens and the media to exercise such freedoms as speech, assembly, and political opposition. We can classify a political sys-

A Zulu in traditional dress casts his vote in the first fully democratic election in the history of South Africa.

tem as a **"liberal democracy"** when *citizens enjoy not only electoral democracy but also these more extensive political rights and civil liberties regarding participation, personal freedoms, and opposition.*

Even a liberal democracy is still less than the literal notion of full *"participatory democracy"*—understood as active rule by all the people. In a liberal democracy, the citizens have extensive rights, but there is still only "contestation" among competing elites, with most citizens exercising minimal or no direct control on policy decisions by the ruling leadership group (see Dahl 1971, 1991; Schumpeter 1950; Schattschneider 1960).

Perhaps we have now established one possible set of sufficient, as well as necessary, conditions for a **democracy**: *governance by leaders whose authority is based on a limited mandate from a universal electorate that selects among genuine alternatives and has some rights to political participation and opposition.*

This is a modest notion of democracy, since it guarantees the people little more than an occasional opportunity to select among the competing elites who govern them. Yet among the first seven political systems in the list on page 151, only Japan and the United States are clearly classified as democracies by this definition. Singapore is more problematic, since the extent to which there is genuine contestation is unclear. While all seven systems encourage some forms of political participation and allow some political opposition, the authority of the political leadership in Cuba, Kuwait, Libya, and (perhaps) Nigeria is not based on its electoral selection, by universal suffrage, among genuine alternatives, for a fixed period of time.

A very expansive conception of democracy might emphasize not only the processes by which political authorities are selected, but also the nature of *outputs* (value allocations) produced by those authorities. For example, Austin Ranney (1990: 111–118) defines democracy as a form of government in which power to make decisions or select public officials is granted to all adult citizens, based on majority rule, and in which "having ascertained the people's preferences, public officials must then put them into effect whether they approve or not" (Ranney 1990: 114). Notice that the first part of Ranney's definition refers to the processes of selecting political authorities and making value allocations, while the second part addresses the actual content of the value allocations, at least in the sense that those allocations must be consistent with what people want.

However, an analytic problem with this policy-output conception of democracy is deciding how to establish whether decision outputs do reflect the "people's preferences." Are they determined by yesterday's opinion polls? By the insights of the public officials? By an assumption that the voters in the previous election were approving the complete array of policies discussed during the campaign? None of these measures seems promising.

In fact, consideration of how the citizen's policy preferences are expressed raises associated questions about the **electoral system**—the *framework by which the citizens' votes select those candidates who receive a limited mandate to govern.* How are the electorate's votes converted into the selection of a particular set of representatives? Do you have a clear answer to how this should be done? Box 7.1 suggests that the best method for this conversion of votes to seats is not as straightforward as it might seem. Could a political system that meets all the other conditions for democracy be faulted because its conversion of votes to seats greatly disadvantages some voters?

Minimally, a process-and-output conception of democracy must incorporate a vision of the effects of the political system as well as the procedures by which value allocations are made. Thus it ensures the population of: (1) participatory rights to select and influence political decision makers empowered for a limited term of office, and (2) broader political and social rights such as freedom of speech, press, assembly, and religion. An extremely broad conception of the "output" aspects of democracy might also include provision of such value allocations as the right to employment, health care, housing, and other forms of social welfare.

This discussion might help you to identify the criteria that *you* think are necessary for an adequate definition of democracy. (It is certainly possible that your definition will differ from any of those suggested here. You should, however, be able to justify your criteria.) Can you now articulate a conceptual definition of democracy and use it to classify the political systems in the list on page 151? Do you think your friends will accept your definition and classification? Would a Kuwaiti or Libyan student accept it? You might be surprised how difficult it is to develop a generally accepted definition of this most widely used political concept.

Defining Nondemocracies

How about nondemocracies? What concepts can be used to characterize those systems that are not democratic?

Dictatorship.　One conventional concept is dictatorship. Is dictatorship more easily defined than democracy? A stringent definition of a "dictator" might be a ruler with absolute power and authority (independent of any consideration of the process through which power was acquired). Can any one individual or even a small group

BOX 7.1

How Much Is Your Vote Worth? Converting Votes into Political Representation (via the Electoral System)

In Chapter 4 (Box 4.1) we considered how much casting a vote is worth to an individual—especially a rational individual who evaluates all the personal costs and benefits connected with that action. At another level, every political system that allows its citizens to vote for elected officials must determine how those votes will be converted into a distribution of political representatives. How much is one vote worth to the political system?

When All Citizens Vote for a Single Office

When there is an election for a single office, such as a national president or a regional chief executive, the most obvious approach is to empower the individual who garners the largest number of votes. But some political systems complicate this straightforward approach by allowing preliminary elections in which some candidates are eliminated (e.g., primary elections in the United States) or in which candidates can volunteer to drop out after a first electoral round (e.g., the French elections for the legislature). Even more countries require that the winner receive a majority of the votes; if no candidate receives a majority on the first round, there is a run-off election between the two top vote getters.

The United States is one of the few presidential democracies that does not allow its citizens to elect their chief executive directly. *Fact:* Your vote for president can count for absolutely nothing, because if your candidate does not gain the largest share of votes in your state, all the state's electoral college votes are cast for another candidate. *Fact:* One presidential candidate can garner the largest share of votes nationally and not be elected, because the winner is the candidate who wins states which hold a majority of the electoral college votes. *Fact:* In 1824 and 1876, the presidential candidate with the largest popular vote was not elected. Does this seem right? *Fact:* If there is no majority in the electoral college, every state gets a single vote in the election of a President. Does it seem right that California, Wyoming, New York and Rhode Island would all have equal impact on the selection of the president?

When All Citizens Vote for a Legislature

The conversion of votes into representatives in a legislature can require some interesting decisions.

First, how many representatives will be elected from each district? It is possible to elect one representative per district, as in the U.S. House of Representatives, but the districts in many political systems have more than one representative. The U.S. Senate has two legislative representatives per district, but many countries vary the number of representatives per district, depending on the population in the district, with as few as one and as many as thirty-nine representatives per district (Taagepera and Shugart 1989: table 12.1). At the extreme, some countries (e.g., the

(continued)

BOX 7.1 *(Continued)*

Netherlands, Israel) treat the entire country as one giant electoral district. Can you think of a sound argument for having all the legislators elected by everyone?

Second, how is the number of votes converted into the number of legislative seats? Table 7.1 presents a possible distribution of votes among candidates for four parties that are distributed ideologically from right (Party A) to left (Party D).

In a *plurality* system (column a), used in most countries with single-member districts, each voter casts a vote for a specific candidate, and the candidate with the largest number of votes wins. The virtue of this approach is that the representative is the candidate preferred by the largest number of voters in the constituency. In column (b) of Table 7.1, can you see a rather serious problem with this plurality victory for Candidate A?

In a system of *proportional representation (PR)*, which has typically been used with multimember districts, candidates from each party are elected in proportion to their party's share of the total district vote. For example, if there were twenty legislative seats in the district, the outcome would be that shown in column (c) of Table 7.1. Can you see how this distribution of seats was determined? The calculations within PR systems can become very complicated if "leftover" votes are transferred into other districts or pooled nationally for certain additional legislative seats.

Most political systems use one of the many variations of either plurality or PR voting, but other calculations are possible. A growing number of countries have attempted to combine favorable aspects of both the PR and plurality approaches. In some systems (e.g., Mexico), there is direct plurality voting for part of the legislature and additional seats are distributed by proportional representation. Recently, "mixed-member proportional" electoral systems have been implemented in such countries as Italy, Japan, and Russia. The particular representative who is elected is the individual preferred by the largest number of voters in the district, but the party's total number of representatives in the legislature is proportional to its national electoral success.

A few political systems (e.g., Australia) employ preferential voting. Voters rank candidates in the order of preference, and then the votes for the candidate with the lowest total are redistributed to those voters' second choice, and so on until a major-

TABLE 7.1
Converting Votes into Elected Officials: Number of Representatives Elected per District in Each Electoral System

	(a) Percentage of Votes	(b) Plurality	(c) PR	(d) Preferential	(e) Approval
Party A	31%	1	6	0 (38%)	0 (46%)
Party B	15%	0	3	0 (0%)1	1 (75%)
Party C	29%	0	6	1 (61%)	0 (69%)
Party D	25%	0	5	0 (0%)1	0 (54%)

Note: Regarding this hypothetical example: In the proportional representation (PR) system, there are twenty seats in the district. In preferential voting, it is assumed that the votes for party B split evenly between A and C, and then all of D's votes go to C. In approval voting, it is assumed that each voter judges the candidates adjacent to his first choice to be acceptable. The percentages in parentheses reflect these assumptions.

BOX 7.1 *(Continued)*

ity candidate appears (see column [d] of the table). Some scholars have argued in favor of approval voting (see column [e]) in which voters can vote for all the candidates they find acceptable, with the winner being the candidate who is acceptable to the largest proportion of the electorate (Brams and Fishburn 1983).

In Table 7.1, each of these four alternative approaches produces a different outcome! Which approach makes most sense to you? As you reflect on the virtues of these broad alternatives, you might notice that every system is flawed in some manner. There is no system that can perfectly mirror the voters' preferences in the composition of a representative legislature. Compared with plurality systems, PR systems tend to enable more parties to gain seats in the legislature, which is good for representing citizens' preferences but might be less desirable for producing a coherent governing majority. It might also be argued that although the candidate of Party B is the first choice of the fewest citizens, he enjoys the broadest support and is the best "consensus candidate."

So, how much is your vote worth? How much should it be worth? How should votes be converted into a fair distribution of representatives? These are intriguing political puzzles.

exercise "absolute" power? Would a system not be a dictatorship if the ruler is unable to exercise absolute power? Alternatively, **dictatorship** might be better defined by *the absence of a limited mandate*—a critical factor in our definition of democracy. That is, if the citizens have no regular and realistic opportunity to replace the political leadership, then the political system is a dictatorship. Clearly, an unpopular ruler or ruling group that has forced the population to accept its authority is dictatorial. However, even a political leadership that has popular support from the majority but does not provide opportunities for the population to renew the mandate in competition against alternative leaders could be defined as dictatorial. This definition seems to characterize the situation in Libya under Qadaffi and in Cuba under Castro.

Authoritarian regime. In the current taxonomies of political scientists, the most common concept applied to nondemocratic systems is *authoritarian regime.* One critical element of authoritarianism, shared with a dictatorship, is the absence of a limited mandate. But **authoritarianism** adds another dimension—*the political actions and decisions of the ruler are not constrained, while the political rights and freedoms of the citizens are significantly limited.* In other words, under authoritarianism, the population has no political rights. An authoritarian regime places severe restrictions on the activities of individuals and groups who desire to influence the allocation of values by the political system. The great majority of the population is not allowed to participate in any political activities except those expressly encouraged by the regime. In most instances, this means that occasional public expressions of support for the system, such as mass rallies, are the only forms of political behavior that are acceptable (Linz 1993).

Citizens are not permitted to question the political institutions, procedures, or value allocations of an authoritarian regime. However, the nonpolitical aspects of people's lives, such as occupation, religion, and social life, are not generally under the direct control of the political system. In some countries, these other areas of life are still significantly controlled, but the control is by traditional societal values or by overriding religious values, not by the political system.

Totalitarian regime.   In a *totalitarian regime,* the definition of *res publica* becomes total. Thus under **totalitarianism**, *the political system's allocation of values and its control penetrate into virtually every aspect of its people's lives.* The totalitarian political system demands complete obedience to its extensive rules regarding culture, economics, religion, and morality. It prescribes and proscribes the behavior and even the thoughts of its population in virtually every domain of existence. Every political system intervenes occasionally in such domains, but the defining characteristic of the totalitarian regime is its constant and pervasive efforts at total control of its population's lives (Friedrich and Brzezinski 1956).

All organizations are subordinated to the totalitarian state. Every activity of the individual citizen is subject to scrutiny by the state, in the name of the public interest. As an example of the penetration of the totalitarian state into all aspects of social life, the North Korean state defines the acceptability of films and plays, determines what and how much of each type of crop will be produced on every farm, discourages or prohibits the activities of organized churches, and decides which families will live in which housing units.

Totalitarian regimes, even more than authoritarian regimes, depend on the use of extensive coercion for their survival. The state employs its military, internal security forces, and other instruments of violence to suppress any citizen or group that challenges its authority. To sustain its pervasive control, the totalitarian regime also makes extensive use of the agents of political socialization, especially the media, the educational system, and cultural forms. Often, the totalitarian state is dominated by a single leader, venerated in a cult of personality and by a single political party. George Orwell's novel *1984* (1949/1967) is a literary vision of the totalitarian state, and recent examples include Cambodia under Pol Pot (Box 5.5), Myanmar (Box 4.5), North Korea, and Sudan.

Some political systems are probably best classified on a continuum between totalitarianism and authoritarianism. These are authoritarian regimes whose political systems extend their control into some nonpolitical domains but do not exercise the totality of control associated with totalitarianism. For example, Saudi Arabia under the Saud family and Iran during the period under Ayatollah Khomeini (1979–1989) are not totalitarian regimes but do assert extensive control over culture, religious practice, and social life. Even further toward authoritarianism on the continuum are political systems dominated by a powerful military or bureaucracy that uses laws and coercion to constrain some aspects of the citizens' lives beyond politics. Examples of such authoritarian regimes are Indonesia under Suharto (1966–1998), Iraq under Saddam Hussein (since the late 1970s), and Congo (Zaire) under Mobuto Sese Seko (1965–1997) [see Box 13.2].

A Democracy–Nondemocracy Continuum

Consideration of several of the cases among the first seven countries named in our list, especially Singapore, Kuwait, and Nigeria, suggests that there are gradations of democracy among political systems. None of these cases is an example of totalitarianism, because many areas of life are free from extensive political control. None of these countries is even fully authoritarian, because citizens have some limited rights to criticize and oppose the leaders (although see Box 15.5 on behavioral controls in Singapore). In all three countries, the citizenry occasionally votes, which can result in turnover within the national legislature. The electoral process determines Singapore's top executive, while Nigeria's leader achieved power in a flawed election, and Kuwait's top leaders are hereditary.

Few, if any, actual political systems are perfect examples of democracy or its opposites. Do you think it is appropriate to think of democracy and dictatorship as two ends of a single continuum? Are democracy and authoritarianism two ends of a continuum? Or democracy and totalitarianism? Not all political analysts are consistent in how they employ these concepts. In this book, at least, dictatorship, authoritarianism, and totalitarianism will all be treated as modes of politics that contrast with democratic regimes. *Dictatorship* will especially emphasize the absence of a limited mandate for the political leaders. *Authoritarianism* will connote a more encompassing array of nondemocratic practices and significant controls over citizens' political behavior. And *totalitarianism* will be used to describe systems whose oppressive control goes far beyond the strictly political sphere, into personal and social life as well.

Notice that the dictatorship dimension differs in an important respect from the authoritarian and totalitarian dimensions. Many authoritarian or totalitarian regimes are dictatorships. However, there are instances where people elect their leaders but the political system substantially limits the people's personal and political freedoms. Thus, as in Singapore, the Ukraine, and Iran, there can be an authoritarian regime with relatively nondictatorial leadership. Indeed, since the early 1990s, many countries that were previously nondemocratic, especially in Latin America, the former Soviet bloc, and Africa, have engaged in serious attempts to establish democratic political systems, although they might fall short of liberal democracies.

What proportion of national political systems are democratic? The precise number of countries in this "wave of democracy" (a key theme in Chapter 11 and in Part Five of this book) ebbs and flows yearly as some countries establish democratic systems while others retreat or revert to nondemocratic systems. Freedom House (1999) is an organization which uses the various conceptualizations of democracies and nondemocracies to analyze this question.

First, Freedom House identifies those countries that meet the minimal conditions for an electoral democracy. Second, those countries that do not meet these conditions can be classified as nondemocracies. Third, Freedom House analyzes the extent to which each country, whether an electoral democracy or not, grants its citizens the *political rights* (e.g., to form political parties promoting genuine alternatives, to allow contestation in elections) and *civil liberties* (e.g., religious and ethnic freedom, press freedom, etc.) that define a liberal democracy.

Freedom House has developed a widely-cited 14-point scale, with a country scoring from 1-7 points on political rights and from 1-7 points on civil liberties. A country's combined score on the two measures can range from 2 points, the most extensive liberal democracy, to a worst score of 14 points in the world's most repressive regimes. Based on actual conditions, a country is classified as "free" (2-5 points), "partly free" (6-11), or "not free" (12-14) (Freedom House 1999; Karatnycky 1999). If a country is an electoral democracy, but its citizens' political rights and civil liberties are assessed to be only partly free or not free, the country is also classified as an "*illiberal democracy*" (Zakaria 1997).

Table 7.2 indicates the classifications of selected countries by Freedom House, circa 1999, and Figure 7.1 (on p. 163) provides a visual representation of the overlapping relationships among these related concepts. According to that analysis, 117 (61 percent) of the 191 countries were electoral democracies in 1999, but twenty-nine (15 percent) of these countries were "illiberal democracies." And only eighty-

TABLE 7.2
**Classification of Selected Counties by Level of Freedom
and Regime Type, Circa 1999**

Country	Level of Freedom (Score)[a]	Regime Type
Sweden	Free (1,1)	Liberal democracy
United States	Free (1,1)	Liberal democracy
Costa Rica	Free (1,2)	Liberal democracy
Germany	Free (1,2)	Liberal democracy
Hungary	Free (1,2)	Liberal democracy
Poland	Free (1,2)	Liberal democracy
Japan	Free (1,2)	Liberal democracy
South Africa	Free (1,2)	Liberal democracy
South Korea	Free (2,2)	Liberal democracy
India	Free (2,3)	Liberal democracy
Thailand	Free (2,3)	Electoral democracy
Argentina	Free (3,3)	Liberal democracy
Brazil	Partly Free (3,4)	Electoral democracy
Mexico	Partly Free (3,4)	Electoral democracy
Russia	Partly Free (4,4)	Electoral democracy
Turkey	Partly Free (4,5)	Electoral democracy
Indonesia	Partly Free (6,4)	Electoral democracy
Nigeria	Partly Free (6,4)	Electoral democracy
Singapore	Partly Free (5,5)	Electoral democracy
Swaziland	Not Free (6,4)	Nondemocracy
Cambodia	Not Free (6,6)	Nondemocracy
Egypt	Not Free (6,6)	Electoral democracy
Yugoslavia (Serbia)	Not Free (6,6)	Nondemocracy
China	Not Free (7,6)	Nondemocracy
Congo	Not Free (7,6)	Nondemocracy
Myanmar	Not Free (7,7)	Nondemocracy
Saudi Arabia	Not Free (7,7)	Nondemocracy
Syria	Not Free (7,7)	Nondemocracy
Vietnam	Not Free (7,7)	Nondemocracy

Source: Karatnycky 1999.
[a] Scores: The first score is for the level of political rights enjoyed by the population, and the second score is for civil liberties. The highest level of rights and liberties is 1 on each score and 7 is the lowest score (Freedom House 1999).

eight (46 percent) of the countries in the world were "liberal democracies" (electoral democracies with full freedoms). These liberal democracies include 2.35 billion people—40 percent of the world's inhabitants (Freedom House 1999).

In contrast, 39 percent of the countries were nondemocratic. Moreover, fully 54 percent of the countries (and 60 percent of the world's population) do not enjoy the full political rights and civil liberties associated with democracy. Of these, 28 percent of the countries are classified as "partly free" (in generally authoritarian regimes ruling 26.5 percent of the world's population). In 26 percent of the countries (ruling 33.5 percent of the world's population), the people are "not free" and live in conditions approaching totalitarianism (Freedom House 1999; Karatnycky 1999).

Now that some of the complexities of defining political systems on a democracy–nondemocracy continuum have been explored, do you have a clearer notion of how you might define and operationalize democracy?

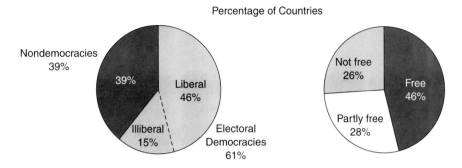

Figure 7.1   Distribution of countries on two analytic dimensions of democratic practices

Sources: Freedom House 1999; Karatnycky 1999.

CONSTITUTIONAL AND NONCONSTITUTIONAL REGIMES

A related classification of political systems also emphasizes aspects of the relationship between the rulers and the ruled. In this schema, the key question is whether the political system abides by the provisions in the state's constitution or fundamental laws. A **constitutional regime** *operates in terms of the rule of law and ensures effective restraints on the power holders,* as defined within the constitution. In contrast, a **nonconstitutional regime** is characterized by *unchecked political power, and the structural arrangements of the constitution are not upheld.* In theory, at least, a state might scrupulously follow a deeply repressive and undemocratic constitution imposed by the political leadership and thus qualify as a constitutional regime. However, those who employ this distinction typically assume that the guarantees within the constitution provide for a generally democratic and humane political order.

Constitutions

At the heart of most political systems is a **constitution**, *a set of statements describing the fundamental rules of the political system.* Most constitutions are composed of a single, written document, in the manner of the U.S. Constitution. However, some political systems do not have such a document; their fundamental rules are embedded in major statutes, precedents, and legal decisions, as in Great Britain's "unwritten constitution" or in Israel's "basic laws."

Although the idea of a constitution has a certain timeless quality associated with it, the constitutions of political systems are always changeable. For example, in the 1970s, Belgium revised a 170-year-old constitution in an attempt to resolve conflicts between its Flemish and Walloon nations. And Sweden rewrote Europe's oldest constitution to alter the structure of the legislature and reduce the power of the king.

The constitutions of more than two-thirds of the contemporary countries have been enacted since 1945. (Box 7.2 discusses the interesting history of the 1947 Japanese constitution.) First, many of these constitutions are in states that achieved independence in the postcolonial period after 1945. Second, there has been a recent burst of constitution writing as more than two dozen states that had been part of the Soviet Union or its Central and East European allies have been attempting to establish new institutions and principles for their political lives.

BOX 7.2

Constitution by Fiat: Japan

One of the most extraordinary episodes of drafting a constitution occurred in Japan. The Japanese operated under the Imperial Meiji Constitution from 1889 until their defeat by the Allies at the end of World War II. After the war, Japan was under the control of the American occupation forces, led by General Douglas MacArthur. Both MacArthur and officials in Washington, D.C., concerned about possible communist influence in Japan, had insisted that the Japanese write a new, democratic constitution. Through a newspaper leak, it became clear that a Japanese commission charged with writing the constitution was unwilling to propose major changes in the Meiji Constitution. Thus in February 1946, MacArthur decided to take decisive action. He convened a group of seventeen American military officers stationed in Tokyo and told them that he wanted a constitution for Japan in one week. The group included four lawyers but no one with constitutional specialization, no political scientists, and no one who was deeply knowledgeable about Japanese culture.

Using their knowledge of the American political system and their imperfect understanding of the British parliamentary system, the group completed the constitution in just eight days! After the English version was completed, it was translated into two forms of Japanese, one in formal bureaucratic language and one in common Japanese. Some of the Americans' perspectives were so alien to Japanese culture and political traditions that there were concepts in the new constitution, such as "civil rights," that were not even words in the Japanese language and required new ideographs. The constitution copied much of the preamble to the U.S. Constitution and referred to George Washington, President Roosevelt, and even Douglas MacArthur. The Japanese political leadership was shocked by and deeply opposed to the new constitution, but they were faced with a variety of even more undesirable threats (especially the possibility that the emperor would be tried as a war criminal). Consequently, the leadership capitulated and accepted the "MacArthur constitution." The Japanese cabinet presented the constitution to the Japanese public as its own. It was passed almost unanimously in the legislature and it became binding in May 1947.

This constitution, written by inexpert foreigners, has been in force in Japan since 1946. It was not amended for nearly fifty years and it seems to have worked, in the sense that the Japanese maintained a stable and working political system in the subsequent decades. Can you explain this constitutional "success"? Perhaps the military officers developed a sound constitutional framework for the governance of contemporary Japan. Perhaps the constitution is primarily a symbolic document and its details are unimportant for the actual functioning of the political order. Or perhaps this was an early example of Japan's postwar skill: taking an American product, reflecting on how to improve upon it, and modifying it into a superior product.

And third, dozens of other countries have abandoned their existing constitutions and ratified new ones in an attempt to rejuvenate their political systems. For example, Nicaragua enacted a new constitution reducing the power of the president, strengthening the legislature, and altering the electoral system in 1994. Mongolia adopted a democratic, post-communist constitution in 1994. In 1997, Thailand adopted a new constitution and Hong Kong implemented its new Basic Law as part of the transition from British colony to Special Administrative Region of China. The process does not always succeed. In the late 1980s, Israel abandoned its most recent effort to draft its first constitution, due to deep disagreements regarding issues of minority rights and religious practices.

While early constitutions tended to be relatively short and general, many recent constitutions are quite detailed. The Nigerian Constitution has 245 articles; the Indian Constitution has 395 articles. The language of constitutions is also increasingly similar due to quite liberal borrowing of ideas and even specific language from the constitutions of other countries. For example, more than three dozen countries have borrowed Abraham Lincoln's felicitous phrasing regarding government "of the people, by the people, and for the people."

Constitutional Regimes

The defining feature of a *constitutional regime* is that the state does attempt to fulfill the provisions of its constitution. The constitution declares the existence of the state and it expresses the most important fundamental rules of the political system. Three sets of rules are crucial. First, the constitution allocates governmental activities, defining what actions are within the domain of *res publica* and what political structures will perform these various actions. Second, it establishes the formal power relationships among the political structures, indicating the conditions under which each is independent or dependent upon the actions of the others. Third, the constitution limits the power of the rulers and guarantees the rights of the ruled, by defining the maximum extent of the state's authority over its citizens and by enumerating citizens' freedoms and benefits from the state.

This third set of rules is most important. A regime becomes more fully a constitutional one to the extent that the political system abides by constitutional limits on the rulers' power and the guarantee of rights to the ruled. Even among constitutional regimes, the limits on the state and the rights of the citizens are not absolute and are not absolutely implemented. Some states justify suspension of major constitutional provisions as a "temporary" response to circumstances that threaten the stability of the society. Such a suspension can last for months or years. A regime becomes less constitutional as there is a greater disparity between the provisions in the constitution and the actual politics of the society. In fact, the disjunction between promise and reality is frequent and extensive in many political systems.

Ultimately, the force of the constitution depends on the will of those with political power to enforce its provisions. The actual drafting of every constitution is either directly or indirectly controlled by those with political power in the society. Many groups in a society might offer interpretations of what the constitution means and how it ought to be applied to particular circumstances—governmental officials, courts, political parties, interest groups. But in the short run, at least, political power in the society establishes whose interpretation of the constitution will prevail and how the constitution's provisions will be implemented. In constitutional regimes, the interpretations are generally reasonable and judicious, and the implementation is fair.

Few constitutions provide a precise description of how the political system actually works. Yet constitutions are not insignificant. In the turbulent debate over the creation of the new constitution for Spain, the distinguished historian Julian Marais insisted, "If the constitution does not inspire respect, admiration and enthusiasm, democracy is not assured." Even if there are major diversions from the provisions of the constitution, it remains a moral yardstick against which to measure actual performance and is a persistent reminder of the high ideals and goals that have been set for the political system.

Nonconstitutional Regimes

Almost every political system occasionally violates or ignores some principle in its constitution. But the political system can be termed a nonconstitutional regime when there is persistent nonenforcement of crucial limits on rulers or rights of the ruled. In this sense, most authoritarian or totalitarian regimes are nonconstitutional.

Several sets of conditions produce nonconstitutional regimes. First, some political systems simply do not have a constitution. Some authoritarian regimes (e.g., Bhutan, Saudi Arabia) are governed by hereditary rulers, religious principles, or traditions that guarantee no rights to the ruled and place few limits on the rulers. Second, in some countries (e.g., Myanmar, Somalia) the rule of law collapses because of the complete disregard of the constitution by the ruling group or because of a collapse of social order through civil war. Third, there are instances where either the entire constitution or major constitutional rights are suspended "temporarily" because of a crisis in the society. In Israel, for example, this temporary suspension of constitutional rights (there is no written constitution) has persisted since independence in 1948.

AREAL DISTRIBUTION OF POWER

With the exception of small political systems serving only a few thousand citizens, most political systems have found it desirable or necessary to create governmental structures at several levels. The *areal distribution of power* describes the allocation of power and functions across these levels of government. National political systems, in particular, can be classified into three major forms of areal distribution of power: (1) unitary states, (2) federations, and (3) confederations.

Unitary State

In a **unitary state** there is *a central government that holds all legitimate power*. While the central government has indivisible sovereignty, it can delegate power or functional responsibilities to territorial units, which are given such names as departments, regions, or prefectures. These peripheral governments serve only at the convenience of the central government, which can revoke their power or functions at any time. More than 70 percent of the current countries are unitary states. Examples include China, France, Japan, the United Kingdom, and most Latin American and Asian political systems.

Why are most contemporary states unitary? The major advantage of a unitary state is the presence of clear, hierarchical authority. While there might be a conflict between the central and the peripheral governments, the center's superior constitutional power is clear, and center-periphery stalemates are uncommon. In addition, because the loyalty of all citizens is focused on the governmental authority embodied in the national government, citizens tend to identify with the country as a whole, rather than regional authorities.

Federation

A **federation** has *a constitutional division of power and functions between a central government and the set of regional governments*, which have such names as states, provinces, or cantons. In contrast to a unitary state, there is an explicit sharing of power among levels of government in a federation, and no level has legal power to dominate any other level in all policy domains. The essence of a federation is coordination, not hierarchy.

There are five major rationales for a federation:

1. *Large size.* Many states become federations to distribute governmental power where there is a huge area to be governed. Fewer than twenty-five states are federations today, but this group includes nearly one-half of the land area of the world. Most of the largest states are federations, including Brazil, Canada, India, Mexico, Nigeria, and the United States. During the constitutional debate in the United States, Thomas Jefferson observed, "Our country is too large to have all its affairs directed by a single government." The assumption here seems to be that responsiveness is higher when government does not become too massive in scale.

2. *The prior existence of strong states.* A federation can be an acceptable compromise when strong peripheral governments create a central government. In the formation of the United States, for example, the already strong state governments were unwilling to give up the bulk of their power to a central government, as in a unitary state. Rather, they agreed to delegate certain functions to the new central government while retaining all other "residual" powers for themselves.

3. *The attempt to create unity or accommodate diversity.* Chapter 5 described the serious problems of conflict between states and nations, especially in the newer states. Federations appear to bond diverse nations into a unified state while still recognizing the different nations' diversity and desire for power. The peripheral governments represent major ethnic, linguistic, religious, or other nation-based characteristics of regions. India is a federation with twenty-five states, most of which are related to linguistic-ethnic dominance in the area and a few of which are related to religious dominance. The Indian Constitution defines a complex pattern of power distribution, with the center responsible for ninety-seven governmental functions, sixty-six functions reserved for the states, and forty-seven functions shared between the two levels.

4. *The desire to concentrate power and resources.* In some instances, a federation is created to combine several states into a stronger political system. In the effort to create Arab unity and to expand the political and economic power of the state, Egypt has several times attempted to forge federations with its neighbors. Thus at various times Egypt has been part of federations with Syria, Yemen, Iraq, and Jordan. For similar reasons, Kenya, Tanzania, and Uganda formed the East African Federation. As in these examples, federations are often short-lived

because the prior states are unwilling to sacrifice sufficient local power and resources to a potent central government.

5. *The desire to disperse political power.* In contrast to the previous rationale, a federation can be established to prevent the overconcentration of power in the central government. After the trauma of Hitler, West Germans formed a federation to impede the emergence of another overly powerful central government. The bulk of legislative power was granted to the central government, but most power to administer and adjudicate the laws is held by the Länder (regional) governments.

Confederation

A **confederation** is *an association in which states delegate some power to a supranational central government but retain primary power.* It is a loose grouping of states in which each state's membership, participation, and compliance to the central government are conditional, depending on the state's perception of its own national interest. Confederations are usually created when states decide that the performance of certain functions is enhanced by structured cooperation with other states. To facilitate such cooperation, permanent supranational machinery is set up. The United Arab Emirates is a confederation of ministates, and the United Nations is a confederal structure containing about 190 member states. Confederations can emphasize economic cooperation, such as the European Union (EU), or military cooperation, such as the North Atlantic Treaty Organization (NATO).

Although confederations can serve many useful functions for member states, their activities and even their very survival are always contingent upon the continuing support of the members. A member state will often refuse to comply with policies that conflict directly with the state's definition of its own national interest. Disagreements among the members can necessitate negotiation and compromise, as in the periodic adjustments within the EU regarding farm subsidies to member states, and in the complex evolution of a common monetary policy. A confederation can wither if the supragovernment is ineffective, as in the case of the Articles of Confederation in colonial America, or if members refuse to support its directives, as in the League of Nations after World War I.

Table 7.3 indicates some of the major advantages and shortcomings of each approach to the areal distribution of power. While each seems to have relative advantages under certain conditions, none is without considerable drawbacks, and none can ensure the effective functioning or even the survival of a political system. The general trend toward the centralization of political power within states has meant that the distinctions between unitary states and federations are less clear than in the past and that confederations have become particularly fragile.

FORMS OF EXECUTIVE–LEGISLATIVE RELATIONS

Another conventional method of classifying and especially of describing political systems is by defining the pattern of power and interaction between the legislative and executive structures. The taxonomy in this section emphasizes the two most common patterns through which the executive and the legislative structures interact to perform the functions of policy making and policy implementation. These

TABLE 7.3
**Relative Strengths and Weaknesses of Areal Distributions
of Power**

Form of Areal Distribution	Strengths	Weaknesses
Unitary state	Clear authority	Hyperconcentration of power
	Decisive control	Weak representation of
	No stalemates between center and periphery	diversity and minorities
Federation	Diversity represented	Duplication and overlap of power
	Checks on center's power	Conflicts over ultimate power
	Unity created	Sluggishness; compromises
Confederation	Facilitation of cooperation	Conditional compliance
	Power retained by subunits	Instability
		Limited power

are the presidential form and the parliamentary form of government. Three other types of executive–legislative arrangements are also examined: the hybrid, council, and assembly systems.

Presidential Government

The crucial feature of **presidential government** is the *separation of executive and legislative structures.* Figure 7.2 portrays the electoral chain of command that is supposed to order the relationships between citizens and major political structures. In separate electoral decisions, the citizens select the chief executive (usually called the president) and the members of the national legislature. This electoral process provides both the president and the legislature with independent mandates to represent the citizens in the governing process. The length of the term of each is predetermined, and thus the tenure in office of each is not dependent on the other (except in the rare case of impeachment of the chief executive).

The separation of executive and legislative powers is explicit and intentional, in order to ensure a system of checks and balances in the policy-making and policy-implementation processes. Primary responsibility for policy making (debating, modifying, and enacting policies as law) resides in the legislature. Although the chief executive can veto legislation, the legislature can override that veto. Primary responsibility for the implementation of policy is with the president, who has control of the government's administrative departments. The president also appoints a cabinet, whose members are responsible for overseeing policy in the government's administrative departments and who are controlled directly by the president.

Although the actions of the executive and the legislature are interdependent, neither depends on the other for its power or its tenure in office. In practice, it is common to find a considerable blurring of functions, and especially for the

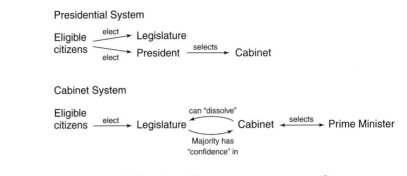

Figure 7.2   Presidential and parliamentary systems of government

president to have substantial involvement in the policy-making function. The United States is the model example of presidential government; this form of government is also found in many Latin American and some African and Asian states, including Colombia, the Ivory Coast, Kenya, Mexico, Sri Lanka, Venezuela, and the Philippines.

Parliamentary (Cabinet) Government

In contrast to the presidential system, the crucial element of the **parliamentary government** is the *fusion of executive and legislative functions and structures.* As is indicated in Figure 7.2, the people elect the legislature (the parliament), whose majority empowers a cabinet, which then empowers one of its members to be the chief executive, typically called a prime minister or premier. The length of the legislature's mandate is often five years, but its term can be shorter under the circumstances described next. The complex relationships among cabinet, legislature, and prime minister merit further detail.

Cabinet and legislature.   The cabinet is a collective leadership group of six to thirty individuals who are, in most systems, also members of the legislature. The cabinet is responsible to the legislature. This means that the cabinet serves only as long as it can maintain the "confidence" of the majority of the members in the legislature. As long as the cabinet does have the support of the legislative majority, it has primary responsibility for both the policy-making and policy-implementation functions. Although policies must be voted into laws by the legislative majority, it is the cabinet that devises, drafts, and implements most policies.

In an intriguing manner, the cabinet and the legislature are at each other's mercy. At any time, the legislative majority can pressure the cabinet to resign, either by a negative vote on a major piece of legislation proposed by the cabinet or by a general motion of "no confidence" in the cabinet. Also at any time, the cabinet can "dissolve" the legislature, requiring immediate new elections. In the subsequent election, voters select a new legislature, whose majority then identifies a cabinet it will support, and the process begins anew. Thus the cabinet and the legislature, rather like two gunfighters standing gun-to-gun in a spaghetti Western, each has the power to eliminate the other but might also be destroyed in the exchange. Since new elections put everyone's position in jeopardy, it is more common for the cabinet to resign or reconstitute itself than for the cabinet to dissolve the legislature.

Legislature and prime minister.   In the parliamentary system, the prime minister (or premier or chancellor or whatever the chief executive is called) is not directly elected by the citizens to be the top leader. The prime minister is the member of the legislature who is supported as chief executive by the majority of the legislature. This executive can be removed at any time by a no-confidence vote of the legislature and might also be obliged to resign if the legislature defeats a major legislative initiative of the prime minister. The prime minister directs the overall thrust of decision and action in the legislative process.

Cabinet and prime minister.   The balance of power between the cabinet and the prime minister can be subtle, although both depend on the majority support of the legislature. Traditionally, the cabinet that had legislative support could select one of its members to serve as prime minister. The prime minister was *primus inter pares* in the cabinet—the first among equals. The prime minister exercised broad policy leadership within a collective decision-making body. If a cabinet majority no longer supported a prime minister, however, the prime minister either resigned or attempted to reconstitute a cabinet that supported him and was supported by the legislative majority.

In many contemporary parliamentary systems, however, there has been a substantial shift of power from the cabinet to the prime minister. In these systems, the electorate selects legislative candidates from a party committed to support a particular prime minister. If a legislative majority can be created, its leader becomes prime minister. The prime minister then appoints the members of the cabinet and clearly dominates the cabinet in the governmental process. In Figure 7.2 the two-headed arrow between cabinet and prime minister indicates these alternate patterns of power.

Thus the parliamentary system is characterized by the fusion of executive and legislative functions because the cabinet and prime minister formulate policies, guide their passage through the legislature, and administer policy through the administrative departments. However, the actual policy process in a parliamentary system depends on whether there is a coherent majority group in the legislature.

A distinction can be made between "stable" and "unstable" parliamentary systems. In a stable parliamentary system, there is a clear majority in the legislature (such a majority may be composed of either one party or a coalition). This majority provides the cabinet and prime minister with sufficient legislative support to enact their policy program, without the problems of stalemate and confusion of accountability that can result from the separation of powers in the presidential system. Australia, Canada, Denmark, Great Britain, and Japan are examples of parliamentary government systems that are usually stable.

In contrast, an unstable parliamentary system often emerges when there is no coherent legislative majority. Instead, policy-making requires agreement within a coalition composed of multiple parties that tend to disagree on some important policy issues. If the legislature votes no confidence in the cabinet or defeats it on a major bill, the cabinet usually resigns. Then one hears that a parliamentary government has "fallen" or that there are efforts to form a "new government" (a new cabinet, actually). The new cabinet might have almost all the same people as members, or it might have a quite different set of individuals, drawing its majority support from different groups within the legislature. In general, prime ministers in unstable parliamentary systems are weaker than those in stable parliamentary systems.

Unstable parliamentary systems have been prevalent where stronger ideological differences and multiple political parties have emerged in contemporary legislatures. Italy has had an average of one cabinet (new government) per year since 1945. During the French Fourth Republic, the parliamentary system was so volatile that the average cabinet served for only eleven months, and the shortest for less than six hours.

Hybrid Systems

An increasing number of political systems attempts to blend desirable aspects of both the presidential and parliamentary systems. These **hybrid systems** *have a prime minister and an elected legislature that can both enact and implement policies, but they also have a president* (elected for a fixed term and having some independent executive powers) who, being a single individual, can act with decisiveness (Elgie, 1999; Shugart and Carey 1992).

Some hybrid systems function more like parliamentary systems: The president has limited power, and most control is exercised by the prime minister and cabinet. In India, for example, the president is elected by the legislature for a five-year term and has notable responsibilities, including the appointment of state governors and the right to take over governance of the states during emergencies. However, the prime minister is the dominant political power in the system, with the president performing mainly ceremonial roles. Germany, Austria, and Ireland are other examples of this style of the hybrid.

In other hybrid systems, there is a more balanced sharing of power between the president and the parliament. In Finland, for example, the presidential executive controls the administration and has oversight powers. While the president does attend meetings on major legislation and both the president and the prime minister must sign a law before it is enacted, the cabinet and legislature undertake most of the legislation. In these more balanced hybrids, the relative power of the president and of the prime minister/cabinet vary, depending on the constitutional rules, the personality of the officeholders, and the political situation in the society. (See Box 7.3 on the French hybrid system.)

Hybrid systems have been implemented in virtually all of the countries that emerged from the Soviet Union and in the post-communist countries of Central and Eastern Europe. Nearly all of these countries have placed relatively greater power in the position of president, including the right to dismiss the prime minister. However, they have also given direct control of the government to a prime minister, who is responsible to the elected legislature. In most of these countries, the president periodically dismisses the prime minister, relieving temporarily the citizens' dissatisfaction with the failures of the political system. But since many of these states face huge problems of governability (see Chapter 14), it is not obvious that the more ambiguous power relationships of the hybrid structure are best.

Council Systems

In **council systems**, *a small group shares collective leadership and is responsible for both executive and legislative functions.* While one member of the group might be deemed the leader for symbolic reasons, all members of the council are equal in constitutional terms, and decisions and actions are based on the will of the council majority or, ideally, on council consensus. In American local government, the weak-mayor–council system and the boards of commissioners/supervisors (prevalent in many counties, school districts, and special districts) are council systems. Also many tribal societies in Africa were traditionally ruled by a council of elders, who collectively made decisions that were binding on the members of the tribe.

In many situations the replacement of the top leader by force results initially in the sharing of power and authority by a small collective leadership group. When the group that has taken power is from the military, this council-type group is called

---

BOX 7.3

A Hybrid System in Action: France

Many recent constitutions establish a hybrid model in which both a president and a prime minister have significant political power. A central issue is whether two independent executives can share power effectively. An early example of this complicated system is the French Fifth Republic, based on the "de Gaulle Constitution" of 1962. France created this hybrid to overcome the highly unstable parliamentary government system of the Fourth Republic. The premier (prime minister) and cabinet are responsible for the day-to-day functioning of the government, as in a parliamentary system, but the president (an office Charles de Gaulle fashioned for himself as a condition for his return to government) has extensive power and the freedom to exercise it. The president is elected popularly for a fixed seven-year term and then selects a premier, who selects a cabinet. The cabinet controls the budget and legislative agenda as in a normal parliamentary system; however, the president can dissolve the legislature while retaining the cabinet. And Article 16 in the constitution provides that the sweeping powers of the presidency may be exercised whenever the president *alone* deems the political situation to be dangerous for the country.

De Gaulle served as the first president of the Fifth Republic, from 1958 to 1969. He was an extraordinarily powerful individual, and he demanded extraordinary power. He established a precedent that the president can act far more extensively than the constitution allows. He dominated every premier who served during his presidency. The presidents after de Gaulle (Pompidou, Giscard d'Estaing, Mitterrand, and Chirac) continued to follow the de Gaulle precedent, exercising considerable power. This approach was reasonably workable during this period, because the majority in the legislature, and thus the cabinet and premier, usually shared the ideological orientation of the president.

(continued)

BOX 7.3 *(Continued)*

Many people felt that the French "dyarchy" (dual rule) would lead to a constitutional crisis as soon as a premier and cabinet challenged the president's extensive power. The first strong test of the French hybrid finally occurred between 1986 and 1988, when Socialist President François Mitterrand was faced with a legislative majority dominated by conservatives. But Mitterrand accepted the situation, appointing the conservatives' leader, Jacques Chirac, as premier. Despite strong ideological differences between the president and the premier-cabinet-legislative majority, there was a reasonable sharing of power and authority, which the French call "cohabitation." President Mitterrand continued to be very active in foreign policy, but allowed the premier to control the domestic policy agenda. From 1993 to 1995, a conservative legislative majority produced a second period of cohabitation. A weakened Mitterrand acknowledged that "it is not the task of the president of the Republic to govern," and his relations with the moderate conservative premier Balladur were generally civil (Safran 1995; 169–172). At the turn of the century, a socialist premier operated effectively with a conservative president. After these varied periods of cohabitation, the powers of the president in the French hybrid seem to be sufficiently limited and institutionalized to survive the conflict inherent in a dyarchy. Through constitutional safeguards and precedents, the hybrid system in every country must establish an effective power balance between its two executives.

a *junta.* There have been many such juntas in Latin America and Africa (e.g., in Algeria since 1992; in Argentina, from 1976 to 1983; in Gambia since 1994; and in Niger since 1996). In many cases, council rule evolves into more dictatorial rule as a single political leader increasingly dominates the others.

Assembly Systems

In **assembly systems,** *collective leadership is exercised by a large group, usually constituted as a legislature.* There might be an executive officer, but the legislature is clearly dominant. Switzerland has an assembly system in which the legislature dominates the collective seven-member executive council that it elects. Most confederations, such as the United Nations and the European Parliament (the elected legislative wing of the European Union), are assembly systems in which legislatures delegate administrative power to an appointed executive. The New England town meeting in American local government is an extreme version of the assembly system, because all citizens directly participate in key decisions and oversee the administration of policy.

In theory, most communist states are assembly systems because the constitution grants most power for policy making to the legislative body. In reality, however, the legislatures in such states have traditionally been rubber stamps that authorize the policies and administration of a single leader or a small collective leadership group, as in China and North Korea. In fact, there are few if any national political systems that operate as true assembly systems, since power for policy making and policy implementation rarely remains dispersed among a large group of relatively equal rulers.

Which Form Is Optimal?

Which form of executive–legislative relations is best? If there were agreement on this question, we might reasonably expect most states to have adopted the same form of government. In fact, however, each form has its strengths and weaknesses.

The parliamentary form offers the advantages of a clear and decisive authority structure for the allocation of public values, from the initial formulation of policy through its administration. But it can be argued that there are too few checks on a coherent legislative majority, which can bulldoze its policies through the system. Conversely, there might be too little capacity for decisive action in a parliamentary system when there is no stable majority. The presidential system offers checks and balances, but it does not ensure consistency between legislation and execution. Also, a presidential system can so balance power between the legislature and the executive that there are damaging stalemates and confusion of accountability.

Because hybrid systems attempt to fuse the strengths of the parliamentary and the presidential forms of government, an increasing number of states are adopting some version of the hybrid. However, a significant risk with these hybrids is the increased potential for major power struggles, especially between the cabinet and prime minister, on one side, and the president, on the other side. A council system has the virtue of distributing power among a manageable number of people, but there is a strong tendency for collective leadership to result in persistent internal power struggles as one or a few members attempt to assert their dominance. Finally, assembly systems are the best approximation of a genuine representative democracy, but they lack the clear and decisive executive leadership that seems to be desired by the populations in most contemporary states.

POLITICAL PARTY SYSTEMS

Another taxonomy for political systems is based on the system of political parties. Party systems are generally classified according to the number of political parties and the interactions among the parties in the governing process. In the comparative study of political parties, four types of party systems are usually distinguished: (1) two-party systems, (2) multiparty systems, (3) dominant-party systems, and (4) one-party systems. The distinguishing features of each type are described in this section, and representative examples are identified in Table 7.4.

Two-Party Systems

A *two-party system* is characterized by the alternation in governmental power of two major political parties. Each party has a realistic possibility of forming a governing majority; they generally alternate in power, although the electoral success of each party varies over time. Significant third parties can exist in two-party systems, but the third party has limited power unless a major party needs its support. Great Britain is an example of a party system in which the two major parties (Labour and Conservative) have quite distinct ideologies.

However, there can be a substantial ideological overlap between the two parties. In both Costa Rica and Honduras, for example, the two major parties often present similar political orientations and objectives.

TABLE 7.4
Examples of Party Systems

Country	Number of Seats in Legislative Body
Costa Rica, Legislative Assembly (1998)	
Democratic Force	2
National Liberation Party	22
> Christian-Social Unity Party	29
Libertarian Movement	2
Other	2
	57
Cuba, National Assembly of People's Power (1998)	
>Cuban Communist Party	601
	601
Hungary, National Assembly (1998)	
Hungarian Socialist Party	134
Alliance of Free Democrats	24
> Hungarian Democratic Forum	17
> Alliance of Young Democrats	148
> Independent Smallholders, Agrarian Workers and Citizens	48
Hungarian Justice and Life Party	14
Others	1
	386
Israel, Knesset (1999)	
Democratic Front	3
One Nation	2
> Yisreal Akhat (Labour coalition)	26
Meretz	10
Arab parties (United Arab, National Democratic Alliance)	7
> Shas	17
> Yisreal Ba-Aliya	6
Merkaz	12
Likud	19
National Religious Party	5
Jewry of Torah	5
National Union	4
Our Home	4
	120
Italy, Chamber of Deputies (1996)	
> Refounded Communists	32
> Olive Tree Alliance (Democratic Party of the Left, Greens, Democratic Union, Italian Renewal)	284
Pole of Freedom Alliance (Forza Italia, National Alliance, Christian Democratic Center)	246
Northern League	59
Others	6
Open	3
	630

TABLE 7.4 *(Continued)*

Country	Number of Seats in Legislative Body
Mexico, Chamber of Deputies (1997)	
Worker's Party (PT)	7
Green Party	8
Party of the Democratic Revolution (PRD)	125
> Institutional Revolutionary Party (PRI)	239
National Action Party (PAN)	121
	500
Singapore, Parliament (1997)	
Workers' Party	1
People's Party	1
> People's Action Party	81
	83
South Africa, Parliament (1999)	
> African National Congress	266
Inkatha Freedom Party	34
Democratic Party	38
United Democratic Movement	14
New National Party	28
Other	20
	400
Sweden, Riksdag (1998)	
> Left-Wing Party	43
> Social Democratic Party	131
Green Party	16
Centre Party	18
People's Party	17
Christian Democratic Party	42
Moderate Rally Party	82
	349
Turkey, National Assembly (1999)	
> Democratic Left Party	136
> Nationalist Movement	129
Virtue (Islamic)	111
> Motherland Party	86
True Path Party	85
Non-partisan	3
	550

Notes: > signifies parties included in governing coalition, in March 2000. For each country, parties are listed in order of general ideological orientation from left to right.
Source: Political Resources on the Net (2000): www.agora.stm.it/elections

Multiparty Systems

As you might expect, a *multiparty system* has more than two parties whose participation can be essential in the formation and activities of government. In parliamentary systems, this means that the creation of a legislative majority (a government) might require a coalition of two or more parties.

Working multiparty systems.   In a "working" multiparty system, there is a relatively clear split between sets of parties capable of forming a governing majority. For example, one or several cooperating center- and right-oriented parties might form one group, with a social democratic or socialist left party constituting another, as in the cases of France, Norway, and Sweden. In 1998, the Swedish electorate retained a government dominated by the Social Democratic Party, which had defeated the center-right coalition previously in 1994 (see Table 7.4; also see, in Chapter 13, Box 13.2). It is also possible to have a working multiparty system in which various parties are willing to cooperate in a governing coalition. A notable example of this situation is Switzerland, where four major parties typically share governing power and it is viewed as undesirable for any one of the parties to govern independently.

Unstable multiparty systems   Multiparty systems are often unstable. In these cases the parties that form the government (the majority coalition) have underlying ideological disagreements, as in Israel, where the Labour Party leads a complicated coalition. And in Turkey, the Democratic Left Party gained cooperation from other parties in order to govern with a minority of legislators. At some point the government's policy on some issue induces a coalition partner to withdraw its support, causing a crisis for the government. In parliamentary systems, such a crisis often leads to the resignation of the government or the dissolution of the legislature. In presidential or assembly systems this situation tends to produce paralysis in the legislature. Clearly, the difficulty of forming a governing majority among multiple parties increases as different parties are more firmly committed to their unique ideological orientations.

Instability is a particular problem where extreme parties (of the left or right) refuse to participate in any coalition. This was generally the case in Italy from World War II until 1994. Typically, the centrist Christian Democratic Party formed the heart of a coalition government, often a minority government, because neither left nor right extreme parties would be part of the government coalition. The system was quite unstable, with governments resigning, on average, more than once per year. Then in 1994, the parties of the right swamped the Popular Party (the renamed Christian Democrats) to form a different, but no more stable majority coalition. While several center-right governments fell during the next two years, a new electoral system was implemented. This system was designed to reduce the number of parties by encouraging the formation of party coalitions, which would compete for 475 seats, with only the remaining 155 seats being allocated by the traditional PR (proportional representation) method (recall Box 7.1). Ironically, fully 251 parties put forth candidates in the 1996 election and no coalition gained a majority of seats in the legislature. The Olive Tree Alliance became the core parties in a left-center government (Table 7.4), and the remnants of the Christian Democratic Party seemed to suffer a total electoral collapse. It is actually possible that, if these alliances become more stable and effective, Italy's multiparty system will begin to operate like a two-party system.

In the initial years of democratic politics in the post-communist states of Central and Eastern Europe, an extreme form of multipartism existed. Many groups formed fledgling political parties and as many as 200 parties competed for political power. Even in 1995, for example, Russia still had forty parties running for seats in the national legislature. When many parties win representation, it has been extraordinarily difficult to form the stable coalitions necessary for coherent policy making. There has been a significant reduction of effective parties in most of the post-communist states. In Hungary, for example, the party system now has only six major parties, three of whom form the governing coalition.

Dominant-Party Systems

In a *dominant-party system,* the same party repeatedly captures enough votes and seats to form the government, although other parties are free to compete. Among the examples in Table 7.4, Singapore provides the most clear-cut case of a dominant party. The People's Action Party wins nearly all the seats in the legislature, although candidates who are not members of the party are allowed to run. In South Africa, the African National Congress has emerged as a dominant party in the initial post-apartheid period, but its capacity to retain this level of power will be tested.

A dominant party can eventually lose support and become a competitor in a multiparty system. This happened to the Congress Party in India, which lost its legislative majority in the late 1970s after nearly thirty years in power. It now might be happening to the Institutional Revolutionary Party (PRI). PRI dominated Mexico's national political system, winning the presidency and a majority in both houses of the legislature in every election from 1929 to 1994. However, the dominance of the PRI is eroding. In some Mexican states, politicians from parties other than the PRI now serve as the chief executive (governor) and control the legislature. The PRI presidential candidate Ernesto Zedillo received less than half the total vote (48.8

percent) in 1994, but was elected when other candidates split the remaining votes. And then in 1997, PRI actually lost its majority in the Chamber of Deputies.

A similar decline seems to have occurred for the Liberal Democratic Party (LDP) in Japan, which was a dominant party for thirty-eight years after the ratification of the MacArthur constitution in 1947 (recall Box 7.2). But scandals involving party leaders and changing attitudes among the Japanese electorate are among the reasons that a non-LDP coalition government was formed after the 1993 election. Disagreements in that coalition resulted in the return to power of a no-longer-dominant LDP with a minority government after the 1996 election. It is unlikely that the LDP will regain its status as a dominant party.

One-Party Systems

In a *one-party system,* the single party of the governing group is the only legal political party. The clearest examples of one-party systems are in states dominated by the Communist Party, such as China, Cuba, and North Korea. In its effort to control all aspects of public life, the state accepts no institutional opposition to its rule, and a second political party would be the most direct and objectionable form of such opposition. Similarly, many authoritarian regimes do not tolerate the existence of any political parties other than the one that represents the state and its vision of political order, as in Iraq.

In some states, multiparty systems are ultimately reduced to one-party systems. First, in states that have not institutionalized the electoral mandate, the party entrenched in power is reluctant to relinquish that power to another group. Second, where the acceptance of political opposition is not strong, the governing group tends to view any party that expresses opposition to its rule as disloyal or even seditious (which means that the party is stirring up resistance or rebellion against the government), rather than as a "loyal opposition." The eventual result can be the abolition of any party other than the single "party of the state/government/society." Among the examples of this evolution to one-party states are the west African states of Ghana and Cameroon.

There are one-party systems that do inject some competition or selection. For example, Tanzania has had a single-party system since its independence in 1963. However, the party offers alternative candidates for each of the 200 seats in the National Assembly. Thus voters in each constituency have at least some choice, since the candidates have different styles and tend to offer slightly different priorities, despite their loyalty to the single party. In some elections, more than half of the members of the Tanzanian legislature who seek reelection are voted out of office.

No-Party Systems

While it is not a party system in the normal sense, the taxonomy should have a category for those political systems that have no political parties. The institution of political parties is usually considered one of the key elements in modern political systems. Historically, there were many political systems that had no organized parties. In addition, some contemporary political systems do not allow political parties. Such countries as Bahrain, Sudan, and Swaziland have banned political parties, either because the rulers do not want organized bases of opposition to their authority or on the grounds that parties divide people's loyalty to the society. The latter argument is a primary justification given for the nonpartisanship (lack of political party affiliations or organization) of candidates for public office in many American local governments.

CLASSIFICATION AND CLARITY

Most theorizing about political systems begins with some classificatory scheme. Classifying political systems in some taxonomy is quite straightforward, especially when the categories are based on clear institutional characteristics (e.g., federations, confederations, and unitary states). But many of the most interesting classifications (e.g., democracies and dictatorships) are challenging because political systems tend to be complex mixtures of characteristics that do not fit tidily into any category. In addition, any classification is time specific, because evolutionary and revolutionary processes can change the nature of a political system.

There are at least three important reasons for classifying political systems. First, such classification can provide us with useful descriptive information about political systems. Most people have a vague sense that other political systems are different from their own, and by describing how various political systems are organized between central and peripheral units or between executives and legislatures, we expand our grasp of alternative forms of governmental structures.

Second, the classification of political systems helps us to undertake political analysis—to identify patterns of similarities and differences among the political systems of the world. Rather than positing that every political system is unique, the development of a taxonomy assumes that some generalizations can emerge from an analysis of these systems. Sets of political systems that share important characteristics can be compared to each other, or compared with sets that do not share those characteristics. Such taxonomies provide us with a basis for thinking more clearly about the kinds of generalizations that we can articulate. Comparative analysis can then increase our confidence regarding what we know about the political world.

Third, the taxonomies in this chapter might encourage us to specify with greater precision what we mean by value-laden terms such as "democracy" and "dictatorship." In this manner, the analytic study of political institutions improves our understanding of how these terms are most appropriately used as thoughtful descriptors rather than as mere rhetorical labels.

Ultimately, the development of greater precision in our use of key political concepts and the increase in our knowledge about the political world can do more than clarify our thinking. They can also enhance our ability to evaluate the nature and desirability of the political structures in our own nation and in other countries, and to decide whether there is a "best" form of government.

Would you argue that one form of areal division of power and one form of executive–legislative relations and the same constitution are best for *all* states? Or might the best institutional arrangements be contingent upon the major goals and key characteristics of the particular political society? As a closing puzzle, if your country were to convene a constitutional convention now, would you argue in favor of retaining all the same governmental forms that exist in your political system? Why, or why not?

FOR FURTHER CONSIDERATION

1. What is your definition of a democratic political system? What are the minimal conditions necessary for a country to be classified as a democracy? If you opt for the definition used in this chapter, explain which elements of the definition are the most essential and the least essential for democracy.

2. In the late eighteenth century, the United States opted for a federal, presidential, two-party system with plurality elections. Given the situation at the beginning of the twenty-first century, what are the major shortcomings with each of these decisions? Speculate what politics in the United States might be like if the country became a unitary state with a parliamentary government or a multi-party system based on proportional representation.

3. Some analysts argue that democracy is not possible unless there are at least two political parties. Provide a critical evaluation of this viewpoint. In theory, might we expect any relationship between the number of parties and the extent to which the political system is democratic?

FOR FURTHER READING

Arendt, Hannah. (1973). *The Origins of Totalitarianism.* New York: Harcourt. The classic study of the forces underlying totalitarian regimes.

Barber, Benjamin. (1984). *Strong Democracy: Participatory Politics for a New Age.* Berkeley: University of California Press. A persuasive argument that democracy can and should be based on active and extensive participation by the citizenry.

Bratton, Michael, and Nicolas van de Walle. (1997). *Democratic Experiments in Africa: Regime Transitions in Comparative Perspective.* New York: Cambridge University Press. Numerous examples are provided of the attempts to establish and sustain liberal democracy in Sub-Saharan Africa, which, due to its history, informal institutions, and elite behavior, has been less successful in this transition than any other region.

Elgie, Robert, Ed. (1999). *Semi-Presidentialism in Europe.* New York: Oxford University Press. An exploration of the manner in which similar forms of executive–legislative structures (hybrids with a directly elected president and a prime minister responsible to the legislature) can result in different patterns of politics and power.

Fulbright, William J. (1989). *The Price of Empire.* New York: Pantheon. The highly respected former chair of the Senate Foreign Relations Committee argues that the United States could reduce government gridlock by changing to a parliamentary system.

Hesse, Joachim Jens, and Vincent Wright, Eds. (1996). *Federalizing Europe?: The Costs, Benefits and Preconditions of Federal Political Systems.* New York: Oxford University Press. From the perspective of developments within the European Union and its member states, the problems and prospects of federal forms of governance are debated.

Lijphart, Arend, Ed. (1992). *Parliamentary versus Presidential Government.* New York: Oxford University Press. A wide-ranging set of readings examining the advantages and disadvantages of the two major forms of executive–legislative relations as well as hybrids.

Peterson, Paul E. (1995). *The Price of Federalism.* Washington, D.C.: Brookings. In the context of a detailed consideration of federalism in the United States, the author analyzes the strengths and problems associated with this form of areal distribution of power.

Stepan, Alfred, and Juan J. Linz. (1996). *Problems of Democratic Transition and Consolidation: Southern Europe, South America and Post-Communist Europe.* Baltimore, MD: Johns Hopkins University Press. Based on illuminating examples from two continents, the authors explore the difficulties associated with the shift from authoritarian or communist regimes to democratic ones.

Wheare, K. C. (1966). *Modern Constitutions.* London: Home University Library. Although first written in 1951, this description of the content and impacts of constitutions is arguably still the best.

CHAPTER 8

Political Economy

In all the political systems of the world, much of politics is economics and most of economics is also politics....For many good reasons, politics and economics have to be held together in the analysis of basic social mechanisms and systems.

—*CHARLES E. LINDBLOM*, Politics and Markets *(1977: 8)*

This book is about the *political* world. But if Lindblom is correct, understanding contemporary politics requires an understanding of its linkages with economics. This combination of politics and economics is called **political economy**. The main aim of this chapter is to provide you with a grasp of political economy. First, the connections between the economic system and the political system are described. Then three different types of political economies are characterized: (1) the *market economy*, (2) the *command economy*, and (3) the *mixed economy*. Finally, we examine how these political economies are related to major "isms" in the political world, especially capitalism, socialism, and communism.

POLITICS AND ECONOMICS

Many of the decisions by the political system can have significant impacts on the economy. Can you think of implications for the economy from such policies of the state as the following?

No state involvement in the construction or repair of highways and roads

State ownership of all factories producing cars

Very high state taxes on the profits of businesses

State financing of all education for all citizens, from preschool through post-doctoral training

Absolutely no state restrictions on the right of foreigners to enter and work in the country

State regulation of the price of all basic foods

Similarly, activities within the economic system can have a major impact on the political system. The political order depends on the economic system to generate goods and services for the survival and prosperity of its citizens. Thus the decisions and actions of the political system can be powerfully influenced by the actions of major economic actors and the performance of the economic system. For example, what policy responses might you predict from the U.S. government to the following economic factors?

A lengthy nationwide strike by air traffic controllers

The proposed sale of the country's major computer company to a Japanese company

The discovery that there are fewer than five years' worth of underground oil reserves within the country's boundaries

A disastrous harvest that reduces the nation's grain output by 50 percent

The more one reflects on modern political systems, the clearer it becomes that the political system and the economic system are inextricably entwined.

Understanding political economy requires a grasp of some basic economic concepts. Economic systems and the concepts used in economics can seem as complicated as political systems and the concepts used in political science. Thus this chapter describes a framework for the economic system that is similar in spirit to Easton's framework for a political system (see Chapter 5). The framework deals only with some core ideas, with considerable simplification and little detail. (If you want the full treatment, read an introductory economics book such as Heyne [1999], or take an introductory economics course.) Even the discussion here involves some complicated abstractions, so hang in there!

A POLITICAL-ECONOMIC FRAMEWORK

The abstract models presented in Figure 8.1 are our starting point for understanding the idea of a political economy. The figure offers an extremely simple characterization of the way in which extraordinarily complex systems of production and exchange operate (see Baumol 1997: ch. 8; Ruffin and Gregory 1997: ch. 6).

Factors, Firms, and Households/Consumers

In the beginning (according to this model), there are three kinds of important productive resources—the three major *factors of production* (A). (See part A of Figure 8.1.) *Land* means the ground plus any raw materials (such as coal ore and bananas) on or in the ground. *Labor* is the productive input of a human (our common understanding of "work"). *Capital* is the nonhuman productive input from other resources (especially financial resources, machinery, and technology). Each factor of production is controlled by an owner who, in the language of economics, is referred to as a *household* (B).

Some actor called a *firm* (C) (in this book, the terms "firm" and "producer" are used interchangeably) attempts to acquire a combination of these productive resources (factors of production) in order to produce a *good* (D1). A good can be a product (e.g., a pencil, a nuclear missile) or a service (e.g., a massage, transportation on an airplane).

A firm might be a single individual who produces a good from her own resources. For example, a masseuse (massage giver) provides a massage through her own labor skills. Or a firm might be a large organization that uses many productive resources (of land and commodities, workers and capital). For example, a firm

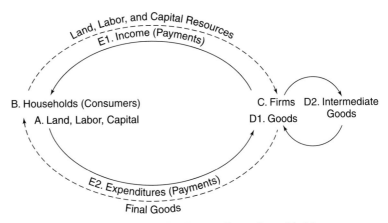

Part A. An Economic Framework: The Income-Expenditures Model

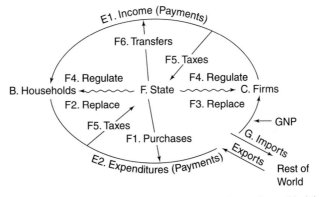

Part B. The State is Integrated into the Income-Expenditures Model,
with the State Having Six Possible Roles.

Figure 8.1 A political economy framework
(part A): An Economic Framework: The Income and Expenditures Model
(part B): The State is Integrated into the Income-Expenditures Model, with the state having
six possible roles:

F1. It can be a consumer, purchasing any good from a firm.

F2. It can replace (that is, be) a household, in the sense that it controls some or
all factors of production.

F3. It can replace (that is, be) a firm, producing any good.

F4. It can regulate the manner in which either households or firms operate by enacting
policies that encourage or prevent certain behaviors by those other economic actors.

F5. It can tax (extract resources from) the payments to any actor.

F6. It can transfer payments to any actor.

NOTE: The gross national product (GNP) is the sum of household expenditures (including investment
via the financial system), government purchases, and exports minus imports.

that produces something as simple as a pencil needs such productive resources as wood, graphite, rubber, machines, and workers. The firm transforms these factors of production into the final good—here, a pencil. Often goods are acquired in order to make more complicated goods; these goods used in the firm's production process are called *intermediate goods* (D2). The pencil firm, for example, has probably acquired such intermediate goods as graphite (which it acquires from another firm that has mined and refined the metal) and wood (which has come from a firm that owns, cuts, and mills trees).

A household has a second role, as a *consumer,* when it wants to acquire a final good. A consumer offers something of value to the firm in exchange for the good that the consumer wants. What emerges between the household/consumer and the firm is a system of *payments* (E1 and E2 in the figure). A firm must pay something to those households that control the relevant productive resource(s) necessary for the firm to produce goods. And a household, in its role as a consumer, must pay something to the firm in order to get the final goods that it wants. Notice that any individual or group can act as either a consumer or a firm, depending on whether the individual or group is transforming productive resources into goods or is acquiring a final good.

The richest merchant in a Bedouin market in Egypt displays the goods she will sell, proudly wearing the chains of gold coins that attest to her entrepreneurial skills as a "firm" in a market economy.

The size of a payment (the price) is established by what one actor is willing to exchange (to sacrifice) in order to acquire a good held by another actor. In simple economies, a payment might involve a straight exchange. The actor who has grown a dozen tomatoes exchanges them with someone who will give her a massage (or whatever else she values enough to give up the tomatoes). In every system there are some of these good-for-good exchanges.

But most systems develop a standard mechanism for exchanges among goods (typically, money). The consumer gives the producer some amount of money in exchange for the final good. For example, a tomato might cost $1 (or an equivalent amount of money in francs or yen) and a massage might be offered for $12.

If firms want to sell more massages than customers want to buy, the price of a massage is likely to come down. This is how *supply and demand* operate: If demand is low relative to supply, the price comes down; and if demand is high relative to supply, the price goes up. In theory, with enough producers and consumers making exchanges, the price of a good reaches a perfect balance point between supply and demand, known as the "equilibrium point" (see Figure 8.2).

The payment by a consumer to a firm (E2) might be different from the payments by the firm for the productive resources necessary to produce that good (E1) (see Figure 8.1). A firm is successful if it is able to sell the good for more than it paid to produce the good. This return to the firm in excess of its payments is called *profit*. If the firm must sell the good for less than the cost of producing it, the firm suffers a "loss." Obviously, firms normally try to increase their profit and to avoid loss.

Getting and Spending

In this way, the system of exchange goes around and around. The households expend their resources on goods and the firms provide the households with income as they pay for productive resources. Ideally, everyone is exchanging things of value for other things that they value even more. As the system becomes more complex, many actors are involved in the production and distribution of goods. In addition

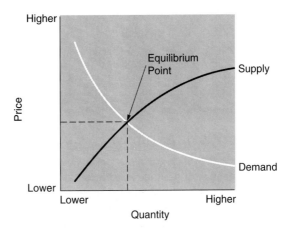

Figure 8.2   The relationship between the supply of a good and the demand for the good

to offering goods for money and exchanging money for desired goods, some actors can operate as brokers, organizing complicated or large-scale exchanges.

As the cycle continues, more and more goods are produced, bought, sold, and consumed by all the actors in the economic system. The complexity of the actual exchanges in most economic systems is beyond comprehension. As an example, see how long a list you can develop (in one minute) of the number of different people who contributed some fraction of the value (the one dollar) that you pay for a tomato at the supermarket. (Think about the actors involved in the production and distribution to you of that tomato.) With sufficient time, you could probably identify hundreds of people who share in the resource that you have sacrificed (i.e., the payment you have provided in exchange for the tomato).

To the extent that others are willing to offer substantial payments in exchange for the factors of production or the goods that you control, you have more resource power. You have many choices regarding the use of your own resources. If you have twelve tomatoes, you could (1) eat them all; (2) eat six and sell/trade six for as much money or goods as you can get; (3) eat two and sell/trade the rest for a loaf of bread and a book of verse; (4) eat two, sell/trade two for a loaf of bread, and use the remaining eight to make sixteen tomato sandwiches that you sell/trade (for as much as you can get); (5) give all the tomatoes to hungry people; or…—the possibilities are extensive. And if you chose approach 2, 3, or 4, you would now have further choices to make with your new bundle of resources.

Presumably, you attempt to pursue a strategy that maximizes your utility (i.e., that results in your most-preferred mixture of goods and resources) and hence enhances your life. Individuals (and groups) can have very different sets of preferences. One person might want to hoard money or food or precious metals; another might want to spend everything on consumption for personal pleasure. One person might actively seek the resources to own a mansion and a Mercedes-Benz, while another person might be happiest with no possessions other than the bare necessities she carries in a backpack. One person might work obsessively to increase her total package of resources, while another person might join a meditation society, giving up all possessions in favor of the contemplative life.

Of course, it's a tough world, and so all people are not equally capable of maximizing their value preferences. An individual's success in getting her preferred mix of goods and resources can be affected by such things as the kinds and amounts of resources she already controls, her skills in producing desired goods, the constraints in her environment, the actions of others, and even luck. Over time, there are likely to be huge differences in the mix of goods and resources controlled by different individuals and groups.

The State (and the World) Join In

We now have our first approximation of an abstract model of the economic system. The cyclical exchange of payments for factors of production and payments for final goods becomes a perpetual motion machine. This model is extremely simplistic. One crucial omission in our description to this point is the absence of the political system. The state (F) is added in part B of Figure 8.1, and the interaction between the economy and the state results in the dynamic processes we term the *political economy*. The state can powerfully affect the economic system in the six general ways labeled F1 through F6 in part B of Figure 8.1. Notice that the state can regulate any economic activity, can replace either a consumer of goods (a household) or a producer of goods (a firm), can tax any actor, and can transfer goods or money to any actor. It will become evident in the next section that the actions of the state regarding the six dimensions of behavior distinguish different types of political economies. (As we talk about the state in this discussion, it is useful to reiterate that the state, like other aggregate actors, is really a complex organizational structure composed of many individuals whose combined decisions and actions constitute the behavior attributed to "the" state.)

Part B of Figure 8.1 also recognizes that there are boundaries that affect the behavior of economic actors. Producers can sell goods outside of the state's boundaries to some consumer in the rest of the world (these are *exports*). Or consumers can purchase goods from producers outside the state's boundaries (these are *imports*). Thus there is a net flow of income into or out of the economic system, based on the levels of imports and exports (G). In addition, a state (the actor's own state or another state) can implement policies that either restrict freedom (e.g., tariff barriers) or facilitate freedom (e.g., conquest of one state by another). In this chapter, the role of political economies in the rest of the world will generally be ignored, but the significant role of such external actors will be emphasized in Chapters 13 through 17. As Figure 8.1 indicates, the total productive effort of the economy is called the *gross national product (GNP)* or *gross domestic product (GDP)* (also see Box 8.1).

Since our model is fairly complicated already, we'll stop here. But other elements of a fully specified model of an economic system are still missing. You can readily find them in an introductory economics text. Two more facts about the model should be pointed out, however. First, part B of Figure 8.1 does not explicitly identify the role of certain financial actors that would be shown in a fuller model. A household can save some of its income rather than spend it all. These savings are put into the financial system. Its investors pay households to use these resources as capital, which the investors offer to firms in exchange for payment.

Second, although the actors are presented as independent individuals in our model, an economic actor, like a political actor, might be an individual or a collectivity. In an actual economy, some actors will combine their resources with those of others in order to enhance their relative advantages in the processes of production and exchange. They might develop cooperative arrangements, forming groups and institutions that attempt to control the use of a resource. Such cooperation might emerge among individual owners of labor, such as a farming collective or a labor union; among those owning a commodity, such as a cartel; or among those controlling capital, such as a syndicate or a diversified corporation.

TWO IDEAL-TYPE POLITICAL ECONOMIES

It is now possible to distinguish the two ideal-type political economies. An *ideal type* is a description of what a certain phenomenon might be like in its pure form. An ideal type is illustrative, but it does not necessarily correspond exactly to any real-world example. The two ideal-type political economies are the *market economy* and the *command economy.*

BOX 8.1

A Gross Product

The total level of production in an economy is usually measured by one of two monetary figures. The *gross national product (GNP)* is the total value of all the final goods produced by a state's economic actors during a certain time period. GNP includes the production of all citizens of the state, whether they are inside the state's boundaries or not. In many analyses, it is now more common to use the second measure, *gross domestic product (GDP).* GDP is the total value of all final goods produced by all people within a state's boundaries, whether or not they are citizens. Although GNP is still the measure referred to most frequently in the United States, many international economic actors now opt for GDP as a more accurate indicator of a country's economic vitality, given the large numbers of noncitizens who produce goods within many countries.

Since these gross products are very influenced by the size of the country, attempts to compare the relative prosperity of the people in different countries have typically divided the productive total by the number of citizens (as "per capita"). As measures of a country's prosperity, both GNP per capita and GDP per capita have at least three important flaws.

First, they do not measure how the prosperity is distributed among the country's economic actors, and thus many citizens have an individual level of prosperity that is very different from their country's average production per capita.

Second, only the goods that actually enter the society's monetary sector are measured, while many other valued goods are ignored. These unmeasured goods include household work and goods in the "underground economy," particularly trade in illegal goods, barter trade, and the black market. In some countries GNP and GDP are particularly misleading because such unmeasured goods are a very significant proportion of total economic activity.

Third, GNP and GDP are often used to compare the prosperity of one country versus another. However, there are huge between-country disparities in the exchange value of money. In comparing two countries, the same amount of money (converting local currencies into an international exchange currency, usually dollars) can buy much more or much less of the same specific goods (e.g., a loaf of bread, a bus ride, a book, a computer). Due to these disparities, there is increasing use of a third prosperity measure that attempts to establish equivalent value, using an index based on "purchasing power parity" (PPP)—that is, correcting monetary levels to reflect the amount of local currency required to buy certain standard goods in that country.

Using PPP indexing, the World Bank (1999: table 1.1) reports that while India's GNP per capita is $370, this equates to $1,660 per capita in "purchasing power." The

BOX 8.1

purchasing power of Japan's $38,160 is actually $24,400. In purchasing power dollars, the economic gap between the wealthier countries and the poorer countries usually decreases. However, it is important to note that when a country attempts to participate in the global economy, and especially when it attempts to import goods, the purchasing power of its currency is directly tied to international exchange rates, not to the price of bread at home (or PPP dollars), and its relative wealth or poverty remains.

Table 8.1 compares how these measures differ for each of 15 countries. Do you notice changes in relative wealth? For most countries, wealth relative to other countries changes less than 20 ranks out of 210 economies. However, in some cases, like the Czech Republic and Japan, the absolute level does change quite strikingly. There are a few instances, like Poland, where the relative position between gross product per capita and the correction for PPP are rather large. What might explain a disparity like that in Poland?

More broadly, which of the measures do you think is the best means of measuring general prosperity? Is there another measure you think would be better than any of these? Why?

TABLE 8.1
Alternative Measures of Economic Prosperity

Country	$GNP/capita	$GNP/capita in PPP$[a]	$GDP/capita	$GDP/capita in PPP$[a]
Japan	38,160 (4)[b]	24,400 (8)[b]	22,700	21,930
Singapore	32,810 (10)	29,080 (4)	21,200	22,604
United States	29,080 (6)	28,740 (2)	28,600	26,977
Czech Republic	5,240 (70)	10,380 (63)	11,100	9,775
Brazil	4,790 (73)	6,350 (90)	5,928	6,300
Mexico	3,700 (81)	8,110 (85)	8,100	6,769
Poland	3,590 (83)	6,510 (46)	6,400	5,442
Turkey	3,310 (91)	6,470 (88)	6,100	5,516
Russia	2,680 (95)	4,280 (104)	5,200	4,531
Costa Rica	2,680 (95)	6,510 (85)	5,500	5,969
Egypt	1,200 (129)	3,080 (134)	2,900	3,829
Indonesia	1,110 (135)	3,390 (125)	3,770	3.971
China	860 (145)	3,070 (135)	2,800	2,935
Congo	670 (156)	1,290 (180)	400	n.a.
India	370 (177)	1,660 (163)	1,600	1,422

Source: $GNP/capita and $GNP/capita at PPP: World Bank 1999: table 1; $GDP/capita and $GDP/capita in PPP: Freedom House 1999.
[a]PPP = purchasing power parity
[b]Ranking among 210 economies

In distinguishing the market economy from the command economy, five fundamental questions will be posed:

1. Who controls the factors of production?
2. Who determines what goods are produced?
3. Who establishes the value attached to different resources and goods?
4. Who decides how resources and goods will be distributed?
5. What is the role of the state?

The answers to these questions (summarized in Table 8.2) establish the nature of the political economy in a society. Let us examine how these five questions are answered for each of the two ideal-type political economies, the market economy and the command economy. (For other approaches that explain political economy, see, e.g., Heyne [1999] and Lindblom [1977].)

The Market Economy: Total Private Control

1.   **Who controls the factors of production?** In the ideal-type **market economy** there is total private control. Every actor has direct, personal control over all her own factors of production (although she cannot control the value attached to those factors). The worker decides who, if anyone, she will offer her work to and the type and amount of resources she will accept in exchange for that work. The owner of land or capital similarly decides the conditions under which she will allow her productive resources to be employed in the productive system. And the firm determines what productive resources it will acquire.

In general, every household and every firm are motivated to maximize the value associated with the resources and goods they control. As an actor operates in this economic order, she continually attempts to expand the total package of resources

TABLE 8.2
Two Ideal-type Political Economies

Key Points	Market Economy	Command Economy
1. Control of factors of production	Every economic actor controls own factors	State owns and controls all factors
2. Production decisions	Sum of all private actors' decisions ("invisible hand" of market); demand oriented	State decisions defined in detailed plan; supply oriented
3. Value established	Exchange value in the market	State sets values attached to all goods
4. Distribution decisions	Choices by private actors	State determines who will receive what products at what levels
5. Role of the state	Generally passive; enforces rules, provides minimal protection to actors	Dominates process; owns, plans, controls, and regulates all economic activity

that she controls. Thus she aims to take actions such that every exchange will increase her accumulated value. To the extent that she can exchange some resources(s) and receive an even greater amount of resources in return, she has increased her total resource base. Of course, it is also possible that she can make bad decisions about what to control and thus reduce her total resource base.

2.   **Who determines what goods are produced?** As all the actors make their own separate decisions in an attempt to maximize their own resources, a pattern emerges regarding what goods are produced. In particular, every firm acts to maximize its profits through the process in which it pays to acquire productive resources and then produces goods that are sold to consumers. The firm's decisions about what goods to produce are based on its assessment of how it can achieve maximum profit. In the phrase of the famous Scottish economist Adam Smith (1723–1790), production is guided by the "invisible hand" of the market. This invisible hand is the summation of the actions of every household and every firm regarding the uses of the factors of production.

If one thinks of an economy in terms of the supply and demand for goods, this system is demand oriented. The most important consideration for a firm that is deciding what to produce is this: What good can I offer that others will demand and for which others will offer the highest payments, in comparison to my costs of production? Thus the firm attempts to assess the demand for various goods in the market and then to transform the factors of production it controls in order to provide whatever good it thinks will maximize its own profit.

3.   **Who establishes the value attached to different resources and goods?** Similarly, the invisible hand of the market establishes value. Each factor of production and the goods that are produced through transformation of these factors are valued at their opportunity cost—the value (e.g., money, good, factor of production) that is sacrificed by someone in the market in exchange for them. Hence nothing has value except to the extent that some other actor will exchange resources to obtain it.

In most circumstances, many actors offer similar resources and goods. The result is vigorous competition among private actors, as everyone tries to gain the maximum payment from others in exchange for her own resources and goods. Ultimately, the value of every resource and good is subject to this competition, based on both its supply and the existing demand for it (recall Figure 8.2). Sometimes production is controlled almost completely by one firm (a monopoly) or a few firms (an oligopoly) that can manipulate the supply and value of goods.

Competition is particularly intense where supply and demand are quite unequal. For example, if five workers will drill holes in metal (supply) and one firm needs two workers with this resource (demand), the firm can bid down the resources it has to pay for the work (this is usually a wage rate, but it can also include other resources, such as work conditions, benefits such as housing or health care, or shares of the firm's profits) by inducing the five workers to undercut each other's wage claim. Conversely, if there are only two workers available with this skill and the firm needs five, the workers can bid up the resources that they will be offered.

A basic economic assumption in a market economy is the continual adjustment of supply and demand toward an equilibrium point. For example, some workers might move to a different place or offer a different labor skill if the wages for drilling holes get too low or there are too few jobs. And a firm might find a substitute for the labor it needs if hole-drilling labor is too expensive or too scarce to enable the firm to make a profit in the market. (Can you think of other supply-demand adjustments that the workers or the firm might make?)

4. **Who decides how resources and goods will be distributed?** Again, it is the invisible hand of the market, rather than anyone in particular, that determines the distribution of resources and goods in the market economy. As everyone pursues her own private interests, actors accumulate dramatically different bundles of resources and goods, depending on their preferences, the resources they control, and their skill and luck in exchanging and transforming resources in the market.

5. **What is the role of the state?** In a market economy, state intervention is minimal. The state is passive in the productive system, allowing private actors to operate in a relatively unconstrained manner. The state is obliged, under the social contract, to prevent private actors from doing violence to each other. Also, the state protects its citizens from the external environment, preventing or resisting the violation of its sovereignty or its citizens' rights by other states. In meeting these responsibilities, the state might purchase some resources, might levy minimal taxes, and might affect firms' import and export activities. But the general principle in the ideal-type market economy is that the state does not have a significant role in the economy.

The Command Economy: Total State Control

1. **Who controls the factors of production?** In the ideal-type **command economy**, the state assumes total control of virtually all the significant factors of production. The state replaces or eliminates the role of private owners of labor, land, and capital whose activities are so crucial in the market economy. The state owns the land, the natural resources, the factories, the machines, and so on. The state even owns labor, in the sense that the state decides the conditions and purposes for which all individuals must offer their labor. Thus it is the state that determines how every factor of production will be used.

2. **Who determines what goods are produced?** In terms of part B of Figure 8.1, the state is the firm that produces virtually all major goods in the system. The state devises a detailed *economic plan* that specifies what levels of each good will be produced from what combination of resources. A political ideal guides this plan for production: the commitment to provide every citizen in the society with the goods that enable each citizen to enjoy a life of material well-being. Thus the state's plan sets production decisions that are supply oriented (in contrast to the demand orientation of the market economy). The state/firm attempts to use productive resources optimally to maximize the supply of appropriate goods available for consumers. Centralized planning guided by a broad vision of social needs, rather than independent decisions by many profit-seeking actors, guides the complex actions resulting in the production of a particular mix of goods.

3. **Who establishes the value attached to different resources and goods?** Since the state controls all the factors of production and is the firm producing all goods, it is also able to set the values (i.e., establish the payments) for all exchanges within its boundaries. Competition is eliminated, since the state, rather than the

market, establishes the payments for every factor of production and every good in the society. Thus the state tells a group of farmers to produce a million tomatoes and then sets the exchange value of those tomatoes. Similarly, the state decides which individuals will have jobs drilling holes and it establishes the wages and benefits they receive for their work. The state is not completely free to set payments—for example, the scarcity of a productive resource can influence its cost—but given availability, value is set primarily by the state's decisions.

4. Who decides how resources and goods will be distributed? The state is equally active in the decisions on the distribution of goods to the population. The state's plan indicates who will receive which goods in what amounts. The plan will specify, for example, that automobile-producing factory X will receive forty-six tons of steel each month, and that a town will receive three tomatoes per family per week. The plan can also indicate precisely where these goods will come from (i.e., steel from factory Y and tomatoes from farm Z).

In the real world, most near-total command economies base their plan on the objective of distributing necessary goods (especially food, shelter, education, health care) to every person on a relatively equal basis. As an ideal type, however, a command economy need not be committed to such egalitarianism. The state could decide that one particular group will receive a very large share of the goods and that other, less favored groups will receive very little. The crucial decisions about distribution of goods are made by those with power in the political system.

5. What is the role of the state? Clearly, the state has a dominant, even an overwhelming role in this type of political economy. The state controls virtually all of the important factors of production, plans the manner in which they will be utilized in the production of goods, establishes the official value of all resources and goods, and decides how the resources of the society will be distributed among individuals. In the command economy, surplus value is accumulated by the state, not by individuals. The state then determines how this surplus value will be used to serve its objectives and to provide goods to certain actors.

KEY PROBLEMS FOR EACH IDEAL-TYPE POLITICAL ECONOMY

There are potential shortcomings in the actual operation of either the market economy or the command economy. It is important to consider a few of the major problems inherent in each type of political economy. These, along with the benefits, are summarized in Table 8.3.

Market Economy

Resource inequality. One major problem with the market economy is that substantial resource inequality tends to emerge. In a market economy, competition is everywhere and it tends to become ruthless. As every actor strives to maximize resources and control over the factors of production, some actors are extremely successful and others are total failures. Most importantly, the market system is indifferent to the problems of those who do not succeed. Over time the rich tend to get

TABLE 8.3
Benefits and Problems of Market and Command Economies

Market Economy	Benefits	Problems
Competition	Energetic and efficient production	Ruthless interactions; huge inequalities in wealth and resources
Demand orientation	Goods' cost and quality responsive to consumers' desires	Creation of demand for and proliferation of goods that have limited social value
No central plan	Local decision and "invisible hand" stimulate innovation, facilitate freedom	Economic cycles of boom and bust, inflation and recession
Command Economy		
No competition	Work for common good; relative equality of wealth and income	Little initiative; shoddy products; low productivity
Supply orientation	Production and distribution for social and individual needs	Oversupply and shortages; lack of coordination
Central plan	Rational use of societal resources	Overcentralized control; limited innovation and lack of responsiveness to changing circumstances

richer (especially if they cooperate a bit) while those with a few resources tend increasingly to lose economic power in the market.

Neither the successful actors nor the state intervene to protect those who fail to capture many resources. Thus some people, and perhaps even large numbers of people, lack the resources to enable them to consume the goods they need for a secure and comfortable life. As inequalities of wealth, power, and status increase, there is greater likelihood of alienation among the less successful and of conflict between the rich and the poor.

Production for profit, not need.   A second problem is that a demand-oriented system of production does not necessarily produce goods that meet human needs. Rather, production decisions are dominated by actors who produce only those goods that they believe will maximize their own resources. Thus there can be a proliferation of extravagant or marginal goods that are profitable, while more essential goods are produced in insufficient amounts because they are less profitable. For example, there might be an abundant supply of quality health care for the rich, while large numbers of poor people lack adequate care because private producers see too little profit in caring for them and the state is passive in the production and regulation of health care.

There also might be wasteful competition as many variations of a good are offered. Considerable resources can be spent manipulating demand for these goods through such techniques as advertising. For example, there might be literally hundreds of different breakfast cereals, most of which are minimally nutritious. A cereal's cost might be based more on the expense of advertising and packaging (to create demand for that particular brand) and on profit (to the producer) than on the factor payments to produce the cereal.

Severe economic cycles. Third, a market economy can experience major economic cycles. There is no guarantee that the very large number of private decisions about production and consumption (the "invisible hand") will mesh in a manner that ensures steady growth and prosperity for the economic system as a whole. The economy is prone to large swings in the direction of either hyperactivity (causing inflation and scarcity) or serious economic decline (causing recession or depression), and the state does not intervene to counteract these swings. Fluctuations between boom and bust, even if infrequent, can be deeply disruptive to the productive system and especially to those actors whose limited resources make them vulnerable to bad times.

Command Economy

Limited incentives for efficiency. The absence of competition in the command political economy can result in problems as serious as those from excessive competition. First, if there is no competitive market of alternative goods, there is minimal initiative to produce goods of high quality. People are obliged to accept

goods that are unexciting or of poor quality. Second, if payments are standardized by the state and there are no major economic incentives for individual initiative and hard work, managers and workers tend to become conservative and even lazy.

Unresponsive production.   The state's emphasis on a supply orientation means that production decisions are not directly responsive to consumer demand. The supply-oriented political economy is guided by the central planners' ideas of what people should want, not what consumers actually do want and will purchase. Thus the plan typically results in substantial oversupply of some goods and severe shortages of others.

Overcentralization and inflexibility.   Command economies are usually so centralized that they lose touch with the differences and complexities of individual firms and consumers. The central planners usually do not receive and react effectively to information regarding miscalculations and mistakes in either the development or the implementation of the state's overall plan. Such rigidity and unresponsiveness make the efficient use of productive resources unlikely. In short, the political economy that combines minimal competition, a weak demand mechanism, and inflexibility is prone to low productivity, inferior goods, and inefficient use of resources.

THE MIXED ECONOMY

Given the potential shortcomings of the ideal-type market and command political economies, is there an alternative? The **mixed economy** can be understood as an attempt to combine the strengths of these two ideal-type economies while also minimizing their shortcomings. As a hybrid, the mixed economy is not a "pure" ideal type. It compromises on each of the five key issues considered earlier.

1.   **Who controls the factors of production?** In a mixed economy, control of the means of production is shared between the state and private actors. The state owns or directly controls some of the major factors of production, such as those relating to key commodities (e.g., coal, oil, steel), to key infrastructure systems (e.g., transportation, telecommunications), and to key financial resources (e.g., the banks). However, a substantial share of the factors of production are controlled by private actors (households).

2.   **Who determines what goods are produced?** Production decisions in the mixed economy are primarily demand oriented, driven by the market mechanism. Most public (state) sector firms are under direct state control, as in a command economy, but they usually must interact and even compete with many private firms when acquiring productive resources and when selling goods to consumers. However, firms and households can be constrained by the state in the mixed economy. The state can regulate the behavior of private actors and it can implement an economic plan that specifies broad guidelines for all actors in the system.

3.   **Who establishes the value attached to different resources and goods?** The value of a good in the mixed economy is established in a manner more akin to that of the market system. Value is generally determined through the market processes of supply and demand, which interact to determine the opportunity costs, and thus

the price, of most goods. But the state does intervene to ensure that national priorities are protected. For example, the state might establish the value of certain factors of production, including wages; it might set guidelines to control the market prices of key goods; it might regulate the manner in which households and firms collaborate and compete; and it might employ taxing and expenditure (purchases [F1] in part B of Figure 8.1) to influence the productive system.

4. **Who decides how resources and goods will be distributed?** Decisions on the distribution of values are the most complicated element of the mixed economy. Private actors are allowed to make decisions and take actions that maximize their profits and their share of the resources. The state then intervenes by a variety of taxation mechanisms (F5), recapturing some of the payments received by every private actor. In turn, the state uses these taxes to purchase goods (F1) or as transfer payments (F6), both of which the state redistributes to certain actors in the social order. The state undertakes only a partial redistribution of resources (unlike the case in the command economy), leaving private actors with considerable resources and freedom to make their own decisions about production and consumption.

5. **What is the role of the state?** In sum, the mixed economy is a middle way between the market and the command political economies. The state's rules, actions, and direct involvements in the productive system moderate and limit the market of private households and firms. The state attempts to blend a demand orientation and a supply orientation, to facilitate some competition but to mitigate the effects of ruthless competition, and to allow private actors to benefit from their skillful use of resources while ensuring a certain level of necessary goods for the less successful actors. The great challenges for the state in a mixed economy concern the difficulties of striking a proper balance between competition and control, between a free market and a planned economy, and between private profit and a sharing of society's resources. Real-world economies are so immensely complex and dynamic that the search for such a balance is continual and in some cases impossible.

POLITICS PLUS POLITICAL ECONOMY: THE OTHER "ISMS"
The Three "Isms"

One set of great "isms" in political analysis includes the ideologies of conservatism, classical liberalism, and socialism (see Chapter 2). Another set of great "isms" explicitly links politics to political economy: these three "isms" are capitalism, communism, and socialism. In twentieth-century politics, these were extremely emotive labels, endowed with powerful ideological content. In their most straightforward form, capitalism, communism, and socialism correspond loosely to market economy, command economy, and mixed economy, respectively.

Capitalism is a system in which private economic actors are quite free from state constraints and the state engages in only the most limited efforts to shift resources among private actors. It is founded on the philosophy of laissez-faire economics celebrated by Adam Smith and it imposes the severe limitations on government activity that are associated with classical liberalism. While the freedom of economic actors from government intervention is critical, there is no assumption that capitalism requires any particular form of political processes to function efficiently (Thurow 1997).

Communism is a system that closely resembles the command political economy described earlier in this chapter. Its centerpiece is the socialization of resources—the notion that the state must maintain control of society's land, labor, and capital. The state must guide the utilization of all these major means of production, by means of a central plan, so that the production and distribution of goods serve the best interests of the entire population. Although it is primarily an economic system, communism usually emphasizes an ideological commitment to economic and social equality among all its citizens. It also typically posits that government and politics, like the economic system, must be guided powerfully by a unified leadership. Communism is generally associated with the theories of Karl Marx and with the economic systems that were developed in such countries as China (1949 to about 1990), Cuba (since 1959), and the former Societ Union (1917–1991).

Socialism is in the middle of the three "isms" and thus its differentiation from the other two is not precise. It is akin to the mixed political economy, since it attempts a more complex balance between state involvement and private control. Some major productive resources are owned or controlled by the state, and the state actively intervenes in the economy, but most production decisions are private, and value is established primarily by supply and demand. While the policies in a socialist state attempt to reduce inequalities significantly, they do not aim for total economic equality. Sweden and Denmark are typical examples of what are known as democratic socialist systems. Socialism is a confusing term, however, because it is also used to describe the system in certain countries, such as Cuba and North Korea, whose regimes can be called Marxist-Leninist socialism, based on the manner in which Marx used the concepts of socialism and communism (recall Chapter 2, and see Box 8.2). And some countries such as China have evolved away from Marxist-Leninist socialism, incorporating significant elements of the market system.

Communism is distinguishable from socialism in an analytic sense, because the communist state (on behalf of "the people") attempts to control virtually all important factors of production in the society and has a fundamental commitment to total economic and social equality among all citizens. (Notice that such egalitarianism is not a necessary condition of the ideal-type command economy.) A socialist system, in comparison to capitalism, tends to use public policy to redistribute societal resources toward those citizens who are less advantaged economically, and the socialist state is substantially more involved in economic planning, regulation, and even ownership of productive means than a state under capitalism (Przeworski 1985).

The Real World

In terms of political economy, there are several notable conclusions among the countries in the contemporary world. First, no country has a political economy that corresponds exactly to either the market economy or the command economy. Since these are ideal types, this fact is not surprising. While it is possible to locate countries generally along a continuum from a "pure" market economy to a "pure" command economy, all actual political economies are mixed. However, this does not mean that all political economies are basically the same—the mix of elements varies a great deal from country to country.

BOX 8.2

Communism versus Socialism in Marxist Theory

It is worth noting that Marx and Marxist theorists use the terms "socialism" and "communism" in a different manner from either the political economy approach of this book or contemporary Western media and politicians. In Marxist theory, communism is a higher stage of political economy that follows socialism. In a *socialist system,* the state strives to achieve social control of resources (of the means of production) by eliminating private property. As private property is eliminated, there will be a reduction in the presence of the different strata (classes) of citizens that are separated by substantial differences in the amount of private property that each controls. (A detailed description of the class approach to explaining politics will be provided in Chapter 9.)

In Marxist theory, *communism* emerges only when all classes (and the inevitable conflict between those classes) cease to exist. Thus most Marxists acknowledge that no "socialist" state (e.g., Cuba) has yet completely eliminated classes and the class struggle; in this sense, communism remains a goal. In the classless society, everyone will work for the good of all, not to gain private value. Thus under socialism everyone provides resources (work) according to ability and receives resources according to that work, while under communism everyone provides according to ability and receives according to need.

This book employs the common Western usage: communism exists if a state has nearly total control over the major factors of production. Given the recent shift away from communism (see Chapter 15), only a few contemporary states (e.g., North Korea) meet this criterion.

Second, the concepts of communism, socialism, and capitalism might be best understood as broader, somewhat ideological labels that signify considerably more than the way in which the political economy is organized. For some, these labels also connote *sociopolitical* orders. Communism is viewed as a system that denies individual freedoms in noneconomic spheres and in which government does not depend on the consent of the governed. Capitalism signifies a system of self-interested individualism that denies the need for collective action to nurture society as a whole, to promote social values and culture, or to protect the ecology (Heilbroner 1994).

Third, every state engages in some regulation of some economic actors and some redistribution of resources. Politics and values play a powerful role in establishing exactly what kinds of interventions the state will undertake and what values and interests the state will serve. Thus understanding the mixed nature of actual political economies entails more than simply comparing the proportion of the GDP controlled by private actors versus the state.

In theory, at least, two countries might have the same overall levels of market freedom and state intervention in the economy (as well as the same level of taxation and the same share of GNP in the public sector) and yet be guided by very different philosophies. In one country the state's role could be to limit the power of large firms, to ensure labor's participation in national economic policy making, and to facilitate domestic consumption. In another country, the state might be no less interventionist, but its involvement might be based on policies that support the growth of large firms, that suppress labor unions, and that channel citizens' resources into savings.

The latter profile is consistent with the political economies of some of the most successful industrializing countries of Asia, such as South Korea, whereas countries such as Spain and Uruguay generally fit the first profile. These issues will be examined in more detail later in the book (in the study of economic development in Chapter 10, and in the comparative analyses of strategies for achieving prosperity in Chapters 13–15). The four examples that follow here suggest some of the features of actual political economies relative to ideal types.

Generally market and capitalist: Switzerland.   The wealthiest country in the world (measured as GNP per capita), Switzerland has a relatively weak central government. This decentralization of political power is linked to a political economy that strongly emphasizes private control and limited government involvement. Switzerland is ranked in the group of countries with the least state regulation of the economy (Freedom House, 1999). Nearly all factors of production are privately owned, and most decisions and actions regarding the use of those resources are in private hands. On the expenditure side, central government spending is less than 15 percent of GNP. Apart from defense expenditures and education, relatively few resources are allocated to the provision of public goods, given the wealth of the society. Although still low, welfare spending rose substantially in the 1990s, generating a national debate about limitations on public expenditure on social programs.

Generally mixed and capitalist: South Korea.   In South Korea, the state has little commitment to use the political economy for direct improvement of its citizens' quality of life. Apart from education, the state does not provide many welfare goods and services to its citizens. Central government expenditure is only about 16 percent of GNP. It is not a purely capitalist system, however, because the state is extremely interventionist in promoting economic development. The state bureaucracy works very closely with firms to implement a comprehensive, collaborative strategy for economic growth. This strategy has particularly favored the development of a few major Korean companies. Government loans, tax credits, and other subsidies are channeled to these companies, which are expected to operate and diversify in directions suggested by the government. In turn, the government has assured the companies of high profits and of a labor force that is well educated, disciplined, and unable to organize effectively for high wages. The state has also employed many hidden subsidies and import restrictions to provide competitive advantages in the international market to its export-oriented firms. (This "developmental state" approach is discussed further in Chapter 10.)

Generally mixed and socialist: Denmark.   The great majority of productive resources in Denmark are privately owned, and the state allows considerable freedom of action to entrepreneurs. However, the state is an active and visible force in the Danish political economy. First, the state enforces strong policies which regulate private economic actors, especially "corporatist" policies that control working conditions and environmental quality. (See Box 8.3 on corporatism.) Second, the state provides an extensive array of welfare services to the population, including income supplement programs, a comprehensive free health care system, state-subsidized housing for the elderly and for low-income groups, free child care and education from infancy through university, and an extensive public transportation system. And third, to finance these programs, the government collects various forms of taxes equal to more than 50 percent of the GNP.

Generally command and communist: Cuba. In response to the global movement toward more market-oriented systems, Cuba has reduced the level of centralized state control over the economy. However, the state still owns and controls the major means of production in Cuba and there is a detailed central economic plan. Thus Cuba is among the eleven countries (of 178) with the highest level of state regulation of the economy (Freedom House, 1999). Agriculture and manufacturing operations remain collectivized. The state promises work for all (although there is unemployment) and workers' wages are controlled by the state. Consistent with the ideals of communism, the state retains a fundamental commitment to egalitarianism

BOX 8.3

From the "Ism" File II: Corporatism

Recently many scholars have referred to the political economy of some states by another "ism," corporatism. *Corporatism* is characterized by extensive economic cooperation between an activist state and large organizations representing major economic actors. The corporatist state identifies a few groups that control major productive resources. These "peak associations" (organizations that represent these big groups) usually include large industries, organized labor, farmers, and major financial institutions. The organizational leaders of the peak associations are given great influence in working with the state to determine answers to key political economy questions regarding production decisions and the distribution of resources.

The idea is that there will be consultation, cooperation, and coordination among the state, big capital, big owners, and big labor, rather than conflict and competition. The peak associations have some autonomy from the state, but they are supposed to work together for common national interests. In short, corporatism blends features of capitalism (e.g., private ownership, private profit) and socialism (e.g., extensive state economic planning, coordination of major factors of production with the state's conception of the national interest).

Italy under Benito Mussolini created the first modern corporate state—one with a strong fascist bent—between 1922 and 1943. Twenty-two corporations were established, including ones for chemical trades, textiles, lumber and wood, credit and insurance, and inland communications. Each corporation had owner, employee, and managerial representatives who met with state officials to develop economic policy (Macridis and Burg 1991: 220–226). France and Japan are among the contemporary states with strong corporatist tendencies (see Schmitter 1993; Wiarda 1996).

through its control and allocation of societal resources. Many state policies are guided by the quest for economic and social egalitarianism. There has been a strong emphasis on state spending on education and health care, and on policies to redistribute land and income and to produce equality between races, between genders, and between urban and rural citizens.

CONCLUDING OBSERVATIONS

This chapter has introduced you to an approach that classifies and characterizes political systems in terms of their political economies. These concepts are abstract and require the fusion of the languages of political science and of economics. They are important concepts because the linkages between the political system and the economic system are fundamental and pervasive in the contemporary political world. Indeed, the two systems have become so interrelated in most states that it is difficult to separate them, except in an analytic sense. There is very substantial variation in the extent to which the political system intervenes in the system of production and distribution of resources. At one extreme, the state can leave every activity to private actors, while at the other extreme, virtually all economic activity is planned and controlled by the state.

In considering a system such as communism or capitalism, you might find it difficult to avoid strong normative judgments. This difficulty is probably due both to your political socialization and to your tendency to identify an "ism" with particular states for which you have strong positive or negative feelings. For example, your evaluative orientations of communism might be negative because you associate it with the governments of North Korea or the former Soviet Union, states that you might have been socialized to distrust. It is certainly reasonable that you will make both analytical *and* normative judgments about the virtues and shortcomings of every form of political economy and every "ism."

Indeed, assessing the appropriateness of a country's political economy might be the most crucial issue in understanding its effectiveness in the contemporary political world. In recent years, the support for communism and the command political economy has substantially declined among the leaders and citizens in many countries. However, as you will see in Part Five, that decline has not necessarily led to the full implementation of a market economy. It has not even meant that most political leaderships and most citizens have abandoned their support for all of the principles associated with a more command-oriented political economy or with communism.

Despite your own political socialization, you might reflect on a fundamental question: Is *every* state, regardless of its current economic and political development, best served by exactly the same political economy? If you allow for variations in the most appropriate form of political economy for countries in the post–cold war world, you leave open many challenging and important questions about political choices, questions that will be considered from a variety of perspectives in the remainder of this book. This exploration begins in Part Four, with chapters that examine crucial issues associated with political decision making, political, social and economic change, and political violence.

FOR FURTHER CONSIDERATION

1. The economic productivity of command political economies has always been inferior to that of market political economies in comparable countries. What, then, might have been the attraction of this approach to many groups and to many countries between the 1950s and the 1970s?

2. What would be the greatest benefit to individuals if the state played virtually no role in its political economy? What would be the most serious problem with such a system?

3. Are there measures other than the growth in GNP per capita that might indicate the success of a political economy? Why are leaders in most states so worried if there is no growth in GNP per capita?

4. Do you agree with those who contend that capitalism is so individualistic that it fails to protect the collective good?

FOR FURTHER READING

Courtois, Stephane, Nicholas Werth, Jean-Louis Panne, Adrzej Paczkowski, Karel Bartooek and Jean-Louis Margolin. (1999). *The Black Book of Communism: Crimes, Terror, Repression*. Trans. by Jonathan Murphy and Mark Cramer. Boston, MA: Harvard University Press. A detailed and profoundly critical analysis of the history of communism in the twentieth century. Its core argument is that a series of regimes and ruthless dictators, ranging from Lenin and Stalin in the Soviet Union to Mao Zedong in China to Pol Pot in Cambodia to Kim Il Sung in North Korea, have led Communist regimes that engaged in brutal "class genocide" in their societies, resulting in as many as 100 million deaths. There are powerful chapter-length analyses of communist regimes on every continent.

Friedman, Milton. (1981). *Capitalism and Freedom.* Chicago: University of Chicago Press. The major contemporary explication of the classical liberal preference for a strong market economy with only limited state intervention.

Heilbroner, Robert. (1994). *Twenty-First Century Capitalism.* New York: Basic Books. An economist and social critic outlines the challenges facing capitalism and the continuing need for the state to guide the market economy and serve the social good.

Johnson, Chalmers. (1982). *MITI and the Japanese Miracle: The Growth of Industrial Policy, 1925–1975.* Stanford, CA: Stanford University Press. Characterizes the innovative manner in which Japan created a highly successful blending of a market political economy with an interventionist and supportive state furthering a well-defined national economic development policy.

Kristol, Irving. (1978). *Two Cheers for Capitalism.* New York: Basic Books. A leading American neoconservative argues that capitalism is superior to alternative forms of political economy.

Lindblom, Charles E. (1977). *Politics and Markets: The World's Political-Economic Systems.* New York: Basic Books. A rich comparative analysis of the relative merits of the political economies of modern socialism and capitalism.

Thurow, Lester. (1997). *The Future of Capitalism.* New York: Viking-Penguin. A leading economist critically assesses the strengths and weaknesses of capitalism as a political economy and as a system which must deliver prosperity to most of its citizens.

Westoby, Adam. (1989). *The Evolution of Communism.* New York: Free Press. A thorough and illuminating history of the development of communist thought and practice

PART FOUR

Political Processes

"You asked us to build a computer which could replace the government."

CHAPTER 9

Politics as a Value Allocation Process

How does politics actually work? Here is one answer:

You may very appropriately want to ask me how we are going to resolve the ever-accelerating dangerous impasse of world-opposed politicians and ideological dogmas. I answer, it will be resolved by the computer. Man has ever-increasing confidence in the computer; witness his unconcerned landings as air transport passengers coming in for a landing in the combined invisibility of fog and night. While no politician or political system can ever afford to yield understandably and enthusiastically to their adversaries and opposers, all politicians can and will yield enthusiastically to the computer's safe flight-controlling capabilities in bringing all of humanity in for a safe landing.

—R. BUCKMINSTER FULLER,
Operating Manual for Spaceship Earth *(1970: 46) [emphasis added]*

This description from R. Buckminster Fuller probably does not match your idea of how most political decisions are currently made. You probably think that self-interest, pressure from interest groups and parties, ideology, and even irrationality are embedded in many of the actual value allocations by a political system. (It is worth noting that Fuller is a futurist who offers a normative vision of how he thinks politics *ought* to work; he is not an analytic political scientist attempting to describe and explain things as they are.)

One of the most obvious yet most fascinating questions in political science is: How does politics work? How does a political system handle the incredibly difficult and complicated value allocations that are the stuff of politics? If someone from another country asked you how major policy decisions are made in your country, what would you say? What are the key points you would emphasize?

Earlier chapters have introduced you to many of the major actors and significant structures in the political world and have indicated how these actors and structures operate. This chapter details three extremely "political" analytic explanations of the value allocation process. These three broad approaches are termed (1) the elite approach, (2) the class approach, and (3) the group approach.

Each approach provides a different explanation of how politics works, how influence is exercised, and what political forces seem to shape political decisions. No country or political system is likely to operate exactly like any of these three analytic approaches. Rather, each approach is a rich illustration of a pattern of power and decision making that is prevalent in some systems at a given point in time. The approaches also share two important analytic features:

1. They are constitutive approaches (as a type of functional analysis; see the Appendix) in the sense that they attempt to define *the* fundamental unit of analysis that explains politics.
2. They explain politics in terms of the interactions among aggregations of individuals who use the political system to pursue their own particular interests.

Our discussion begins with the elite approach.

THE ELITE APPROACH
Key Concepts

Two key concepts are central to the explanation of the value allocation process using the **elite approach**. First, **politics** is defined in a straightforward manner as *the struggle for power*. Second, the *political world* is characterized by *political stratification*.

Political stratification means that the population is segmented into separate groups that are in layers (or "strata") with higher or lower power. In the elite approach, there are only two major strata. The stratum of the population that does more of what there is to do (in the policy process) and that gets more of what there is to get (in the allocation of values) is called the **political elite**. The stratum that does less and gets less is called *the mass*.

Elite theory can be visually represented by a power pyramid, as shown in Figure 9.1. Such a depiction emphasizes that the elite is composed of a relatively small number of individuals who are in a dominant position on top of the large mass. Notice that there is a third stratum between the elite and the mass. This is *the under-*

Figure 9.1   Characterization of an elite system

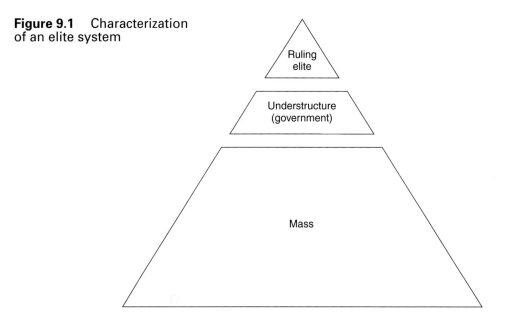

Ruling elite

Understructure (government)

Mass

structure, composed of political officials and state administrators who carry out the policy directives of the elite.

Major Theorists

The elite approach has been particularly grounded in the writings of European political theorists of the late nineteenth century. Among the scholars most strongly associated with this are the Italians Roberto Michels, Wilfredo Pareto, and Gaetano Mosca. In *The Ruling Class* (1896/1939), Mosca provides one of the fullest explications of the elite approach. He analyzes the political histories of a variety of political systems and concludes that they all have two strata, the political class (the elite) and the nonpolitical class (the mass). The political class controls all political functions, holds virtually all political power, and dominates the allocation of values. The basis of elite power has varied across time and location, but Mosca identifies broad historical stages during which the primary basis of elite domination has been military power, then religious control, then economic power, and most recently, technical knowledge. According to Mosca, the major role of the political system is as an instrument of the political class, serving the elite's interests in the allocation of values.

A well-known American application of the elite approach is *The Power Elite* (1956) by C. Wright Mills. Mills concludes that political power in American society resides in the controlling positions in the hierarchies of the society's most powerful institutions. In particular, Mills identifies three key groups that compose the American power elite: (1) the "warlords" in the military establishment, (2) the "corporation chieftains" in the economic sector, and (3) the "political directorate" composed of those in the top positions in the political system. Mills observes that the members of the elite share crucial values about how society in general, and the political system in particular, ought to operate. The members of the elite tend to come from similar social and educational backgrounds, to circulate among major positions in each of the three key institutional structures, and to have long-standing personal relationships with each other. Like other elite theorists, Mills does not claim the elite is a conspiracy that continually plots to retain control. But some of its active members do meet periodically to discuss common interests, and most of its members will act in concert during times of crisis (see also Domhoff 1998).

Most elite theorists focus on the elite itself—the identity and socialization of elite members, and how the elite maintains its domination through a variety of techniques, such as the manipulation of symbols, the strategic distribution of resources, control of the state, and the use of force. There is a normative element in the discussions of many elite theorists, indicating their disapproval of a system in which there is a high concentration of political power to serve only a small minority within society. But others respond that elite theory merely reveals the inevitable tendency for a few people to take control and to dominate the political order, while those in the mass willingly subordinate themselves to a few who are capable of giving coherence to political society.

The Value Allocation Process

The value allocation process is explained primarily in terms of the actions of the elite. Some members of the elite decide that a particular public policy decision is in the elite's interest. A discussion then occurs within the elite, to determine whether this policy should be enacted and how it should be implemented. If there is general consensus among those members of the elite who are concerned about the decision, representatives of the elite instruct the relevant members of the understructure to perform the policy-making and policy-implementation activities that serve the elite's interests.

In the elite explanation of the policy process, the active elites are subject to little direct influence from the mass or even from the understructure of governmental officials. The mass is politically apathetic and impotent, and policy is imposed on this large proportion of the population. The understructure follows the directives of the elite because its members depend on the elite's power and resources as the basis of their own political positions and authority.

The Prevalence of Elite-based Political Systems

How many countries have elitist political systems? As noted in Chapter 7, more than half of contemporary countries are authoritarian or totalitarian systems. It seems reasonable to infer that these systems are dominated by an elite in the manner described by the elite approach.

However, the issue might be more complicated. Is it true that all the key conditions of elitism are met in every nondemocratic country? This is an empirical question that could be examined in specific political systems (e.g., El Salvador, Saudi Arabia, Singapore, or Congo). Here are a few of the analytic questions that might be addressed:

1. Does the political leadership act with unanimity on all major issues?
2. Is there active and effective political participation by non-elite groups?
3. Are some major political decisions responsive to non-elite demands, even when the decisions are contrary to the elite's interests?
4. Is there dramatic inequality in the distribution of resources between the elite and the mass?

While definitive answers to these issues are very difficult, our knowledge of political systems suggests that many are generally characterized by elite rule. (Consider the brief description of Swaziland in Box 9.1.) In many contemporary states, the power to make crucial political decisions and the benefits from those decisions do seem predominantly concentrated in the hands of a small elite.

The issue can also be considered in a different way. Is it possible that a country classified as a democracy is actually run by an elite? That is, even if a political system meets such basic criteria of democracy as a limited mandate and freedom to criticize and oppose the leadership (recall Chapter 7), does this necessarily mean that the system is not elitist?

This question underlies a fierce debate among analysts on whether the elite approach best describes politics, even in many "democratic" political systems. Some, like C. Wright Mills (1956), provide arguments and evidence that there is elite rule even in most democracies. In this view, a small proportion of the population dominates most significant political decisions and enjoys a hugely disproportionate share of the benefits from the value allocations made by the government. Box 9.2, on the local political system in Oakland, California, suggests that a powerful few can dominate a city's development decisions.

Such empirical assessments of the elite approach, whether of a single city or an entire country, are highly controversial and ideologically charged, since they represent a direct attack on the existence of democracy. Moreover, a definite proof of the elite approach in most political systems would be a massive undertaking, requiring the documentation of systematic elite dominance on a large number of key decisions across a variety of issue areas.

THE CLASS APPROACH

The **class approach** shares certain fundamental concepts with the elite approach, but it offers a very different explanation of the continuing dynamic processes of politics. The most important shared concept is the notion of *stratification*, the basic fact of *structured inequality* in the distribution of values in society.

The strata identified in the class approach are called classes, the second key concept. *Class* is an analytic concept that denotes a large group of individuals who are

---

BOX 9.1

Elite Politics in Swaziland

One of the many contemporary examples of elite politics is Swaziland, a small African country between Mozambique and South Africa. While Swaziland was a British colonial protectorate (1902–1968), a local king (Sobuza II) became a hero of his people by leading the movement for independence (from 1921). After independence in 1968, Sobuza became the ruling monarch of the new country. A British-style parliament with competing parties was installed. There have been periodic elections for parliament since that time, with universal suffrage among the 700,000 adults in the population. There were competitive parties in three parliamentary elections, although the king's party dominated in each election.

Yet everyone in Swaziland has always understood that real political power is concentrated in King Sobuza and his small council of advisers. Consistent with the elite approach, virtually all major political decisions are made by this group, and there is little or no consultation with others in the society. Indeed, in 1973 the king banned the opposition groups and declared that European government forms were "un-Swazi." Since then there has been a nonpartisan parliament that affirms the king's decisions.

When Sobuza died in 1982, there was a power struggle among members of the royal family and the king's advisory council. In 1986 one of the young princes was installed as King Mswati III. The new king then dissolved the advisory council, removed many of his rivals from positions of authority, and elevated his own set of trusted advisers to positions of decision-making power. Under King Mswati III, as under King Sobuza, both policy making and the major sectors of the economy (the mines and most farmlands) are directly controlled by a king's council. Overall, two key criteria of elite politics are met: (1) The mass of people in Swaziland have little

(continued)

BOX 9.1 *(Continued)*

direct impact on the policies or politics of the state, and (2) there is substantial inequality in the distribution of resources between the few rich and the many poor. Indeed, Swaziland ranks second among 80 countries assessed on the basis of the highest proportion (54.5%) of national income held by the richest 10 percent of the population (World Bank 1998). Swaziland has one of the world's highest infant mortality rates (about one in ten), and its citizens' life expectancy is only thirty-nine years (Kranzdorf 1997: table 6.1; Ramsey 1999: 164; World Bank 1998: table 1a).

A day after being called back from high school in England and being crowned as the ruler of Swaziland, King Mswati III attends a party in the palace. The 18-year-old king moved quickly to establish rule under his personal control.

similar in their possession of or control over some fundamental value. The most fundamental value that distinguishes classes differs for different class theorists. Karl Marx (1818–1883), the best-known class theorist, differentiates classes primarily on the basis of a group's relationship to the major factors of production in the economic system (Marx 1867/1981: ch. 52). At the simplest level, Marx divides society into two classes: (1) the *capitalist class,* which includes those who own significant amounts of the major factors of production in the society (especially financial resources, raw materials, and capital—the physical facilities to manufacture goods); and (2) the *proletariat class,* which includes those who own little more than their own labor.

Analysts have suggested a number of modifications to refine Marx's distinctions between classes. Some argue that in most modern societies it is control (rather than ownership) of the means of production that tends to be important in determining the power of individuals and groups. Others observe that in certain social systems, other values, such as status, kinship, ethnicity, religion, and tradition-based author-

BOX 9.2

Elite Domination of Development in Oakland

When the Planning Commission in Oakland, California, reported that large areas of the downtown and adjacent districts were blighted and required redevelopment, the residents and property owners in the area were threatened and outraged. (This discussion relies on Hayes 1972.) The City Council even passed a resolution declaring that there was no blight in Oakland. But Oakland's economic elite could see that its members would realize great benefits from redevelopment. Thus they initiated a strategy to ensure that their redevelopment plan would be implemented.

First, the city's real estate board hired costly outside consultants to advise the city's business leaders on how to accomplish their objectives. Then the elite persuaded the newly elected mayor to appoint a committee to lay the groundwork for redevelopment. This committee (called OCCUR, the Oakland Citizens' Committee for Urban Renewal) was led by a top manager from a major local industry, the executive vice president of the home builders association, the past and current presidents of the real estate board, a corporate attorney, and the manager of a large department store.

OCCUR raised, refined, and promoted redevelopment proposals and coordinated the public and private activities necessary for their enactment and implementation. The committee soon offered a comprehensive plan for redevelopment and conservation in all areas of the city. The City Council rejected the plan. Over the next four years, OCCUR mounted an extensive campaign to ensure support for the plan from the council and other local groups. The national association of large real estate developers sent its president to assist the process. The local chamber of commerce prepared a promotional film on redevelopment that was shown to scores of local groups. Oakland's major newspaper ran countless articles and editorials in support of redevelopment. The council was even provided with a chartered airplane trip to successful urban renewal projects in cities around the United States. By this point, the council had initiated the first of several large redevelopment projects proposed by the business elite.

Overall, these projects displaced the poor, increased the tax burden on the middle class, provided subsidized new facilities for major local and national business corporations, and generated huge profits for the local building, real estate, and banking elites. This apparently democratic process of policy making can be described in terms of elite theory. The economic elite dominated the formulation of policies, guided their passage, and reaped a very large share of the benefits from those decisions. The political understructure implemented the policies formulated by the elite, and the mass of citizens—politically ineffective and relatively passive—benefited little from the outcome.

ity, might distinguish different strata within the class system. Still others suggest that possession of significant data resources and knowledge has become the crucial resource distinguishing classes in postindustrial, information-based societies. Class theorists identify more than two major class strata in most contemporary societies, with each class characterized by its particular levels of social, political, and economic power (see, e.g., Dahrendorf 1959; Esping-Andersen 1990; Poulantzas 1973).

Figure 9.2 portrays three attempts to represent visually the relationships among classes. These representations reveal different conceptions of the size of classes, the number of classes, the extent of precise differentiation between classes, and the extent of hierarchy among the classes. While part A of the figure shows a characterization similar to the elite approach in its hierarchical and pyramidal form, the clear separation between classes is also emphasized. Part B highlights the overlapping nature of the classes. Here the boundaries between classes are permeable rather

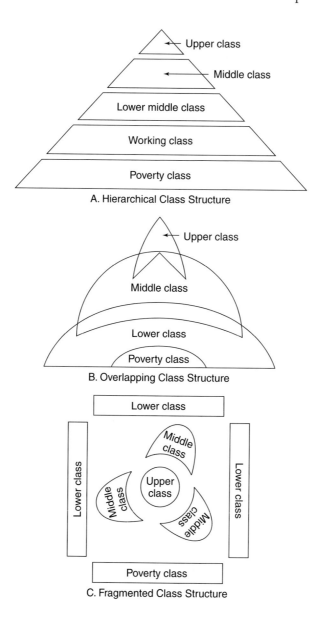

A. Hierarchical Class Structure

B. Overlapping Class Structure

C. Fragmented Class Structure

Figure 9.2   Different characterizations of class structures
SOURCE: Based on Bill and Hardgrave 1981: 181.

than distinct, and some members of "lower" classes have as much or even more political power than those in the class above them (see Lenski 1966: 284). The interactive and even reciprocal nature of power in interclass relations is emphasized in part C of Figure 9.2. Although there is still substantial inequality in this system, and the higher classes clearly dominate the lower classes, there is more interdependence among classes, and the lower classes do affect the actions and domination of the higher classes by means of a variety of constraints and obligations.

The third crucial concept of the class approach is *class conflict*. It is assumed that classes lower in the class system can increase their share of key values only at the expense of the classes above them. Given the fundamental inequalities in the distribution of values, struggle between classes is inevitable. The higher classes employ various strategies, and ultimately coercion, in order to prevent a significant loss of values (and of relative advantage) to the classes below them. Lower classes find that only violence enables their class to increase its relative share of values. Thus class conflict is systematic and ubiquitous, although its most visible and violent manifestations (such as strikes, riots, and rebellion) might be suppressed for periods of time if the higher classes are effective in their distribution of benefits and use of coercion.

Most class analysts do not explain in detail how policy decisions are actually made. Like elite theorists, class analysts assume that the common interests shared by members of a class will result in general consensus on what public policy decisions should be enacted. And, similar to the elite approach, the political system is viewed as a set of structures that are subordinate to the dominant class. Thus the policies and actions of the state serve the preferences of that class and preserve the existing distribution of values.

The class approach centers on the examination of the tactics of class domination and the dynamics of the class struggle. Not every value allocation by the state is coercive or of direct benefit only to the dominant class. The state might implement policies to shorten the length of the working day or to increase health care benefits to the middle classes. Such policies either ameliorate the worst conditions that might provoke violence or provide certain classes with advantages over classes below them. In such uses of public policy, benefits are provided to some classes in an effort to buy their support or their acquiescence, or at least to dampen their propensity for conflict.

Despite such strategies, the systematic inequalities in fundamental values generate continuing conflict between classes in the society. Periodically, this conflict explodes into class violence. Ultimately, in an episode of the class war, a lower class succeeds in overthrowing the highest class. At this point a new class gains dominance in the system, including control over the political system and superiority in the distribution of values. In the view of Marx and many other class theorists, major class conflict can end only when the elimination of dominant classes reduces the system to a single class, and hence a classless society. In the absence of class inequalities, the state serves all groups and there is no cause for further conflict among groups.

THE GROUP APPROACH

The **group approach** offers a very different account of the political process, although it also describes politics in terms of the interactions among aggregations of individuals. This approach is grounded in the concept of the *group,* which is any aggregate of individuals who interact to pursue a common interest. A political group, as an analytic concept, exists whenever individuals have a shared interest regarding some allocation of values by the political system.

The explanation of politics as a complex web of group interactions has many historical roots, but this approach is particularly identified with American social scientists. For many, the crucial work in this area is *The Process of Government* (1908/1967), by American political scientist Arthur Bentley. Other scholars who have provided major elaborations of this approach include David Truman (1951) and Robert Dahl (1961, 1967, 1971), who is the modern political scientist most strongly associated with the development and defense of the group approach.

According to this approach, any particular individual can belong to many different groups. Individuals are not stratified into large, permanent groups as described by the elite and class approaches, because the aggregation of people who share common identity on one political interest is not the same as the people who are part of groups regarding other political interests. Table 9.1 shows six hypothetical people whose group memberships overlap in different ways, depending on the issue. The group approach begins with the assumption that an individual's group memberships are multiple and nonreinforcing.

The second important notion of the group approach is that *many different political resources* might influence those who make value allocations for the political system. As discussed in Chapter 3, the kinds of resources that might be used to influence political decisions include money, numbers of supporters/voters, monopoly of expertise, political skill, access to information, and status. A key assumption of the group approach is that every individual (and hence every political group) has some political resources with which he can attempt to influence policy decisions.

In the group approach, *politics* can be understood as *the interaction among groups that are pursuing their political interests.* The political process is a giant sys-

TABLE 9.1
Group Memberships of Six Hypothetical Individuals in the United States

Groups	Individuals					
	Person 1	Person 2	Person 3	Person 4	Person 5	Person 6
Democratic Party	✓				✓	
Republican Party		✓				
AFL–CIO union	✓					
Christian Coalition			✓			✓
Mothers Against Drunk Driving		✓			✓	✓
National Abortion Rights Action League	✓					
National Rifle Association	✓		✓			
Parent–Teacher Association	✓	✓				

Note: Each checkmark (✓) indicates a group with which the individual is affiliated. This distribution supports the concept of nonreinforcing group memberships. An individual shares group membership with different people across various groups.

tem of interacting groups and the role of the state is to manage the interactions within this system of groups. The particular functions of the government are (1) to establish rules of the game for the group struggle, (2) to determine the interests of competing groups and the levels of political resources mobilized by those groups, (3) to find a public policy that approximately balances the positions of all active groups in terms of their interests and resources, (4) to enact these balance points as public policy decisions, and (5) to enforce the resulting value allocations.

The state is not merely a cash register or a weighing machine that totals the value of each group's influence resources. First, the state can place greater emphasis on some broad objectives rather than others. For example, it might emphasize assistance to the most disadvantaged groups by enacting some policies and rules that help those groups gain skills (e.g., extra educational or occupational opportunities). Or it might emphasize procedures and decisions that support the most advantaged groups, since those groups are perceived to be crucial to the stability and prosperity of the political economy. In addition, certain state actors have their own personal and institutional interests (e.g., for political support, for growth of their unit's power, for personal wealth). When such interests are relevant, state actors can become active as groups that participate in the decision process (with obvious advantages because they are inside "the system"). But government, as an analytic construct in the group approach, is best understood as a neutral arbiter in the competition among groups. Hence, public policy is defined as the balance of the group struggle at a given moment in time (see Box 9.3).

The group approach explicitly rejects the notion that a small elite dominates the resource allocation process. Rather, many different groups become active in the political process on a narrow range of issues relevant to their interests. Mobilized

Individuals and groups can influence the policy-makiing process in some political systems, as in this New England town meeting.

BOX 9.3

Two Analyses Applying the Group Politics Approach

Health Care Policy as a Hypothetical Example

To illustrate how the group approach explains the political process, let's develop a greatly oversimplified example of policy formation in a society like the United States. Our example is in the policy domain of health care provision. At one policy extreme, all health care (doctors, hospital services, drugs, and so on) might be provided by the private market system and each individual would receive the health care he desires and can pay for. At the other extreme, state agencies might provide all health care services to every citizen, free of any direct charge. Between these extremes, the state might engage in many activities, such as providing care for certain health problems, providing care only to certain groups (for example, the elderly, the poor), subsidizing care, or regulating the manner and prices by which private firms provide care.

1. Identify a few groups that you think would have the largest stake in decisions in this policy area.

2. On a continuum of possible policy outcomes, locate the preferred policy decision of each group.

3. Estimate the level of political resources each group is likely to employ to influence the decision regarding this policy (represented as a "weight" on the continuum).

4. Find the equilibrium point that balances the "weights" of the political resources mobilized by all groups.

5. Describe this equilibrium point in terms of a public policy decision that corresponds to this position on the policy continuum. According to the group approach, the decision corresponding to this point will be the state's "authoritative allocation of values" (recall Chapter 5).

Figure 9.3 offers one estimation of a public policy outcome in the health care policy example. The key groups who mobilize resources include the following:

1. *The professional association of doctors.* Objective: an essentially private health care system in which consumers have free choice among providers and where prices, provision standards, and levels of service are determined primarily by individual doctors in a free market. Considerable political resources: money, strong interest, lobbyists, ability to withhold necessary services; but increasing fragmentation within the profession regarding health care policy.

2. *The health insurance companies.* Objective: a mainly private health care system, with some state regulation of prices, in which insurance companies can profitably sell health care insurance to nearly all individuals and groups. Substantial political resources: money, organization, numerous lobbyists, high interest, access to policy makers.

BOX 9.3 *(Continued)*

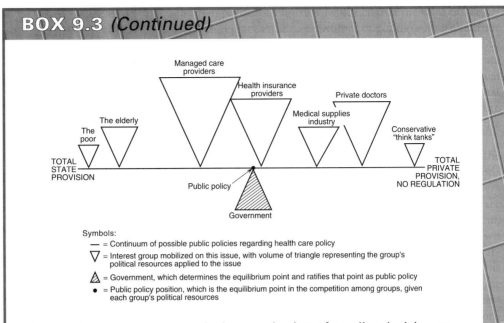

Symbols:
— = Continuum of possible public policies regarding health care policy
▽ = Interest group mobilized on this issue, with volume of triangle representing the group's political resources applied to the issue
△ = Government, which determines the equilibrium point and ratifies that point as public policy
● = Public policy position, which is the equilibrium point in the competition among groups, given each group's political resources

Figure 9.3 A group approach characterization of a policy decision on health care provision.

3. *Managed care providers.* Objective: domination over private doctors and health insurers in a market where the state regulates prices, providers, and consumer choice and where state subsidies advantage large-scale, rationed-service providers. Very substantial political resources: extensive financial resources, many lobbyists, effective organization that provides increasingly concentrated actors with bargaining power over doctors, insurance providers, and even the state.

4. *The relatively poor citizens.* Objective: quality health care, provided directly by the state or at least subsidized by the taxation system and with regulated prices. Limited political resources: interest in the issue, numbers who could mobilize their votes during elections, but usually are not well organized.

5. *The medical supplies industry.* Objective: higher profits from minimal state regulation of the production and sale of large quantities of pharmaceuticals and other medical equipment, except for regulation of quality. Notable political resources: financial power, strong interest, a few highly organized producers, professional lobbyists.

6. *The elderly.* Objective: subsidized or free health care for their group. Moderate political resources: high interest, a large voting bloc that can be mobilized, a general societal sense of responsibility and empathy for the needs of the elderly.

7. *Conservative "think tanks."* Objective: Limit state involvement in health care, as an important component of a broader ideological commitment to promote a market system for the provision of all important goods. Modest political

(continued)

BOX 9.3 *(Continued)*

resources: access to many policy makers, visibility in the media and other set-tings where policy issues are discussed.

There are likely to be other groups with substantial stakes in this decision, such as nurses groups, public and private hospitals, taxpayers in higher tax brackets, and companies that provide health care benefits in their wage agreements. However, in the simplified case provided above, the weights for key groups in Figure 9.3 suggest that the equilibrium point among these groups would result in a policy that involves a complex mix of both private provision and also state support and regulation to man-age the market and to subsidize the health care of at least some services and/or groups.

Do you think that this analysis would have been different in the United States thirty years ago? (Among the differences in group politics that you might con-sider: private doctors were a much more dominant actor in this policy domain, there were few significant managed care providers, and the elderly were not such a formidable political group. Also, the policy environment was different, with rel-atively strong public opinion opposing any state involvement that might be termed "socialized medicine.")

An Actual Development Decision in New Haven, Connecticut

The two Lebov brothers were wealthy local businessmen in New Haven, Con-necticut, who acquired sixty-five prefabricated metal houses from military surplus. (This section is based on Robert Dahl's seminal advocacy of the group politics approach, *Who Governs?* [1961: 192–199].) They received permission from the city's building department to erect these houses on a site that was zoned for industry in a neighborhood called "The Hill." Their proposal also had the support of the mayor and the city's lawyer.

But the (mainly) Italian-American residents of the working-class neighborhood were outraged. They viewed the metal houses as an "instant slum" that would threaten the property values of their modest but well-kept houses and would bring African-American residents to The Hill. Miss Mary Grava emerged as the improb-able leader of the residents' opposition to the project. An elderly spinster, she had never been very involved in politics. She was tireless in contacting people who might influence the city's decision. She mobilized the residents to telephone members of the City Council and others in city government, and played Republican politicians against Democratic politicians in order to gain support from both groups for the neighborhood's opposition to the metal houses.

Under severe pressure from the neighborhood, the council drafted legislation to stop construction of the metal houses. But the Lebov brothers began building anyway, with added support from the local newspaper, which saw the houses as affordable housing for needy low-income families. The city's lawyer ruled that the council had no legal power to stop construction. The council nonetheless voted to

BOX 9.3 *(Continued)*

stop the project. The mayor vetoed the council's legislation. In response, The Hill residents organized a neighborhood association led by Mary Grava's brother, who happened also to be the mayor's godfather. This local association widened its base, gaining support from the middle-class League of Women Voters (which wanted to expand its membership among ethnic working-class groups), from the current mayor's chief Republican rival on the council, and from the Democratic candidate for mayor. The council overrode the mayor's veto. After an arson fire destroyed one of the metal houses, the fire inspector withdrew his support for the project. Ultimately, the metal houses were never placed in the neighborhood.

For Robert Dahl, this is a compelling example of how a group can emerge when it cares deeply about an issue and can concert its limited political resources to influence policy on the issue. In this case, "just plain folks" had fought city hall and had beaten the rich developers, the mayor, and the city's lawyer.

groups use their political resources to affect the decision. While a group might not always win, its participation can affect the policy decisions made in the area.

Critics of the group approach argue that some groups *are* likely to win almost every time they play the game of politics because they have a huge advantage in their political resources, such as wealth, access to decision makers, and political skill. Even though "the little people" might occasionally win a particular episode, the powerful groups in the system are persistent winners and big winners, and the system perpetuates very substantial inequalities in the distribution of benefits (Bachrach and Baratz 1962; Parenti 1996). Indeed, even in the metal houses case discussed in Box 9.3, the biggest losers are probably the poor families in New Haven for whom this housing would have been a substantial improvement over their existing conditions.

THE THREE APPROACHES COMPARED
Which Approach Is Correct?

The three approaches offer powerful answers to the basic political questions of who gets what, why, when, and how. Which of these three approaches is correct? Is one the most accurate explanation of politics for all political systems? For most political systems at a given historical moment? Do different approaches account for the politics of particular systems? For particular kinds of issues?

Advocates of each position offer both theoretical and empirical evidence to show that the politics of actual systems correspond to the description provided in their approach. As an indirect method of providing support for their approach, advocates also provide considerable evidence indicating the inaccuracies and contradictions of the other approaches. As you might suspect, the debate has been most acrimonious between, on the one hand, supporters of the group approach and, on the other, supporters of the elite and class approaches, which both assume persistent stratification and deep inequality. Some scholars contend that virtually all political systems, even "democratic" ones, are elitist, in the sense that the policy process is guided by and generally supports the interests of a dominant elite (Domhoff 1998). In the United States, the debate has been most intensive among those who study power at the local level, prompted by the dispute four decades ago between such "elitists" as sociologist Floyd Hunter (1953) and such "pluralists" (supporters of the group approach) as political scientist Robert Dahl (1961).

Political scientists and other social scientists have yet to establish a critical test that reveals which of the approaches best describes or explains politics. After hundreds of studies in various political systems at the local, regional, and national level, the disagreements among the advocates of the three approaches remain as deep as ever. How might you decide which approach provides the greatest insight into the politics of a particular political system? Here are some key conceptual and empirical questions that you might consider in assessing the validity of each approach:

The Elite Approach

Are there criteria by which a small elite can be clearly identified, in both an analytic sense and in an empirical study?

Is there evidence of actual collaboration among the elite in the formulation of preferred public policy?

How often (if at all) does the elite lose on policy decisions of significance to its members?

Does the overall pattern of policy decisions clearly benefit the elite? At the expense of the mass?

Are there no instances where the elite truly loses on a policy decision of concern to its members?

Is the mass of citizens uninformed, inactive, and impotent regarding its society's politics?

Is the competition among elites so limited that it does not undermine their overall cooperation?

Is the understructure of government actors almost always responsive to the will and values of the elite?

Does the same elite determine policy in all areas?

The Class Approach

Does the same fundamental value separate virtually all people in a society into a few distinct strata?

Are the group identities of most people reinforcing rather than cross-cutting?

Is the concept of class still valid if most people do not identify themselves with the classes specified by the analyst?

Does the state almost always operate to serve the interests of a dominant class group?

Are the relationships among most groups characterized primarily by conflict?

In their political activities, are most groups limited by force or other mechanisms of coercion?

Are most significant social changes directly attributable to violence?

The Group Approach

Is there clear evidence that large groups of people do not share major political interests with a single broad group?

Does every group "win some and lose some" on policy decisions that matter to the group, or are there persistent winners and persistent losers?

Does the state apply rules and policies fairly and equally to all groups?

Can the competition among groups be fair if there are huge inequalities in the levels of political resources available to different individuals and groups?

Does one political resource—money—dominate (or convert into) all other major resources in the competition to influence policy making?

Essential Similarities and Differences

In attempting to explain the value allocation process, the elite, class, and group approaches all focus on the interactions among aggregates of individuals. The elite and class approaches share certain crucial premises. For both approaches, the fundamental feature of society is stratification—the unequal distribution of values across distinct groups. Also in both approaches, the government is one of the key mechanisms controlled by the dominant group, and the government's policy decisions are intended to maintain that group's domination. Thus in the elite and class approaches, the political system and the value allocation process operate of, by, and for the dominant group.

But the elite and class approach differ in their conceptions of the nature of the groups and their interactions. For the elite approach there are two broad groups, the elite and the mass. For the class approach there can be more than two distinct class groups. Most discussion by elite theorists focuses on the elite—its membership, the basis of elite domination, and the strategies employed by the elite to maintain its control. The mass is assumed to be inactive politically and is rarely subjected to detailed analysis.

In contrast, most class theorists emphasize the dynamic interactions among the classes. There is substantial political energy inherent in the lower classes, and they are the active agents of major political change. The class approach attempts to explain why class conflict is inevitable, how it manifests itself, and how it produces transformations in the sociopolitical system. In short, the elite approach tends to provide a top–down perspective in a two-group system, whereas the class approach often takes a bottom–up perspective, emphasizing the dynamic processes of conflict and change among multiple groups.

The group approach differs fundamentally from both the elite and class approaches, beginning with its rejection of the notion of social stratification. Rather, the group approach conceptualizes a sociopolitical world composed of many groups, with multiple (and hence nonreinforcing) group memberships among individuals. Different groups emerge on each particular political issue, and each group has an array of resources that can be organized in order to influence decisions on that issue.

For the group approach, the government is a relatively neutral referee in the process by which various groups compete to influence public policy decisions, rather than the instrument of only one particular group or class. The state ensures that the policy competition among groups is fair and that all participants accept the outcome of any given competition. According to the group approach, there is a dispersion of power, of resources, and of benefits from policy decisions, rather than a pattern of "structured inequality." Overall, different people, as members of many different groups, prevail on particular issues. Everyone wins some and loses some, but the losers can always win on the next issue.

Vigorous and often hostile debate has persisted among the advocates of these three conceptions of how politics works. This debate is deep and serious, for it reflects fundamental disagreements about the very nature of society and politics. The elite and class approaches are based on a *coercive view of society.* Conflict and change are ubiquitous features of the relations among groups. Social coherence is maintained by means of power and constraint, of domination by the most powerful class and its agent, the state. In contrast, the group approach reflects an *integrative view of society.* Society is essentially stable and harmonious, in the sense that there is a moving equilibrium maintained by a "fair" competitive game, refereed by the state and played by many groups who accept the rules and the outcomes. Social coherence is grounded in cooperation and consensus (see Dahrendorf 1959).

FOR FURTHER CONSIDERATION

1. What do you think is the single most important flaw in the assumptions or knowledge claims of the elite approach? The class approach? The group approach?

2. How might a class approach theorist challenge the hypothetical and actual cases of group politics presented in Box 9.3? How might a group theorist account for the cases in Boxes 9.1 and 9.2?

3. In a sense, all political systems are elitist, since a few govern and many are governed. Does this observation seem accurate? Is it a persuasive basis for confirming the validity of the elite approach?

4. Are you and your peers characterized by nonreinforcing group memberships in the manner claimed by the group approach? List six groups that have a political agenda and with which you have a membership or a strong identity. Ask two or three friends to provide you with a similar list. How much overlap is there in your group affiliations? Does this seem to support the group approach tenet of nonoverlapping memberships? (To undertake a fuller test, you would need to survey many individuals from a variety of backgrounds.)

FOR FURTHER READING

Balulis, Joseph, and Vickie Sullivan, Eds. (1996). *Shakespeare's Political Pageant: Essays in Politics and Literature.* Lanham, MD: Rowan & Littlefield. These articles offer a rich exploration of how the interplay of politics, power, and human nature is illuminated in the extraordinary plays of William Shakespeare.

Burki, Shahid J. (1991). *Pakistan under the Military: Eleven Years of Zia ul-Haq.* Boulder, CO: Westview Press. A detailed description of elite rule in Pakistan under an authoritarian regime.

Curtis, Gerald L. (1999). *The Logic of Japanese Politics: Leaders, Institutions, and the Limits of Change.* New York: Columbia University Press. A fascinating account of how contemporary Japanese politics works, emphasizing competition among individuals and groups rather than consensus-building, the more widely accepted explanatory framework.

Dahl, Robert. (1961). *Who Governs? Democracy in an American City.* New Haven, CT: Yale University Press. This remains the classic theoretical and empirical statement of the group approach to explaining politics.

Domhoff, G. William. (1998). *Who Rules in America?: Power and Politics in the Year 2000.* Mountain View, CA: Mayfield. Updates Mills's *The Power Elite,* using more data and an elaborated theoretical base, and reaching similar conclusions.

Ibsen, Henrik. (1882/1964). *Enemy of the People.* In *Six Plays by Ibsen.* Trans. by Eva Le Gallienne. New York: Random House. A classic Norwegian play revealing the political processes by which self-interest and greed overwhelm the efforts of a good citizen to prevent his town from a policy decision that will result in grave environmental damage.

Mills, C. Wright. (1956). *The Power Elite.* New York: Oxford University Press. A widely cited study that identifies the elite system underlying American national politics.

Rubin, Barry. (1987). *Third World Coup Makers, Dictators, Strongmen, and Populist Tyrants.* New York: McGraw-Hill. Portraits of political leaders and the elitist regimes that they have dominated.

Tuohy, Carolyn Hughes. (1999). *Accidental Logics: The Dynamics of Change in the Health Care Arena in the United States, Britain and Canada.* New York: Oxford University Press. An interesting description of group politics in the policy process in one important area—health care—which reveals the forces of continuity and change in three political systems.

Yang, Benjamin. (1997). *Deng: A Political Biography.* Armonk, NY: M.E. Sharpe. A compelling characterization of Deng Xiaoping, the shrewd leader who followed Mao Zedong to power in China, this book also provides an intriguing and illuminating account of an elite political system in action.

CHAPTER 10

Change and Political Development

Oman is a medium-sized country east of Saudi Arabia, at a strategic point on the Persian Gulf. Although Oman has a long history of trading with other countries, its rulers attempted to maintain an extremely traditional society, even in the late twentieth century. But the sultan who ruled between 1932 and 1970, Said ibn Taimur, faced a strong challenge after 1964, when vast oil deposits were discovered in Oman. Fearful that this huge wealth would corrupt his people, the sultan took extraordinary steps to prevent modernization. He declared a moratorium on the building of roads, schools, houses, even hospitals. All ten Omani doctors were forced to practice abroad because the sultan distrusted modern medicine. Many objects of modernity were prohibited, including sunglasses, flashlights, and European shoes. One could be imprisoned for traveling after dark with any light other than a kerosene lantern. The gates of the capital were locked after sunset, and no one was allowed to enter or leave. The sultan even confined his son, Prince Qabus, to a house far from the capital, because he feared the ideas that his son had brought back from his education in England.

But there was a group of Omani citizens who had some experience of Western culture, through education, travel, or working with foreigners. These people increasingly chafed under the sultan's "backward" rule. Encouraged by the influential British elite in Oman, this group took action in 1970, overthrowing the sultan and replacing him with Prince Qabus. The (now) Sultan Qabus and his advisers moved swiftly to bring improvements in the areas that his father had blocked. There has been a massive school building program (from 16 to 490 schools) and Sultan Qabus University opened in 1986. Hospitals and many health clinics are operating, and an extensive road system has been built. Females are now being educated, and many Western consumer goods are purchased. Indeed, among 143 countries, only the United States now has more television sets per capita than Oman (WABF 1997). On a comprehensive measure of "human development" (described in Chapter 13), Oman now ranks seventy-one out of 174 countries, at the top of the "medium" level on the index, just above Russia and just below Turkey (United Nations Development Programme 1999). Many Omanis now have a lifestyle that attempts to balance the behaviors and morals of traditional Islamic culture and the material possessions of a wealthy, highly modernized society. (This discussion is based on Spencer 1998.)

CHANGE

The recent history of Oman indicates the virtual impossibility of preventing change in any contemporary society. This chapter examines the question of change within the political world. In particular, there is discussion of the nature and processes of development in a society and within its political system.

A few cultures have generally avoided the processes of change and modernization. The Tasaday of the Philippines and the Masai of the Serengeti Plain in East Africa live in a manner that has changed little from the ways of their ancestors of fifty generations ago. The Masai, for example, continue to raise their cattle, ignoring the Kenya–Tanzania border and resisting the attempts of the Kenyan government to alter their long-standing cultural patterns of family and tribal life. But even the Masai have been affected by the modernization surrounding them. It has brought health care and disease, money from tourists and reduced land for grazing herds, education and cultural confusion. In the modern world, there seems nowhere to hide from the forces of change.

The Greek philosopher Heraclitus articulated this view in the fifth century B.C.E. His famous dictum, "You can never step in the same river twice," is an extreme version of the viewpoint that everything is in constant flux. From this perspective, change is inevitable. It is presumed that just as individuals undergo a developmental sequence of birth, growth, maturity, decay, and death, social organisms (groups, organizations, societies) also have some form of evolutionary development.

On the opposite side of the debate about the inevitability of change is the wry French observation, *plus ça change, plus c'est la même chose.* This translates loosely as "The more things change, the more they remain the same." Do you believe this? Is this a wise commentary about the human condition? An erroneous cliché?

There is debate about the desirability of change, as well as its inevitability. One normative position, most aligned with modern rationalism, is that change is generally a positive force in human society. Change is the mechanism of growth, development, and progress, all of which are assumed to increase knowledge, extend control over the environment, and thus improve the human condition. This view is reflected in the ideas of Sir Isaac Newton (1642–1727), Immanuel Kant (1724–1804), and Charles Darwin (1809–1882). In the contemporary world, it is especially prevalent among those who believe in the benefits of science and technology.

In contrast, some take the normative position that change and development have significant negative effects, perhaps so many that change is undesirable. Plato (c. 428–347 B.C.E.), Jean-Jacques Rousseau (1712–1778), and Sigmund Freud (1856–1939) are among those who argue that knowledge, civilization, and excessive control over the environment result in a loss of innocence, goodness, and happiness, and create the capacity for great harm and destruction. Material progress has been achieved at the cost of moral and spiritual decline. In this view, the human capacity to increase our supply of food and material goods cannot be separated from our development of repressive and destructive forms of human interaction and technologies (e.g., weapons, chemicals) that degrade the environment and eliminate certain species of life, including, possibly, human beings. Most people now recognize the paradox that change and development simultaneously increase *and* reduce the quality of life. And most accept the serious problems and dangers associated with progress, in order to enjoy the material benefits.

DEVELOPMENT
Characteristics of "More Developed" Social Systems

Contemporary changes of social, economic, and political systems are usually discussed in terms of *development* or *modernization*. While both of these concepts can be slippery, social scientific research usually employs the concept of development, because modernization is particularly fuzzy (see Box 10.1). The designation of a social system as being more developed (or more modern) indicates that certain key characteristics are evident at relatively high levels. The concept of development can also be used to refer to the processes through which these characteristics become more pronounced.

Several packages of characteristics are general indicators of the more developed social systems. These characteristics tap social, cultural, economic, political, and personal dimensions, and can be classified in various ways. For simplicity, we can specify three packages of dimensions that are particularly associated with more developed social systems (Bill and Hardgrave 1981: 63):

1. The *organizational* dimension: emphasis on specialization, interdependency, and differentiation of roles and functions in groups, organizations, and societies.

2. The *technological* dimension: use of increasingly complex and sophisticated artifacts to control the environment and to produce goods and services.

3. The *attitudinal* dimension: cognitive, affective, and evaluative orientations that are dominated by increased knowledge, rationality, secular values, and individualism.

Virtually every state attaches high importance to economic development—the core of the technological dimension. The expansion of available goods and services in the society offers the promise of a life that, for at least some of the citizens, is more secure and more comfortable. Thus most states attempt to identify and implement strategies that facilitate economic growth, which is usually measured as the national economic product (described in Box 8.1 as gross national product or gross domestic product).

BOX 10.1

What Makes Millie Thoroughly Modern?

Suppose you were asked whether you like "modern music." What does that mean? What kind of music does it bring to mind? Atonal? Rock and roll? Electronic? Hip hop? The determination of what is "modern" is extremely difficult. It depends very much on the particular historical moment and on the values and culture of the analyst. What seemed modern in the United States thirty years ago does not seem so modern now, given a world of rapid social and technological change. For example, the United States in 1970 was a world virtually without personal computers, CDs, VCRs, cable television, AIDS, the Internet, or the global economy.

For some purposes the key indicator of economic development is an overall measure of productive capacity (as in total GNP or GDP per capita), and for other purposes the emphasis is on the rate of growth in one of these dimensions.

Not all states, however, are equally interested in increasing all aspects of the organizational and attitudinal dimensions. The example of Oman reflects the concerns of some individuals in every developing society: that many of the social changes associated with development can have negative effects on deeply revered social and cultural values. In some countries these negative changes are referred to as "Westernization" and are reflected in attitudinal changes favoring greater secularism, individualism, and materialism. This is often an important concern of groups promoting Islamic fundamentalism and has also been a key consideration in some rapidly developing countries such as China. In this and later chapters we shall consider other instances of states where there is deep disagreement about the benefits of change in the attitudinal dimension.

Indeed, even economic development is questioned by those alarmed about the negative effects of growth on the environment. Concern for the environment centers in both *depletion of the earth's resources* (e.g., the destruction of the rain forests and the overcultivation of the land to increase agricultural production) and *degradation of the environment* (e.g., severe air and water pollution associated with industrial processes and consumerism).

Despite these concerns, most states are characterized by efforts to increase their level of development. Both public sector and private sector actors devise strategies to foster at least some aspects of a more developed system. Many social indicators reflect the extent of development that has occurred in the organizational, technological, and attitudinal dimensions. These include greater urbanization, growth in productive capacity, higher consumption of power, expanded communications, more extensive social networks, higher caloric intake, decreased death rates, increased education levels, higher literacy rates, and greater social mobility.

Can we define with precision what constitutes a "developed country"? No. There are no agreed upon measures for distinguishing sharply between systems that are modern/developed and those that are not. Currently, the most common distinction is between the "developed countries" and the "developing countries"—a difference based mainly on a single measure of economic development (GNP or GDP per capita). Chapter 13 explains this book's criteria for categorizing levels of development, combining economic development with the three dimensions of social development discussed earlier. For the present discussion, the more developed countries can be understood to be those that are relatively high on urbanization, literacy, productive output, complexity, specialization, and secularization.

The Process of Development

Stage typologies. Many scholars have attempted to define the process(es) through which development and modernization occur. One approach is to define a series of stages or phases that each society passes through. Best known are the simple typologies, many of which have only two or three stages. These stages are given such labels as *traditional* and *modern, mechanical* and *organic, folk* and *urban, less developed* and *more developed.* These labels are so broad that they provide minimal conceptual clarity.

Karl Marx proposed a more complex typology, in which most societies pass through six stages of development; a society's particular stage of development depends on the existing distribution of control over the major productive resources in the society. Marx posited an initial stage of *primitive communism,* in which all individuals share control jointly over any available productive resources. The development process then continues through a series of stages in which there are increasingly subtle forms of domination by some classes over others: *slavery,* then *feudalism,* and then *capitalism.* Eventually, capitalist systems are transformed into *socialist* and finally to *communist* systems, an ultimate stage in which differentiated social classes and inequality in control of resources are eliminated (recall Chapters 2 and 8).

Response to key challenges. Most explanations of the process of development do not incorporate Marx's conviction that history or logic reveals a single, inevitable sequence of stages. Rather, analysts identify a series of key challenges in the developmental process. Different processes are possible, depending on the sequence in which the challenges occur, the particular response that is made, and crucial features of the society and its environment. Some of the key challenges can be the tension between traditional ideas and values and modern ones; the transition from a rural, agrarian society to an urban, industrial society; the transfer of social and political power from traditional elites to modernizing ones; the fit among geographical territory, national identities, and state boundaries. Barrington Moore (1966), whose approach is discussed in Box 10.2, is one theorist who explains modernization in terms of the pattern of responses to key challenges facing the society; others include Black (1966) and Rustow (1967).

Individual-level change.   Most analyses of development, whether emphasizing stages, sequences, or international political economy, focus on the macro-level struc-

BOX 10.2

Barrington Moore's Explanation of Development

Barrington Moore's study, *The Social Origins of Dictatorship and Democracy* (1966), illustrates one approach to the study of societal development. A social historian, Moore analyzes the changing patterns of relations among key groups in a society. He places particular attention on the actions of the landed aristocracy and peasants in the rural areas. He also examines the role of the bourgeoisie (those who operate factories, shops, and commercial establishments) and of governmental bureaucracies. He details eight historical case studies—China, England, France, Germany, India, Japan, Russia, and the United States—and concludes with analytic generalizations.

Moore's key questions about development concern the shift from agrarian society to modern industrial society. Does the landed aristocracy take the lead in the commercialization of agriculture? Are the peasants cohesive and do they support or resist state authority? Is the urban bourgeoisie strong and effective in economic development? Whose interests do the governmental bureaucracies represent?

Moore distinguishes three different modes of modernization, depending on the dominant actions and evolving relationships among the key groups. There are *bourgeois revolutions,* which are driven by the modernizing efforts of the urban bourgeoisie who dominate the urban workers and gain control of the rural sector, as in England, France, and the United States. There are *revolutions from above,* in which development is effected by a coalition of the landed aristocracy and strong governmental bureaucracies, as in Germany and Japan. There are *peasant revolutions,* in which the peasants are more cohesive than the upper classes or the bourgeoisie, resist the powerful state apparatus, and eventually overthrow the old regime, as in Russia and China. And finally there are some societies where no groups have been able to lead a modernizing revolution, as in India.

Moore's most powerful assertion is his conclusion: that all forms of development and modernization are essentially revolutions from above, that the great majority of the population does not want these changes, and the changes are implemented by a ruthless minority at great cost to the large majority. But Moore also argues that, despite the widespread suffering generated during the developmental process, the costs (in terms of cumulative hardship to the population) of going without a modernizing revolution are even more severe for the people of a state in the contemporary world.

tural dynamics—that is, on the nature of the organizational and technological dimensions of social systems. But attention to the attitudinal dimension shifts the analysis to micro-level dynamics. This perspective emphasizes the social-psychological factors that might account for variations in rates and patterns of development. Such analyses are similar to the political behavior studies described in Chapters 2 through 4 (e.g., the political culture analyses, pp. 31-33, and Pye's study of the Burmese leaders in Box 4.5), although the focus here is on a broader array of beliefs (not just political beliefs) and on the implications of such beliefs for modernization and development. While the approaches have often characterized the attitudes of groups and nations, most of the research actually focuses on the distinctive patterns of political beliefs of *individuals* within a given nation (Inkeles and Smith 1974; Inkeles et al. 1985; Inkeles, 1996; McClelland 1961).

In the attempt to establish the attitudinal traits associated with modernity, the work of Alex Inkeles and his colleagues (Inkeles and Smith 1974; Inkeles et al. 1985) is noteworthy. This group gathered extensive survey data from more than 5,500 men in six developing countries (Argentina, Bangladesh, Chile, India, the "Oriental" Jews of Israel, and Nigeria). Statistical analyses have produced a set of seven qualities that the researchers believe constitute a "syndrome of modernity"—that is, the general traits of a modern person in a developing society:

1. Openness to new experiences, regarding both people and behaviors
2. A shift in allegiance from those individuals in traditional authority structures (e.g., parents, religious leaders) to those representing modern institutions (e.g., government leaders)
3. Confidence in modern technologies (e.g., science, medicine) and a less fatalistic attitude about life
4. Desire for social mobility for oneself and one's children
5. Belief in the value of planning and punctuality
6. Interest in local politics and community affairs
7. Interest in news, especially national and international affairs

Inkeles and his colleagues conclude that there is remarkable similarity in these clusters of beliefs among the modern men in all six societies they studied. On this basis, they claim that there is a "unity of mankind in terms of psychic structure" (Inkeles et al. 1985: 102); in other words, that the same traits are present in modern individuals in virtually all cultures. Some believe that this uniformity of ideas is one part of a broader set of forces that are homogenizing everyone into a global economy, a global culture, and a global information network (Barber 1995). Karl Deutsch (1961: 497) terms these individual-level changes as *social mobilization,* defined as "the process in which major clusters of old social, economic, and psychological commitments are eroded or broken and people become available for new patterns of socialization and behavior." In general, such social mobilization does seem to be associated with elements of broader social development, including increased education, exposure to modern media, and work within modern industrial or bureaucratic organizations (Inkeles et al. 1985).

In the large literature on the traditional and modern personality, many issues are unresolved. For example, most studies have not established the existence of a single syndrome of modernity that exists across all cultures. Also, it is unclear whether the rate of economic or political development is associated with the presence of modern attitudes among a certain proportion of the population. Indeed, in cases of Islamic fundamentalism as in Iran, it seems that leaders who display some of the activist and outward-oriented psychological traits associated with the syndrome of modernity are actually working to return the society to its traditional pattern of attitudes and actions (Banuazizi 1987).

In most developing societies, some people and groups enthusiastically embrace the new beliefs and new behaviors while others cling tenaciously to the old ones. Box 10.3 summarizes a powerful literary account of the trauma experienced by some individuals when tradition and modernity collide. You probably think it is obvious that development and modernization involve an interplay among emerging modern individual-level behavior (both beliefs and actions), group behavior, and societal development. Virtually all the researchers agree with you. But there are still many interesting and generally unanswered questions: Why do old patterns erode? Which kinds of people are most inclined to accept new patterns? Are there certain sectors or a certain proportion of the population whose social mobilization is necessary before macro-level change occurs? What macro-level conditions seem particularly conducive to individual-level change? And most broadly, what are the causal linkages between psychological modernity and societal development?

Civil society.   The attitudinal changes in individuals are most crucial when they create new patterns of interaction at the group or societal level. Thus a key consideration in assessing the nature of development at the societal level is the extent to which a "civil society" has emerged. Certain values, present as prevalent behavioral styles, are centrally associated with the existence of civil society. These include tolerance of differences in opinions and behaviors, willingness to cooperate with others, propensity to negotiate in order to approach consensus and avoid violence in the resolution of differences, and a sense of solidarity with others. Some analysts conclude that, while a society could certainly be "developed" without being a civil society, the prevalence of these values is crucial for sustaining effective democracy (Diamond et al., 1997; Stepan and Linz 1996; Putnam 1993).

Culture and change.   Some studies of development have emphasized the importance of culture in the broad processes of change. Since Max Weber's classic study (1958a) of the linkage between the culture of the Protestant religion and the rise of capitalist political economies, there have been continuing efforts to clarify the relationship between broad cultural systems and economic development. Some, like Weber, have argued that Protestantism has motivated people to make substantial, even irrational, sacrifices of material consumption and the pleasures of life in order to work extraordinarily hard and accumulate wealth rather than spending it. Similarly, it is contended the religions of developing European societies have promoted passivity to hardships, a feature associated with transformation to a modern society and economy (Davis 1987: 223–234).

Weber (1951, 1958b) also has tried to apply his cultural explanation to India and China in order to account for the absence of development there. But the dramatic surge of economic development among the Asian newly industrialized economies during the 1980s and early 1990s (to be discussed later in this chapter), following the earlier pattern in Japan, stimulated interest in trying to explain the developmental success of these

BOX 10.3

How Ideas Undermine Culture: Things Fall Apart in Nigeria

You might be able to understand individual-level change intuitively if you think about what happens to a society when it is infused with major threats to existing values via education, new religions, television, and travel. As a popular post–World War I song asked about the returning soldiers, "How are you going to keep 'em down on the farm, after they've seen Paree?" The erosion of traditional values and behaviors can be rapid or slow. But as the Oman case suggested, it is difficult to prevent change in the face of major unsettling forces. The Islamic religion explicitly recognizes the importance of personal values in shaping culture. As one Koranic verse observes, "Lo! Allah changeth not the condition of a people until they first change what is in their hearts."

A rich illustration of these change processes is Chinua Achebe's 1959 novel, *Things Fall Apart.* Achebe's novel describes the dramatic and traumatic changes experienced by the Ibo people of Nigeria at the turn of the twentieth century. The key theme is the conflict between the binding power of the Ibo's traditional views of life and religion and the disruptive ideas introduced into the culture by the Christian missionaries and British colonial administrators. The story centers on the members of one Ibo village who are increasingly divided between those who continue to be guided by traditional patterns of behavior and religion and those who no longer accept those traditions.

The major character, Okonkwo, is a great farmer and a strong leader. He follows the traditional patterns very rigidly, even participating in the murder, decreed by tribal law, of a boy he has treated like a son for years. This murder so alienates his own son that the son becomes one of the first in the village to be persuaded by the missionaries to convert to Christianity. Okonkwo continues to follow the traditions of his tribe, resulting in a series of major setbacks, including being banished for seven years and losing his land and his possessions. Eventually, Okonkwo's anger and frustration at the collapse of Ibo village life leads him to murder a messenger of the colonial administrator. Rather than be executed by the white men, he finally does violate a basic Ibo law by committing suicide.

Before Okonkwo dies, his friend Obierika articulates how these external ideas have caused the collapse of the village (and of Ibo) society. In a key passage, he says:

> Our own men and our sons have joined the ranks of the stranger. They have joined his religion and they help to uphold his government.
>
> If we should try to drive out the white men in Umuofia we should find it easy. There are only two of them. But what of our own people who are following their way and have been given power? They would go to Umuru and bring the soldiers….[The white man] says our customs are bad; and our own brothers who have taken up his religion also say that our customs are bad. How do you think we can fight when our own brothers have turned against us? The white man is very clever. He came quietly and peaceably with his religion. We were amused at his foolishness and allowed him to stay. Now he has won our brothers and our clan can no longer act like one. He has put a knife on the things that held us together and we have fallen apart. (Achebe 1959: 161–162)

countries. Because these countries have had substantially higher levels of development than other countries attempting to employ their strategy, these explanations have emphasized how culture has *facilitated* development in Asia (Davis 1987; Huntington 1987: 21–28, 1991; Pye 1985; and see Chapter 15, especially Box 15.3).

The Dynamics of Economic Development

The actual economic development of a country is the product of a complex set of actions by both major players (e.g., the government, large corporations, international banks) and small players (e.g., individuals as consumers and workers, small businesses) that is staggering in scale and incomprehensible in nature.

In the abstract, however, the discussion of political economy in Chapter 8 (look again at Figure 8.1) provides the key to understanding what is happening. Economic development occurs as more and more households and firms are engaged in ever-higher levels of production and consumption. More goods (and, ideally, more diverse and complex goods) are produced, more income and expenditures are exchanged, and thus the GNP gets larger relative to the number of people sharing in the carnival of production and consumption. Given the presence of the rest of the world (Figure 8.1B), a political economy is normally healthier and more vibrant if it not only is growing but also can bring in more income via exports than it sends out via imports. Public and private actors in every country are attempting to accomplish these development goals through their decisions and actions.

Chapter 8 explored some of the general challenges facing every political economy in the quest for economic development. The underlying puzzle is: What should the political system do in order to facilitate economic development? In the latter half of the twentieth century, two competing visions guided the answer to this question in many contemporary political economies.

Statism.   Between the 1950s and the 1980s, many countries (e.g., Brazil, Mexico, India, Tanzania) implemented versions of **statism.** This approach emphasizes the importance of strong actions by the state to support the system of production and distribution of goods. The state provides an extensive infrastructure for economic exchanges (e.g., transportation, power), regulates the actions of firms and households, protects firms from external competition, and distributes many free or subsidized goods and services, especially to less advantaged groups. Many important areas of production are publicly owned and are operated as state enterprises. The political economies of many communist countries (e.g., Bulgaria, China, Cuba) were extreme forms of the statist approach.

Neoliberalism.   Alternatively, many countries have applied variations of **neoliberalism.** Grounded in the market political economy model (see Chapter 8), the neoliberal approach severely limits state action, which is seen to undermine and distort the efficiency of the free market. Public expenditure is minimal, there is little government regulation of the economy, and direct foreign investment and free trade across state boundaries are encouraged. Beginning in the mid-1970s, an increasing number of countries adopted variations of the neoliberal approach. This includes many regimes, such as Brazil, Kenya, and Mexico, who reformed their systems in the direction of neoliberalism due to the disappointing levels of economic growth they achieved with the statist approach and due to pressure from the international banking community (Stepan and Linz 1996). It also includes many countries that abandoned the strong statism associated with a command political economy (e.g., China, Poland, Zimbabwe).

The Asian "developmental-state" approach. Some countries adopted a hybrid development strategy, combining elements of both the statist and the neoliberal approaches, that has been particularly effective in achieving a high level of economic growth in the last two decades. Based on the Japanese approach, this *"developmental-state" approach* is grounded in three broad strategies:

1. *An export-oriented market/state political economy.* Like a market political economy, aggressive capitalism is favored, and there are minimal governmental constraints on firms. However, the state is very interventionist, providing strong support for firms through its insulation of the political economy from "politics," its shaping of the labor force via education, and its taxing and spending policies, which facilitate investment, promote the export of goods, and discourage high levels of domestic consumption.

2. *Targeting market niches.* Firms and the state work cooperatively to produce particular goods that can be successfully sold in the international marketplace. Initially, modest-quality goods are sold at or below cost in order to capture a share of the market and gain consumer support. Gradually, prices and quality are increased. The balance of production shifts slowly from simpler, more labor-intensive goods such as textiles, shoes, and toys to more complex goods requiring sophisticated production technologies such as shipbuilding, electronics, and automobiles. The state's policies (e.g., tariffs) protect producers against imported goods, although investment of foreign capital is usually encouraged.

3. *Agrarian support.* Government policy strongly encourages efficient domestic food production, even if self-sufficiency in food is not attainable. This element can include redistribution of land to small private farmers, price support subsidies on domestic food production, and tariffs on imported foods (Johnson 1985; Simone and Feraru 1995).

During the period of rapid economic expansion, the political regimes in these countries were generally effective in maintaining stability and in providing an infrastructure for development. The state is repressive, restricting political freedoms and discouraging group politics. To ensure a disciplined and docile labor force, the state's policies have prevented political action by trade unions or other economically-based interest groups. Apart from educational expenditure (to produce well-trained workers), most of these states distributed only modest levels of surplus resources to citizens in the form of public goods and services. As these countries became more prosperous, some of them also became less repressive, allowing their citizens to participate actively in a more pluralist politics.

Most of the initial developmental state success stories have been in Asia, first Japan, and more recently Singapore, South Korea, Taiwan, and to a lesser extent Malaysia and Indonesia (see Chapter 15 for additional discussion of the NICs—the newly industrializing countries). Other developing countries that have attempted variations of the strategy have had mixed success, with some achieving relatively high levels of multiyear economic growth (e.g., Argentina, Chile) but others failing to sustain such growth (e.g., Brazil, India, and Mexico). Some of these countries can be classified as NICs because they have established a large, modern industrial sector that produces advanced manufactured goods for export. But for many countries, the level, rate, and persistence of economic development have been quite limited. In most cases, economic development is narrowly based and heavily dependent on external actors, loans, and markets. Labor is difficult to control. The rural sector produces insufficient food to feed the population. Large landholders and peasants conflict violently over the distribution of land. A cosmopolitan elite enjoys a high standard of living, but huge segments of the population continue to live in deep poverty.

Moreover, in the late 1990s, things seemed to go awry even in the more successful NICs in Asia. Beginning in Thailand with currency problems in July 1997, the booming economies of Asia suddenly and unexpectedly fell into a severe decline. In most Asian countries, these declines were evident in negative GDP growth, high unemployment levels, and the huge loss of value of such assets as property and stocks. (More details are provided in Chapter 15.) Although some countries with rapid economic growth seemed to avoid severe problems (e.g., China, Singapore), the economic "crisis" in Asia was soon followed by similar problems in other rapidly developing countries in Latin America (Mahon 1999).

The breadth and depth of these negative economic conditions, even in Japan, resulted in widespread reconsideration of the flaws as well as the potential benefits of the developmental state model. There was recognition of a variety of problems, such as overprotection of favored firms by the state, inadequate regulation of the banking system and currency, and unrestrained speculation in land and stock. Within three to four years, some of these economies regained their economic momentum, but others struggled to recover. The economic turbulence has produced renewed uncertainty in many developing countries about whether the developmental state approach is the best way to maximize broad economic growth and economic stability.

Dependency within the international political economy.   With the exception of a few of the NICs that have sustained or regained economic prosperity, most countries that have attempted to develop economically in the postcolonial period have enjoyed only modest success. Some analysts posit that the difficulties facing the less developed countries are due to their vulnerability to, and perhaps their dependency on, the countries that are highly developed. This view is most explicit in a set of explanations of development known generally as the dependency approach or as world-systems theory.

The **dependency approach**, which has both ideological and descriptive elements, argues that the "late developers" of the Third World cannot follow the same processes that produced strong economic growth in the now-developed countries. The world system within which they are attempting to develop is quite different from the one that faced the now—developed countries (Isbister 1998).

According to the *ideological* element, the key problem is a long history of exploitation by the more developed "capitalist/imperialist" states. These states have manipulated and controlled the political economies of the developing countries for decades or even centuries by means of their economic, military, and political domination of the global system. Indeed, one of the main reasons the capitalist states have sustained their prosperity in the second half of the twentieth century is that they are still able to exploit the political economies of developing countries, especially through their overall control of capital, markets and prices, and technology. Thus they continue to reap huge profits at the expense of the less developed countries. In this view, the activities of the developed countries have not merely retarded the progress of the late developers, they have actually "deformed" (distorted and ruined) their efforts at development.

The *descriptive* element of the dependency approach provides a similar analysis, but without heaping blame exclusively on all the capitalist states. Rather, it posits an economic hierarchy in which many economic actors take advantage of those below them in the global economic system. At the top of the heap is a **core**, composed of the states, firms (especially multinational firms such as Siemens, Matsushita, General Motors), and financial institutions of the most developed countries (e.g., Germany, Japan, the United States). At the bottom of the heap are the villages of the developing countries, at the edge of the *periphery*. Many actors engage in exploitation. The resources of the villages are exploited by local and regional economic actors, who are in turn exploited by national economic actors, who are also exploited, by the powerful core actors. There is also a middle group of states (a *semiperiphery* including such countries as Brazil, Mexico, South Africa, Taiwan) whose national economic actors are able to take advantage of the periphery and to limit the level of exploitation by the core states.

Within most developing countries, certain modern sectors and some prosperous actors do emerge, because these sectors and actors cooperate with the international capitalists. But development in such countries is extremely uneven. Organizational and technological development are evident mainly within the state (especially in its bureaucracy and repressive military) and within a few limited sectors of the economy. A large proportion of the population, however, remains trapped in conditions of underdevelopment and poverty (Cardoso and Faletto 1979; Heredia 1998). For example, in Evans's (1979) analysis of development in Brazil, there is an alliance of three key actors: (1) the multinational corporations, (2) the Brazilian capitalist class, and (3) the Brazilian state apparatus. Only the groups in the alliance, and especially the multinationals, gain most of the benefits derived from Brazil's rich resources, whereas the great majority of the population remains poor and backward.

In general, the states of the periphery remain suppliers of raw materials and providers of cheap labor for core states. The economic choices and options available to these developing states are severely constrained by other actors in the international environment. Small movements up the chain of exploitation are possible; but dependency and low economic development are continuing conditions for most in the periphery (Isbister 1998; So 1990; Wallerstein 1974, 1980, 1991; Wilber and Jameson 1995).

Look again at the photograph at the beginning of this chapter. Why are these men smiling? Probably because they got free Pepsis. But the bigger story is that a major U.S.-based multinational corporation has just won a fierce political battle against Indian politicians and local cola manufacturers. Pepsi was granted franchising licenses in India, despite arguments from locals that a major, foreign soft drink company would squash local producers and extract massive profits from the huge Indian market.

It is clear that the process of development is substantially affected by the international political economy. However, many analysts dispute the validity of the dependency approach. First, some question its assertion that the behavior of the developed capitalist countries is mainly ruthless and exploitative (Almond 1987;

Weatherby 1997b). Second, it is argued that the rapid economic development of the NICs seems to contradict key contentions of the dependency approach. The success of many Asian developing countries, relative to those in Africa and Latin America, has led some to suggest that cultural factors might be more crucial to development than is the level of dependence on foreign capital (Fallows 1993; Huntington 1987, 1991). Third, many observe that serious internal problems, especially extensive corruption and conflicts between nationality groups, are major limitations on development in many countries (Isbister 1998). And fourth, many of the highest rates of economic growth during the 1990s actually occurred in some developing countries rather than in the more developed countries (World Bank 1998: table 11).

In response to such arguments, dependency theorists observe that economic actors from the core have become more active in exploiting cheap labor in the periphery, as well as its natural resources. They note that this can generate a higher growth rate for a few years, but that it is unlikely to be sustained for very long, as revealed by the economic declines in many growth economies in the late 1990s. Moreover, growth is extremely uneven—many developing countries experienced minimal growth, and even in developing countries with high growth rates, most of the actual benefits are enjoyed by elites, not by the great majority of the population. Worldwide, the disparity in income between the top 20 percent and the bottom 20 percent of the population has doubled in the last three decades, to a ratio of 60:1 (World Bank 1999; United Nations Development Programme 1999).

Dependency theorists claim that, at best, the patterns of dependency and deep inequalities within the world system became more complicated in the 1990s. The dependency approach continues to raise controversial and significant questions about the obstacles to development and about the level and distribution of benefits to a developing country when advanced industrial countries and their corporations are extensively involved in its political economy. The flow of foreign investment capital into the developing countries has been growing rapidly, reaching more than $200 billion per year by the mid-1990s. But if the developing countries become more reliant on international capital, who will benefit most? Will the gap between the rich countries and the poor countries be reduced? Will the patterns of dependency merely take a new form? These questions are part of the broad contemporary debate about economic development.

POLITICAL DEVELOPMENT

To this point, the discussion has broadly considered development in all spheres of human activity, and particularly the economic sphere. Let us now turn our attention to the specifically *political* aspect of development. **Political development** refers to the emergence of more extensive capabilities in the political system, and especially the political structures of the central government, to manage its internal operations and to respond to its environment.

Characteristics of Political Development

The study of modernization and development of the political system also begins with attempts to list the defining characteristics of development. Some scholars (e.g., Cutright 1963) define political development as the establishment of the rule of law, legitimate elections, and representative institutions. What do you think of this definition of a developed political system? Many scholars object that this conception is extremely biased. Why? What concept do such characteristics seem to measure?

Recent attempts to define the key characteristics of more developed political systems emphasize these four dimensions:

1. *Concentration of power in the central state.* Traditional sources of political authority weaken, and most power and authority are increasingly centralized in a single state-level governmental system. The citizens recognize the right of the state to allocate public values and their own responsibility to accept those allocations as authoritative. The legal-formal apparatus of government (e.g., constitutions, laws) is established.

2. *"Modern" forms of political organization.* Specialized political structures emerge to fulfill most key political functions. There are complex, organized political institutions such as legislatures, executives, political parties, and political interest groups. The actions of these institutions are generally guided by such bureaucratic principles as rationality and efficiency.

3. *"Modern" forms of political behavior.* Individuals develop a strong identity with the political system and the nation-state as the entities, beyond familial groups, that receive their primary loyalty and support. Active political roles become widespread as individuals become participants in the processes of politics, as voters, communicators, and so on (recall Table 3.1).

4. *Expanded capabilities of the political system.* The system becomes better able to generate support, to respond to demands from its population, and to control the environment. Overall, its organization is more stable and coherent, its structures are more efficient, and its actions more effectively serve its goals and objectives.

A "capabilities analysis" of the political system (item 4) is arguably the best set of indicators of the level of political development. Almond and Powell (2000) posit that as a political system improves in any of five key capabilities, it achieves a higher level of political development:

1. *Extractive:* using human and material resources from the environment
2. *Regulative:* controlling individual and group actions
3. *Responsive:* making decisions and policies that react to demands for value allocations
4. *Distributive:* allocating values through institutionalized structures and procedures
5. *Symbolic:* manipulating images and meanings, and distributing nonmaterial rewards and values

The Process of Political Development

The process of political development is a topic of great interest to those attempting to shape their society as well as to those attempting to analyze the political world. From one perspective, political development occurs primarily in response to development of the economic and social systems. Increases in the elements of modernization, such as greater economic development, urbanization, and social mobilization, create a need for a more developed political system, which provides the infrastructure for complex economic activities and serves the needs of a modern citizenry.

This is the causal framework characterized in Model A of Figure 10.1. Political development is essentially a **dependent variable**. (The **dependent variable**, as is explained in the Appendix, is the phenomenon that changes because of the impact of other significant forces, which are the **independent variables**.) In this view, the elements of modernization (the independent variables) provide the material and human resources that make a developed political system possible. Greater economic capability produces goods that the political system can distribute. An urban population with increasingly modern beliefs is more willing to accept the authority of government and to participate meaningfully in politics. In short, the political system develops more complex and specialized structures as a response to changes that are occurring in the society and the economy.

This view of political development is generally based on analyses of political systems that developed in the eighteenth and nineteenth centuries. But consideration of societies whose development has occurred primarily during the last fifty years has revealed the growing power and impact of the political system as a causal force for change. From this second perspective, the political system is the crucial force that causes development of the social and economic systems.

Obviously, development in the political, social, economic, and other domains are interdependent. But Model B of Figure 10.1 emphasizes the central importance of the political system as an agent of change—as the *independent* variable—in relation to other societal characteristics. As Kwame Nkrumah, the first president of Ghana, observed: "Seek ye first the political kingdom, and all else shall be added unto you." This widely quoted, nearly religious invocation assumes that if the political system is developed first, it can then serve as the instrument through which social and economic development are achieved. Value allocation decisions by the

Figure 10.1 Models of development

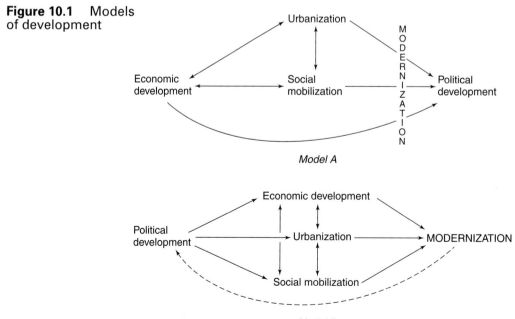

Model A

Model B

political leadership can guide or even determine the direction of changes in individual and group behavior, the political economy, and the society.

According to Model B, when a new political elite takes control, it is the political system over which the elite has most direct control. By explicit policy decisions and actions, an assertive leadership group can create modern forms of political organization and encourage modern forms of political behavior. The leaders can, for example, enact policies that establish new governmental structures, diminish the power of traditional authority sources, empower governmental bureaucracies to perform particular functions, create political parties, mobilize certain groups into the political process, or assert state control over human and natural resources.

Given its direct control over the political system, the political leadership can also employ these structures, processes, and public policies to modernize other domains of social and economic life, such as the political economy, the educational system, the culture, national identity, the media, and religious practices. The efforts of Chairman Mao in China and of Pol Pot in Cambodia are examples from earlier chapters of the explicit use of the political system as a powerful instrument to change many aspects of the society. Kemal Atatürk's efforts in Turkey are another example (see Box 10.4).

Political Development as Democratization

Earlier in this chapter it was noted that some scholars treat political development and political democracy synonymously. Given our core concept that development is based on the capacity of the political system to handle certain basic functions, there are political systems that are developed but nondemocratic (e.g., Cuba). However, a very positive normative value can be attributed to democratization as an important goal of political development.

The 1990s are notable not only for the high proportion of political system deaths (Chapter 5) but also for efforts to establish democratic political regimes in more countries than at any other time in history. Chapter 7 noted that there were 117 electoral democracies (61 percent of all countries) at century's end (Freedom House 1999). The processes of democratization have been strong in many of the postcommunist states that emerged from the former Soviet Union and in Central and Eastern Europe, and in a variety of previously military regimes in Latin America, Asia, and Africa (e.g., Argentina, Chile, Liberia, and South Korea). Many countries in this last group have been described as "protected democracies" because the military has played a leading role in maintaining democratic practices (Loveman 1994).

In general, a country's transition to democracy requires (1) tolerance of political opposition, (2) free elections among genuine alternative candidates, and (3) acceptance by political leaders of the results of the election as well as a limit on the time that the leaders' mandate is in force (see Chapter 7). Indeed, a key benefit of the processes of democracy is that they enable politicians and policy advocates to "lose peacefully" (Mansbridge 1991: 6).

Huntington (1991) suggests that there have been three long waves of democratization among modern states. The first occurred between the 1820s and 1926, when about thirty states established liberal democracies. Some of these then "reversed" (democracy was abandoned), until a second wave produced thirty-six democratic governments between 1945 and 1962. After another period of reversal, the third wave began in 1974 and the number has now more than doubled, to about ninety states. Of course, the total number of states has also expanded dramatically during

BOX 10.4

Political Development and Modernization in Turkey

The modernization effort in Turkey is an example of "seeking the political king-dom first." Historically, the area of the Turkish nation was part of the large Ottoman Empire ruled by a sultan. After World War I an army commander named Mustafa Kemal led a fierce military struggle for national independence. Victory resulted in the creation of the sovereign state of Turkey in 1922. Mustafa Kemal, who seized political power in the new republic, was committed to rapid modern-ization. At the time, Turkey had very traditional political, economic, and social sys-tems, with Islamic law dominating the actions of the 98 percent Muslim population. The new leader decided that the key to modernization was to reduce the hold of Islam on the people.

In a stroke of symbolic politics, he began his modernization drive at the per-sonal level. He changed his name to Mustafa Kemal Atatürk, the addition meaning "father of the Turks." (Kemal was also a fortunate name, since it means "perfect one.") Atatürk initially focused on political development, establishing a new state based on the principles of independence and democracy. A constitution was approved in 1924, executive power was granted to a president, the sultan was exiled, a legislature was elected, and a single political party was established. Atatürk thus created a political system with modern structures of governance and modern forms of political participation. This political system then became the instrument for Atatürk's broader efforts to reform Turkey.

From 1925 until his death in 1938, Atatürk employed his great political power to implement three major sets of public policies that were meant to modernize Turkey and to separate it from the traditional Muslim world. First, he promulgated laws that prohibited the wearing of religious garments in everyday life, abolished religious schools, and closed religious tombs as places of worship. Second, he encouraged the emergence and empowerment of a nationalist elite, by such steps as creating a new Turkish language and banning the public use of other languages, replacing the Ottoman script with the Latin alphabet, and establishing Turkish lit-eracy programs, especially in urban areas. Third, he established a new civil code (copied from Switzerland) to govern the legal relations between individuals and col-lectivities, relegating Shari'a law and the Koran to peripheral status in guiding pub-lic life. For example, he reduced the subordinate role of women, encouraging them to work, providing them with rights of divorce and inheritance, allowing them to vote and hold public office, and banning polygamy.

Many changes prompted by Atatürk are evident in Turkey. While 70 percent of the population lived in villages in 1964, Turkey is now 65 percent urban. The econ-omy was 75 percent agrarian in 1978 and is now 70 percent industrial and has diver-sified considerably. Turkey's 64 million people remain 99 percent Muslim, but the country now has the most educated and modern women in the Muslim world. From 1993 to 1996, Tansu Çiller was Turkey's first female prime minister. While gender inequality remains, about one-fourth of Turkish professionals are now women and the proportion of female doctors in Turkey is higher than in the United States.

BOX 10.4

Politically, the attempt to create an effective multiparty democracy in Turkey remains unfinished. There have been periods of serious social instability and governmental corruption, and three periods of military rule since 1960, although the military returned power to civilians in each case once order was restored. The military has not intervened directly since 1982, when a new constitution was adopted by popular vote and a parliament was elected from among four main political parties.

Then, in 1996, an Islamic party (the Welfare Party) came to power for the first time since Atatürk. Although the Prime Minister reaffirmed his commitment to the secular society established by Atatürk, his government began to promote numerous policy changes based on Islamic principles and practices. The military responded with stern warnings, shows of force, and demands that the Islamic policies be abandoned. A crisis was averted in 1997 when the Welfare Party resigned from power and was replaced by a government led by a party committed to secularism. The situation remains unstable because there is considerable support in the society for a more prominent role for Islam and for parties that promote religious policies. If those parties become too successful or their supporters become too assertive, the military might fulfill its threat to seize power in defense of a modern, secular Turkey.

Thus Atatürk's strong policies have not totally transformed Turkey, but they are an illuminating example of the use of political power to achieve considerable modernization and development within a society. At this point, the military remains the ultimate guarantor of democracy, stability, and secularism in Turkey.

---

this period, but the proportions of states that are liberal democracies and/or electoral democracies (recall Chapter 7) have increased in the most recent wave.

Why is there an expansion of democracies? A variety of explanations has been offered (Huntington 1991). One reason might be that there is a *contagion effect:* When some countries make the transition to democracy, citizens in other countries also place high value on this form of government, and they are successful in demanding that their leaders also implement democratic reforms.

In other cases, the *breakdown of authoritarian and totalitarian regimes* has provided a window of opportunity for such demands and a situation in which the old regime does not have the resources to suppress the pressure for change. This seems to have been particularly important in the states of the former Soviet Union and Central and Eastern Europe, as well as in Algeria, Argentina, Benin, Chile, and Jordan (Stepan and Linz 1996).

In still other cases, the level of *economic development* seems crucial. Many scholars conclude that democracy seems most viable in relatively wealthy countries or, conversely, that poverty is a serious obstacle to sustaining democratic government (Diamond et al. 1997). Greater wealth might reassure both citizens and leaders that the increased participation and demands associated with democratization can now be handled without serious political decay because sufficient resources are available to meet those demands. In this way, the tendencies toward democracy have increased in such states as South Korea and Taiwan.

A key factor in the transition to democracy is the presence of *political leadership* committed to democracy. Either such leaders, primarily from new elites, can decide that democratization is a valued goal to be pursued (as with South Africa's Nelson Mandela) or existing elites can conclude that allowing increased democratization is the best means to maintain their positions of power (as with Boris Yeltsin in Russia) (Diamond et al. 1997; Sorensen 1997).

The behavior of *external actors* can also be a highly relevant factor in the shift toward democracy. In the late 1980s it became clear that the Soviet Union under Mikhail Gorbachev would not intervene to support unpopular totalitarian leadership in East European states. In the same period, the United States applied increasing pressure to implement democratic practices on some governments to which it was providing economic and military aid. Also, the Catholic Church reduced its doctrinal emphasis on obedience to governmental authority, undermining citizen acquiescence to authoritarian regimes in such Catholic countries as Argentina and Brazil. Since the 1990s, an increasingly important force for political reform has been the World Bank and other international actors who insist that countries introduce democratic reforms as a condition for economic assistance (Maxfield 1997).

Political Institutionalization and Political Decay

If the theory that democratization comes in waves is correct, the current expansion will also crest and then recede. Many of the states that are being swept up in this wave might lack the political institutionalization, the broad support of the politically active groups, or the level of economic development necessary to sustain viable democracy. There is some evidence that the wave is already receding, especially in "frail democracies," a pattern most visible in the parts of Central and Eastern Europe and Africa that are reverting to authoritarian regimes. Researchers are particularly interested in developing theories about the necessary and sufficient conditions for the maintenance of a democratic political system. Such stabilization and institutionalization is often referred to as the "consolidation" of democracy (Diamond et al. 1997; Linz and Stepan 1996; Schedler 1998).

If democratic development can recede, it raises the broader question of whether political development in general might decline. The example of Turkey suggests that even when the forms of the political system appear to be modernized, the changes might lack "staying power." Samuel Huntington (1968, 1987) offers incisive commentary regarding the illusion of political development. He observes that many studies have assumed a fundamental compatibility among economic, social, and political development, believing there would be a steady progress in all domains from a traditional society to a modern one. But in many political systems, there has been a deterioration of political structures, processes, and roles, and this reversal of political development has not necessarily been associated with a decline of economic or social development.

Huntington (1968) argues that political development must be measured not by the outward forms of political structures or democratic practices, but by **political institutionalization**—that is, *by the extent that political organizations and procedures have acquired value in the eyes of the population and the stability to withstand significant pressure.* Like the capabilities analysis described earlier in the chapter, political institutionalization is measured by the political system's capacity to regulate its citizens, respond flexibly to citizen demands, extract and distribute resources efficiently, and adapt to changing circumstances.

Rather than assuming inevitable progress in political development, Huntington sees **political decay**—*a significant decline in the capabilities of the political system, and especially its capacity to maintain order*— as always being a possibility. Features of the modernization process, such as social mobilization, economic growth, urbanization, education, and so on, are inherently destabilizing. Social mobilization can undermine the traditional values and beliefs that sustained social order; economic growth produces new resources over which there is competition; urbanization concentrates heterogeneous groups into large, densely packed masses; and increases in education and communications make these masses aware of the many resources and values that they do not currently enjoy.

These circumstances can generate a huge increase in the volume and nature of demands directed at the political system. Groups begin to demand that the state provide them with many values, such as better education, decent health care and housing, good jobs, a free and open political process. Most developing political systems lack the capacity to extract the requisite resources from the political economy and lack the authority to persuade the citizens to accept value allocations that they judge insufficient.

In the face of growing citizen dissatisfaction with the political system, Huntington argues, a common strategy for the political leaders is an attempt to "buy off" the population by increasing their political participation and mobilization rather than providing tangible (scarce and costly) goods and services. Such increased political activity might satisfy people in the short run, but it soon generates even higher levels of demands that cannot be met. At this point, rising social, political, and economic frustrations erupt into political demonstrations and protests, and even riots and rebellion.

Given low levels of support and excessive citizen demands, the political system must employ other mechanisms to maintain social order.

- In some cases, a charismatic leader emerges. The leader gains the support and obedience of the people, but only by personalizing power and thus weakening the overall processes through which power and political structures are institutionalized.

- In some cases, the one organization in most societies that *is* institutionalized—the military—forcibly takes over political power, under the justification of restoring order.

- In some cases, no individuals or institutions have the capacity to reestablish social peace, and widespread disorder and violence result.

What can be done to achieve political institutionalization? Huntington (1968) suggests two general strategies. In the most direct approach, the political system acts to increase the value and stability of political institutions. For example, traditional authority structures (e.g., chiefs, religious leaders, tribal councils) might be adapted to the modern system. Or there might be a long incubation period under colonial rule while new political structures and processes slowly gain value and stability. Or political parties might be created as a locus of legitimacy and a basis of stable governance. The problem with creating or transforming institutions, according to Huntington, is that this very approach has already been attempted and has failed in many developing states.

This Samburu herdsman in a remote area of Kenya seems to balance tradition and modernity with ease.

In the second approach to institutionalization, the political system substantially limits the processes of political participation and social mobilization. Doing this requires instituting policies that minimize visible political issues by limiting the activities of political parties and the media, the open competition among political elites, and citizen participation in politics. More fundamentally, the political system can manipulate citizens' political beliefs and actions by controlling the educational system and the media.

A third approach to institutionalization, one not suggested by Huntington, is to mobilize the population but to encourage only those forms of participation that support the political order. That is, the political system mobilizes individuals and groups to "serve the people," not to make demands on the political system. This is the ultimate form of U.S. President John F. Kennedy's famous inaugural exhortation, "Ask not what your country can do for you; ask what you can do for your country." Mao Zedong attempted this third approach in China. For a while, people were inspired to work with zeal despite minimal resources and skills. However, by the period of the Cultural Revolution (1962–1968), the political system lost control. Mao encouraged an overmobilized segment of the population (led by the Red Guards) to revitalize the revolutionary spirit of the society. But their methods were primarily persecution, violence, and disruption. Skilled people were ridiculed and forced to do menial work, while unskilled party loyalists were given positions requiring organizational and technical knowledge that they did not possess. The result was chaos in all spheres of Chinese society and a severe decline in economic productivity.

Notice that neither of the latter two approaches are particularly compatible with democratization, even if they do support political institutionalization. Indeed, in Huntington's (1968) analysis (see Figure 10.2), the political leadership must balance participation and demands, on the one hand, against political institutionalization and system capabilities (capacity), on the other. As the modernization process generates social mobilization and economic development, there is a tolerable range for the ratio between participation and institutionalization. If the system overemphasizes institutionalization, there is what Huntington terms *political order;* if participation is overemphasized, there is *political decay.*

From this very choice of terms (*order* rather than *repression, decay* rather than *activism*), it should be evident which overemphasis Huntington believes is preferable. Recall Huntington's insistence (quoted in Box 5.3) on the primacy of order over liberty. What do you think of Huntington's preferences and assumptions here? If stability is preferred so absolutely, what kinds of objectionable actions by the state might be justified?

ACHIEVING POLITICAL DEVELOPMENT

Ultimately, all political systems aim to increase their capabilities and thus to increase their level of political development. There is general consensus that a more developed political system should enable the political actors to accomplish their objectives more fully. But there is considerable disagreement about the specific shape that political development should take.

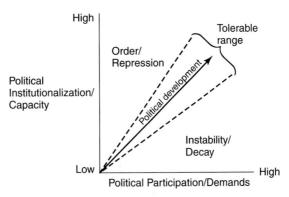

Figure 10.2   Political institutionalization and political decay
SOURCE: Based on Huntington 1968.

In general, most people assume that political development in other countries should result in political systems and political economies that resemble those in their own country. It is debatable, however, whether all states should or even can follow the same developmental path. Some, perhaps most, newly developing countries might have basic value systems, cultures, histories, economies, or social systems that are not compatible with the patterns of development or the political structures and processes that "worked" in other countries, especially those that emerged in earlier eras.

The leaders in most developing countries try to assess whether the prior experiences and development strategy of some other state provide a model for their own development. This process might help the developing country to benefit from the successes and avoid the mistakes of that country. Even if a model is selected that does seem compatible with the developing country's own goals and unique characteristics, achieving political development and political institutionalization are extremely difficult in the contemporary world. In addition to all the problems discussed in this chapter, the remainder of this book will continually illustrate the extent to which the choices and actions of states are influenced and sometimes controlled by other states in the international system. This is a particular problem for states with low capabilities and minimal stability—that is, in states that lack political institutionalization.

Huntington is certainly correct that the challenges to political development are great. There have been periods of major political instability even in some European and Latin American countries—and these countries had the advantage of a long period in which the structures of a modern state could evolve into more complex and effective forms and in which the citizens could come to accept and value their political system.

In contrast, most states in the contemporary political world began creating their own modern political systems after 1945. While these systems have the appearance of modernity—complex, specialized political structures, widespread political participation, and so on—many lack the stability and value that come with a long evolutionary development. The fundamental dilemma for the political elites in these states is how to allocate public values effectively while maintaining political order, expanding political participation, and strengthening the political economy.

How much political participation and opposition should be allowed? How large should the domain of *res publica* be? To what extent and by what policies should the state control the political economy? What levels of what values should be allocated to particular groups? All states continually deal with these issues. But in the absence of strong political institutionalization, determining and implementing appropriate answers to these issues can be nearly impossible.

FOR FURTHER CONSIDERATION

1. Most people in Western societies have been socialized to believe that change is associated with progress and is generally a good thing. However, the ideology of conservatism (as outlined in Chapter 2) does not make this assumption. What are the conservative's views about change? More broadly, can you specify types of change that would not necessarily be positive for a given political system?

2. The success or failure of the developmental state strategy in certain developing countries is sometimes attributed to elements of culture. What factors other than culture might affect a country's capacity for rapid development? How important do you think a society's culture might be? Why?

3. Many countries have recently established democratic political processes. Is political decay inevitable in most of these countries? Why or why not? What strategies, general and specific, seem most promising in the attempt to avoid serious political decay?

4. Write a dialogue between two analysts: one contends that the dependency approach offers the best explanation for the failure of many countries to achieve development, while the second analyst argues that other factors best explain why some countries have limited development.

FOR FURTHER READING

Achebe, Chinua. (1969). *Arrow of God.* New York: Doubleday. In themes similar to those in Achebe's highly acclaimed *Things Fall Apart* (1959) [Box 10.3], this novel describes how West African villagers' beliefs in their local gods are undermined by a Christian missionary, leading to the disintegration of their cultural traditions.

Bornstein, David. (1996). *The Price of a Dream: The Story of the Grameen Bank, the Banking Program that Is Changing the Lives of the Poor.* New York: Simon and Schuster. As suggested by the subtitle, the Grameen Bank has gained international acclaim for its program of small loans which transform poor individuals into entrepreneurs. This book describes the philosophy of the Grameen Bank and provides examples of its development activities in Bangladesh.

Diamond, Larry, Marc Plattner, Yun-han Chu, and Mung-mao Tien. Eds. (1997). *Consolidating the Third Wave Democracies.* Baltimore, MD: Johns Hopkins University Press. In two volumes (*Themes and Perspectives; Regional Challenges*), a diverse set of top scholars thoughtfully and comprehensively assess the issues and empirical realities associated with efforts to "consolidate" (institutionalize) liberal democracy in countries in every region of the world.

Huntington, Samuel P. (1991). *The Third Wave: Democratization in the Late Twentieth Century.* Norman: University of Oklahoma Press. The wide-ranging assessment of contemporary transitions to democracy by one of the major scholars of comparative development. The general argument about political institutionalization and political decay discussed in this chapter is fully elaborated in his earlier sweeping study, *Political Order in Changing Societies* (New Haven, CT: Yale University Press, 1968).

Johnson, Chalmers. (1995). *Japan: Who Governs? The Rise of the Developmental State.* New York: W.W. Norton. An elaboration of his important earlier analyses of the Japanese development strategy (Johnson 1982), this book provides a broader framework characterizing the government-industry cooperation that produced the "Japanese miracle" and has become the basis of the development approach taken by other Asian NICs.

Lipset, Seymour Martin. (1988). *Revolution and Counterrevolution: Change and Persistence in Social Structures.* Rev. ed. Rutgers, NJ: Transaction Books. Provocative essays on the processes of change and development, with a particular emphasis on the effects of culture.

So, Alvin Y. (1990). *Social Change and Development: Modernization, Dependency, and World-System Theories.* Newbury Park, CA: Sage. A thoughtful description and comparison of the three key theories of development (in the subtitle), with an effort to characterize the evolution of each theory and to identify their points of convergence.

Sorensen, George. (1997). *Democracy and Democratization: Processes and Prospects in a Changing World.* 2d ed. Boulder, CO: Westview Press. A wide-ranging discussion of the spread of democratic processes in many countries, defining the patterns and conditions under which democracy is viable and the likely evolution of various democratic systems.

Weiner, Myron, and Samuel P. Huntington. (1987). *Understanding Political Development.* Boston: Little, Brown. A series of important essays on such aspects of political development as participation, culture, dependency theory, ethnonationalism, and the role of the state.

Bosnian civilians run for cover in the capital as Serbian troops shell the town.

CHAPTER 11

Political Violence

Yesterday in the political world:

Eight Algerian soldiers were killed in an attack on a military camp east of Algiers by Islamic militants opposing the government.

More than 20,000 people fled their villages in Northern Liberia as rebels looted and burned down their towns.

American and British warplanes bombed an Iraqi radar site, killing nineteen and seriously wounding eleven.

Despite a ceasefire, more than fifty died in fighting between Ugandan and Rwandan troops in Congo.

A white supremacist on a shooting rampage was shot to death after killing one and wounding five near a Jewish community center in California.

Israeli agents are suspected in the bombing death of the commander of the Islamic group Hezbollah in Lebanon.

Marxist rebels kidnapped for ransom the Roman Catholic Bishop of a large town in Colombia.

A roadside bomb planted by the Tamil Tigers killed nine policemen and wounded twenty-four other people in a small, Sri Lankan coastal town.

South Korean police used tear gas and water cannons to disperse thousands of students in Seoul who were marching in support of unification with North Korea.

Eleven Israeli soldiers were injured when a Palestinian drove his car into a crowd in a market town in the West Bank; the driver was shot and killed.

Russian soldiers engaged in an intense fire fight with rebels in the province of Dagestan, killing more than 200 as 14 soldiers also die.

An Indian plane shot down a Pakistani surveillance plane near the Indian border, killing all sixteen on board.

Such incidents of violence are often at the center of our awareness of the political world. On a given day, the media rarely report that the great majority of countries and billions of people experienced no bombings, kidnappings, riots, or revolutionary acts that had an explicit or implicit political motivation. Rather, the media are likely to report on the few settings that do experience armed conflict, riots, assassinations, terrorist incidents, and so on. In part, this selective reporting reflects our general fascination with the horror of violence. And in part it indicates our underlying sense that such political violence is extraordinary, or even an aberration, from politics-as-usual.

Violence is excluded from some definitions of politics, such as the group approach, since violence is viewed as a breakdown of politics, understood as consensus building and conflict resolution. For example, one textbook defines politics as "bloodless conflict" (Donovan, Morgan, and Potholm 1984). However, other definitions, including the class approach, treat conflict and violence as one possible, and perhaps even inevitable, form of politics. Indeed, some approaches argue that political violence can be a positive force, producing necessary change and constructive outcomes. The purpose of this chapter is to discuss the nature and dynamics of political violence.

VIOLENCE

Before the discussion can unfold, we need to consider briefly the concept of violence itself. The most common notion is that *violence* entails the use of physical force, usually with the purpose of injuring or damaging the object of the violence. In the political world, the tools of such violence can range from flying fists and feet to clubs and bullets to nerve gas and nuclear missiles.

But notice that some analysts take a much broader view of violence. First, the threat of violence might sometimes be understood as a form of violence, even if the violent act is not actually committed. If someone points a gun in your face and you give him your money, you will probably view this interaction as a violent one, even if the gun is never fired. In parallel, then, if a state points many nuclear missiles at the state across its border, would you classify this as an act of violence? Is it a violent act if an interest group threatens to blow up a public building unless its demands are met? Is it a violent act if a group shouts down a speaker at a public rally? Do you think that such acts of intimidation and threat of force have a violent element, even if there is no actual physical injury or damage?

Second, an even broader view of violence includes various forms of subjugation and manipulation that do not involve even the threat of direct physical harm. For example, consider a group that is an "underclass" within a society. The group is subjected to discrimination in education, in health care, in jobs, in housing. This intentional pattern of systematic deprivation continues over time. The group is not targeted for any specific physical violence, but the economic and cultural systems provide the group with minimal opportunities to gain a significant share of the values in the society. Some would classify such oppression as a form of violence by the dominant group(s) against the fundamental rights of this group as it pursues the goals of life, liberty, and happiness. The extensive use of propaganda techniques might be considered an even subtler form of violence against those people.

This chapter focuses on **political violence**, defined as *the use of actual physical violence or very serious threats of such violence to achieve political goals*. As you assess the role of violence in politics, however, you should also consider the other ways in which the world of politics generates actions and impacts that "do violence" to many people. Although the resort to physical force is quite evident in politics, the more subtle forms of coercion and manipulation are more extensive, if less visible.

POLITICAL SOCIETY

For Thomas Hobbes (1588–1679), the formation of political society is an attempt to overcome the frequent reliance on force and violence in human interaction. Life in the state of nature, described by Hobbes as "solitary, poor, nasty, brutish, and short," is pervaded by interpersonal violence. Consequently, individuals submit to the social contract in an attempt to submit force to reason—to ensure that force becomes the *ultima ratio* (final resort), not the *prima ratio* (first resort) in human interactions. In essence, individuals cede to the state a monopoly over the legitimate use of violence, sacrificing their own right to do violence in exchange for a similar sacrifice from others.

Some individuals and groups argue that the existing political society and its social contract have no authority over their actions and that they are therefore not morally bound to refrain from engaging in "justifiable" violence. Indeed, those who commit political violence virtually always offer a justification for their actions. Among the most common rationales for political violence are the preservation of values, the restoration of order, self-defense, and retribution. Broadly, all such justifications are based on a claim either that their group has never accepted the right of a particular government to command their obedience or that the political system has failed to act properly (it has gone too far or it has not gone far enough in its value allocations).

TYPES OF POLITICAL VIOLENCE

A simple taxonomy of political violence can be based on specifying the actor who is the source of the violence, and the target of that violence. Either party may be a state or an individual/group. Figure 11.1 categorizes the four types of political violence that result. In this chapter we discuss three of these types, deferring the discussion of war to Chapter 12, which examines the relations between states. While the categories in Figure 11.1 help organize and clarify our discussion, this taxonomy is imperfect and the boundaries between categories are imprecise because the states, groups, or individuals who engage in political violence often are motivated by multiple objectives and employ complex strategies.

| | **Target** | |
Source	**Individual/Group**	**State**
Individual/Group	Crime Terrorism Nation-based conflict Class conflict	Riots/Rebellion Separatist violence Coup Revolution
State	Order maintenance Establishment violence	War

Figure 11.1   Types of political violence

State Violence against Individuals or Groups

Given the state's monopoly of the legitimate use of violence, there are many instances where the application of political violence by the state seems justifiable. The state typically characterizes its own use of violence as an *order maintenance* activity. In many instances the state acts as police officer, judge, and executor of punishment when individuals or groups seem to have violated the society's legal system. The state's agents might arrest, try, and punish an actor who breaks a criminal law, such as by robbery, or a civil law, such as by tax fraud. In such cases, most citizens are likely to support the state's efforts to create and maintain public order.

But some uses of violence by the state are more problematical. Recall Lenin's definition of the state as "a body of armed men, weapons, and prisons" (in Chapter 5). Because the state has the capacity to define the nature and severity of all "crimes," it is possible for it to be highly repressive and discriminatory in its use of state violence. Thus excessive reliance on force and oppressive laws can be viewed as *establishment violence* rather than as the state's legitimate use of violence to maintain public order.

The boundary between a crime against society and a crime against the existing political order can blur. In some countries, a "political crime" is no more than opposition to the actions of the current political leadership. Thus political opponents become "enemies of the people," and are subject to constraints on freedom of action, deprivation of resources, imprisonment, and death. The state can also institute systematic policies of violence against certain groups who are not overt opponents of the regime but who are blamed for problems faced by the state and thus are made scapegoats.

A key instrument of state power against its enemies is its security forces. These forces include official groups such as the regular military and the secret police, and violence can be applied by unofficial armed groups (e.g., the Serbian paramilitary forces) or civilian vigilante groups (e.g., the Iranian Revolutionary Guards). Another form of state power is judicial systems and prison systems, which punish those whose behaviors displease the state. According to Amnesty International, a group that monitors violations of individual civil rights by agents of the state, political prisoners are being subjected to establishment violence in the majority of contemporary states. In addition, the state can cause great suffering or even death to individuals through its power to withhold access to such rewards as good jobs, shelter, and welfare services.

In the contemporary world, there is extensive attention to certain forms of political violence, especially violence between states (war) and individual/group violence (such as terrorism and civil war). This attention is understandable because such violence is dramatic and terrifying. But, according to an extensive analysis by political scientist R. J. Rummel (2000) of "death by government," the death toll from establishment violence far outweighs the deaths from war in the twentieth century. These data are summarized in Table 11.1.

According to Rummel, the deaths of more than 203 million people in the twentieth century are directly attributable to government violence and war. The most staggering aspect of these data is that fully 83 percent of these deaths are establishment violence. That is, while about 34 million people have been killed in the wars

TABLE 11.1
Death by Government in the Twentieth Century

	Total Deaths (Millions)			Percentage of Total Deaths
	Domestic	Foreign	All	
Establishment Violence	129.9	39.3	169.2	83.3%
By communist governments	101.9	8.3	110.2	54.2
By other totalitarian goverments	2.1	26.1	28.2	14.0
By authoritarian governments	25.7	3.0	28.7	14.1
By democratic governments	0.2	1.9	2.1	1.0
War	4.8	29.2	34.2	16.7
TOTAL	134.7	68.5	203.2	100.0%

Source: Adapted from Rummel 2000: Table 1.6.

of the twentieth century, it is (conservatively) estimated that governments killed almost 170 million of their own citizens—the people they are supposed to serve. According to Rummel, almost all of these deaths through establishment violence have been the work of nondemocratic governments. More than half of the deaths (54.2 percent) are attributable to communist regimes, about 28 percent are the responsibility of other totalitarian governments, and almost 29 percent are by authoritarian governments (Rummel 2000: Table 1.6; Figure 1.4).

Rummel particularly emphasizes the massive death totals attributable to the twentieth century's "bloodiest dictators." Among those political leaders who killed the largest numbers of their citizens are Joseph Stalin (whose Soviet regime killed 42.6 million between 1929–1953), Mao Zedong in China (37.8 million from 1923–1976), the elimination of more than 20.9 million by Hitler and the German Nazi regime (1933–1945, recall Box 2.3), and the deaths by execution and starvation of 2.4 million Cambodians under Pol Pot's regime (recall Box 5.5). If you need evidence regarding the fundamental importance of the state in determining the quality of citizens' lives, the 170 million deaths attributable to the citizens' own governments should be compelling.

Individual Violence against an Individual

In most instances when an individual is the source of violence and another individual is the target, the violence is not explicitly political. Most such violence (e.g., murder, robbery, rape, assault, and certain crimes against property, such as burglary and arson) is best characterized as *ordinary crime*. Only the state (and its agents) have a legitimate right to use violence, and thus an individual who does violence independent of the state is normally in violation of the law. Thus such violence has a political component in the sense that the state is usually involved in determining what behavior is criminal, and then in apprehending violators, judging them, and punishing them.

Analyzing individuals' motivation in violent ordinary crimes is complicated by the fact that in most societies, members of deprived or subordinate groups tend to engage in these crimes far more frequently than members of the more advantaged classes. Can you think of ways in which this pattern might suggest that the commission of some violent crimes has, at least in part, a subtle political origin?

Occasionally one individual commits violence against another individual in a situation where the motivation is personal as well as political. In such cases, neither the source nor the target is acting primarily as the representative of some larger political group. In a famous American example from 1804, Vice President Aaron Burr shot and killed Alexander Hamilton in a duel that had its origins in a personal and political disagreement between the two men (see Box 11.1). Each of the American presidents who was assassinated (Abraham Lincoln in 1865, James A. Garfield in 1881, and John F. Kennedy in 1963) was shot by an individual who was apparently acting on political motives, but acting alone.

Group Violence against an Individual

In many situations where an individual is targeted for political violence, including most assassinations, the actual source of violence is a group, even when the violent act is performed by an individual. Box 5.3 described the assassinations of two prime ministers of India, Indira Gandhi and then, only seven years later, her son Rajiv Gandhi. While Indira Gandhi was killed by only two guards and Rajiv Gandhi by one woman, in each case the assassins believed that they were acting on behalf of the political interests of their nation (the Sikhs and the Sri Lankan Tamils, respectively). Similarly, Israeli Prime Minister Yitzhak Rabin was assassinated in 1995 by an individual who belonged to Kach, an extreme right-wing Jewish religious group, in an attempt to undermine the "land-for-peace" agreement between Israel and the Palestinians. And the Armenian Prime Minister was among six members of government shot to death by five anti-Armenian gunmen who invaded the parliament building in 1999.

Terrorism.   When the target of premeditated violence serving an underlying political objective is an "innocent," the act is usually termed **terrorism**. Bombs can be planted in public places such as pubs or airplanes, civilians can be kidnapped or murdered, harmful chemicals can be placed in food, water, or air. Many terrorist acts are committed by residents of the country in which the terrorism occurs, as in the 1995 bombing of the U.S. federal government building in Oklahoma City. Particular attention often focuses on "international terrorism"—incidents where the terrorism is committed by individuals from another country. Since the early 1980s, there have been about 300–400 international terrorist acts per year. Recent years have been characterized by fewer acts of terrorism but higher numbers of deaths, with 273 terrorist acts and 741 killed in 1998, for example (U.S. Department of State 1999: 77).

Why harm innocents? The motives of political terrorists vary, but several rationales guide most such acts. First, one common motive is to use the terrorist act as a means to gain international publicity for the group's cause. Unlike those committing ordinary crimes, terrorists typically claim credit for their violent actions and hope for extensive media coverage. A second motive is to secure financial resources for the group's political activities or to demand the release of imprisoned members. Many of the acts of violence entailing hostages and ransom demands are of this type. While innocents are the direct target of these actions, some existing state is usually the ultimate target. (Recall the perspective of Abu Nidal in Box 4.4.) Thus a third objective of terrorist violence can be to promote revolution—a strategy discussed later in this chapter.

BOX 11.1

Politics Will Be the Death of Me

After a long and extraordinary career in politics, Alexander Hamilton (1757–1804) took up the life of a country gentleman in 1800. But the seminal Founding Father, cowriter of the *Federalist Papers,* and first U.S. Secretary of the Treasury was unable to withdraw from the political world. He was alarmed by the growing dominance of the Jeffersonian Republicans over his own Federalist Party. In Hamilton's view, the Republicans were undermining values in which he believed deeply—a powerful and independent judiciary, a strong national government and military, and an evolution away from slavery in the United States.

Hamilton was increasingly displeased with the policy responses of the Federalists. He toyed with the idea of reentering politics to establish a new political party, the Christian Constitutional Society, which would appeal to people's religious sensibilities and their concern for collective good rather than their selfish, individual interests. He was dismayed when the Federalists in his home state of New York decided for strategic reasons to support Jefferson's vice president, Aaron Burr, in the election for governor of New York. Hamilton had never liked Burr, either for his political views or for his personal style. Hamilton was vocal in his opposition to Burr, who failed to win the governorship.

Shortly after the election, Burr sent a note to Hamilton demanding an explanation for negative remarks that Burr believed Hamilton had made about him. Burr cited remarks overheard by others in which Hamilton is purported to have said that he "looked upon Mr. Burr to be a dangerous man, and one who ought not to be trusted with the reins of government" and other, unquoted opinions that Burr claimed were "even more despicable" (McDonald 1979: 359–360).

At that time, the *code duello* required that a gentleman was obliged to explain or apologize for remarks that caused affront to another gentleman. The code further allowed the aggrieved party to challenge the other man to a duel in order to obtain "satisfaction." In such cases, men of honor would normally duel with pistols, intentionally miss each other, shake hands, and consider the disagreement resolved.

Hamilton did not deny his disdain for Burr or Burr's politics, but he refused to explain or apologize, on the grounds that the charges against him were too vague. When negotiations between the representatives of Hamilton and Burr broke down, Burr challenged Hamilton to a duel. As a gentleman, Hamilton could not decline. On the early morning of July 11, 1804, Burr and Hamilton met in the woods. After Hamilton shot in the air, Burr shot Hamilton through the liver. Carried back to his home, Hamilton forgave Burr, repented his sins, and died after thirty-six hours in great pain (based on McDonald 1979).

Usually, the politics of death are impersonal. The killer and the killed know each other only as types. But there are a considerable number of instances where personal animosities and grudges, with political undertones or overtones, are

(continued)

BOX 11.1 *(Continued)*

resolved violently. Murders of political rivals, such as assassinations of leaders, are among the most dramatic moments in the political life of a country. A deadly conflict like that between Hamilton and Burr might seem odd to you—today, people are more civilized than these "gentlemen." When individuals (especially boys and men) have personal–political differences, they now resolve them through discussion and compromise, not with weapons and violence. Don't they?

Alexander Hamilton is mortally wounded in his 1804 duel with Aaron Burr, the ultimate resolution of their political dispute.

In the late 1990s, an ominous change emerged: an increasing proportion of terrorist acts are committed by those who neither claim responsibility nor make specific demands. Analysts suggest several reasons for this more anonymous terrorism. First, the risk of revealing one's identity is now far greater, as law enforcement agencies have become more effective in tracing and apprehending terrorists. Second, more acts are being classified as "rage terrorism"—violence provoked by a diffuse anger against a world that seems too threatening and complex and that is seething with interpersonal and intergroup hostility. In either case, the terrorist can gain satisfaction from the profound public anxiety associated with what seems an act of random, senseless violence (Marquand 1996).

There are ambiguities in the assessment of terrorism. One problem is that in many acts labeled "terrorism," the targets are not truly "innocents," but rather are agents of the enemy state. For example, a Palestinian group bombed and killed 241 U.S. Marines in their barracks in Beirut, Lebanon, in 1984 and a bomb killed 19 in a Marine housing complex in Dharan, Saudi Arabia, in June 1996. In each case, U.S. spokespersons termed the attack "terrorism;" yet Marines can hardly be construed as innocents. Another common target of terrorists is police officers or judges who are accused of having done violence to individuals associated with the terrorist group or those sympathetic to its cause. In such cases, the political violence can be terrible, but one must decide whether group violence against agents of the state is appropriately defined as terrorism.

Ironically, some groups labeled terrorists are actually employees of a political system, which uses them as "death squads" to eliminate opponents and to keep the citizens in line. And some terrorist groups are mercenaries, who are subsidized by one state to perform violent acts against a rival state. In such cases, the actor actually causing the political violence is best understood as a state, not a group. Such actions can be labeled *state-sponsored terrorism.*

With the proliferation of groups employing terrorist tactics, the wry observation has been made that "one person's terrorist is another person's freedom fighter." The root problem with using terrorism as an analytic concept is that it has become a powerful and negative label in political rhetoric. In the manipulative language of politics, the label is sometimes used regardless of the innocence of the victim, the identity of the actual sponsor of the violence, or the justifiability of the ends. It communicates a disgust for extreme political violence against innocent individuals, but it can also be used to discredit any group that uses violent means to achieve its political ends or to condemn a group whose political ends, as much as its means, are unacceptable. Ultimately, the issue centers in moral and political values: Are there *any* circumstances in which group political violence against individuals is justifiable? If so, what kinds of violence are acceptable under what circumstances?

Group Violence against a Group

Nation-based violence. When one group engages in political violence against another group, it is usually motivated by a deep animosity based on some element of the two groups' identities, such as ethnic or religious differences. Such nation-based violence is the source of most of the political violence occurring in the post–cold war period. Nearly all of the major military conflicts during this period have been within, not between, countries (Sivard 1996: 17). Nationality groups are increasingly mobilized to demand political autonomy, a process that is termed **ethnonationalism** (Connor 1994). Many of the groups are prepared to use political violence against other groups with whom they share territorial boundaries, generating an ethnic conflict that can be termed a "war of identity."

In some cases, one or more groups attempt to establish their own sovereign state based on national identity, a situation discussed later in the chapter as separatist violence. However, in many instances the nation-based groups are struggling against each other for political and cultural domination rather than for separation. The continuing violence between Hindus and Muslims in India (Box 5.3) is a revealing example of how the antipathy between nationality groups can poison the relations between them as they attempt to share a country, or even a remote village. Box 5.1 described the prolonged civil war (beginning in 1975) in the southern African country of Angola. More than 500,000 Angolans have died in the violence among three rival groups, each representing a different linguistic/ethnic region, that are attempting to control the entire country. In a strikingly similar pattern, the central African country of Chad has experienced a continuing nation-based internal war, with an estimated 400,000 deaths since independence in 1960. And the toll from a civil war in Sudan since 1983, between the Islamic north and the mainly Christian and animist south, is more than 1.5 million people—at least one in five southern Sudanese.

When group political violence entails the murder of many members of one ethnic group by its rival, the term *genocide* can be applied. The political system is often a partner in such situations, since its machinery of violence is employed by the dominant group. When the state organizes the campaign against an ethnic group, such genocide can be classified in Figure 11.1 as establishment violence. Twentieth-century examples of genocide include the killing of Armenians by the Turks (in 1915), of 6 million Jews by Hitler's Germany (1933–1945), of the Tutsis by the Hutus in Rwanda (1963–1964) and of the Hutus by the Tutsis in neighboring Burundi (1988), and of the Hmong by the Laotians (1976–1979). In the 1990s, the killing of nearly one million Tutsis in Rwanda and the Serbs's brutal destruction of civilian populations of Bosnians and of ethnic Albanians (in Kosovo), accompanied by their language of "ethnic cleansing," has renewed international concern about the prevention of genocide and the punishment of those who are responsible for it. Table 11.2 is suggestive of the massive toll in death and displaced refugees caused by some of the major ethnic conflicts during the last decade.

Class conflict.   In some cases, intergroup violence might be attributable to an underlying *class conflict* (Chapter 9). Often this class conflict is linked to an ethnic or religious cleavage. In Lebanon, Northern Ireland, and Sri Lanka, for example, one of the groups in the conflict has dominant social, economic, and political power over the others. Thus class theorists argue that the "real" conflict in many settings is not actually due to religion or language or ethnicity, but is the inevitable class struggle that emerges from stratification and inequality. Of course, class conflict can occur between any strata, such as the peasant class against the landlord class or the

TABLE 11.2
Deaths and Refugees Resulting from Recent Major Ethnic Conflicts

Country	Number Killed	Displaced Refugees
Sudan	1,500,000	4,300,000 +
Afghanistan	1,050,000	6,200,000
Rwanda	800,000	3,500,000 +
Myanmar	500,000	1,000,000 +
Colombia	250,000	1,000,000 +
Iraq	250,000	1,500,000 +
Algeria	100,000	105,000 +
Sri Lanka	70,000	900,000 +
Kashmir (India/Pakistan)	50,000	213,000

Source: Wright 1999: A15

capitalist class against the worker class, independent of any nation-based cleavage that might reinforce the distinction between conflicting classes. The group-based political violence in some Latin American countries, such as Colombia, Guatemala, and Mexico, seems best interpreted as a struggle between deeply unequal classes.

Individual or Group Violence against the State

Individual or group political violence directed against the political system can stem from several bases. At one extreme, such violence might be a spontaneous outburst of frustration with a person's or group's life conditions. At the other extreme, there might be such deep-seated hostility against the existing political system that the individual or group undertakes a lengthy series of violent actions in order to overthrow that political system.

Riot and rebellion. When political, social, or economic conditions become intolerable, frustration can escalate into demonstrations and civil disobedience and then into riots.

Riots are a sporadic and relatively disorganized form of such violence. They can involve group violence against property, against agents of the political system, against perceived opponents in the society, or against random targets. Riots often arise spontaneously out of a specific incident that is a catalyst for latent frustration. A riot might begin with an action by the police, such as the shooting of an individual, or with an economic problem, such as a sudden large increase in the price of basic foodstuffs. Once riots begin to occur, such political violence can spread as others within the society are motivated to demonstrate their dissatisfaction with the political system or social conditions.

Riots are expressions of frustration in which there is an implicit or explicit demand for redress of grievances. There is an expectation that the political system will perceive the nature of the grievances and will enact public policy that is responsive to the unmet demands. The basic demands might involve opposition to or support for certain public policies or political leaders. Black South Africans engaged in many riots in the ultimately successful opposition to apartheid during the 1980s. Similarly, widespread rioting by Indonesians led in 1998 to the fall of Suharto, ruler for more than thirty years.

Such political violence might be termed a *rebellion* when riots become more frequent, premeditated, and widespread and involve more people. At this point, many of those engaged in violence have lost faith in the likelihood that the system will respond to their problems. It is such a deterioration of citizen support and escalation of political action into political violence that is at the heart of Samuel Huntington's description of political decay (in Chapter 10).

The Palestinian Intifada ("uprising") is an example of a rebellion. Some leaders of the Palestinian movement decided that such a rebellion would be an effective intermediate strategy, since neither negotiations nor terrorism had resulted in their gaining an independent state on lands held by Israel. When the Intifada began in 1987, people of all ages were encouraged to participate in limited political violence, mainly using rocks but no firearms. The idea was that world opinion would be sympathetic to the underdog rock throwers who would be dealt with quite violently by the powerful Israeli military. Some scholars conclude that the Intifada is

Citizens' frustrations with the policies of the state can trigger public demonstrations that lead to violent confrontations, as in this street battle between South Korean students and workers and the state's riot police.

a key reason why Israel agreed to negotiate a home rule settlement with the Palestinians (Khalidi 1993).

Separatist violence.   At the heart of most nation-based violence is a struggle for autonomy—for the nationality group's right to control its own political and cultural destiny. Given the heightened politicization of nationality differences in the post–cold war world, when the desire for autonomy is strong and the existing political system seems unresponsive, groups increasingly engage in *separatist violence* to achieve their goal. If the separatist group is small and lacks political resources, the probable forms of political violence are acts of terrorism or attacks against specific individuals or structures within the political system. This characterizes the actions of the Irish Republican Army (IRA) throughout much of the twentieth century, as it attempted to separate Northern Ireland from the United Kingdom and establish a united Republic of Ireland. Targets of the IRA's bombs and murders have usually been the British "occupying army" and members of the Protestant paramilitary groups in Northern Ireland. Similar forms of separatist violence have characterized recent activities by Kurdish separatists against Turkey and Iraq, by East Timorese against Indonesia, by Chechens against Russia, by Sudan's southern Christians and animists against the Islamic rulers in the north, and by both Sikhs and Kashmiris against India.

In most colonial settings, violent uprisings against the colonial power have usually been one element in the political struggle for independence. In some cases, organization of the separatist violence has been weak or nonexistent. But in most cases, the separatist violence has been coordinated by an organized group, such as the Mau Mau versus the British in Kenya (1950s), the Muslim League versus the British and Hindus in the Indian subcontinent (late 1940s), and the Vietminh/Vietcong versus the French and then the Americans in Vietnam (1940s–1970s).

A **civil war** is the likely form of the political violence when *a significant proportion of the population in a region actively supports a separatist movement and political violence emerges on a large scale.* In the United States, the political leaders of the slaveholding Southern states decided that they no longer wished to maintain their participation in the American federation, and they announced that their states were seceding (withdrawing formal membership) from the federation. The central government rejected their request to secede, forcing eleven Southern states to declare their independence, create a confederation, and initiate a military struggle against the central government. In the bloody Civil War (1861–1865), the Union forces of the central government ultimately defeated the army of the Confederacy and forced the Southern states to remain in the federation.

A similar civil war occurred in Nigeria (1967–1970). The Ibo tribe, differing from other major tribes in religion, language, and political traditions, attempted to secede from the federation and create a separate state called Biafra. After four years of civil war and nearly one million deaths, the central government's army was victorious, and Biafra was stillborn as a state. In contrast, the Bengalis were successful in their separatist civil war against the central government of Pakistan (recall Box 5.3), and thus the new nation-state of Bangladesh was created (in 1971).

The devastating struggle among the Serbs, Bosnians, Croatians, and other nationality groups since the breakup of Yugoslavia in 1991 is a graphic example of separatist violence. Antipathy based on these groups' differences in ethnicity, history, language, and religion all reinforce their separate national identities (see Box 15.3). The widespread separatist violence resulted from the groups' efforts to determine precisely what states would emerge and where the boundaries between the states would be.

Coup. A **coup** occurs when *the top leader or part of the leadership group is replaced by violence or the explicit threat of violence.* There is no intention to overthrow the entire political-economic order, although the opposition to the existing leadership can be based on differences in policy preferences as well as on personal rivalry. This is a common form of leadership turnover in political systems that have no institutionalized procedures for leadership succession. Political violence against the top leadership group is typically organized by other members of the political leadership, by a rival political group, or by the military. In the postcolonial period, coups have been especially common in Latin American and African states. An extreme example is Bolivia, where 190 coups occurred over a 156-year period. Despite the enthusiasm with which many countries are democratizing their political systems in the post–cold war period, coups continue. Coups in the 1990s ousted the leaders of Algeria, Afghanistan, Burundi, Comoros, Congo (Brazzaville), Congo (former Zaire), Ethiopia, Gambia, Liberia, Mali, Niger, Pakistan, Sierra Leone, Somalia, Tajikistan, and Thailand.

Revolution. As Lennon (John, of the Beatles, that is) observed, "You say you want a revolution, well you know, we all want to change the world." In contrast to the other forms of political violence against the state, the explicit object of revolution is to destroy the existing political system. In a **revolution** there is *a rapid and fundamental transformation of the state organization and the class structure* (Skocpol 1979). The ultimate goal is to establish a new political system with a fundamentally different distribution of value allocations. The extent of transformation that must occur for "revolutionary" changes in the state organization, class structure, or distribution of values is sometimes difficult to specify (for reasons similar to those discussed in Chapter 5 for determining whether a political system has "died").

In many instances new leadership takes power, claiming that it will serve a new ideology and will allocate power and resources to new/different groups. When Colonel Muammar Qaddafi overthrew the hereditary king and installed a new revolutionary council committed to total egalitarianism (in 1969), it was clear that there had been a revolutionary change in the Libyan political system. But there are many instances where it is not clear whether the essential features of the political system have dramatically changed. This situation can occur either because the attempt to transform the political system is a charade or because it falls far short of its objectives. This issue will be considered further at the end of this section, in discussing the outcomes of the revolution. First, let us describe four broad strategies that can be employed to achieve a revolution.

Strategy 1: Terrorism. As a revolutionary strategy, *terrorism* involves selective acts of violence, usually by small organized cells of political activists. While an "innocent" might be the apparent target of this political violence, the state is the actual target. Terrorism is a strategy for a group that lacks sufficient membership and resources to sustain a direct struggle against the existing state.

Terrorists use violence to disrupt public life, by such means as bombings in public places, interrupting basic services such as electricity and food distribution, and disabling key political actors within the regime. Terrorists believe that these tactics might further their revolutionary objectives in two ways. First, the acts of terrorism might provoke harsh and repressive order-maintenance actions by the state, such as large-scale detention of citizens and crackdowns on opposition groups and opposition media. In this situation, terrorists assume, many citizens will become alienated as they see the "true" repressive nature of the political system. Second, terrorist acts might prevent the political system from effective allocation of such values as distribution of food, provision of transportation, and, most fundamentally, maintenance of public order. It is assumed that either repressive or ineffective state behavior will undermine citizen support for the system and decrease resistance to (and possibly even increase support for) revolutionary change.

The anticolonial resistance in Algeria is a clear example of the successful use of terrorism. A mixture of random public bombings, disruptions of infrastructure services, and violence against the agents of the colonial French led to a dramatic decline in the quality of life and provoked highly repressive responses from the political and military authorities. As conditions deteriorated, France decided to abandon the ungovernable country, whose anticolonial/terrorist leadership, under Ben Bella, formed a new political system. (Pontecorvo's powerful film, *The Battle of Algiers,* documents this period.)

Obviously, terrorism, like other revolutionary strategies, does not always produce the expected results. Often the terrorists are crushed without achieving any of their objectives, as was the case with terrorist groups in the United States in the 1960s, including the Weathermen and the Symbionese Liberation Army. And sometimes the repression evoked by terrorism merely makes things worse. The leftist terrorists in Iran were successful in destabilizing Shah Reza Pahlavi's regime, but it was the Islamic fundamentalists supporting the Ayatollah Khomeini who succeeded in grasping political power and forming a new fundamentalist political system even more unappeal-

BOX 11.2

Terrorism Makes It Worse: Uruguay

Between 1903 and the early 1960s, Uruguay became widely respected as the exemplary Latin American democracy (this discussion is based on Goodwin 2000). A stable two-party system was the basis of a liberal democratic government that facilitated increasing social welfare and economic prosperity. But political decay emerged in the 1960s, grounded in economic decline, high inflation, and governmental incompetence and corruption. These failures spawned the Tupamaros, an urban guerrilla group that engaged in widespread violence and terrorism to overthrow the state and establish a more just political order. This terrorism completely undermined the citizens' confidence that the political system could maintain order. The civilian government was overthrown, not by the Tupamaros but by the conservative military in a 1973 coup.

The Uruguayan military dictatorship then launched a massive campaign to suppress not only the Tupamaros, but all civilian opposition. During this period, Uruguay became known as "the torture chamber of Latin America," with widespread human and civil rights abuses. By 1979 more than 1 in 100 of all Uruguayans were political prisoners, estimated to be the highest proportion in the world. And one-sixth of the population (a half million people) were in exile. The economic crisis worsened under the military regime, with inflation of more than 60 percent and unemployment higher than 30 percent. When the military promoted a referendum on a new constitution in 1980, 60 percent of the population rejected it.

Eventually the military allowed elections, returning governmental power to civilian rule in March 1985. In a second election in 1989, the opposition political party regained power and the transfer of authority was smooth. Soon, political interest groups became active, press freedom was reestablished, and the independence of the judiciary was assured. Even the Tupamaros reemerged, not as a guerrilla movement but as a political party championing the interests of the poor.

There is considerable optimism that Uruguay has returned to its earlier, democratic ways. It has been classified as a "free," liberal democracy by Freedom House (1999) since 1985. Its population of 3.3 million enjoy nearly universal literacy and gook health care, and the society and economy have opened substantially as a consequence of Uruguay's membership in the regional free trade association (Mercosur). However, the military remains in the background, watching quietly for signs of disorder. The military vetoed the candidacy of the most popular presidential candidate in the 1994 election. And its security service continues extensive surveillance of key political and labor leaders as well as the media. The impacts of terrorism on democratic practice are still evident after nearly three decades.

ing to the leftists than the Shah's. The situation in Uruguay (see Box 11.2) is another example of revolutionary terrorism that backfired. Nonetheless, terrorism continues to be the only feasible strategy for certain revolutionary groups without widespread popular support, such as the Sendero Luminoso in Peru and FARC in Colombia.

Strategy 2: Revolution from above. The essence of the *revolution from above* is the swift overthrow of the elite. There are three key characteristics in revolution from above (Johnson 1966). First, activity is centered primarily in the urban capital. Second, some members of the existing political elite are usually supportive of the revolution and thus the existing political structures have to some extent been infiltrated by those who intend to create a new political system. Third, toleration or support of the revolution by the armed forces is important.

In this form of revolution, the old regime is eliminated in a few minutes or a few days. The revolutionaries might storm the leader's residence and capture or execute key figures of the old regime. Sometimes the revolutionary group takes control while the leader is away from the capital on business or pleasure. In either case, the new leadership uses the media to declare the elimination of the old leadership and the creation of a new political order, and then it proceeds to create new political institutions. A slow penetration of the new political system into the hinterlands outside the capital city follows.

Historically, many revolutions most closely resemble the revolution from above. The Russian Revolution is a version of this strategy, although the armed forces did not acquiesce to the change. This led to Trotsky's observation that if the forces of coercion are split, there will be civil war rather than a decisive revolutionary victory. Other twentieth-century examples of revolution from above include Gamal Abdel Nasser's replacement of King Farouk in Egypt (1952), Muammar Qaddafi's victory over King Idris in Libya (1969), the execution of communist Premier Nicholae Ceausescu in Romania (1989), and the flight of socialist leaders Mengistu Mariam in Ethiopia and Said Barre in Somalia (1991).

Strategy 3: Guerrilla war. The strategy of revolutionary guerrilla warfare has been highly refined in the twentieth century, especially during the Chinese Revolution. Guerrilla war contrasts with the revolution-from-above strategy in four crucial ways. First and most important, the essence of **guerrilla war** is *a long, protracted campaign of political violence against the state from rural bases,* although the fighting can be in both rural and urban areas. Second, it is a direct struggle against the military. The strategy, rather like that of the young boxer Muhammad Ali, is to "float like a butterfly and sting like a bee." The guerrilla's forces persistently harass the regime's army by fighting in a hit-and-run style, suddenly attacking an exposed point and then literally disappearing into the population and the countryside.

Third, there is an extensive and continuing effort to win the support of the peasants, mixing two techniques: (1) propaganda—promises of land reform and exhortations for resistance against domestic traitors and foreign invaders, and (2) terror—disrupting the village stability, eliminating local leaders loyal to the government, demanding food and shelter, and dragooning locals into the guerrilla army. China's Mao Zedong observed that if he had ten points to give for success in the revolution, he would award three points to the urban dwellers and the military and seven to the peasants, for "without the poor peasants, there can be no revolution."

Fourth, guerrilla warfare creates new political institutions *prior* to the collapse of the old regime. Ultimately, the guerrilla army defeats the regime's military and marches victoriously into the capital city, the previous leadership having fled or been killed. The leadership and political institutions developed in the countryside are empowered in the urban capital.

Many of the successful Third World revolutions in the last fifty years have employed the strategy of guerrilla warfare. With the Chinese Revolution as the model (victory in 1949), this strategy has been the method of revolutionary political violence in Cuba under Fidel Castro (1959), in Vietnam under Ho Chi Minh and his successors (1975), in Zimbabwe (formerly Rhodesia) under Robert Mugabe (1980), and in Nicaragua under the Sandinistas (1979). It is evident in recent struggles in Afghanistan, Algeria, Colombia, and Congo. Guerrilla war directly contradicts two key principles of the Marxist-Leninist-Trotskyist conception of revolution. First, it undermines the principle that revolution emanates from the urban proletariat. Second, it rejects the view that revolution cannot be made against the elite's armed forces.

Strategy 4: "Democratic" revolution. There is also a strategy for *democratic revolutionary change.* In this case, legal, nonviolent political action is effectively mounted to achieve a fundamental transformation of the political system. In one form, the population uses the democratic electoral process to select a new leadership elite, which then dismantles the existing political system and creates a new one. This form might describe the rise of Hitler and the establishment of the *Third Reich* in Germany (1933), the election of Salvador Allende's Marxist government in Chile (1970), and the election of the anti-Sandinista coalition in Nicaragua (1990).

In a second form of democratic revolution, widespread but generally nonviolent resistance to a regime forces the elite to resign. The new leadership, although not initially elected, implements fundamental transformations in the political system. This occurred in such Soviet bloc states as Czechoslovakia, East Germany, and Poland in the late 1980s. When Soviet leader Gorbachev indicated that the Soviet Union would no longer support unpopular leadership groups, citizens in these states participated in mass demonstrations against the existing communist governments. With a minimum of violence, the regimes rapidly collapsed and the repressive, one-party communist states were replaced by more democratic, multiparty systems. (The revolutions in Central and Eastern Europe are discussed further in Chapter 15.)

The conditions for revolution. The conditions under which political revolution occurs is an issue that has fascinated many people, especially those who want to analyze revolution and those who want to lead a successful revolution. Many different explanations are offered to account for the occurrence of revolution. The most widely cited studies of major historical revolutions include those by Hannah Arendt (1963), Crane Brinton (1957), Chalmers Johnson (1966), Barrington Moore (1966), and Theda Skocpol (1979). The revolutions in postcolonial states are analyzed in works by Joel Migdahl (1974) and Eric Wolf (1969).

One long-standing explanation of revolution is the "theory of rising expectations," associated with Alexis de Tocqueville (1835/1945), James Davies (1971), and others. In this view, the key cause of revolution is a sudden growth in the disparity between the values that the population expects to enjoy from the government and the actual value distribution the population receives. Contemporary research calls this the "J-curve" theory because, as is indicated in Figure 11.2, the disparity resembles an inverted J. At the point where this gap between expected and actual values becomes substantial, political violence emerges and can escalate into rebellion and then revolution. Although this explanation is intuitively appealing, most scholars find the empirical research testing the J-curve to be unconvincing. In particular, it has been difficult to establish the size of the gap that provokes revolutionary violence, and the approach does not specify which or how economic, social, and political conditions are crucial.

Although the various theories of revolution present evident differences in the specific causes and dynamic process, most theories of contemporary revolutions share certain commonalities (Hagopian 1984: ch. 6). First, the state has experienced *broad, destabilizing forces* that have affected the culture, the economy, or the political system. These might include the decline of traditional social and religious values, the emergence of a modern state, a transformation of the economic system, social mobilization (recall Chapter 10), or the global expansion of capitalism into a world economic system. Second, there are more *direct and immediate forces of disruption,* such as violent conflict with another state, major economic decline, serious financial problems for the state, or incompetence or division within the ruling elite.

The outcome of revolution. Since the ultimate objective of revolution is a fundamental transformation in the political system, an assessment of the outcomes of revolutions is at least as important as an analysis of causes and processes. Many scholars still distinguish the three postrevolutionary phases identified by Crane Brinton (1957), based on his extraordinary study of the French Revolution of 1789:

1. *Rule of the moderates.* After the revolution, the leadership group that comes to power attempts to fashion a new political order, but not to use governmental power to transform drastically the social and economic system. Often the moderates are committed to increasing the democratic nature of politics in the society.

2. *Rule of the radicals.* The moderates are displaced by more ideological and aggressive political groups. These radical groups want to use political power to implement a far more extensive transformation of society, including greater centralization of political and economic power in the state. The radicals also direct substantial and continuing political violence against any groups who are viewed as obstacles to this transformation.

3. *Reaction and moderation.* At some point, a new set of moderates regains control from the radical groups. There are various reasons why the radicals might lose control: They might destroy each other through internal struggles over power or ideology; the revolutionary violence might become so extreme that there is insuf-

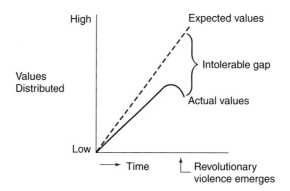

Figure 11.2   "J-curve" description of revolution
SOURCE: Derived from Davies 1971.

ficient popular support to sustain the radicals; or the new entrenched elite might begin to enjoy the privileges associated with power and lose its revolutionary fervor. At this point, the "old regime" is dead, but the resulting political system is far less extreme than that during the rule of the radicals.

Brinton's three-phase model of outcomes is grounded in the French Revolution; but it does not fit many revolutions, especially those in the post–World War II world. First, in many recent revolutions, initial rule by moderates is either fleeting or nonexistent. The groups who seize power after many of the revolutionary guerrilla wars in peasant societies come to power committed to move quickly into a phase that resembles the rule by radicals. This was certainly true in such postrevolutionary states as Cambodia, China, Cuba, and Vietnam. Extremist groups have also taken immediate control in many countries where religious fundamentalist groups seized power, as in Iran, Libya, and the Sudan.

Second, in many states, the third-phase shift to moderation either is limited or emerges only very gradually. Rather, the new society forged during the radical phase is institutionalized, at least for as long as the revolutionary leadership remains in power. Sometimes there is an alternation between periods of significant revisionism and renewed radicalism. Fidel Castro reveals the persistent commitment to radicalism of most such leaders with his 1992 comment: "The revolution is like a bicycle; it has brakes but no reverse." However, with the death or replacement of the initial radical leadership, moderate leadership does seem to emerge in many post–cold war states. This has been the case in China, Iran, Mozambique, and Vietnam, among others. In an era of expanding democratization, the key question is whether a transformation to more democratic and moderate politics will follow phase three.

EVALUATING POLITICAL VIOLENCE: MEANS AND ENDS

Political violence must be understood as a failure of institutionalized political action. A strong and persuasive normative perspective contends that political violence is unacceptable, deviant behavior. Conservative ideology provides the most explicit condemnation of such violence. For the conservative, the only legacy of violence is to undermine order in the society. Moreover, the resort to violence is part of an erroneous belief that radical social change can lead to lasting improvements. As Englishman Edmund Burke (1729–1797) observed: "Time is required to produce that union of minds which alone can produce all the good we aim at. Our patience will achieve more than our force" (Burke 1790/1955: 197).

A contrary perspective argues that political violence is often the best or even the only mechanism for liberation from oppression and tyranny. This view contends that most societies are controlled by dominant elites who manipulate the state to serve their interests, not the collective good. If a government and its leaders refuse to be constrained by a limited mandate and are not responsive to the citizens, then the people have the right to overthrow them by any available means. Although this perspective is mainly associated with class theorists and Marxist ideology, the counterpoint to Burke is provided by another English political thinker, classical liberal John Locke (1632–1704), who argued that citizens create government to protect their rights to life, liberty, and property. If the existing government does not serve these purposes well, argued Locke, the people can and must revolt in order to replace tyranny and create a new and better government (Locke 1690/1963: 466).

Political violence can be either a source of progress or a source of nearly universal suffering and chaos. Clearly, there are fundamental issues about means and ends tied up with one's personal assessment of political violence. On the one hand, if the maintenance of public order and political institutionalization are valued goals, one must consider whether the resort to political violence undermines longer-term prospects for peaceful, orderly governance. Many cynics would share Italian novelist Ignazio Silone's (1937) assessment: "Every revolution begins as a movement of liberation but ends as tyranny." On the other hand, if you value social and political justice, it is important to consider whether the processes of political violence can be a legitimate means of last resort to ensure such justice. Those who justify some forms of political violence might sympathize with African-American Eldridge Cleaver's claim that "a slave who dies of natural causes will not balance two dead flies of the scale of eternity."

There are no tidy answers to the question of whether or when political violence is justifiable. Perhaps one way to organize your own assessment of political violence is to reflect on three basic questions:

1. Are the means of political violence unacceptable under all circumstances?

2. If you answered no, could an outcome emerge from the use of political violence that is so preferable to the existing situation that establishing the precedent of using political violence is justifiable?

3. If you answered yes to question 2, what specific circumstances would be necessary to justify the resort to political violence?

In the current technological era, the mechanisms for violence are more efficient, powerful, and horrifying than at any time in human history. The implications of this fact are especially evident in the relations between states, which is a topic of Chapter 12. But even subnational political groups can now inflict massive and destructive political violence. Thus, questions about the balance between liberation and destruction have never been more pressing at any time in human history.

FOR FURTHER CONSIDERATION

1. Is the state more to be feared than its enemies? Assess the implications of the predominance during the twentieth century of "death by government" in which the state is the actor and the state's citizens are its target.

2. Summarize the key elements of a three-way debate between an absolute pacifist, a committed revolutionary, and yourself regarding the conditions under which political violence is justifiable.

3. It is suggested that much of the contemporary political violence is nation based. Analyze the nation-based conflicts about which you have some awareness. Is most of the violence caused by fundamental antipathy between two nationality groups due to differences in ethnicity, religion, language, and so on? Or is

the violence primarily motivated by other issues, such as inequality and class conflict, quest for power, or some other cause?

4. Must every revolution end in tyranny (à la Ignazio Silone)? Can you identify a revolution that, by the criteria you establish, can be viewed as a success?

FOR FURTHER READING

Aguila, Juan D. del. (1988). *Cuba: Dilemmas of a Revolution.* Boulder, CO: Westview Press. Pessimistic observations of a famous revolution by a former minister of the Castro government, now an exile.

Goldstone, Jack A., Ed. (1994). *Revolutions: Theoretical, Comparative and Historical Studies.* 2d ed. San Diego, CA: Harcourt Brace. A readable set of articles that includes both detailed case studies of revolutions and more analytic work that attempts to develop generalizations about revolutionary violence.

Gourevitch, Philip. (1998). *We Wish to Inform You that Tomorrow We Will be Killed with our Families: Stories from Rwanda.* New York: Farrar & Giroux. A gripping exploration of the manner in which ethnonationalism was used to mobilize the Hutu people to massacre almost one million Tutsis and Hutu moderates in Rwanda in the mid-1990s, while the international community was unwilling to intervene to prevent the genocide.

Hoffman, Bruce. (1998). *Inside Terrorism.* New York: Columbia University Press. A broad-ranging and troubling exploration of terrorism, with particular attention to the recent evolution of strategies and goals of terrorists.

Johnson, Chalmers. (1966). *Revolutionary Change.* Boston: Little, Brown. A thorough and interesting characterization of the different forms of revolution.

Walter, Barbara F., and Jack Snyder, Eds. (1999). *Civil Wars, Insecurity, and Intervention.* New York: Columbia University Press. Centering on thoughtful case studies of the recent civil wars in Bosnia, Cambodia, Somalia, and Rwanda, important scholars analyze why the international community has not been particularly effective in preventing either the outbreak or the resolution of civil wars.

Weiss, Peter. (1965). *Marat-Sade: The Persecution and Assassination of Jean-Paul Marat as Performed by the Inmates of the Asylum at Charenton under the Direction of the Marquis de Sade.* New York: Atheneum. A brilliant play (and a dazzling film with the same title directed by Peter Brooks) offering a debate about revolution between Jean-Paul Marat, a leader of the French Revolution who attempts to retain his idealism about revolutionary change despite having become a victim of the "rule of radicals," and the Marquis de Sade, the ultimate cynic. Their debate occurs as a play-within-a-play, in an asylum where both have been committed.

PART 5

Politics Among States

Let's hook up! The political leaders of the countries in the Association of Southeast Asian Nations (ASEAN) offer a picture of unity and cooperation during an informal summit meeting in the Philipppines. The countries represented are (from the left): Laos, Indonesia, Malaysia, Myanmar, Philippines, Singapore, Thailand, Cambodia, Brunei, and Vietnam.

CHAPTER 12

Politics between States

Imagine an island state, Buena, blessed with temperate climate and rich natural resources that provide sufficient food and other necessities for the population. A few hundred miles to the south is a similar island, Malo; but Malo is cold and windy and has few resources to support its population. Each island is located about fifty miles off a large landmass composed of several states.

If you knew nothing more about either state, could you make any educated guesses about the political and economic relations of each with the other state and with the states on the large landmass?

In considering the relations between these states, many issues might emerge, including these: Is either island state more needful of trading relations with outsiders? Does either state have strong reasons to protect itself from intervention by outsiders? How could such protection be accomplished? If either state establishes a military, what kind of forces would make most sense? What kind of political alliance would each state be most likely to forge (with states on the landmass or with each other)?

One traditional method of thinking analytically about states is based on precisely these kinds of assessments. This method of **geopolitics** assumes that the geography of a state—that is, its physical characteristics (e.g., location, topography) and its natural and human resources (e.g., population size, fossil fuel resources, arable land, water)—might significantly affect the politics of the state (Parker 1998).

While only a few argue that "geography is destiny," it does seem reasonable to assume that a state's geography can be the source of both opportunities and constraints on its actions. Consider, for example, the effects on a state of conditions such as insufficient domestic food production, abundant fossil fuel resources, a small population relative to land area, the absence of any natural barriers separating the state from surrounding states, being snowbound eight months per year, enormous variation in yearly rainfall, or strategic location in a major international shipping lane.

It should also be obvious that other important features within its boundaries besides physical setting and resources might powerfully affect the state's behavior toward other political systems. Among the important features are the state's political culture, the style of its major political leaders, and the nature of its political structures.

The poet John Donne wrote, "No man is an island, entire of itself, every man is a piece of a continent." In the contemporary political world, it is clear that not even an island is insulated from the world around it. Indeed, our imaginary Buena and Malo (or actual islands such as Cuba, the Falkland Islands, Great Britain, Haiti, or Japan) will find that their politics are heavily dependent on what other states are doing. In the model of the political system in Chapter 5, this point is made explicitly in the concept of the extrasocietal environment. The behavior of every political system is affected not only by its own characteristics but also by the actions of some political systems outside its boundaries, as well as by other types of external systems, such as economic, cultural, demographic, and social systems in other states or in the international system as a whole.

Most contemporary states expend much, and in some cases most, of their political energy on their relations with other states. When we analyze the decisions and actions of the individual state relative to other states, it is termed the study of *foreign policy.* When the *interactions* among two or more states are studied, such decisions and actions are termed *international relations.*

This chapter examines the relations between the political system and its extrasocietal environment, with particular emphasis on the interactions among states. First, the major goals pursued by all states are detailed. Second, there is a discussion of the means by which states can attempt to facilitate cooperation and resolve conflict with each other. Third, key forms of interstate competition, such as balance of power and colonial domination, are examined. The final section of the chapter considers the nature and causes of political violence between states.

THE GOALS OF STATES
Realist and Idealist Perspectives on the State's "Motives"

To understand how states behave in relation to other states, one reasonable approach is to identify what motivates states. From this perspective, states can be analyzed, almost like individuals, as having motives and values that they attempt to pursue in the international environment. However, the context within which the states exist is different than that for individuals, because most analysts assume that the politics between states occurs in an international system that is *anarchic.* This does not mean that the system is chaotic. Rather, it means that there is no overarching authority that can impose order and "good behavior" on all the states in their relations with each other. Scholars attempt to explain how and why states interact in the ways that they do, in the absence of such an authority. Among the theoretical perspectives that posit different motivations of states, two perspectives have especially influenced international relations theory: political realism and political idealism.

Political realism assumes that people are naturally disposed to behave selfishly. This same selfishness extends to the behavior of the states that people form. In the international system, there is no supreme authority that protects the states from each other. Thus the fundamental goal of each state is to ensure its own security and survival. Its security increases to the extent it maximizes its own power (e.g., economic power, knowledge power, and especially military power), relative to the power of every other state. States are in constant competition for power, especially because power is a "zero-sum" commodity—that is, an increase in power for one actor results in an equivalent decrease for another. There is no expectation that another state can be trusted, will avoid violence, or will act ethically. A state makes treaties or breaks them, makes war or cooperates with other countries for only one reason: to maximize its security goals.

In contrast, the crucial assumption of **political idealism** is that human nature *is* basically good. People, and the states they construct, can be altruistic and cooperative. States have many goals, and aggressive, power-maximizing behavior is not inevitable. If a state's actions reduce the welfare of people in any country or increase interstate conflict and war, it is usually because of poorly designed institutions (e.g., governments, economic systems, legal systems), not because people are evil or selfish. For the political idealist, it is possible to establish an international system in which well-designed institutions can facilitate cooperative behavior among states creating a situation that is "positive sum"—everyone is better off.

It is obvious that realism and idealism (and their recent elaborations, neorealism and neoliberalism, respectively) lead to very different explanations of a state's behavior toward other states (Kegley 1995; Keohane and Nye 1989; Waltz 1979). They also provide contrasting prescriptions about how a state ought to respond to the actions of another state. Are you strongly oriented toward the realist or the idealist perspective? You might consider how the assumptions of realism or idealism alter one's interpretations of the topics in this chapter.

Major Goals

What major goals might a state pursue? The political system of each state attributes different levels of relative importance to the wide variety of goals. However, crucial political goals of virtually all political systems can be subsumed under three overarching goals: *security, stability,* and *prosperity.* Each of these three goals includes component goals that the political system might act to serve. The significance of each component goal and the capacity of the political system to achieve each goal depend on many factors. These include the state's relative tendency toward a realist or idealist orientation and other elements noted earlier (e.g., the state's geopolitical situation, history, culture, leaders, political structures, and interactions with other states). Figure 12.1 illustrates this framework of basic goals. In the lists that follow, major components of each overarching goal are presented in the general order of their priority for most states.

Security

1. *Survival* is the fundamental element of security. It entails the very existence of the state, such that other states do not conquer it and absorb it.
2. *Autonomy* refers to the capacity of the state to act within its own boundaries without intervention into or control of its affairs by other states.
3. *Influence* involves the state's ability to alter the actions of other states in desired ways, by means of persuasion or the use of inducements.
4. *Prestige* is the desirable situation wherein other states admire and respect the state.
5. *Dominance* is the use of power or violence to enable the state to impose direct control over other states.

Stability

1. *Order maintenance* is the capacity of the state to ensure social peace for its citizens through the prevention of individual and group violation of societal norms, especially those involving violence.

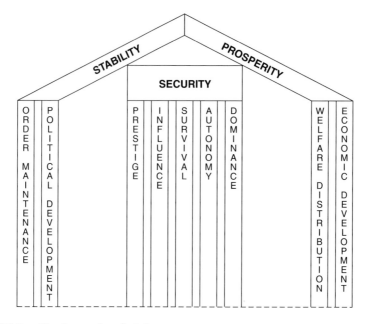

Figure 12.1 Basic goals of states

2. *Political development* refers, as in Samuel Huntington's conception of institutionalization (recall Chapter 10), to the concentration of political authority in a state that has strong capabilities to make and enforce effective policies and to gain support from its citizens.

Prosperity

1. *Economic development* refers both to (a) the increasing scale, complexity, and specialization of the productive system and of the goods produced; and (b) the capacity of the political economy to obtain, manage, and transform resources into valued goods.

2. *Welfare distribution* refers to the private or public allocation of adequate and increasing levels of valued goods to enhance the quality of life of the citizenry.

Few, if any, states can fully achieve their desired level on even one of these nine major goals, and the pursuit of multiple goals entails difficult trade-offs. In an obvious example, expansion of the welfare goods and services allocated to the citizenry is costly and absorbs resources that might otherwise be reinvested in the economic system to facilitate economic development. This trade-off is often referred to as the fundamental policy choice of "growth versus welfare." Also, resources allocated to the military for major security goals are not available for either welfare or for economic development. The policy trade-off between security and welfare is often characterized by the phrase "guns versus butter."

Notice that Figure 12.1 gives particular priority to security goals. While survival must be a fundamental goal of a country, the centrality of security goals in the diagram can be interpreted as particularly influenced by realist thinking. It is certainly possible that in some states the prosperity goals or the stability goals might be more important than some of the security goals, such as dominance. Of the nine major goals listed in Figure 12.1, which sets do you think are most complementary? Most competitive?

The politics between most states, most of the time, are characterized by cooperation or competition. The next two sections explore these dominant patterns in international relations. In most instances, there are more benefits and fewer costs to a state if it pursues its goals without the use of force against other states. However, the competition between states can escalate into conflict. Thus the final section examines those crucial situations where conflict resolution fails, resulting in interstate violence.

MECHANISMS OF COOPERATION BETWEEN STATES
Diplomacy and Interstate Agreements

Do you agree with the proposition that, under most circumstances, a state is likely to accomplish more of its goals at lower costs if it can develop mutually advantageous cooperative arrangements with other states? From the neoliberal (contemporary idealist) perspective, a state will have an inherent preference to establish arrangements through which such cooperation be nurtured. Realists are likely to be more cynical about such cooperation, viewing such agreements as strategic ones to be made or broken as they serve the state's national interest.

States formalize and coordinate their interactions through many mechanisms, the most widespread being *diplomacy*. Diplomatic practices developed so that a state's own skilled representatives could engage in regular discussion and negotiation with the representatives of other states. Thus most states maintain an array of actors (e.g., ambassadors, cultural attachés) and institutions (e.g., embassies, trade delegations) whose objectives are to further interests shared with other states and to resolve potential problems by means of "normal diplomatic channels" and informal communications.

The essence of traditional diplomacy is sensitive and strategic face-to-face discussions between diplomats on behalf of their countries. However, modern communications technologies (e.g., videoconferencing) have provided new modes of interactions between leaders as well as diplomats, who can deal with each other directly, even if not in person. An interesting example of these new hybrids is "teleplomacy"—the use of broadcast television as a means for high-level communications between states. In an example during the Gulf War, Libya's leader, Muammar Qaddafi, telephoned Cable News Network (CNN) and requested that he be allowed to propose a peace settlement on television. CNN staff hung up on Qaddafi several times, assuming it was a crank call. Finally, the Libyan ambassador contacted CNN to verify that it was Qaddafi on the telephone. Now CNN recognized its opportunity for a scoop. Soon Qaddafi was explaining his plan to the world on live television from his tent in Tripoli.

More explicit cooperation among states is usually established by bilateral (between two states) or multilateral (among three or more states) agreements. Distinctions are sometimes made between three forms of these agreements: alliances, treaties, and regimes. *Alliances* are informal or formal agreements between states that they will cooperate or assist each other militarily, economically, or politically. **Treaties** are also interstate agreements which deal with the same areas but tend to be more formal and legalistic, and there is a stronger expectation of compliance.

These agreements can range from a rather straightforward arrangement for a cultural exchange between two friendly nations to a complex nuclear-arms reduction pact between many hostile states. Most alliances and treaties involve a limited set of countries. For example, the North American Free Trade Agreement (NAFTA) is a treaty between three neighboring states to cooperate on a complex set of trade arrangements. And the European Union (EU), described in Box 12.1, is an example of a multistate, multipurpose confederation for economic, political, cultural, and military cooperation among fifteen European nations with a combined population of more than 350 million. Examples of security pacts are the North Atlantic Treaty Organization (NATO) and the Strategic Arms Reduction Treaties (START II, 1993, between the United States and Russia).

Some of the agreements are also called **international regimes** to signify *a set of norms, rules, and procedures, accepted by many countries, that guide their behavior regarding a particular issue* area such as international trade (e.g., the World Trade Organization [WTO, previously GATT]), or arms control (e.g., the Nuclear Non-proliferation Treaty, 1968, now including 163 countries), or environmental protection (e.g., the Montreal Protocol on the ozone layer). Many international regimes establish a permanent organization through which the member states can enact, modify, and implement the agreements.

The direct, day-to-day interactions among most states are substantially governed by alliances, treaties, and regimes. Like other forms of international cooperation, such agreements are binding only as long as the participating states are willing to abide by the conditions of the agreement or are willing to submit disputes to some form of resolution. But such agreements can collapse.

- First, some participants might find their national goals are not well served and the agreement is ignored or violated. Thus, for example, the needs of particular Organization of Petroleum Exporting Countries (OPEC) member states for additional revenue have resulted in violations of the interstate agreements on production and pricing.

- Second, participants can disagree on what actions are acceptable. After the Persian Gulf War, the United States (usually backed by the United Nations) repeatedly accused Iraq of violating elements of the peace treaty relating to the dismantling of its chemical and nuclear weapons capabilities, while Iraq insisted that it was complying with the agreements and that the United States was violating Iraq's sovereignty.

- Third, fulfillment of the key objectives in an agreement might be impossible. For example, the Treaty of Locarno (1925) between Britain and Italy failed in its attempt to deter Germany from violating the borders of France and Belgium, because Britain and Italy were not strong enough to counteract the reemergence and assertion of Germany's military power, and Italy's national interest eventually became more pro-German.

International Law

The broadest attempt to formalize and constrain the interactions among states is **international law**. In 1625 Hugo Grotius, the "father" of international law, published *De jure belli et pacis* (On the Laws of War and Peace) (Grotius 1625/1957).

BOX 12.1

The More We Are Together: The European Union

According to some observers, the Soviet Union is dead and the United States is in long-term decline, but there is a new giant emerging in the world. It was born in the 1950s, when West European countries battered by World War II developed three cooperative communities regarding interstate trade, atomic energy, and coal and steel production. The underlying objectives were mutual self-help in economic redevelopment and military defense. It has evolved from a loose alliance into a powerful confederation that is the largest and wealthiest single consumer market in the world.

The original "Six" (Belgium, France, Germany, Italy, Luxembourg, and the Netherlands) added six more countries during the 1970s and 1980s (Denmark, Greece, Ireland, Portugal, Spain, and the United Kingdom) and three more during the 1990s (Austria, Finland, and Sweden). At least fifteen other European countries, including Hungary, Turkey, and Poland, are somewhere in the membership application process. This European Union (EU) now includes more than 375 million people and a combined GNP of more than $7 trillion per year, greater in both population and economic product than its nearest rival, the NAFTA (North American Free Trade Agreement) group of Canada, Mexico, and the United States.

In the vision of its strongest proponents, the EU is becoming a true *supranational organization*—an international organization with autonomous policy-making and implementation powers over national states that have ceded considerable sovereignty and have agreed to abide by its collective decisions, even when those decisions are not in the state's own national interest. The scope of EU decisions will cover a vast array of policies that would normally be controlled by national political systems. In economic terms, this means that the EU is a single economic market in which people, money, and goods flow freely without regard to national borders. In military terms, there will be a common foreign policy and joint armed forces under a single command. And in political terms, the goal is a "United States of Europe" with an elected European Parliament that passes legislation binding on all citizens, a Council of Ministers operating as a collective executive under a president, a Court of Justice serving as the interpreter and enforcer of laws that supersede the laws of individual countries, and a large administrative branch of Eurocrats applying the laws.

All of the key elements of the EU are now in place, including the elected European Parliament of more than 600 delegates and all the other institutions previously described. As examples of the shared policies, there is now a common European passport and a common currency, the euro. Every country has been obliged to convert to the metric system. And labor and capital move freely between countries. However, some member countries are not prepared to concede a substantial share of their sovereignty to the EU, resisting compliance on key issues that are perceived to affect their national interest. There have been continuing problems with fiscal policy, tax structure, and agricultural policy. Disagreements on foreign policy have also been evident, especially regarding the level of military involvement in the Gulf War and in the conflicts between Serbia and both Bosnia and the ethnic Albanians of Kosovo.

(continued)

BOX 12.1 (Continued)

After its indecisive response to the Gulf War, Belgium's Foreign Minister Mark Eyskens observed that Europe "is an economic giant, a political dwarf, and a military worm" (Kegley and Wittkopf 1997: 165). The EU's role as an economic giant is somewhat tempered by the ongoing squabbles among member states unwilling to sacrifice sovereignty to it. If it does achieve political and military unanimity of action as well, the EU will be the undisputed superpower in the world.

Despite its failure to achieve complete union and unanimity of action in all cases, it is clear that the EU is now a formidable player in international politics (see Box 13.3 on the relative power of the EU, Japan, and the United States). Ironically, as more European countries achieve membership, the power of the EU might be diluted rather than enhanced because it will be more difficult to achieve consensus on major issues. The evolution of cooperative arrangements within the EU is one of the most fascinating and important developments for international relations in the early, twenty-first century world. (Discussion based on Nugent 1999; Kegley and Wittkopf 1995.)

This document emphasized **natural law**—sensible forms of behavior that ought to guide the relations among states and restrain hostile or destructive interactions.

Unfortunately, "sensible" action is often defined by a state's political needs and is uncommon when deep disagreements or violence emerge between states. Thus, by the nineteenth century, natural law had been supplanted by **positivist law—** *explicit written agreements which define both appropriate and unacceptable behaviors between states*, in the form of international treaties or conventions. Positivist laws have attempted to adjudicate geographic boundaries (e.g., the three-mile limit on the waters around states), to regulate states' use of environmental resources (e.g., laws limiting whale hunting in international waters), and to establish states' right and limits over nonnational resources (e.g., the law of outer space).

The treaties and conventions of positivist law even attempt to distinguish acceptable from unacceptable behavior during conflicts between states. For example, the Helsinki Agreement binds the combatants to use no glass-filled projectiles or other forms of violence that produce "unnecessary suffering." The Geneva Convention on "fair" war prohibits the use of poison gases and insists that captured soldiers be treated with dignity, although it does not preclude most of the terrible forms of suffering or death that a soldier can experience before she becomes a prisoner. Recently, there has been particular attention to the use of international law to arrest and prosecute political leaders and others who are directly responsible for the deaths of large numbers of people from other nationality groups, as in the actions against the leaders of the Kurds (Abdullah Ocalan) and of the Serbs (Slobodan Milosevic), each accused of "crimes against humanity" (Gutman and Rieff 1999). While positivist law has the great advantage of being formulated in explicit written agreements, such agreements ultimately depend on the willingness of states to comply. Some states refuse to sign particular agreements, sometimes signatories openly violate the agreements, and states often deny accusations that they have violated the agreements.

The International Court of Justice (the World Court) at The Hague can rule on alleged violations of positivist law, but the court has jurisdiction and binding decision authority only if both parties to the dispute accept its ruling. The court has occasionally provided a valuable mechanism for conflict resolution. But when the political or economic stakes are high or even when emotional elements of the disagreement are intense, states typically refuse to accept the court's jurisdiction or to be bound by its judgments.

One study found that the World Court considered only sixty-four cases during the forty-five years ending in 1991, that advisory opinions were given in only nineteen cases, and that very few cases actually concerned violent conflicts between states (Riggs and Plano 1994). And only 29 percent of the United Nations' 184 member states have agreed to accept automatically the court's jurisdiction in matters affecting them; most of these have added qualifications to their acceptance. The United States is among the member states that reject the court's jurisdiction, as in a 1984 case regarding covert U.S. actions against the Nicaraguan government (such as mining Nicaraguan harbors). In fact, juridical resolution between states is more likely to be found in the domestic court system of one of the disputants rather than in an international court.

An intriguing question: Is it reasonable for a state to refuse the court's jurisdiction? What do you think would happen to international politics if all states automatically accepted the court's jurisdiction?

International Organizations

International organizations is a broad term for many of the overarching institutional mechanisms whose objectives are to influence the behavior and policies of states. Some of these international organizations attempt to prevent or resolve conflict among states, although most focus on a specific issue area within the full range of economic, social, environmental, cultural, and political concerns that have global significance. There are two primary types of international organizations.

The first type are international NGOs (INGOs), a transnational version of **NGOs**—nongovernmental organizations. NGOs are associations which are not actually part of the governmental apparatus in a country, but which work actively to promote public policies and even to provide services, programs and information that might otherwise be provided by government. Between 1960 and 2000, the number of INGOs active in at least three countries rose from 1,000 to more than 30,000. This includes about 5,000 major INGOs with global reach that distribute important services and sometimes have a significant impact on the policies of states (Weiss 1996). The members of these INGOs are committed to furthering issues with transnational dimensions (e.g., Amnesty International's concern with protection of human rights, the animal preservation goals of the World Wildlife Federation, the humanitarian medical services provided by Doctors without Borders, and the lobbying to control destructive technologies by the Union of Concerned Scientists). Although their issues tend to be regional or global, the actions and effectiveness of these INGOs can be analyzed in the same framework applied to national interest groups (in Chapter 3).

Second, there is an extremely important group of actors called **intergovernmental organizations (IGOs)** whose members are states, not private groups or individuals. Although there are currently less than 300 IGOs, they have vast potential to shape the relations among states, some or all of whom are their members.

States jointly establish these IGOs to provide a forum of communication between states, to implement policies that respond to problems transcending national boundaries, to enact international laws and treaties, and to intervene in disputes between states. Some of the treaties, alliances, and international regimes discussed earlier in this chapter (e.g., the European Union, NAFTA, NATO) can be classified as IGOs.

The most powerful and wide-ranging IGOs in the twentieth century have been two major international organizations—the League of Nations and the United Nations. The League of Nations was formed in 1921 as a mechanism for collective security against aggression. But aggression by Italy in Ethiopia and by Japan in Manchuria in the 1930s revealed that the League lacked the diplomatic, political, or military power to achieve its goal.

After World War II, the United Nations was created (in 1946) as another attempt at international organization. While the United Nations (UN) has a mixed record of success and failure in its central objective of keeping the peace, it *has* improved the international political climate during its more than fifty-year history. At the least, the United Nations has been a highly effective setting within which rivals can engage in continuing diplomacy. UN officials and representatives from various countries can attempt to mediate conflicts and prevent escalation to war. The UN can also pass resolutions that might constrain certain countries from acting in opposition to the moral force of international public opinion.

Most directly, a *United Nations peacekeeping force* can intervene between combatants. This is a multinational military and civilian force, authorized by the Security Council with the consent of the disputing parties. The peacekeeping force literally stands between the combatants and uses force only in defense. During the cold war the United States and the Soviet Union used their veto power in the Security Council to block many peacekeeping initiatives that the UN might have undertaken. Nonetheless, more than a dozen UN peacekeeping operations were deployed between 1948 and 1988, including forces between India and Pakistan in 1949 and again since 1965, in the Congo in 1960, between the Greeks and the Turks in Cyprus since 1964, and on the border between Israel and Lebanon since 1978. In such cases, the UN troops patrol a cease-fire line while the states attempt to negotiate a peace agreement. Ironically, while the presence of the UN usually prevents the escalation of political violence, it also lowers the incentives for the opponents to reach a workable peace agreement. For example, the UN forces have been trying to keep the peace between India and Pakistan in the border region of Kashmir for more than fifty years.

By its various actions, the United Nations has contributed to what former UN Secretary-General Dag Hammarskjold (1953–1961) termed "preventive diplomacy"—limiting the extensive political and military involvement of major powers during conflicts between other countries. In 1988 the UN peacekeeping operations were awarded the Nobel Peace Prize.

In the post–cold war period (beginning in the late 1980s), the UN's role seems to be expanding. The source of one global police force, the Soviet Union, has disintegrated. The other, the United States, has promoted a "new world order" in which collective military action by many countries is supposed to enforce the global peace. The UN is the obvious choice to organize and implement such collective military action. Thus more UN peacekeeping operations have been deployed in the post–cold war period than in the preceding forty years.

Significantly, most of the post–cold war operations differ from the previous ones, in that their central objective is to maintain *internal* peace among factions within a country. Of seven peacekeeping missions established in 1991 and 1992, for example, the primary objective in five (Angola, El Salvador, the Western Sahara, Cambodia, and Somalia) was to prevent political violence among groups within the country. Another mission was an attempt to limit the violence in what began as an internal conflict as new states emerged from the former Yugoslavia (see Box 15.3). It has been particularly difficult for the UN forces to end the violence in these internal conflicts where both borders and the identity of combatants are ambiguous.

The UN also provides many nonmilitary services that enhance states' security, stability, and prosperity. In a quiet manner, its committees, agencies, and commissions, such as the World Health Organization (WHO), the United Nations Educational, Scientific, and Cultural Organization (UNESCO), and the United Nations Conference on Trade and Development (UNCTAD), attempt to mitigate global problems and enhance the quality of human life in such areas as human rights, agricultural development, environmental protection, refugees, children's health, and disaster relief. Such efforts are one important way to reduce human suffering and thus reduce the conditions that might cause political violence.

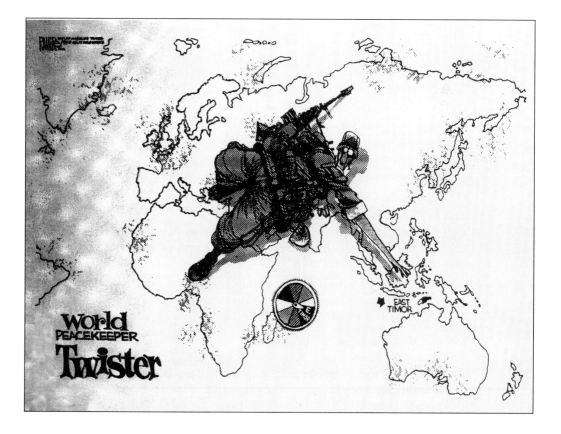

The continuing level of political violence in the international system underscores the fact that the UN lacks the power to prevent all interstate conflict. Many states withdraw their support (financial and political) when UN actions are at variance with the states' perceptions of their national interest. However, through its agencies, its debates and resolutions, its continuous open forum for formal and informal communications between states, and its peacekeeping operations, the UN does contribute to greater cooperation and reduced conflict among states.

COMPETITION AMONG STATES
Balance of Power

When the competing interests between states are stronger than their mutual interests, the states are unlikely to agree on a cooperative strategy. From the realist perspective, in particular, states should expect this pattern to be the most crucial feature of the international system. In such situations, another way in which direct conflict can be avoided is if a **balance of power** emerges. This occurs if there *is a rough equality in the power resources (political, economic, and especially military) that can be exercised by sets of competing states*. The situation can be understood as one in which an actor is prevented from taking advantage of others because of the power that other actors have to retaliate.

The term balance of power is widely used and has many meanings, but there are a few key elements in the classic notion of balance of power, which is especially associated with the political realist perspective (described earlier in this chapter; see also Kaplan 1957; Morgenthau 1948).

1. It is an attempt to maintain a general stability in the relations among states and to preserve the status quo.

2. It assumes that peace can be ensured only by a balancing of contending states, because potential aggressors will be deterred only by overwhelming opposing power.

3. There are typically a few (usually four to six) major power states that are decisive in ensuring that the balance is sustained.

4. These states, and others, constantly create shifting alliances, based only on self-interest and system equilibrium, never on friendship or ideology.

5. To prevent actions that seem to threaten the overall balance of the system, one or more power states must intervene in the affairs of a single state or the relations between states.

6. There will be periodic political violence and war, because states must use force to preserve themselves and because the system is not always in such balance that all conflict between states is deterred.

Since the emergence of modern states in the seventeenth century, there have usually been only a few states that, at any point in time, had both the desire and the power to project their interests over many other states. Some scholars characterize international relations during most of the period from the Peace of Westphalia in 1648 to the beginning of World War I in 1914 as a period of classic balance-of-power politics. This description applies primarily to the shifting alliances and actions of the European states, which tended to be the most significant actors in international politics during these 300 years. Great Britain often played a major role as the "balancer." As Winston Churchill (1948) observed, "For 400 years the foreign policy of England has been to oppose the strongest, most aggressive, most dominating power on the continent, in joining the weaker states."

However, by the late nineteenth century there were changes in the international system that made balance-of-power politics less possible. The growing importance of both ideology and nationalism were especially significant, because these factors hindered the ease with which alliances between states were made and broken. This was most clear in the deep antipathy that developed between France and Germany, who would inevitably be on opposite sides of any conflict.

The driving force of ideology became even more evident after World War II, with the hostility between the U.S. bloc and the Soviet bloc. The old pattern of flexible, nonideological balancing between a handful of independent states had broken down. In addition, the arena of between-state power struggles expanded from its narrow European base to a worldwide one. And the newer technologies of war reduced the ease with which war could be employed and controlled as a tool of foreign policy.

After World War II, the classic balance-of-power system was replaced by a different form, in which there were two major power blocs. In this *bipolar* balance-of-power system, the United States and its allies were generally balanced against the Soviet Union and its allies. The groups associated with each superpower were rather rigid in their ideological antipathy to the other bloc and were inflexible in their alliance formation. But the two blocs did prevent each other from achieving *hegemony* (i.e., clear domination of the international system).

From the early 1970s until the breakup of the Soviet Union in 1991, the international system became increasingly *multipolar*. During these two decades there was a decline in the coherence of the U.S. bloc and the Soviet bloc, as powerful actors such as China, Japan, Western Europe, and groupings of "nonaligned" states began to act with greater independence. Although multipolar, this was not a classic balance-of-power system, since alliance formation remained rather inflexible and guided by ideology. At the same time, the United States and the Soviet Union continued to be the preeminent global powers and to engage in a massive buildup of military capability and nuclear weapons.

In the "post–cold war era" (since 1991), the state system remains somewhat transitional. Although the system continues to have multipolar elements, the military and economic dominance of the United States suggests a unipolar period in which the international system is generally controlled by a single "hegemon." While the U.S. attempts to utilize the United Nations in peacekeeping roles have been characterized above, the United States has often taken a very leading role in establishing collective military action, through the United Nations (e.g., in the 1990 Gulf War) or through NATO (e.g., the 1999 actions against the Serbs in Kosovo) or it has operated rather unilaterally (e.g., the lengthy bombing campaign against Iraq when the U.N. weapons inspection program collapsed in 1998).

Balance of Terror

The enormous destructive capacity of modern military technologies was a key element that undermined traditional balance-of-power politics. War became far less controllable as an instrument of foreign policy between major states when each had the capacity to wreak massive devastation on the other and to risk equal destruction at home. For a state with nuclear weapons, the power of its enemies was balanced if it possessed so much military and nuclear capacity that it was confident other states were unwilling to bear the costs of attacking it.

The problem with this strategy of nuclear deterrence is that each state fears vulnerability: Does the rival have a numerical superiority in weapons or firepower? Does the rival have a technically superior system for attack or defense? Could a rival's first strike destroy one's own capacity for second-strike retaliation?

To overcome such uncertainties about mutual deterrence, a state expands its destructive capacity, numbers of weapons, and technical sophistication to a point where it has great confidence that under any conditions of conflict it can inflict catastrophic and unacceptable damage on a rival. Thus the balance of power evolved into a balance of terror, a system of *mutually assured destruction (MAD)*. Even at this point, the fear of technological breakthroughs by rivals and the inherent desire for superiority induce each state to expand its military capability to an extraordinary, and excessive, magnitude. In the 1970s and 1980s, this continued expansion of military power and destructive capacity resulted in an arms race that produced nuclear arsenals capable of massive, even total, annihilation of humankind. In short, balance-of-power politics became a dangerous and possibly irrational mechanism for regulating the relations among powerful states in the nuclear age.

In the post–cold war period, significant reductions in nuclear weapons have been negotiated between the United States and Russia (the country that inherited most Soviet nuclear power). However, both have retained weapons far in excess of MAD. And although the likelihood of a nuclear war between these two cold warriors has shrunk, the number of countries with the potential to deploy nuclear weapons is growing, creating new forms of instability in the balance of terror.

Domination and Dependence

While all states enjoy sovereign equality, it is obvious that some states are far more powerful than others. Few relations between states are perfectly symmetrical, in the sense that neither state enjoys greater ability to influence or control the actions of the other. This section discusses the situation in which one state has very substantial power over another. The capacity of one state to alter the actions of another state can be based on different forms of leverage, although there are three primary mechanisms of control:

1. *Economic* leverage is based on the advantageous trade, financial interactions, or economic aid that the state can provide (or withhold from) another state.

2. *Military* leverage can be applied either negatively, via the use or threat of military action against a state, or positively, via military assistance in the form of protection, provision of military resources, or training.

3. *Political* leverage is derived from the ability of a state to affect the actions of another state by the application of its political resources, such as its negotiating skills, its effective political institutions, or its influence in interstate relations.

Colonialism/imperialism. In the twentieth century, particular attention has focused on extremely uneven patterns of dominance and dependence between states, and especially on the relations usually termed **colonialism** or *imperialism*. Various goals might motivate a state to attain mastery over another state. First, the subordinate state can provide resources, both human and physical, for the dominant state. Second, the subordinate state can be a controlled market for the products of the dominant state. Third, the subordinate state can serve important strategic functions, either as a buffer between the dominant state and its rivals or as a staging area for the dominant state's political or military objectives. Fourth, a state with a missionary zeal might dominate another state to ensure that its values (usually political or religious) guide the subordinate state. Fifth, a state might want to dominate another state to gain international prestige.

While all forms of colonial domination entail a mix of economic, military, and political control, dominant states have employed different emphases.

1. In the *segregationist* style of colonialism, the exploitation by the dominant state is quite explicit. There is little or no attempt to improve the economic, political, or social systems in the subordinate state. This style generally characterized the relations of Belgium, Germany, and Portugal with their African and Asian colonial territories.

2. In the *assimilationist* style, there is some attempt to transform the subordinate state into an external extension of the dominant state. While the subordinate state is still being exploited, the institutions, knowledge, and culture of the dominant state are introduced to the elite of the subordinate state and become a basis for political, economic, and cultural development. This style is particularly associated with French colonialism in Africa and Asia and with Soviet colonialism.

3. In the style of *indirect rule,* the dominant state uses the traditional leaders and institutions of governance and culture in the subordinate state as intermediaries in its control, but it also introduces the modern forms of the dominant state that will eventually supplant traditional forms. The British approach to its vast empire (prior to the independence movement after 1945) is the classic example of indirect rule, and this mode of colonialism also seems to correspond to the style used by the United States in some Latin American and Pacific Rim states.

Neocolonialism. In the half century since World War II, most states have, willingly or reluctantly, granted independence to their colonial holdings. But it is not the case that political independence has necessarily ended these states' subordination to strong states. The label **neocolonialism** is given to new forms of domination and dependence that are nearly as powerful as those under colonialism. These new forms were described in Chapter 10 in the discussion of dependency approaches to explaining the lack of development in many of the states gaining political independence in the postcolonial era (i.e., after 1945).

Despite official withdrawal by the dominant state, especially of its direct political and military presence, domination has been maintained, especially by economic leverage. Through the use of foreign aid, loans, technology transfer, military support, and economic intervention, the dominant state can continue to control many of the actions of a supposedly independent state. The actions of the dominant state become relatively invisible, and its interests are served by a subtle alliance of a small internal elite, transnational corporations and other transnational actors, such as the International Monetary Fund (Maxfield 1997; So 1990). The recent history of the Republic of Congo (Box 12.2) exemplifies the impacts of colonialism and neocolonialism on vulnerable Third World states.

BOX 12.2

The Faces of Colonialism: Congo/Zaire/Congo

The Congo is a large, resource-rich state (one-fourth the size of the United States) located in the center of the African continent. It encompasses more than 30 million people and 250 ethnic groups. King Leopold of Belgium sponsored expeditions down the Congo River and in 1879 claimed the area as his own private kingdom. Leopold's companies extracted the natural resources ruthlessly and treated the people with brutality. In 1908 the area was placed under Belgian colonial administration, as the "Belgian Congo." Military forces were used to "pacify" the population and local men were forced into virtual slavery as workers in the mines and on the plantations. The colonial regime provided only minimal education to the population and encouraged Catholic missionaries to teach the population the great virtue of obedience to authority.

The Belgians continued to exploit the resources of the Congo until internal unrest and the general liberation of African colonies made it clear that the time of Belgian colonial rule in the Congo was over. Within about one year after substantial resistance to Belgian rule emerged, Belgium granted the Congo its independence on June 30, 1960. Belgium withdrew its military and administrative personnel, and most of its financial and technical support.

Unprepared for self-rule, and without the Belgians' order-maintaining institutions, the Congolese elite broke into competing factions and the country collapsed into civil war when the wealthy province of Katanga attempted to secede. The remaining Belgians fled, leaving the country in chaos. The United Nations sent in a peacekeeping force, and the Soviet Union also began to provide support for some groups in the Congo. With assistance from Western countries (and the apparent assistance of the U.S. Central Intelligence Agency [CIA]), an army leader, Joseph Mobutu, led the army of the central government to victory over Katanga and assassinated the prime minister.

In 1965 Mobutu, now army chief of staff, led a coup that overthrew the civilian government, and installed himself as the leader in a one-party, authoritarian system that ruled for more than three decades. Mobutu "Africanized" his society, changing his own name to Mobutu Sese Seko ("all powerful one") and the country's name to Zaire. Another insurrection in Shaba (previously Katanga) was defeated in 1977. Despite the repressive rule of Mobutu, the clear evidence of widespread corruption, and the persistent failure of the economy, his staunch anticommunism won him substantial economic and military support from the United States.

After "independence," Mobutu's victories over Katanga/Shaba and his long tenure in office depended on foreign aid, loans, technology transfer, and military support from Western countries, especially the United States. Zaire relied heavily on foreign corporations to build and maintain its mines, factories, and infrastructure facilities. But volatility in the world prices of key export commodities and the massive diversion of funds to Mobutu and his cronies from state-owned mines (e.g., copper, cobalt, diamonds) resulted in huge state deficits.

The International Monetary Fund (or IMF, the consortium of First World banking institutions) loaned Zaire enormous amounts and repeatedly restructured Zaire's debt of more than $4 billion (the largest in Africa). But the IMF has demanded "conditionality"—

BOX 12.2

the requirement that Zaire accept crucial economic policies, including devaluation of the currency, cutting real wages, and drastically reducing social welfare programs. There were extended periods when Zaire was obliged to allow its national banking system to be run by a six-person group of Europeans sent in by the IMF.

The combination of internal corruption and exploitation by foreign economic interests left little for the people. The level of education continued to decline, the country could no longer feed itself, and the infrastructure system (e.g., roads, water supply, telecommunications) was in shambles. The real wages of urban workers had fallen to less than one-tenth of what they were at independence. Surrounded by the appalling poverty of most of the population, Mobutu was rumored to be the wealthiest person in Sub-Saharan Africa, with holdings of more than $10 billion.

With the cold war over, even the United States found Mobutu an embarrassment and tried to pressure him into democratic reforms. Mobutu responded with a promise in 1990 to begin a transition from single-party rule to democracy. He finally allowed elections in 1993, but when his own candidate for prime minister was defeated, he ordered the armed forces to prevent the winning candidates from taking office. Instead, he installed a puppet government and sustained Zaire's "kleptocracy" (rule by thieves). The multinational corporations, however, still found much in Zaire to appreciate and they maintained their business dealings with Mobutu.

After years of deepening political decay, Mobutu's end came suddenly. A low level guerrilla war, which had been waged against Mobutu for many years, was substantially expanded after more than 1.2 million Hutus fled from the ethnic chaos in two neighboring (Tutsi-controlled) countries, Burundi and Rwanda. When the Hutus settled in refugee camps in eastern Zaire, they were attacked by the Zairean guerrillas, who were mainly Tutsis, and large numbers of additional Zairean Tutsis joined in the political violence. When the Hutus had been expelled, the enlarged rebel army focused on the civil war.

By early 1997, neither the alienated citizenry nor the Army, demoralized and undisciplined after years of low pay in a corrupt society, were willing to risk their lives for Mobutu. The United Nations, the United States and the multinationals also abandoned Mobutu. Facing little opposition, the rebels advanced rapidly to the west, reaching the capital city of Kinshasa by May 1997. As Mobutu fled the country, the rebel leader, Laurent Kabila, declared himself president and renamed the country as the Republic of Congo. However, other Congolese groups refused to accept Kabila's rule and have engaged in a widespread and destructive civil war to topple him. The conflict became regionalized with the involvement of troops and military aid from six other African countries, including Rwanda, Uganda, and Zimbabwe.

Despite these changes of leaders and even country name, the Congo's economic and political systems remain deeply dependent on Western capital. After ninety years under a brutal and exploitive colonial system, forty years of "independence" have brought no blossoming of democratic politics, no sharing of the society's abundant resources among its people, no economic development. Rather, contemporary Congo is a tragic product of colonialism and neocolonialism as well as its own internal failings, a state characterized by poverty, corruption, oppression, economic chaos, and dependence on foreign states and foreign economic actors.

Some analysts such as Immanuel Wallerstein (1980; 1991) take this perspective a step further, arguing that individual dominant states have been replaced by a *world system* of domination and dependence. As noted in Chapter 10, a handful of powerful "core" states have the capacity to manipulate the international political economy to their enormous advantage. These core states (especially the United States, the members of the European Union, and Japan) can use their superior technology, financial resources, diversified economy, and skilled labor to control the production and sale of most modern goods and services in the international market. States on the "periphery" (especially many developing countries) mainly provide labor, raw materials, and simple goods for export and are subject to systematic exploitation by and subordination to the core states.

One of the most ideologically charged issues in international politics is the extent to which a few states do reap enormous benefits through their domination of many less developed countries. The dependency approach provides both an explanation for underdevelopment (Chapter 10) and a rationale for demands that the prosperous states redistribute their resources to those states that have been exploited. It also posits that the patterns of dominance and dependence that were established under colonialism have become global and systemic.

Competition in the Post–Cold War World

The disintegration of the Soviet Union is regarded as the crucial event ending the cold war era. The international system that is evolving in the new conditions of the post–cold war period is premised on the disappearance of the bipolar balance-of-power system dominated by a conflict between the U.S. bloc and the Soviet bloc. Several major trends are likely to be important in this evolution.

First, a *more complex and multipolar international system* has emerged. Although the United States remains a dominant military power, five or more major countries or blocs constitute potential poles in this new system, which is based on both military and economic power. China, Germany/European Union, Japan, Russia, and the United States are among the most obvious power bases in the emerging system. These states and many others will jockey for position in a more fluid set of alliances and interstate relationships. There is disagreement among scholars regarding the extent to which this multipolar system will result in more international conflict than the bipolar system. However, empirical research suggests that in the twentieth century, unlike the nineteenth century, aggressive competition and military conflict have been more likely as the international system becomes highly diffuse and multipolar (Brecher and Wilkenfeld 1997; Kegley and Wittkopf 1997: ch. 15; Russett and Starr 1996).

Second, *military power* remains a significant factor in the relations among states. While the lessening of cold war tensions has resulted in a reduction in worldwide military expenditure, more than $567 billion per year is still being spent on defense (Sivard 1996: 44). It is quite likely that regional conflicts will be more frequent in a diffuse, multipolar world in which ethnonationalism is rampant. As was discussed earlier in the chapter, it is not obvious that the UN or any other actors have the will and capacity to prevent interstate conflicts.

Third, intense *economic competition* will split the developed countries that were allies during the cold war. In fact, competition among the major powers will pivot more on economic issues than on military or ideological issues. In the global economy, regional groupings have formed, and the major economic competition might be among three groups: North America under leadership from the United States, the European Union, and an East Asian group under Japanese leadership. Other regional economic groups have formed in South America and among the Muslim states of Central Asia.

Fourth, the state-centered system is evolving toward one in which *transnational entities* are extraordinarily important. Most of these powerful new actors are multinational corporations (MNCs) such as General Motors, Exxon, IBM, Toyota Motor, British Petroleum, Daimler Benz, and Samsung. In terms of comparative economic power (measured as gross economic product in 1990), only 63 of the top 100 economic units in the world are countries and 37 are multinational corporations (Kegley and Wittkopf 1997: table 7.3). The transnational system also includes other important nonstate actors (i.e., actors whose members and interests are independent of any particular state), such as the International Monetary Fund, OPEC, and NATO, as well as the many other international government organizations (IGOs) and nongovernmental organizations (NGOs) discussed earlier in this chapter.

State boundaries have little significance for transnational actors. The MNC shifts its resources and its operations from country to country in a single-minded pursuit of profit maximization within the global economy. Although located in a home country, MNCs have operations in other host countries as well. The loyalty of the MNC to the prosperity and security goals of its home country may sometimes be limited or nonexistent. The MNC operates without significant, direct participation in or control by any government and it can avoid many of the laws and taxes of any state (Keohane and Nye 1989; Russett and Starr 1996; United Nations Commission on Transnational Corporations 1991). (See Box 12.3.)

To this point, states still retain direct control of most legitimate military power and constrain the behavior of most actors within their boundaries. But increasingly, MNCs and other transnational actors hold international economic power, shape global culture and communications, and operate outside the legal control of states. Some analysts conclude that the emerging international order is now dominated by "imperial corporations" whose earth-spanning systems of production and distribution of goods, finance, technologies, and communications enable them to transcend sovereign states and shape the global system (Barnet and Cavanagh 1994; Falk 1993). For these reasons, some predict that a key conflict in the early twenty-first century will be between the MNCs or between MNCs and states (Heilbroner 1993; United Nations Commission on Transnational Corporations 1991). Do you think it would be desirable to have an international system dominated by transnational actors rather than by states? Would the relentless pursuit of profit produce a more peaceful or a more just world than the relentless pursuit of national interest and state power?

VIOLENCE BETWEEN STATES

When you think of violence between states, you probably think of war. War is sustained, organized violence between states. But there are other forms of violence, short of war, that a state might employ when interstate cooperation or equilibrium breaks down. A state can threaten to use force, it can display force, or it can actually use limited force (Gochman and Maoz 1984).

BOX 12.3

Here, There, and Everywhere: Portrait of an MNC

In 1926 four large British companies involved in chemicals (e.g., explosives, dyes) combined to form Imperial Chemical Industries (ICI). During the next seven decades the company evolved into a major multinational corporation (MNC), dramatically extending its global reach and expanding its product array. Its total annual sales of more than $23 billion placed it among the top 100 economic entities in the world, with an annual product higher than the GNP of more than two-thirds of the world's countries (Kegley and Wittkopf 1993: table 6.1).

One crucial feature of major MNCs is their **globalization**. Operating in many countries enables an MNC to move its activities in order to exploit opportunities and avoid problems in any host country, and even in the home country. For example, until the mid-1970s, ICI had about two-thirds of its work force and its capital in Britain (the home country). But a weakening British economy and costly labor due to problems with Britain's powerful unions caused ICI to spread its operations around the globe.

Within ten years ICI had dramatically increased its active involvement in the political economies of many countries. It shifted its emphasis in production and sales to countries promising the highest profits and best growth potential. It now has factories in more than forty countries and selling companies in more than sixty, including virtually every West and East European country, the United States, Canada, six major Latin American countries, twelve Asian and Middle Eastern countries, thirteen countries in Sub-Saharan Africa, and extensive operations in Australia and New Zealand. Thus by the 1980s ICI had been dubbed "International" Chemical Industries.

A second feature of most MNCs is *product diversification,* also to reduce their dependence on any single country or good. ICI produces and sells goods in ten major product areas: agriculture, fibers, general chemicals, organic chemicals, industrial explosives, oil, paints, petrochemicals, pharmaceuticals, and plastics. No product area constitutes more than 17 percent of the overall sales, a reflection of the balanced diversification of this huge corporation.

When the 1973–1974 oil crisis occurred (raising the cost of petroleum), ICI's profits in several petroleum-based product areas (e.g., petrochemicals, plastics) collapsed. ICI immediately cut back dramatically on its operations in these areas, resuming production in those areas only when profit ratios were favorable again. It quickly redirected its efforts, investing heavily in the development of its own oil division, which became a high profit area within only a few years.

MNCs such as ICI have the capacity and willingness to shift their production activities from country to country and to alter the complex mix of goods they produce in order to serve their profit drive. The indictment of MNCs includes the criticisms that they monopolize the production and distribution of important goods in the world marketplace, widen the gap between rich and poor nations, and challenge the sovereignty and autonomy of the state (Kegley and Wittkopf 1997: 192). From the perspective of national governments, labor, and consumers, such MNCs can seem to be everywhere and nowhere and can seem uncontrollable. Thus "the MNC remains one of the most controversial actors in the international political economy" (Jenkins 1993: 606). (Discussion based on Clarke 1985.)

Threat of Force

States frequently communicate with each other, and their messages are typically friendly or neutral. However, when there is a clear conflict of interest between states, the messages can become quite hostile. Although usually couched in more sophisticated language, these messages are not unlike those between belligerent children: Stop that! If you don't do X, I'll do Y and you won't like it!

These hostile messages can be quite vague or can warn of particular actions that will be taken. As the conflict escalates, these messages are more likely to involve a *threat of force* or violence that will be forthcoming if the other state does not behave as the first state demands (recall the discussion of coercive power in Box 6.2). A state might threaten to declare war or to use its regular military forces (e.g., threatening a blockade or attack of the other state's territory). These strategies, also called *coercive diplomacy,* can be quite effective. Most states do not want a disagreement to escalate into the use of force, and thus they attempt to behave in a manner that satisfies the threatening state.

Display of Force

A more serious step is the actual *display of force*. A state can place its military or its weapons systems in a state of alert. Tension between states increases when one state moves its military forces into a threatening position. Typically, it is the militarily stronger protagonist that engages in a display of force. For example, the United States has often been accused of "gunboat diplomacy" because of its historical tendency to position its naval forces off the shore of a country (especially in Latin America) with which it has a major policy disagreement.

Interactions between states that involve either a threat of force or a display of force so serious that there is a risk of war are sometimes characterized as *crises*. These military confrontations have been increasing in number and intensity since World War I, with nearly six major crises per year between 1918 and 1988. Moreover, the proportion of crises that do escalate into a conflict involving force has also increased over the seventy-year period and is now greater than one in three crises. The incidence of crises is higher in the developing countries than in the more developed countries, between states that share a border, and where ethnonationalism and/or ongoing rivalry is a factor (Brecher and Wilkenfeld 1997). A larger number of crises signifies rising tensions within the international system. One of the challenges in the post–cold war system is to reduce the number of crises and to manage these low-level conflicts to prevent their escalation.

Use of Force

There is no precise point at which a *limited use of force* becomes a war. However, there are a variety of situations where the use of violence between states seems less than war (Gochman and Maoz 1984):

> In a *blockade,* the military (e.g., ships, troops, munitions) of one state is used to seal off territory (e.g., border crossings, harbors), preventing entry or exit by the rival state.

> In *state-sponsored terrorism,* the state provides financial or material support to groups committing occasional acts of political violence within the rival state (Chapter 11).

A state can engage in a brief, *single use of force,* such as a bombing raid, firing of munitions into the enemy state, or rapid invasion for a specific purpose (e.g., the sabotage of a facility).

In a *clash,* there is a brief engagement between the armed forces of two states, as in a border skirmish.

In a *low-intensity conflict (LIC),* a group uses force in a rival's territory, in a manner that is sporadic and prolonged, but does not involve full-scale military conflict (Klare 1988). The concept is particularly applied to situations in which a government, or a powerful external state, directs persistent uses of violent force against groups resisting the government, such as ethnonationalists or guerrillas. The source of violence can be regular military units, but often it is a police action by paramilitary groups or mercenaries. Despite the label, the violence associated with low-intensity conflict *is* intense for those involved, especially the targets.

War

War is *interstate violence that is sustained and organized*, and (usually) involves hostilities between the regular military forces of the states. Such violence is the ultimate mechanism for resolving conflict between states. Chapter 11 indicated that, for those who define politics as conflict resolution, war represents the utter failure of politics. But many probably agree with Karl von Clausewitz's (1833/1967: 87) famous dictum, "War is a political instrument, a continuation of political activity by other means." Thus war is the use of violence by one state to achieve its political goals at the expense of another state.

Robert Ardrey (1966: 27), a well-known ethologist (a person who studies animal behavior to better understand human behavior), wryly observes that "human war has been the most successful of all our cultural traditions." That is, history is marked by recurrent episodes of organized violence among groups, nations, and

Congolese army soldiers of President Kabila engage in a firefight with rebels loyal to former President Lissouba in one of his regional strongholds, Southwestern Congo.

states. Indeed, world history is usually presented to us as a subject dominated by wars, which are treated as the exceptional and notable phenomena through time.

The elimination of war is not among the accomplishments of the modern world. The comprehensive analysis of major interstate wars between 1816 and 1980 found good news: Wars are less frequent, are considerably shorter, and involve fewer states. But the bad news is that the number of wars "in progress" at any given time has increased substantially since 1900 and the total number of war deaths has risen astronomically (Singer 1991; Sivard 1996). Moreover, the post–cold war context has not significantly reduced the number of major armed conflicts. In the period 1990–1996, ninety countries were free of major armed conflict. But fifty countries experienced civil war during the period, thirteen countries were engaged in interstate wars, wars of independence were occurring in three countries, and ten more countries had combinations of these various types of conflicts. Thus fully 46 percent of the world's countries suffered the enormous costs of a major armed conflict during this brief seven years (Smith 1997).

Who does all this fighting? Are some states fighters? Box 12.4 challenges you to identify the most conflict-prone states.

Few of the major conflicts at the turn of the century are *conventional wars*— that is, wars that entail the direct, sustained confrontation of the military forces of two or more states within a defined space, usually occurring on the soil of one of the combatants. Recent conflicts that do generally fit the definition of a conventional war include the Argentina-United Kingdom War (Falklands War, 1982), the Iran-Iraq War (1980–1988), the Iraq-Kuwait War (Persian Gulf War, 1990), the Equador-Peru War (1995), and the Ethiopia-Eritrea War (1999-).

But many contemporary conflicts are more complex and the combatants more fluid. The conflict in Congo (Box 12.2) seems a prototype of the contemporary unconventional war. At one level, it is an internal, civil war between the military forces loyal to President Laurent Kabila and several large, paramilitary groups who do not accept his authority. Some of the cleavages underlying the conflict are regional, some are ethnonationalist, and some are merely based on personal animosity and ambition in a situation where no one has a legitimate mandate to rule. But the conflict has also involved non-Congolese combatants and groups who entered the country as a result of the ethnic violence in neighboring Rwanda and Burundi. The fighting has further expanded into an internationalized conflict, with the entry of military forces of Burundi, Rwanda, and Uganda in opposition to Kabila. In response, Angola, Namibia, and Zimbabwe have provided military support to Kabila. The United Nations has also sent some peacekeeping forces, but has been reluctant to commit a major role, despite international recognition that the situation in the Congo could provoke Africa's first "world war." The active participation of armed forces from countries other than the disputants has been particularly evident in conflicts between developing countries during the post-colonial period (e.g., Syria and Israel in Lebanon 1975–2000).

The changing nature of many contemporary wars is most evident in the enormous increase in the proportion of civilian deaths. Whereas in World War I there was only one civilian death for every eight military deaths, in World War II there were two civilian deaths for every military death. In the 1990s, nine out of every ten war deaths were *civilians,* and the wars going on in 1990 have been killing more than half a million civilians each year (Sivard 1996: 7, 17). Even more distressing is the huge increase in the total number of deaths in war. Ruth Leger

BOX 12.4

*Top Ten List: States That Are **Bad!***

Some people seem especially prone to getting into fights while others seem able to avoid conflict completely. There seem to be similar differences among states. What states do you think have been most likely, over a long period of their history, to get into the most violent disputes with other states?

One study by Gochman and Maoz (1984) analyzed the frequency with which countries engaged in interstate conflict between 1816 and 1976. Their analysis focused on fourteen types of "militarized interstate disputes." These included the threats of force, displays of force, and uses of force described earlier in this chapter. A state is considered to be in a dispute whether it is the initiator or the target of the conflict. Since some countries have considerably longer histories as states, the analysis measured disputes per year of the state's existence.

So who are the most dispute-prone states? Before you look at the list below, make some informed guesses about which states are in the "top ten."

The states most likely to enter into disputes with other states, rated from highest to lowest, are:

1. Israel (1.55 disputes per year)
2. United Kingdom (1.12)
3. India (1.07)
4. United States (.99)
5. Pakistan (.90)

6. Germany (.82)
7. Russia/Soviet Union (.82)
8. France (.80)
9. China (.60)
10. Italy (.50)

Are you surprised by the composition of the top ten? Do you notice any pattern or commonalities among these states? Many inferences have been made from analyses of such data. First, a limited number of states engage in most of the disputes. Of more than a hundred states in the analyses, thirty initiated more than 70 percent of all disputes and were the primary targets of more than 60 percent of the disputes. Second, major powers in the international system are, in general, far more dispute prone than minor states. However, the postcolonial, middle-power states of Israel, India, and Pakistan also have very high levels of disputes. Third, among these ten most dispute-prone states, nine (except Pakistan) are more frequently initiators of disputes than the targets of a dispute. And fourth, the states that most often initiate disputes are also the ones most likely to join ongoing disputes involving other countries.

In short, it is evident that some states are fighters and are far more likely than other states to be involved in interstate violence.

Sivard (1991: 20) notes: "The twentieth century in particular has been a stand-out in the history of warfare. Wars now are shockingly more destructive and deadly. So far, in the 90 years of this century, there have been over four times as many war deaths as in the 400 years preceding."

Worldwide, the more than $700 billion per year being spent to support the security objectives of states could, if redirected to the prosperity goals of those states, greatly enhance the quality of life for the citizens in those states. The problem, of course, is that the policy makers believe that security goals have highest priority and that security is the *sine qua non* for fulfilling prosperity goals. And, in an era of high-tech warfare, virtually no one feels truly secure; this insecurity leads every state to push itself and its rivals into an accelerating, unending, and potentially devastating expansion of the capacity for massive political violence.

What Causes War?

Are there fundamental causes of war? Studies have attempted to determine whether there are some attributes of a state or its population that result in a greater propensity of the state to engage in war. Such attributes include the state's size, its economic system, its political system, its cultural features, its geographic position, its wealth, its religion, and its rate of modernization. Many studies have attempted to isolate the key characteristics of more "warlike" states, but the findings of such analyses are inconclusive, and there are always unique contingencies associated with particular wars. Certain traits, however, do seem to be associated with more warlike states. Kegley and Wittkopf (1997: 353–366) offer seven propositions that are generally supported by the empirical research:

1. *Newer nations* are more likely to initiate war than are mature states.
2. War is more likely in states which have effectively *socialized their citizens to accept the government's actions* on behalf of the national interest and accept its right to wage war.
3. The most warlike states are *relatively poor,* but are not the very poorest states.
4. States that are most *highly militarized,* and especially those that are rapidly expanding their military power, are more warlike.
5. Countries whose political culture reflects a high degree of *nationalism* are more warlike.
6. Communist countries and capitalist countries are as likely to participate in war.
7. Democracies are as likely as nondemocracies to be involved in war, although stable democracies rarely fight against each other.

At the "ultimate" level, however, three broad alternative explanations of war are usually offered.

1. War can be attributed to scarcity in *nature.* Because the consumption goals of states are greater than the natural resources available, states undertake war to protect or capture resources from other states. Thus states struggle with each other for the control of such resources as people, food, minerals, and strategic locations.
2. War can be attributed to the inadequacy of *institutions.* In this view, neither the existing sociopolitical structure nor the rules governing the conduct among states

are adequate to prevent states from using force to achieve their objectives. Thus states are guided by self-interest, and there are no conflict resolution mechanisms that prevent the occasional explosion of large-scale interstate violence.

3. War can be explained by *human nature.* From this perspective, humans are innately aggressive, as a biological species. Humans are virtually the only species that engages in widespread killing of its own kind. And humans, it is claimed, are acquisitive, competitive, and selfish by nature, rather than by nurture. Thus war becomes a predictable group-level manifestation of these inherent qualities. A variation on this explanation emphasizes the critical importance of an aggressive leader who draws his country into war (Stoessinger 1993).

The first and second explanations are clearly associated with the idealist perspective outlined earlier. And the third reflects the essence of political realism. Each of the three explanations of war also suggests possible "solutions" that might eliminate war.

1. If the problem is scarcity of natural resources, one might look to *technological solutions,* as states develop new techniques for more efficient exploitation of natural resources and for the development of substitutes for scarce resources.

2. If the problem is inadequate institutions, the need is for *social engineering*—for the creation of organizational arrangements that more effectively structure the relations among individuals and states. In the political domain, this might ultimately entail the creation of a viable world government.

3. If the problem is human nature, the solution is found in *human engineering,* by means of comprehensive political socialization or perhaps even genetic manipulation to create a population with the "proper" qualities.

There is some evidence in support of each of these three general explanations of the causes of war. But there is also sufficient counterevidence so that none of the three positions is compelling as a complete explanation. Neither abundance of natural resources nor advanced technology has ensured the absence of intergroup violence. And while there are societies whose members have not been driven by human nature into warlike behavior against their neighbors, no set of human institutions has been shown inevitably to generate war or perpetuate peace between states. While the complete elimination of war might be impossible, it does seem that a combination of material abundance, effective institutions, and thorough socialization could reduce the incidence of war. The question is whether this combination can be identified and implemented by political actors.

Is War Justifiable?

Chapter 11 probed your views about the conditions under which political violence might be legitimate. The same issues are germane on an even larger scale regarding the justification of war. Despite the massive human and financial costs of war, few would support the proposition that there are absolutely no conditions under which war is justified. But what are the circumstances that justify war?

A classic justification for war is the doctrine of *self-defense,* a position associated with St. Augustine (354–430 A.D.). A victim of an unprovoked attack has the right to use violence as a means of protection. Apart from total pacifists, there are few who would reject the principle of self-defense as a legitimate rationale for violence. But the application of this principle might be subject to considerable disagreement, especially in the relations among states. Here are some examples: Might state A engage in nonviolent actions that are so provocative that state B is justified in responding with violence? What if the initial violence against state B is by an actor from state A who does not have the sanction or the explicit support of state A? What if the violence by state A was unintentional? What if the initial violence is within the territory of state A but is perceived as directly harmful to citizens or interests of state B? What if state B uses violence to prevent state A from the (expected) use of far more substantial violence? What if the violent response of state B is of far greater magnitude than the violence by state A? Wars sometimes develop because there are such patterns of misperception, accident, preemption, and incremental escalation (Schelling 1960).

Frequently, however, war is justified on the more ambiguous rationale, associated with St. Ambrose (339–397 A.D.), of the *defense of universal principles.* In this view, "man has a moral duty to employ force to resist active wickedness, for to refrain from hindering evil when possible is tantamount to promoting it." In the contemporary world, however, it is difficult to identify truly universal principles in whose defense war is always justifiable. Even the interpretations of "active wickedness" and "evil" are not shared across all cultures. Obviously, not all citizens in every state were persuaded either by Iraqi Saddam Hussein's Gulf War justification for a *jihad* (holy war) against the infidels (those who do not believe in Mohammed) or by U.S. President Reagan's mid-1980s justification for military action against the minions of the Soviet Union's "evil empire."

In most cases of international political violence, a justification based on universal principles is invoked. State power is used against other states in the name of many principles, such as freedom, social justice, human rights, self-determination, territorial integrity, egalitarianism, religious freedom, religious orthodoxy, anticommunism, communism, and so on. But all states do not accept a single vision of natural law that provides universal principles to govern international relations. Moreover, the international system itself has not implemented powerful and effective institutional mechanisms for conflict avoidance. Thus occasional outbreaks of interstate conflict and war are inevitable.

The crucial point is that the context of international politics is essentially *amoral.* Recognition of this fact is the key to understanding most behavior in international relations, whether diplomatic activities, alliances, or war. At some points, a state's actions in the international environment are constrained by *its* views of morality and universal principles. But at other points, a state's decision makers might decide that virtually any action is acceptable, if the action seems to further the state's achievement of its security, stability, and prosperity goals. If either view is correct, what are the chances that contemporary states will ever meet the requirement of the UN Charter that the states "settle their international disputes by peaceful means in such a manner that international peace and security, and justice, are not endangered"?

FOR FURTHER CONSIDERATION

1. In the post–cold war period, the bipolar international system dominated by the equilibrium between the United States and the Soviet Union has ended. A new pattern must structure the relations among states. What is the most desirable

pattern that might be established? What is the least desirable? What seems most likely for the international system in the first decades of the twenty-first century?

2. Which of Kegley and Wittkopf's (1997) seven propositions about war is most surprising to you? Why? What proposition do you think might be added to the list?

3. Can the United Nations, or *any* multinational body, be so effective in imposing an international order that interstate war becomes highly unlikely?

4. Who, if anyone, can judge whether there are appropriate conditions under which a country's sovereignty can be violated? What might such conditions be?

FOR FURTHER READING

Barnet, Richard J., and John Cavanagh. (1994). *Global Dreams: Imperial Corporations and the New World Order.* New York: Simon & Schuster. A rich, insightful, and often scathing analysis of the enormous power and impacts of the MNCs on the international system and the lives of citizens in many countries.

Brecher, Michael, and Jonathan Wilkenfeld. (1997). *A Study of Crisis.* Ann Arbor, MI: University of Michigan Press. A comprehensive, usable database from the International Crisis Behavior project provides valuable information on 412 crises between 1929 and 1992, following the authors' thoughtful analyses of and generalizations about the patterns of interstate crises.

Claude, Inis L. (1984). *Swords into Plowshares: The Problems and Progress of International Organization.* 4th ed. New York: McGraw-Hill. A classic study of the development and roles of the United Nations.

Dougherty, James E., and Robert L. Pfaltzgraff. (1990). *Contending Theories of International Relations.* 3d ed. New York: Harper & Row. A readable and comprehensible explanation and assessment of the major theories of international relations.

Freedman, Lawrence, Ed. (1994). *War.* New York: Oxford University Press. A splendid collection of readings, ranging from the greatest classical treatments of the reasons for and the nature of war to significant contemporary analyses.

Gutman, Roy, and David Rieff, Eds. (1999). *Crimes of War: What the Public Should Know.* New York: W.W. Norton. Authorities on the laws of war and experienced members of the media offer diverse and enlightening discussions on the legal and ethical issues regarding war crimes and international humanitarian law, with powerful commentaries on such cases as Cambodia, Chechnya, and Rwanda, and dramatic illustrations by photojournalists.

Nugent, Neill. (1999). *The Government and Politics of the European Union.* 4th. ed. Durham, NC: Duke University Press. A thorough description of the most significant regional alliance in the global system (and the subject of Box 12.1).

Parker, Geoffrey. (1998). *Geopolitics: Past, Present and Future.* New York: Continuum Publishers. The emergence, development, and explanatory power of geopolitical thinking is explained, with particular emphasis on relevant themes of contemporary interstate relations, including ethnonationalism, globalization, inequality, and environmental degradation.

Pastor, Robert A. Ed. (1999). *A Century's Journey: How the Great Powers Shape the World.* New York: Basic Books. Noted scholars explore the foreign policy behavior and resulting international impacts during the twentieth-century of each of seven major powers— China, France, Germany, Great Britain, Japan, Russia, and the United States. The authors illuminate the pervasive influence of these powers on the relations between states, the international political economy, and the international system.

Sassoon, Siegfried. (1968). *Collected Poems: 1908–1956.* London: Faber & Faber. The deeply moving poems about war by a young British intellectual who suffered the horrific experiences of European trench warfare during World War I.

Sivard, Ruth Leger. (Annually). *World Military and Social Expenditures.* Washington, DC: World Priorities. A revealing yearly discussion and assessment providing comparative data, for most states in the world, reflecting the current aspects of military expenditure, war, and arms control, and social dimensions measuring education, health, and poverty.

Small, Melvin, and J. David Singer. (1982). *Resort to Arms: International and Civil Wars, 1816–1980.* Beverly Hills, CA: Sage. Analyses of political violence based on the largest available data set on interstate conflict between 1816 and 1980, generated by a research group at the University of Michigan. See also J. David Singer and Melvin Small, *Wages of War, 1816–1965* (New York: Wiley, 1972).

Stearns, Jill. (1998). *Gender and International Relations: An Introduction.* New Brunswick, NJ: Rutgers University Press. A comprehensible and thoughtful explanation of feminist perspectives on international relations theory, an approach which particularly challenges the key assumptions and interpretations of realist theory on such core topics as interstate relations, violence and militarism, and international political economy.

Stoessinger, John G. (1993). *Why Nations Go to War.* 6th ed. New York: St. Martin's Press. A rich set of descriptive case studies of twentieth-century wars, particularly emphasizing individual behavior and motives, including World War I, Korea, Vietnam, India–Paistan, Israel–Arabs, and Iran–Iraq.

Walzer, Michael. (1992). *Just and Unjust War.* 2d ed. New York: Basic Books. A political philosopher presents a careful argument about the morality of war, grounded in the context of numerous actual wars.

CHAPTER 13

The Developed Countries

AN INTRODUCTION TO THE NEXT THREE CHAPTERS: GROUPING THE STATES IN THE CONTEMPORARY WORLD

Chapters 13 through 15 aim at the near impossible: to characterize the key features of politics, both within and between the more than 190 countries in the contemporary political world. As you discovered in Part One, a central goal of political analysis is to develop general descriptions and explanations of political phenomena. To generalize about all these countries, it is necessary to use a taxonomic system that allows discussion of a few groups that include most states.

Given the complexity and variations among states, however, no taxonomy is fully satisfactory. The situation is further complicated by the extensive and rapid transformations that are occurring in many states in the post–cold war world. In particular, the former Soviet Union and its East European allies have made dramatic efforts to alter fundamentally their economic and political systems. Certain other newly industrializing countries, especially in Asia and Latin America, are also undergoing especially rapid development.

To discuss the world's states within a general framework, these chapters use a taxonomy that groups countries according to their level of development. As with many current classifications, one dimension of the taxonomy is the country's level of economic development. But the broader issues of development discussed in Chapter 10 suggest a second dimension for the classification, based on a country's level of social development.

1. **Economic development.** The most conventional indicator of economic development measures the value of goods produced in a country, divided by the population of the country. Chapter 10 defined the two most widely used indicators, GNP (gross national product) per capita and GDP (gross domestic product) per capita. Although not perfect, these are the best available overall measures of countries' relative level of economic development. On the basis of GNP per capita, the World Bank (1999) distinguishes thirty-four "high-income countries," with GNP per capita greater than $9,655 per year; eighty-eight "middle-income countries" (the MICs), with GNP per capita between $9,655 and $785; and sixty-one "low-income countries" (the LICs), with GNP per capita below $785. A further distinction is made between upper and lower middle-income countries, with a break point of $3,125.

2. **Social development.** To enrich the classificatory scheme, this book employs a second dimension that is not explicitly economic. This also taps a country's level of development but is grounded in the more subjective and nonquantifiable dimensions of development. Here the criteria are the extent to which the country is characterized by the types of organizational, technological, and attitudinal development discussed in Chapter 10. Every country is a mix of complex and simple organizational structures, high and low technologies, modern and traditional attitudes. But in relative terms, there are very substantial cross-national differences in countries' general levels on these social components of development, and it is these differences that constitute the second dimension of the taxonomy. The specific indicators in this index, which is scored from 0–30, measure the country's level of adult literacy, extent of urbanization, and average number of televisions per household. In the aggregate, these measures reflect some key underlying aspects of relative level of social development, as reflected in the pervasiveness of knowledge, urban lifestyles, and modern communications in the environment of the population. Figure 13.1 locates a selection of countries on the two dimensions and suggests labels for clusters of countries.

The Developed Countries

The countries in the upper-right part of Figure 13.1 are among those usually referred to as the *developed countries*. Most of this chapter will explore key aspects of these countries. The developed countries group includes most of the countries with the

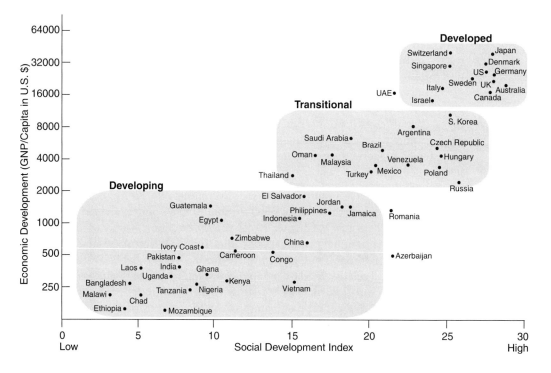

Figure 13.1   Classification of selected countries based on economic and social development.

highest levels of GNP per capita in the world. These states are also relatively high on the social dimensions of development. They are generally urbanized and secularized countries, with highly specialized and institutionalized organizational systems. Their technological infrastructure is advanced, and most people are frequently and directly involved with high technologies of communications, transportation, and information. These developed countries are also sometimes referred to as (1) the *industrialized countries,* because of their large manufacturing sector; or (2) the *postindustrial societies,* because of the growing dominance of the knowledge-based and service-based sectors of their economies.

The Developing Countries

Social scientists, political actors, and the media frequently refer to a large group of countries as the *developing countries.* This term is used in this book to designate a very large set of more than 125 countries. As you would expect, these countries have lower levels of economic development and are relatively less developed on the technological, organizational, and attitudinal dimensions than the developed countries. Thus in Figure 13.1 the developing countries are located on the lower half of the figure and are especially clustered in the lower-left quadrant. Chapter 14 will focus on key themes associated with the pursuit of prosperity, security, and stability in these developing countries.

By the late 1950s, many of these countries were generally called "The Third World." Initially, this term was applied to those states that, by their own definition, were "nonaligned." This meant that the country's leaders claimed it was not under the domination of either the United States and its allies or the Soviet Union and its allies. Others used the term "Third World" even more broadly, to refer to almost all countries other than the developed countries, those in the Soviet bloc, and a few "newly industrializing countries " (NICs). Currently, many commentators still refer to a large and undefined set of countries as the Third World, although other analysts conclude that the concept covers such a diversity of countries that it is no longer an appropriate term (Lewis 1999). It is certainly true that the developing countries are a diverse group and that the states in this category, however defined, vary substantially. Chapter 14 will suggest other criteria by which the developing countries can be further categorized into subsets, such as regional clusters.

The Transitional Developed Countries

The more developed countries and the developing countries are rather standard categories in analyses by governmental agencies and social scientists. But there are countries in Figure 13.1 that are along the boundaries between these two broad groupings and thus are particularly difficult to classify. At this point, the levels of economic and/or social development in these countries put them "in the middle." These countries arguably seem different from most developing countries, yet they are not as fully developed as the developed countries. While all the countries in the world are always in transition, this book labels these countries-in-the-middle of Figure 13.1 as *transitional countries* to connote their middle range, and sometimes their high rate of change, on one or both dimensions of development.

Chapter 15 distinguishes and examines in detail two subsets of transitional countries. Each of these subsets is made up of countries that seem to have some important commonalities regarding their economic situation and/or their political culture. The decision to focus on these countries is also based on the interesting nature of the challenges these sets of countries face and their approaches to achieving their goals.

One subset is composed of most of the countries that emerged after the breakup of the Soviet Union and also its former European allies in the Warsaw Pact. We call this group the *post-communist developed countries (PCDCs)*. The group includes most states created from the former Soviet Union (e.g., Belarus, Estonia, Georgia, Russia, and Ukraine) and most Central and East European states (e.g., Bulgaria, Hungary, Poland, and the Slovak Republic). These states are quite high on most dimensions of social development, especially in the attitudinal and organizational domains, and most have moderately high (by world standards) levels of economic development. Most are engaged in efforts at substantial transition of their economic systems from command-oriented to market-based and of their political systems toward democratization. This is the set of countries currently referred to by the World Bank as the "transitional economies" (World Bank 1999).

The second group of transitional countries is often termed the *newly industrializing countries (NICs)* because the capacity of the economic system in each NIC has advanced beyond that of most developing countries. NICs have established strong, export-centered economies in which substantial value is added to goods during the production process. Most NICs are included in one of two subgroups with distinctive regional and political cultural differences—one group is in East Asia (e.g., Malaysia, South Korea) and the other group is in Latin America (e.g., Argentina, Brazil, Mexico). On the economic dimension and increasingly on the social dimension, the NICs are reaching levels of development that approach those of some of the developed countries. The analysis in Chapter 15 centers particularly on the leading Asian NICs, because their successful development strategy has become a model for many developing countries (Chapter 10).

Thus Chapters 13 through 15 examine the developed countries, the developing countries, and the transitional countries. Each chapter describes critical issues for countries in each group as they attempt to achieve the key goals of prosperity, stability, and security. In the attempt to provide you with a broad understanding, general patterns within each group are emphasized and similarities are highlighted; but you should recognize that:

- there are substantial differences among states within each group, especially among the large number of states lumped together as the developing countries.

- each state has unique features that will be lost in such generalized discussion.

- in some instances, a trait is more similar among certain states across groups, rather than among all the states within one group.

As these qualifications suggest, this method of grouping countries for analysis and generalizations is not perfect. Indeed, there is no classificatory scheme currently agreed upon by most analysts. Box 13.1 notes some of the issues associated with any taxonomy of countries, such as the one employed in Part Five of this book. Thus as you read these chapters, you should assess the extent to which this classificatory scheme provides a useful means of grouping and discussing the more than 180 countries listed in Table 13.1. This chapter begins this exploration, focusing on the more developed countries.

BOX 13.1

Who's In, Who's Out?

As Figure 13.1 suggests, the boundaries between groups of countries are not precise. It is reasonable to question why certain countries are included in or excluded from a particular category in the figure and the analysis.

The most direct answer is that these decisions are somewhat arbitrary. Like any taxonomy (see the Appendix), there is an attempt to create groups that can be distinguished analytically, are based on some specifiable criteria, and seem to make sense. However, when classifying entities as complicated as countries, it is inevitable that not every country will fit neatly into a category. Classification can be especially difficult at the "edges" between groups.

For example, the inclusion or exclusion of a particular country in the NIC category can be problematic. While a few Asian NICs (e.g., Singapore, South Korea, and Taiwan) defined this category, it has become more ambiguous as an increasing number of countries, in Asia and also in Latin America, reflect more of the basic characteristics of the category. Should one include Costa Rica or Jamaica or Indonesia among the NICs? Based on the criteria used in this book, such countries have been judged too low on economic development; but other analyses do classify these and other countries, including India, South Africa, Suriname, Turkey, and Trinidad and Tobago, as NICs (McCormack 1995). Whatever criteria one employs, some countries that are emerging from the large group of developing countries are difficult to classify.

There is also considerable diversity among the *post-communist developed countries.* Not all the countries that were part of the Soviet Union or its bloc in Eastern Europe have sufficient levels of both economic and social development to be treated as "developed" countries. This group, which includes such countries as Albania, Kyrgyzstan, and Tajikistan, seems best understood as part of the developing countries.

There are other anomalies: A few oil rich ministates like the United Arab Emirates have economic levels comparable to the developed countries; some former Soviet states (e.g., Azerbaijan) retain the considerable social development from their history as part of the Soviet Union but have quite low economic development; Singapore, one of the original NICs, now has levels of development that place it clearly among the developed countries; and so on. The assumption underlying the clustering of countries in Chapters 13 through 15 is that discussing them as distinguishable subsets will illuminate interesting and important issues about the quest for prosperity, security, and stability in the contemporary political world. It is certainly appropriate for you to consider whether certain countries should be in or out of the categories in Chapters 13 through 15. These categories are acceptable if their use provides clarification and insight and, ideally, if they facilitate the development of generalizations and theory. As a political analyst, *you* should assess the utility of this taxonomy, relative to alternative ways of grouping countries for analysis.

IMAGES OF THE DEVELOPED COUNTRIES

When you think of countries in the developed world, what images come to mind?

Anyone reading this book has probably lived in at least one of the more developed countries listed in Table 13.1. As a result, the images you select for "life in the developed world" will be somewhat more accurate than those you might offer for countries in other parts of the world.

Among other things, you might envision large and tall cities, extensive use of high technologies such as computers and VCRs, representative government and electoral politics, an ethic of individualism, a generally high standard of living, freedom of speech, quality medical care, rock and roll, and....

What traits do *you* think best characterize life in the developed countries? As you try to provide your own list, you might become aware of how difficult it is to capture complex reality with straightforward descriptors. The life of a poor farmer in rural Mississippi is rather different from that of a wealthy banker in Zurich or that of a secretary in Yokohama or that of an unemployed factory worker in Milan or that of a teenager in the New Zealand countryside.

The list of such differences could be extended. This is a further reminder that the generalizations offered in these chapters will, at best, capture broad tendencies that oversimplify the diversity of political situations. Given that shortcoming, we begin with a brief discussion of the political culture of the developed countries.

TABLE 13.1
Classification of Countries

Classification	Countries		
Developed Countries	Australia	Iceland	New Zealand
	Austria	Ireland	Norway
	Belgium	Israel	Portugal
	Canada	Italy	Singapore
	Denmark	Japan	Spain
	Finland	Liechtenstein	Sweden
	France	Luxembourg	Switzerland
	Germany	Monaco	United Kingdom
	Greece	Netherlands	United States
Post-communist Developed Countries (PCDCs)	Belarus	Hungary	Russia
	Bulgaria	Kazakhstan	Serbia/Yugoslavia
	Croatia	Latvia	Slovak Republic
	Czech Republic	Lithuania	Slovenia
	Estonia	Poland	Ukraine
	Georgia	Romania	Uzbekistan
Newly Industrializing Countries (NICs)	Argentina	Mauritius	Thailand[a]
	Brazil	Mexico	Turkey[a]
	Chile	South Africa	Uruguay
	Malaysia[a]	South Korea	Venezuela
	Malta	Taiwan	

POLITICAL CULTURE

Each of the developed countries contains a variety of political (sub)cultures. While the political cultures vary across country and time, they can be characterized broadly in terms of the tension and balance between elements of the three ideologies outlined in Chapter 2: classical liberalism, conservatism, and democratic socialism.

Classical liberal ideology is the basis of the assertion, by some groups in the developed countries, that their governments have grown far too large and too interventionist. To promote greater individual and economic freedom, they believe governments in the developed countries should reduce their regulation of the economy and of behavior in private life. This perspective shares with conservatism an antagonism toward the extensive use of government taxing and spending policies to redistribute wealth in the direction of greater equality. But those influenced by conservatism do advocate a strong role for government in preserving the global preeminence of the developed countries through military strength and foreign policy, in supporting economic entrepreneurship, and in maintaining order within societies that seem increasingly disorderly. Conservatives also urge that government policies

TABLE 13.1 (continued)

Classification	Countries		
Developing Countries: "Third World"	Albania[d]	Ghana	Peru
	Algeria	Grenada	Philippines[c]
	Angola	Guatemala	Qatar[e]
	Antigua and Barbuda	Guyana	Saint Christopher– Nevis
	Armenia[d]	Honduras	Saint Lucia
	Azerbaijan[d]	India[c]	Saint Vincent and the Grenadines
	Bahamas	Indonesia[c]	
	Bahrain[e]	Iran	Saudi Arabia[e]
	Barbados	Iraq	Seychelles
	Belize	Ivory Coast	Sierra Leone
	Bolivia	Jamaica	Solomon Islands
	Bosnia and Herzegovina[d]	Jordan	Sri Lanka
		Kenya	Sudan
	Brunei	Kuwait[e]	Suriname
	Cameroon	Kyrgyzstan[d]	Swaziland
	China	Lebanon	Syria
	Colombia	Libya[e]	Tajikistan[d]
	Congo Rep.	Marshall Islands	Trinidad and Tobago
	Costa Rica[c]	Micronesia	
	Cuba	Moldova[d]	Tunisia
	Cyprus	Morocco	Turkmenistan[d]
	Dominica	Nicaragua	United Arab Emirates[e]
	Dominican Republic	Nigeria	
	Ecuador	North Korea	Vietnam
	Egypt	Oman[e]	Yemen
	El Salvador	Pakistan	Zimbabwe
	Fiji	Panama	
	Gabon	Papua New Guinea	
		Paraguay	

(continued)

TABLE 13.1   (continued)

Classification	Countries		
Developing Countries	Afghanistan	Ethiopia	Nepal
Fourth World[b]	Bangladesh	Gambia	Niger
	Benin	Guinea	Rwanda
	Bhutan	Guinea-Bissau	Samoa
	Botswana	Haiti	São Tomé and
	Burkina Faso	Kiribati	Principe
	Burundi	Laos	Senegal
	Cambodia	Lesotho	Sudan
	Cape Verde	Liberia	Somalia
	Central African	Malagasy Republic	Tanzania
	Republic	Malawi	Togo
	Chad	Maldives	Tuvalu
	Comoros	Mali	Uganda
	Congo (Zaire)	Mauritania	Vanuatu
	Dijibouti	Mongolia	Yemen
	Equatorial Guinea	Mozambique	Zambia
	Eritrea	Myanmar	

[a]This country could also be classified as Developing Country: Third World.
[b]All of these countries could also be classified as Developing Country: Third World.
[c]This country is sometimes classified among the NICs (newly industrializing countries).
[d]This country is sometimes classified among the post communist developed countries.
[e]This country has high wealth per capita.

support the traditional family, religious, and moral values that they believe are being undermined by modern culture.

In contrast, those influenced by democratic socialism advocate an activist state whose policies mitigate negative effects of the market-oriented political economies in the developed countries and increase opportunities for disadvantaged citizens. This ideology also leads to support for government policies that use the country's substantial economic development to contribute to a "welfare state," in which inequality is reduced and all citizens receive adequate education, health care, shelter, and security against economic hardship. Those influenced by democratic socialism further argue that the state must take the lead in providing social goods, such as environmental protection, and infrastructure needs, such as transportation systems.

In the developed countries, there are strong and articulate advocates of each of these three ideologies, and elements of each ideology influence both the belief systems of individuals and the collective political cultures of these countries. As every developed country pursues the major political goals of prosperity, stability, and security, its policy decisions are influenced by the current ideological balance within its political culture, as well as by such factors as its history, culture, economic situation, leadership, and distribution of political power. In most of the developed countries, the period after 1945 was characterized by relatively greater support for policies associated with democratic socialism; from the mid-1970s the balance shifted toward conservative and classical liberal values.

By the late 1990s, some leaders, especially British Prime Minister Tony Blair and German Chancellor Gerhard Schroeder, were advocating a *third way*. This is presented as an ideological blend of elements of both classical liberalism and democratic socialism. This third way advocates a reduced level of state intervention in the political economy, allowing the market to dominate the system of production and distribution of goods, and there is little enthusiasm for extensive social welfare programs by the government. Yet there is also a willingness to use public policy to provide quality education and health care, to prevent any groups from being marginalized in the society, to protect the environment, and to support humanitarian values internationally (Dahrendorf 1999). Our exploration of the politics in the developed countries begins with an examination of the key approaches these countries take to achieve prosperity.

GOAL: PROSPERITY

In the developed countries, the goal of prosperity (and its components of economic development and welfare distribution) is pursued with great energy. The emphasis is on sustaining a high level of economic development, under the assumption that this will generate an expanding economic base that directly provides more material benefits to the population and enables government to distribute greater welfare to the citizens.

Mixed Economy

To achieve prosperity, these countries have relied on a mixed political economy. There is considerable private ownership and control of productive resources (land, labor, and capital) and substantial freedom in their use. Private actors are encouraged to use their resources aggressively in order to acquire desired goods and resources, to produce goods, and to maximize their profit. Chapter 8 characterized the state's key roles in the mixed political economy: regulating the free market, providing guidance and incentives for production decisions, and redistributing some money and goods to the less advantaged individuals in the society.

A central policy issue in most of the developed countries is the appropriate level of state activity in the political economy. Should the state reduce the taxes and state regulation imposed on private actors, under the assumption that the market economy is most likely to stimulate greater production and higher economic growth? Or should more of the surplus be captured by the state, which then redistributes it as welfare to the poor and the underclass, who suffer most in an economic downturn? This choice is sometimes posed in a rather simplistic manner as "growth versus welfare."

There is considerable variation in the extent to which the free market dominates in the political economy of particular developed countries. One broad comparative measure of the public-private mix is the percentage of the gross domestic product (GDP, which is defined in Box 8.1) that is in the public sector. Table 13.2 indicates that the proportion of productive capacity (measured as GDP) that is directly under state control varies enormously, from nearly 60 percent in Sweden to 31 percent in the United States. The mixed political economy designation seems especially appropriate for countries in which public expenditure is about 40 percent or more of total GDP, including ten of the seventeen states in the table.

Mixed systems are evident in the Scandinavian states, the "Benelux" states (Belgium, the Netherlands, and Luxembourg), many major West European countries,

TABLE 13.2
Total Public Expenditure as a Percentage of Gross Domestic
Product in Selected Developed Countries

Country	Percentage of GDP (1999)
Sweden	59.6%
France	53.9
Denmark	53.8
Austria	49.4
Italy	49.4
Finland	49.0
Netherlands	47.5
Norway	47.2
Germany	46.9
Canada	41.8
Greece	41.7
Spain	40.8
United Kingdom	40.3
Japan	38.4
Australia	33.6
United States	31.2

Source: Organization for Economic Cooperation and Development, *Economic Outlook* (June 1999):
annex table 28.

and Canada. When political power is held by those oriented to social democratic ideology, taxation is more aggressive, and more revenue is reallocated either as transfer payments or as subsidized goods and services (e.g., health care, housing, educational and cultural opportunities) to the citizens. The state is also more active in protecting individuals and groups against firms whose actions are contrary to the public interest (e.g., price fixing, unsafe working conditions, environmental degradation). In some of these social democracies, the public sector retains control or ownership of some major productive resources that have strategic importance for the political economy and the society. In the international marketplace, domestic producers and workers are protected from aggressive or "unfair" foreign competition by means of tariffs and quotas on imports and subsidies for domestic production and consumption. These mixed economies are sometimes called **social market systems**, because the state encourages the operation of an extensive free-market economy but is also committed to social welfare distribution and income redistribution. The example of Sweden is presented in Box 13.2.

When the political elite is more committed to conservatism or classical liberalism, market incentives are extended to encourage efficient production for private profit, and the state shifts toward leaner, more limited government with lower taxes and a balanced budget. Social welfare services are reduced toward a basic "safety net" with which the state protects individuals only from the harshest consequences of poverty. Government also reduces its constraints on economic activity (e.g, fewer antitrust actions, less protection of unions, industry deregulation). Private ownership and control of the productive system are extended, particularly by **privatiza-**

BOX 13.2

The Social Market System: Sweden

Sweden is an example of the more progressive form of the social market system. A relatively homogeneous country of 8.3 million, the state is committed to capitalism, with more than 90 percent of the economy in private hands. Economic policy facilitates the growth and extension of Swedish goods in the world market. Sweden's prosperous economy ranks tenth in the world on GNP per capita (World Bank 1999).

At the same time, Sweden has one of the most expansive welfare states among the developed countries. About one-third of the national economic output is spent on social programs. Among the universal benefits available to citizens at little or no direct cost are health care, education, day care, maternity/paternity leave, job training, and public transportation. Those suffering economic hardship receive substantial income supplements and support for amenities such as housing. As one example of Sweden's social welfarism, the state provides complete nursing home care to any elderly citizen for less than 5 percent of the actual costs. The regulatory policies of the state are also expansive in both economic and social life (e.g., environmental protection, working conditions). The state has even banned parental spanking to protect children against physical abuse.

Many celebrate Sweden as the model social democracy. A vigorous, multiparty parliamentary system operates under a constitutional monarchy, and there is high citizen involvement in the political process. Citizens are satisfied with the quality of life in their country. Sweden has one of the most equal distributions of wealth and income in the world. And it has one of the highest scores on quality of life indices such as the one in Table 13.3.

One cost of social welfare has been high taxes. Total taxes paid by citizens and firms are about 57 percent of GDP, in comparison with about 38 percent in Germany and 30 percent in the United States. This tax burden reduces Swedes' disposable income and, along with regulatory policies, has made Swedish goods less competitive in the international market. In 1991, the Swedes followed many other electorates in the developed countries that had turned to governments of retrenchment. The Social Democrats, the governing party in Parliament for fifty-three of the previous fifty-nine years, were replaced by a minority governing coalition of center and right parties that have lowered taxes and reduced the public sector. But by 1994, the Swedes had returned the Social Democrats to power. And again, in 1998, despite troubling levels of budget deficits and unemployment, the Social Democrats retained their control of both the prime minister's position and the legislature (as the largest party, with support from another, more leftist socialist party). Thus Sweden's government and citizens continue to support one of the most social of the social market states.

tion (i.e., the selling off of state-owned firms and the use of private firms to provide public goods and services). Most states also reduce tariffs or quotas on imported goods and cut subsidies on domestic production in order to encourage companies to be strong and competitive in the international market.

The developed countries in which a larger proportion of economic activity remains in the private sector, usually designated as *market economies,* include Australia, Japan, Switzerland, the United Kingdom, and the United States.

The array of final goods that the public sector produces also varies among these states. Some sectors, such as education, public safety, utilities, and national defense, are primarily the responsibility of the public sector in all the states. In the mixed political economies that are more committed to the social market, the state also tends to be very active in the provision of health care, housing, transportation, and income support.

Influenced by the strength of classical liberal and third-way ideas, most countries have reduced the direct participation of the state in the political economy, and the percentages in Table 13.2 are considerably lower than ten years ago.

Performance

The developed countries assess their prosperity primarily in terms of economic activity, usually measured as GNP (or GDP) per capita, and there is particular interest in the rate of change in GNP per capita over time. Former U.S. Secretary of State George Schultz reflected a widely shared view among leaders in the developed countries when he stated: "The immediate international imperative is…adequate growth. Without that, no one's objectives are achievable." But some accuse the developed countries of "growthmania," claiming that quality of life and citizen satisfaction are better measures of performance than an increasing GNP.

Table 13.3 provides comparative data on GNP per capita for most developed countries. If one accepts the idea that the value of a society's total production of goods (relative to population size) is a reasonable indicator of its prosperity, these countries do enjoy considerable prosperity. In a rank ordering of GNP per capita among 133 major countries in the world, the top three are Switzerland, Japan, and Norway. Eighteen of the top twenty states are developed countries. The only other states in the top twenty are Singapore and an oil-rich ministate, the United Arab Emirates.

A *"human development index"* (HDI) is the second measure of prosperity in Table 13.3. This measure is computed by the United Nations Development Programme (1998) to reflect the quality of life enjoyed by citizens in a country. It is a composite index that gives equal weight to three indicators: "life expectancy, representing a long and healthy life; educational attainment, representing knowledge; and real GDP (per capita, in purchasing power parity dollars), representing a decent standard of living" (United Nations Human Development Programme 1996: 12). A score of 100 on the index would indicate that all the country's citizens have attained the desirable level of health, education, and living standards, and the scores range from 100 to 0.0. Broadly, a score of 80 or above currently represents a high level of human development (64 countries), scores in the 79–50 range are attributed "medium" levels of human development (65 countries), and a score below 50 indicates a relatively low level (44 countries) (UN Development Programme 1998: Table 5). A more comprehensive quality-of-life index might include many other indicators in addition to the three employed by the United Nations (see, e.g., Estes 1988). If you were attempting to create a comparative measure of the quality of life across many countries, what indicators would *you* include?

TABLE 13.3
Prosperity Measures for Selected Developed Countries

State	GNP/Capita ($U.S.)	Human Development Index
Switzerland	$43,060	93.0
Japan	38,160	94.0
Norway	36,100	94.3
Denmark	34,890	92.8
United States	29,090	94.3
Germany	28,280	92.5
France	26,300	94.6
Sweden	26,210	93.6
Netherlands	25,830	94.1
United Kingdom	20,870	93.2
Australia	20,650	93.2
Italy	20,170	92.2
Canada	19,640	96.0
Israel	16,180	91.3
Spain	14,490	91.3
Greece	11,640	92.4
Portugal	11,010	89.2

Sources: GNP/capita: World Bank 1999: table 1.1; human development index: United Nations Development Programme 1998: table 1.1.

The developed countries in Table 13.3 have very high scores on the human development index. Every country scores above 85.0, with most scoring greater than 90.0, and thus all achieve "high" scores. Canada currently has the highest score in the world (96.0), followed by France (94.6), Norway (94.3), and the United States (94.3). Portugal has the lowest score—89.2— among the more developed countries. Thus on both a basic measure of economic production and on a quality-of-life index that adds measures of literacy and health, the developed countries seem relatively successful in achieving their overall prosperity goals.

Challenges

Erratic economic growth.   Despite the clear accomplishments of most of the developed countries, there are problems evident in the quest for prosperity. Most of these states have periods of solid economic growth (about 4 percent or more per year), and they averaged 2.3 percent annual growth in GNP/capita between 1965–1997 (World Bank 1999: table 1.4). However, there are also extended periods, such as in the early 1980s and again in the early 1990s, when many of the states have not sustained the high levels of economic growth that are essential to their own definition of prosperity. Either there is low growth or, more seriously, there are periods of recession (a negative change in a key economic growth measure). Some underlying problems seem to contribute to the problem of economic growth.

First, increases in *productivity* have been lower than is desirable if the goods that are produced are to generate adequate levels of profit. Several explanations of low productivity gains in the developed countries have been proposed. Some suggest that government regulations and taxes on firms stifle the firms' incentives for expansion and shrink their profit margins. Some emphasize the firms' failure to develop and fully exploit new technologies. Still others claim that the state-controlled areas of the economy are the problem, because they lack the drive for profit that vitalizes the private market sectors.

Second, many of these countries have experienced periods of significant *inflation,* which occurs when there is high demand for productive resources or goods. While high demand might seem good for the economy, high inflation undermines economic stability, planning, and development. It can also result in domestically-produced goods that are more costly, and thus less competitive in the world market. And if high demand for goods is financed by extensive borrowing, then increasing levels of private and government debt can also undermine the value of the currency.

Most importantly, the economies of the developed countries suffer from the increasingly *competitive international economic system.* Economic actors have less direct control of resources and markets than they did when their states were colonial powers (Chapter 12). These firms also face increasing competition from the newly industrializing economies, from the post-communist developed countries, and from developing countries that have substantially lower production costs. Even more importantly, there is growing competition *among* the developed countries, as their firms attempt to sell goods in one another's markets and to other countries. Box 13.3 suggests the comparative strengths of Japan, the European Union, and the United States in this economic competition among the developed countries, which might be the crucial issue for these countries in the current global system.

A combination of low productivity, inflation, and international competition can result in a reduction of income in the national economy, lower levels of production, higher levels of unemployment, trade deficits and balance of payments problems with other states, and other factors that slow the national economic machine. In recent years, even such strong countries as Germany and Japan have had problems sustaining economic growth in the competitive international economic marketplace.

Inequality of prosperity.   Another problem in some developed countries is the unequal distribution of their prosperity. Economic inequalities can be measured in various ways. One widely used measure, the "Gini index" of wealth distribution, computes a score in which a perfectly equal distribution of wealth in the population would equal 0.00 and a completely unequal distribution would score 1.00. As the Gini index increases, and especially as it is higher than about .40, the distribution is very unequal. A second measure of economic inequality is the ratio of the country's personal income that is held by the top 20 percent of the population relative to the lowest 20 percent.

Table 13.4 provides these data on economic inequality for the populations in the developed countries. In global comparisons (as you will see in Table 14.4), the developed countries have relatively less wealth inequality than most countries in the contemporary world. The ratio of income inequality between richest and poorest households is more than 5:1 in the majority of the developed countries. More broadly, the poorest 40 percent of households in these countries get only 18 percent of the total income. This suggests that the wealth differences between those in the top and bottom fifths of the income distribution are substantial but not huge.

Prosperity seems to be distributed most equally in some of developed countries, especially the social market systems, including Denmark, Sweden, and Belgium.

BOX 13.3

When This Battle Is Over, Who Will Wear the Crown?

With the end of the cold war against the Soviet Union, the developed countries have turned their attention from military domination to economic domination. This is a new game, with new stakes and different rules. Ironically, the major players were teammates in the military game: Japan, Western Europe, and the United States. Many analysts are attempting to determine which player will prevail in this global battle for economic hegemony. Which one do you think will win? Why? Political economist Lester Thurow provides a comprehensive handicapping of this new competition in *Head to Head: Coming Economic Battles Among Japan, Europe and America* (Thurow 1992). In his analysis, each competitor has impressive assets and serious shortcomings.

Japan

The positives: The current leader in global economic competition, Japan has the world's largest trade surplus. Among its greatest strengths is a superb educational system, which is particularly distinguished for the fine education provided to the less able half of its population. Japan's cohesive national culture facilitates cooperation and purposeful shared action to achieve its collective goals. The state and industry collaborate very effectively, employing the developmental state model (Chapter 10) to target investment and resources for maximum economic return.

The problems: Japan must reduce the protectionist trade policies that have been central in its drive to create the ultimate export-driven economy. This is necessary to prevent a serious backlash in which it is shut out of its important markets in Europe and North America. This might also deal with the "rich Japan, poor Japanese" problem by relieving the frustration of its own population to policies that stifle domestic consumption and limit their enjoyment of Japan's prosperity. For more effective overseas expansion, Japan must overcome its cultural insularity, developing better strategies for cooperating and compromising with governments and workers in other cultures. And it must revise both its educational system and its research and development policies to encourage greater innovation and inventiveness. The growing economic power of Japan's neighbors, the NICs and China, might provide opportunities for Japan's continued economic expansion, but is more likely to constitute dangers.

Europe

The positives: With its combination of many cultures and skills, Europe is the excellent all-rounder. It can draw on such strengths as German technological and scientific expertise, British economic and financial acumen, and Italian aesthetics. Its population is well educated, generally prosperous, and comfortable with its institutionalized, highly pluralist political order. Its citizens are confident that their governments' social market systems will protect their welfare and ensure them of a

(continued)

BOX 13.3 *(Continued)*

secure life. The European Union (EU) of 375 million people is now the world's largest single market, with an annual GNP of more than $7 billion, making Europe the richest economic actor in the global system (recall Box 12.1).

The problems: The EU is a source of strength, but the move to complete integration is an unresolved challenge. Some member states continue to guard their sovereignty jealously and are unwilling to sacrifice national interest for collective good. There are also long-standing nation-based animosities between some countries. The attempts by the EU to establish fully its stated goals of complete economic, military, and political unification could become a source of continuing tension and even major conflict between the countries of Europe. The puzzle of integration is made more complex by the evolution of Eastern and Central Europe. Many post-communist countries desire membership in the EU, but could be a serious drag on its political coherence and economic vitality. Even without membership, the turmoil and violence in that region will have many negative consequences for Western Europe.

The United States

The positives: The United States has the largest national political economy, with vast resources and a big internal market. The NAFTA trade agreement with Canada and Mexico further expands its regional economic options. The United States remains the world leader in the development and use of high technology, which partly accounts for its continued capacity for productivity gains. Its extensive commitment to higher education has produced a very large pool of what is arguably the world's best-trained and most-skilled knowledge workers. Its political system is deeply institutionalized, and its public policies allow freedom and profit incentives to economic actors.

The problems: Its role as the world's only military superpower provides it with considerable leverage in international relations. But the United States spent $4 trillion to win the cold war, and its continuing high level of global military involvement results in massive expenditures that limit the resources available for economic competition. Although about half the population receives an excellent college education, nearly half of the adults end their schooling with a dreadful education that prevents most of them from contributing importantly to a postindustrial economy. NAFTA might create explosive policy problems as the United States deals with the large number of Americans who are not knowledge workers and whose skills will make them noncompetitive with the low-wage workers of Mexico. And compared to their rivals, Americans are big spenders and poor savers. The mix of high consumption, low investment, and a willingness to mortgage the future have produced the world's largest debtor nation, with a cumulative debt of nearly $5 trillion.

And the winner is:

No one is certain who will win this economic battle. Although some analysts argue that all can win, most conclude that there will be very significant differentials among the competitors. After his detailed analysis, Thurow concludes that the winner will be "the House of Europe," whose overall balance and more limited problems provide it with the winning edge. (Based on Thurow 1992.)

The developed countries have the highest levels of economic prosperity in the world, but some also have substantial inequality in the distribution of that prosperity, with significant numbers of very poor people like this homeless man.

These countries have among the most equal distributions of income in the world, as measured by the Gini index. To a significant degree, this level of equality is attributable to the effects of sustained public policies which, as in Sweden's social market system, provide a diversity of services and subsidies. The political cultures in these states also tend to be more accepting of governmental actions which redistribute prosperity to insure a better quality of life for all citizens.

Not everyone in the developed countries enjoys a life of material well being. About 100 million people in these countries live below the poverty line and 100 million are homeless (United Nations Development Programme 1998: 27). There are higher proportions of the relatively poor in certain developed countries, especially those where the values of classical liberalism and conservatism are dominant in the policy-making process. Such states tend to distribute relatively less welfare through the provision of human services and there is less concern in the society for reducing inequalities. The governments in these countries are especially unlikely to provide broad welfare support to politically marginalized groups and to noncitizens. The United States and Switzerland, for example, rank among the bottom half of the world's countries on measures of equal wealth distribution. In the United States,

TABLE 13.4
Income Inequality in Selected Developed Countries

State	Gini Index of Income Inequality	Ratio of Household Income, Highest to Lowest 20 Percent of Households
United States	40.1	9.4 to 1
Switzerland	36.1	5.9 to 1
Israel	35.5	6.2 to 1
Australia	33.7	5.8 to 1
France	32.7	5.6 to 1
United Kingdom	32.6	5.6 to 1
Spain	32.5	5.4 to 1
Canada	31.5	5.2 to 1
Netherlands	31.5	5.0 to 1
Italy	31.2	5.1 to 1
Japan	n.a.	4.3 to 1
Germany	28.1	4.1 to 1
Belgium	25.0	3.6 to 1
Sweden	25.0	3.6 to 1
Denmark	24.7	3.6 to 1

Source: World Bank 1999: table 2.8.

the poorest 20 percent of households (which also tend to have more members) have only about one-ninth as much disposable income as the wealthiest 20 percent of households. About one in eight US citizens is "in poverty" according to the government's own statistics, and one in five children is born poor. Such substantial and persistent inequality can produce a permanent *underclass* of citizens who are also disadvantaged in education, job skills, housing, health care, and, most broadly, quality of life (Wilson 1987; 1996).

These challenges of sustaining economic growth and distributing prosperity are continual. No developed country has permanently solved them and they remain at the heart of the political debate in virtually all of these countries. Nevertheless, the developed countries have a better overall record than any other set of countries in the world in delivering higher levels of prosperity to most citizens.

GOAL: STABILITY

The developed countries have been generally successful in achieving their stability goals of political institutionalization and order maintenance. Within a framework of representative democracy, the politics of these states is characterized by the group approach, with multiple competing elites and groups. There are substantial pressures on some of the governments, where existing economic and social problems are exacerbated by vigorous group politics. But overall these states enjoy relatively high levels of social and political stability while allowing widespread participation in the political process.

Chapters 6 and 7 described the variation in the political structures of different developed countries. Most have a cabinet government, based on coalitions formed from a multiparty system. Some are very stable, with alternating left then right governments (Great Britain) or coalitions (Canada, Denmark, and Germany). Others experience substantial instability, due to the fragmented nature of the party system (Greece, Israel, and Italy). While there are some hybrids, with an elected president in addition to the cabinet and prime minister (France), the United States is an exception as a presidential government with a two-party system, and Switzerland is an exception as a council system. Many countries have dual executives, often with a constitutional monarch.

Political power is distributed rather than being concentrated in a single governmental structure. Most are unitary states, although a few are federations (e.g., Canada, the United States, and Germany). Even in the unitary states, policy implementation for many human and welfare services is the responsibility of local governments. The national legislatures are important actors in the policy process, with most being unicameral or having one dominant chamber. These countries have large, efficient bureaucracies and relatively independent judiciaries. Chapter 3 indicated that the developed countries allow a diversity of modes of political participation by their citizens and that most countries have considerable political involvement, at least in terms of elections and interest in politics.

Political Institutionalization

The developed countries have high levels of political institutionalization—that is, substantial value and stability are attached to political structures and processes. They are all constitutional democracies, and thus leaders and policies are constrained by the rule of law and the rights of the ruled are guaranteed by law and tradition. Individuals and groups have substantial freedom to criticize and oppose the government and to engage in a wide variety of nonviolent political actions to change leaders and policies. Leaders operate with a limited mandate, leadership succession is regularized, and the selection of many public officials is based on citizen elections and genuine alternatives.

The governments in some of the developed countries have evolved over centuries by means of gradual and generally nonviolent mechanisms of political change. This pattern applies to such states as Belgium, Canada, Denmark, Great Britain, Sweden, Switzerland, and the United States. The distribution and uses of political power have changed as new groups gain admission to and influence in the political system, extending participation steadily until mass representative democracy is created. This "politics of inclusion" has drawn important groups into the political process and built their support for the political system, reducing their need to use extraconstitutional mechanisms such as violence to capture political power (see Box 13.4). While this emphasis on the relative absence of violence is accurate, it is useful to recall Barrington Moore's observation, discussed in Box 10.2, that development in virtually all societies has involved a considerable amount of violence against some groups.

Some developed countries have substantially restructured their political system in the last sixty years. Many created new constitutional systems after their involvement in World War II had undermined the legitimacy of the previous political regime, as in Austria, France, Italy, Japan, and Germany. Despite the relatively short period during which these political systems could acquire value and stability, democratic political processes appear to be firmly established. While many have

BOX 13.4

Building Political Institutionalization by Political Inclusion: The British Case

Great Britain is an excellent example of the evolutionary approach to building political institutionalization. Britain has the longest-lived modern political system in the world. During a period of nearly 800 years (after 1215) the powers of the hereditary monarch (the king or queen) were established, then constrained, and finally limited markedly. Now, in the twenty-first century, the monarch exercises some formal political functions but has virtually no direct political power. The monarch still dissolves Parliament for new elections, summons an individual to form a government and become prime minister, and delivers the opening speech in Parliament that sets the year's legislative agenda. But by convention, these activities are done in a politically neutral manner, with the monarch serving a symbolic role, merely implementing the decisions of the real executive power base, the prime minister and the cabinet.

In parallel, the political power of the legislative bodies, the House of Lords and the House of Commons, was gradually extended after 1215. The elective Commons, which began as a weak second house, slowly gained equality and then clear dominance over the Lords, whose membership has been mainly by heredity. The Commons, which directly represents the population, has emerged as the powerful house that selects the executive leaders (cabinet and prime minister) and authorizes legislation, an indication of the increasing influence of the citizens over the political process. In 1999, the Commons ended the hereditary nature of the House of Lords, limiting its members to "life peers"—individuals appointed for life on the basis of merit (not heredity), in a set of appointments technically made by the monarch but actually controlled by the Commons.

Over the same period, the electorate expanded steadily, with new classes of citizens being enfranchised as wealth, gender, and age barriers to political participation were dropped. The Reform Act in 1832 increased the electorate from 500,000 to 813,000. Another Reform Act in 1867 increased it 82 percent, from 1,358,000 to 2,477,000. Legislation in 1884 reduced property requirements for voting so that virtually every working man could vote for members of the House of Commons, and also for the local council. In 1918 all adult men were allowed to vote, as well as women over 30 (if married or property owning!). In 1928 voting rights were extended to all adult women, and the voting age for men and women was reduced to 18 in 1969 (Norton 1998).

The political parties also changed, becoming more representative of and responsive to the major groups in the society. As new groups entered the electorate, each party altered its program to include policies meant to attract the groups' support. Most important, the Labour Party, which explicitly represented the interests of the working class and the trade unions, emerged after 1906 and soon became one of the two major parties. The Labour government of 1945–1951 enacted an extensive set of policy decisions, which implemented the British welfare state and greatly benefited the working class and lower class.

BOX 13.4 *(Continued)*

The great majority of the British population believes that the governmental bureaucracy serving it is honest and efficient and that the politicians have been relatively responsive to citizen needs and interests. (Recall the data on the British political culture in Chapter 2.) The period since 1945 has been difficult for Britain, as it has declined from a major world power to a marginal actor in international politics with a struggling economy. Thus there have been periods of substantial political unrest and occasional outbreaks of internal violence by groups (especially ethnic minorities and workers in declining industries) who are frustrated by the failure of the political system to serve their interests. There has also been a sharp decline in support for the monarchy, which has traditionally been a unifying force. Still, the British political system is highly institutionalized, with strong support from its population, stability, and effective performance of its functions.

had relatively strong leftist or socialist parties, even those parties are generally committed to working within the democratic parliamentary system.

Order Maintenance

The developed countries have had varying levels of success in meeting the stability goal of order maintenance. This goal can be interpreted as the *absence of disorder* in the political, social, and personal domains. As discussed in Chapters 3 and 11, explicitly political violence includes such modes as illegal demonstrations, riots, rebellions, coups, and revolutions. Failure to maintain public order is also reflected in social disorder, such as murder, rape, robbery, white-collar crime, and organized crime, as well as in personal disorders, such as suicide and substance abuse (alcohol, drugs).

These countries are neither the most orderly nor the most disorderly in the political world. Overall, most citizens in most developed countries enjoy secure lives. The differences among the states can be very substantial, and it is difficult to generalize. The Netherlands, Norway, and Japan, for example, have relatively low levels of social disorder such as violent crime. Yet Japan has one of the highest suicide rates in the world, alcohol abuse is high in Norway, and drug abuse is high in the Netherlands. The United States and France, in contrast, are relatively high on most measures of social and personal disorder. These are among the increasing number of developed countries with substantial problems related to substance abuse and drug-related crime.

While the homicide rate in the United States is not dramatically higher than the rate in a few of the other developed countries (e.g., Canada), its murder-by-handgun rate is "exceptional": 11,000 handgun murders per year, a part of the 37,000 deaths per year caused by gunfire. In contrast, less than 100 people per year are murdered with handguns in virtually every other developed country. Continuing problems with violent nationalist groups (as in Britain and Israel) or with extremist political groups (as in Germany) result in higher levels of political disorder in some countries.

What explanation(s) do you think best accounts for the fact that some of the developed countries seem to have such high levels of social and personal disorder?

Challenges to Stability

Value conflicts and disputes.   Since the developed countries allow open group politics, disagreements about specific policies and even about fundamental values can become such active issues that they produce instability. Some enduring value conflicts center on disputes regarding the circumstances in which the *state regulation of individual behavior* is legitimate. Such regulation might be justified to preserve social peace, to promote the collective good, to protect the rights and freedom of others, or to protect the individual from himself and others.

In the United States, for example, state constraints on private behavior generate particular controversy between conservatives and others in such areas as the following:

Abortion

Development and use of private land

Discrimination/ preferences (based on age, gender, ethnicity)

Educational curriculum (religious instruction, sex education, evolution versus creationism)

Free speech (in the media, on the Internet)

Ownership and use of firearms

Sexual conduct

Substance abuse (alcohol, drugs)

Another source of instability in many developed countries is the conflict among *nationality groups.* Some countries have a long tradition of containing several nations, such as Canada's English-speaking and French-speaking populations, or the Walloons and Flemish in Belgium. Some countries have substantially increased their cultural diversity in recent decades, either because of immigration from their former colonial states (as in Britain and France) or because of the immigration of large numbers of foreign workers (as in Germany, Switzerland, and the United States). A few states, such as Israel, have a deeply entrenched antipathy between their largest nationality groups.

For both cultural and economic reasons, the value conflicts between nationality groups have been intensifying. Up to this point, most of the discrimination and violence have been directed against the minority groups and especially noncitizens (e.g., physical violence against foreign guest workers and political asylum seekers in Germany). "Anti-foreigner" politics have become a powerful force in some countries (e.g., the Freedom Party in Austria). This has generated counterdemands for policies supporting multiculturalism and protection/promotion of minority rights (e.g., bilingualism and the movement to partition Canada, affirmative action in the United States). Thus the rights and restrictions on noncitizens are volatile policy issues in many developed countries.

As previously described, there is also intense political debate regarding the degree to which the state should have an active role in the *political economy* and should distribute generous welfare benefits to various groups in the society. Many groups have strong ideological concerns or vested interests associated with government policies on taxing, public spending, and regulation of the economy. Thus there is active and sometimes rancorous conflict over these issues among a diversity of interest groups who demand that public policy be shaped to serve their particular agenda.

Hyperpluralism and political polarization.   Resolving such value conflicts among competing groups and making difficult policy decisions are among the defining characteristics of politics. The political elites and the governments are generally committed to working within the framework of representative democracy and group politics. They are generally successful in establishing compromises on issues that might become highly politicized.

However, where value conflicts are intense and many groups are mobilized, efforts to maintain political order are particularly difficult. Chapter 9 suggested that the processes of group politics are not well suited to situations in which there are many mobilized groups with strong and irreconcilable preferences. The risk is **hyperpluralism**, a situation in which many effective groups are able to pressure the government to respond to their policy demands. As the government attempts to satisfy all these different group demands, public policy can become contradictory or muddled. Even worse, the government might find itself trying to accommodate so many interests that it becomes somewhat paralyzed, unable to respond in the face of competing demands (Edwards, Wattenberg, and Lineberry 1998: 268–270). If key groups become very dissatisfied with government unresponsiveness and paralysis, they can make increasingly strident political demands, engage in aggres-

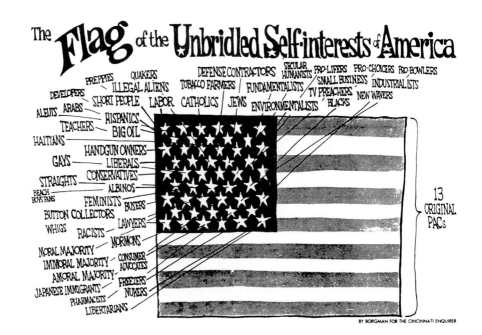

BY BORGMAN FOR THE CINCINNATI ENQUIRER

sive political actions in support of their respective policy preferences, and produce high levels of political instability.

The risks of instability are especially great when there is substantial political polarization within the society. In such cases, center parties and centrist policies are only weakly supported by the citizens, and politics becomes a battleground between large, mobilized groups of the right and the left. Conflict resolution and decision making become extremely difficult for the political system, since it is often impossible to satisfy both sides. Such polarization and instability occur periodically in such countries as Britain, France, Italy, and Japan.

A few states have concluded that the threats to stability are so great that democratic processes must be restrained. For example, Israel, faced with an extensive, combative political resistance from its minority Arab population (e.g., the Intifada, 1987–1992), reacted aggressively to maintain order and prevent hyperpluralism. However, the governments of most developed countries tolerate hyperpluralism and political disorder rather than becoming too repressive in the pursuit of stability goals. Thus Britain, France, Italy, the United States, and other states have periodically experienced rather high levels of civil disorder during the past forty years. Other states, such as the Netherlands, Norway, and Switzerland, have reduced the incidence of serious disorder by nurturing a cultural style of social tolerance or by developing political institutions that accommodate competing groups (Eckstein 1966; Lijphart 1978; 1984). Most analysts conclude that these factors are not a fundamental risk to political stability, because political institutionalization is strong in the developed countries.

Domination and control.   A far more critical assessment of order maintenance in many of the developed countries is offered by some analysts. They describe societies in which states control their citizens by coercion rather than consensus, combining limited welfare distribution, extensive political socialization, and effective restraints on public life by the state's agents (e.g., the police, the bureaucracy, the judicial system). Some class and elite theorists also argue that each more developed country is controlled by a "hegemonic elite"—an extraordinarily powerful group that sustains its domination over a long period of time (Domhoff 1998; Esping-Andersen 1990; Poulantzas 1973). These theorists insist that politics in the developed countries is not a fair competition among groups, that the state is not a neutral referee, and that most public policies enable certain groups to maintain their advantaged position in society (Chapter 9).

It is clear that the developed countries do have powerful and effective institutions which can shape the political process, control groups, and contain the level of instability. And the group politics explanation offers a problematic account of how democratic politics can work when there are huge inequalities in political resources available to different groups (Dahl 1961; Parenti 1996). There is no doubt that certain institutions and individuals (such as media baron Rupert Murdoch, described in Box 13.5) have extraordinary powers to shape political life in the developed countries. Yet most analysts and most citizens see no compelling evidence that these political systems are controlled by self-serving, nondemocratic elites. Radical (Marxist) theorists interpret such citizen views as tragic evidence that the state *can* fool most of the people all of the time. One of the great (and perhaps impossible) challenges for political scientists is to develop an indisputable empirical analysis of how political power is exercised, how values are allocated, and how order is maintained in the developed countries.

GOAL: SECURITY

During the twentieth century, the developed countries enjoyed moderate success in the pursuit of their basic security goals, especially survival and freedom. However, the first half of the century was marked by two massive multistate wars among the developed countries. While most of the states survived intact (there are notable exceptions, including Austria-Hungary after World War I and Germany after World War II), many states were devastated in human, material, and political terms by these wars. Arguably, the greatest security victory of the developed countries in the second half of the century was the collapse of the communist state in the Soviet Union, their major adversary. At the beginning of the twenty-first century, these countries are still establishing new arrangements for security in the altered, post–cold war international system.

The Era of Colonialism

Some developed countries have been extremely successful at extending their influence or control over other states in order to enhance their own security goals. Belgium, France, Germany, Japan, Portugal, Spain, and the United States are among the developed countries that dominated vast colonial territories until the mid-twentieth century. Great Britain was the leading colonial power, controlling more than one-fourth of the world's population (in 1945). Colonialism was a means by which many of these countries furthered virtually all of their security goals. While their colonial holdings are now independent states, the dominance of the developed countries often continues through neocolonialism, as Chapter 12 described. From the perspective of many developing countries, the developed countries have very much "had it their own way" in promoting their security interests and projecting their will in the international political arena.

The Cold War Period

From World War II until the late 1980s, the security goals and security-oriented actions of virtually all of the developed countries were powerfully influenced by the international struggle between the United States and the Soviet Union, generally called *the cold war.*

During the cold war period, U.S. policy was based on the assumption that the main threat to the security of the developed countries was the Soviet Union, its allies, and the worldwide expansion of communism. The freedom, influence, and even survival of the developed countries depended on strong military power to balance the Soviet bloc. As the leading advocate of this bipolar balance-of-power perspective, the United States had a foreign policy based on at least two core elements.

First, the United States used military power in an attempt to deter Soviet military activity outside of the Soviet Union and its European satellites. The United States was the key actor in NATO, a mutual security pact among the developed countries, and it was prepared to undertake military actions anywhere in the world where Soviet activities threatened its conception of international stability. The United States also developed a massive capacity for nuclear war. The nuclear arsenals of the United States and the Soviet Union created a balance of terror in which neither side was willing to initiate direct military hostilities against the other (Chapter 12).

BOX 13.5

Media Mogul Murdoch

Information is one of the critical resources that can shape politics in any society. If the control and dissemination of information is concentrated into the hands of a few major actors, the possibility of elite domination increases. Rupert Murdoch, an Australian (and naturalized American), stands tall among a small group of media moguls who are shifting global media power toward private actors (Hachten 1999). Some other very influential members of this group include Emilio Azcarraga of Mexico (Televisa) and Ted Turner of the United States (CNN, TBS [Turner Broadcasting System]).

Murdoch started with ownership of two Australian newspapers. He then began a forty-year process of leveraging his holdings to acquire additional media resources in other parts of the world. He purchased control of the *Sun,* a London tabloid that he pushed to top ratings with a strong dose of sensationalism and sex. His next moves were to acquire a major London publishing house and the prestigious *London Times* newspaper. He pursued the same strategy with the media of United States, even acquiring U.S. citizenship so that he could legally own an American television station. He purchased newspapers, including the *Boston Herald* and the *Star* tabloid, Fox broadcasting (Fox television and Twentieth-Century Fox films), *TV Guide,* the Harper-Collins publishing house, and the Barnes and Noble bookstore chain.

Murdoch's next major step was the founding of BSkyB, a multichannel satellite network initially serving only Great Britain with news, sports, and entertainment. In 1993, he acquired Star TV, the major Asian satellite system broadcasting in Mandarin Chinese, Hindi, and English to thirty-eight countries. He is now the world's largest distributor of videocassettes and owns television stations reaching 40 percent of American families. He is also gaining more leverage in other areas of popular culture, such as control of professional sports teams (e.g., the Los Angeles Dodgers, the Manchester City Football Club).

Murdoch's dream of a communications empire with global reach is close to realization as he works to link these major systems and add satellite news service to southern Africa and cable television service to Latin America. His current net personal income of more than $200 million per year is derived from the $1 billion yearly profit of his communications corporation.

Does Murdoch have any personal values that influence the content of the messages transmitted by his media? While he denies substantive influence, he is a staunch political conservative. His newspapers and television networks are openly supportive of conservative candidates and policies and antagonistic to most of those on the left, especially the British trade unions and the Kennedy family politicians in America. In 1992, for example, Murdoch purchased the story of Gennifer Flowers, who claimed that she had engaged in a twelve-year affair with Bill Clinton, then candidate for U.S. president, and Murdoch's vast array of media relentlessly circulated the story.

BOX 13.5 *(Continued)*

After helping Murdoch gain a waiver allowing him to own the *New York Post* newspaper as well as a New York television station, then-Governor Mario Cuomo observed that while other newspapers might provide a politician with one editorial, "With Murdoch, he gives you the whole paper, page 1 to page 96, every day for six months—for you or against you." While most of the content of Murdoch's media is not explicitly political, there can be little doubt that his information and "infotainment" empire help shape the ideas and views of many people. (Discussion based on Barber 1995; Shawcross 1991.)

Secondly, the United States applied its considerable military, economic, and political power to affect the actions of many developing countries. It provided support to pro-American, anticommunist regimes (e.g., Congo/Zaire, El Salvador, South Korea) and to many nonaligned Third World states, and it attempted to destabilize leftist or pro-Soviet regimes (e.g., Cuba, Grenada, North Korea). This policy was generally successful, but suffered its most catastrophic setback in the direct U.S. military involvement and ultimate defeat in Vietnam (1964–1975).

Not all political elites in the developed countries shared the U.S. perception of a clear bipolar struggle between the forces of good and evil. Some states (e.g., Austria, Finland, and Switzerland) maintained a position of neutrality. Others (e.g., Denmark, France, Greece, Italy, New Zealand, and Sweden) emphasized a more conciliatory policy of détente ("relaxation" of tensions) with the Soviet bloc, based on the view that both blocs had common interests in maintaining their superior position internationally and preventing a global nuclear war. This latter view became more widespread by the late 1980s, due to Soviet leader Mikhail Gorbachev's effective peace initiatives.

Challenges to Security in the Post–Cold War Period

By 1990, with a speed that stunned the world, the Soviet bloc countries and even the Soviet Union were transformed (see Chapter 15). These countries moved away from communism and in the direction of democratic politics and market political economies. They sought economic cooperation rather than military conflict with the United States and Western Europe. The cold war seemed to end with the unification of East and West Germany (1990) and particularly with the breakup of the Soviet Union (1991) into fifteen countries.

The global military power of the United States is now unmatched. But the costs of maintaining such massive military power for fifty years have taken a serious toll on the economic strength of the United States and on its willingness to serve as the world's "police." Although the United States still takes an active role, there is now greater emphasis on alternative security arrangements among the developed countries, such as collective security through the United Nations or NATO, and on regional security agreements. As they reformulate their approaches to security, they are influenced by at least four major security challenges.

Instability in the post-communist developed countries.   For the developed countries, especially those in Europe, the good news is that the threat of war against the formidable Soviet bloc has disappeared. But the less good news is that some states of the former Soviet bloc remain sources of insecurity. First, the military power of the Soviet bloc has not been eliminated; rather, much of it is now controlled by a set of less stable regimes. Second, there has been economic and political instability and ethnic conflict in some post-communist developed countries, particularly the former Yugoslavia and Russia (see Chapter 15). Thus all developed countries that border these countries face major spillover problems that undermine regional security.

Disorder in the developing countries.   During the cold war period, most major political violence occurred in developing countries. Given the growing ethnonationalism and increasing economic and political expectations in most developing countries, the incidence of disorder will increase. In each situation, governments of the developed countries must weigh the security benefits from stabilizing a distant part of the international system against the substantial costs of intervening and the difficulty (impossibility?) of maintaining stability in many of those countries. Thus the developed countries are grappling with complex decisions on when, how, and for what purposes to intervene.

Proliferation of weapons.   Significant reductions in the military equipment of Russia and the United States have occurred during the post–cold war period (e.g., START II). However, this period is also characterized by the expansion of military power in many states, the sale of weapons of mass destruction to all who can pay for them and the spread of nuclear weapons to more countries. Equally serious, because they are the cause of most casualties in political violence, is the widespread distribution of "light weapons" (e.g., guns, mortars, land mines) to large numbers of irregular forces (Klare 1997). Firms from the developed countries still lead the world in production and sales of military hardware, but the number of suppliers is expanding and the developed countries must take the lead in the development of effective strategies to prevent the further proliferation of all these kinds of weapons.

International economic relations.   In the absence of a common military enemy, economic competition becomes a source of more conflict. As noted earlier, the most powerful actors at the center of this global economic competition are the developed countries themselves (Box 13.3), as well as multinational corporations (Chapter 12). But the newly industrializing economies (see Chapter 15) and even the developing countries also intensify this competition. Fierce global economic competition could be the greatest source of insecurity for the more developed countries in the post–cold war period (Thurow 1992).

THE DEVELOPED COUNTRIES OVERALL

In terms of pursuit of the broad goals of prosperity, stability, and security, the more developed countries generally have the highest levels of "success" in the world. These states have the most developed systems of economic production, especially when measured by gross national product per capita. In the last four decades these states have evolved political economies that effectively mix capitalism and democratic socialism. The majority of productive resources remain under private control, but in most developed countries the state has established a substantial program of welfare distribution to the citizenry. Most of their citizens enjoy a higher standard of living than people in any other part of the world.

By exercising their considerable economic, military, and political power in the international system, the developed countries have also met their security goals. They have a strong record of survival, influence, and even control over other political systems. For many of the assertive developed countries, the approach to international balance-of-power politics was most extreme during the period of colonialism. The leading developed countries still exercise their power quite energetically to maintain their advantages in the international system.

In the pursuit of security goals, the greatest recent success of the developed countries is their "victory" in the cold war against the Soviet Union and its global promotion of communism. But security issues are more ambiguous in the post–cold war era. The Soviet threat, which encouraged cooperation among the developed countries and shaped the international system after 1945, disappeared by the early 1990s. They must now develop strategies in response to interstate conflicts based on different economic, political, and ideological issues. If they are ineffective, the risk is a return to the intensive conflict among themselves that caused two devastating world wars.

The success of the developed countries in achieving prosperity and security is not unqualified. While most citizens enjoy a high material standard of living, others live in relative poverty and despair, and such inequalities might be the Achilles' heel of their prosperity. Also, critics, especially in developing countries, argue that the developed countries have maintained their prosperity by exploitation—historically, of the poor within their own societies, and more recently and more systematically, of the population and resources of other states, by means of neocolonialism and military intervention (see Chapter 14). They have not reached the top by being passive or generous.

The developed countries, perhaps because of their prosperity and security, have maintained a relatively open, fair, and stable group politics. Democracy and political equality do not prevent enormous inequalities in political influence and political power. And there are tensions between the commitment to individual freedom and limited government, on the one hand, and state intervention to increase equality of outcomes, on the other. While pluralism has occasionally been severely strained, there is tolerance of a wide range of political beliefs and actions. Many individuals and groups are able to mobilize their political resources to influence the processes of government and decision making, and citizens do have the right to select among leadership elites at regular intervals. In comparison with other countries in the past fifty years, the developed countries receive high marks for their maintenance of constitutional, participatory politics.

FOR FURTHER CONSIDERATION

1. How would you further classify the developed countries into two or more subsets? What criteria would you employ?
2. In the post–cold war period, what is the greatest threat to the stability of the developed countries? What is the most appropriate strategy to reduce that threat?

3. Consider the issue of hyperpluralism. Do you think that a country can be *too* democratic? What are several of the strongest arguments on each side of this question?

4. Write a script or role-play (with others) a situation in which a classical liberal, a conservative, and a democratic socialist discuss the virtues and failings of a particular developed country.

5. If you were to create a "quality-of-life" index, what measures would you include? Rank order the importance you would attach to the various measures and explain why you have given those rankings.

6. How should the desirable level of distribution of prosperity among citizens in a society be determined? Should the state do anything to ensure that prosperity is distributed more equally among its citizens? What actions by the state are appropriate and might be effective?

FOR FURTHER READING

Allison, Graham. (1971). *The Essence of Decision: Explaining the Cuban Missile Crisis.* Boston: Little, Brown. Applies three important analytic frameworks to explain how democratic governments make decisions—in this case, the U.S. decision regarding a response to the placement of Soviet missiles on Cuba in 1962.

Almond, Gabriel, and G. Bingham Powell, Eds. (2000). *Comparative Politics Today: A World View.* 7th ed. New York: Addison Wesley Longman. Solid case-by-case studies of selected developed countries (England, France, Germany, Japan, and the United States) as well as Brazil, China, Egypt, India, Mexico, and Nigeria, employing Almond's structural-functional concepts (recall Chapter 5).

Burgess, Anthony. (1970). *A Clockwork Orange.* Harmondsworth, England: Penguin. A dystopian novel describing a near-future Britain in which youth gangs rule the mean streets of a divided and amoral society. It is the source of a chilling film by Stanley Kubrick.

Castles, Francis G. (1998). *Comparative Public Policy: Patterns of Post-war Transformation.* Northampton, MA: Edward Elgar Publishing Company. A rich, comparative characterization of how the governments of twenty-one developed countries have attempted to create effective policies to deal with the challenges of the last half of the twentieth century, with particular attention to issues of both the distribution of welfare and the control of the political economy.

Dinnerstein, Leonard, and David Reimers. (1999). *Ethnic Americans: A History of Immigration.* 4th ed. New York: Columbia University Press. The complex dynamics and processes of the American governmental and citizen response to waves of immigrants, with particular attention on the most recent waves of the last two decades, are thoughtfully explored.

Kennedy, Paul. (1987). *The Rise and Fall of the Great Powers.* New York: Random House. A sweeping analysis of how countries such as the United Kingdom and the United States become the strongest in the world, and then decline.

Pinder, John. (1999). *The Building of the European Union.* 3rd ed. New York: Oxford University Press. A sound exploration of the institutions, processes, and challenges of the European Union as it attempts to extend its roles, power, and effectiveness in the complex post–cold war world.

Thurow, Lester C. (1992). *Head to Head: Coming Economic Battles among Japan, Europe and America.* New York: William Morrow. A rich study of the post–cold war shift in which the key conflicts will be economic ones among the developed countries.

Wolferen, Karel van. (1989). *The Enigma of Japanese Power: People and Politics in a Stateless Nation.* New York: Knopf. A fascinating characterization of the linkages between culture and politics in contemporary Japan. The author's argument that Japan's politics are different from those in other democratic states, despite similar political structures, evoked very strong negative reactions from the Japanese.

School days in Cairo. Education is a top priority in many countries that are attempting to achieve both social and economic development.

The Developing Countries

THIRD WORLD IMAGES

What is your image of the many *developing countries* that are sometimes called the *Third World* ? It might be of dusty villages where poor and uneducated people scrape out a subsistence diet from their small farms. It might be of large cities where some live and work in modern, technologically advanced settings but are surrounded by a huge, dense population living in abject poverty and squalor. It might be of a huge state attempting to govern one billion people or of a small island state with a population of less than 50,000. It might be of a country successfully adapting European political forms of representative democracy, popular participation, and freedom of opposition, or of a despotism where the small leadership clique ruthlessly eliminates all opposition and where leadership change occurs only by political violence.

Developmental Classification

Somewhere among the 140 states and more than 4.8 billion people of the developing countries, all of these images are accurate. Even the definitions that place particular countries in this group are somewhat varied. Classification as a developing country can be based on a strictly economic definition such as GNP per capita, which is used, for example, by the World Bank. Virtually all of the states considered in this chapter are included among the World Bank's two subgroups of developing countries (middle income and low income), with GNP per capita ranging from $80 per year to about $9,655 per year (see Chapter 13).

Chapter 13 explained why this book uses a classification that also considers a state's overall level of social development. Figure 13.1 displayed graphically the large and diverse cluster of developing countries considered in the present chapter. The post-communist developed countries and the NICs (newly industrializing countries) of Asia and Latin America will be explored more fully in Chapter 15. However, those transitional developed countries that are most comparable to the developing countries are occasionally included in the discussions in this chapter. As Chapter 13 noted, there are several labels applied to the developing countries. The concept *Third World* was originally devised to refer to a large group of states that were at the margins of an international system dominated by two powerful blocs, led by the United States and Soviet Union (Mittleman 1993: 908–910). Soon, many commentators considered every country outside the two superpower blocs, or even every developing country, to be part of the Third World. At this point, some analysts reject the term on the grounds that it has become too ambiguous and covers such a diversity of countries (Lewis 1999).

The developing countries are also sometimes referred to as the *South,* which contrasts them with the North, the geographical location of the great majority of the developed countries. Chapter 13 also noted that the United Nations, among others, sometimes refers to a *Fourth World,* which includes more than half a billion people in the four dozen least developed Third World states (United Nations Development Programme 1995). Fourth World states show the fewest signs of progress toward overcoming the development gap in relation to other countries. In Fourth World countries, most people live close to subsistence, hard-pressed to provide themselves with the basic essentials of food, clothing, and shelter.

Such labels as "developing country," "Third World," "Fourth World," and "South" are best understood as a potentially useful shorthand. These labels denote certain common traits attributed to states that, relative to the developed countries and even most transitional countries discussed in Chapter 15, are less economically developed, are less modern, and have a lower overall standard of living. Most also have high birthrates (sometimes higher than economic growth rates) and youthful populations (in more than forty developing countries, at least 45 percent of the population is below the age of 15).

This chapter attempts to specify dominant patterns and general trends among the developing countries. Since these states are very diverse, generalizations about the developing countries oversimplify political reality and are subject to qualifications. These states differ in developmental styles and approaches to politics. Also, they do not share a single political culture; rather, they encompass many different histories, traditions, religions, and political ideologies.

As you read this chapter, and especially as you formulate your own understanding about the developing countries, be sensitive to the variation across these states and, in many cases, within each state. Just as the most developed countries have some people living in abject poverty and primitive conditions, even the poorest developing countries have advanced technology and some citizens enjoying enormous wealth and a high standard of living.

Regional Classification

Although this chapter generalizes across all developing countries, Table 14.1 reveals that there is a region-based clustering, based on economic development levels, that is worth considering. Excluding the world's ministates, most developing countries in Sub-Saharan Africa and Asia are low-income countries, and most countries in Latin America and in the Islamic Middle East and North Africa are middle-income countries. For comparative purposes, the table also indicates the economic development levels of the transitional countries that will be assessed in Chapter 15. It is useful to summarize some broad regional differences among the developing countries.

Latin America.   The countries in this subset tend to be relatively advanced on both economic and social development, with a modern, technological sector. Direct colonial control of these states was early, with most of them having been granted independence before the mid-nineteenth century. In most, there is a strong national identity that corresponds to the geographic boundaries of the state, and the state has considerable political institutionalization. There are also other well-institutionalized structures in the society, particularly the armed forces and the church, and there is a long-standing upper-class elite. Finally, most of these states are highly urbanized, and it is estimated that more than 80 percent of the population in Latin America now live in cities.

There is one distinctive sub-subset in Latin America, composed of the Caribbean states. These hundreds of islands are extremely diverse in culture and geography. In comparison with the rest of the Latin American region, these island states tend to have longer colonial legacies, to be less developed and less urban, and

TABLE 14.1
Distribution of Developing and Transitional Developed Countries, by Economic Development Level (GNP per Capita) and Region

Sub-Saharan Africa	Asia	Latin America	North Africa and Middle East	Other
		Low-Income Countries ($80–$785)		
Rwanda				
Mozambique				
Ethiopia				
Tanzania				
Burundi				
Sierra Leone				
Congo (Zaire)				
Malawi				
Liberia				
Chad				
Uganda	Nepal			
Madagascar	Bangladesh	Haiti		
Niger				
Kenya	Afghanistan			
Mali	Mongolia			
Nigeria	India		Yemen	
Burkina Faso	Laos			
Sudan				
Togo				
Somalia				
Gambia		Nicaragua		
Zambia				Tajikistan
Benin				
Cent. Afr. Rep.				
Ghana	Pakistan			
				Guinea
		Honduras		
Senegal				Azerbaijan
Ivory Coast				
Congo Rep.				Moldova
Angola				
Cameroon				Kyrgyz Rep.
Lesotho				Armenia

(continued)

TABLE 14.1 (continued)

Sub-Saharan Africa	Asia	Latin America	North Africa and Middle East	Other
Middle-Income Countries (Lower: $785–3,125)				
		Bolivia		Macedonia
Zimbabwe	China			
	Indonesia		Egypt	Albania
	Sri Lanka			
	Philippines		Syria	
			Morocco	Uzbekistan
	Papua New Guinea	Guatemala		Kazakhstan
		Ecuador		Bulgaria
		Cuba		Romania
		Dominican Rep.	Jordan	Lithuania
		El Salvador		
		Jamaica	Iraq	
		Paraguay	Algeria	
		Colombia	Tunisia	
Namibia	North Korea			Ukraine
		Peru		Belarus
				Latvia
	Thailand	Costa Rica		Croatia
				Russian Fed.
			Iran	Estonia
Middle-Income Countries (Upper: $3,125–9,655)				
		Panama		Slovak Rep.
		Venezuela		Poland
South Africa	Mauritius	Brazil	Lebanon	Czech Rep.
	Malaysia	Chile	Libya	Hungary
		Puerto Rico	Turkey	
		Mexico		
		Uruguay	Oman	
			Saudi Arabia	
		Argentina		
High-Income Countries ($9,655+)				
			Kuwait	Slovenia
	South Korea		United Arab	
	Singapore		Emirates	

to have an ethnic-cultural heritage that is African and Asian (and, secondarily English and French) more than Indian and Hispanic (the heritages that predominate in the rest of Latin America). A second sub-subset in Latin America might distinguish the half-dozen states which have achieved sufficient overall development to be classified as NICs. This group includes Argentina, Chile, and Uruguay and perhaps Brazil, Mexico, and Venezuela.

Asia. A second regional group consists of most of the states in Asia. This vast region covers one-third of the world's land and contains about two-thirds of its people. The area is characterized by great ethnic, cultural, and geographic diversity. It is dominated in human and historical-cultural terms by China (with 1.27 billion people) and India (with 1.02 billion). The group of low-income countries includes India and several other populous South Asian states (e.g., Bangladesh and Pakistan) as well as some smaller East Asian countries, most of which have a recent history of Communist political regimes (e.g., Cambodia, Vietnam). China and Indonesia are among the East Asian countries whose somewhat greater economic development places them among the middle-income countries. Asia also is the region from which the leading NICs (e.g., South Korea, Taiwan) emerged (Chapter 15).

Asian developing countries are predominantly rural and agrarian, and there is a significant gap between the traditional society and the smaller modernized and technologically advanced sectors in the major cities. India and most of South Asia have experienced considerable and direct European colonial influence since the seventeenth century. Colonialism occurred later for much of East Asia, an area that has also been affected by the looming presence of China. There are substantial nationality differences in most contemporary Asian states, based on diverse ethnic, religious, and linguistic traditions. Political structures and the political economy also vary substantially from state to state.

North Africa and the Middle East. This region includes the dozen states and ministates of southwest Asia (e.g., Afghanistan, Iran, Saudi Arabia) as well as the five North African states that are on the Mediterranean Sea and are dominated by the Sahara Desert (Algeria, Egypt, Libya, Morocco, and Tunisia). Most of the peoples of North Africa and the Middle East are Islamic in religion and culture and mainly Arabic in ethnicity and language (although not Iran). The area has major geopolitical importance, both for its strategic location, including its waterways, and for its petroleum resources. Much of the region was controlled by the Ottoman Empire between 1453 and 1918. In the nineteenth and twentieth centuries, European colonial power was exercised mainly through indirect economic and military involvement. Despite some brief periods of direct colonial rule, European values and structures did not penetrate most of these states, and many remain socially conservative and somewhat tribal-feudal.

Sub-Saharan Africa. Despite its substantial natural resources, Sub-Saharan Africa (the African continent excluding the states of North Africa listed previously) is the poorest and least economically developed region in the world. About two-thirds of the world's poorest countries (as measured by GNP per capita) are in this region. After the abolition of the slave trade, the experiences with colonialism in most of these states were late, occurring between the 1880s and the 1950s, and were extremely intensive and exploitative. These countries are generally in a neocolonial situation, with limited control over their own resources and a dependency on foreign financial and technological assistance. Few have a strong sense of national unity, because colonial powers created states that arbitrarily merged many nationality groups who had no historical commonality. More than two-thirds of the population in these countries is rural, although there is an increasing migration to cities. In most countries, the authority of the central, modern state is weak, and central political, social, and economic structures lack institutionalization.

GOAL: PROSPERITY

All developing countries strive for the benefits of prosperity associated with economic development and welfare distribution. While the developing countries employ the same economic strategies as the developed countries and the NICs, many of them have had only limited success in achieving prosperity. Table 14.2 presents our two prosperity measures for selected developing countries.

Although GNP per capita can be difficult to determine in the many developing countries with less extensive cash-based economies, it is still the common mea-

TABLE 14.2
Prosperity Measures For Selected Developing Countries and Newly Industrializing Countries (NICs)

State	GNP/Capita ($US)	Human Development Index
Argentina*	8,950	88.8
Saudi Arabia	7,150	77.8
Uruguay*	6,130	88.5
Oman	4,950	77.1
Brazil*	4,790	80.9
Malaysia*	4,530	83.4
Mexico*	3,700	85.5
South Africa	3,210	71.7
Thailand*	2,740	83.8
Costa Rica	2,680	88.9
Colombia	2,180	85.0
El Salvador	1,810	60.4
Jordan	1,520	72.9
Algeria	1,500	74.6
Morocco	1,260	55.7
Philippines	1,200	67.7
Egypt	1,200	61.2
Indonesia	1,110	67.9
China	860	65.0
Zimbabwe	720	50.7
Ivory Coast	710	36.8
Cameroon	620	48.1
Pakistan	500	45.3
Laos	400	46.5
Ghana	390	47.3
India	370	45.1
Bangladesh	360	37.1
Kenya	340	46.3
Vietnam	310	56.0
Nigeria	280	39.1
Tanzania	210	35.8
Congo (Zaire)	110	38.3
Ethiopia	110	25.2

Sources: GNP/capita: World Bank 1999: table 1.1; human development index: United Nations Development Programme 1998: table 1.
* = classified as a Newly Industrializing Country in this book

sure of prosperity. A striking aspect of the table is the low GNP/capita levels in many countries, especially in comparison to the developed countries (recall Table 13.3). Almost every developing country with a relatively high GNP/capita is either an oil-rich state or a country now defined as a NIC. A very low GNP per capita suggests limited production of goods within the society, but it does not reveal the additional factor that these goods are often very unequally distributed and that even the most basic goods are minimally available to many people. For example, about one third of the population, 1.3 billion people, live below the absolute poverty line. More than 840 million experience chronic hunger, eating less than the daily subsistence level of calories, and one-third of children are malnourished and underweight. One billion are illiterate; 1.5 billion lack basic health care or access to clean water (Evans and Long 1997: 58–61; Knickerbocker 1999; Kurian 1998: 381).

Can you place these stark statistics in a human context? They are graphic illustrations of the life conditions that are also represented by the low Human Development Index scores of many developing countries (Table 14.2), with the very lowest scores predominantly from Africa and Asia. The emerging NICs (e.g., Malaysia, Mexico, Thailand, and Uruguay) tend to have the highest HDI scores among developing countries, scores approaching those of some of the more developed countries.

The sixty low income developing countries in Table 13.1 have an average GNP/capita of only $350 per year and GNP in all developing countries in the table averages less than $1,300 per capita. GNP/capita for the entire population of the developing countries averages less than $800. Can you see why these numbers are different? (Hint: consider the unit that is being measured).

There is a broad correlation between GNP per capita and quality-of-life scores in Table 14.2, but the relationship is far from perfect. The divergence between the two measures is most striking in a few examples, such as Vietnam, where the score on the Human Development Index is substantially higher than might be expected on the basis of its GNP per capita, possibly because of this socialist state's efforts to provide education and health services to the entire population. In contrast, GNP-per-capita levels in some Middle Eastern and North African countries are relatively high in comparison with their scores on the quality-of-life measure. What do you think might account for this?

These data suggest that a few developing countries are on a positive path toward high levels of economic development. But for many developing countries, prosperity is an elusive (impossible?) dream as much as it is a goal on which steady improvements can be assumed. These states attempt to prosper in a competitive global economy in which they face substantial disadvantages. Before assessing their strategies for development, certain key obstacles to prosperity must be considered.

Obstacles to Prosperity

High birthrates. On average, each woman in the developing world has more than 3 children. Since death rates have dropped faster than birthrates, the population of the developing countries continues to grow at about 1.4 percent per year (see Box 14.1). Currently, more than 40 percent of the women in the developing countries, the source of 95 percent of the world's children, do not have easy access to family planning. If, from this moment, every female has only two children who reach adulthood, the world's population will not stabilize until it reaches about 8 billion. Even

BOX 14.1

Can the Population Bomb Be Disarmed?

Before we hit 2000, we reached 6 billion....The world population reached 6 billion in late 1999 and is currently adding nearly 80 million new people per year. The population of the developing countries has expanded from less than 2 billion in 1950 to 4.8 billion in 2000. Among these are 3 billion under 25 years of age who are ready to enter their prime childbearing years. Although birth rates in almost all countries have declined in the last few years, the developing world is still projected to be home to 6 billion in 2015 and 8 billion by 2054. Of the nearly 4 billion births between 2000 and 2050 worldwide, 19 out of 20 births and virtually all population growth will occur in the developing countries. Already, China and India *each* has a larger population than the combined populations of all the developed countries (Mitchell 1998).

For some analysts, the large and growing population in most developing countries is the major cause of many problems—economic stagnation, famine, nationality conflicts, global warming, and desertification. This rapid increase has many consequences for the developing countries, including the need for more than 1.2 billion new jobs, hundreds of millions of new schools and houses, and a major increase in food production. An underlying concern is that the sheer number of people is becoming so large that the regenerating capacity of the earth will be overwhelmed by the depletion of resources and degradation of the environment (e.g., cutting down the rain forests, polluting the water and the air, depleting fossil fuels). Thus some observers term this situation a *"population bomb"* that can wreak havoc on humanity as extensive as nuclear bombs could (Ehrlich and Ehrlich 1990).

Governments in developing countries offer extraordinarily different policy responses to overpopulation. Some countries have essentially taken a *Darwinian* approach to population control. Lacking either the will or the capacity to attack the problem, they allow the natural forces of famine and disease to cull their populations. They provide neither effective birth-control programs nor adequate prenatal and postnatal care; health care provision is meager and there are few successful policies to boost agricultural productivity. Recurrent images of shocking levels of famine, disease, and death appear from Bangladesh, Ethiopia, Somalia, and other countries. Overall, more than 200 million people have died in the past twenty years from hunger-related diseases.

The most common policy response to overpopulation is to offer *mild incentives* for birth control. The Mexican government, for example, implemented an extensive public relations campaign on television, radio, billboards, and print media, attempting to persuade its largely Catholic population that "small families live better." India is among the developing countries that distribute free birth-control devices; however, since more than two-thirds of the village women in India are illiterate, many do not use the oral contraceptives properly.

A few countries implement *aggressive public policies* to limit population. China is best known for its combination of rewards and sanctions. The government authorizes each couple to have only one child. If a couple has a second child, that child is not qualified to receive most of the free welfare benefits, such as health care. If the

BOX 14.1 *(Continued)*

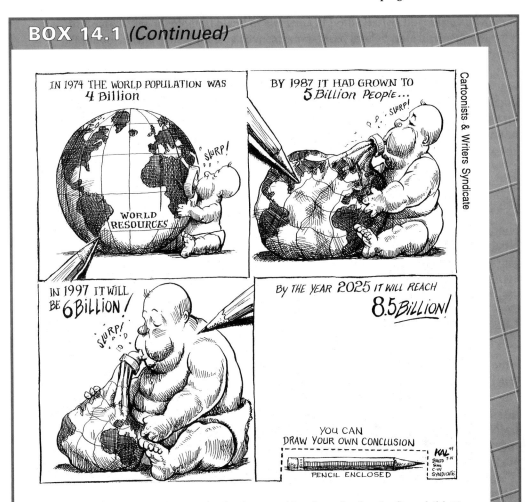

couple has a third child, the couple also loses welfare benefits for the first child. Since many Chinese have a strong culturally based bias toward male children, special cash "rewards" are given to families that have a single female child. The government offers abortions to any women who request them. It also authorizes certain women to monitor the menstruation of all women in their workplace, farm, or village to ensure that there are no pregnancies among women who do not have approval to have a baby. A woman with an unapproved pregnancy is subjected to substantial peer pressure to get an abortion, since the baby will be the financial responsibility of the entire work group, without additional compensation from the state.

In the last decade, the birth rates in many developing countries have dropped significantly. And some analysts argue that technological innovations have outpaced and will continue to outpace the problems of an expanding population, or that it is morally wrong to limit people's right to bear children (see, e.g., Simon 1992). Nonetheless, most analysts agree that the population increases in the developing countries continue to pose serious global threats to the environment and that the failure of governments to deal with the population problem is undermining their pursuit of prosperity, stability, and security.

the goal of stability at 8 billion by 2050 seems unlikely. It requires an aggressive and widely accepted global approach to population control, based on programs costing more than $20 billion per year, substantially more than current spending. The UN recently estimated that global population could grow to about 9.4 billion by the mid-twenty-first century (Kegley and Wittkopf 1997: 282–289; Mitchell 1998).

As noted previously, prosperity is typically measured as GDP/GNP *per capita* or as income *per capita* to indicate the levels of goods and income that are available to each person in the society. Unless production increases more rapidly than population, more food must be produced, more schools and housing built, more health care provided just to maintain the existing, quite low standard of living. Unless governments in many developing countries take decisive action to limit population, there will be few or no surplus resources for economic expansion and an increased level of welfare distribution.

Inefficiency and corruption.   The search for prosperity is also thwarted by high levels of inefficiency, corruption, or both (see, e.g., Isbister 1998). One source of organizational inefficiency is the limited availability and ineffective use of modern technologies. Many developing countries have been unable to maintain efficient economic infrastructure systems, such as those for transportation, communications, or information. Another major source of productive inefficiency is the absence of Weberian bureaucracies (as defined in Chapter 6) in most of these states. The functioning of the political economy is complicated or disrupted because predictable behavior and the following of rules cannot be assumed from those who work in public and private organizations.

An even more serious obstacle to prosperity is corruption. Corruption exists in every society—major scandals involving government officials and businesspeople seem to occur with increasing frequency in many developed countries. Yet corruption seems especially pervasive in public and private organizations in the developing countries. Chapter 6 noted that *baksheesh* (literally, "something given"), *chai* (literally, "tea"), and *mordida* (literally, "the bite") are among the words which signify the private payoffs that too frequently are expected by organizational personnel (both high-ranking and lower-level) whose actions are necessary to fulfill one's objectives. Widespread corruption demoralizes the population and drains the productive energy from the political economy.

Dependence on primary commodities for export.   A strong, developed economy is diversified, producing a wide variety of goods for domestic use and for export. Exports are especially important because they are the primary source of foreign exchange capital—the funds used to pay for imports (e.g., imported food, oil, consumer goods, machinery) and to pay the interest on foreign debts. During the colonial period, most developing countries relied on the export of a few primary commodities (raw materials and agricultural products) to generate capital. In turn, they imported most manufactured goods and advanced services from the more developed countries.

Virtually all developing countries have been systematically disadvantaged historically by the reliance on a few primary commodities to support economic development, since the prices for those primary goods have fluctuated greatly and decreased in value (relative to manufactured goods) over time. The developing countries have substantially diversified their mix of exports in the last several decades—

the percentage of manufactured products increased from 24 percent in 1970 to 58 percent in 1990 (Kegley and Wittkopf 1995: table 8.1). But some developing countries, especially in Sub-Saharan Africa and the Caribbean, still depend heavily on the export of primary commodities.

Neocolonialism.   The discussions of the dependency approach in Chapter 10 and of colonialism and neocolonialism in Chapter 12 (including the example in Box 12.2 of Congo/Zaire) both reveal that political independence does not necessarily end the subordination of many developing countries. Rather, economic, cultural, and military domination by the governments and institutions of the developed countries can continue as *neocolonialism*—a more unofficial and indirect, but no less extensive, control of the resources, economic systems, and markets of developing countries (Wallerstein 1980; Weatherby 1997: 34–39).

Whether or not the interactions are labeled neocolonialism, both firms and resources in the developing countries are often linked directly to political, financial, and business elites of the more developed countries. The developed countries are the major source of the financial capital, advanced technologies, and product distribution systems that many firms in developing countries need in order to compete in the international marketplace. Thus these firms establish economic arrangements (described in the next section) with more developed countries, international financial institutions, and multinational corporations (MNCs). It is debatable whether developing countries have much choice about whether to enter these dependency arrangements, given a history of resource exploitation and current economic underdevelopment (Evans 1987).

Strategies for Prosperity

Industrialization.   Industrialization is the classic strategy of many developing countries attempting to increase economic development and hence prosperity. The aim is to use labor and capital to transform commodities into intermediate goods (e.g., trees to lumber, ore to steel, water to electricity) and then into more refined and valuable goods (e.g., furniture, radios, trucks). A contemporary variant of industrialization emphasizes service-based goods (e.g., data entry, tourism) and knowledge-based goods (e.g., banking, computer software) rather than the production of traditional "hard" goods. Whatever the balance of goods, the production of more, more diverse, and more desirable goods over time generates economic growth. Achieving these changes requires a well-organized system of resource control, a trained and disciplined urban work force, effective technologies, and an efficient infrastructure for distributing goods.

One key decision regarding industrialization involves the balance between two different emphases. The first strategy emphasizes *import substitution*—the production and exchange of goods within the country to provide people's wants without relying on imports. The second strategy encourages *export promotion*—the production of goods that can be sold to the rest of the world to earn foreign-exchange capital.

Also, a developing country can choose to foster industrialization by means of greater state control or market dominance of the political economy (Chapter 8). After independence, many developing countries opted for a *statist approach*—more extensive state control of the political economy—assuming that economic dependency and underdevelopment could best be overcome by a strong centralized effort to plan and control the production and distribution of goods in the society. In this approach, the state's role is expansive—it owns major industries (nationalization), controls production decisions, regulates prices and wages, protects domestic producers from foreign competition, and encourages import substitution.

By the late 1980s, many developing countries rejected this approach in favor of a strategy of *market-oriented development* (described as neoliberalism in Chapter 10). There are several key features of this strategy. First, government regulation of both industry and agriculture is dramatically reduced and many government-owned industries are privatized (sold to private entrepreneurs). Second, there is an emphasis on export promotion, but with the elimination of trade controls (e.g., tariffs, quotas) in favor of international free trade. Third, instead of relying on foreign loans, the economy is opened to direct foreign investment and active participation by multinational corporations. Fourth, a combination of tax cuts and substantial reductions in public spending, especially on welfare services, further limits the government's role.

Agricultural development.   The transition from subsistence farming to commercial agriculture can be an alternative or complement to industrialization in the quest for prosperity. *Commercial agriculture* means that people produce a surplus of food that can be sold or exchanged in a market. Ideally, production exceeds the need of the rural-sector population, thereby providing extra food to support a growing urban population. Equally important is the growth of food for export, since this generates capital that can be reinvested in either rural or urban economic development. The successful transition to commercial agriculture requires several elements: (1) techniques that increase crop yields and overcome such natural hardships as drought and pestilence, (2) stable and attractive prices within a reliable market, and (3) an efficient system of distribution. These elements might be enhanced by technology and by either state control or private control of agricultural development.

New technologies. Some farms have increased productivity by substituting new technologies for traditional approaches to agriculture. Since the 1960s, one major initiative has been the "green revolution," using chemical fertilizers, pesticides, and hybrid grains that provide higher yields. Along with mechanization and better irrigation systems, the green revolution doubled average yields for rice, corn, and wheat between 1960 and 1996. Although population rose dramatically during the same period, total grain production did increase a bit faster than the mouths needing feeding (Herring 1996).

State control. As with industrial development, the political regimes of some developing countries have established extensive state control over agriculture. The farmland is organized into large state farms where technology is shared and labor is grouped into production teams. The state's economic plan sets quotas and prices for certain crops and provides the system for distributing agricultural goods. This approach has been most fully implemented in command economies, such as Cambodia, China, Cuba, and Tanzania. It has had limited success, however, because most rural people resist social restructuring and are not motivated to work as hard for the general welfare as for their own profit. For these reasons, nearly all developing countries have now abolished state farms, encouraging market-based production of cash crops by private farmers or local collectives (Isbister 1998).

Private control. In most developing countries, farmland is now privately owned. It is assumed that private farmers will maximize crop yields in the pursuit of food for consumption and for profit in the market. Often, most of the very productive land is owned by members of the national elite or by multinational corporations. In Zimbabwe, for example, 4,500 white farmers own as much land as 7 million black peasant farmers and control virtually all of the superior land (Kranzdorf 1997: 177). Small, privately owned farms are common in some areas of the developing world where large landholdings were never widespread (e.g., Nigeria) or where land-reform policies have given local people the farmland that was previously controlled either by the state (e.g., China) or by large landholders (e.g., Kenya, Peru).

Collaboration with foreign capital.   A third strategy in the search for prosperity is to embrace the foreign devils—to make explicit deals allowing powerful actors in the international political economy to have direct access to the developing country's resources and markets. These countries need capital (particularly financial resources) to invest in the productive system, to purchase imports, and to distribute welfare benefits to a needy population. Since their level of economic growth is often too low to serve all these needs, developing countries typically look to the developed countries (and their major national and multinational corporations and financial institutions) for capital. This capital can be derived from foreign aid, direct foreign investment, or loans.

Foreign aid. Foreign aid can take many forms, but most aid from the developed countries to the developing countries has been in the forms of shared technology, unconditional grants, and loans with no expectation of full repayment. Many developing countries argue that the developed world "owes" them such aid, as compensation for decades or even centuries of colonial and neocolonial exploitation that greatly benefited the developed countries and left the developing countries with depleted resources and severe underdevelopment. A few developing countries still call for a *new international economic order* (NIEO) in which the developed countries: provide aid, knowledge, and technology transfer; cancel debts for previous loans; and pay "reparations" for prior exploitation of resources.

The developed countries have little enthusiasm for these kinds of aid, since they might shift significant wealth *away* from their countries. Increasingly, they provide aid with strings attached that serve their own self-interest: economic (to obtain resources, to open markets for their own goods and services); political (to establish alliances or a political sphere of influence, to exclude ideological rivals); or military (to deploy strategic military power).

Direct foreign investment. The current emphasis of the developed countries, consistent with the ideology of market-oriented development, is to promote direct foreign investment, not to provide aid. That is, external actors invest in the firms of the country and are allowed to set up their own firms within the country. Most developing countries now take a pragmatic approach and attempt to negotiate the most favorable terms possible for obtaining capital and technology from these external economic actors (i.e., more developed countries, multinational corporations, and transnational institutions such as the World Bank). They accept substantial foreign involvement in their economy on the assumption that capital, jobs, and other economic benefits will "trickle down" to their population or that their country can insist on a significant share of the foreigners' profits (Maxfield 1997).

Loans and debt. Faced with the problem of insufficient resources for economic growth and welfare distribution, another approach to development is to implement quick fixes. Most developing countries resort to borrowing funds from the international financial community, composed primarily of major banks and coordinated by the International Monetary Fund and the World Bank. Loans offer an enticing

short-run solution for financing economic growth and distributing welfare benefits to the population. Unfortunately, loans require repayment. The country's political economy is soon saddled not only with current needs for surplus to support
growth and welfare, but also with a large debt obligation from previous borrowing.

As a consequence of their extensive loans, many developing countries are now
deeply indebted to the financial institutions of the developed countries. Their total
external debt increased twentyfold during the 1970s and then tripled again from
1980 to 1993. The states of the developing world now have a staggering outstanding debt of more than $2 trillion. Repayment of such debt is a debilitating additional
burden for a state facing the difficult challenge of generating economic surplus to

TABLE 14.3
**Economic Indicators for Selected Developing Countries and Newly
Industrializing Countries**

State	GNP/Capita, Average Annual Growth Rate, 1985–1995 (percent)	Inflation, Average Annual Rate, 1985–1994	Debt Service as Percentage of Exports, 1997
Algeria	−2.4 %	22%	97%
Argentina *	1.8	317	59
Armenia	−15.1	134	6
Bangladesh	2.1	7	11
Brazil *	−0.8	900	57
Chad	0.6	2	12
Chile *	6.1	18	20
China	8.3	10	9
Costa Rica	2.8	18	12
Egypt, Arab Republic	1.1	16	9
Ghana	1.4	29	30
India	3.2	10	20
Indonesia	6.0	9	30
Kenya	0.1	12	22
Malaysia *	5.7	3	8
Mexico *	0.1	40	32
Morocco	0.9	5	27
Nicaragua	−5.4	1,311	32
Nigeria	1.2	30	8
Pakistan	1.2	9	35
Peru	−1.6	492	31
Philippines	1.5	10	9
Rwanda	−5.4	5	13
Saudi Arabia	−1.9	1	0
South Korea *	7.7	7	n.a.
Turkey	2.2	66	18
Zimbabwe	−0.6	20	22

Source: World Bank 1996: tables 1, 2, and 17; World Bank 1999: tables 1.4, 4.19.
* = country classified as a Newly Industrializing Country in this book.

finance current welfare and future growth. Table 14.3 reveals that many countries must expend more than 30 percent of their export earnings to service their debts.

Even worse, some governments resort to printing huge amounts of money to cover their expenses. But in the absence of a strong economy to back the money, it becomes worth less and less both internationally and at home, producing a serious inflationary spiral. Inflation rates in some developing countries have been quite high and occasionally staggering. The annual inflation rate throughout Latin America from 1980 to 1992 was about 230 percent per year, and a few countries had crushing rates in some years. For example, until it stabilized in 1995, Brazil's annual inflation rate for the previous ten-year period was 900 percent and in Peru it was 492 percent (World Bank 1996: table 2). Obviously, personal finances, let alone maintenance of a coherent plan of national economic development, are impossible in the face of such hyperinflation. There is now evidence of stabilization, with average inflation in Latin America falling from 196 percent in 1991 to less than 20 percent at the end of the decade (World Bank 1999).

Overall Performance

Both individual cases and aggregate statistics provide useful information about the recent performance of developing countries in the overall pursuit of prosperity. Table 14.3 displays individual examples which reveal the varied success of developing countries in their pursuit of prosperity. Although each country has its own unique configuration, certain broad patterns are evident:

A few states, such as China and Malaysia, have enjoyed strong economic growth with only moderate inflation and little reliance on borrowing.

A second pattern, reflected by such states as Chile and Indonesia, is a solid level of economic growth tempered by some inflation and major loan obligations.

A common pattern, as in Costa Rica, Ghana, India, and Pakistan, is of limited but positive growth, significant inflation, and substantial debt repayment.

Another group, which includes Kenya, Mexico, and Morocco, has virtually no economic growth, despite inflation and the burden of debt.

Some countries, such as Algeria, Rwanda, Saudi Arabia, and Zimbabwe actually experienced negative growth during the decade, worsened in some cases by double-digit inflation.

Armenia, Brazil, Nicaragua, and Peru reflect the nightmare of negative growth and hyperinflation.

Aggregate data provide a broader perspective. Since population growth has been outstripping economic growth in some developing countries, the annual GNP-per-capita growth rate between 1990 and 1997 is actually *negative* in the Middle East and North Africa (-1.8 percent) and in Sub-Saharan Africa (-2 percent), and is only slightly positive in Latin America and the Caribbean (1.1 percent). Only eastern Asia and the Pacific (5.5 percent) and southern Asia (2.2 percent) achieved substantial real economic growth during the period (World Bank 1998: table 1).

These differences between countries and regions are one aspect of "uneven development." The distribution of prosperity at the *individual* level is also substantially uneven. In many developing countries, both the decisions of the political system regarding the allocation of values and also the effects of pressures and demands from the international financial community have resulted in an array of policies that have generally shifted resources *away* from the most disadvantaged sectors of the population, especially the poor.

Table 14.4 reports the level of inequality in the distribution of wealth in selected countries, based on the two measures described in Chapter 13, the Gini index of income inequality and the ratio of income held by the top 20 percent of the population relative to the lowest 20 percent. Most of the countries with huge inequalities in the distribution of prosperity are developing countries. Twenty-three of the thirty countries with the world's most unequal distributions of wealth are developing countries. And if one includes six newly industrializing countries (the NICs are discussed more fully in Chapter 15) that are just emerging from the developing country category, developing countries constitute twenty-nine of these thirty countries. (In this analysis, only South Africa is arguably not a developing country.) These countries have extremely high Gini index scores, ranging from 62.9 in Sierra Leone to 43.4 in Madagasgar. The pattern is similar on the measure of income ratios, where developing countries again are a highly disproportionate share of the countries with the greatest inequality in the distribution of wealth. The richest 20 percent often control ten to twenty-five times more wealth than the poorest 20 percent of the population. It should be noted that a small proportion of the quartile of the world's countries with the most *equal* distributions of wealth are developing countries. This set includes Bangladesh, India, Laos, Pakistan, and Sri Lanka.

This inequality in wealth has occurred in many developing countries which have experienced limited or negative economic growth and have implemented cuts in government spending on education, health, and welfare. The result is that more than one billion people in the developing countries have experienced a substantial *decline* in

TABLE 14.4
INCOME INEQUALITY IN SELECTED COUNTRIES

Country	Gini Index of Inequality In Income Distribution	Gini Rank among 96 Countries	Ratio of Wealth, Top/Bottom 20%
Sierra Leone	62.9	1	57.6 to 1
Brazil*	60.1	2	25.7 to 1
South Africa	59.3	5	22.3 to 1
Kenya	57.5	6	18.3 to 1
Colombia	57.2	7	19.8 to 1
Chile*	56.5	9	17.4 to 1
Mexico*	53.7	16	16.2 to 1
Malaysia*	48.4	19	11.7 to 1
Russia	48.0	20	12.6 to 1
Costa Rica	47.0	22	13.0 to 1
Thailand*	46.2	25	9.4 to 1
Nigeria	45.0	27	12.4 to 1
China	41.5	34	8.6 to 1
United States	40.1	39	9.4 to 1
Morocco	39.2	42	7.0 to 1
Indonesia	36.5	43	5.6 to 1
Switzerland	36.1	46	5.9 to 1
Israel	35.5	51	6.2 to 1
Ghana	32.7	56	5.0 to 1
United Kingdom	32.6	62	5.6 to 1
Egypt	32.0	64	6.8 to 1
Canada	31.5	65	5.2 to 1
India	29.7	73	6.1 to 1
Belarus	28.8	75	4.4 to 1
Germany	28.1	80	4.1 to 1
Hungary	27.9	84	3.9 to 1
Poland	27.2	80	3.9 to 1
Czech Republic	26.6	92	3.6 to 1
Finland	25.6	84	3.6 to 1
Norway	25.2	93	3.5 to 1
Belgium	25.0	94	3.6 to 1
Sweden	25.0	94	3.6 to 1
Denmark	24.7	95	3.6 to 1
Austria	23.1	90	3.2 to 1
Slovak Republic	19.5	96	2.6 to 1

Source: World Bank 1999: Table 2.8.
On the Gini index, perfect equality among all cases in the distribution of income would have a score of 0.0, while total inequality in the distribution would have a score of 100.0. The data are for 96 countries, while approximately 80 other countries are not analyzed by the World Bank. Among those countries not analyzed, but given attention in this book are: Argentina, Cambodia, Congo, Cuba, Iran, Iraq, Japan, Myanmar, Oman, Singapore, Swaziland, Taiwan, Turkey, and Uruguay.

*= country classified as a Newly Industrializing Country in this book.

their standard of living since the late 1980s. In Latin America, for example, the average income per person in 1993 was 5 percent lower than in 1980 and fully 46 percent of the population was in poverty (Naim 1995). In general, the decline in living standards has been even more precipitous for many people in Sub-Saharan Africa. Minimally, developing countries need to feed their own populations. Yet one in four people suffer chronic hunger, and the level of deaths from the effects of hunger is tragic: about 42 deaths per minute, 2,500 per hour, 60,000 per day, and 22 million per year (Evans and Long 1997: 59).

In order to better grasp the nature of this economic performance, it is useful to explore how, in general, the strategies of industrialization, agricultural development, and collaboration with foreign capital have contributed to it.

Industrialization.   At the least, the pursuit of industrialization in many developing countries has reduced their dependence on a few primary commodities and increased their output of manufactured goods. The market-oriented development approach, which generated substantial growth in the Asian NICs (see Chapters 10 and 15), has met with variable success in other developing countries. It has generated solid, sustained economic growth in a few countries, especially in some other Asian countries such as Indonesia and Thailand.

Elsewhere, the impacts of market-oriented, manufacturing-based development have been more mixed or negative. In Latin America, the approach has generated economic growth and reduced inflation in some countries, especially such emerging NICs as Argentina, Brazil, Chile, and Mexico (see Chapter 15). However, in most of Latin America, real wages have decreased, unemployment has risen, income inequality is greater, and there is widespread unhappiness with these market-based economic policies and the political leaders who have implemented them. In some developing countries in Africa and South Asia, the market-based approach to industrialization has not only resulted in negative impacts on the living standards of many people, but has also produced minimal or even negative growth rates. Given such problematical results from market-oriented industrialization, some leaders, particularly in Latin America, are attempting to formulate a new policy approach. Similar to the "third way" ideas in the developed countries, this approach not only encourages expansion of the free market, but also fosters improvements in the quality of life of all groups in the society. This focus on enhancing the lives of citizens emphasizes the provision of significantly more welfare distribution, social services, and jobs for those most disadvantaged by the market approach, especially the poor (Conger 1998).

An associated risk with strategies that place primary emphasis on industrialization has been the "mutual poisoning" of both the rural and the urban sectors (Schumacher 1973: 167). Many of the most productive workers migrate to urban areas from the rural sector, which then has a far more limited workforce to produce food. Those remaining in the rural sector revert toward subsistence agriculture and cannot produce sufficient food for those in the cities. Thus, rather than exporting food for surplus capital, the country is required to import food. At the same time, the overpopulated urban sector is overwhelmed with people whose demands for good jobs, shelter, amenities, and even food cannot be handled by the political economy.

Agricultural development.   Emphasis on commercial agriculture has contributed importantly to economic growth in a few developing countries; but most countries have made only limited advances toward prosperity through a strategy emphasizing agricultural development. Small farms still produce half of the food grown in developing countries. Many states are now attempting to encourage entrepreneurial small farmers by subsidizing the prices of farm products and providing an efficient infrastructure for distribution, marketing, and export. While such state support has been successful in some countries, notably in China (Goldman 1993), small private farms still produce little more than is necessary for family subsistence in most developing countries with a large rural population and low market prices (e.g., Bangladesh, Ghana, Indonesia, and Kenya). Ironically, some of the most successful small farmers are those producing lucrative but illegal cash crops such as coca and opium rather than those producing legal crops, whose international prices tend to fluctuate greatly.

Many large commercial farms are relatively efficient, with production directed primarily to the export market. But in many cases, the political elite and private (national or foreign) elites collude. Thus the profits are captured primarily by these elites and are not used for national economic development or welfare (e.g., in Chile, Congo, El Salvador, and the Philippines). Moreover, some states have been so committed to shifting production to agricultural goods for export that production for domestic needs deteriorates and the country must import basic foods for its own population.

In addition, the technologically based production gains in agriculture due to the green revolution seem to have reached certain limits. First, the costs of its components, especially fertilizers and pesticides, rose dramatically. Second, unanticipated negative consequences from high-tech farming emerged. The example of Indonesia (Box 14.2) is indicative of the problems associated with overreliance on hybrid grains and chemicals. Despite the global rise in yields previously noted, grain output per person in the developing world actually fell by more than 10 percent between 1984 and 1994 (Brown 1994). Increasingly, farmers are attempting to balance the use of modern technology with more traditional methods to stabilize agricultural productivity.

The pressures to provide food and fuel for a growing population have caused many rural people to engage in extensive deforestation, overgrazing, and aggressive farming techniques that exhaust the soil, destroy forests, and harm ecologically sensitive areas. These actions, in a vicious cycle with serious droughts and flooding in some regions, have resulted in a substantial reduction in the amount of productive farmland (Brown et al. 2000). The environmental consequences are frightening. It is estimated that during the 1990s, mainly in the developing countries, 6.25 million square miles of timberland disappeared, 250 billion tons of arable topsoil vanished from croplands, and deserts claimed 5.3 million square miles (an area about one and one-half the size of the United States) (Population Institute 1992).

Even in some developing countries where commercial agriculture has been successful, increases in food production barely exceed population growth. The key puzzle seems to be how to encourage high levels of productivity in a manner that preserves the environment, feeds the domestic population, and produces surplus for export. An approach that achieves all three of these objectives would enable a developing country to support its own population while also creating a financial surplus for economic growth and welfare distribution. In most developing countries, this puzzle remains unsolved.

Collaboration with foreign capital. Beneath the rhetoric of loans, direct foreign investment, trade agreements, and joint ventures is a reality: The distribution of benefits from an agreement between a developing country and a developed country or a multinational corporation usually reflects the underlying inequalities in

BOX 14.2

Something Can Be Done! Appropriate Technology and Agricultural Self-Help

Many developing countries are now engaged in agricultural self-help programs, based on the use of natural farming techniques and "appropriate technologies." In Indonesia, for example, the green revolution based on hybrid rice breeds and chemicals had dramatically increased rice yields in the 1970s, but then turned into a disaster. By the early 1980s, huge areas were devastated by insect infestation. The new farming technologies were the problem. First, eliminating traditional methods of crop rotation allowed the insect population, especially brown hoppers, to explode. Second, the new rice breeds were far less resistant to infestation. And third, the increasing use of pesticides actually increased the ratio of pests to "good" insects.

In 1986, Indonesia's President Suharto implemented aggressive policies that reversed the high-tech strategies of the green revolution. Laws prohibited the use of fifty-seven pesticides and allowed the remaining eight to be used only in very limited amounts. Government workers instructed the farmers to return to crop-rotation strategies, to use biological sprays that protect the good insects, and to limit severely the use of chemical fertilizers in favor of natural fertilizers such as dung and clover. By the mid-1990s, pesticide use was down nearly 80 percent and Indonesia's crop yields had rebounded.

Many developing countries have implemented small-scale projects that have improved their agricultural productivity with environmental sensitivity. A tree-planting program since 1990 in Niger (sponsored by CARE [Cooperative for American Relief to Everywhere]) has produced more than 400 miles of trees in rows that now protect the soil from wind and erosion. As the trees mature, crop yields have already increased more than 20 percent. Small farmers in neighboring Burkina Faso have been taught to use a simple level (provided by Oxfam [Oxford Committee for Famine Relief]) in order to survey their flat croplands. Groups of farmers then build low rock walls and dams that direct rainwater into areas where it moistens land for planting and then replenishes groundwater and wells, both of which irrigate crops and provide well water for year-round vegetable gardens.

political and economic power. Few countries can afford to reject such foreign capital, even though some interpret it as a mode of neocolonialism. (See Box 14.3.)

Faced with debt repayment, the flight of capital, and the growing role of multinational corporations in their economies, the developing countries sent $150 billion more to the developing countries than they received from them through export earnings, new loans, and private investment between 1985 and 1990 (Raymond 1991). When extensions on loan repayment or additional loans are requested, the financial institutions of the developed countries have insisted on "structural adjustment programs." These programs (described more fully in the discussion on economic security later in the chapter) require governments in the developing countries

BOX 14.3

Just Say No! China under Mao

Some developing countries have refused to collaborate with the developed countries, insisting that their national self-interest is better served by preserving autonomy rather than by accepting assistance. A notable example is China during most of Mao Zedong's rule (1948–1976). Mao argued that to achieve political and economic self-sufficiency, China must not accept outside aid and, in the process, become dependent upon the aid givers. He was so committed to this policy of independence that during a catastrophic drought (1960–1962) the Chinese even declined humanitarian aid from the International Red Cross while 20 million Chinese starved to death. But even Mao had periods of reliance on the Soviet Union, and the current Chinese leadership is energetically soliciting external involvement in China's economic development.

Few developing countries have had the resource diversity and political will to attempt self-reliance. At most, they have temporarily resisted external demands regarding loan repayment to international lenders or more favorable treatment of multinational corporations operating within their boundaries.

to open their economy to even greater direct foreign investment and to cut state spending dramatically.

The balance sheet.   The pursuit of prosperity has produced extremely uneven results. There are some clear positives. First, economic diversification and growth have occurred in many countries, especially in some that successfully implemented market-oriented approaches to industrialization and agricultural development in recent years. Some of those that have sustained high levels of economic development are now classified as the NICs and are an inspiration and a possible model for other developing countries. Secondly, the overall economic growth rates per capita for developing countries in the 1990s have averaged more than 5 percent per year, compared to a rate of only 2.1 percent in the developed countries (World Bank 1999: table 1a). Indeed, low income countries had higher average annual growth in GNP per capita than middle income countries or high income countries for the thirty-year period 1965–1996 (World Bank 1998: table 1.4). And thirdly, the "average person in the developing world" is living longer, is healthier and better educated, and has more material possessions than at any prior time.

However, the glass of prosperity can also be viewed as half empty. First, the financial, industrial, and commercial-agricultural sectors in most developing countries continue to be characterized by high levels of dependency on the developed countries and multinational corporations. While almost two-thirds of developing countries' total exports are now manufactured goods (excluding oil-exporting countries), most countries still must borrow money to pay for imports, to support limited welfare distribution, and to repay their foreign loans. They remain net importers of capital, technology, manufactured goods, oil, and even food. Secondly, the gap in the level of general prosperity in the developing countries, relative to the more developed countries, continues to broaden. Per capita GNP is less than one-twentieth as large, life expectancy is about fourteen years shorter, and life is far less comfortable for the average person (Sivard 1996: table III).

Thirdly, the economic growth is very uneven across developing countries. It is noted above that growth is particularly concentrated in East Asia and somewhat in South Asia, while other areas of the developing world have languished on the overall growth indicators. Moreover, inflation between 1980 and 2000 has been high enough in many developing countries to eliminate most or all of the apparent growth in GNP per capita when the real value of currency is considered (World Bank 1999). Thus, a focus on growth rates alone can deflect attention from a broader notion that the essence of prosperity is economic and social betterment for most of the population. Growth statistics can merely reflect increased total output without any necessary changes resulting in an enhanced life for most citizens. There are serious shortcomings in the pursuit of prosperity during a period when, despite apparent economic advancement, one billion people in the developing world experience a deterioration in their standard of living.

Prognosis

Many developing countries are rich in human and natural resources. Yet most have not been able to sustain a solid level of economic development or to distribute a modest level of welfare to most of the population, let alone both. This seems unlikely to change in a period guided by market-oriented political economies, an increase in direct foreign economic involvement, and pressure to reduce government spending on citizens' welfare. Most developing countries continue to vary their mix of the three broad strategies of industrialization, agricultural development, and foreign involvement as they search for an approach best suited to their particular political and economic situation. In the immediate future, the general pattern in most will remain economic underdevelopment and minimal welfare for the majority of people. The perplexing question for their leaders is how to convert their resources into prosperity, given underdevelopment, a disadvantaged position in a harshly competitive international environment, and the substantial challenges to their security and stability described in the next sections.

GOAL: SECURITY

The developing countries search for security in the face of pervasive insecurity. Their problems are grounded in low levels of political and economic development, which reduce their capacity to control their own population and resources. Such incapacity makes a state vulnerable to intervention by other states. Paradoxically, this relative weakness can also lead a state to be more aggressive in its interstate relations, both as a defensive reaction to perceived threats and as a means to divert its citizens' attention from internal problems. Our analysis of the search for security in the developing countries begins with a focus on interstate violence.

Interstate Violence

At any given time, most developing countries are *not* involved in violent interstate disputes. However, most wars since 1950 and most interstate violence are in the developing world, often between neighboring states (Cruikshanks 1997; Gochman and Maoz 1984). There are many reasons why interstate violence between *adjacent* developing countries is so frequent.

1. Many of the *geographic boundaries* between current states do not correspond to the boundaries of historically established nations. Thus conflict develops in an attempt to realign borders with nations.
2. Differences in the *cultures* of two states, especially those differences grounded in nationality, political ideology, or religious belief, can produce animosities so deep that violence erupts.
3. States often look covetously at valuable *resources* in neighboring states and sometimes attempt to gain control of those resources by force.
4. States with severe *internal problems* can use other states as scapegoats, redirecting internal frustration into violence against those states.
5. Conflict is encouraged by the *actions of other states* that are attempting to serve their own national interests.

In the developing countries, most interstate conflicts entail a combination of these reasons. The Iran–Iraq War, described in Box 14.4, is a revealing example of the interrelated themes of nationality, resources, ideology, internal problems, and external influences that are often at the core of such interstate violence. Only occasionally do these conflicts expand, as in this case, into a war (e.g., Cambodia–Vietnam, Chad–Libya, China–India, Eritrea–Ethiopia, India–Pakistan). It is more common for the conflict to take the form of a militarized dispute (short of war) between developing countries that share a border (e.g., Argentina–Chile, Bolivia–Paraguay, Cambodia–Thailand, Equador–Peru, India–Pakistan, Rwanda–Uganda) (Gochman and Maoz 1984).

Some of the conflicts between a developing country and a developed country are also between adjoining states. The most frequent of these conflicts has been the five wars and many militarized disputes since 1948 between Israel and the neighboring Arab states, especially Syria, Egypt, and Jordan. The conflicts between the apartheid regime of South Africa and its neighbors (e.g., Angola, Namibia) can also

---

BOX 14.4

The Third World War

The brutal war between Iran and Iraq, which raged from 1980 to the 1988 cease-fire, is characteristic of the complex causes of interstate violence between neighboring countries in the developing world, even among states that share a common culture—in this case, Islam. Iraq's effort to regain total control of the Shatt al Arab was the manifest reason for the war, which began officially when Iraq invaded Iran in September 1980. The Shatt al Arab, a narrow strait between the two countries, has strategic value as a trade outlet to the Persian Gulf. In addition, these five factors are partial causes of the long-standing hostilities that resulted in war:

1. There is historical, nation-based hostility between the Iranians, whose ethnicity is Persian, and the Iraqis, who are predominantly Arabic.

2. There have been periodic disputes along the Iran–Iraq border, which was established after World War I, because of the attempts by the Kurdish nationality (whose region, Kurdistan, is along the border) to establish autonomy from the Iraqis, and also because of Iranian support for separatist political violence by the Kurds.

3. The Kurdistan area has valuable oil resources that both Iraq and Iran want to control.

4. The Iranian revolution (January 1979) brought to power a fundamentalist Shia Muslim regime under the Ayatollah Khomeini. The Shia Muslims are deeply antagonistic to the religion of the Sunni Muslim minority, who rule a Shia majority in Iraq. There was also a history of personal animosity between Khomeini and Iraq's President Saddam Hussein.

5. Internal political difficulties in each country, and especially major economic problems in Iran after the revolution, provoked each state to redirect the frustrations of its population against the enemy across the border.

Moreover, the actions and intentions of many other states were also significant factors that caused and sustained the Iran–Iraq War. For example, Egypt and other Arab states supported Iraq's war effort because of their desire to prevent

be interpreted as examples of interstate violence between a developed country and a less developed country. Military intervention might also occur under the rationale of stabilizing a neighboring regime, as in the Soviet Union's involvement in Afghanistan (1979–1987).

In most instances of interstate conflict between a developing country and a *non-adjoining* state during the postcolonial period, the other combatant has been a more developed country. A developed country might intervene with force to protect its strategic, economic, or ideological interests in an internal war, as the United States did in Haiti in 1994 and France did in the Central African Republic in 1996. Often, the developed country engages in low-intensity conflict (see Chapter 12) to support or undermine one side in a civil war or revolutionary war. Occasionally the conflict

BOX 14.4 *(Continued)*

Islamic fundamentalism from spreading to their state. Syria, an Arab country that had long been in conflict with Iraq, was a primary supporter of non-Arabic Iran. When Shah Reza Pahlavi's pro-American Iranian government was replaced by a strongly anti-American Iran under Khomeini, who was deeply resentful of U.S. support for the Shah, the United States began to aid Iraq. The U.S. shift toward Iraq caused the Soviet Union to limit its long-standing support for Iraq. And some arms-producing states, such as Brazil and France, sold large quantities of weapons to Iran and Iraq.

The war was devastating to the human and economic resources of both Iran and Iraq, including more than one million casualties. After the cease-fire in August 1988 stopped the fighting, Iran withdrew from international military struggle and focused on pursuing its prosperity and stability goals. It slowly normalized its relations with other states and achieved slight economic growth. However, the cease-fire provided no solution to the complex conflicts in the region. Disputes regarding borders, resources, and religion were again among the complex reasons that Iraq invaded Kuwait in 1990. This time, the United States organized a major multinational military response against Iraq, which suffered another massive toll, with high casualties (estimates range greatly, between 10,000 and 500,000) and extensive destruction of its infrastructure. However, Iraq, under its defiant and dictatorial leader Saddam Hussein, continued to provoke military reaction. As part of the settlement after the Gulf War, the international community insisted that Iraq allow an international team to inspect all of its facilities to ensure it was not holding or producing "weapons of mass destruction," whether nuclear weapons or chemical and biological weapons.

Protracted diplomatic negotiations did not resolve disagreement between United Nations' weapons inspectors and Iraq, which claimed that many of the inspections were a violation of its sovereignty. To punish the Iraqis for resisting the inspections, the United States initiated daily airstrikes on various Iraqi targets, claiming it was bombing "military installations." Months of such bombing did not force Iraq to become more cooperative. Even after two devastating wars with its neighbors and the more developed countries, Iraq remained unbowed, combative with its neighbors, and aggressive against its Kurdish population

escalates into a conventional war (e.g., between the United States and North Vietnam in the 1960s, between the United Kingdom and Argentina in 1982, and between U.S.-led military forces and Iraq in 1991).

Typically, the developing country will claim that its aggression against a developed country is self-defense, even if it seems to initiate the hostilities. From the perspective of many developing countries, the entire period of colonialism and neocolonialism has involved the sustained use of military, economic, and psychological violence against them by the developed countries. Thus Third World people sometimes directed violence against the agents of the developed countries during the colonial period, especially during wars of liberation. And in the postcolonial period, developing countries have occasionally used political violence against a developed country that is perceived to be a source of oppression—as exemplified by Libya's and Syria's apparent sponsorship of terrorist activities against Europeans and Americans in the 1980s.

A striking feature of the post–cold war period has been the increasing presence of the United Nations peacekeeping forces to provide security (see Chapter 12). In 1996, for example, fifteen of the nineteen active UN peacekeeping operations were in developing countries (Kegley and Wittkopf 1997: 499). Unlike most of the earlier UN operations, these recent ones are often attempts to maintain internal stability within a developing country rather than to intervene in an interstate dispute. In El Salvador and Cambodia, for example, the UN forces' objective was to protect and implement peace agreements that had already been signed by belligerent internal groups. Despite differences in outward forms, most UN peacekeeping missions are explicit efforts, primarily organized and funded by the developed countries, to ensure the stability of "zones of turmoil" in the developing world. An emerging form of intervention, problematic from the perspective of a state's sovereignty, is the use of external force on humanitarian grounds—to protect an ethnic minority that is the target of widespread, violent treatment by the state (Falk 1999).

Economic Security

The search for security is often extremely costly. Many developing countries devote a substantial amount of their limited resources to military expenditure. A few statistics illuminate this fact. The developing countries currently spend $70 million per day on arms, ammunition, and other military hardware. Since 1960, total military spending by the developing countries has increased sixfold in constant dollars and the number of people in their armed forces has nearly doubled. In 1994 alone, the developing countries spent $110 billion on their armed forces (Kegley and Wittkopf 1997: 384; Sivard 1996: 44).

Obviously, these huge military expenditures can enhance security and stability. But empirical analyses suggest that greater military might is actually associated with a *higher* probability that a state will be involved in interstate conflict (Bremer 1980). Moreover, expenditures on the military represent resources that are not available for economic development and social welfare. For every $1.00 that is spent on education and health care, $1.70 is spent on the military. It has been estimated that each dollar spent on arms in the developing countries reduces domestic investment by twenty-five cents and agricultural output by twenty cents (Klare 1987).

The fragility of the economic systems in many developing countries is also a crucial element in the quest for security, because a state's goal of autonomy—of controlling its own destiny—depends in part on its capacity to resist external manipulation of its political economy. When the developed countries and multinational corporations provide economic and technological assistance, they expect substantial influence and benefits, such as advantageous terms for establishing firms, favorable trade relations, and rights to undertake strategic military activities within the state. And when the developing countries owe more than $2 trillion to the financial institutions of the developed world, intervention and control by the international financial community are inevitable.

This intervention has come most explicitly from the IMF (International Monetary Fund), a consortium of financial institutions based in the more developed countries that sets economic policy and monitors the behavior of lenders and debtors. To grant additional loans or to reschedule payments on existing loans, the IMF requires "conditionality"—the debtor state must fulfill specific conditions set by the IMF. The IMF's conditions often include implementation of a *structural adjustment program* (SAP). The intent of an SAP is to accelerate the developing country's transition from a statist political economy to a free-market system and to open the country to the global economy. SAPs typically require an overall reduction in public spending, with particularly severe reductions in the distribution of welfare services to its population, as well as currency devaluation, cuts in wages, and privatization of state-owned firms. The country must also facilitate direct foreign investment and freer trade by lowering its barriers to the entry of capital and goods. The political and financial elites in nearly all developing countries seem to believe that their interests are best served by cooperation with the developed countries and the international financial community, and that loss of some control over their political economy and even over their policy process is an acceptable cost.

Some developing countries are now attempting to organize their own regional free-trade zones to increase their autonomy from the more developed countries. Such trade zones have emerged among states representing half of Latin America's population ("Mercosur"), including Argentina, Brazil, Paraguay, and Uruguay, and among a set of Islamic states with 300 million people, including Iran, Kazakhstan, Pakistan, and Turkey. For the foreseeable future, however, virtually every developing country will need some economic aid, goods, markets, and technology from the developed world.

This continuing need for support from the developed countries was captured in a paradoxical comment by Kenya's President Daniel Arap Moi: "No country can maintain its independence without assistance from outside." In the contemporary political world, no state can survive as an independent entity. But the developing countries are particularly dependent upon outside assistance in many forms, especially economic and technological. Because they are susceptible to influence, manipulation, or even control by other states, few of them can escape this economic component of their insecurity.

GOAL: STABILITY

Many developing countries find that achieving stability is as elusive as achieving prosperity and security. They have not been able to establish structures that maintain social order and ensure stable functioning of the political system through time.

Challenges to Political System Effectiveness

Recall (from Chapter 10) Kwame Nkrumah's credo: "Seek ye first the political kingdom and all else shall be added unto you." This perspective places primary importance on the political system as the crucial instrument for achieving the developing country's goals. It is assumed that the leaders will effectively use the policies and structures of the state to create the conditions to increase the country's prosperity, security, and stability.

However, in many developing countries the political system proves to be a flawed instrument for goal achievement, because the state's effectiveness and stability are challenged by a variety of factors. In most states, the problems stem from some of the same circumstances that threaten prosperity and security:

1. The citizens of many developing countries have *little shared culture* or purpose. Rather, historical nationality cleavages grounded in ethnicity, religion, and language become the basis for intensive competition and conflict over value allocations (Barber 1996; Huntington 1997).

2. *Other actors in the international environment,* particularly states and major economic institutions (such as multinational corporations), often use the developing country to achieve their own goals. Typically, their actions reduce the state's political capabilities (Chapter 10) and its capacity to sustain economic development and internal security (Isbister 1998).

3. Most developing countries provide an *inadequate level of material well-being* to satisfy most of the population. The problem is grounded in the country's lack of economic capacity to produce sufficient goods which, in turn, would provide a decent standard of living and support welfare distribution by the state. But Table 14.4 revealed that the problem is even worse: In general, these states have the world's most unequal distributions of wealth. As those representative examples indicated, the disparity between rich and poor can be huge, and it is especially visible in urban areas. The economic elite, and often the political elite, enjoy a very high standard of living, an island of luxury in a sea of desperately poor people. Insufficient prosperity is always a potential source of political frustration, conflict, and instability, and severe inequality in the distribution of the existing resources makes the situation even more volatile.

Other obstacles to the search for stability are more direct consequences of the political situation:

1. Most of these states *lack a tradition of limited mandate*—an institutionalized, nonviolent procedure for the periodic transfer of power from one government leader to another. In the last decades of the twentieth century, the top political leader in many developing countries was more likely to be replaced by political violence, such as a coup or an assassination, than by a genuine election. In one of the most extreme examples, Bolivia experienced 190 coups in the 156 years ending in 1982. And during the 1980s, only 3 of 170 leaders in Sub-Saharan Africa left power voluntarily.

Election day in Nigeria. As developing countries attempt to institutionalize democracy, the military must achieve the delicate balance of maintaning order and protecting democratic practices without taking control of the government during the inevitable periods of instability.

2. More broadly, the legitimacy of the political structures and leaders in many developing countries remains problematic. In other words, these countries *lack political institutionalization*—the infusion of value into political structures and roles rather than into personalized bases of power (Chapter 10). The political institutions in most developing countries (South American states are the general exception) have existed for fewer than sixty years. Modern political forms have been established—they are usually either a copy of the institutions of the former colonial master state or a hybrid between the colonial power's institutions and the traditional governing forms in the society. When subjected to the (inevitable) internal and external pressures, these political institutions function ineffectively or break down in political decay (Aguero and Stark 1998; Bratton and van de Walle 1997; Sorensen 1996; Stepan and Linz 1996).

The Decline of Political Order

Political decay. Samuel Huntington's (1968) model of political decay, described in detail in Chapter 10, is based on the problems of instability he identified in developing countries. The postcolonial history of Ghana (see Box 14.4), like the case studies of Cambodia, Congo, India, and Uruguay in this book, includes episodes of serious political decay. In such states, the combined effects of national independence, some modernization, some economic development, increasing social mobilization, and political leaders' rhetoric generate high expectations among the population regarding increased prosperity and a higher standard of living.

Since the political economy is usually unable to deliver sufficient goods (jobs, housing, health care, food, and so on) to meet these expectations or even to sustain a reasonable level of economic development, support declines for the political leadership and institutions. The leaders attempt different strategies: (1) some request trust and patience, promising that the system will eventually provide the desired goods; (2) some attempt to substitute symbolic rewards such as greater political participation, which generates some support if the citizens feel they have a genuine role in their state's political destiny; and (3) some impose repressive policies and force against any groups or media that criticize the political system.

In most developing countries, a major casualty of these strategies is democratic processes (Bratton and van de Walle 1997; Sorensen 1996). The people lose patience with promises and the politically active groups are frustrated when their demands are not met. In many cases, the leadership does reassert order through increasingly authoritarian practices. If the state's repressive policies are ineffective, there is a spread of political violence—strikes, riots, terrorism, and rebellion. In

BOX 14.5

A Case of Political Decay: Ghana

Historically, the Gold Coast of West Africa was dominated by the Kingdom of the Asante tribes and had trade linkages with many European powers. The British conquered the area only in 1901, gaining colonial control of the region. As the new state of Ghana, it was the first colonial territory in Sub-Saharan Africa to gain its independence, in 1957. Its early leader, Kwame Nkrumah, became an articulate spokesman for African freedom and independence in the postcolonial era.

In the decade before independence, an active multiparty system was created and democratic elections were held. Nkrumah and his Convention Peoples Party (CPP) won the first postindependence election. But significant problems arose immediately, including economic shortfalls associated with world cocoa prices and widespread corruption and inefficiency within the CPP and the government bureaucracy.

Unfortunately, everyone lacked experience with the parliamentary style of government-versus-opposition. Other parties and groups vehemently criticized the failures of the CPP ("a party of incompetents") and the extensive powers exercised by Nkrumah ("a dictator"). These criticisms embarrassed, threatened, and angered Nkrumah and the CPP, and so they passed laws restricting opposition activities. Opponents protested verbally and then physically. The government responded with even more repressive measures, arguing that any opposition was unpatriotic.

The government became more and more autocratic. An election in 1960 was obviously rigged, and a referendum of support for the government in 1964 was a farce. By the 1965 election, legal opposition was virtually eliminated and all CPP candidates were declared elected. Both the economy and social order were in collapse and Nkrumah was behaving like a dictator. In 1966 the army intervened, overthrowing Nkrumah and installing a "temporary" military junta.

some cases, as political decay increases, social order can collapse into nation-based violence, separatist violence, or revolution. In other cases, external intervention (e.g., the UN, another country) reestablishes democratic practices. But most frequently, a new, even more "forceful" leadership elite (often from the military) emerges (Huntington 1968; Onwumechili 1999; Stepan and Linz 1996).

Military regimes. There are three reasons why the military tends to emerge in the attempt to restore order under conditions of actual or potential political decay. First, a key norm within the military is a *commitment to order* and an abhorrence of social disorder. This norm induces the military to act when civilian (or even other military) leadership has failed to maintain order because of a major crisis, a breakdown in the transfer of political power, or evidence of serious political decay. Second, the military has the capacity to *exercise power effectively* since it is the most highly institutionalized and disciplined societal structure in a developing country. Third, the military has the *capacity to subdue disorder,* since it usually controls the greatest concentration of force and violence in the society (Macridis and Burg 1991: 133–135).

BOX 14.5 *(Continued)*

Since 1966 Ghana has alternated between civilian governments and military coups. In 1972, 1978, 1979, and 1981, military officers took control of the government in the face of civilian incompetence and corruption. A young air force officer, Flight Lieutenant Jerry Rawlings, led the last two coups. By 1981 Rawlings had become convinced that his leadership and solutions were superior to those of civilian governments. Despite several assassination and coup attempts, he has ruled continuously since 1981. Opposition parties are now active and Freedom House has classified Ghana as "partly free" since 1992. Under pressure from the international community, Rawlings submitted to an election in 1996. He used state power to shape the election and was narrowly reelected.

Whereas Nkrumah attempted to install a command economy, Rawlings has used political power with equal purposefulness to shift to a market economy. He collaborated with the International Monetary Fund to secure loans, implement a structural adjustment program, denationalize most public corporations, and radically cut public services. Ghana's economic performance has somewhat improved under Rawlings in the sense that GNP per capita is now growing slightly, at an average of about 1.4 percent per year and inflation is being "held down" to an average of about 30 percent (see Table 14.3).

If Rawlings does build a strong economy, his epitaph as a ruler will be positive. To this point, however, his rule has not dramatically altered the persistent motifs of politics in Ghana: high inflation and unemployment, corruption and mismanagement, dependency on external political and economic power, curfews, detention without trial, closed borders, and authoritarianism. Ghana, the state that was going to be a model for postindependence Africa, has instead provided a depressing model of economic stagnation and recurrent political decay.

As in the example of Ghana (Box 14.4, and recall Box 5.5 on Cambodia and Box 4.5 on Myanmar), the emergence of strong military leadership is a recurrent pattern in the developing world. At one point in the early 1980s, military regimes were in power in fifteen of the twenty-two major Latin American states and in twenty of the twenty-six major Sub-Saharan African states. By the mid-1990s, the military in most developing countries had accepted the professional norm that it should support the civilian regime and prevent nondemocratic practices but that it should not seize power. Thus a substantial number of developing countries are now "protected democracies" in which a strong military protects the political leadership and democratic processes in exchange for public policies supported by the military, social stability, and the maintenance of the privileged status of the military in society (Loveman 1994). However, members of the military in some countries are still inclined to take political power when they perceive political decay, especially in Africa and South Asia (e.g., Nigeria in 1998; Pakistan in 1999). When members of the military do take political power, they might claim that they are restoring democracy, but they usually establish an authoritarian regime.

Internal war.   When political decay becomes so extensive that no groups, not even the military, can maintain order, internal war—either civil or revolutionary— becomes more likely. Given the economic and political conditions outlined earlier, it is understandable why some populations are susceptible to ideologies that promise a dramatic improvement in the distribution of values. In some states (e.g., Cambodia, Peru, the Philippines), variations of Marxism continue to appeal to frustrated groups who are persuaded their situation fits Marx's revolutionary call that the people have nothing to lose but their chains.

While the appeal of Marxist ideology has diminished in many developing countries, fundamental power struggles and deep inequalities among groups remain. Conflict is fueled by some combination of ethnonationalist, class, and regional cleavages. During the 1990s, rival groups competing for power and control of resources reduced Afghanistan, Burundi, Congo, Liberia, Sierra Leone, and Somalia to anarchy. In a particularly volatile combination, four decades of conflict among government forces, leftist guerrillas, and drug traffickers has resulted in 35,000 deaths in Colombia, as well as 22,000 deaths in Peru during the 1980s.

Major internal violence in developing countries is almost always supported by other states, which pursue their own national interests while providing financial or military assistance to combatants. Thus virtually every civil or revolutionary war in the developing world mobilizes overt and covert support from other states: Syria and Israel invade Lebanon; Uganda, Rwanda, and Burundi intervene in Congo; Libya, France, and the United States assist factions in the civil war in Chad; the United Nations intervenes in Angola, Cambodia, East Timor (Indonesia), El Salvador, and Somalia. Indeed, a key element in the pervasive insecurity *and* instability of developing countries is the ease with which other states can pursue their own policy goals within the context of internal violence in these states.

Democratization

Chapter 10 analyzed the wave of democratization sweeping the world. This trend has been evident among developing countries in all regions. The post–cold war period has generated additional pressure in developing countries to shift away from authoritarian and military regimes toward regimes with an elected leadership, a multiparty system, and open, pluralist politics. This pressure has particularly come from the international financial community and from internal groups which mobilize to demand their political rights.

The spread of democratization is most dramatic in *Latin America*. In 2000, every country in the Western Hemisphere except Cuba had an electoral democracy. During the 1990s some, such as Brazil and Peru, weathered serious episodes of political decay that earlier would almost certainly have resulted in a military coup. Others, including Argentina, Haiti, and Venezuela, defeated coup attempts. Thus Freedom House (1999) currently classifies twenty-three of the Latin American countries as fully free democracies. Nine additional countries are only "partly free" (including Brazil, Colombia, Guatemala, Haiti, Mexico, and Peru), and Cuba is "not free." According to the Freedom House classification, a country that is "not free" substantially limits its citizens' political rights (e.g., to form political parties which represent a significant range of voter choice and to engage in vigorous, open political opposition to the leaders) and it does not uphold its citizens' civil liberties (e.g., protection of religious, ethnic, economic, linguistic, and other rights). "Partly free" means that there are significant political restrictions and violations of civil liberties, even though it might be an electoral democracy (recall page 161).

The countries of *Sub-Saharan Africa* are characterized by their highest level of democratization since independence. One analyst concludes that slightly more than half of these countries exhibit promising democratic reforms (Matloff 1996). However, Freedom House classifies less than one-third of the countries in Sub-Saharan Africa as electoral democracies. In its assessment, nine of the 53 countries (17 percent) are "free," and twenty-one (40 percent) are "partly free," while twenty-three (43 percent) are "not free" (Karatnycky 1999). In *Asia*, the spread of democratization is also mixed. China emphatically reversed its movement toward democracy at Tiananmen Square in 1989. China, Cambodia, Myanmar, North Korea, and Vietnam are among seven major Asian developing countries that are classified as "not free." Six more (including Bangladesh, Indonesia, Malaysia, and Pakistan) are only "partly free." India remains the world's largest democracy, although it has been battered by political decay, including parliamentary deadlock, assassination, and extensive violence among Hindus, Muslims, and Sikhs. Electoral democracies are also functioning in Mongolia and the Philippines, and in the Asian NICs of Taiwan, Thailand, Singapore, and South Korea, although some are fragile and under persistent pressure. Even many of the developing countries of the *Islamic Middle East* and *North Africa* have introduced elements of democratic politics. Most countries now elect their political leadership (e.g., Egypt, Iran, and Morocco), while others at least have a democratically elected legislature (e.g., Jordan). However, democratic structures are not deeply entrenched, and Freedom House does not classify any of these states as electoral democracies (Karatnycky 1999). When democratic processes threaten the elites, those processes are still usually reversed by elite action, as occurred in Algeria and Syria. According to Freedom House (1999), only Jordan, Kuwait, and Morocco are "partly free," and fourteen of these states are judged to be "not free."

Overall, democratization has expanded substantially in developing countries. Most regimes have granted some political rights to individuals and groups and have begun a process of elite accountability by promising elections. An increasing number have held elections, and while the old elites have retained power in many cases, especially in Africa, there are also many countries, especially in Latin America, where power has passed to former opposition groups.

Nonetheless, the staying power of the current wave of democracy (discussed in Chapter 7) might already be ebbing in the developing countries. An analysis of democratization in Sub-Saharan Africa concludes, in contrast to the one by Matloff (1996) previously discussed, that although democratic practices are evident in many countries, only eight African democracies are actually "taking root" (Drogin 1996). For example, when Zimbabwe conducted a "democratic" election in 1996, Robert Mugabe, who has been president since independence in 1960, had significant advantages besides incumbency. His government controlled all media and all campaign funds, and both candidates opposing him withdrew before the vote (one was arrested). Not surprisingly, Mugabe won easily, and his party won 147 of the 150 legislative seats. Even in Latin America, there is some evidence of a resurgence of popular support for leadership that is strong and decisive but also authoritarian. For example, with support from the majority of citizens, Peruvian President Alberto Fujimori suspended the Constitution and seized power from the legislature in a creative political action in 1992 called a *self-coup* (autogolpe) and Venezuelan President Hugo Chavez launched a more limited takeover of power in 1999.

Thus the positive developments regarding the expansion of democratization in developing countries are balanced against three negative factors. First, these societies face the major destabilizing forces discussed in this chapter. Second, the elites in many developing countries do not have a genuine commitment to democratic practice. And third, democratic regimes in the developing countries often have limited political institutionalization. Many of these countries still move in and out of the "free" category. Even if the elites do have good intentions to extend democracy, it seems inevitable that some, and perhaps many, of these countries will retreat from democratic governance and experience further rounds of some combination of economic decline, political decay, corruption, military intervention, and authoritarianism. "Hero" by well-known Egyptian cartoonist Toughan (page 377)reflects some of the demoralizing obstacles to political and economic development experienced by citizens in many developing countries..

Political Approaches

For those who do first "seek the political kingdom" as the primary instrument for achieving political and economic goals, the fundamental question is: What approach will increase the likelihood of prosperity, security, and stability? Developing countries pursue these goals within various political frameworks, which can be categorized in different ways. One useful method for categorizing these frameworks is to consider the political approach taken regarding two basic issues: resource equality and democratic participation.

Resource equality concerns the extent to which the political system attempts to produce an equal distribution of key economic and social values (e.g., wealth, income, status, housing, health care, education, and jobs). The state's authoritative allocation of these values can result in either greater equality or greater inequality. While a command political economy can most directly use public policy to distribute economic values in a certain way, any type of political economy can implement policies aimed at increasing or decreasing equality. And many public policy decisions shape the broader level of egalitarianism in the society.

© Cartoon News

The issue of *democratic participation* concerns the extent to which the people are mobilized into active and meaningful involvement in the political process. As was discussed in Chapter 7, a political system is more democratic when there is greater citizen participation in the selection of political leaders from among genuine alternatives and when individuals have a greater capacity to discuss and influence issues in the public domain. At one theoretical extreme, a single person has all the political power in a country and all others are prevented from any political action. At the opposite extreme, every citizen has an equal role in political decisions and actions.

Obviously, there is no actual political system located on either end of the continuum (for either resource equality or democratic participation). Figure 14.1 indicates four ideal-type political approaches that have different orientations toward the desired mix of equality and democracy: (1) conservative authoritarianism, (2) modernizing authoritarianism, (3) revolutionary socialism, and (4) constitutional democracy. The characteristic features of each are described next.

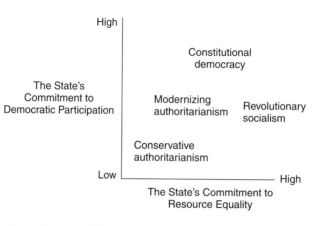

Figure 14.1   Ideal-type political approaches

Conservative authoritarianism.   Conservative authoritarian regimes have little or no commitment to resource equality. There is an effort to preserve the traditional socioeconomic order and culture. Certain groups enjoy great advantages in the distribution of economic and social power; these groups might be defined by lineage, ethnicity, class, religion, or some other trait. The socioeconomic elite, with support from the government apparatus, exercises substantial control over the political economy; this elite might also exercise great political power. Most people are allowed little or no role in the political process. Political repression of the mass can be based on traditional practices, especially those associated with religion, or on state actions, especially those implemented by such agents of the state as the police and the military. In fact, many of these regimes are dominated by an elite drawn from the military or religious leaders.

Higher political stability tends to occur in conservative authoritarian states where there are limited economic resources to distribute, where there is no ideology of egalitarianism, and where those groups engaged in order maintenance are well organized and loyal to the elite. As these conditions become less strong in the political system, the probability of instability increases. Contemporary examples of such political systems are Afghanistan, Nepal, Saudi Arabia, Somalia, and Tajikistan.

Modernizing authoritarianism.   Modernizing authoritarian regimes differ from conservative authoritarianism primarily in their elite's willingness to recognize that development is inevitable and perhaps even desirable. These states can have well-institutionalized organizational structures in the public sector, and technocratic elites within the bureaucracy can be a key group within the ruling coalition. Typically, most of the political economy is under private control, although the state works cooperatively with economic actors.

Substantial economic and social inequalities remain, and no direct attempt is made to reduce them. Rather, there is an assumption that economic development will have an indirect, trickle-down effect and will raise the absolute level of economic and social power of the less advantaged. Many of these states claim to be evolving slowly toward democracy, as another effect of development. Minimal levels of popular political participation are allowed, although state policies regulate political behavior and restrain opposition. There is a strong emphasis on stability, and considerable state resources are allocated to create strong capabilities for order maintenance. As with conservative authoritarianism, military leaders are often a prominent part of the political elite. Modernizing authoritarianism characterizes such regimes as China, Egypt, Indonesia, Kenya, Morocco, Nigeria, and Syria.

Revolutionary socialism.   Revolutionary socialist regimes have a strong commitment to economic and social equality but provide a very limited political role for the large majority of the population. The leadership contends that a small political elite is essential, since leaders must be decisive and unconstrained if they are to reduce the massive inequalities in the society. Thus the leadership acts on behalf of the population, asserting totalitarian control over the political economy and the society.

Revolutionary socialism emphasizes the political mobilization of the population, which is expected to support the policies of the elite. There is an extensive program of political socialization through the educational system, social and occupational groups, culture, and the media. The people are indoctrinated to recognize the political implications of virtually every action. The objective is to create citizens who want to "serve the people" rather than pursue self-interest, and who serve collective interests as a matter of value preference rather than because they fear sanctions. In practice, these states do employ repression and sanctions as well as positive socialization and peer pressure in the attempt to induce desirable behavior from the citizens.

China during the period under Mao Zedong is a clear example of revolutionary socialism. There are few current examples of this approach, although its features are evident in the regimes in Cuba, Libya, and North Korea. The military regimes in Myanmar and in Peru (between 1968 and 1976) are examples of revolutionary socialism in a non-communist system. Cases in which the political system has emphasized sanctions and repression of the masses include Laos and Cambodia under the Pol Pot regime (described in Box 5.5).

Constitutional democracy.   Constitutional democracies emphasize an open politics in which citizens are allowed considerable freedom to undertake many modes of political participation. As a constitutional regime, political actors and political decisions are constrained by the rule of law, which guarantees the rights of the ruled and limits the powers of the rulers. And as a democratic regime, the leaders are directly accountable to the citizens and receive a limited mandate by means of an electoral system with genuine alternatives. Open political opposition is allowed, the media are relatively free to assess political actions, and public involvement in the political process is facilitated.

The political leadership is not committed to using public policy to achieve economic equality. A state-regulated but relatively free economic order is viewed as the best means to generate resources for the benefit of all. Thus the political system facilitates the operation of a mixed political economy, a substantial part of which is privately controlled. The state engages in some welfare distribution, particularly to those in greatest need, and there might be public policies to encourage modest increases in social equality.

Botswana, India, Jamaica, Malta, Venezuela, and Costa Rica (see Box 14.6) are states that have generally maintained constitutional democracies in the last thirty years. As previously noted, many developing countries evolved toward more complete con-

BOX 14.6

A Third World Democracy That Works: Costa Rica

Costa Rica is one of the few developing countries that has sustained a constitutional democracy for decades. This Central American country of 3.6 million has a small (fifty-seven-member) unicameral legislature and a president elected for one four-year term. There is an efficient (if large) public bureaucracy, a relatively independent judiciary, and a stable party system dominated by two parties, which are generally pragmatic rather than ideological. For most of the twentieth century the state and the society have enjoyed high levels of political and social order. There is freedom of expression, a free press, and active political opposition. For those promoting constitutional democracy in the developing countries, the obvious question is: How has Costa Rica done it?

Costa Rica has had a few intrinsic advantages. The great majority of the population shares ethnicity and language, and there is no large subservient class of nonwhite laborers. Still, Costa Rica shares many features with other Latin American states that have not been able to sustain democratic politics:

It is small and hence a manageable size (but this factor has not helped neighbors Panama, Nicaragua, and El Salvador).

It has only limited natural resources, and its export economy has relied on a few commodities such as coffee, bananas, and sugar.

It was part of the Spanish colonial empire, then was under the general hemispheric dominance of the United States after its independence in 1821.

It has a small, wealthy upper class that controls the large plantations, a substantial middle class, and a significant number of poor and unskilled people who live primarily in rural areas.

Catholicism is the state religion.

Its population is about half urban and half rural (only highly urban Mexico is an exception to this pattern in Central America).

The success of Costa Rica as a constitutional democracy is based less on fortuitous conditions than on sensible policies and continuing commitment to democ-

stitutional democracy during the 1990s. Constitutional democracies in developing countries do still face substantial pressure during the inevitable periods when there are problems in achieving prosperity, security, or stability. Operating within democratic processes, the political system must attempt to satisfy groups on the left, which demand greater egalitarianism, and groups on the right, which demand greater economic freedom and a stronger government role in maintaining political and social order.

BOX 14.6 *(Continued)*

ratic processes. The norms and the procedures of the political system encourage efforts to achieve political consensus within a framework of participatory government. The constitution prohibits the president from serving a second term, balances the power of the executive and legislative branches, and encourages cooperation within a legislature that often does not have a single-party majority.

Consistent with the ideal-type constitutional democracy in Figure 14.1, the Costa Rican state does not have a strong commitment to use public policy to equalize resources. The political economy is oriented toward the market system. The government has balanced some controls on the private sector and protection of workers' rights with policies that encourage and subsidize private farmers and business entrepreneurs. Economic and social inequalities remain.

However, a tradition of reformist policies has gradually expanded social welfare and reduced inequalities. Costa Rica has the second highest Human Development Index score among all countries in Central and South America. Public expenditure is allocated to subsidize extensive health services, public education, and financial support for the elderly (e.g., pensions, social security). Since the late 1880s the state has provided free and compulsory education to all children. And after a brief civil war in 1948, Costa Rica replaced its military with a small national police, spending less than 2 percent of central government expenditure on military support (compared with 13 percent in Guatemala, 8 percent in Nicaragua, and 7 percent in Honduras) (Goodwin 1998: 28–45).

Costa Rica has faced considerable destabilizing forces in the last decade. While Costa Ricans enjoy the highest standard of living in Central America and rank eighth on per-capita GNP among twenty-two major Latin American countries (World Bank 1999: table 1.1), Costa Rica's fragile export economy is still reliant on agricultural commodities. The economy has sputtered as a consequence of inflation and a large level of domestic and foreign debt. In the 1990s, Costa Rica had to cope with spillovers from the instability and natural disasters in neighboring Panama and Nicaragua and substantial numbers of refugees. Yet its balanced social policies and accommodating political culture have helped generate strong support for the legitimacy of its political system from all major groups within the society. Costa Rica continues to provide hope, if not a model that can be duplicated, for other developing countries that aspire to political democracy. (This discussion relies on Goodwin 2000: 27–29.)

Which route?   Every state attempts to attain the broad goals of prosperity, security, and stability. But in terms of the dimensions depicted in Figure 14.1, there are fundamental choices about the approach by which these goals will be pursued. The rhetoric of political leaders in most developing countries (but not in conservative authoritarian regimes) implies a vision in which their society ultimately achieves the upper-right corner in Figure 14.1—a state characterized by both high levels of political democracy and considerable social and economic equality. The key question is: What is the most effective route to reach that "ideal location"?

The route taken by a state will be influenced by many factors that the state's leaders cannot control in the short run. These factors relate to many of the themes in this book: a country's relations with other states, its political culture, its geopolitical situation, its nationality composition, its history of political institutions and leaders, and so on. Within these constraints, political choices can be made regarding the route. One set of major choices centers in the structure of the political economy, especially the level and nature of state involvement in the economic system. Figure 14.1 reflects two other key choices. Modernizing authoritarianism, revolutionary socialism, and constitutional democracy place different emphases on the balance between attaining political democracy and achieving social and economic equality.

The most explicit trade-off between the two sets of objectives is evident between constitutional democracy and revolutionary socialism—between, on the one hand, greater individual and political freedom and, on the other hand, a strong interventionist state that promotes egalitarianism of social and material conditions rather than personal freedom. Modernizing authoritarian regimes tend to move slowly (sometimes very slowly, and sometimes backward) in both directions, and in most cases do not promote either democracy or egalitarianism aggressively.

When leaders in developing countries look for exemplary successes in reaching the upper-right corner in Figure 14.1, few cases can serve as models. The assessment of an "enlightened" leader who would like to achieve the ideal (and who has a pragmatic grasp of the recent histories of most developing countries) might follow these lines:

> Revolutionary socialism is best justified if our economic conditions are desperate. The strong interventionist state can try to "bootstrap" development by organizing the population and by installing a command economy that limits external economic control and makes best use of societal resources. Despite extensive efforts at political mobilization and socialization, maintaining stability in this system requires stringent restrictions on personal freedom and repressive social policies. And the economic performance of command economies has been mediocre, leading to an equality of poverty. Few populations have sustained enthusiasm and support for this approach. Indeed, most governments seem to have abandoned it.

> Constitutional democracies have the desirable feature of allowing greater personal freedom and stimulating more economic initiative. The market-oriented political economy is vibrant but becomes dependent on the direct involvement of the multinational corporations and the developed countries, which enjoy many of the economic benefits from this neocolonial situation. It also tends to produce very uneven economic development across regions, economic sectors, and population groups. There is usually an increase in inequality between rich and poor, advantaged and disadvantaged. These conditions, in conjunction with a commitment to democratic political processes, tend to produce considerable political and social instability. A government committed to democratic processes will have trouble delivering prosperity, will then lose electoral support, and might not be able to prevent political decay. At the least, I will be removed from office; at worst, there is a significant prob-

ability that the government will face a military coup, civil war, internal revolutionary political violence, and/or direct foreign intervention.

Modernizing authoritarianism is a compromise with the fewest risks and the lowest potential gains regarding either goal. Material conditions improve marginally for most of the population, but there has been minimal reduction in social and economic inequality. The Asian newly industrializing countries (NICs) have used a version of this approach to achieve prosperity and stability, although political democracy follows only at a slow pace. The most problematic factor, however, is that many other developing countries in other regions have attempted a version of modernizing authoritarianism without duplicating even the economic growth of the Asian NICs. In other cultures, this approach seems to produce short-run stability but little significant progress toward democracy or social and economic equality. And even the Asian NICs had serious economic problems in the late 1990s. At the turn of the century, the economies of most modernizing authoritarian states still seem dependent on the developed countries, international finance, and the multinational corporations. And the politics of many of these regimes seems to rely on repression as an antidote for the recurrent political decay.

What should we do? And, more fundamentally, what can we do? The problems we face are not just management problems of choosing and implementing a strategy. We are not free and unconstrained. The problems created by diversity and conflict within this country are substantial. And the problems caused by external actors, especially those from certain developed countries and some hostile states in this region, are enormous, and sometimes overwhelming.

CONCLUDING OBSERVATIONS: IT'S GOT TO GET BETTER(?)

In political forms, as in goals, there are no fundamental differences between the developing countries and the more developed countries. The selection of a particular political approach or political economy in any developing country is dependent on many factors, especially historical patterns, geopolitical conditions, and current circumstances. Similarly, a few political economies are command economies, others are almost total market economies, and most implement some form of a mixed market system. There are constitutional democracies and there are totalitarian dictatorships. *Economic* underdevelopment is obviously the main factor distinguishing the developing countries from the developed countries. But the conditions of *political* underdevelopment are the pivotal problem if the political system is to be the crucial instrument for social and economic change.

Regardless of the political approach selected, virtually all developing countries face difficult challenges as they attempt to use the political system to achieve prosperity and security. Most have valuable natural resources and a population that is willing to apply its energies to achieve these goals. However, their underdevelopment places them at an enormous disadvantage in the post–cold war world, where political, military, and economic patterns are now globalized and where states are even more single-minded in the pursuit of national self-interest.

For many of these states, especially the low-income developing countries, it is possible that no political approach and no form of political economy can simultaneously achieve all these major goals. The leaders of any developing country must make very difficult decisions about how to gain partial success on some of their goals. Some objectives will have to be sacrificed in the quest for others, and there is no assurance that any objective can be accomplished.

In the contemporary political world, the obstacles are formidable, and determining the best strategy is baffling. At every turn, the underlying political choices are fundamental: freedom versus security, economic development versus welfare, political equality versus economic equality, democracy versus efficiency, aid versus independence, market economy versus command economy, guns versus butter,…

A poem by Robert Graves (1966: 211) begins:*

> Every choice is always the wrong choice,
>
> Every vote cast is always cast away—
>
> How can truth hover between alternatives?

These lines must seem especially profound to political actors pursuing the goals of prosperity, security, and stability in developing countries.

* Robert Graves, "Whole Love." Excerpt from *Poems Selected by Himself* by Robert Graves (Middlesex: Penguin, 1966), p. 211, by permission of Carcanet Press Limited, London.

FOR FURTHER CONSIDERATION

1. Assess the claim that the label "Third World" has no meaning, either analytical or political, in the post-cold war world.
2. Are the problems in achieving economic development in the developing countries attributable primarily to the actions of the developed countries or are they best explained by domestic circumstances in these countries?
3. Specify the conditions in a real (or imaginary) developing country. In that context, provide a response to the comments of the "enlightened" developing country leader presented near the end of this chapter. Given your country's conditions, what political and economic arrangements make most sense for progressing on the key development goals you emphasize?
4. Is political violence in the developing countries likely to be greater or less during the next ten years compared to the past ten years? Why?
5. In addition to greater economic prosperity, what conditions seem most likely to sustain the shift to democratization in many developing countries? In particular, what forms or arrangements of political structures are most important?

FOR FURTHER READING

Bill, James A., and Robert Springborg. (1997). *Politics in the Middle East*. 4th ed. New York: Addison Wesley. A sound comparative introduction to political systems in the area.

Ehrlich, Paul R., and Anne H. Ehrlich. (1990). *The Population Explosion*. New York: Simon & Schuster. Updating the earlier arguments in *The Population Bomb*, the Ehrlichs mount a powerful case that overpopulation in the developing world will lead to actions that result in catastrophic deterioration of the planet's resources.

Esposito, John L., and John O. Voll. (1996). *Islam and Democracy.* New York: Oxford University Press. Interesting case studies, including Algeria, Egypt, and Iran, are employed to develop a sensitive analysis of the ways in which Islamic countries adapt to democratic principles and to the forces of secularism.

Isbister, John. (1998). *Promises Not Kept: The Betrayal of Change in the Third World.* 4th ed. W. Hartford, CT: Kumarian Press. A sensible and balanced analysis of the difficulties that have prevented most developing countries from achieving sustained development, exploring both the external and the internal obstacles to prosperity.

Krasner, Stephen D. (1985). *Structural Conflict: The Third World against Global Liberalism.* Berkeley: University of California Press. A challenging critique of the political and economic domination of the developing countries by the more developed countries.

Li, Cheng. (1997). *Rediscovering China: Dynamics and Dilemmas of Reform.* Lanham, MD: Rowan Littlefield. An insightful description of the powerful changes sweeping China at both the individual and the institutional level, based on Li's personal observations and interviews.

Mehta, Ved. (1993). *A Portrait of India.* New Haven, CT: Yale University Press. A sensitive characterization of one of the most complex and intriguing developing countries.

O'Donnell, Guillermo, Philippe Schmitter, and Laurence Whitehead, Eds. (1986). *Transitions from Authoritarian Rule.* Baltimore: Johns Hopkins University Press. Important case studies regarding the development and decline of rule by the military and technocrats, especially in Latin American countries.

Odwumechili, Chuka. (1999). *African Democratization and Military Coups.* Westport, CT: Praeger. A sobering and occasionally encouraging characterization of forty years of struggle to establish democracy in African countries and to limit the tendency toward violent takeovers and authoritarian rule by the military.

Ogden, Suzanne. (1995). *China's Unresolved Issues: Politics, Development and Culture.* 3d ed. Englewood Cliffs, NJ: Prentice-Hall. A thorough and readable text on Chinese politics, which particularly emphasizes the linkages among political structures, political ideology, and political economy.

Simon, Julian. (1992). *The Ultimate Resource.* Princeton, NJ: Princeton University Press. A powerful critique of those, like the Ehrlichs, who predict disaster due to overpopulation and environmental degradation. It argues that the ultimate resource (people producing knowledge and then applying it as technology) will outstrip problems.

Skidmore, Thomas, and Peter Smith. (1997). *Modern Latin America.* 4th ed. New York: Oxford University Press. A helpful comparative introduction to society and politics in Latin America.

Weatherby, Joseph N., et al., Eds. (1997). *The Other World: Issues and Politics of the Developing World.* 3d ed. New York: Longman. Thoughtful general chapters on colonialism, development, and conflict resolution precede informative chapters focusing on each region of developing countries.

Weiss, Thomas G., and Meryl A. Kessler, Eds. (1991). *Third World Security in the Post–Cold War Era.* Boulder, CO: Westview Press. Diverse essays, guided by a regional framework, on the quest for security by various developing countries.

World Bank. (Yearly). *World Development Report.* New York: Oxford University Press. Systematic yearly statistics on the economic, financial, and demographic aspects of development for more than 180 states. Each annual issue also emphasizes a key theme (e.g., 1990 on poverty, 1991 on environment, 1997 on the role of the state, 1998 on knowledge for development), with a strong emphasis on the developing countries.

A whole new world! A Russian veteran casts his vote, selecting from more than fifty political parties, under the disapproving gaze of V. I. Lenin, who had established one-party rule by the Communist Party of the Soviet Union.

CHAPTER 15

The Transitional Developed Countries

Even in a dynamic world, the forces of change seem especially powerful in certain countries, including the two groups of *transitional developed countries* whose characteristics were defined in Chapter 13: (1) the post-communist developed countries (PCDCs) of the former Soviet bloc; and (2) the newly industrializing countries (NICs). The specific countries in each group are listed in Table 15.1. The countries in these two groups generally have lower levels of development than the developed countries (discussed in Chapter 13). These countries can also be distinguished from most other developing countries (in Chapter 14) because they are relatively higher on the economic and/or the social dimension of development. They are singled out for examination in this chapter because many appear to be in a particularly notable periods of transition. It is possible that the changes in these countries will ultimately result in levels of economic and social development comparable to that in the most developed countries. But there are significant obstacles that might prevent their achievement of such levels in the near future and some of these countries are most likely to be very similar to other developing countries. Thus they are revealing case studies of "countries-in-the-middle" within our framework of analysis. This chapter explores broad patterns of change and obstacles faced by each subset.

The Post-Communist Developed Countries

The post-communist developed countries is a category which includes many of the states that emerged after the breakup of the Soviet Union in 1991 (e.g., Estonia, Georgia, Latvia, Russia, Ukraine) and the states that evolved from the Soviet Union's previous allies in Central and Eastern Europe (e.g., the Czech Republic, Hungary, Poland, Slovenia). The nineteen states in this analytic category have a population of about 400 million. This discussion generally excludes the eight (of twenty-seven) countries from this region that are classified as low-income countries by the World Bank (e.g., Azerbaijan, Moldova, Tajikistan).

The PCDCs are currently engaged in a process of substantial economic and political transformation. The period from the late 1940s to the late 1980s was dominated by an effort to achieve prosperity, stability, and security under the structure of a command political economy and the totalitarian political regime of communism. By the late 1980s, this effort was abandoned as these states attempted to transform themselves into more market-oriented political economies and to implement democratic politics. The sweeping changes in these countries precipitated the shift in the international system to the post–cold war period (described in Chapter 12).

TABLE 15.1
Transitional Developed Countries

Country	Population	Former State
Post-Communist Developed Countries		
Belarus	10,200,000	Soviet Union
Bulgaria	8,910,000	
Croatia	4,500,000	Yugoslavia
Czech Republic	10,000,000	Czechoslovakia
Estonia	1,573,000	Soviet Union
Georgia	5,549,000	Soviet Union
Hungary	10,588,000	
Kazakhstan	16,538,000	Soviet Union
Latvia	2,681,000	Soviet Union
Lithuania	3,690,000	Soviet Union
Poland	37,799,000	
Romania	23,397,000	
Russia	147,386,000	Soviet Union
Serbia	9,000,000	Yugoslavia
Slovak Republic	5,000,000	Czechoslovakia
Slovenia	2,000,000	Yugoslavia
Ukraine	51,704,000	Soviet Union
Uzbekistan	19,906,000	Soviet Union
Post-Communist Less Developed Countries		
Albania	3,335,000	
Armenia	3,305,000	Soviet Union
Azerbaijan	7,145,000	Soviet Union
Bosnia and Herzogovina	4,500,000	Yugoslavia
Kyrgyzstan	4,372,000	Soviet Union
Moldova	4,341,000	Soviet Union
Tajikistan	5,112,000	Soviet Union
Turkmenistan	3,621,000	Soviet Union
Newly Industrializing Countries: Asia		
Malaysia	18,845,000	
Singapore	2,721,000	
South Korea	43,045,000	
Taiwan	20,454,000	
Thailand	58,722,000	
Newly Industrializing Countries: Latin America		
Argentina	34,628,000	
Brazil	162,661,000	
Chile	14,333,000	
Mexico	95,773,000	
Uruguay	3,239,000	
Venezuela	21,983,000	

Figure 13.1 reflects that these countries are relatively advanced on the social development dimension. Their populations are educated and mainly urban, and high technologies are penetrating the economy and private life. Their economic development is more difficult to assess by the standard GNP per capita measure because the performance of their political economies was significantly depressed during the 1990s, a period of fundamental change.

A new complexity has emerged in most of the PCDCs. Democratic political processes have been adopted but are institutionalized to quite varied degrees. While some citizens support the shift to a market economy, others are dissatisfied with the effects of this change on themselves or on their society. In their quest for prosperity, stability, and security, the PCDCs are attempting to find a reasonable balance between these newer forms of politics and economics and the "traditional" communist approaches. The next sections describe key elements of both the newer forms and also the communist approaches that shaped these political systems for between forty and eighty years (and ending about 1990).

POLITICAL CULTURE

The peoples of the PCDCs have a rich and complicated history shaped by many political cultures. Most of the former Soviet Union was ruled autocratically by the Russian Czars for three centuries before the Russian Revolution of 1917. The rest of the region was controlled for much of the same period by great empires, including the Ottoman Turkish Empire in Eastern Europe (e.g., Bulgaria, Macedonia, Romania) and the Austrian (Hapsburg) Empire in Central Europe (e.g., Czech Republic, Hungary, Poland). Only in the late nineteenth century did independent states emerge in Central and Eastern Europe. The political cultures of these states are strongly influenced by their history of oppressive rule and by the multiple nationalities that live within the boundaries of most of the states.

Under Communism

The dominant influence on political culture in these states from 1945 to 1985 was *Marxist-Leninist socialism* (Chapter 2). This political philosophy began with Karl Marx (1818–1883) and evolved after the Russian Revolution through the decisions of such Soviet leaders as V. I. Lenin (in power 1917–1924), Joseph Stalin (1927–1953), and Mikhail Gorbachev (1985–1991). Marxism-Leninism is supposed to be a "scientific" description of reality, but it also provides a normative perspective (i.e., a prescription of how things *should* be).

This political culture has four central concepts. First, consistent with the class approach (described in Chapter 9), individual societies and the international system have historically been subject to patterns of *stratification and class struggle.* Over time, lower classes overthrow the oppressive class above them, and the political economy is then transformed.

Second, the ultimate goal is a political economy producing *equality* in the control of and benefits from societal resources, regardless of a person's status, role, age, gender, ethnicity, or any other such factor. This equality produces a classless society, guided by Marx's well-known phrase: from each according to his ability, to each according to his need.

Third, however, until a classless society is achieved, politics must be *guided by an ideological elite.* This vanguard, the Communist Party, controls the state, makes all policy decisions, and monitors the behavior of all actors to ensure that the necessary changes are made in the political economy and in individuals' political beliefs and actions. Lenin called this phase "the dictatorship of the proletariat."

Fourth, when the transformation to communism is complete, the coercive state is no longer necessary and a true *people's democracy* is established. The state will, in the language of Engels, "wither away," to be replaced by "the administration of things" and by widespread democratic participation in politics at the local level.

Post-Communism

Opposition to Marxist-Leninist political culture always existed in these countries, although it was generally repressed by the state and the Communist Party until the 1980s. By the post-communist period, beginning in the early 1990s, there was a substantial shift of popular support and political power toward those favoring alternative visions of political culture. The alternative visions differ in some of their emphases, but generally share the belief that the political system must be based on genuine democratic participation, including civil rights and personal freedom. The monopoly of power by the Communist Party is rejected in favor of a system based on group politics with multiple competing groups. The post-communist political culture also insists that the political economy must abandon extensive state control and state ownership, shifting toward a market political economy and allowing greater freedom of action to firms and to individuals.

During the current period of transition for their political systems and political economies, there are serious tensions within the political cultures of these countries. Many people are attracted to the tenets of the post-communist political culture, which envisions individual freedom and economic prosperity. However, there are differences of opinion on several issues, including the extent to which the state should continue to redistribute society's resources in order to increase equality and the extent to which ethnic diversity should be tolerated by the dominant ethnic group.

Even more importantly, key elements of Marxist-Leninist political culture, the basis of the citizens' political socialization and reality for more than forty years (and for nearly seventy years in the Soviet Union), continue to have a strong hold on some people, especially those whose self-interest is best served by that political culture and those disaffected with the post-communist period. For example, the problems associated with the post-communist system have been so severe in Russia that the majority of citizens indicated in 1999 that they preferred the system in place during the communist period (circa 1985) to the current system (VCIOM 1999). There is considerably less recollection of the "good old days" in the countries where economic prosperity has been most widely enjoyed, especially in Central Europe (see below).

Both the tensions between these viewpoints and also people's actual experiences under both the communist and post-communist periods substantially affect their current beliefs about the best means to pursue the basic goals of prosperity, stability, and security. The next three sections characterize these countries' strategies and performance during both periods.

GOAL: PROSPERITY
Under Communism

These states claimed that the main purpose of communist economic development was to allow for the equal distribution of abundant goods and material welfare to the entire population. The principal strategy for achieving prosperity was the *command economy*, as described in Chapter 8. The state and the Communist Party, guided by a comprehensive plan, attempted to control the use of society's valued resources, so that the production system benefited all "the people" rather than the very few rich and privileged.

Performance.   Measured by GNP per capita, these countries' economic performance under communism ranked them in the upper one-third of the world's states in the late 1980s. Most ranked between fifteenth (the former East Germany) and forty-ninth (the former Yugoslavia). Relative to the more developed countries (with which they compared themselves), GNP per capita in these states was disappointing. However, these countries did have relatively high scores on most quality-of-life indices (such as the Human Development Index), measures that correspond more closely than GNP per capita to the Marxist-Leninist political culture's own definition of prosperity. At the individual level, virtually every citizen had access to inexpensive or free health care, education, food, and shelter, and most had economic security against such problems as illness and old age.

Problems.   Although basic goods were distributed to most people, the overall quality of goods was poor and there were persistent shortages of many goods and services. Among the many explanations for low productivity and low-quality goods, three inherent problems with command political economies seemed particularly important (recall Chapter 8):

1. *Inadequate incentives.* Contrary to the Marxist ideal, workers were less inclined to work hard for the good of all the people, rather than for their own private benefit. Since there were few wage incentives, many workers had minimal motivation to work efficiently or to produce high-quality goods and services. Also, managers were cautious, because the penalties for failing to follow the economic plan were greater than the rewards for successful innovation.
2. *Overcentralization.* The states' large central planning bureaucracies were rigid and unable to foresee the precise needs of producers and consumers. Thus the economic activities based on these plans were not responsive either to short-term opportunities and problems or to particular local circumstances.
3. *Inadequate capital investment.* While the development of heavy industry and military equipment was emphasized, there was insufficient capital investment in machinery and modern technologies (e.g., computers) to stimulate productivity gains in agriculture, light industry, and consumer goods (Blasi, Kroumova and Kruse 1997; Goldman 1994).

Post-Communism

Many countries (e.g., Hungary, Poland, and Yugoslavia) had begun economic innovations in the 1980s, introducing elements of a market and encouraging some profit seeking by firms. Soviet leader Mikhail Gorbachev accelerated these changes with his support for economic *perestroika* ("restructuring") (Goldman 1994; Medvedev 2000).

In most of the PCDCs, the leaders who came to power in the early 1990s attempted to achieve a rapid transition to a market political economy. Similar strategies have been followed in most countries. Central planning has been abandoned. Private firms are allowed to form and to produce goods for profit. The prices of most goods are determined by supply and demand. Many state-owned enterprises have been sold to private actors ("privatized") or shut down. Firms must operate in the competitive international economic system and deal with powerful transnational corporations and financial actors. Currencies are being adjusted to their real value.

While this general approach has been adopted in most PCDCs, countries have varied considerably in the speed and depth with which these changes have been implemented. Some countries (e.g., Czech Republic, Poland, Romania) opted for radical market reforms (sometimes termed *"shock therapy"*), attempting to introduce the market political economy quickly and extensively. Other countries (e.g., Hungary, Russia, Slovenia) chose a more gradual (*"reformist"*) approach based on much slower implementation of changes in the political economy (Rutland 1999). The gradualists assumed that the massive negative impacts of radical reforms—a substantial decline in gross national product, high unemployment, inflation, and personal economic hardship—would be unacceptable and would generate serious political and economic instability.

Performance.   Regardless of approach, most PCDCs experienced the feared negative effects at quite high levels during the early 1990s. Virtually every country suffered a substantial net decline in economic output (GNP/GDP) per capita between 1990 and 1994. In the late 1990s, yearly economic growth reemerged in many of the PCDCs. Economic output per capita for most of the PCDCs ranges broadly between about $5,000 and $1,000 (Table 15.2). Table 15.3 indicates the extent to which there was overall economic growth or decline during the decade. In only two of the thirteen PCDCs in the table was there any net growth, and the average annual decline was very steep in half of the countries. While the problems in Russia were particularly severe, its disastrous failure to achieve the transition to a market economy, briefly characterized in Box 15.1, dominated the situation in the region.

PCDCs experienced quite different levels of economic decline and are now growing at different rates. There is no simple explanation for the varying levels of economic performance in these transitional states during the first post-communist decade. Several factors seem important. First, these countries began the transition to market economies at varying points of economic development, and the less developed economies have generally been less successful in adapting. Second, the countries that undertook radical change have been more effective in shrinking the role of inefficient state enterprises and of expanding private sector activity. Third, an unanticipated problem with the gradualist approach has been "crony capitalism"— the tendency for the old communist party elite to use their connections in order to reemerge as the new economic elite. These insiders gained control of many of the most lucrative state assets when they were privatized, often at bargain prices, and then exploited those assets for personal gain (Aron 1998; Kroumova and Kruse 1997; Rupnik 1999).

TABLE 15.2
Prosperity Measures for Selected Transitional Developed Countries

State	GNP/Capita ($U.S.)	Human Development Index
Singapore	$32,490	89.6
South Korea	10,550	89.4
Slovenia	9,680	88.7
Argentina	8,570	88.8
Uruguay	6,020	88.5
Czech Republic	5,200	88.4
Brazil	4,720	80.9
Malaysia	4,680	83.4
Hungary	4,430	85.7
Mexico	3,680	85.5
Poland	3,590	85.1
Venezuela	3,450	86.0
Estonia	3,330	75.8
Thailand	2,800	83.8
Russia	2,740	76.9
Latvia	2,430	70.4
Bulgaria	1,140	78.9
Ukraine	1,040	66.5

Sources: GNP/capita: World Bank 1999: table 1; human development index: United Nations Development Programme 1998: table 1.1.

TABLE 15.3
Economic Decline in Selected Post-Communist Developed Countries During the 1990s

Country	Average annual growth/decline in gross domestic product per capita (1990–1997)	Percentage Change in Human Development Index 1992 to 1995
Belarus	−6.5 %	−4.9 %
Bulgaria	−3.5	−4.3
Czech Republic	−1.0	1.1
Estonia	−4.3	−10.5
Georgia	−26.2	−14.7
Hungary	−0.4	−0.7
Kazakhstan	−10.5	−8.4
Poland	3.9	2.3
Romania	0.0	2.6
Russia	−9.0	−7.7
Slovak Republic	0.4	0.1
Ukraine	−13.6	−16.3
Uzbekistan	−3.5	−0.4

Source: World Bank 1999: table 11; United Nations Development Programme 1993, 1998: table 1.

BOX 15.1

Russian Roulette: Economic Transformation with all Chambers Loaded

Russia's transition to a market economy has received the greatest international attention, not because its transition is typical of that in most other PCDCs, but because Russia is the most prominent country in the region, given its size and international significance. Although the leaders did not opt for shock therapy, the Russian economy was privatized steadily in the early 1990s. By 1996, 72 percent of large and midsized enterprises and nearly 90 percent of small shops and retail stores were under private ownership.

However, the political leadership was unwilling or unable to implement fundamental economic reform. About two-thirds of the private ownership of enterprises moved into the hands of insiders from the old regime (especially senior bureaucrats and other powerful Communist party members) whose agenda was to acquire the society's economic assets at bargain prices and then exploit those assets ruthlessly in get-rich-quick schemes (a system termed "crony capitalism"). The state did not privatize some of the most inefficient enterprises, which the state continued to operate at significant losses. Domestic production shrunk steadily. Corruption pervaded every aspect of economic life. Overall, the state was ineffective in guiding the economy, controlling public spending, or extracting taxes.

Table 15.4 provides some data reflecting the substantial decline in the Russian political economy during the initial years after the changes were introduced. Real GDP per capita plunged 50 percent between 1989 and 1999 and economic crises became recurrent. Despite massive loans from the World Bank, Russia's budget deficit became huge (e.g., between 1985 and 1991 it increased from 2 percent to 30 percent of GDP). There was hyperinflation (e.g., prices increased twenty-sixfold in 1992 alone), direct foreign investment dried up, and the value of the currency plummeted. Many people worked for months without being paid. Indeed, the economy had disintegrated to such an extent by the late 1990s that, by one estimate, about 80 percent of the country's business transactions were being conducted in barter trade (Goldman 1998).

TABLE 15.4
Changes in the Russian Economy, 1992–1995

Types of Change	Year			
	1992	1993	1994	1995
Percent change in real income	−47.%	+10.%	+16.%	−13.%
Percent change in gross domestic product	−14.%	−9.%	−13.%	−4.%
Inflation rate	2600.%	940.%	320.%	130.%
Unemployment rate	4.9%	5.1%	7.1%	8.2%

Sources: World Bank 1996: A2; Harmon 1996: A6.

BOX 15.1 *(Continued)*

VLADIMIR MOCHALOV

Cartoonists & Writers Syndicate

The impacts on the citizens were severe. The state could no longer afford to provide social services to a population increasingly ravaged by unemployment and inflation. While only 2 percent of the Russian people were in absolute poverty in 1988, fully 44 percent were in poverty in 1995 (World Bank 1999: table 1c). A huge increase in the inequality of wealth is reflected in the dramatic rise in the Gini inequality index (from 31.0 to 48.0) in less than a decade. By 1996, the richest one-tenth of the Russian population was earning fourteen times the wages of the poorest one-tenth. By the late 1990s, many Russians felt that they must have experienced the worst effects of the economic transition and that things would begin to improve. Then another major economic crisis occurred in 1998, marked by a 70 percent loss of value of the ruble, a return of hyperinflation, and the imposition of stringent controls by the international financial community. The percent of the Russian people living below the subsistence level increased from 22 percent to 35 percent (55 million people) in less than one year (July 1998 to June 1999).

Despite an overwhelming array of problems in Russian society at the end of the 1990s (e.g., severe political decay, corruption, crime, environmental degradation), it is not surprising that the three top problems identified by the citizens were directly related to economic performance: price increases, rising unemployment, and the "crisis in the economy" (VCIOM 1999). Peoples' daily lives and the political economy were in such disarray at the end of the 1990s that only one in four Russians (27 percent) disagreed on a survey with the conclusion that it would be better (for Russia) had "everything in this country remained as it was prior to 1985" [that is, when the country was still communist and authoritarian] (VCIOM 1999). In the view of many, a decade of economic transition in Russian had produced disastrous results. (This discussion based on Blasi, Kroumova, and Kruse 1997; Goldman 1998; Millar 1999; Roberts and Sherlock 1999; Weir 1999.)

In every PCDC, the dismantling of the command political economy has had significant effects on many individuals. The real income of most people dropped substantially, cuts in welfare services have been deep, and unemployment has soared. Inflation averaging higher than 100 percent per year occurred in all but two of the PCDCs, and inflation rates of greater than 1,000 percent in a single year have been common in countries of the former Soviet Union (e.g., 2,200 percent in Belarus in 1994) (World Bank 1996: table A3). Indeed, the *average* yearly inflation between 1990 and 1997 was more than 50 percent in such countries as Ukraine (800 percent), Belarus (564 percent), Russia (397 percent), Estonia (92 percent), and Bulgaria (78 percent) (World Bank 1998: Table 11).

The quality of life in these countries has also dropped, at least in the short run. As Table 15.5 indicates, the number of people in absolute poverty increased enormously in the region in less than a decade—from 14 million people just prior to the "fall of communism" in 1988 (4 percent of the population) to 147 million in 1996 (fully 40 percent of the population). As with the economic growth data, the effects of the transition to a market economy varied greatly across PCDCs. Absolute poverty was almost nonexistent and unchanged over the period in some countries, such as the Czech Republic and Hungary. However, it more than doubled in Poland to 14 percent, increased almost sevenfold in Romania to 39 percent, expanded dramatically from 1 percent to almost 30 percent in the Baltic states, and exploded in such countries as Russia (2 percent to 44 percent) and the Ukraine (2 percent to 63 percent).

Even scores on the Human Development Index, which is stabilized by longer-term levels of education and health, declined for many of the post-communist developed countries (Table 15.3). The top HDI scores among PCDCs (in the high 80s) are primarily in the Central European countries (e.g., Slovenia, the Czech Republic, Hungary, and Poland). Many of the countries of Eastern Europe (e.g., Bulgaria, Romania) and the Western parts of the former Soviet Union (e.g., Belarus, Estonia, Russia) have scores in the mid-70s, and other countries that emerged from the for-

TABLE 15.5
Level of Poverty in Selected Post-Communist Developed Countries, 1988 and 1995

Country	Percent of population in poverty		Total number of poor (millions)	
	1988	1995	1988	1995
Moldova	4%	66%	0.2	2.9
Ukraine	2	63	1.0	32.7
Central Asian States	15	53	6.5	25.0
Russia	2	44	2.2	66.1
Romania	6	39	1.3	8.9
The Baltic States	1	29	0.1	2.3
Poland	6	14	2.1	5.3
Hungary	1	2	0.1	0.2
Czech Republic	0	0	0.0	0.0
All PCDCs	4	40	13.6	147.1

Source: World Bank 1999: Table 1c

mer Soviet Union, especially in Central Asia (e.g., Turkmenistan, Uzbekistan), have rather low human development index scores (mainly in the low 60s).

Challenges.   Now that they are attempting to implement political economies which function under the same dynamics as those in the most developed countries, the post-communist developed countries face all the formidable challenges to sustaining prosperity that confront those countries, as detailed in Chapter 13. However, these challenges are greatly compounded in the PCDCs because the people and organizations in these states have more than two generations of experience under the nearly antithetical framework of the command political economy and the political culture of Marxism-Leninism. Certain key challenges are especially critical in the current period.

First, economic actors must learn *how to function with free market mechanisms* (e.g., capital markets, business contracts, and business law), which did not exist under the command economy. At present, many of these economic systems are also hampered by extremely ineffective systems of taxation (e.g., tax evasion is widespread) and considerable illegal economic behavior (e.g., extensive black markets) (Kramer 1998).

Second, many of the states must *establish strategies which loosen the control of the state and the former communist elites over the economy.* Some countries have been reluctant to shrink the state sector very rapidly because the closure of state enterprises eliminates many jobs and the subsidized goods (e.g., food, electricity) that they produced. However, in a free market system, inefficient enterprises are supposed to fail if they cannot achieve profitability and the subsidies on goods are supposed to be minimized. Moreover, some PCDCs have extensive regulatory and bureaucratic obstacles to the formation of private firms, even though they profess support for the establishment of such firms. And, as previously noted, the former communist elites have not been prevented from exploiting privatized state assets in some PCDCs.

Third, these states must *determine an appropriate level of welfare distribution* for various groups in society. The PCDCs have neither the ideological commitment nor the financial resources to sustain the high levels of welfare distributed under communism. At a time when many citizens face extraordinary economic hardship, the state has eliminated its extensive transfer payments to the financially disadvantaged and its deep subsidies for food, shelter, health care, education, transportation, and so on. The material living conditions of many people have declined significantly since the abandonment of the command economy. Yet the prosperity of some individuals and groups has risen dramatically, creating highly visible inequalities. For a people socialized to believe in the virtue of egalitarianism and accustomed to relative equality in their material lives, these severe hardships and growing inequalities are a highly disruptive element in the transition to a market political economy.

Fourth, the states must *prevent economic change from being undermined by the vigorous new group politics* that has emerged. These states suffer the disadvantage, relative to the NICs discussed later in this chapter, of experiencing political reform *prior* to economic reform. Thus the hardships associated with economic change have led to a highly volatile politics. Politicians blame each other for the kinds of economic problems previously described and many citizens use their new democratic voting rights to reject leaders and parties associated with the most recent negative impacts from economic transitions. This results in substantial political instability and makes economic reforms difficult for any political leadership to sustain (Linz and Stepan 1996; but also see Weyland 1999).

At present, significant economic development in most PCDCs requires a combination of farsighted economic policies, responsive social policies, hard work and tolerance from a citizenry receiving minimal rewards, cooperation and economic support from the more developed countries, and considerable good fortune. All this is more than most of these states can realistically expect. Prosperity remains an illusive goal.

GOAL: STABILITY
Under Communism

Under communist political regimes, a basic assumption was: prosperity + equality = stability. That is, social and political stability would result because the people would be pleased by the relatively equal distribution of abundant goods and services. Under communism, only partial success was achieved. On the one hand, these states did achieve substantially higher levels of equality than was the case in either the MDCs or their own pre-communist period (Kolosi and Wnuk-Lipinski 1983). Education and welfare goods, such as housing and health care, were either free or largely subsidized. Table 14.4 revealed that even in the mid-1990s, many of the PCDCs had more equal distributions of wealth than most countries in the world. At that time, eight PCDCs were among the fourteen countries with the world's most equal wealth distributions. Of all the PCDCs, only Russia (20) and Estonia (40) are ranked in the top half of the world's most unequal wealth distributions among 96 countries ranked on the Gini index (World Bank 1999: table 5). However, the economic transitions discussed below are, among other things, now increasing substantially the income inequalities in the PCDCs.

On the other hand, certain groups, such as professionals, urban citizens, and certain ethnic groups, were favored in the distribution of material goods and status. And the greatest benefits were enjoyed by Communist Party members, especially those near the top of the hierarchy. Novelist George Orwell's ironic observation in *Animal Farm* (1945/1964) that "everyone is equal, but some are more equal than others" aptly applied to citizens in these states.

In terms of the stability equation, however, the key problem was the insufficient *level* of prosperity, not the degree of inequality. The failure of the economy to generate material abundance was a major source of citizen dissatisfaction. These states promised far more material well-being than they were able to deliver, causing alienation in some of the population and undermining support for the political system.

Instruments of social control.   To ensure stability in the absence of prosperity, these states imposed a pervasive system of controls over many aspects of people's lives, based on four key instruments.

First, *rewards and sanctions* were a major part of order maintenance. Those who were obedient and supported the system could gain such benefits as Communist Party membership, higher priority for desired goods, job advancement, and status rewards such as plaques and public recognition. In contrast, an extensive system of surveillance was employed to ensure that those who failed to obey the norms and rules of the communist system lost basic welfare benefits, and those who committed serious offenses were imprisoned.

Second, the state used the agents of *political socialization* to reinforce the values of loyalty, obedience, and service to the society throughout a person's life. The educational system and mass social organizations (e.g., youth clubs) that required participation were especially important. And the state owned all television, radio, and news media, which presented high-quality, selective content intended to educate, entertain, and socialize.

Third, *Communist Party* membership, an honor extended to only about 10 percent of the population, included the responsibilities to encourage friends and workmates to support party policy and to report anyone's inappropriate behavior.

Finally, the *governmental apparatus,* and especially the huge bureaucracy, the police, and the military, shaped many aspects of social and organizational life as it administered policy in day-to-day activities.

Performance.   Overall, these mechanisms of control resulted in a high level of stability under communist regimes. There were occasional outbreaks of collective violence, as in the uprisings in Hungary in 1956, Czechoslovakia in 1968, and Poland in 1956, 1968, and the 1980s. But such outbreaks were firmly suppressed, and the normal pattern of collective life was stable, with the Party and the state in firm control.

In some periods, these states were appropriately characterized by imagery of a totalitarian, "police state" atmosphere. But overall, the people behaved in accordance with the rules of the regime, because the mechanisms of control were effective and because the people did accept a life that, although dull, was safe and secure. Violent antisocial behavior—that is, crimes against people (e.g., murder, rape, and assault) and crimes against property (e.g., burglary and theft) —was at much lower rates than in the more developed countries. This difference is shown in Table 15.6, which provides comparative crime data from 1987 for the United States and the Soviet Union, shortly before its breakup. While crime was low in such oppressively stable systems, individual frustration did manifest itself at the personal level. Substance abuse (e.g., alcoholism) and family problems (e.g., divorce, child abuse) were relatively high (Goldman 1996).

TABLE 15.6
Crime Rates in the Soviet Union and the United States, 1987

Type of Crime	Cases per 100,000 Population	
	Soviet Union	**United States**
Aggravated assault	13	350
Rape[a]	6	37
Property crimes	191	4,906
Violent robbery	4	NA
Murder[a]	6	8
Overall crime rate	657	5,550

[a]Soviet figures include "attempted rape" and "attempted murder" while U.S. figures include only rape and murder.
Source: *Los Angeles Times,* February 15, 1989, based on reports of the Soviet Foreign Ministry and the U.S. Federal Bureau of Investigation.

Opposition to the Communist Party became more open and personal freedoms expanded significantly during the 1980s, with an enormous boost from Mikhail Gorbachev's policy of *glasnost*—a tolerance of public discussion and criticism of the political, economic, and social system. In the late 1980s, it became evident that Gorbachev would not use the military or economic power of the Soviet Union to support an unpopular political regime in any country in the region.

Box 15.2 details key events in the extraordinary year 1989. With the world watching, the streets of East Germany, Czechoslovakia, and other states filled with citizens demanding political and human rights. After decades of repression, the Communist Party leaderships capitulated in country after country, lacking either the will or the capacity to retain power. Except in Romania (where events corresponded to a revolution from above), the dramatic changes occurred with so little violence that they are best described as "democratic revolutions" (see Chapter 11). By December 1991, after a brief, failed coup attempt by Communist Party conservatives, even the Soviet Union had been transformed into fifteen independent countries.

BOX 15.2

That's the Way the Curtain Crumbles: 1989 in Central and Eastern Europe

In 1989 there was a series of tumultuous changes in Central and Eastern Europe. Events occurred at a dizzying pace, and each incident had impacts in other states. Some of the most notable events:

January and February

Hungary's Parliament legalizes freedom of assembly, and the Communist Party allows the creation of legal, independent political parties. In Poland tens of thousands of citizens openly insist on their political and economic rights, staging demonstrations and wildcat strikes.

March, April, and May

The pivotal event, again in Hungary, is the dismantling of parts of the barbed-wire fence that separated Hungary from Austria, the first physical break in "the Iron Curtain"—a system of travel restrictions, guards, walls, fences, and other obstacles that physically prevented East Europeans from free entry into Western Europe. The Soviets begin to cut their troop levels in Eastern Europe, and most people conclude that Gorbachev's Soviet Union will not interfere with reforms. Public protests intensify and broaden, particularly in Poland and Czechoslovakia.

June and July

In Poland the independent trade-union movement (Solidarity) deals the Communist Party a devastating defeat in legislative elections, creating a formal political

Post-Communism

In most countries, the new leaders who emerged after 1989 were committed to sweeping transformations of the political system, as well as the political economy. These countries crafted and ratified new post-communist constitutions—ones that established democratic, multiparty political systems with widespread participation in place of one-party authoritarianism. But the mechanisms of social control that these states had relied on to maintain stability—the political culture, the Communist Party, a massive state bureaucracy, selectively totalitarian methods, and Soviet military power—were now discredited or gone. In the absence of these control mechanisms, the fundamental political, economic, and social transitions occurring in these states have resulted in powerful challenges to the new political institutions and their capacity to maintain stability.

Nationality conflicts. A few nationality groups, such as the Poles and the East Germans (who were reunited with their West German brothers and sisters), now

---

BOX 15.2 *(Continued)*

opposition in the legislature. Moderates take control of the Hungarian Communist Party and attempt to negotiate with opposition groups.

August, September, and October

Central and East Europeans, including more than 30,000 East Germans, flow into Western Europe via the new openings in Hungary's borders. There are massive demonstrations in East Germany, and the party chief (Erich Honecker) resigns after eighteen years. In Poland a new government is formed in which non-communists are the majority. Hungary establishes a "free republic" and plans multiparty elections in early 1990.

November and December

East Germany removes restrictions on foreign travel in an attempt to discourage the massive illegal exodus. Then, on November 9, it opens the Berlin Wall, the most dramatic and notorious symbol of the Iron Curtain. A million East and West Germans begin an exuberant reunion in the streets of West Berlin. A new East German government is formed in which the interim president and one-fourth of the cabinet are non-communists. Free elections are promised for May (and then changed to March) 1990. After massive demonstrations, several reformations of the Czech government are attempted, leading to the replacement of the Communist Party leader, the prime minister, and the president, and the installation of the first non-communist dominated government in forty-one years. Public demonstrations in Bulgaria force the government to promise free elections by June 1990. Violence explodes in Romania as the state's security police kill hundreds of demonstrators. After a brief civil war, a reformist group takes political control in Romania and executes Nicolae Ceauşescu, the hard-line party leader since 1965.

live in ethnically homogeneous states. However, *ethnonationalism* (recall Chapter 5) threatens the existence of many PCDCs which have two or more significant nationality groups within their borders. In most of the countries, marginalized ethnic groups are increasingly active in demanding greater autonomy. The major nationality group typically responds by aggressively asserting its domination. Thus internal ethnic conflict has exploded into violence in such PCDCs as Georgia, Russia (in Chechnya and Dagestan), and Ukraine. In 1993, Czechoslovakia broke into two states based on its two main ethnic groups (Czechs and Slovaks). And Yugoslavia, a complex multiethnic state under communism, has been transformed into a brutal battleground as different nation-based groups fight to define the boundaries of a set of new states (see Box 15.3).

Democracy and instability.   Throughout the area, fragile democratic political systems replaced systems that were undemocratic but highly institutionalized. Many of these new constitutional regimes are hybrids (Chapter 7) that distribute power between an elected president and a legislature-plus-prime minister selected through proportional representation (PR) voting. In marked contrast to their communist predecessors, judiciaries are attempting to fulfill an independent role.

Many political parties have formed and are trying to establish broad-based support. In some cases, dozens of political parties still contest each election. In recent

Chechen rebels threaten Russian prisoners of war captured during a bloody battle during the Chechens' ethnonationalist struggle for regional autonomy.

elections, for example, Russians selected a legislature from among more than forty parties and the Bulgarians and Poles have coped with more than two hundred parties. In most countries, there are three clusters of political parties:

> One cluster includes the *liberal* parties. These parties are particularly supportive of a rapid transition to a market economy, with minimal state intervention and maximum incentives for private entrepreneurs and free markets.

> A second cluster is composed of *nationalist* parties whose members are particularly concerned with promoting the interests of those individuals included in their definition of the nation and are antagonistic toward those outside this group.

> The third cluster is composed of former supporters of the Communist Party who have redefined themselves as *"reformers"* (and do not use the term communist to describe their parties or policies). These post-communist communists accept the gradual transition to a market economy but argue that the free market must be given a more "social face." They remain committed to egalitarian principles and a strong state role in the provision of social welfare goods (e.g., health services, housing), in the protection of jobs, and in continued state management of some key industries and services.

At the beginning of the twenty-first century, some of the PCDCs seem to have successfully made the transition to liberal democracy. In countries such as the Czech Republic, Hungary, Poland, and the Baltic states, political discourse is wide-ranging and unconstrained, and virtually all political parties and groups accept the outcome of actively contested elections among genuine alternatives. Other countries, particularly those in Eastern Europe as well as Russia, are now electoral democracies; but democratic practices and individual rights are not institutionalized and are substantially limited because of deep cleavages within the population over such critical issues as economic reform, welfare distribution, or ethnic conflict. A few of the PCDCs (e.g., Georgia, Serbia, Ukraine) have resisted the transition to democratic politics in the sense that the citizens have elected reform Communists who still rule in an authoritarian manner.

Hybrid political systems with many parties, such as those that have been formed in the PCDCs, are inherently unstable. Faced with severe economic problems and intense public debates on economic and social policies, these countries are experiencing recurrent patterns of stalemate, crisis, and government turnover. In Russia, for example, President Yeltsin dismissed four successive prime ministers in the 18 months before his resignation in 2000. It is common for the public mood to swing against whichever parties are in power, whether their ideology and policies are liberal, nationalist, or reform communist. Elections tend to produce a majority of votes *against* the parties in power, but do not usually provide a strong mandate to a cohesive alternative party or coalition.

Socioeconomic disruption.   The free-wheeling economic system and disappearance of traditional mechanisms of social control have had some negative byproducts for stability. Despite the equality of wealth under communist regimes previously described, substantial *inequalities in prosperity* and incomes have rapidly emerged. Russia, for example, shifted in less than a decade from having a more equal income distribution than 75 percent of the world's countries to being more equal

Out of Many, One; and Then Many Again: Yugoslavia

Like many countries, Yugoslavia was forged from many nationalities by the heat of history, military might, and strong leadership. Historically, the Balkan area included many ministates that had been dominated by the Austrian Hapsburg Empire and the Ottoman Turkish Empire. The first Yugoslav state, formed after World War I had diminished the former imperial powers, was a royal dictatorship called the "Kingdom of the Serbs, Croats, and Slovenes," renamed Yugoslavia ("Land of the South Slavs") in 1929. The lack of shared national identity among the various ethnic groups became most obvious during World War II. In a brutal civil war, the Slavs killed more of one another in interethnic fighting than were killed in Yugoslavia by the invading Nazis. The area was divided among the Germans, Italians, Albanians, Hungarians, and Bulgarians; Croatia declared independence and became an ally of the Germans.

After the war, Josip Broz Tito, a shrewd and charismatic leader of the resistance to the Nazis, took political power. Tito united the various groups (six republics and two autonomous regions) into a federation that was fragile at first but eventually gained stability and relative prosperity. He installed a collective executive that shared power among the various ethnic groups. Although Tito was a communist, he established an economy that allowed substantially more enterprise and initiative than the command economies in other East European states. Tito also established an independent foreign policy, making political and economic alliances with West European states as well as with members of the Soviet bloc.

The country remained stable after Tito's death in 1980, but then the turbulence in Eastern Europe in the late 1980s reawakened the nationalist animosities within Yugoslavia. The key protagonists were 9 million Serbs (generally Greek Orthodox, pro-communist), 4.5 million Croats (Catholic, non-communist), 2 million Slovenes (Catholic, non-communist, and the most prosperous group in the country), 4.5 million Bosnians (Muslim), 2 million Macedonians (Greek Orthodox, with strong links to northern Greece), and 600,000 Montenegrans (Greek Orthodox, pro-Serbian, and with a history under their own king).

In 1991 the Croats and the Slovenes each rejected the authority of the central government, located in Belgrade in the Serbian region, and each declared independence. Each group fought against the Serb-dominated Yugoslav armed forces, briefly in Slovenia and for nearly a year in Croatia, until the United Nations arranged a cease-fire in April 1992. The major foreign powers and the United Nations recognized the sovereignty of Croatia and Slovenia.

But Bosnia did not gain immediate recognition when it declared independence in March 1992. Serbs, about one-third of the population within Bosnia, launched a bloody civil war as Bosnians and Serbs each attempted to secure as much of the region of Bosnia-Hercegovina as possible for their emerging states. In devastating town-to-town fighting, Serbian and Bosnian paramilitary groups murdered and bru-

BOX 15.3

The Balkans, *circa* 2000

talized each other and many civilians. Eventually, a settlement was imposed by the United Nations and more developed countries, based on a complex three-person presidency representing all key ethnic groups.

The next explosion of violence was in Kosovo, an impoverished province in southern Serbia, in which 90 percent of the population are ethnic Albanians. The ethnic Albanians' desire for autonomy resulted in a revolutionary guerilla war led by the Kosovo Liberation Army (KLA). Fighting with the Serb rulers became extensive in 1998, and once again the United Nations attempted to intervene. While this unsuccessful effort was underway, Serbian President Slobodan Milosevic encouraged the local Serbs to engage in another round of ethnic cleansing. Within

(continued)

BOX 15.3 *(Continued)*

months, the great majority of ethnic Albanians were either dead or in exile. NATO intervened with massive airstrikes in Kosovo and in Serbia. By late 1999, NATO reestablished the rights of the ethnic Albanians to inhabit the area, and they returned, turning their hostility on the Serbs in residence.

At the turn of the century, virtually the entire Balkan region as well as all the minicountries that emerged from the former Yugoslavia are unstable and prone to violence. Albania had its government overturned by a coup in 1997, lost control of its northern areas to rebel groups, and its reform Communist government claimed parts of Macedonia as well as Kosovo. Bulgaria faced antagonism from the Serbs for cooperating with NATO in the Kosovo conflict. The multiple presidents of Bosnia-Hercegovina could not cooperate, as each sided with the ethnic group and country with which his group is associated. Croatia pursued an intensely nationalistic domestic and foreign policy under an authoritarian ruler. Macedonia is surrounded by hostile states with whom it has ethnic overlaps. Yugoslavia/Serbia is the region's major catalyst of violence and protagonist under Milosevic, who faces increasing internal opposition as well as international condemnation. Only Romania and Greece (entrenched in multi-issued conflict with Turkey) had avoided the Balkan morass.

Gloomy analysts predict that the turmoil will continue until, if ever, the region completes an ethnic ordering in which borders coincide with nationality identity. This ethnic ordering has already produced hundreds of thousands of refugees and more than one-quarter million people dead through brutal killings in the last decade. Ominously, this exceedingly complex turf war over the boundaries of new states-information is still far from resolved (Brown 1999; Rupnik 1999).

than only 20 percent of the countries. In the entire region, the Gini inequality index rose sharply in the 1990s, at an average of 1.5 points per year, to an index score of 33 (World Bank 1999: 6). For a population socialized to value egalitarianism, these rapid increases in visible inequality have been extremely disturbing to many people.

Moreover, *social disorder* is dramatically evident in the high incidence of crime. Countries that were accustomed to minimal rates of violent crime are now reeling from an explosion of crimes against both people and property. In the first five years of post-communism, for example, reported serious crimes increased 270 percent in Romania, 222 percent in Bulgaria, and 105 percent in Poland (Murphy 1995). In Russia, more than 4,000 mafia crime groups are engaged in widespread extortion, auto theft, drug peddling, burglary, and other criminal activities. In contrast to the data in Table 15.6, the Russian murder rate is now more than double that in the United States. In many regions, the police are either ineffective or corrupt, and citizens live in fear of organized crime, random criminal violence, and even the police (McFaul 1998). The disorder has also spilled over into political violence in some countries, including bombings and assassinations, as occurred with the murders of the prime minister and eight other ministers in the Armenian parliament building in late 1999.

Overall. Some post-communist developed countries, such as Estonia, Hungary, and Poland, seem to have attained sufficient economic strength, political institutionalization, and nationality identity to maintain stability. And in nearly all of these states, political leaders have accepted the transfers of governmental authority occurring through relatively open elections. But the substantial changes in the post-communist period eliminated the high levels of stability evident under communism. In many of the PCDCs, citizens' demands and expectations now far exceed the capacity of the political systems to deliver the goods. Amoral individualism is widely evident, there are insufficient state resources to distribute an adequate level of welfare goods, and the old forms of social control have disappeared. In the absence of deep political institutionalization, the conditions seem ripe for the kinds of political disorder and violence described in such analyses as Huntington's conception of political decay (Chapter 10) and the J-curve theory of Davies (Chapter 11).

GOAL: SECURITY

The fundamental goal of all states is survival. By that standard, the 1990s was a disaster for the Soviet Union and its allies in Central and Eastern Europe. In December 1991 the Soviet Union disappeared, replaced by fifteen states that are based on historical ethnic and regional boundaries. East Germany, the economically strongest state, also disappeared, having merged with West Germany in 1990. Yugoslavia fractured into multiple states, and Czechoslovakia split in two. All this seems rather remarkable for a "Soviet Empire" that was judged an adversary equal to the powerful United States during the four-decade cold war. Assessing the security situation in the Soviet Union and Eastern Europe during the cold war aids our understanding of the dramatic changes that have occurred and the new security issues that these states now face.

Under Communism

History and geopolitics.   Between its foundation in 1917 and its demise in 1991, the Soviet Union placed exceptionally high importance on security goals. In Halford John Mackinder's (1962) famous nineteenth-century geopolitical analysis, Eastern Europe and Russia were the essential "heartland"—control of that region would ensure world dominance. These areas have been battlefields for the last 200 years, including devastating invasions by the French under Napoleon and by the Germans under Hitler.

After World War II, the Soviet Union perceived itself to be surrounded by increasingly hostile, anticommunist threats to its survival. To the east, Japan, a historical military adversary, evolved into a major capitalist world power. To the southeast, China, with its huge population and alternative vision of communism, displayed growing combativeness. To the southwest, the militancy of Islamic fundamentalism presented an explicit and growing danger, given its antipathy to communism and the prevalence of Islamic peoples in the southwestern regions in the Soviet Union. To the west were the major capitalist powers, with their own deep animosity to the communist systems and with NATO's devastating military (including nuclear) capabilities stretched along almost half of the Soviet bloc's border.

Military power.   To protect itself against all these real or perceived threats to its survival, the Soviet Union aimed for unchallengeable military power. In order to create a buffer zone between itself and its rivals, it gained control over territory on all sides, annexing some areas into the Soviet Union and creating a bloc of subservient states in Central and Eastern Europe. This Soviet bloc then built what was arguably the world's most powerful military for conventional warfare, and the Soviet Union was not far behind the United States and its European allies in air power and nuclear capabilities.

In the bipolar international system, both the Soviet bloc and the United States continually expanded military capacity and weapons technologies. This rivalry spawned a huge military buildup and arms race and resulted in the mutually assured destruction (MAD) discussed in Chapter 12. Soviet leaders from Stalin to Gorbachev opted for guns over butter, spending 9 percent to 15 percent of the GNP on defense in the late 1980s (compared with about 6 percent in the United States). Such high military expenditure substantially reduced the societal resources available for economic growth and distribution of welfare and is arguably the main reason for the demise of the Soviet system (Medvedev 2000).

Post-Communism

Obviously, the disintegration of the Soviet Union and the transformation of Central and Eastern Europe have fundamentally altered the security situation for the states in the region. The states' collective security system (the Warsaw Pact) collapsed. Even worse, some former allies (e.g., Czech Republic, Hungary, Poland) have now joined the old enemy, NATO, despite strong opposition from Russia. In addition, some PCDCs fear Russia will attempt to reassert itself as the dominant regional power, using economic or military power to limit the autonomy of other states, reminiscent of its imperial style in the nineteenth century (Kurth 1999). On the international stage, Russia maintains its formidable military machine, including a large standing army and the second largest nuclear arsenal in the world, with more than 6,000 strategic nuclear warheads (Powaski 1999). In short, these changes have increased both the complexity of international relations in the region and also the insecurity of Russia and other former Soviet buffer states that are outside of NATO.

The many disjunctions between nationality groups and state borders described in the previous section are a second source of interstate conflict between the PCDCs. Most of these countries have actively discriminated against the members of nationality groups from neighboring states who are "trapped" within the boundaries of their state. When the state faces severe economic problems and political instability, there is increased likelihood that such nationality issues will produce tensions, scapegoating, and violence both within and between states. The conflicts in the former Yugoslavia (described in Box 15.3) are a compelling example of the disorder and violence spawned by ethnonationalism within a post-communist developed country.

In economic terms, the security of some of these states is threatened by the most developed countries. In the transition to a market economy, many of these states have been dependent on the expertise, capital, and technology of the most developed countries, the multinational corporations, and the international financial community. The possibility remains that some states might slide into a form of neocolonial dependency, as economically powerful external actors take advantage of their educated labor forces, extensive natural resources, and markets.

In retrospect, the international system had become relatively secure under the strong bipolar security regime dominated by the United States and the Soviet Union. The breakup of the Soviet Union transferred control of its vast military capabilities from a single conservative and stable state to a dozen unpredictable and unstable states. Such shifts substantially increased the insecurity of all states, especially those within and adjacent to the region. According to balance-of-power analyses, the current evolution toward a more diffuse, multipolar international system will increase insecurity in the relations among states (see Chapter 12). In the post–cold war world, one of the major challenges for all countries, including the post-communist developed countries, is how to adapt to the end of the bipolar system.

The Newly Industrializing Countries

During the past several decades, one group of countries has been particularly successful in achieving the transformation from developing to developed countries. These countries have been labeled the NICs —the newly industrializing countries (some, such as the World Bank, also refer to them as the NIEs—the newly industrializing economies). A NIC is distinguished by its economic transition into a major exporter of manufactured goods and by its sustained high economic growth rate, relative to population growth.

To this point, only several Asian NICs—Singapore, South Korea, and Taiwan—have been fully successful on both dimensions. Certain Latin American countries, especially Argentina and Uruguay, have also advanced considerably toward achieving the level of development and sustained growth characteristic of the leading NICs. There is a larger set of countries, mainly in Asia (e.g., Malaysia) and Latin America (e.g., Brazil, Mexico, Venezuela), that seem to be reaching the levels of development that place them in this group. The NICs are clearly above most other developing countries in the analytic framework presented in Figure 13.1. This section discusses the key political and economic transitions that are occurring in the NICs. There is particular attention to the leading Asian NICs, because many other developing countries have attempted to model aspects of their own developmental strategies on these important examples.

POLITICAL CULTURE

Generally, the Asian NICs share a social and political culture that is influenced by such ethical-religious philosophies as Buddhism, Taoism, and most notably Confucianism. Indeed, many analysts have concluded that Asian cultural norms, and Confucianism in particular, are the critical factor that accounts for the notable success of the NIC approach in Asian countries, relative to developing countries in Latin America or other regions (Fallows 1993; Huntington 1991; Pye 1985; but also see The Economist 1998). These norms emphasize hard work, acceptance of authority, and subordination of personal needs to collective goals. Box 15.4 explores the critical linkages between Asian political culture and economic development.

The political culture in Latin American NICs has some similarities to the cultural norms of the Asian NICs. The Catholic Church is an important institution which traditionally encouraged obedience to a hierarchical authority system and subordination of current rewards to eventual benefits. Similarly, Latin American social structure has generally been based on hierarchical class strata and a dominant ruling class whose members are in charge of the economic and political systems. However, in comparison to Asia, Latin American cultural norms generally place less importance on mass education, hard work, and the pursuit of collective goals at the expense of those goals which serve oneself and one's kin.

BOX 15.4

Confucius says...Culture and Development

Important scholars like Max Weber (1958a) and R. H. Tawney (1938) have linked crucial elements of a society's cultural norms with success in implementing capitalist economics. Recently, analysts have asked: how can we explain the particular recent success of the leading Asian NICs in achieving economic development, given a global system that seems to advantage the more developed countries (recall the dependency approach discussion in Chapter 10)? Many answers have emphasized the powerful positive influences of Confucian cultural norms. Based on the teachings of a fifth-century B.C.E. Chinese intellectual, *Confucianism* stresses that individual action must be based on what is best for the group and for society as a whole. Harmony and cooperation are always to be sought, and disunity and conflict must be avoided. Society is shaped by a series of superior–subordinate relationships in which obedience must be offered: by subject to ruler, by child to parent, by younger to elder, and by female to male.

In political terms, Confucianism places the highest value on *order, stability, and discipline* within a framework of hierarchical authority. The ruler, the parent, and the boss must be obeyed unquestioningly. The individual's responsibilities and public duty have priority over his individual rights and interests. Such principles powerfully support a political system in which authoritarianism is natural and acceptable. The political elite is justified in taking any action that maintains harmony and order or that serves the broader interests of the society, regardless of the costs to individuals or interest groups (e.g., political parties, unions, students). Other key cultural norms include the beliefs that making and saving money are virtuous and that individuals (traditionally, males) should achieve the highest possible level of education and learning.

Analysts suggest that this combination of norms has encouraged behaviors that facilitated capitalist development in the late twentieth century. These facilitative behaviors include the discipline and loyalty of employees to the firm, the subordination of personal needs and prosperity to enhance the goals of the nation, the high propensity to save (and invest), and the acceptance of close linkages between the state and the economic elite (Fallows 1993). Obviously, many other factors are also critical for economic development, including the availability of necessary resources, the activities of economic competitors, the quality of economic and political leadership, the security of the country, and so on (Economist 1998). But most agree that Confucian cultural norms have been a very positive force in the economic transition of the Asian NICs.

Both regions have considerable experience with authoritarian political leadership. The Latin American region is particularly associated with a popular acceptance of leaders, often from military background ("caudillos"), who exert extremely strict control over the political system and even aspects of the social system. Latin American political cultures have typically assumed that there would be political competition, but that it would be hegemonic, involving the alternation between elites rather than open competition among truly opposing forces (Aguero and Stark 1998). In contrast, Asian political cultures have placed considerably less premium upon political competition and group struggle, given the value attached to consensus and hierarchy. Thus political authoritarianism has been especially consistent with traditional Asian norms.

GOAL: PROSPERITY

The most successful NICs, particularly those in Asia, have pursued prosperity by employing variations on the *developmental state strategy* which was outlined in Chapter 10. The three key elements of this strategy are: (1) reliance on a market political economy, guided by an active state whose bureaucracy operates under minimal political pressures and implements policies that support private firms, export-oriented trade, and direct foreign investment; (2) cooperation between firms and government under a powerful planning agency to target niches in which export goods can be sold profitably; and (3) government support of the agrarian sector, including the redistribution of land and encouragement of commercial agriculture.

This strategy, based on the approach used by the Japanese after World War II, emphasizes the primacy of economic development (Fallows 1993; Johnson 1996; Simone and Feraru 1995). Government actions likely to result in political or social development are generally deferred in the Asian NICs, except where such changes directly promote the transition of the economy. State expenditure supports development of the infrastructure for the economy (e.g., transportation systems, communications networks) and education, although there has been minimal distribution of resources for poverty-linked socialwelfare services. Government policy encourages savings and investment rather than consumerism, and it limits wage rates for workers. Only recently, as economic development reached high levels has there been a shift toward policies which allow citizens to acquire more consumer goods and which increase the level of welfare distribution to less advantaged citizens.

While the broad strategy of the Asian NICs is similar, there are significant differences. For example, the South Korean government supported the development of a few very large firms, called *chaebols* (e.g., Hyundai, Goldstar, and Samsung), which produce a vast diversity of manufactured goods. In contrast, the Taiwanese government encouraged many small firms with specialized product bases. Singapore emphasized service industries (building on its existing strength in shipping and developing such knowledge industries as financial services) and has allowed more extensive involvement of external multinational corporations.

The governments in most Latin American NICs have been less interventionist than those in the Asian NICs. For example, governments in the Latin American NICs have generally been less active in agrarian reform and rural land redistribution, less controlling regarding the role of multinational corporations in their economies, and less restrictive of trade union activities. Another geopolitical difference is that the Latin American NICs have a more substantial endowment of natural resources and agricultural goods. Thus the governments have generally attempted to balance their development policies to support not only manufacturing and service industries, but also the extraction and processing of natural resources and foods. The vast economic system of the United States has exerted even greater influence on development in Latin America than has the Japanese economy in Asia. Additionally, a more lengthy period of active electoral politics has had numerous consequences in the Latin American NICs, including more extensive distribution of social welfare goods by the state to secure votes.

Performance.   The economic performance of the NICs has been strong, as measured by rates of growth in GNP/GDP per capita. Table 14.3 reflected these variations in rates of economic growth for selected NICs. Figures 15.1a displays some of these growth rates in more detail. In general, all the NICs have enjoyed increases in both GDP per capita and Human Development Index scores (Figure 15.1b). It is also clear that, although the Latin American NICs generally began at higher levels than the Asian NICs in 1960, the increases on both measures have been more consistent and at a higher rate of improvement for the Asian NICs.

The leading Asian NICs have sustained economic growth rates averaging about 7 percent annually during the last two decades, placing them among the fastest-growing economies in the world. They have positive trade surpluses and high levels of capital accumulation. Their firms now compete effectively in the international marketplace across a wide range of goods. Only a few Latin American NICs, such as Chile, have approached these admirable rates of persistent growth. Most Latin American NICs have had more sporadic periods of economic growth, with overall growth at rates higher than that in most developing countries, but not exceptional .

Most individuals in the NICs have experienced an improvement in the quality of their lives during the past two decades. As one indicator, the Human Development Index scores of leading NICs (e.g., Singapore, Chile, South Korea, Argentina, and Uruguay) are in the 89–88 range, placing them among the top one-fifth of the world's countries (recall Table 15.2). Many of their citizens now enjoy a level of material possessions and services (e.g., health care, education) that is approaching that in some of the more developed countries. The emerging NICs, such as Venezuela, Mexico, Thailand, Malaysia, and Brazil, are in the next subset among the world's countries, with HDI scores in the 86–80 range.

For the NICs, as for many countries, average scores on GNP/capita and even on the HDI, can be somewhat misleading. Like many of the developing countries discussed in Chapter 14, the distribution of prosperity in some of the NICs, particularly those in Latin America, is highly unequal, as revealed in Table 14.4. Brazil, for example, has the second highest level of wealth inequality in the world (after Sierra Leone), among the 96 countries that were ranked. Chile is also in the "top 10," and Mexico is seventeenth in inequality. In most of the Latin American NICs, a proportion of the population enjoys a extremely high standard of living, but large numbers of people remain very poor and experience a harshness of life comparable to that of many people in the developing countries. Compared to the Asian NICs, such inequality is much greater in the Latin American NICs, which have a long history of a social system with a wealthy elite class and a large poverty class (Birdsall 1998). Table 14.4 indicates that most Asian NICs have considerably more equal distributions of wealth than most other developing countries.

In the mid-1990s, it appeared that not only the original Asian "tigers" (e.g., Singapore, South Korea, and Taiwan) but also a second wave of "little dragons" (e.g., Malaysia and Thailand) were on a fast track of rapid and sustained economic development. Then the economies of most Asian NICs experienced a severe decline. It began with a currency crisis in Thailand in July 1997, which was soon followed by a broad and sharp disintegration of most East Asian economies. Currencies lost value, stock markets collapsed, banks and other major firms went into bankruptcy, direct foreign investment dried up. Within only fifteen months, $1 trillion in loans had defaulted, $2 trillion in stock market value had disappeared, and $3 trillion of economic growth in

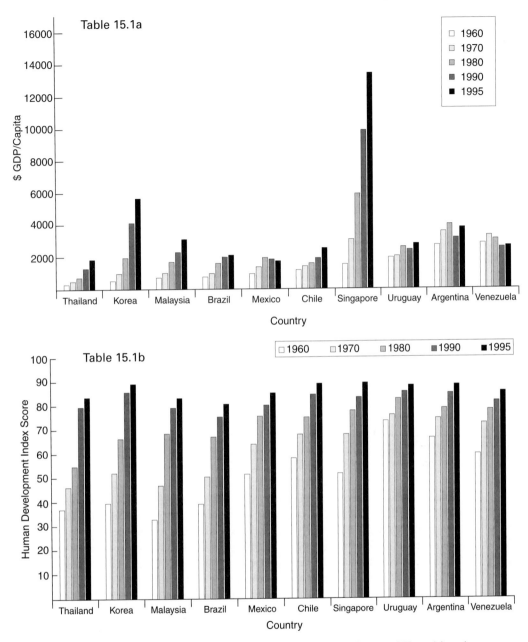

Figure 15.1   Changes in Prosperity measures for Selected Transitional
Developed Countries, 1960-1995
Source: United Nations Development Programme 1998: Table 5

gross domestic product was lost (Winters 1998). To limit the damage to the global economic order, more than $150 billion in rescue loan packages was quickly sent to the
Asian NICs via the International Monetary Fund. The economic disruptions negatively affected almost every economy in East Asia and then the economies of other
"emerging markets," particularly in such transitional countries as Brazil and Russia.

A worldwide debate sought to explain what had happened. Among the main factors cited to account for the economic collapse in the Asian NICs are: (1) *crony capitalism*—powerful government and private sector actors (e.g., banks) make deals, initiate projects, and provide funding to each other in ways that are not based on sound financial practices; powerful elites mutually exploit the economic resources of the country (recall the previous description of a related process in many PCDCs); (2) the *volatile international financial system*, which allowed investment in companies, projects, and currencies to shift within and between countries at rapid speed and in huge amounts; or (3) the emotional, even *irrational actions of many investors* who overinvested in the NIC economies and then withdrew resources massively in a growing panic. Some of the Asian NICs were less vulnerable to the collapse, and most recovered their economic momentum by the end of the decade. However, the "magic" of the NICs as invulnerable engines of economic growth had been shattered (Mahon 1999; Winters 1998). And ramifications from the financial crisis in Asia led to a round of serious economic setbacks in the Latin American NICs as well.

Generally, the Latin American NICs have been subject to periodic economic declines (e.g., the Mexican "peso crisis" of 1994) and periods of hyperinflation, like their less developed regional neighbors (recall Chapter 14). And, like many other economies in Latin America, the NICs have been reliant on loans and support from global financial institutions. Thus the International Monetary Fund has required the NICs to submit to the same kinds of structural adjustment programs, which have resulted in periods of substantial decline in the living standards of large numbers of the population, especially in Brazil and Mexico (Mahon 1999). The Asian NICs generally avoided such economic turbulence until the crisis of 1987, which generated their most severe levels of hardship and unemployment in recent decades.

GOAL: STABILITY

The governments in the Asian NICs have been particularly concerned about maintaining a highly stable and orderly social system. As Box 15.4 indicated, conflictual politics, social disorder, and labor agitation are viewed as serious impediments to economic development, as well as contrary to Confucian cultural norms about appropriate social relations. A further reason that the Asian NICs value stability is the assumption that the economic system thrives in an environment of order and predictability. Thus, until recently, governments in the Asian NICs have been centralized, authoritarian, and repressive (Simone and Feraru 1995).

For example, Taiwan was under martial law from 1949 to 1987. In South Korea, the period from 1948 to 1987 was dominated by three autocratic presidents, Syngman Rhee, General Park Chung Hee, and Chun Doo Hwan. Singapore was ruled with harsh firmness for thirty-one years (1959–1990) by a single prime minister, Lee Kuan Yew, and his People's Action Party has been so dominant that Singapore is essentially a one-party system. As described in Box 15.5, Singapore has become a worldwide exemplar of a strategy in which government policy is used extensively to "encourage" a stable and orderly society. The less developed Asian NICs have been less successful in maintaining order and are characterized by more complex, multiparty politics and less political stability. Thailand, for example, has suffered nearly twenty successful or attempted coups since 1932.

BOX 15.5

Welcome to the Brave New World: Singapore

Singapore has used government policy expansively to influence the social life of its citizens. A small island of 3 million people located off Malaysia, Singapore gained independence from Britain in 1963 and became a republic in 1965. Prime Minister Lee Kuan Yew exercised singular power for thirty-one years (until 1990) and guided the country to remarkable economic success. Its annual economic growth rate has averaged 8.3 percent since 1965. Its GNP per capita has risen to rank fourth in the world, placing it among the leading more developed countries in terms of its overall prosperity.

Singapore is also notable for the remarkable set of social-control policies instituted by Prime Minister Lee and the parliament he dominated for three decades. For example, to deal with traffic congestion, the government maintains a strict quota on the number of cars imported. An individual who purchases a new car must pay import duties and registration taxes that triple the car's market price. To reduce the massive yearly auto-registration fee, the driver can save $10,000 per year by purchasing a special red license that allows only nighttime and weekend driving. The high toll-road charges and other auto fees are used to subsidize an effective system of mass transit.

To promote financial responsibility and personal savings by its citizens, the government places 34 percent of each worker's wages in a special fund, and the worker can use these forced savings only to buy government stocks, to purchase a house, or for retirement.

The state uses the media and the schools to support extensive campaigns to discourage certain behaviors, such as spitting in public, long hair on men, and littering. The stiff penalties imposed to enforce its social-control policies received worldwide attention in 1994 with the "flogging" of American teenager Michael Faye for spraying graffiti on automobiles. For many offenses, there are heavy on-the-spot fines: in U.S. dollar equivalents, $124 for driving without a seatbelt, $250 for littering, $310 for eating on a subway, $310 for smoking in a restaurant. To prevent speeding, all taxicabs are equipped with a bell that begins to ring loudly as soon as the legal speed limit is exceeded, and trucks have a yellow light on top that flashes when the truck is driven too fast. Technological surveillance includes computerized camera systems that record the license plates of cars that violate traffic laws, and odor-activated videocameras in elevators that record anyone who urinates in the elevator (the person is also locked in). There is even a law against failing to flush after use of a public urinal.

Singapore also instituted a set of not-so-subtle eugenics/population-control policies. Women of less than high school education are given a government-subsidized home mortgage, but they lose the subsidy if they have a third child. To increase the low population "productivity" of college graduates, the government's Social Development Unit offers a computer-matching service for educated singles. One program, eventually discontinued, offered these smart singles a government-funded vacation at a romantic seaside holiday camp.

(continued)

BOX 15.5 *(Continued)*

Because of such extensive policies of social control, Singapore has been subjected to jokes and serious criticism about its limitations on civil liberties. But no one denies that the country is exceptionally orderly, clean, and efficient. (This discussion is based on Sesser 1992.)

In the Latin American NICs, as previously noted, Catholicism and a well-entrenched social class system have had effects somewhat similar to Confucianism in encouraging obedience to authority and an acceptance of hierarchy. Strong leaders and extensive control of the political system by a hegemonic class elite are also characteristic of most of these countries in the second half of the twentieth century. Chile, Uruguay (recall Box 11.2), and Argentina have alternated between periods of rule by a civilian government and by authoritarian military regimes that, in most cases, came to power by violence and ruled repressively. Mexico has been dominated nationally by a single, socially conservative political party, PRI, since 1929. Only Venezuela has generally avoided authoritarianism, with four decades of civilian rule by governments that have accepted a limited mandate.

Thus there has been a tendency for many NICs to have more the appearance than the reality of popular elections with multiple parties and genuine alternatives, tolerance of government opposition, civil liberties, and representative legislatures with significant power. However, by the late 1980s and early 1990s, all the NICs had begun a process of democratization, which is proceeding at varying rates in different countries. In 1992, for example, Taiwan held its first truly competitive legislative election in the more than fifty years since the political elite had fled China after losing the civil war to Mao Zedong. In the same year, South Korea also held its first fair and actively contested presidential election with a genuine multiparty system. Argentina, Chile, and Uruguay have experienced the reemergence of a vigorous and competitive democratic politics in the 1990s. Even PRI in Mexico has lost its one-party dominance of the national political system, having already become only one of several key parties competing for power at the regional level (recall Chapter 7).

Along with the positive effects, the combination of democratization and greater prosperity has generated forces of instability in many NICs. In general, the NICs which have achieved the highest levels of economic development now seem most able to cope with these forces. They have adapted best to the expansion of political democratization and to the instability associated with competitive group politics, social change, and vigorous public debates over such issues as the allocation of resources and the shape of the political economy. These transitions challenge the government to find a policy mix that maintains social order through a balance of liberalization and repression. There can be wide swings in the successes and set-backs associated with these transitions, as reflected in the recent history of Brazil described in Box 15.6.

BOX 15.6

Order and Progress in Brazil: Sometimes

The motto on the Brazilian flag is "Order and Progress." The vision of order and progress has guided much of Brazilian policy since the founding of the republic in 1889, but recent circumstances have cast doubt on its ability to realize this vision. Brazil is the fifth largest country (in area) in the world, with a population of 164 million and vast natural resources. In many ways Brazil reflects the promise of development in the twenty-first century—but it also epitomizes the troubles associated with that quest.

Progress

From the mid-1960s to the mid-1970s, the Brazilian state took the lead in guiding industrialization, both emphasizing import substitution and promoting exports. The involvement of international capital and foreign corporations was encouraged. The results were impressive. Brazil's economic development was praised worldwide as a "miracle," with yearly growth averaging 10 percent. Brazil's economy is larger than that of all the rest of South America and is now the eleventh largest in the world. It is a leader among the developing countries in the production of many goods, including such agricultural exports as coffee, sugar, and cocoa, such minerals as tin, gold, iron ore, and bauxite, and such industrial goods as textiles, cement, automobiles, weapons, and machinery.

(continued)

BOX 15.6 *(Continued)*

Order

Politically, Brazil is a constitutional democracy. The government is a federal republic, with an elected president who has dominant power over the bicameral National Congress. It has a multiparty system, universal and compulsory voting, an independent judiciary, and a relatively free press. The large state bureaucracy has maintained social and political order, with minimal class-based conflict, and Brazil is often cited as one of the world's most successful multiracial societies. A strong military ensures the security and sovereignty of Brazil.

Progress?

The economic miracle was built on a weak, statist base, fueled by debt-led growth and deeply dependent on external support for finance capital, technology, and markets. Much of the growth was in the 600 state-owned companies, many of which were extremely inefficient and eventually went bankrupt. The emphasis on industrial development has had many negative consequences: The agricultural sector has atrophied, resulting in 2 million landless peasants and the need to import basic foods; in urban areas, the upper and middle classes have received most of the benefits of uneven development and there are large numbers of working poor and unemployed. More than 40 percent of Brazilians (60 million people) live in absolute poverty.

Brazil has the second widest gap between rich and poor of all major countries in the world. After years of miracle growth, the economy came close to collapse between the early 1980s and the mid-1990s. The average annual growth rate for the period from 1985 to 1994 was –04 percent, coupled with hyperinflation. The inflation rate averaged about 370 percent per year during this period, reaching a staggering high of 2,864 percent in 1990. New economic policies since 1995 have controlled inflation, privatized many state-owned enterprises and brought hope of a return to sustained economic growth. But one in four adults is unemployed and more than one-third of the population lives in absolute poverty. Brazil's foreign debt is the largest in the transitional countries or developing world, reaching $179 billion in 1996. Consequently, under structural adjustment pressures from the international banking community, reductions in social spending leave almost half of Brazil's huge population with a miserable standard of living.

Order?

Since 1930 the military has deposed six top political leaders from office. The military, supported by the middle class, seized power most recently in a 1964 coup against an elected government that was judged too sympathetic to the needs of the many rural and urban poor. The military government was repressive and ruthless, crushing leftist opposition, censoring the press, and compiling one of South America's worst records of human rights abuses. An elected president took office in 1985 after twenty-one years of authoritarian military rule and a new constitution was implemented in 1988. Since that time the recurrent economic problems have provoked a huge rise in social disorder. Crime rates have shot up; urban riots are frequent, especially in the

BOX 15.6 *(Continued)*

During a massive demonstration on the main street of Brasilia against the neoliberal economic policies of the government, protestors carry a symbolic coffin with the message: "Bury FHC (President Fernando Henrique Cardoso) before he buries you."

huge shantytowns surrounding the cosmopolitan cities; and there is violence between peasants and landholders, who are disputing the government's announced but unfilled promises of land reform. Shortly after one president (Collor de Mello) was forced to resign due to a massive corruption scandal, a new president, Fernando Henrique Cardoso assumed office in 1995. As an indicator of their disgust with government, one in three Brazilians abstained in the presidential election and blank votes outnumbered votes cast for any Senate candidate in twenty-two of the twenty-six states. Cordoso, reelected in 1998, faces a fractious legislature composed of nineteen political parties whose members are primarily loyal to their regional political bosses. And his economic policies have generated extensive public protest. The Brazilian flag flaps ironically over the building where these politicians attempt to govern. (This discussion is based on Goodwin 2000: 64–70; Margolis 1992; World Bank 1998.)

Democratization, the structural adjustment policies (SAPs) imposed by the international financial community (described in Chapter 14), and the recurring periods of economic crisis produce negative impacts on many groups, and especially the poor. Political violence can be the response from such economically and politically marginalized groups as the peasants in the Chiapas region of Mexico, students and labor union members in South Korea, and the Indian populations in Brazil. Moreover, instability that occurs across the borders from a NIC can spill over into disruption and violence in that NIC, as in Chile (from Peru), Malaysia (from Indonesia), South Korea (from North Korea), or Venezuela (from Columbia).

The economic crisis in the Asian NICs during the late 1990s, which also spilled over to many Latin American NICs, was a strong test of political institutionalization: to what extent would governments tolerate much slippage in stability before implementing repressive policies? To what extent would citizens tolerate attempts by government to reduce their new economic and political liberties? While governments in the least advanced NICs, such as Malaysia, did tighten down considerably on civil rights and political freedoms, most of the NICs in both regions displayed considerable tolerance and resilience in the face of difficult economic and political circumstances. The challenges to stability confronting these transitional countries will continue to be serious and persistent in the first decade of the twenty-first century.

GOAL: SECURITY

The borders of Latin America were established in the nineteenth century and have been relatively stable for more than 150 years. While there are occasional political disagreements between the Latin American NICs and their neighbors in recent decades, these rarely reach the level of militarized disputes (as described in Box 12.4). Interstate war involving these states was rare in the twentieth century. While the NICs' considerable military strength could be deployed for protection against neighboring states, it has been more actively engaged in maintaining internal order, either by supporting the political leadership or by overthrowing it and seizing political power.

Some of the most significant threats to security have been from the former colonial powers that did limit the NICs' autonomy and freedom of action, particularly the United States, Spain, and Great Britain. Indeed, the most notable conventional war since 1950 that involves a Latin American NIC is the Falklands War between Argentina and Great Britain in 1982. This conflict resulted from the attempt by the Argentinian military government to seize islands off its coast that remained under the colonial dominion of Britain. Argentina's defeat in a short war, like the deep penetration into Latin American economies by the developed countries and their financial institutions, was a reminder that dependency and subordination persist in the postcolonial period.

Despite their effective policies for internal stability, the Asian NICs operate in a region where there are significant external threats to security. Japan occupied most of these countries in a brutal manner during World War II (and, in the case of Korea, from 1905). South Korea has the particular challenge of dealing with the huge differences in political economy and ideology in relation to its militaristic brothers and sisters in North Korea, a conflict which exploded into the Korean War from 1950-1953. Recently, tensions have been high, with South Korean attacks on North Korean military ships and airplanes and the possible development of nuclear weapons capabilities by North Korea. Taiwan is treated by much of the international community as a breakaway province that must ultimately be reunited with China, and a serious conflict between Taiwan and China would result in severe regional instability. And from a broader perspective, every Asian NIC perceives Japan, China, and/or Russia as major powers in the region that might have geopolitical designs on it.

With the exception of South Korea, none of the Asian NICs has sufficient military power to resist the advances of a strong country. Thus most have relied on the protection of an interested "big brother" (e.g., Great Britain, the United States) or the international security regime (e.g., the United Nations) to provide sufficient military power to protect their borders. And the Asian economic crisis was a clear indicator that these transitional countries are all extensively integrated into the global economy, resulting in considerable economic dependence on key actors such as the European Union, Japan, the United States, and International Monetary Fund.

The Future of the Transitional Developed Countries

While the two sets of countries discussed in this chapter are quite different from each other, most of these countries-in-transition share an uncertain future. Many are currently confronted with development dynamics that could disrupt the relative stability and whatever prosperity they have enjoyed.

The *post-communist developed countries* are attempting to make the most dramatic transformations, having abandoned political institutions, a political culture, and a political economy that provided generations of citizens with stability and security, although with disappointing levels of prosperity. Similar to some countries in the developing world, the PCDCs are engaged in a simultaneous transition to democratic politics and to a market economy. Coping with both forms of change at once can be overwhelming. And, perhaps even more than for most citizens in developing countries, the citizens in the post-communist developed countries have higher expectations of the standard of living that should be provided. Thus there is a particular risk of an intolerable gap between expectations and reality in the achievement of prosperity, stability, and security.

Shifts to a market political economy and a democratic political system require extensive institutional adaptation and citizen tolerance. The most favorable prognosis might apply to those PCDCs that began the process with the highest levels of economic development and greater population homogeneity. This group includes the Baltic states, Czech Republic, Hungary, Poland, and Slovenia. The practices of liberal democracy seem to be functioning relatively well in these countries, the expansion of the private sector has been strong, and the probability of improvements in prosperity and quality of life seems high.

Political leadership and the political system are generally under more pressure in those countries where the levels of prosperity and stability have been particularly disappointing in the post-communist period. In countries such as Bulgaria and most of the states emerging from the Soviet Union and Yugoslavia, the politics have been volatile or there has been a reliance on authoritarian leadership. Economic assets have not been distributed fairly. And the situation is compounded by a weakening of economic safety nets, which further heightens conflicts between groups. At this point, many citizens in all the PCDCs are struggling to achieve personal success in a setting of economic and social dislocation and hardship.

The *NICs* are clearly in a more advantageous position. Singapore is already comparable to the more developed countries in prosperity, stability, and security, and several others (e.g., South Korea, Taiwan) soon will be. These leading NICs are also similar to the more developed countries regarding the continuing challenges that they must address to sustain high achievement of these goals (recall Chapter 13).

For most of the emerging NICs, current efforts at transition to a fully developed economic system and to political democracy will result in a mix of positive and negative effects. Economic growth and development offer the promise of rising standards of living for a larger proportion of the population through the products generated by the market and the distribution of welfare by the state. As their political economies become more diversified and resilient, the emerging NICs should also have increased control over their own destiny in the global economy. Deepening democratization should provide the citizenry with greater freedom of action and thought and increase the citizens' positive support for the political system, thus reducing the level of order maintenance required for stability. There is now a stronger civil society, based on a community of interest groups who will resist a return to the kinds of authoritarian politics that have been prevalent in most of the NICs in both Latin America and Asia.

The dynamics in the transitional developed countries are complex, and positive political, economic, and social outcomes are not inevitable. The sudden and precipitous decline in the economic fortunes of many Asian NICs in the late 1990s is compelling evidence that economic growth is reversible and that its foundations can be substantially less solid than they appear. Few of these transitional countries have escaped crony capitalism, overspeculation in currencies, property, and stocks, and dependency on the global economy.

There are many promising signs that democratic practices are becoming institutionalized and that economic growth can be achieved. However, the transitions to full democratization and economic development entail considerable disruption and dislocation. It is evident that no one fully understands how to sustain economic growth in the current international environment and thus prosperity in the transitional countries is vulnerable to many forces that the leaders cannot control. Most of the countries examined in this chapter are likely to confront periods when false steps, disruptions from the external environment, or bad luck could severely challenge their pursuit of prosperity, security, and stability.

FOR FURTHER CONSIDERATION

1. What seems to be the most serious obstacle in converting a command political economy into a market political economy in post-communist developed countries? How can this obstacle be reduced or overcome? In the absence of prosperity, is democratic politics doomed to failure?
2. Are the greatest threats to the security of the post-communist developed countries due to internal or external factors?

3. Develop an argument for or against including any of the NICs within the group of more developed countries considered in Chapter 13.
4. Is there any element in the NIC development strategy that seems particularly difficult to implement in countries outside of Asia?
5. Explore similarities and differences between Confucian culture and Latin American Catholic culture as mechanisms for social order.

FOR FURTHER READING

Blasi, Joseph R., Maya Kroumova, and Douglas Kruse. (1997). *Kremlin Capitalism: Privatizing the Russian Economy*. Ithaca, NY: Cornell University Press. A revealing and readable characterization of the rather disastrous strategies employed by the Russians under Yeltsin in the attempt to privatize the economy,

Fallows, James. (1993). *Looking at the Sun: The Rise of the New East Asian Economic and Political System.* New York: Pantheon. A readable and insightful analysis of the interplay among political culture, politics, and political economy in the Asian NICs.

Flynn, Norman. (2000). *Miracle to Meltdown in Asia*. New York: Oxford University Press. The rise and sudden crisis in the Asian NICs are thoughtfully analyzed, with particular attention to the balance of power between the market, cronyism, and authoritarianism in governing the state and guiding the political economy.

Laquer, Walter. (1994). *The Dream that Failed.* New York: Oxford University Press. A renowned historian traces the rise and fall of the Soviet Union, from the Bolshevik revolution to the collapse of Mikhail Gorbachev's leadership.

Medvedev, Roy. (2000). *Where is Russia Going?* Translated by George Shriver. New York: Columbia University Press. A lengthy but insightful exploration of the difficulties during the Yeltsin era of what Medvedev, a key advisor to both Gorbachev and Yeltsin, believes has been a too-radical transition to a market economy.

Simone, Vera, and Anne Thompson Feraru. (1995). *The Asian Pacific: Political and Economic Development in a Global Context.* New York: Longman. A thorough comparative study of the political and economic development of the fifteen countries of East and Southeast Asia, with particularly strong treatment of China, Japan, and the Asian NICs.

Thomas, Robert. (1999). *The Politics of Serbia in the 1990s.* New York: Columbia University Press. An interesting approach to understanding the political dynamics and power struggles in Serbia, the key protagonist in the chaotic Balkans, emphasizing an analysis of what was being said (as well as done) by the key actors, especially Milosevic.

Zaslavskaya, Tatayana. (1990). *The Second Socialist Revolution: An Alternative Soviet Strategy.* Bloomington: Indiana University Press. An interesting study by a Soviet sociologist of the obstacles to implementing change during the Gorbachev period, emphasizing public opinion and political culture.

The Reverend Jesse Jackson marches in support of democracy in Haiti and in support of the broad goal of justice for all.

CHAPTER

16

The Last Chapter: Looking Backward, Looking Forward

Profound and powerful forces are shaking and remaking our world. And the urgent question of our time is whether we can make change our friend and not our enemy.

—U.S. President Bill Clinton

It is not easy to understand the political world.

First, the scale of political phenomena is vast. There is an international political system, at least 190 national political systems, and tens of thousands more local political systems. There are also the political beliefs and actions of the more than 6 billion individuals in all those political systems. How would you estimate the number of politically relevant actions on a single day? It is surely in the trillions.

Second, the range of political phenomena is immense. Politics affects every action and thought that touches on the authoritative allocation of values and meanings—in your life at school, in the workplace, at leisure, in your home.

Third, political phenomena are often complex, changeable, unpredictable, even paradoxical. The attempt to generalize about the political world is both fascinating and frustrating. Einstein's observation that politics is more difficult than physics is an apt characterization of the challenges facing those who attempt to understand the political world.

This book has provided you with some conceptual tools and substantive information aimed at improving your ability to understand the political world. A basic premise has been that it is possible to formulate some generalizations about politics. Not every political event is unique, not every political system is one-of-a-kind, and not every person's political behavior is random. To this point, the study of politics, as political science, has mainly provided descriptive taxonomies and only a modest level of explanation. But the application of more systematic methods and more rigorous thinking does seem to improve our insights about politics. Most of our reflections on the political world have related to four essential themes: political outputs, political structures, political processes, and political change. Let's review them briefly.

POLITICAL OUTPUTS

What is the domain of politics? One crucial task is to define the essence of politics and the range of phenomena that are political. This book has employed the widely used definition of the political system as that set of activities through which values are authoritatively allocated for the collectivity. The crucial element in this definition is political outputs—those decisions and actions by the political system that determine the differential distribution of rewards and sanctions to individuals and groups.

The first central issue is: *What values will be allocated?* All societies are generally concerned with achieving prosperity, security, and stability. In the pursuit of these broad objectives, which value allocations are appropriately handled through the political process? In each society it is politics that defines *res publica*—things of the people. This definition sets the boundaries within which political action and decision are appropriate.

Some political systems assert extensive control over virtually every aspect of the lives of their citizens, while others intervene only minimally into personal, social, and economic life. Thus different political systems reach dramatically different answers to political questions such as these:

What (if any) religious instruction will occur in the schools?

Who will decide the value of a person's labor?

What (if any) level of health care is the right of all citizens and how will health care be financed?

Who owns land and what limits are placed on its use (abuse)?

How will people be protected from physical harm by others?

What things is a person forbidden to say, to read, to view?

The second central issue is: *Who will benefit from and who will be burdened by* the particular configuration of value allocations? Most values are scarce and their very "value" is often subject to significant disagreement. Thus there are few value allocations by the political system that are truly *Pareto optimal*—that is, an action that makes some individual or group better off and no one worse off. Usually an allocation that is favorable for some produces a negative outcome for others. In virtually all cases, the result of a particular value allocation is that some receive greater benefits (or lower burdens) relative to others.

For most individuals, politics tends to be personal. That is, most people are concerned primarily with the impact that policies will have on their own lives. For them the essential question regarding any value allocation is: *How does this decision affect me/my loved ones/my group?* The individual wonders if he will pay higher taxes, receive increased health care benefits, be protected from cultural works he perceives as offensive, and be given access to a broader range of imported products.

As a political analyst, you must also assess the broader effects of political decisions and actions on groups, on countries, and even on the international system. What groups or classes will experience a disproportionate share of the increased benefits or burdens from a public policy decision that increases the taxes on fuel, that restricts imports of a product, that alters eligibility rules for a welfare service, that decreases expenditure on nuclear weapons, that lowers the priority of prosecuting racial discrimination cases, or that implements collectivization of agriculture? Such concerns are at the core of the essential political question: *Who gets what?*

POLITICAL STRUCTURES

How do people organize themselves politically? In the late twentieth century there are only a few societies that continue to operate without explicit, complex political structures. To understand the political world, one must have a clear knowledge of the structural arrangements through which political decisions are made and implemented.

At the *formal-legal* level, the study of political structures focuses on the nature of the state, the basic actor in international politics. The state exercises sovereign power over its people and its territory; it has primary responsibility for making and carrying out political decisions. Among other things, the state formulates the basic laws, often embodied in a constitution, that define acceptable political behavior for individuals and groups as well as for the state itself. A state can decide to grant some of its legal power to another political entity, such as a regional federation or an international organization.

The *institutional approach* is explicitly concerned with the nature of political structures. This approach attempts to characterize different forms of executives, legislatures, judiciaries, bureaucracies, political parties and party systems, electoral systems, areal distributions of power, and the like. The key substantive interests of the institutional approach include explaining how political structures are organized, what responsibilities are associated with each role within a structure, and how the various roles and structures interact.

Finally, the more *analytic approach* to political structures attempts to develop conceptual models based on abstractions that represent the forms and relationships among those structures. The concept of a political system operating within an intrasocietal and extrasocietal environment has been the most widely used analytic framework for characterizing political structures.

POLITICAL PROCESSES

There are both micro-level and macro-level dimensions to the study of political processes. The *micro-level political processes* concern how the individual understands the political world and how the individual acts politically. First, the political beliefs of a person can be characterized and the configuration of these beliefs can be summarized as his belief system. Similarly, the forms and frequency of political actions performed by individuals can be described. Second, these patterns of political beliefs and actions can be compared across individuals in the search for generalizations about micropolitical processes. Third are the explanations of these processes—attempts to identify the factors that cause individuals to hold certain political beliefs and to act politically in some ways rather than others. This process entails an analysis of the agents of political socialization, the cultural and political milieu within which the individual exists, and the individual's own physical and psychological characteristics.

Macro-level political processes are the politically relevant interactions among many individuals, groups, and organizations. The themes of power, authority, influence, bargaining, decision making, conflict, and conflict resolution are central. This is the "stuff of politics" for most of those who are interested in understanding the political world. These processes take many forms, as political groups emerge and attempt to influence the selection of political actors and public policies; as political demands, supports, and other types of political information are communicated; as value allocation decisions are made by the political system; as public policies are implemented; and as goods and services are produced and distributed in the political economy. When states interact in the international environment, these processes include the patterns of cooperation, equilibrium, domination and dependence, and violence. The elite, class, and group approaches are three general forms for explaining the fundamental dynamics of macro-level political processes.

POLITICAL CHANGE

The political world is changing rapidly and constantly at the end of the twentieth century, more than ever before. Citizens and elites in every country are grappling with the implications of such trends as the globalization of the world economy, the evolution of democratic politics, and the explosion of scientific and technical knowledge. New technologies of production, communications, transportation, and warfare have created an interdependent global village in which every state is subjected to powerful forces of change. Among the key political questions about these potential transformations are the direction, rate, and controllability of change.

Direction

Chapter 10 explored the changes that occur when social mobilization, economic development, urbanization, and political development interact. In most states the exposure to organizational and technological knowledge increases specialization, rationalization, and predictability in the structures and processes of the political system, as well as other systems.

However, political development is more susceptible to reversal into political decay than the "modernizing" transformations in the social, economic, and cultural systems. Democracy can break down, political leaders can trample constitutional restraints, bureaucracies can be racked by inefficiency and corruption, party systems can collapse, groups can resort to political violence. The last fifty years provide ample evidence that the direction of political change is not necessarily toward greater order and rationality.

Rate

Even in the twentieth century there are still a few groups, such as the Bushmen of the Kalahari Desert in southern Africa and the Masai in Kenya and Tanzania, whose social and political lives have remained almost unchanged over hundreds of years. A few contemporary political systems, such as those of Britain and the United States, have changed only gradually over hundreds of years. But the rate of change in most current political systems is quite high. Sudden and fundamental (revolutionary) change has always been possible and has become far more likely today. Even in the absence of revolution, the dynamics of the modern world tend to transform most political systems at a very high rate. The impacts, structures, and processes of most political systems have changed more during the past 50 years than in the preceding 500. The rate of political change is likely to continue to accelerate. Can you think of circumstances that would slow the rate of political change in a particular state?

Controllability

The leaders of every political system attempt to use governmental policies to control the changes that occur both within the system and in its environment. Earlier chapters have provided dramatic examples of the capacity of strong political leadership to control such changes: Mao Zedong in China, Kemal Atatürk in Turkey, Pol Pot in Cambodia. To achieve its goals, a leadership needs some combination of political will, political skills, effective political structures, group support, relevant resources, and luck.

There are many reasons why the leaders of a political system usually have only modest capacity to control change. First, there might be an insufficiency in such elements as will, skill, support, and resources. Second, in complex systems, powerful forces of inertia offer resistance to change. Third, unanticipated effects of action can be more significant than the intended changes. Fourth, attempts to control change can be undermined by the actions of the array of national and international actors as they pursue their own objectives.

The recent developments in countries that emerged from the former Soviet bloc provide dramatic examples of how these powerful forces can affect change. Even with the extraordinary political leaders cited previously, changes ultimately evolved in ways that they neither anticipated nor desired. In short, despite the formidable powers that can be harnessed by these leaders, it is perhaps more remarkable that significant change can *ever* be controlled than that leaders often fail to achieve their objectives.

INTO THE TWENTY-FIRST CENTURY: UNDERSTANDING AND ACTION

Novelist Charles Dickens opens *A Tale of Two Cities* with the famous observation: "It was the best of times, it was the worst of times. It was the age of wisdom, it was the age of foolishness....It was the spring of hope, it was the winter of despair." Many people might find this to be an apt description of the political world at the beginning of the twenty-first century. The danger of a nuclear war between the United States and the Soviet Union has become a historical anecdote, democracy is spreading to more political systems than ever, and technology enables us to produce a remarkable array of material products. More people live longer and with a higher quality of life than at any point in history.

At the same time, people also seem to accept the inevitability of widespread political violence, human suffering, and environmental degradation. While some are optimistic about changes in the post–cold war period, others see little evidence that it is going to be less violent or less destructive than in the past. As we move into the twenty-first century, three broad challenges loom especially large.

Challenge 1: The Quest for Harmony with Our Technology

Technology (i.e., applied knowledge) is the most remarkable change agent in the contemporary world. In its many forms, it has vastly expanded human powers of control and production. But new technologies are also closely linked to many substantial changes in personal and social life, in political and economic life, and to the environment. While many people assume that technologically driven change necessarily enhances the quality of our lives, the reality is considerably more complicated.

A computer can serve as the eyes and ears of a disabled person or as the guiding system of a missile. A therapeutic wonder drug can be distributed to all who need it or sold only to the wealthy few for a very high profit. Genetic engineering can develop a new breed of rice or a new breed of people. Moreover, major technologies often generate effects that were neither intended nor desired. A nuclear power plant is not built with the expectation that its radioactive materials will cause severe health problems to local residents. Vast electronic networks can link us to a global community but also reduce our personal interactions with our friends and workmates. Extensive databanks of personal information increase the efficiency of our transactions with business and government, but they also provide many actors with access to detailed information about our private behavior.

This huge expansion of technological capacity occurred during a century in which humans killed far more of their race than at any time in history. Do you think that this is a coincidence? In addition to the sheer efficiency of war technologies, can you think of other ways in which new technologies have contributed to the increase in political violence?

The fact is that every technology offers a variety of possible uses and impacts, which are determined largely by human choices. Many of these choices are motivated by particularistic interests (e.g., domination, profit, convenience) rather than by concern for the collective good. Thus these choices are political, both because they affect public life and because they should be guided by wise public policy (Abramson, Arterton, and Orren 1988; Andersen and Danziger 1995). Box 16.1 explores some of the political implications of communications technologies—arguably the most pervasive change agent in the contemporary world.

In most countries, few constraints have been placed on the development and application of advanced technologies. However, faced with the extraordinary range of technological impacts, many governments are intensifying their attempts to manage technology. Policies have been implemented in such areas as protecting individual privacy against electronic surveillance, improving the safeguards against technologically based accidents, and assisting those unemployed due to technological changes in the workplace. In some of the most dramatic examples, promising informal and formal international agreements have been reached to prevent the proliferation of nuclear weapons and the manufacture of chemical and biological weapons. Despite these efforts, more countries than ever have the capacity to destroy using nuclear weapons and other technologies of war, increasing numbers of workers are permanently unemployed, and we spend more time interacting with electronic equipment than with each other. Thus the key political challenge is to develop local, national, and international strategies that will guide important technologies to serve the collective good and to do minimal damage.

Challenge 2: The Quest for Harmony with Planet Earth

One central focus of this book has been to examine the efforts of political systems to control their environments, both internal and external. Political and economic development and contemporary technology have created increased capacity for control of the environment but also for its unparalleled destruction. Such "environmental degradation" includes both the poisoning of the ecosystem by generating more wastes than the earth can absorb and the consumption of the earth's resources at a high rate.

Massive oil spills, ozone-layer depletion, contamination from nuclear waste, rapid deforestation, and the like tend to elicit a resigned response of "so it goes." For a majority of people, especially those in the developing countries, protection of the environment remains a secondary goal relative to increasing material prosperity. For example, croplands are depleted through the attempt to grow too much too fast in a battle against hunger; air quality is sacrificed to ensure that export-oriented industries will produce at a profitable unit cost; the benefits of trees to the biosphere are sacrificed to meet the immediate need for fuel or shelter. Even most citizens in the developed countries, where there is more concern for environmental quality, are not prepared to reduce their high consumption levels or to pay the full costs of repairing the damage caused by their lifestyle.

Is there hope for the human ecology? Individuals and countries must agree to sacrifice their short-term benefits in order to improve the prospects for longer-term environmental health. Individuals must recognize that their own decisions and actions are linked to those of many other actors and produce cumulative impacts on the environment. There are now, both locally and globally, groups such as Greenpeace and the Green parties that promote more environmentally sensitive behavior.

Many countries are showing willingness to share responsibility in curbing certain practices, as in the 1985 international Convention on Prevention of Marine Pollution by Dumping of Wastes and Other Matter and the 1991 Protocol on ozone-destroying chlorofluorocarbons, the first international treaty to ban a non-military commodity. Such agreements are a hopeful sign, although they are sometimes violated and still cover only a few environmental risks.

More broadly, some UN agencies advocate a worldwide program of "sustainable development," which would require substantial restraints on growth and resource use by the developed countries and an expanded but limited use of resources to allow modest prosperity among the developing countries' poor (World Commission on Environment and Development 1987).

Some observers are pessimistic about the willingness of people and countries to accept such restraints on their quest for material abundance. Richard Falk, an international relations scholar, asserts that the current system of states is incapable of generating the cooperation necessary to prevent environmental disaster. Thus Falk proposes the establishment of international agencies with wide-ranging powers to set detailed standards for environmental protection; to monitor the behavior of countries, their citizens, and their corporations; and to enforce compliance (Falk 1975, 1995; Haas, Keohane, and Levy 1993). The most pessimistic analysts argue that *no* political arrangements will induce people to save the planet, except perhaps a worldwide authoritarian regime whose top priority is environmental issues (Hardin 1995).

Challenge 3: The Quest for Harmony with One Another

At the signing of the Declaration of Independence, Benjamin Franklin observed: "We must indeed all hang together, or, most assuredly, we shall all hang separately." Franklin was referring to the need for cooperation among the separate states of the emerging United States in the late eighteenth century. His insight applies with even

BOX 16.1

Will the Communications Revolution Revolutionize Politics?

Just one generation ago, the large majority of citizens in even the most technologically advanced countries did not have the types of media that you probably take for granted today—personal computers, VCRs, commercial cable television, fax machines, modems, electronic mail, and satellite communication systems. In many countries, even televisions and telephones were available only to a small proportion of the population. Given the astounding expansion of communications media during the last several decades, it is not unreasonable to talk of a revolution in communications technologies.

As these technologies have become more widely available, intriguing questions have emerged: What effect does all this technology have on politics? Has it revolutionized politics—that is, has it fundamentally transformed the manner in which political power is distributed and exercised? In a world of electoral campaigning via television ads, "sound-bite" news, "spin doctors," and "mediagenic" politicians, it is clear that the new communications technologies have substantially altered politics, even if the changes are not yet transformational (Neuman 1999).

First, the new communications media have greatly expanded the means of information exchange between political elites. Direct dialogue has been facilitated by multisite telephone conferencing, electronic mail, and satellite technology. Elites can more easily assess the situation and attitudes of both allies and rivals by monitoring television and radio broadcasts. Sophisticated surveillance technologies have also vastly expanded the elite's capacity to monitor others, both within and outside the country.

Second, the emergence of global networks controlled by a few multinational corporations might be the dominant trend in the next several decades. Despite the proliferation of the media and media sources and the possibility for many individuals and groups to transmit information, the huge media conglomerates will likely shape the world of communications (recall Box 13.5 on Rupert Murdoch). Howard Frederick (1993: 124) predicts that within a few years "five to ten corporate giants will control most of the world's important newspapers, magazines, books, radio and television outlets, cinema, recording industries, and videocassettes." This concentration and globalization of major communication sources could have profound effects, creating a shared global culture and furthering the integration of economic and political life (Barber 1995).

Third, the media have made far more information about politics easily accessible to the citizens than at any previous time. In some countries an individual has access to hundreds of hours of "news" *every day.* Such news (not all of it political, of course) can be a rich source of information as well as analyses and criticisms regarding the political world. For example, as much as 40 percent of total television broadcast hours in many countries is devoted to news programming (e.g., Argentina, Canada, India, Poland, Russia, Zimbabwe) (Lippman 1992). Most of the democracies of Europe and North America now televise the proceedings of their national legislatures. The most dramatic recent expansion of information power has benefited those information-haves

BOX 16.1 *(Continued)*

It's "Cyber-Ted!" Senator Kennedy updates his home page on the World Wide Web, which provides citizens with information about his current political actions and policies.

with access to the Internet and other multimedia resources. Through digital libraries, web pages, CD-ROMs, and the like, individuals can undertake precise searches for relevant political information in the vast, global information environment.

A key question is whether the recent changes—the enormous volume of information about politics and the greater diversity of sources—significantly increase citizens' knowledge and interest in the political world and encourage their more active participation in the political process. To this point, the evidence is mixed. Consistent with the adage that you can lead a horse to (a huge body of) water but can't make it drink, no clear linkage has yet been established between the explosion of sources of information and greater absorption of political knowledge by most citizens.

Fourth, the new media make it far more difficult for a government to control the information available to its citizens. From radio to cross-border television to regional satellite transmissions to computer-based information networks, national borders have been obliterated as barriers to the movement of information. When asked what had caused the remarkable collapse of communism in Central and Eastern Europe in the late 1980s, then President Lech Walesa of Poland pointed to a television set and proclaimed, "It all came from there."

All political regimes attempt to manipulate information as a means of social control. When the citizenry has access to news and information broadcasts from

(continued)

BOX 16.1 *(Continued)*

other countries and when foreign media are persistently probing the situation within the country, even an authoritarian regime has reduced capacity to deceive its own population and to prevent outsiders from witnessing its repression and cruelty. The news media have been a key factor in the recent wave of democratization—enhancing citizens' ability to communicate with others within their society, increasing their awareness of the rights and privileges enjoyed in other countries, and emboldening them in the knowledge that "the whole world is watching" as they publicly demand their political and social rights.

Fifth, the new technologies open the possibility of "electronic democracy." Citizens will use computers to vote electronically. Television, interactive cable systems, and the internet might be employed to enable government to convey facts and issues related to a policy decision to citizens in their homes, for citizens to participate in questions and discussion, and then for citizens to register their approval or even to vote on a policy choice from their remote location (Abramson, Arterton, and Orren 1988). However, it is not obvious that government decision makers will facilitate the implementation of such systems, since their own decision-making discretion is reduced by such electronic plebescites.

Sixth, the new communication technologies can affect the political and social values of many people, especially those in more traditional societies. The increasing availability of foreign media exposes people to information and ideas that challenge their cultural base, including their understandings about the political world (Ito 1990; Malik 1989). As each individual can choose among several hundred cable television channels, many are likely to find a reference group and a national identity (recall Chapter 5) whose values are at variance with the dominant values of their states.

Electronic networks, such as electronic mail and computer bulletin boards, extend this changing political identity even further. For those who are part of these electronic networks, the traditional community, as a set of individuals with whom one shares values and face-to-face interactions, might disappear. Instead, the high-tech citizen's group identity and interactions could be primarily with a network of individuals who are geographically dispersed. As a result, a very different form of group politics might emerge in high-tech societies. Until now, groups have emerged through personal interactions and then taken their demands directly to political officials, government offices, or into the streets. Increasingly, action by "virtual" groups might dominate, existing primarily in blizzards of e-mail messages originating from isolated keyboards throughout the city, region, or world and directed at the mailbox of a political decision maker. Hundreds of electronic political networks already exist, such as GreenNet based in London and PeaceNet based in San Francisco. However, it is unclear whether these virtual groups will have the same capacity to effect change as the mass mobilization of people in direct political action.

Do you think government will be more or less able to control its citizens in a world with a huge proliferation of media sources and with individuals' own communications increasingly mediated by electronic technologies?

greater force to the relations among individuals, groups, and states as we enter the twenty-first century.

The globalization of communications and the economy are shrinking the planet. Economic enterprises, interpersonal networks, and personal reference groups are expanding beyond the boundaries of any political jurisdiction. These developments could increase our sense of common destiny and shared values, and, as a consequence, increase our capacity for cooperation across states and nations.

However, greater interaction among states and nations might also generate antipathy. Familiarity might breed contempt as increased knowledge of other groups accentuates the importance of differences. For example, indifference could be replaced by a sense that the behavior or values of another group are a threat that requires a response. The possibility of conflict might also increase as groups that are extremely unequal in resources and power become more aware of each other. There is no compelling short-run evidence that either globalization or the end of the cold war has substantially reduced the overall level of political violence, and each might be a cause of increased nation-based violence.

At the height of the rioting in Los Angeles during the spring of 1992, Rodney King (victim of the police beating that was the catalyst for the riot) made his first public appearance to ask: "Can we all just get along?" This plaintive question applies equally to the groups, nations, and countries that are both the components of the social world and the source of continuing political violence. One hopeful sign is the increasing efforts of the United Nations and other multinational agencies to resolve conflicts and restore social peace. Clearly, the ultimate challenge is to develop both personal and global strategies for sharing benefits and burdens and for getting along.

CHOOSING A FUTURE

As we think about the political world, fundamental questions are never far below the surface. Many of these questions entail the conflict among such desirable values as individual freedom, social order, material abundance, social justice, democracy, and happiness. Each individual and each political system makes decisions about the importance attached to these values and then attempts to create the political conditions under which the values are achieved.

The comparison of different political systems has highlighted variations in collective judgments about the relative importance attached to major political goals and, perhaps even more, in the relative success of various political systems in achieving their objectives. The contrast can be especially dramatic, as when two bordering states employ different approaches in pursuit of their goals. The juxtapositions between North Korea and South Korea, Iraq and Turkey, and the United States and Mexico provide particularly stark contrasts.

As we enter the twenty-first century, some people enjoy astonishing material abundance while one-fifth of the world's population lives on a subsistence diet and 15 million people each year die from the effects of hunger. Contemporary political systems spend more than $25,000 per soldier per year on the military and less than $1,000 per student per year on education (Sivard 1996: 6). Citizens in some countries enjoy almost unlimited personal freedom while in other countries they languish under totalitarian constraints. Political choices account for these circumstances.

There has never been such awareness of what is possible and such sensitivity about the gap between expectations and reality as in the current period. Global communications, a global economy, and a decline in authoritarian regimes have combined to make 6 billion people far more aware of what they have (and what they don't have) in comparison to others around the world.

Indeed, as more individuals, groups, and states increase their expectations and hence their demands, the possibility of satisfying everyone diminishes. A widely quoted statistic is that the United States, with about 5 percent of the world's population, has been accustomed to using about 25 percent of the planet's resources. Obviously, as even a few countries approach these consumption levels and as most countries try to consume their own "fair share," the worldwide consumption of resources will accelerate environmental degradation.

Ultimately, *political choices* will determine whether individuals, states, and the international system will implement public policies that ensure life, liberty, and happiness for most people, that constitute a more protective approach to natural resources, and that employ technologies safely and humanely.

Although people have become aware of what they want, the changing conditions do not necessarily increase their understanding of how to meet their wants or of the costs and trade-offs involved in pursuing their values. Thus one potential contribution of education in general, and the study of political science in particular, might be to enhance your critical thinking skills. Such skills are now the key to personal and national success in goal achievement, according to Robert Reich, Presi-

Can the young people who will take power in the next century provide the understanding and leadership necessary to enable humankind to live in peace and prosperity?

dent Clinton's former secretary of labor. In *The Work of Nations: Preparing Ourselves for Twenty-First-Century Capitalism*, Reich (1992: 154) argues that the "standard of living of a nation's people increasingly depends on what they contribute to the world economy—on the value of their skills and insights." Thus citizens must be able to identify false assumptions and inadequate concepts, select significant information, and assess its longer-term consequences.

Many people look to their political system as a major source of solutions in the complex, post–cold war world. But many also seem to believe that political systems are a major source of obstacles preventing their achievement of goals. A central objective of this book has been to increase your understanding of the political world. The discussions and many examples are meant to help you (in Popper's expression from Chapter 1) "to see more clearly than before." You should now have a more informed opinion about whether political *science* is feasible. Even more importantly, you should have a clearer opinion about whether political analysis contributes to the pursuit of political good.

Voltaire observed, "If we believe absurdities, we shall commit atrocities." The political world is full of disagreement, hyperbole, and ruthless competition. Political science cannot necessarily make the world a better place; its primary role is to increase our understanding about how politics works. Such understanding can be the basis of insights: about different conceptions of how politics should be organized, about the basis of any real political disagreements that require response, about mechanisms for conflict resolution, and about how to organize ourselves in the pursuit of specific (private, group, or national) interests within a framework of the common good.

As individuals, we often feel powerless in the face of the massive power mobilized in the political world. But every individual—even you!—can affect what happens. The democratic ideals that are widely celebrated in the political world are based on the assumption that people, individually and collectively, can make a difference. First, if you approach political questions with knowledge, insight, and sensitivity, you can better understand how to think and act in the political world. Second, you can communicate your own political demands and supports in order to influence the policies that are made by actors in the political system. Third, you can become a political activist, as a shaper of public opinion, a leader of a political group, or a public official. The American novelist F. Scott Fitzgerald observed, "One should be able to see that things are hopeless and yet be determined to make them otherwise." In the political world, things are not yet hopeless, unless people like you fail to think, to understand, and to act.

APPENDIX   Political Analysis

The mind rests in explanation.
-Aristotle

This book began with the claim that, in a democracy, men are more likely to vote than women. You were encouraged in Chapter 1 to read this appendix on political analysis as you considered this question about the relationship between gender and voting and as you assessed the data in Table 1.1. Chapter 1 defined *political analysis* as the attempt to describe and explain political phenomena. The following sections introduce you to some of the basic analytic tools for political analysis— that is, for conceptualizing, collecting, and analyzing data about actual political phenomena. After a brief discussion of the different types of data that are used in political analysis, we shall consider how to read data like those in Table 1.1 and how to draw a tentative inference based on those data. Most of the Appendix describes four broad approaches used for political analysis: taxonomic analysis, formal analysis, functional analysis, and relational analysis.

DATA IN POLITICAL ANALYSIS

Many political analyses rely on the assessment of data. Data is a general concept that refers to virtually anything that provides a bit of information. The term data can be defined as any observations, facts, statistics, or other forms of information that attempt to measure or represent some aspect of reality. The data used in political analysis can be characterized on different dimensions, including the style of measurement, the level of analysis, the composition, and the time dimension.

1. *Style of measurement*
   a. *Nominal data* measure by applying names to phenomena that have some common characteristic. Examples: male voters or female voters; Conservative, Labour, or Liberal parties in Britain; democratic, authoritarian, or totalitarian governments.
   b. *Ordinal data* rank phenomena in an order, such as from higher to lower, bigger to smaller, greater to lesser. Examples: more developed countries or less developed countries; voters who are older than 65, voters between 35 and 65, or voters younger than 35; political party systems that have one major party, two major parties, or many parties.

   c. *Interval data* are like ordinal data, but they also have a numerically equal distance between any two adjacent measures. In other words, the distance from 5 to 6 is the same as the distance from 81 to 82. Example: The Bush presidency of 1989-1993 (four years) was exactly half as long as the Reagan presidency of 1981-1989 (eight years).

   d. *Ratio data* are like interval data, but they also have a real zero point. Examples: a country's total expenditure on defense in a specific year; the number of citizens participating in antigovernment rallies; the percentage of seats in the legislature held by a particular political party.

2. *Level of analysis.* Political data can be measured at various levels of analysis. Examples: at the level of the individual, the strength of a particular individual's loyalty to a political party; at the group level, the percentage of Asian-Americans who vote; for a geographic area, the number of parliamentary seats in Wales.

3. *Composition.* Data can measure a single phenomenon, such as a political leader's age or a country's percentage of yes votes on a set of related issues at the United Nations; or they can be aggregate measures that combine phenomena, such as the percentage of total votes cast for conservative political parties in an election or a country's average annual rate of inflation over ten years.

4. *Time dimension*

   a. *Cross-sectional data* measure a single point in time. Example: a person's vote for president in 2000.

   b. *Longitudinal data* measure several points through time. Example: a person's votes for president in 1980, 1984, 1988, 1992, 1996, and 2000.

The example of voting in the 1976 presidential election in Chapter 1 uses data that are nominal (men versus women), ratio (percentages), and aggregated (for many people) in a cross-sectional analysis (only one election). You might think of data as dry statistics, but the data in political analysis are rooted in real-world events. If properly analyzed, relevant data can increase our political knowledge on an endless list of questions. Examples: Are countries that spend the greatest amount on military preparedness more likely to avoid war? Is religion or social class a better predictor of whether a Scot will vote for the Labour Party? How much longer is average life expectancy in rich countries than in poor countries?

ON READING TABLES

Table A.1 (which shows the same data as Table 1.1 in Chapter 1) provides data from selected presidential elections in the United States. Does this table help you to clarify the relationship between gender and voting level in democracies? Since political analysis often includes data presented in tables, it is useful to know the basic steps for reading tables. When you examine a table like Table A.1, the first thing is to establish precisely what the data are about. The title of the table and the names given to the variables (the key concepts measured in the table) indicate what the analyst who created the table thinks that it reveals. But the analyst can be misleading or mistaken, so it is worthwhile to assess whether the phenomena measured by the data correspond to the labels given to the variables, whether the data seem relevant to the analytic question, and whether the data seem accurate.

TABLE A.1
Analysis of Table 1.1: Participation of Eligible
Voters in the 1976 and 1996 U.S. Presidential
Elections by Gender

	1976	
	Men	**Women**
Voted	a. 77%	b. 67%
Did not vote	c. 23%	d. 33%

Yule's $Q = +.24$

	1996	
	Men	**Women**
Voted	a. 53%	b. 56%
Did not vote	c. 47%	d. 44%

Yule's $Q = -.06$

Next you should examine the data in the table. What do the data measure? Table A.1 provides data on the percentage of men and women who did or did not vote in the election of the U.S. president in 1976 and 1996. How are such tabular data read? Are either of the two following statements supported by the 1976 data in the table?

1. Twenty-three percent of those who did not vote were men.
2. Thirty-three percent of the women did not vote.

It is useful, especially when there are percentages in a table, to examine how the columns (up and down) and the rows (across) are formed. In the case of percentages, find any direction(s) in which the data add to 100 percent. In this table, the columns add to 100 percent. Thus statement 2 is supported by the table and statement 1 is not. Can you see why this is so?

In many cases the analyst uses more sophisticated techniques than tables in order to assess the relationships between variables. Later in this appendix, in the discussion of relational modes of analysis, the use of statistical techniques to examine these relationships will be considered. That section will explain the meaning of the Yule's Q statistics in Table A.1.

The use of statistics and other quantitative techniques can be helpful in political analysis. The more demanding task for the analyst is to use careful judgment to decide whether the relationship identified by such techniques has *substantive* significance. The key question is: Do the tables, statistics, and so on provide useful insights about political processes or about how political phenomena are associated?

MODES OF POLITICAL ANALYSIS

Chapter 1 indicated that political science has little theory in the strictest sense of the term; that is, it does not have a set of precise, systematically related generalizations. However, most contemporary political analysis does strive to make our understanding of politics more general, precise, and systematic. Such efforts at theory building involve primarily the ordering of empirical data, using one of these four modes of political analysis: taxonomic, formal, functional, or relational.

Taxonomic Analysis

Aristotle (384-322 B.C.E.), the father of political analysis, was interested in distinguishing different types of Greek city-states. He classified them by using a concept derived from earlier work by Herodotus (c. 484-425 B.C.E.): the size of the ruling group. Aristotle defined three categories: The city-state might be ruled by one person, by a few people, or by many people.

This is an example of **taxonomic analysis.** Its objective is the orderly arrangement of some political phenomena by developing a set of distinct categories. Most political analysis begins with a taxonomy—a set of categories that classify data into different types. The categories within a taxonomy establish the crucial concepts that define the analysis. The criteria for naming the types and for classifying phenomena into each type are arbitrary, in the sense that they are established by the analyst on the basis of substantive concerns. But the categories ought to be exhaustive (all cases are classified), mutually exclusive (no case fits into more than one category), and comparable (all categories are distinguished by the same criteria). Relevant data might be of any type, although they are usually nominal or ordinal.

Aristotle's three categories of city-states are sufficient to create a taxonomy. But to enrich his analysis, Aristotle also employed a second concept: the group(s) whose interests are served by the ruler. His two categories were (1) the ruler(s) could rule in the general interest, or (2) the ruler(s) could rule in self-interest. Thus Aristotle's taxonomy of governments had two central concepts, each based on nominal data, resulting in the six categories displayed in Table A.2. Aristotle then provided names for each category in the taxonomy. For example, he labeled as a **monarchy** any city-state in which one person ruled in the general interest; if a few ruled in their own interest, the system was called an **oligarchy.** Notice that Aristotle labeled the most perverse case, where many attempt to rule in self-interest, a *democracy!*

Aristotle used his taxonomy for political analysis by placing each Greek city-state in one of the six categories. Athens, for example, was classified as an aristocracy. Notice that a taxonomy organizes data, but it does not answer the *how* and

TABLE A.2
Aristotle's Taxonomy of Political Systems

How Many Rule?	In Whose Interest?	
	General	**Self**
One	Monarchy	Tyranny
A few	Aristocracy	Oligarchy
Many	Polity	Democracy

why questions. To explore such questions (e.g., Is a prosperous middle class more likely in an oligarchy? Under what conditions does a polity transform into a democracy?), the analyst must move beyond taxonomic analysis.

Formal Analysis

Suppose you want to travel around New York City on the subway. If you are unfamiliar with New York, you will probably use a subway map. The map indicates the spatial relationships among different subway stations and identifies the stations where one subway line connects with another one.

A subway map is an example of the product of formal analysis. A **formal analysis** specifies abstract forms that correspond to the reality in which the analyst is interested. The analyst attempts to "model" reality, by defining and interrelating concepts so that the linkages among the concepts in the formal analysis reflect the dynamics and interactions among the actual phenomena. Some formal analyses have the same physical form as the actual phenomena being modeled, such as a miniaturized version of an automobile engine. But most formal analyses use symbol systems as abstract representations of the phenomena, such as a subway map, a schematic drawing of the circuitry in a radio, or a mathematical formula for the trajectory of an object moving through space.

Most formal analyses of political phenomena are recent. Some political scientists have attempted to devise schematic diagrams that represent how some aspect of politics works. In one well-known example, David Easton (1965) developed an abstract diagram, composed of boxes and arrows, which attempts to characterize the flow of activities by which decision makers in the political system establish public policies. Their decisions are influenced by the resources available in the environment and the pressures they experience from various groups. This "political system model" is explained in detail in Chapter 5.

An array of formal analyses called *rational-choice theory* (or *public-choice theory*) has become an important approach in political science. Applications of rational choice theory can be quite complex, but these approaches share two basic features. First, they are attempts at representing political processes primarily by means of mathematical formulations or systems of symbolic notation. From the perspective of advancing a science of politics, such formal theories are given special prominence, because they aim to be general, systematic, abstract, and testable in actual settings.

Second, it is assumed that political actors (e.g., voters, legislators, political parties) behave purposefully. The approach does not assume that all political actors behave with complete rationality all of the time, but it does assume that their behavior is goal oriented and calculating. Both their preferences for various outcomes and their calculation of the costs, benefits, and likely success of different strategies to achieve those outcomes can be formulated as quantified indicators or as systems of symbols (Mueller 1993).

To introduce the rational-choice approach in a nontechnical manner, we offer several simple examples grounded in the logic of the approach. In Box 4.1, the approach is employed to assess whether it is rational for an individual to vote in a U.S. presidential election. The following paragraph describes another brief example (without the mathematics) of how the approach is applied.

Political scientist William Riker (1962) has posited the theory of the "minimum winning coalition." This is a mathematical representation of the well-known saying, "To the victors go the spoils." That is, it assumes that the benefits of any policy decision in a legislature will tend to be distributed among those who have voted in favor of the decision. However, Riker argues, as the size of the coalition voting for the policy becomes larger, the benefits must be distributed among more people (or the groups each person represents) and thus there is a smaller share of benefits available to each coalition member. In order to assure each coalition member of the largest possible share of benefits, there is a tendency to create a coalition that has just enough participants to ensure victory—hence the idea of a minimum winning coalition. This concept is developed as a formal theory through specification of mathematical equations that relate the size of the decision-making group, the size of the coalition, and the amount of resources available for distribution. (For an empirical analysis of national legislatures that challenges Riker's theory, see Strom 1989.)

Functional Analysis

Suppose someone asks you how a car works. You are likely to discuss the key structural components of a car's engine and power train, such as its carburetor, pistons, and driveshaft. You might then detail the processes of the internal combustion engine, noting how an ignited fuel expands in an enclosed area, pushing a series of mechanisms into directed motion. This style of description and explanation is the basis of functional analysis. **Functional analysis** describes the contributions of a certain element (process or structure) to the activities of the phenomenon under study.

In political science, one widely used form of functional analysis identifies certain functions (i.e., processes) that occur within a political system, and it describes how and by what structures the functions are performed. Some scholars, such as Gabriel Almond (1960), have defined certain functions, including political communication, rule adjudication, and interest articulation, that must be performed in every political system.

Applications of functional analysis are described in Chapters 5, 10, and 11. As a brief example here, we can consider the interest articulation function. Individuals might want their government to spend more on preschool care or to protect their right to own handguns. The processes by which individuals communicate these specific interests to others in the political world are called *interest articulation.* According to functional analysis, this communication of political needs and wants is a necessary function in every effective political system. Most functional analysts also describe and explain how structures perform such functions as interest articulation. Thus interest groups emerge to amplify the shared interests of many individuals. For example, the National Rifle Association uses various strategies to promote many individuals' concerns about gun ownership to those who make and implement government policies on firearms.

Related to functional analysis is *constitutive analysis.* Constitutive analysis assumes that political functions can be explained primarily in terms of one fundamental concept. (Indeed, every scientific discipline strives to discover, ultimately, the fundamental structure or process that accounts for more complex phenomena.) Among the concepts that have been proposed as the central one to explain politics are the interactions between groups, classes, or roles.

Constitutive theories are discussed in various chapters, especially in Chapter 9, which presents the elite, class, and group approaches to explaining politics. As an example, Karl Marx's theory of politics pivots on one key concept: class. In every historical period, society is divided into a set of classes, based on the distribution of economic power. The structure of classes determines political and social relations, as well as economic relations. In political terms, the class structure determines who wields political power, for what purposes, and for whose benefit. The role of the state and the dynamics of political change are also explained in terms of class relations.

Relational Analysis

Box 1.3 (in Chapter 1) and Table A.1 consider the question of voting differences between men and women: Is there some relationship between an individual's gender and the likelihood that she or he votes? This is typical of the kinds of questions addressed by relational analysis.

The central goal of **relational analysis** is to discover and explicate the systematic connections between phenomena. Many interesting questions about politics can be addressed by relational analysis. The basic question is always: Are political phenomena linked? For example: Are democratic countries more stable than nondemocratic countries? Are older people more politically conservative than younger people? Are states dominated by Islam more warlike than states dominated by Hinduism? What conditions are associated with victory by revolutionary forces?

Both formal analysis and functional analysis also assume connections, but relational analysis tries merely to identify the connections between phenomena. It does not attempt to model or schematize the connections, as does formal analysis. And it does not focus on crucial functions, as does functional analysis. There are two levels of relational analysis: (1) correlational analysis and (2) causal analysis. To determine whether there is a systematic association between variables, most correlational and causal analyses use various statistical techniques. These statistics provide a mathematical appraisal of the extent to which change in one phenomenon is systematically related to changes in one or more other phenomena. Box A.1 provides further information about such statistics.

Correlational analysis. Correlational analysis determines whether there is a statistically probable relationship between two variables. It does not presume, as does causal analysis (discussed in the next section), that one variable actually is the agent that causes change to occur in another variable. It merely assesses the strength and direction of an association between variables. Many empirical attempts to understand politics begin with the establishment of a correlation between political phenomena.

For example, evaluation of the linkage between gender and voting in Table A.1 is an example of correlational analysis. The table and the Yule's Q statistic both seem to support the tentative conclusion that, for 1976 at least, there seems to be a modest correlation (i.e., a systematic, statistically probable association) between gender and voting. While this seems correct, there are obvious problems with using this election as the basis for a broader generalization about gender and voting. It examines only a single election. The relationship is not evident in the 1996 electoral data. In fact, women outvoted men in every U.S. presidential election after 1980. You

BOX A.1

Assessing Relations between Phenomena

To interpret most quantitative analyses in political science (and most other social sciences), you need to understand a bit about the meaning of the most commonly used statistics (e.g., Pearson's *r*, regression analysis, factor analysis). Ideally, you will take some statistics coursework so that you understand the logic and assumptions of the statistics being employed.

The simplest relational statistics (e.g., Pearson's *r, tau beta,* Spearman's *rho)* usually range in value between + 1.00, which indicates a perfect positive relationship between the variables, and − 1.00, which indicates a perfect negative relationship between the variables. Many of these simple statistics will also have a *significance* level—an indication of how likely it is that the observed relation between variables might have occurred by chance. This is normally measured in terms of this chance probability: .05, .01, .001. The smaller the probability of a chance relationship, the greater the analyst's confidence that the variables are actually associated.

In the case of two variables, a + 1.00 correlation would look like graph *A* in Figure A.1: As one variable increases one unit in value, the other variable increases at a corresponding rate. For example, you would find a + 1.00 correlation if each $100,000 spent on congressional political campaigns increased voter turnout by 1 percent. A − 1.00 correlation would look like graph *B*. Rarely do real-world phenomena in political science come even close to a perfect positive or negative correlation.

A correlation statistic close to .00 means that there is virtually no linear relationship between the two variables, as in graph *C*. For example, you are likely to find that campaign expenditure levels have no consistent relationships with turnout rates. Political phenomena are often extremely complex and subject to many influences and thus they typically have little or no systematic relationship with other factors that you might consider. Thus in many political analyses, the statistical associations are low or statistically insignificant. The strongest statistical relationships for interesting political data are usually at moderate levels of correlation, in the range of ± .10 to ± .35, as in graph *D*.

You can look at simple arrays of data, like those in Table A.1, and draw your own conclusions. Graphical representations (like the four scattergrams in Figure A.1) are another straightforward way to assess data. Each point in the figures represents one case, located at its appropriate value on each of the two variables in the analysis. This visual mapping of cases can provide useful insights about the nature of the relationship between two variables.

As the data become more complex, statistics can help inform your judgment. Table A.1 indicates that the correlation between gender and voting in the 1976 election data is + .24, using a very simple correlation statistic for 2 × 2 tables called "Yule's Q." The correlation of + .24 suggests that in these data there is a moderate, systematic relationship between male gender and higher probability of voting. In the 1996 data, the relationship between gender and voting appears less pronounced,

BOX A.1 *(Continued)*

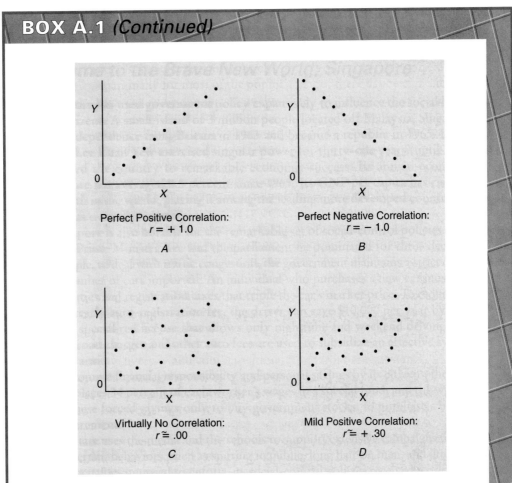

Figure A.1
Correlation relationships between two hypothetical variables, x and y

and this judgment is supported by the Yule's Q of − .06, which indicates that there is virtually no systematic relationship.

While most statistics of association require a calculator or a computer, you can calculate Yule's Q yourself for any 2 × 2 table: (1) multiply the values of the two cells on each diagonal: $a \times d$ and $b \times c$; (2) subtract the two products: $ad - bc$; (3) add the two products: $ad + bc$; (4) divide $ad - bc$ by $ad + bc$; (5) the result of this division should be a correlation score, ranging between + 1.00 and − 1.00. The formula for Yule's Q is thus: $(ad - bc)/(ad + bc)$. (Unlike the case in most correlation statistics, a positive Yule's Q means that the ad diagonal is stronger than the bc diagonal).

Beyond simple statistics and graphs, political scientists have an array of sophisticated data-analysis techniques to examine questions using quantitative data. Most of the techniques are elaborations on the basic idea of examining whether the values on phenomena seem to be systematically related to each other.

might pursue this research on U.S. elections by asking: Is this a new trend or a temporary deviation from a fifty-year pattern?

Moreover, a generalization about democracies might also consider elections other than the presidency and certainly should analyze other democracies. For example, any generalization might take into account an analysis of British and German national elections since 1970, in which there is no correlation between gender and voting rates (Walker 1988: table 1). A further problem with the evident pattern between gender and voting in the 1976 data will be explored later in this section.

Causal analysis. Causal analysis goes beyond correlational analysis, because it explicitly identifies one phenomenon as the effective agent that brings about changes in another phenomenon. Much of the language in political analysis is loosely causal, implying that there is a cause-and-effect relationship between two variables. However, causal analysis is the only approach that attempts an explicit empirical test of cause and effect. Causal analysis presents the "if X, then Y" mode of explanation described in Chapter 1. Here X is the *independent variable* that, given a certain value, actually causes Y, the *dependent variable*, to change in a particular way.

An example of causal analysis links the electoral system and the number of political parties. In his book *Political Parties,* French political scientist Maurice Duverger (1954) contends that the type of electoral system *causes* the number of effective parties to increase or decrease. In particular, he hypothesizes the following:

1. Plurality electoral systems (in which the candidate who receives the most votes wins) reduce the number of major political parties toward two.

2. Electoral systems with proportional representation (in which candidates are elected to the legislature in proportion to their party's share of the total vote) and with multimember districts (more than one legislator per district) allow more than two major parties (recall Box 7.1).

Political analysts have tested Duverger's hypotheses using data from various electoral systems (e.g., Riker 1982; Taagepera and Shugart 1989: chap. 13). Table A.3 presents data from twenty democratic countries for the period from 1945 to 1965. Do you think the data in Table A.3 support Duverger's hypothesis? Why?

TABLE A.3
Relationship between Number of Political Parties and Type of Electoral System

| | Electoral System[a] | |
Number of Parties[b]	Plurality	Other
Two	23	4
More than two	7	73
Yule's $Q = +.97$		

Note: Based on data from twenty Western democracies, in elections of legislative representatives, between 1945 and 1965.
[a]In plurality, or "first-past-the-post systems," the party/candidate with the largest number of votes wins a seat in the legislature, and all other parties/candidates gain no seats. In other systems there is some form of proportional representation or vote transfer.
[b]Number of political parties with at least 5 percent of the seats in the legislature.
Source: Rae 1971.

DRAWING CONCLUSIONS
FROM EMPIRICAL ANALYSES

The purpose of empirical analysis is to increase our knowledge about politics. It is especially important that the analyst draw appropriate conclusions. In political analysis, as in politics, things are often not what they seem. Let's consider some of the potential problems, using the causal analysis of electoral systems and party systems as an example. You probably concluded that the data in Table A.3 support Duverger's hypothesis. Do we now know that the electoral system causes different types of party systems? Yes, maybe....

YES: There is certainly some persuasive empirical evidence for such a conclusion. And, on logical grounds, it does seem reasonable that the electoral system might cause variations in the number of parties that survive over time.

MAYBE: However, the political analyst must always be cautious in drawing conclusions and making generalizations. Several questions should be considered.

1. Are the data and methods appropriate? Did the analysis use accurate, relevant data and the correct analytic techniques? Is the sample of nations or the time period examined typical? Does this generalization also hold for non-European nations? Were systems divided between "plurality" and "other" in a manner consistent with Duverger's hypothesis?

2. Are the analyst's inferences about cause and effect persuasive? Might the dependent variable (in this case the number of political parties) actually have a significant effect on the presumed independent variable (the electoral system)? That is, since the parties in most legislatures have the power to establish the electoral system, certain parties might try to implement an electoral system that perpetuates their power via the existing party system.

3. Are there plausible rival hypotheses? That is, is there another independent variable, not considered in this analysis, that might better account for the pattern of values on the dependent variable? It is possible that both the number of parties and the electoral system are related primarily because each is correlated with the third variable. For example, the number of fundamental issues that divide the electorate might have the greatest effect on the number of major parties, if one party emerges for each pattern of positions on the fundamental issues (Taagepera and Shugart 1989).

When political scientists use the scientific method, any of these kinds of "problems" with a conclusion might be raised by other analysts. The data, the methods, or the inferences might not stand up to such scrutiny. In our examination of Duverger's claims about the causal relationship between electoral systems and number of parties, none of the three problems just listed seems to undermine the analysis. Until one of these types of criticisms is supported persuasively, we can have some confidence that the generalization about the causal relationship is correct—that electoral systems do seem to cause certain types of party systems to evolve over time.

But the gender and voting analysis based on the 1976 election data in Table A.1 is an example of how an initial causal inference can be challenged. The three potential problems must be considered in an assessment of whether the data reveal that gender differences do cause different probability of voting.

1. The data and methods do seem appropriate. However, a generalization (even limited to the United States) would certainly require more than a single case.

2. The posited cause-and-effect relationship seems reasonable. This is the only possible direction of causality, since voting certainly cannot "cause" gender. Also there are reasonable explanations for why men might vote at higher rates than women. Can you think of at least one?

3. However, to make a compelling argument that the data reveal causality, it would be necessary to ensure that there is no other causal agent (i.e., no plausible rival hypothesis) that better explains voting levels or that creates the apparent relationship between gender and voting. While the analyst can never disprove every competing hypothesis, it is important to examine and reject the most plausible ones.

Let's reexamine the 1976 voter turnout data in Table A.1. Can you propose another explanation of the incidence of voting in the United States that is as plausible as gender? Among those you might suggest are age, social class, occupation, interest in politics, identification with a political party, and education level. Table A.4 provides the relevant data on one of these—education level—for our analysis of voting in 1976. Do these data alter your judgment about the importance of gender?

One reasonable interpretation of Table A.4 is that the 1976 election revealed a considerable difference between men and women in the incidence of voting among those with minimal education, but that there is virtually no difference in the level of voting between men and women who have a college education. In the absence of further analysis (and many further analyses could be attempted), these data about education seem to reduce the power of gender as an adequate causal explanation of voting. One might infer, at least on the basis of Table A.4, that both education and gender were important in 1976 but that gender impact was powerfully altered by education level. This closer look should suggest to you that if you were developing a causal theory of voter turnout, you would need to consider many variables and diverse data.

This example reveals a common challenge for most of the interesting questions addressed by causal analyses of politics: There are almost always clusters of plausible explanatory factors that seem interrelated. For example: What accounts for the decision to vote for the right-wing People's Party in Austria—class, education, family experiences, occupation, wealth, beliefs about society, attitudes toward governmental leaders, or something else? What factors lead a group to undertake revolutionary violence—political oppression, poverty, corrupt government officials, charismatic leadership, unequal distribution of wealth, foreign domination, or something else?

TABLE A.4
Participation of Eligible Voters in the 1976 U.S.
Presidential Election, by Gender and Education Level

Education Level	Percentage Who Voted	
	Men	**Women**
Grade school	72%	50%
High school	69	64
College	86	84

KNOWLEDGE AND POLITICS REVISITED

Chapter 1 suggested a number of ways of knowing things about the political world. Your understanding of politics does not need to be grounded in the scientific method and in empirical analysis. Insight and understanding about politics might be based on the method of authority or the method of personal thought, or they might be derived from other sources such as literature, films, or art.

In the attempt to develop precise and valid generalizations about politics, however, most contemporary political scientists use some form of the scientific method and some of the modes of political analysis described in preceding sections. Whatever types of data and modes of analysis they use, political scientists generally accept the notion that all aspects of their research should be subject to scrutiny and challenge by other analysts. Most also agree that their hypotheses, inferences, generalizations, and theories must be subject to some empirical test of validity. Although various sources of knowledge can provide you with insights about politics, this book emphasizes the modes of political analysis described in this appendix as the best means for broad understanding of the political world.

Glossary

Adjudication: Every society creates and enforces rules and laws regarding the proper forms of behavior for individuals and groups. The adjudication function attempts to interpret and apply the relevant rules or laws to a given situation. Most political systems have established judicial structures (e.g., criminal courts) whose primary role is adjudication.

Administration: The general term used to describe the machinery and processes through which rules and policies of an organization are applied and implemented. It is a core function of political systems and is usually one of the four basic institutional structures (along with executives, legislatures and judiciaries). (See also *Bureaucracy*).

Assembly system: A form of collective leadership in which a large group, usually constituted as a legislature, is clearly dominant over the executive. Examples: the United Nations; the European Parliament.

Associational interest group: A type of political interest group organized specifically to further the political objectives of its members. Examples: the British Medical Association; Common Cause. (See also *Interest group*)

Authoritarian regime: A political system in which the ruler is not constrained by a limited mandate to rule and has an absolute right to make policy decisions. The political rights of the population are severely restricted. However non-political aspects of life, including occupation, religion, and social life, are not under the extensive control of the political system.

Authoritarianism: A political system generally characterized by little or no commitment to equality or democratic participation, and by a strong emphasis on order and stability. The political behavior of the population is severely constrained. In many countries, authoritarian regimes are dominated by a military elite.

Authority: 1. A source of knowledge about the political world. The method of authority involves the appeal to any document, tradition, or person that is believed to possess the controlling explanation regarding a particular issue. 2. The legitimacy attached to the decisions of the political system, in the sense that people willingly accept those decisions as binding, independent of their own self-interest.

Balance of power: A configuration of power among a set of states in which there is a broad equality in the power resources (political, economic, and especially military) that can be exercised by competing states. Through a system of shifting alliances, no state or group of states is able to achieve a preponderance of power. Thus stability and the status quo are usually sustained, since states will intervene to prevent a serious imbalance that might lead to domination.

Bureaucracy: Although often used as a synonym for administration, bureaucracy has been defined, especially by Max Weber (1956), as a particular structure and style through which administration can operate. Structurally, bureaucracy is characterized by hierarchical organization and a highly specialized division of labor. Members of the bureaucracy behave according to specific rules of action so that treatment of each case is relatively predictable and non-discriminatory. (See also *Administration*).

Capitalism: One of the great "isms," explicitly linking politics to political economy, capitalism is a system which corresponds loosely to a market economy. In this system, private economic actors are generally free from state constraints and the state engages in only limited efforts to shift resources among private actors. Capitalism is founded on the philosophy of laissez-faire economics. There is no assumption that capitalism requires a particular form of political processes to function efficiently.

Causal analysis: A type of relational analysis, causal analysis goes beyond correlational analysis because it explicitly identifies one phenomena as the effective agent that brings about changes in another phenomena. Causal analysis presents the "if X, then Y" mode of explanation where X is the independent variable that, given a certain value, actually causes Y, the dependent variable, to change in a particular way.

Civil war: A form of political violence that occurs when a significant proportion of the population within a region actively supports a separatist movement and political violence emerges on a large scale. Examples: Sudan (the late 1990s); U.S. Civil War (1861–1865).

Class approach: An analytic explanation of the value allocation process (politics) based on a core notion of stratification—structured inequality in the distribution of key values in society. The class approach centers in an examination of the tactics of class domination and the dynamics of class struggle. Class theory is particularly associated with the writings of Karl Marx (1867) and later forms of Marxist theories.

Classical liberalism: One of the major Western political ideologies. In classical liberalism the highest value is placed on each individualís natural rights to life, liberty, and property and the freedom of the individual to pursue these rights as an independent actor. Government plays a very limited role under classical liberalism, which celebrates a laissez-faire economy and discourages government attempts to create material equality (although equality of opportunity is important). Political thinkers associated with classical liberal thought include John Locke (1632–1704), Adam Smith (1723–1790), and John Stuart Mill (1806–1873).

Colonialism: A situation of dominance and subordination in the relations between two states. One state asserts substantial power and control over the other, based on military, economic, and/or political power. The goals of the dominant state might include: to extract resources, to control a market for its products; to use the strategic location; to instill its own values into members of the subordinate state; or for international prestige. Most areas that were colonial holdings became independent in the decades after 1945.

Command economy: A type of political economy in which the state assumes total control of virtually all significant factors of production. The state replaces or eliminates the role of private owners of land, labor, and capital, makes all production decisions, and determines the value of all goods. The state owns, plans, controls, and regulates all major economic activity. (Compare to *Market economy*.)

Communism: One of the major "isms" linking politics and political economy, communism is a system that closely is closely associated with the command political economy. Based on the theories of Karl Marx (1867) and others, the key to communism is the socialization of resources—the notion that the state must maintain control of society's land, labor, and capital. Although it is primarily an economic system, communism also emphasizes an ideological commitment to economic and social equality among all of its citizens. It also posits that until such equality is achieved, government and politics must be guided powerfully by a unified leadership. Examples: Cuba; the former Soviet Union.

Comparative politics: One of the four major subfields within political science, comparative politics focuses on the similarities and differences in political processes and structures, either cross-nationally or by comparing differences within a single system, such as comparing the welfare policies of the fifty American states. A few of the many subjects for comparison are public policies, legislatures, and political parties.

Confederation: A loose association of states. In a confederation, each state delegates some power to a supranational central government, but still retains primary power and its compliance is always conditional. Confederations are usually created when states decide that the performance of certain functions is enhanced by structured cooperation with other states. Example: the United Nations.

Conservatism: One of the major Western political ideologies, at the core of conservatism is the commitment to sustain traditional values and forms of behavior and to maintain social order. Tradition and religion, rather than reason, are viewed as the most reliable sources for guiding society. There is loyalty to the nation and antipathy to egalitarianism. The writings of Edmund Burke (1790) provide a good example of conservative thought.

Constitution: A set of statements which describes the fundamental rules of a political system, including a characterization of the core activities of major political structures. Most constitutions are a single, written document, such as the United States Constitution, but some are embedded primarily in major statutes, precedents, and legal decisions.

Constitutional regime: A political system that operates in terms of the rule of law, as defined within the constitution, and that ensures effective restraints on the power holders. The defining feature of a constitutional regime is that the state does attempt to fulfill the provisions of its constitution.

Core state: From the perspective of dependency theory, which describes a world system of domination and dependence, a limited number of powerful "core" states have the capacity to manipulate and control the other states and actors in the international political economy to their own enormous advantage. At present, Germany, Japan, and the United States are identified as core states.

Corporatism: A corporatist state is characterized by extensive economic cooperation between an activist state and a set of large organizations which represent actors that control major productive resources. In the hope that there will be cooperation and consultation (rather than conflict) among the state, big capital, big owners, and big labor, the leaders of these groups are given great influence in working with the state to make and implement policy on key political economy issues.

Correlational analysis: A form of relational analysis that determines whether there is a statistically probable relationship between two variables. The analysis does not conclude that one variable is actually the agent that causes change to occur in another variable (as in causal analysis) but merely assesses the strength and direction of the association between variables. Correlational analysis is often a key step in any empirical attempt to understand politics.

Council systems: A political system in which a small group shares collective leadership and is responsible for both executive and legislative functions. All members of the council have relatively equal power, so decisions and actions are based on the will of the council majority or council consensus. Examples: mayor-council systems and boards of supervisors in many American local governments.

Coup: A coup occurs when the top political leader or leadership group is replaced by violence or the explicit threat of violence. A coup is a common form of leadership turnover in political systems that have no accepted and enforceable procedures for leadership succession. Examples: replacement of Wahid in Pakistan (1999); ouster of Suharto in Indonesia (1998).

Democracy: A political system in which governance is accomplished by leaders whose authority is based on a limited mandate and who are elected by a universal electorate. Such an "electoral" democracy becomes a "liberal" democracy when the population selects among genuine alternatives and also has significant rights to political participation, expression, and opposition.

Democratic Socialism: A variation of socialist ideology that treats greater egalitarianism as its primary goal, but also assumes that its goals can and should be implemented by a government that comes to power and rules by democratic means, not by violence and repression. Under democratic socialism the government might own some of the major economic resources and regulate much of the economy, but it does not attempt to plan and control all aspects of the economic system (See also Socialism).

Democratization: The effort to institutionalize democratic political regimes more fully and deeply, especially in countries with limited democratic processes. Analyses often try to measure the extent of democratic consolidation and to specify the political, economic, and social conditions conducive to further democratization.

Dependency approach: The dependency approach in political science essentially claims that an economic and political hierarchy exists in which many actors take advantage of those with less power and resources. At the top of the hierarchy are the most developed countries, and the poor people and the villages of the developing countries are at the bottom. Some analysts claim that many of the difficulties facing the less developed countries stem from their vulnerability to, and dependence on, the more highly developed countries.

Dependent variable: The Y variable whose value changes as a result of changes in some other specified (independent) variables. Causal analysis presents the "if X, then Y" mode of explanation, where X is the independent variable that, given a certain value, actually causes Y, the dependent variable, to alter in value in a particular way.

Dictatorship: A political system in which political leaders are not subject to a limited mandate, but have absolute power and authority. The citizens have no regular and realistic opportunity to replace such political leadership in a nonviolent manner.

Dual Executive: A political system in which one actor, the head of state, performs the more ceremonial aspects of top leadership and embodies the nation, while another actor, the head of government, is responsible for the more political aspects of the executive role. (See also *Executive.*) Example: The United Kingdom has Queen Elizabeth (head of state) and Prime Minister Blair (head of government).

Economic development: Economic development occurs as more and more households and firms within a country are engaged in ever-higher levels of production and consumption. Based on greater control of the environment and resources, more (and more complex) goods are produced and exchanged, and the GNP gets larger relative to the number of people sharing in the market.

Electoral system: The framework by which the votes of citizens are converted into specific selections of candidates who have a mandate to hold office. There are many variations, some based on selection proportional to votes cast (PR) and others based on the selection of the candidate with most (plurality) or at least half (majority) of the votes.

Elite approach: An analytic explanation of the value allocation process (politics) in which the political world is characterized by political stratification, the segmentation of the population into separate groups with greater or less power. In the elite approach, there are only two major strata—those that do more of what there is to do (in the policy process) and that get more of the resources that are available, and those that do less and get less. These two groups are called the political elite and the mass, respectively. Key elite theorists include Gaetano Mosca (1896) and Wilfredo Pareto (1988).

Ethnonationalism: A powerful attitude of identity with and support for others perceived to share a key nation-based trait (e.g., ethnicity, religion, common geography). There is often animosity between groups with different nationality identities. This animosity has become a particular problem producing conflict and violence, both within and between states, because the nationality identities of many people are not coterminous with the borders of their state.

Executive: The branch of the political system composed of a leader or group of leaders who are responsible for defining and managing the implementation of public policy. A broad definition of the executive includes not only the chief executive (e.g., mayor, governor, prime minister, president, queen), but also the entire administrative system.

Fascism: A political ideology that places fundamental importance on the unity and harmony of government and society and is defined particularly by its opposition to forces that might weaken that collective unity. It further assumes that the top leader is the embodiment of the natural will and that all individuals and groups must obey the will of the leader. It is both antisocialist and antidemocratic. Facism has had major impact on twentieth-century history and is particularly associated with such regimes as those of Adolf Hitler ("Nazism") in Germany (1932–1945) and Benito Mussolini in Italy (1922–1943).

Federation: A political system in which there is a constitutional division of power and functions between a central government and a set of regional governments, usually known as states, provinces, or cantons. Power is shared among the levels of government and no level has legal power to dominate any other level in all policy domains. Examples: Brazil, Canada, Mexico, the United States).

Formal Analysis: This form of analysis specifies abstract forms that correspond to the reality in which the analyst is interested. The formal analyst attempts to "model" reality. Most formal analyses use symbol systems as abstract representations of the phenomenon under study, such as a subway map, or a schematic drawing of the circuitry in a radio.

Functional analysis: This form of analysis describes the contributions of a certain element (process or structure) to the activities of the phenomenon under study. For example, one form of functional analysis identifies certain functions or processes (e.g., political communication, rule adjudication) that occur within a political system and describes how and by what structures the functions are performed.

Geopolitics: An analytical method which assumes that the geography of a state—its particular geographical location and also its physical characteristics, natural resources, and human resources—can significantly affect the domestic and foreign policy actions of the state.

Globalization: The expanding interconnectedness of economic and social systems in the world, as well as the increasing homogeneity of material resources, culture, and ideas among the world's peoples. It is claimed that these linkages are altering the actions and beliefs of many individuals and groups and even affecting large organizations and governments. These linkages result from such factors as improved telecommunications technologies, the expansion of multinational corporations and the spread of their products to wider markets, and the growth of a world culture and cross-national identities.

Group approach: An analytic explanation of the value allocation process (politics) which is grounded in the concept of the group—any aggregate of individuals who interact to pursue a common interest. Within this approach, politics can be understood as the interaction among groups that are pursuing their political interests, and policy decisions are the outcome of that group process. It is assumed that any particular individual can belong to many different groups and has some political resources which can be used in an attempt to influence policy decisions.

Guerrilla war: The essence of a guerrilla war is violent opposition to an existing regime by means of a long, protracted campaign primarily from rural bases. Fighting is typically in a hit-and-run style, with extensive efforts to win the support of the peasants and the creation of new political institutions prior to collapse of the old regime.

Hegemony: The existence of an extraordinarily powerful group (a "hegemonic elite") or country ("hegemon") that sustains its domination over other actors for a long period of time.

Hybrid systems: A political system that attempts to blend the desirable aspects of both the presidential and cabinet systems of government. Hybrid systems have a prime minister and an elected legislature that can both enact and implement policies, but they also have a president, who may have relatively equal power with the cabinet or may have key specific, but limited, powers. Examples: France, Russia.

Hyperpluralism: A situation in which many effective groups are able to pressure the government to respond to their policy demands. As the government tries to satisfy all these different demands, public policy can become contradictory or muddled. At worst, government may become paralyzed, unable to respond in the face of strong competing demands.

Independent variable: The variable in a cause-and-effect hypothesis or explanation that produces change in another variable. In the "if X, then Y" mode of explanation, X is the independent variable that, given a certain value, actually causes Y, the dependent variable, to change in a particular way.

Interest group: A group which directly attempts to influence the allocation of public values or other actions of those in the political system. It may undertake political action, provide goods or services to political actors, or provide data and information to those within the political system in its attempts to achieve its political objectives. It may also exert influence through compliance or noncompliance with the government policy process.

Intergovernmental organizations (IGOs): A political actor whose members are states, not private groups or individuals. IGOs can shape the cooperative relations among states, some or all of whom are their members. States form IGOs to provide a forum of communication between states, to enact international laws and treaties, and to intervene in disputes between states. Examples: European Union, NAFTA, NATO.

International law: A broad attempt to establish principles and rules which formalize and constrain the interactions among states. Positivist law, or written agreements between states in the form of international treaties or conventions, is the basis for international law.

International organization: A broad term which refers to many of the cross-national institutions whose objectives are to influence the behavior and policies of states. The two primary forms of international organizations are NGOs (nongovernmental organizations) and IGOs (intergovernmental organizations). Example: the United Nations.

International regime: A set of norms, rules, and procedures which are accepted by many countries and guide their behavior with each other in a particular issue domain. Examples: the World Trade Organization (WTO) on trade relations, the Nuclear Nonproliferation Treaty.

International relations: One of the four major subfields within political science, work in international relations examines the political relations between countries and the dynamics within the worldwide system of states. Subjects of analysis include foreign policy, interstate conflict and conflict resolution, and international law.

Judicial review: In political systems where the judiciary is relatively independent, the judiciary can interpret or even revoke the policy decisions and actions taken by the other political structures, thus exercising the power of judicial review. In the United States, for example, the Supreme Court exercises the power of judicial review when it declares that a law passed by Congress is unconstitutional.

Judiciary: An important branch of most political systems, the judiciary is the system of courts and personnel that determine whether the laws of the society have been transgressed, and, if so, whether and what type of sanctions ought to be imposed on the transgressor.

Legislature: The political structure in which, typically, policy issues are discussed and assessed and public policies are enacted by a set of elected or appointed legislators. Although a particular legislature may not exercise these powers, most have three broad roles (1) enacting legislation; (2) representing the citizenry; and (3) overseeing the executive.

Liberal democracy: A political system that is not only an electoral democracy (periodic elections, limited mandate) but also insures extensive political rights (e.g., parties promoting genuine alternatives, opposition) and civil liberties (e.g., freedom of expression, religion, and the media).

Macropolitics: The politically relevant behaviors and interactions that occur among large groups, institutions, or states. These phenomena are distinguished analytically from those of micropolitics, which particularly focus on the political behavior of individuals and small groups.

Market economy: A type of political economy in which there is near-total private control of land, labor, and capital. Every actor has direct control over his or her own factors of production, and production decisions are essentially the sum of all private actors' decisions. The exchange value of goods is decided by the market. The state is generally quite passive in a market economy, enforcing rules and providing minimal protection to economic actors. (Compare to *Command economy.)*

Marxist-Leninist socialism: A variant of socialist ideology, heavily influenced by the writings of Karl Marx and the interpretations by V. I. Lenin. It begins with three assumptions regarding the changes necessary to produce the key goals of equality and social justice: (1) it might be necessary to use violence to overthrow the old economic order; (2) a powerful government is necessary to restructure the economic system; and (3) a small dictatorial leadership group must manage the government and effect the economic and social changes. This group will be unnecessary when equality is achieved and can be replaced by decentralized citizen-run politics. (See also socialism.)

Micropolitics: An analytic focus on individual and small group political processes, with a particular emphasis on how the individual understands the political world and how the individual acts politically.

Mixed economy: A political economy that attempts to combine the strengths of both market and command economies, while also minimizing their shortcomings. Control of the means of production is shared between the state and private actors. The state's rules, actions, and direct involvement in the economic system guide some production, distribution, and pricing decisions, and also moderate and limit the market behavior of private households and firms.

Monarchy: 1. A political system with a hereditary sovereign, often called a king or queen. 2. Analytically, a political system in which one person exercises a very large proportion of political control.

Nation: A nation is a sociopolitical unit defined by a deeply shared fundamental identification among a set of people. This common identity can be based on such elements as shared ethnicity, language, descent, culture, religion, or geographic space. The nation is a major group, beyond the family, with whom the individual identifies very powerfully.

Natural law: Natural law refers to sensible, widely-accepted norms of behavior that ought to guide the relations among states and individuals and that should restrain hostile or destructive interactions.

Neocolonialism: According to this analytic perspective, new forms of domination and dependence between states have emerged in the decades (after World War II) since the end of colonialism. Although direct occupation by colonial powers was ended at independence, domination has been extended in some cases by the manipulation of such power resources as economic aid, technology transfer, military support, and economic intervention.

Neoliberalism: An approach to economic development that emphasizes a reliance on a local and global free market that is guided by entrepreneurs, who shape decisions about production and distribution of goods. The state plays a minimal role in the political economy, and public spending is focussed on infrastructure support (e.g., transportation, education) rather than welfare distribution.

Nonconstitutional regime: A political system in which there is persistent nonenforcement of crucial limits on the rulers and/or protection of the rights of the ruled, especially those limits and rights specified in a constitution and other key legal documents. Most authoritarian or totalitarian regimes are nonconstitutional.

Non-governmental organization (NGO): National or transnational associations, which are not part of the governmental/state apparatus, but which are committed to the promotion of an issue with national or international (INGO) policy dimensions. Members are groups and individuals who combine their knowledge, financial, and political resources to pursue a shared objective. Examples: Amnesty International's monitoring of human rights; Medecins sans Frontiers (Doctors without Borders) provisions of medical assistance.

Normative political knowledge: This type of knowledge addresses questions about what ought to be, rather than simply providing descriptions and explanations of what is. Examples of normative questions include: "Should there be limits on free speech?" or "How much and what types of health care should the state provide?"

Oligarchy: Literally, rule by the few. Hence, a political system in which a small number of actors dominate the resource allocation process, usually serving their own interests.

Parliamentary (cabinet) government: A political system in which the executive and legislative functions and structures are fused. The people elect the legislature (parliament), whose majority empowers a cabinet, which then empowers one of its members to be the chief executive, usually called a prime minister or premier. The cabinet devises, drafts, and implements most policies, although they must be enacted by the legislative majority. Examples: Italy, the United Kindom.

Participatory democracy: Democracy in its classic sense, as government of and by all the people. There is active, direct participation by all citizens in the authoritative allocation of values.

Party system: The configuration of political parties in a political system. Party systems are generally classified according to the number of political parties and nature of the interactions among the parties in the governing process.

Political analysis: The attempt to describe and explain political phenomena. Most contemporary political analysis strives to make our understanding of politics more general, precise, and systematic, and ultimately to generate and test theories.

Political belief system: The configuration of an individual's political orientations across an array of political issues. Many political beliefs are evaluative orientations, which synthesize facts (cognitive orientations) and feelings (affective orientations) into a judgment (evaluative orientation) about some political phenomena.

Political culture: The general configuration of a particular people's (e.g., a nation or a country) political beliefs. It characterizes those cognitive, affective and evaluative orientations that are dominant among that people. Many explanations of political behavior and political processes are grounded in interpretations of political culture.

Political decay: The phenomena that occur when there is a decline in the capacity of the political system, and especially its effectiveness in maintaining order. It can be manifest in such collective behavior as demonstrations, protests, rebellion and other forms of political violence. It is often associated with extensive demands that the political system cannot meet and with the loss of citizen support for the political system. According to Samuel Huntington (1968), the probability of political decay increases as a state has a lower level of political institutionalization.

Political development: The specifically political aspects of development and modernization. It can refer either to a set of characteristics of the political system or the process through which those characteristics are increased. The key characteristics of more developed political systems can include: (1) the concentration of power in the central state; (2) "modern" forms of political organization, such as institutionalized party systems and effective bureaucracies; (3) complex and extensive forms of individual and group political behavior; and (4) expanded capabilities of the political system to maintain order, manage the environment, meet the demands of the citizens, and so on.

Political group: An aggregation of individuals who interact to pursue a common political objective—a policy or action that might be taken by a governmental or private actor (e.g., a legislature, a corporation). Examples: the National Rifle Association, Greenpeace.

Political economy: The combination, in theory or in practice, of politics and economics. The political system and the economic system are inextricably intertwined, because many of the decisions made by the political system have significant impacts on the economy and activities within the economic system have major impacts on the state. Two ideal-type political economies are the market economy and the command economy

Political elite: A general term for those individuals who have relatively high levels of power, influence, interest, knowledge and involvement in political life. According to the elite approach to politics, the political elite is the stratum of the population that does more of what there is to do (in the policy process) and gets more of what there is to get (in the allocation of values).

Political idealism: A perspective, especially in international relations theory, which posits that human nature is basically good and thus that states have a natural tendency to be cooperative and even altruistic. Thus political institutions can be shaped to facilitate the emergence of these cooperative, nonviolent tendencies in the relations among states.

Political ideology: A comprehensive set of beliefs about the political world, including a specification of desirable political goals and the best way to achieve those goals. These systems of beliefs are generally based on particular assumptions about human nature, the relation of the individual to society, and the desirability of equality.

Political institutionalization: The extent that political organizations and procedures have acquired value in the eyes of the population and the stability to withstand significant pressure. Political institutionalization is measured by the political system's capacity to regulate its citizens, respond flexibly to citizen demands, extract and distribute resources efficiently, and adapt to changing circumstances.

Political participation: The term applied to all modes of the political actions by individuals and groups. The broad goal of political participation is to influence the actions or selection of political rulers. Modes of political participation for an individual range from listening to political discourse to voting to taking part in a demonstration to holding political office.

Political party: An organized group which attempts to capture political power directly by placing its members in government office. The political party is the broadest institution in most political systems that links individuals and groups to the state and it can organize the activities of those participating in government. It also aggregates political interests into a comprehensible set of policy goals.

Political realism: A perspective, especially in international relations theory, which assumes that people are naturally disposed to behave selfishly and that this self-interested orientation extends to the behavior of states. In this view, the fundamental goal of each state is to ensure its own security and survival by maximizing its power. Interstate conflict is likely to be a recurring event, and states sometimes use balance of power strategies to limit the frequency of major conflicts.

Political resources: Something that can influence the actions and decisions of political actors. Examples of an effective political resource, given a particular situation, are: social status, money, legality, special knowledge or skills, ability to mobilize large numbers of people, visibility in the media, control of productive capabilities. According to the group approach, political resources are of many forms and widely distributed. According to the class and elite approaches, one or a few types of political resources are critical and control of those resources tends to be concentrated in a limited group.

Political science: A set of techniques, concepts, and approaches whose objective is to increase the clarity and accuracy of our understandings about political phenomena. This academic discipline is labeled a "science" in the United States because most political scientists use the scientific method to establish shared knowledge about the political world.

Political socialization: The process through which individuals acquire their cognitive, affective and evaluative orientations toward the political world. Some of the most important agents (sources) of political socialization are the family, the schools, peer groups, the media, and culture.

Political society: Political society is formed when individuals cede to the state a monopoly over the legitimate use of violence, sacrificing their own right to do violence to others in exchange for a similar sacrifice from others. This agreement among individuals is termed the social contract by Hobbes.

Political system: A (formal) theoretical concept that attempts to model the fundamental structures, processes, and institutions of politics. According to David Easton (1965), the defining feature of the political system is its authoritative allocation of values for the collectivity.

Political theory: A broad subfield of political science that focuses on the ideas and debates regarding major political issues. One central orientation is to address normative questions, such as the appropriateness of different forms of political leadership or the rationale for political authority. As well as normative approaches, political theory can also be understood more broadly as knowledge claims about political phenomena which are grounded in axiomatic thinking (e.g., rational choice theory) or the scientific method (e.g., empirical political theory).

Political violence: The use of physical violence, or very serious threats of such violence, to achieve political goals. The modes of political violence can range from nuclear war to assassination to riots. Some analysts also define as political violence other activities that do not entail physical violence, such as racial epithets or ethnic discrimination.

Politics: Politics is defined in a variety of ways, but all definitions share the central idea that politics is the process through which power and influence are used in the promotion of certain values and interests. Politics can be thought of as the determination of who gets what, when, and how in a given society.

Positivist law: Explicit written agreements, often enacted by legislatures and interpreted by judiciaries, that specify appropriate and unlawful behaviors, as well as the sanctions for the latter. In the form of treaties or conventions between states, positivist law is the basis of international law.

Power: Although power is difficult to define, there is general agreement that power is exercised when A (one actor) induces B (another actor) to behave in a manner in which B would not otherwise behave. One taxonomy classifying the forms of power includes force (coercive power), exchange (economic power), and mutuality (integrative power).

Presidential government: A political system in which there is a separation of executive and legislative power and structures. This is meant to ensure a system of checks and balances in the policy process, with the legislature taking primary responsibility for policy-making and the president (the executive) taking primary responsibility for policy-implementation (although in practice these distinctions may be blurred). The president and the members of the legislature are elected independently, for fixed terms. Examples: Mexico, the United States.

Privatization: The selling off of state-owned firms to private actors and/or the use of private firms to provide public goods and services.

Rational-choice theory: An array of formal analyses that share two basic features: (1) they are attempts to represent political processes primarily by means of mathematical formulations or systems of symbolic notation; and (2) it is assumed that the behavior of political actors is goal-oriented, based on self-interest, and calculating. Examples: game theory; minimum winning coalition theory.

Relational analysis: Approaches to political analysis which specify the systematic connections between sets of phenomena, revealing either patterns of association (correlation) or of causality.

Representative democracy: A form of electoral democracy in which citizens elect people to represent them in the governing process and to allocate values on their behalf for the collectivity. Also known as a republic.

Revolution: A rapid and fundamental transformation of the state organization and of the allocation of values in a society. A revolution often involves the use of force and violence to destroy the existing political system.

Social market system: A political-economic system in which the state encourages the operation of an extensive free market economy but is also committed to social welfare distribution and some income redistribution, within the context of a democratic political process. Contemporary examples: Germany, Sweden.

Social welfarism: A set of ideological orientations and public policies which aim to insure that all citizens receive an adequate quality of life in such domains as education, health care, housing, and employment opportunities. A social welfare state is usually characterized by relatively high taxes, more extensive resource allocations (e.g., transfer payments or subsidized goods and services), and more active state intervention to protect citizens against the behaviors of those firms or others whose actions reduce the quality of life. Example: Sweden.

Socialism: One of the major Western political ideologies. In the socialist perspective, the most important goal is to provide a high quality, relatively equal standard of living for all. Each individual is encouraged to increase the collective good of all, in an environment that encourages cooperation and sharing. Government plays a crucial role as it attempts to use its allocation of values and control of resources to increase the material, social and political equality of all citizens. Two major variations of socialism include Marxist-Leninist socialism and democratic socialism.

Sovereignty: The premise that each state has complete authority and is the ultimate source of law within its own boundaries. It assumes the equality before the law of all states and that each state has the right to protect its territory against any aggression or intervention.

State: The concept of the "state" has various meanings in political science. 1. The legal notion of the state is that it is a "territorially bound sovereign entity." 2. In the general language of political science, "state" usually refers to the organizational units, institutions, and individuals that perform the political functions for a national territorial entity, such as France or Nigeria. 3. The state can also be defined as the entity with a monopoly on the legitimate use of violence to enforce the laws and decisions of the society.

Statism: One approach defining effective strategies for facilitating economic development. The statist approach emphasizes the importance of strong state action to support and guide the production and distribution of goods by the political economy. The state typically plans and regulates major aspects of the political economy and might own and operate key economic sectors.

Taxonomy: Most political analysis begins with a taxonomy—a set of categories that classify phenomena/data into different types. Categories should be exhaustive, mutually exclusive, and differentiated by consistent criteria. The categories of a taxonomy establish the crucial concepts that structure the analysis.

Territorial integrity: A concept closely associated with sovereignty, territorial integrity is a premise of international law which holds that a state has the right to resist and reject any aggression, invasion, or intervention within its territorial boundaries.

Terrorism: Premeditated violence, serving an underlying political objective, in which the target of violence is an "innocent." As a revolutionary strategy, terrorism involves selective acts of violence, usually by small organized cells of political activists.

Totalitarianism: A political regime which demands complete obedience to its extensive rules regarding not only politics, but virtually all aspects of life, including culture, economics, religion, and morality. A totalitarian political system might prescribe and proscribe the behavior and thoughts of its population in every domain of existence. Examples: contemporary North Korea, the Soviet Union under Joseph Stalin.

Transnationalism: A system of institutions and relationships in which key actors' loyalties and identities are not linked to any particular country. Many of these powerful actors are multinational corporations (MNCs) such as General Motors, Exxon and IBM, and other important transnational actors include the International Monetary Fund, OPEC, NATO, and other IGOs and NGOs. Increasingly, MNCs and other transnational actors hold international economic power, shape global culture and communications and operate outside the legal control of states.

Treaty: A formal agreement between states that they will cooperate or assist each other militarily, economically, or politically. A treaty carries a stronger expectation of compliance than an alliance. Example: North Atlantic Treaty Organization, Nuclear Nonproliferation Treaty.

Unitary state: A political system in which the central government holds all legitimate power. The central government may delegate power or functional responsibilities to territorial units (often called departments, regions, or prefectures), but those delegated powers and functions can be revoked at any time. Examples: China, France, Japan, United Kingdom.

War: Interstate violence that is sustained, organized, and usually involves hostilities between the regular military forces of the states. War is the ultimate mechanism for attempting to resolve power struggles and conflict between states. Examples: Iran-Iraq War, Korean War.

References

Abrahamian, Ervand. (1993). *Khomeinism: Essays on the Islamic Republic.* Berkeley, CA: University of California Press.

Abramson, Jeffrey F., Christopher Arterton, and Gary Orren. (1988). *The Electronic Commonwealth: The Impact of New Media Technologies on Democratic Politics.* New York: Basic Books.

Achebe, Chinua. (1959). *Things Fall Apart.* New York: Fawcett.

Adorno, T. W., Else Frenkel-Brunswick, Daniel Levinson, and R. Nevitt Sanford. (1950). *The Authoritarian Personality.* New York: Harper & Row.

Agnew, John. (1987). *Place and Politics: The Geographical Mediation of State and Society.* London: Allen & Unwin.

Aguero, Felipe, and Jeffrey Stark, Eds. (1998). *Fault Lines of Democracy in Post-Transition Latin America.* Miami, FL: North-South Center Press.

Alexander, William. (1987). "People and Food in the Other World." In *The Other World,* ed. Joseph Weatherby et al., pp. 34–58. White Plains, NY: Longman.

Allison, Graham. (1971). *The Essence of Decision: Explaining the Cuban Missile Crisis.* Boston: Little, Brown.

Almond, Gabriel. (1987). "The Development of Development." In *Understanding Political Development,* ed. Myron Weiner and Samuel Huntington, pp. 437–490. Boston: Little, Brown.

Almond, Gabriel, and G. Bingham Powell, Eds. (2000). *Comparative Politics Today: A World View.* 7th ed. New York: HarperCollins.

Almond, Gabriel, and Sidney Verba. (1963). *The Civic Culture.* Princeton, NJ: Princeton University Press.

Andersen, Kim Viborg, and James N. Danziger. (1995). "Impacts of IT on Capabilities, Interactions, Orientations and Values." In *Information Systems and the Political World,* ed. K. V. Andersen, pp. 65–78. Amsterdam: IOS Press.

Ardrey, Robert. (1966). *The Territorial Imperative.* New York: Atheneum.

Arendt, Hannah. (1963). *On Revolution.* New York: Viking Press.

Aron, Leon. (1998). "The Strange Case of Russian Capitalism." Columbia International Affairs Online. www.cc.columbia.edu/sec/dlc/ciao/wps/ar101.

Aspin, Les. (1992). "National Security in the 1990s: Defining a New Basis for the U.S. Military Forces." Statement to the Atlantic Council of the United States, January 6.

Bachrach, Peter, and Morton Baratz. (1962). "The Two Faces of Power," *American Political Science Review* 56 (December): 947–952.

Bagdikian, Ben. (2000). *The Media Monopoly.* 6th ed. Boston, MA: Beacon.

Banfield, Edward. (1974). *The Unheavenly City Revisited.* Boston: Little, Brown.

Banuazizi, Ali. (1987). "Social-Psychological Approaches to Political Development." In *Understanding Political Development,* ed. Myron Weiner and Samuel Huntington, pp. 281–316. Boston: Little, Brown.

Barber, Benjamin R. (1995). *Jihad versus McWorld.* New York: Random House.

Barber, James David. (1992). *Presidential Character.* 4th ed. Englewood Cliffs, NJ: Prentice-Hall.

Barnes, Samuel, et al. (1979). *Political Action: Mass Participation in Five Western Democracies.* Beverly Hills, CA: Sage.

Barnet, Richard J., and John Cavanagh. (1994). *Global Dreams: Imperial Corporations and the New World Order.* New York: Simon & Schuster.

Barnett, Michael N. (1998). *Dialogues in Arab Politics: Negotiations in Regional Order.* New York: Columbia University Press.

Baumol, William. (1997). *Economics.* 7th ed. Fort Worth, TX: Harcourt Brace.

Bennett, W. Lance. (1996). *News: The Politics of Illusion.* 3d ed. New York: Longman.

Bentley, Arthur. (1908/1967). *The Process of Government.* Cambridge: Harvard University Press.

Bill, James, and Robert Hardgrave. (1981). *Comparative Politics: Quest for Theory.* Lanham, MD: University Press of America.

Birdsall, Nancy. (1998). "Life is Unfair: Inequality in the World." *Foreign Policy* (Summer): 76–93.

Birnbaum, Jeffrey H. (1993). *The Lobbyists: How Influence Peddlers Get Their Way in Washington.* New York: Times Books.

Black, Cyril. (1966). *The Dynamics of Modernization.* New York: Harper & Row.

Blasi, Joseph R., Maya Kroumova, and Douglas Kruse. (1997). *Kremlin Capitalism: Privatizing the Russian Economy.* Ithaca, NY: Cornell University Press.

Boulding, Kenneth E. (1989). *Three Faces of Power.* Newbury Park, CA: Sage.

———. (1993). "Power." In *The Oxford Companion to Politics of the World,* ed. Joel Krieger, pp. 739–740. New York: Oxford University Press.

Brams, Steven J., and Peter Fishburn. (1983). *Approval Voting.* Cambridge, MA: Birkhauser Boston.

Bratton, Michael, and Nicolas van de Walle. (1997). *Democratic Experiments in Africa: Regime Transitions in Comparative Perspective.* New York: Cambridge University Press.

Brecher, Michael, (1993). *Crises in World Politics: Theory and Reality.* Oxford, England: Butterworth-Heineman.

Brecher, Michael, and Jonathan Wilkenfeld. (1997). *A Study of Crisis.* Ann Arbor, MI: University of Michigan Press.

Bremer, Stuart. (1980). "National Capabilities and War Proneness." In *Correlates of War, II,* ed. J. David Singer, pp. 57–82. New York: Free Press.

Brinton, Crane. (1957). *The Anatomy of Revolution.* Rev. ed. New York: Vintage.

Broomfield, John H. (1982). *Mostly about Bengal.* New Delhi: Manohar.

Brown, Justin. 1999. "Lowdown on a High Strung Corner of Europe." *Christian Science Monitor* (March 16, 1999): 12–13.

Brown, Lester, et al. (2000). *2000 States of the World.* New York: Norton.

Brown, Lester R., Christopher Glavin, and Sandra Postel. (1992). *Saving the Planet: How to Shape an Environmentally Sustainable Global Economy.* Washington, DC: Worldwatch Institute.

Burke, Edmund. (1790/1955). *The Works of Edmund Burke.* New York: Harper & Row.

Burns, James MacGregor. (1992). *Leadership.* New York: HarperCollins.

Cantril, Hadley. (1965). The *Pattern of Human Concerns.* New Brunswick, NJ: Rutgers University Press.

Cardoso, F. H., and E. Faletto. (1979). *Dependency and Development in Latin America.* Berkeley: University of California Press.

Castles, Francis G. (1998). *Comparative Public Policy: Patterns of Post-war Transformation.* Northampton, MA: Edward Elgar Publishing.

Central Intelligence Agency. (2000). *World Factbook 1999.* http://www.odci.gov/cia/cia-home.html

Churchill, Winston. (1948). *The Second World War: The Gathering Storm.* Boston: Houghton Mifflin.

Clarke, Ian. (1985). *The Spatial Organization of Multinational Corporations.* London: Croom Helm.

Clausewitz, Karl von. (1833/1967). *On War.* Ed. and trans. Michael Howard and Peter Paret. Princeton, NJ: Princeton University Press.

Conger, Lucy. (1998). "A Fourth Way?: The Latin American Alternative to Neoliberalism." *Current History* 97 (November 1998): 380–384.

Connor, Walker. (1994). *Ethnonationalism: The Quest for Understanding.* Princeton, NJ: Princeton University Press.

Converse, Philip. (1964). "The Nature of Belief Systems in Mass Publics." In *Ideology and Discontent,* ed. David Apter, pp. 224–240. Glencoe, IL: Free Press.

Conway, M. Margaret, Gertrude A. Steuernagel, and David W. Ahern. (1997). *Women and Political Participation: Cultural Change in the Political Arena.* Washington, DC: Congressional Quarterly Press.

Curtis, Gerald L. (1999). *The Logic of Japanese Politics: Leaders, Institutions and the Limits of Change.* NY: Columbia University Press.

Crozier, Michel, Samuel Huntington, and Joji Watanuki. (1975). *The Crisis of Democracy.* New York: New York University Press.

Cruikshanks, Randall. (1997). "Conflict Resolution in the Other World." In *The Other World: Issues and Politics of the Developing World,* 3d ed., Joseph Weatherby et al., pp. 73–104. White Plains, NY: Longman.

Cutright, Phillips. (1963). "National Political Development: Measurement and Analysis." *American Sociological Review* XX: 253–264.

Cyert, Richard, and James March. (1963). *A Behavioral Theory of the Firm.* Englewood Cliffs, NJ: Prentice-Hall.

Dahl, Robert. (1961). *Who Governs? Democracy an American City.* New Haven, CT: Yale University Press.

———. (1967). *Pluralist Democracy in the United States.* Chicago: Rand McNally.

———. (1971). *Polyarchy: Participation and Opposition.* New Haven, CT: Yale University Press.

———. (1991). *Modern Political Analysis.* 5th ed. Englewood Cliffs, NJ: Prentice-Hall.

Dahrendorf, Ralf. (1959). *Class and Class Conflict in Industrial Society.* Stanford, CA: Stanford University Press.

Dahrendorf, Ralf. (1999). "The Third Way and Liberty." *Foreign Affairs* 78: 5 (September/October): 13–17.

Dalton, Russell. (2001). *Citizen Politics in Western Democracies.* 3d ed. New York: Seven Bridges Press.

Danziger, James N. (1986). "Computing and the Political World." *Computers and the Social Sciences* 2: 183–200.

David, Peter. (1988). "The Arab East: A World against Itself." *The Economist,* February 6, pp. 3–30.

Davies, James C. (1971). "Toward a Theory of Revolution." In *When Men Revolt and Why,* ed. James C. Davies, pp. 134–147. New York: Free Press.

Davis, Richard. (1997). *New Media in American Politics.* Boulder, CO: Westview.

Davis, Winston. (1987). "Religion and Development: Weber and the East Asian Experience." In *Understanding Political Development,* ed. Myron Weiner and Samuel Huntington, pp. 221–280. Boston: Little, Brown.

Derbyshire, Denis. (1996). *Political Systems of the World,* 2d ed. New York: St. Martin's.

Der Spiegel. (1985). "Interview with Abu Nidal." Trans. into English from *Der Spiegel* (42) in *Comparative Politics,* ed. Christian Soe, pp. 85–89. Guilford, CT: Dushkin.

Deutsch, Karl. (1961). "Social Mobilization and Political Development." *American Political Science Review* 55 (September): 493–511.

Diamond, Larry. (1996). "Is the Third Wave Over?" *Journal of Democracy* (July): 20–37.

Diamond, Larry, Marc Plattner, Yun-han Chu, and Mung-mao Tien, Eds. (1997). *Consolidating the Third Wave Democracies: Themes and Perspectives.* Baltimore, MD: Johns Hopkins University Press.

Domhoff, G. William. (1998). *Who Rules America? Power and Politics in Year 2000.* Mountain View, CA: Mayfield.

Donovan, John, Richard Morgan, and Christian Potholm. (1984). *People, Power and Politics.* New York: Random House.

Doremus, Paul N., William W. Keller, Louis Pauly, and Simon Reich. (1998). *The Myth of the Global Corporation.* Princeton, NJ: Princeton University Press.

Doxey, John. (1997). "A Soft Coup in Turkey." *The New Leader* LXXX, March 10, pp. 12–13.

Dunleavy, Patrick, and Christopher Husbands. (1985). *British Democracy at the Crossroads.* London: Allen & Unwin.

Duverger, Maurice. (1954). *Political Parties.* New York: Wiley.

Easton, David. (1953). *The Political System.* New York: Knopf.

———. (1965). *A Framework for Political Analysis.* Englewood Cliffs, NJ: Prentice-Hall.

Eckstein, Harry. (1966). *Division and Cohesion in Democracy: A Study of Norway.* Princeton, NJ: Princeton University Press.

The Economist (1998). "What Would Confucius Say Now?" *The Economist,* July 25, 1998: 23–24, 28.

Edwards, George, Martin Wattenberg, and Robert Lineberry. (1998). *Government in America.* 8th ed. New York: Addison-Wesley.

Ehrlich, Paul R., and Anne H. Ehrlich. (1990). *The Population Explosion.* New York: Simon & Schuster.

Elgie, Robert, Ed. (1999). *Semi-Presidentialism in Europe.* New York: Oxford University Press.

Erikson, Erik. (1958). *Young Man Luther.* New York: Norton.

———. (1969). *Gandhi's Truth.* New York: Norton.

Esping-Andersen, Gosta. (1990). *The Three Worlds of Welfare Capitalism.* Princeton, NJ: Princeton University Press.

Estes, Richard. (1988). *Trends in World Social Development.* New York: Praeger.

Evans, Emmit B., Jr., and Dianne Long. (1997). "Development." In *The Other World: Issues and Politics of the Developing World,* 3d ed., ed. Joseph Weatherby et al., pp. 50–72. White Plains, NY: Longman.

Evans, Peter. (1979). *Dependent Development: The Alliance of Multinational, State and Local Capital in Brazil.* Princeton, NJ: Princeton University Press.

———. (1987). "Foreign Capital and the Third World State." In *Understanding Political Development,* ed. Myron Weiner and Samuel Huntington, pp. 319–352. Boston: Little, Brown.

Evans, Peter, Dietrich Rueschmeyer, and Theda Skocpol, Eds. (1985). *Bringing the State Back In.* New York: Cambridge University Press.

Fagen, Richard. (1964). *Cuba: The Political Content of Adult Education.* Stanford, CA: Hoover Institute.

Falk, Richard A. (1975). *A Study of Future Worlds.* New York: Free Press.

———. (1993). "Sovereignty." In *The Oxford Companion to Politics of the World,* ed. Joel Krieger, pp. 851–854. New York: Oxford University Press.

———. (1995). *On Humane Governance: Toward a New Global Politics.* University Park, PA: Pennsylvania State University Press.

Fallows, James. (1995). *Looking at the Sun: The Rise of the New East Asian Economic and Political System.* New York: Random House.

Fendrich, James. (1993). *Ideal Citizen: The Legacy of the Civil Rights Movement.* Albany, NY: SUNY Press.

Flanigan, William, and Nancy Zingale. (1999). *Political Behavior of the American Electorate.* 9th ed. Washington, DC: Congressional Quarterly Press.

Francis, David R. (1994). "Global Changes Test Lenders." *Christian Science Monitor*, October 6, p. 8.

Frederick, Howard H. (1993). *Global Communication and International Relations.* Belmont, CA: Wadsworth.

Freedom House. (1993). *Freedom of the World 1992–93.* New York: Freedom House.

———. (1994a). *Freedom of the World 1993–94.* New York: Freedom House.

———. (1996). *Freedom of the World 1995–96.* New York: Freedom House.

———. (1999). *Freedom of the World: 1998–99.* New Brunswick, NJ: Transaction Books.

———. (1999). *Press Freedom Survey 1999.* http://freedomhouse.org/pfs1999

Fuller, R. Buckminster. (1970). *Operating Manual for Spaceship Earth.* New York: Pocket Books.

Genovese, Michael A., Ed. (1993). *Women as National Leaders.* Newbury Park, CA: Sage.

George, Alexander, and Julliette George. (1956). *Woodrow Wilson and Colonel House.* New York: Dover.

Gochman, Charles S., and Zeev Maoz. (1984). "Militarized Interstate Disputes, 1816–1976." *Journal of Conflict Resolution* 18 (December): 588–615.

Goldman, Marshall I. (1992). *What Went Wrong with Perestroika.* New York: Norton.

———. (1998). "The Cashless Society." *Current History* (October): 319–324.

Goldman, Minton F. (1998). *Russia, the Eurasian Republics, and Central/Eastern Europe.* 7th ed. New York: McGraw Hill.

Gooden, Reginald. (1997). "Latin America." In *The Other World: Issues and Politics of the Developing World,* 3d ed., ed. Joseph Weatherby et al., pp. 105–149. White Plains, NY: Longman.

Goodwin, Paul. (1998). *Latin America.* 8th ed. New York: McGraw Hill.

Graber, Doris A. (1996). *Mass Media and American Politics.* 5th ed. Washington, DC: Congressional Quarterly Press.

———. (1994). *Processing the News: How People Tame the Information Tide.* 3d ed. New York: Longman.

Graves, Robert. (1966). *Robert Graves: Poems Selected by Himself.* Middlesex, England: Penguin.

Greenstein, Fred. (1987). *Personality and Politics.* Princeton, NJ: Princeton University Press.

Grotius, Hugo. (1625/1957). *De Jure Belli et Pacis [On the Laws of War and Peace].* New York: Macmillan.

Haas, Peter M., Robert O. Keohane, and Marc A. Levy, Eds. (1993). *Institutions for the Earth: Sources of Effective International Environmental Protection.* Cambridge, MA: MIT Press.

Hachten, William A. (1999). *The World News Prism: Changing Media of International Communication.* 5th ed. Ames: Iowa State University Press.

Hagopian, Mark. (1984). *Regimes, Movements and Ideology.* New York: Longman.

Hallin, Daniel. (1989). *The Uncensored War.* Berkeley, CA: University of California Press.

Hardin, Garrett E. (1995). *Living within Limits: Ecology, Economics and Population Taboos.* New York: Oxford University Press.

Harmon, Amy. (1996). "Yeltsin Victory Appears to be Fueling Long-Awaited Russian Recovery." *Los Angeles Times,* July 6, p. A6.

Hastie, Reid. (1986). "A Primer of Information-Processing Theory for the Political Scientist." *In Political Cognition,* ed. Richard R. Lau and David O. Sears. Hillsdale, NJ: Lawrence Erlbaum Associates.

Hayes, Edward. (1972). *Power Structure and Urban Policy.* New York: McGraw-Hill.

Hearnshaw, F. J. C. (1933). *Conservatism in England.* London: Macmillan.

Hearst, Patricia. (1982). *Every Secret Thing.* Garden City, NY: Doubleday.

Heilbroner, Robert. (1993). "The Multinational Corporation and the Nation-State." In *At Issue: Politics in the World Arena,* ed. Steven L. Speigel, pp. 338–352. New York: St. Martin's Press.

———. (1994). *Twenty-First Century Capitalism.* New York: W.W. Norton.

Hemphill, Michael R., and Larry David Smith. (1990). "The Working American's Elegy: The Rhetoric of Bruce Springsteen." In *Politics in Familiar Contexts,* ed. Robert L. Savage and Dan Nimmo, pp. 199–214. Norwood, NJ: Ablex.

Heredia, Blanca. (1997). "Prosper or Perish?: Development in the Age of Global Capital." *Current History* 96 (November 1997): 383–388.

Herring, Paul. (1996). "Food Science's Frontier." *Christian Science Monitor.* November 13, pp. 1, 9.

Heyne, Paul. (1999). *The Economic Way of Thinking.* 9th ed. New York: Prentice-Hall.

Hobbes, Thomas. (1651/1958). *Leviathan.* Oxford, England: Clarendon.

Holsti, Ole, and James Rosenau. (1984). *American Leadership in World Affairs: Vietnam and the Breakdown of Consensus.* Boston: Allen & Unwin.

Hopf, Ted. (1991). "Polarity, the Offense-Defense Balance, and War." *American Political Science Review* 85 (June): 475–493.

Hunter, Floyd. (1953). *Community Power Structure.* Chapel Hill: University of North Carolina Press.

Huntington, Samuel P. (1968). *Political Order in Changing Societies.* New Haven, CT: Yale University Press.

———. (1987). "The Goals of Development." In *Understanding Political Development,* ed. Myron Weiner and Samuel Huntington, pp. 3–32. Boston: Little, Brown.

———. (1991). *The Third Wave: Democratization in the Late Twentieth Century.* Norman: University of Oklahoma Press.

———. (1996). *Clash of Civilizations and the Remaking of the World Order.* New York: Simon & Schuster.

Huxley, Aldous. (1932). *Brave New World.* London: Chatto & Windus.

Inglehart, Ron. (1989). *Culture Shift in Advanced Industrial Societies.* Princeton, NJ: Princeton University Press.

———. (1997). *Modernization and Post-Modernization.* Princeton, NJ: Princeton University Press.

Inkeles, Alex. (1996). *National Character: A Psycho-Social Perspective.* New Brunswick, NJ: Transaction.

Inkeles, Alex, and David Smith. (1976). *Becoming Modern: Individual Change in Six Developing Countries.* Cambridge: Harvard University Press.

Inkeles, Alex, et al. (1985). *Exploring Individual Modernity.* New York: Columbia University Press.

Isbister, John. (1998). *Promises Not Kept: The Betrayal of Change in the Third World.* 4th ed. W. Hartford, CT: Kumarian Press.

Iyengar, Shanto. (1994). *Is Anyone Responsible? How Television Frames Political Issues.* Chicago: University of Chicago Press.

———. (Ed.). (1996). *Does the Media Govern? Politicians, Voters and Reporters in America.* Thousand Oaks, CA: Sage.

Jenkins, Barbara. (1993). "Multinational Corporations." In *The Oxford Companion to Politics of the World,* ed. Joel Krieger, pp. 806–808. New York: Oxford University Press.

Jennings, M. Kent, and Richard Niemi. (1981). *Generations and Politics.* Boston: Little, Brown.

Jennings, M. Kent, and Jan Ven Deth, Eds. (1989). *Continuities in Political Action.* Berlin: de Gruyter.

Johnson, Chalmers. (1966). *Revolutionary Change.* Boston: Little, Brown.

———. (1985). *MITI and the Japanese Economic Miracle.* Stanford, CA: Stanford University Press.

———. (1996). *Japan: Who Governs? The Rise of the Developmental State.* New York: W.W. Norton.

Kaplan, Morton. (1957). *System and Process in International Politics.* New York: Wiley.

Kapstein, Ethan, Robert Keohane, and Richard Haass. (1999). *Is Global Capitalism Working?* New York: W.W. Norton.

Karatnycky, Adrian. (1999). "The Decline of Illiberal Democracy." *Journal of Democracy* 10 (January 1999): 112–125.

Kegley, Charles W., Jr., Ed. (1995). *Controversies in International Relations: Realism and the Neoliberal Challenge.* New York: St. Martin's Press.

Kegley, Charles W., and Eugene Wittkopf. (1993). *World Politics: Trend and Transformation.* 4th ed. New York: St. Martin's Press.

———. (1995). *World Politics: Trend and Transformation.* 5th ed. New York: St. Martin's Press.

———. (1998). *World Politics: Trend and Transformation.* 7th ed. New York: St. Martin's Press.

Kellerman, Barbara. (1984). "Leadership as a Political Act." In *Leadership: Multidisciplinary Perspectives,* ed. Barbara Kellerman, pp. 63–92. Englewood Cliffs, NJ: Prentice-Hall.

Kellner, Douglas. (1990). *Television and the Crisis of Democracy.* Boulder, CO: Westview Press.

Keohane, Robert, and Joseph S. Nye. (1989). *Power and Interdependence: World Politics in Transition.* 2d ed. Glenview, IL: Scott, Foresman.

Kerpelman, Larry. (1972). *Activists and Nonactivists: A Psychological Study of American College Students.* New York: Behavioral Publisher.

Khalidi, Rashid I. (1993). "Intifada." In *The Oxford Companion to Politics of the World,* ed. Joel Krieger, pp. 463–464. New York: Oxford University Press.

Klare, Michael T. (1987). "The Arms Trade: Changing Patterns in the 1980s." *Third World Quarterly* 9 (October): 1257–1281.

———. (1988). "Low-Intensity Conflict." *Christianity and Crisis,* February, pp. 11–14.

———. (1997). "The New Arms Race: Light Weapons and International Security." *Current History* 96 (April): 173–78.

Knickerbocker, Brad. (1999). "Welcome to Earth: Population 6 Billion." *Christian Science Monitor* (September 30, 1999): 15-18.

Kolinsky, E. W. (1993). "Green Revolution." In *The Oxford Companion to Politics of the World,* ed. Joel Krieger, pp. 366–367. New York: Oxford University Press.

Kolosi, Tamas, and Edmund Wnuk-Lipinski, Eds. (1983). *Equality and Inequality under Socialism: Poland and Hungary Compared.* Beverly Hills, CA: Sage.

Korzenny, Felipe, and Stella Ting-Toomey, Eds. (1992). *Mass Media Effects across Cultures.* Newbury Park, CA: Sage.

Kramer, John M. (1998). "The Politics of Corruption." *Current History* (October): 329–334.

Kranzdorf, Richard. (1997). "Sub-Saharan Africa." In *The Other World: Issues and Politics of the Developing World,* 3d ed., ed. Joseph Weatherby et al., pp. 150–189. White Plains, NY: Longman.

Krasner, Stephen. (1978). *Defending the National Interest: Raw Materials, Investments and U.S. Foreign Policy.* Princeton, NJ: Princeton University Press.

Kuhn, Thomas. (1970). *The Structure of Scientific Revolutions.* 2d ed. Chicago: University of Chicago Press.

Kurdle, Robert T. (1987). "The Several Faces of the Multinational Corporation." In *International Political Economy,* ed. Jeffrey Frieden and David A. Lake, pp. 230–241. New York: St. Martin's Press.

Kurian, George Thomas. (1998). *The Fitzroy-Dearborn Book of World Rankings.* Chicago, IL: Fitzroy-Dearborn.

Kurth, James. (1999). "The Baltics: Between Russia and the West." *Current History* 98 (October 1999): 334–339.

La Franchi, Howard. (1999). "Another Latin Strongman Emerges." *Christian Science Monitor* (September 2, 1999): 1, 9.

Larkey, Edward. (1990). "Rock Music and Cultural Theory in the German Democratic Republic." In *Politics in Familiar Contexts,* ed. Robert L. Savage and Dan Nimmo, pp. 215–224. Norwood, NJ: Ablex.

Lasswell, Harold. (1960). *Psychopathology and Politics.* New York: Viking.

———. (1977). "Propaganda." In *Harold Lasswell on Political Sociology,* ed. Dwaine Marvick. Chicago: University of Chicago Press. (Originally published in *Encyclopedia of Social Sciences,* 1934.)

Lau, Richard R. (1986). "Political Schemata, Candidate Evaluations and Voting Behavior." In *Political Cognition,* ed. Richard R. Lau and David O. Sears. Hillsdale, NJ: Lawrence Erlbaum.

Lenski, Gerhard. (1966). *Power and Privilege: A Theory of Social Stratification.* New York: McGraw-Hill.

Lewis, Martin. (1999). "Is There a Third World?" *Current History* 98 (November 1999): 355–358.

Lijphart, Arend. (1978). *Democracy in Plural Societies.* New Haven, CT: Yale University Press.

———. (1984). *Democracies: Patterns of Majoritarian and Consensual Government in Twenty-One Countries.* New Haven, CT: Yale University Press.

———. (1999). *Patterns of Democracy: Government Forms and Performance in Thirty-six Countries.* New Haven, CT: Yale University Press.

Lindblom, Charles E. (1977). *Politics and Markets: The World's Political-Economic Systems.* New York: Basic Books.

Linz, Juan J. (1993). "Authoritarianism." In *The Oxford Companion to Politics of the World,* ed. Joel Krieger, pp. 60–64. New York: Oxford University Press.

Linz, Juan J., and Alfred Stepan. (1978). *The Breakdown of Democratic Regimes.* Baltimore: Johns Hopkins University Press.

Linz, Juan, and Alfred Stepan. (1996). *Problems of Democratic Transition and Consolidation: Southern Europe, South America and Post-Communist Europe.* Baltimore, MD: Johns Hopkins University Press.

Lippman, John. (1992). "Tuning in the Global Village." *Los Angeles Times,* October 20, special supplement, pp. H1–H12.

Locke, John. (1690/1963). *Two Treatises on Government.* New York: New American Library.

Long, Dianne. (1997). "The Other World." In *The Other World: Issues and Politics of the Developing World,* 3rd ed., ed. Joseph Weatherby et al., pp. 3–21. White Plains, NY: Longman.

Loveman, Brian. (1994). "'Protected Democracies' and Military Guardianship: Political Transitions in Latin American, 1978–1993," *Journal of InterAmerican Studies and World Affairs* 36 (Summer 1994): 114–130.

Lovenduski, Joni, and Pippa Norris, Eds. (1994). *Gender and Party Politics.* London: Sage.

Lukes, Steven. (1974). *Power: A Radical View.* London: Macmillan.

Machiavelli, Niccolò. (1517/1977). *The Prince.* Trans. and ed. Robert M. Adams. New York: Norton.

Mackinder, Halford John. (1962). *Democratic Ideals and Reality.* Ed. Anthony Pearce. New York: Norton.

Macridis, Roy, and Steven Burg. (1997). *Introduction to Comparative Politics: Regimes and Change.* 2d ed. New York: AddisonWesley.

Mahon, James E. (1999). "Economic Crisis in Latin America: Global Contagion, Local Pain." *Current History* 98 (March): 105–110.

Mansbridge, Jane. (1991). "Politics," in National Research Council, *The Transition to Democracy: Proceedings of a Workshop.* Washington, DC: National Academy Press.

March, James G., and Johann P. Olsen. (1989). *Rediscovering Institutions: The Organizational Basis of Politics.* New York: Free Press.

Margolis, Mac. (1992). "Black Is for Progress." *World Monitor,* December, pp. 38–43.

Marquand, Robert. (1996). "The Age of Anonymous Terrorism." *Christian Science Monitor,* July 29, pp. 1, 8.

Marx, Karl. (1867/1981). *Capital.* Trans. David Fernbach. New York: Vintage.

Marx, Karl, and Frederich Engels. (1848/1978). "The Communist Manifesto." In *The Marx-Engels Reader,* 2d ed., ed. Robert Tucker, pp. 482–500. New York: Norton.

Maslow, Abraham. (1954). *Motivation and Personality.* New York: Harper & Row.

——. (1968). *Toward a Psychology of Being.* Princeton, NJ: Van Nostrand.

Masters, Roger D. (1992). "How Television Has Transformed American Politics." *Public Affairs Report,* November, pp. 7–9. Berkeley, CA: Institute for Governmental Studies.

Matloff, Judith. (1996). "Democracy, of a Sort, Sweeps Africa." *Christian Science Monitor,* August 7, pp. 10–11.

Maxfield, Sylvia. (1997). *Gatekeepers of Growth: The International Political Economy of Central Banking in Developing Countries.* Princeton, NJ: Princeton University Press.

Mazlish, Bruce. (1973). *In Search of Nixon.* Baltimore: Penguin.

——. (1984). "History, Psychology and Leadership." In *Leadership: Multidisciplinary Perspectives,* ed. Barbara Kellerman, pp. 1–22. Englewood Cliffs, NJ: Prentice-Hall.

McClelland, David. (1961). *The Achieving Society.* Princeton, NJ: Van Nostrand.

McCloskey, Herbert, and Dennis Chong. (1985). "Similarities and Differences between Left-Wing and Right-Wing Radicals." *British Journal of Political Science* 15: 329–363.

McDonald, Forrest. (1979). *Alexander Hamilton: A Biography.* New York: Norton.

McFaul, Michael. (1998). "Russia's Summer of Discontent." Current History 97 (October): 307–312.

McQuail, Denis, and Sven Windahl. (1981). *Communication Models for the Study of Mass Communications.* New York: Longman.

Medvedev, Roy. (2000). *Where is Russia Going?* Trans. George Shriver. New York: Columbia University Press.

Menkhaus, Ken, and John Prendergast. (1999). "Conflict and Crisis in the Greater Horn of Africa." *Current History* 97 (May): 213–217.

Merkl, Peter H., Ed. (1986). *Political Violence and Terror:* Motifs and Motivations. Berkeley: University of California Press.

Mewes, Horst. (1987). "The Green Party Comes of Age." In *Comparative Politics* 87/88, ed. Christian Soe, pp. 110–118. New York: McGraw Hill.

Migdahl, Joel. (1974). *Peasants, Politics and Revolution: Pressures toward Political and Social Change in the Third World.* Princeton, NJ: Princeton University Press.

——. (1987). "Strong States, Weak States: Power and Accommodation." In *Understanding Political Development,* ed. Myron Weiner and Samuel Huntington, pp. 391–434. Boston: Little, Brown.

Milbrath, Lester, and M. L. Goel. (1982). *Political Participation.* Lanham, MD: University Press of America.

Millar, James R. (1999). "The De-development of Russia." *Current History* 98 (October): 322–327.

Milgram, Stanley. (1974). *Obedience to Authority.* New York: Harper & Row.

Mills, C. Wright. (1956). *The Power Elite.* New York: Oxford University Press.

Mitchell, Jennifer D. (1998). "Before the Next Doubling." *World Watch* (January/February): 20-27.

Mittleman, James H. (1993). "Third World." In *The Oxford Companion to Politics of the World,* ed. Joel Krieger, pp. 908–910. New York: Oxford University Press.

Moore, Barrington. (1966). *The Social Origins of Dictatorship and Democracy.* Cambridge: Harvard University Press.

Morgenthau, Hans J. (1985). *Politics Among Nations.* 6th ed. Revised by Kenneth W. Thompson. New York: Knopf.

Mosca, Gaetano. (1896/1939). *The Ruling Class.* Trans. Hannah Kahn. New York: McGraw-Hill.

Mueller, Dennis. (1993). *The Public Choice Approach to Politics.* Northhampton, MA: Edward Elgar Publishers.

Murphy, Dean. (1995). "East Europe P.D. Blues." *Los Angeles Times,* February 28, pp. H1, H4.

Nelson, Joan. (1987). "Political Participation." In *Understanding Political Development*, ed. Myron Weiner and Samuel Huntington, pp. 103–159. Boston: Little, Brown.

———. (1993). "Political Participation." In *The Oxford Companion to Politics of the World*, ed. Joel Krieger, pp. 720–722. New York: Oxford University Press.

Neuman, W. Russell. (1999). *The Gordian Knot: Political Gridlock on the Information Highway*. Cambridge, MA: MIT Press.

Neuman, W. Russell, Marion Just, and Ann Crigler. (1992). *Common Knowledge: News and the Construction of Meaning*. Chicago: University of Chicago Press.

Niemi, Richard. (1974). *How Family Members Perceive Each Other*. New Haven, CT: Yale University Press.

Niemi, Richard G., and Herbert Weissberg. (1993). *Controversies in Voting Behavior*. 3d ed. Washington, DC: Congressional Quarterly Press.

Nimmo, Dan, and James E. Combs. (1990). *Mediated Political Realities*. 2d ed. White Plains, NY: Longman.

Nixon, Richard M. (1982). *Leaders*. New York: Warner Books.

Nordlinger, Eric A. (1977). *Soliders in Politics: Military Coups and Government*. Englewood Cliffs, NJ: Prentice-Hall.

———. (1987). "Taking the State Seriously." In *Understanding Political Development*, ed. Myron Weiner and Samuel Huntington, pp. 353–390. Boston: Little, Brown.

Norton, James. (1997). *India and South Asia*. 3d ed. Guildford, CT: Brown and Benchmark.

Norton, Philip. (1998). *The British Polity*. 4th ed. New York: Longman.

Nugent, Neill. (1999). *The Government and Politics of the European Union*. 4th ed. Durham, NC: Duke University Press.

O'Connor, Robert. (1978). "Political Activism and Moral Reasoning: Political and Apolitical Students in Great Britain and France." *British Journal of Political Science* 4: 53–78.

O'Donnell, Guillermo. (1973). *Modernization and Bureaucratic Authoritarianism: Studies in South American Politics*. Berkeley, CA: Institute of International Studies.

Odwumechili, Chuka. (1999). *African Democratization and Military Coups*. Westport, CN: Praeger (1999).

Organization for Economic Cooperation and Development. (1999). *Economic Outlook* (microfiche) (June). Paris: OECD.

Orwell, George. (1945/1964). *Animal Farm*. Middlesex, England: Penguin.

———. (1949/1967). 1984. Middlesex, England: Penguin.

Parenti, Michael. (1992). *Inventing Reality: The Politics of the Mass Media*. 3d ed. New York: St. Martin's Press.

———. (1996). *Democracy for the Few*. 7th ed. New York: St. Martin's Press.

Pareto, Wilfred. (1988). *The Physiology and Pathology of Power in All Political Organizations Throughout History*. Albuqueque, NM: Institute for Economic and World Strategic Studies.

Pateman, Carole. (1980). "The Civic Culture: A Philosophic Critique." In *The Civic Culture Revisited*, ed. Gabriel Almond and Sidney Verba, pp. 57–102. Boston: Little, Brown.

Petracca, Mark P. (1992). "The Rediscovery of Interest Group Politics." In *The Politics of Interests*, ed. Mark P. Petracca, pp. 3–31. Boulder, CO: Westview Press.

Popper, Karl. (1963). *The Open Society and Its Enemies*, vol. 2. New York: Harper & Row.

Population Institute. (1992, September). Untitled pamphlet. Washington, DC: Population Institute.

Poulantzas, Nicos. (1973). *Political Power and Social Classes*. London: Sheed and Ward.

Powaski, Ronald. (1999). "Russia: Nuclear Menace Within." *Current History* 98 (October 1999): 340–345.

Przeworski, Adam. (1985). *Capitalism and Social Democracy*. Cambridge: Cambridge University Press.

———. (1993). "Socialism and Social Democracy." In *The Oxford Companion to Politics of the World,* ed. Joel Krieger, pp. 832–838. New York: Oxford University Press.

Putnam, Robert. (1993). *Making Democracy Work: Civic Traditions in Modern Italy.* Princeton, NJ: Princeton University Press.

Pye, Lucian W. (1962). *Politics, Personality and Nation-Building.* New Haven, CT: Yale University Press.

———. (1985). *Asian Power and Politics: The Cultural Dimensions of Authority.* Cambridge, MA: Belknap Press.

Rae, Douglas. (1971). *The Political Consequences of Electoral Laws.* New Haven, CT: Yale University Press.

Ramsey, Jeff. (1999). *Africa.* 8th ed. New York: McGraw Hill.

Randall, Vicky. (1998). *Political Change and Underdevelopment: A Critical Introduction to Third World Politics.* NC: Duke University Press.

Ranney, Austin. (1995). *Governing: An Introduction to Political Science.* 7th ed. Englewood Cliffs, NJ: Prentice-Hall.

Raymond, Nicholas. (1991). "The 'Lost Decade' of Development: The Role of Debt, Trade and Structural Adjustment." *The US National Committee for World Food Day,* October, pp. 1–14.

"Reforms Lagging, Hopes Dying." (1996). *The Economist,* November 30, pp. 311–315.

Reich, Robert. (1992). *The Work of Nations: Preparing Ourselves for Twenty-First-Century Capitalism.* New York: Vintage.

Reppy, Susan. (1984). "The Automobile Air Bag." In *Controversy,* 2d ed., ed. Dorothy Nelkin, pp. 161–174. Beverly Hills, CA: Sage.

Rigby, T. H. (1999). "New Top Elites for Old in Russian Politics." *British Journal of Political Science* 29: 323–343.

Riggs, Robert E., and Jack C. Plano. (1994). *The United Nations: International Organization and World Politics.* 2d ed. Belmont, CA: Wadsworth.

Riker, William. (1962). *The Theory of Political Coalitions.* New Haven, CT: Yale University Press.

———. (1982). "The Two Party System and Duverger's Law." *American Political Science Review* 76 (4): 753–766.

Riker, William, and Peter Ordeshook. (1973). *An Introduction to Positive Political Theory.* Englewood Cliffs, NJ: Prentice-Hall.

Roach, Colleen. (1993). "Information and Culture in War and Peace: An Overview." In *Information and Culture in War and Peace,* ed. Coleen Roach, pp. 1–40. Baldwin Park, CA: Sage.

Roberts, Cynthia, and Thomas Sherlock. (1999). "Bringing the Russian State Back In: Explanations of the Derailed Transition to Market Democracy." *Comparative Politics* (July 1999): 477–492.

Rokeach, Milton. (1960). *The Open and Closed Mind.* New York: Basic Books.

Rosenau, James, and Ole Holsti. (1986). "Consensus Lost, Consensus Regained?" *International Studies Quarterly:* (December) 375–409.

Rosenberg, Shawn. (1988). *Reason, Ideology and Politics.* Cambridge, England: Polity Press.

Rosenblum, Mort, and Doug Williamson. (1987). *Squandering Eden: Africa at the Edge.* San Diego, CA: Harcourt.

Ruffin, Roy, and Paul Gregory. (1997). *Principles of Economics.* 6th ed. New York: Addison Wesley.

Rummel, R. J. (2000). *Death By Government.* http://www2.hawaii.edu/%7Erummel/DBG.

Rupnik, Jacques (1999). "The Post-Communist Divide." *Journal of Democracy* : (July) 57–62.

Russett, Bruce. (1965). *Trends in World Politics.* New York: Macmillan.

Russett, Bruce, and Harvey Starr. (1996). *World Politics: The Menu for Choice.* 5th ed. New York: Freeman.

Rustow, Dankwart. (1967). *A World of Nations: Problems of Political Modernization.* Washington, DC: Brookings.

Rutland, Peter. (1999). "The Revolutions of 1989 Revisited." *Current History* 98 (April): 147–152.

Sabato, Larry. (1991). *Feeding Frenzy: How Attack Journalism Has Transformed American Politics.* New York: Free Press.

Safran, William. (1998). *The French Polity.* 5th ed. New York: Addison-Wesley-Longman.

Salisbury, Robert H. (1990). "The Paradox of Interest Groups in Washington, DC: More Groups and Less Clout." In *The New American Political System,* rev. ed., ed. Anthony King. Washington, DC: American Enterprise Institute.

Salisbury, Robert H., John P. Heinz, Robert L. Nelson, and Edward O. Laumann. (1991). "Triangles, Networks and Hollow Cores: The Complex Geometry of Washington Interest Representation." In *The Politics of Interests,* ed. Mark P. Petracca, pp. 130–149. Boulder, CO: Westview Press.

Sassen, Saskia. (1996). *Losing Control?: Sovereignty in the Age of Globalization.* New York: Columbia University Press.

Savage, Robert L., and Dan Nimmo, Eds. (1990). *Politics in Familiar Contexts: Projecting Politics through Popular Media.* Norwood, NJ: Ablex.

Schattschneider, E. E. (1960). *The Semi-Sovereign People.* New York: Holt, Rinehart & Winston.

Schedler, Andreas. (1998). "What is Democratic Consolidation?" *Journal of Democracy:* {March} 91–107.

Schelling, Thomas. (1960). *The Strategy of Conflict.* Cambridge: Harvard University Press.

Schiller, Herbert I. (1976). *Communication and Cultural Domination.* White Plains, NY: Sharpe.

Schmitter, Philippe C. (1993). "Corporatism." In *The Oxford Companion to Politics of the World,* ed. Joel Krieger, pp. 195–198. New York: Oxford University Press.

Schmitter, Phillipe, and Gerhard Lembruch, Eds. (1979). *Trends toward Corporatist Intermediation.* Beverly Hills, CA: Sage.

Schumacher, E. E. (1973). *Small Is Beautiful.* New York: Harper & Row.

Schumpeter, Joseph. (1950). *Capitalism, Socialism and Democracy.* 3d ed. New York: Harper & Row.

Segre, Claudio G. (1993). "Fascism." In *The Oxford Companion to Politics of the World,* ed. Joel Krieger, pp. 294–296. New York: Oxford University Press.

Sesser, Stan. (1992). "A Nation of Contradictions." *New Yorker,* January 13, pp. 37–68.

Shawcross, William. (1991). *Murdoch.* New York: Simon & Schuster.

Shugart, Matthew Soberg, and John M. Carey. (1992). *Presidents and Assemblies: Constitutional Design and Electoral Dynamics.* New York: Cambridge University Press.

Siebert, Fred S., Theodore Peterson, and Wilbur Schramm. (1956). *Four Theories of the Press.* Urban, IL: University of Illinois Press.

Silone, Ignazio. (1937). *Bread and Wine.* Trans. Gwenda David. New York: Harper & Row.

Simon, Julian L. (1992). *Population and Development in Poor Countries.* Princeton, NJ: Princeton University Press.

Simone, Vera, and Anne Thompson Feraru. (1995). *The Asian Pacific: Political and Economic Development in a Global Context.* New York: Longman.

Singer, J. David. (1991). "Peace in the Global System: Displacement, Interregnum or Transformation?" In *The Long Postwar Peace,* ed. Charles W. Kegley, pp. 56–84. New York: HarperCollins.

Sivard, Ruth Leger. (1991). *World Military and Social Expenditures 1991.* Washington, DC: World Priorities.

———. (1993). *World Military and Social Expenditures 1993.* Washington, DC: World Priorities.

————. (1996). *World Military and Social Expenditures 1996.* Washington, D.C.: World Priorities.

Skinner, B. F. (1948). *Walden Two.* New York: Macmillan.

Skocpol, Theda. (1979). *States and Social Revolutions: A Comparative Analysis of France, Russia and China.* New York: Cambridge University Press.

Small, Melvin, and J. David Singer. (1982). *Resort to Arms: International and Civil Wars, 1816–1980.* Beverly Hills, CA: Sage.

Smith, Dan. (1997) *The State of War and Peace Atlas.* London: Penguin.

Sniderman, Paul M. (1975). *Personality and Democratic Politics.* Berkeley: University of California Press.

————. (1993). "The New Look in Public Opinion Research." In *Political Science: The State of the Discipline II,* ed. Ada W. Finifter, pp. 219–245. Washington, DC: American Political Science Association.

Sniderman, Paul M., Joseph Fletcher, Peter H. Russell, Philip E. Tetlock, and Brian J. Gaines. (1991). "The Fallacy of Democratic Elitism: Elite Competition and Commitment to Civil Liberties." *British Journal of Political Science* 21: 349–370.

So, Alvin Y. (1990). *Social Change and Development: Modernization, Dependency, and World-System Theories.* Newbury Park, CA: Sage.

Sophocles. (1967). *Antigone.* Trans. E. F. Watling. Middlesex, England: Penguin.

Sorensen, George. (1997). *Democracy and Democratization: Processes and Prospects in a Changing World.* 2d ed. Boulder, CO: Westview Press.

Sparks, Colin, and Colleen Roach, Eds. (1990). "Farewell to NWICO?" *Media, Culture and Society* 12. London: Sage.

Spencer, William. (1998). *The Middle East.* 7th ed. New York: McGraw Hill.

Stearns, Jill. (1998). *Gender and International Relations: An Introduction.* New Brunswick, NJ: Rutgers University Press.

Stepan, Alfred, and Juan J. Linz. (1996). *Problems of Democratic Transition and Consolidation: Southern Europe, South America and Post-Communist Europe.* Baltimore, MD: Johns Hopkins University Press.

Stoessinger, John G. (1993). *Why Nations Go to War.* 6th ed. New York: St. Martin's Press.

Strauss, Leo. (1959). *What Is Political Philosophy?* New York: Free Press.

Strom, Kaare. (1989). *Minority Government and Majority Rule.* New York: Cambridge University Press.

Taagepera, Rein, and Matthew S. Shugart. (1989). *Seats and Votes.* New Haven, CT: Yale University Press.

"Taiwan and Korea: Two Paths to Prosperity." (1990). *The Economist,* July 14, pp. 204–207.

Tawney, R. T. (1938). *Religion and the Rise of Capitalism: A Historical Study.* Middlesex, England: Penguin.

Tetlock, Philip. (1984). "Cognitive Style and Political Belief Systems in the British House of Commons." *Journal of Personality and Social Psychology* 46: 365–375.

Thompson, Leonard. (1966). *Politics in the Republic of South Africa.* Boston: Little, Brown.

Thoreau, Henry David. (1849/1981). *Walden and Other Writings.* Ed. J. W. Krutch. New York: Bantam.

Thurow, Lester C. (1992). *Head to Head: Coming Economic Battles among Japan, Europe and America.* New York: William Morrow.

————. (1997). *The Future of Capitalism.* New York: Viking-Penguin.

Tocqueville, Alexis de. (1835/1945). *Democracy in America.* New York: Knopf.

Todaro, Michael. (1997). *Economic Development in the Third World.* 6th ed. White Plains, NY: Longman.

Toma, Peter. (1988). *Socialist Authority: The Hungarian Experience.* New York: Praeger.

Truman, David. (1951). *The Governmental Process.* New York: Knopf.

United Nations. (1991). *United Nations Demographic Yearbook 1990.* New York: United Nations.

United Nations Commission on Transnational Corporations. (1991). *Recent Developments Related to Transnational Corporations and International Economic Relations.* New York: United Nations.

United Nations Committee on Trade and Development. (1992). *Least Developed Countries, 1991.* New York: United Nations.

United Nations Development Programme. (1990). *World Military Expenditures and Arms Transfers, 1989.* Washington, DC: U.S. Government Printing Office.

———. (1994). *Human Development Report 1994.* New York: Oxford University Press.

———. (1996). *Human Development Report 1996.* New York: Oxford University Press.

———. (1999). *Human Development Report 1999.* New York: Oxford University Press.

U.S. Arms Control and Disarmament Agency. (1992). *World Military Expenditures and Arms Transfers, 1990.* Washington, DC: U.S. Government Printing Office.

———. (1994). *World Military Expenditures and Arms Transfers, 1991–1993.* Washington, DC: U.S. Government Printing Office.

U.S. Department of State. (1996). *Patterns of Global Terrorism 1995.* Washington, DC: U.S. Department of State.

VCIOM. (1999). *Russian Center for Public Opinion and Market Research.* "Russian Citizen Survey" (March): www.russiavotes.org

Verba, Sidney, and Norman Nie. (1972). *Participation in America.* New York: Harper & Row.

———. (1975). "Political Participation." In *Handbook of Political Science,* vol. 4, ed. Fred Greenstein and Nelson Polsby. Reading, MA: Addison-Wesley.

Verba, Sidney, Norman Nie, and Jae-on Kim. (1978). *Participation and Political Equality: A Seven-Nation Comparison.* London: Cambridge University Press.

Verba, Sidney, Kay Schlozman, and Henry Brady. (1995). *Voice and Equality: Civic Voluntarism in American Politics.* Cambridge, MA: Harvard University Press.

WABF. (2000). *World Almanac and Books and Facts.* Mahwah, NJ: World Almanac Books.

Walker, Nancy. (1988). "What We Know about Women Voters in Britain, France and West Germany." *Public Opinion,* May–June, pp. 49–55.

Wallensteen, Peter. (1993). "The Security Council in Armed Conflicts, 1986–1991." In *States in Armed Conflict, 1990–1991,* ed. Birger Heldt, pp. 11–28. Sweden: Uppsala University, Department of Peace and Conflict Research.

Wallerstein, Immanuel. (1974). *The Modern World System.* New York: Academic Press.

———. (1980). *The World System II.* New York: Academic Press.

———. (1991). *Geopolitics and Geoculture: Essays on the Changing World System.* New York: Cambridge University Press.

Waltz, Kenneth. (1979). *Theory of International Politics.* Reading, MA: Addison-Wesley.

———. (1995). "Realist Thoughts and Neorealist Theory" pp. 67–83 in Charles W. Kegley (ed.), *Controversies in International Relations Theory: Realism and the Neoliberal Challenge.* New York: St. Martin's Press.

Wattenberg, Martin. (1991). *The Rise of Candidate-Centered Politics.* Cambridge: Harvard University Press.

Weatherby, Joseph. (1997a). "The Middle East and North Africa." In *The Other World: Issues and Politics of the Developing World,* 3d ed., ed. Joseph Weatherby et al., pp. 227–272. New York: Longman.

———. (1997b). "The Old and the New: Colonialism, Neocolonialism and Nationalism." In *The Other World: Issues and Politics of the Developing World,* 3rd ed., ed. Joseph Weatherby et al., pp. 22–49. New York: Longman.

Weber, Max. (1951). *The Religion of China: Confucianism and Taoism.* Ed. Hans H. Gerth. New York: Free Press.

———. (1958a). From *Max Weber: Essays in Sociology.* Ed. Hans H. Gerth and C. Wright Mills. New York: Oxford University Press.

———. (1958b). *The Religion of India: The Sociology of Hinduism and Buddhism.* Trans. Hans Gerth and Don Martindale. New York: Free Press.

Weir, Fred. (1999). "The Tunnel is Long." *Christian Science Monitor* (August 17, 1999): 1, 9.

Weiss, Thomas, Ed. (1996). *NGOs, the UN and Global Governance.* Boulder, CO: Lynne Rienner Publishers.

Wen, Chihua. (1995). *The Red Mirror: Children of China's Cultural Revolution.* Boulder, CO: Westview Press.

Weyland, Kurt. (1999). "Neoliberal Populism in Latin American and Eastern Europe." *Comparative Politics* (July 1999): 379–400.

Wiarda, Howard J. (1996). *Corporatism and Comparative Politics.* Armonk, NY: M.E. Sharpe.

Wilber, Charles, and Kenneth Jameson, Eds. (1995). *The Political Economy of Development and Underdevelopment.* 6th ed. New York: McGraw-Hill.

Wills, Garry. (1982). *The Kennedy Imprisonment.* Boston: Little, Brown.

Wilson, Edward O. (1978). *On Human Nature.* Cambridge: Harvard University Press.

Wilson, Graham K. (1991). "American Interest Groups in Comparative Perspective." In *The Politics of Interests,* ed. Mark P. Petracca, pp. 80–95. Boulder, CO: Westview Press.

Wilson, William Julius. (1987). *The Truly Disadvantaged.* Chicago: University of Chicago Press.

———. (1996). *When Work Disappears.* New York: Knopf.

Winters, Jeffrey A. (1998). "Asia and the 'Magic' of the Marketplace." *Current History* 97 (December 1998): 418–25.

Wolf, Edward. (1985). "State of the Earth 1985." *Natural History* 94 (April): 51–88.

Wolf, Eric. (1969). *Peasant Wars of the Twentieth Century.* New York: Harper & Row.

Wolin, Sheldon. (1960). *Politics and Vision.* Boston: Little, Brown.

Woo-Cumings, Meredith. Ed. (1999). *The Developmental State.* New York: Cornell University Press.

World Bank. (1983). *World Tables,* vols. 1 and 2. 3d ed. Oxford: Oxford University Press.

———. (1992). *World Development Report 1992.* New York: Oxford University Press.

———. (1994). *World Development Report 1994.* New York: Oxford University Press.

———. (1996). *World Development Report 1996.* New York: Oxford University Press.

———. (1999). *World Development Report 1998-99.* New York: Oxford University Press.World Commission on Environment and Development. (1987). Our Common Future. New York: Oxford University Press.

World Values Survey, 1990–1991. (1994). Ann Arbor, MI: Inter-University Consortium for Political Research.

Woshinsky, Oliver. (1995). *Culture and Politics.* Englewood Cliffs, NJ: Prentice-Hall.

Wright, Erik Olin. (1989). *The Debate on Classes.* London: Verso.

Wright, Robin. (1999). "Wars of Identity." *Los Angeles Times* (April 3, 1999): A 15.

Wrong, Dennis. (1980). *Power: Its Forms, Bases and Uses.* New York: Harper & Row.

Zakaria, Fareed. (1997). "The Rise of Illiberal Democracy." *Foreign Affairs.* 76 (Novenmer/December): 23-46

Zaller, John R. (1992). *The Nature and Origins of Mass Opinion.* New York: Cambridge University Press.

Zarycky, George. (1994). "And Now the Hard Part." *Freedom Review* 25 (January–February): 42–46.

Zelikow, Philip. (1987). "The United States and the Use of Force: A Historical Summary."In *Democracy, Strategy and Vietnam,* ed. George Osburn, Asa Clark, Daniel Kaufman, and Douglas Lute, pp. 31–81. Lexington, MA: Lexington Books.

SELECTED INTERNET SITES

The Internet offers an almost overwhelming number of sites containing information about the political world. The following are a few sites, from a variety of perspectives, that you might find useful in exploring topics of interest. The available sites evolve constantly, and some of those listed below will probably have transformed or disappeared when you try them. Go surfin'!.

Search Engines

http://dir.yahoo.com/Social_Science/Political_Science/
The Yahoo search engine's branch for focussed searches of information about politics and political science issues.

http://lycos.com
The Lycos search engine remains one of the more effective ones for locating useful information on a specified topic.

Sites from Major International Agencies or NGOs.

http://www.unsystem.org
The official web site for the United Nations organizations, which are listed alphabetically.

http://www.undp.org
The web site for United Nations Development Programme, a key unit of the U.N. that specializes in issues of economic and political development.

http://europa.eu.int/index.htm
The official website of the European Union, with extensive information about both the EU and member states, in all EU languages.

http://wto.org/
The World Trade Organization, which coordinates trade policy for more than 135 countries, offers this website to provide key documents and agreements as well as sections which articulate/justify the WTO philosophy of open trade relations among countries.

http://imf.org/
The key documents and agreements among all states and for particular members of the International Monetary Fund (IMF), an organization which includes more than 180 countries who cooperate to sustain a smoothly functioning system of interstate trade and to provide loans and other financial assistance to countries.

http://worldbank.org
The official site of the World Bank, an international consortium of banks and other major financial institutions, there are extensive economic data available, including selections from the annual World Development Report, as well as information on issues of development and trade.

http://world.localgov.org/
The International Local Government Home Page provides links to local government and community sites in many countries.

Sites from the United States Government Agencies

http://www.odci.gov/index.html
Operated by the Central Intelligence Agency, this site includes the very useful World Factbook, with considerable data on every country in the world, as well as the Handbook of International Economic Statistics and other useful sources.

http://www.state.gov/www/ind.html
Operated by the U.S. Department of State, there are country reports and information on international organizations, human rights, and numerous other topics related to foreign policy and international relations.

http://www.loc.gov
U.S. Library of Congress site, with analyses and facts on more than 100 countries' political, economic and social systems.

Media Sources

http://www.cnn.com/WORLD
The site for CNN, the 24-hour news channel, with world news updated frequently.

http://www.news.bbc.co.uk
Current news of the world from the British Broadcasting System (BBC).

http://www.itn.co.uk
World news and British news from Independent Television News, based in London.

http://www.presseweb.ch/
"Webdo" is a Swiss-based link that enables you to access current articles in a diverse set of newspapers from many countries and in a variety of languages.

http://www.nytimes.com
Key articles and information daily from one of the premier newspapers in the United States.

Sites from Interest Groups and Scholarly Sources

http://www.atlapedia.com/
Atlapedia provides diverse statistical information and various maps for each country, as well as recent political history.

http://www.africanews.org/
This site includes key stories from more than 40 African newspapers and news-magazines, as well as other information about each country and links to important documents.

http://www.arab.net
Rich information on the government, culture, business, geography and so on of every country in the Middle East and North Africa are provided, as well as providing coverage of current news and issues.

http://www.asean.or.id/
As the official website of the Association of South East Asian Nations, there are information and documents relevant to ASEAN, news about countries in the region, as well as somewhat self-serving web pages constructed by each member state.

http://www.europeanforum.bot-consult.se/cup/country.htm
The European Forum for Democracy and Solidarity offers country-by-country information on politics and economics for the post-communist developed countries.

http://home.tampabay.rr.com/latinoconnect/
The Latino Connection provides numerous links to political, cultural, and societal information about each country in Central and South America.

http://www.ipl.org.ar
The Internet Public Library provides links to numerous reference books, newspaper and magazines, by region and by country.

http://www.politicalresources.net/
A very useful and accessible site, with information on many countries, including up-to-date data on party systems and the web sites of most parties from each country.

http://www.lib.uconn.edu/PoliSci/polisci.htm
The "Political Science Virtual Library" has links to many political science departments, journals, and other sources of information.

http://www.ifex.org
The International Freedom of Expression Exchange represents more than 50 groups committed to human rights and civil liberties and describes current situations of concern.

html http://nsi.org/Terrorism.html
The website of the National Security Institute provides links regarding terrorism, including data and details of terrorism acts and policy and legislation regarding terrorism.

http://www.constitution.org/cons/natlcons.htm
The constitutions of many countries are provided, often in English, by the Constitution Society, which also provides commentary (usually rather conservative) about the country.

http://www.cfcsc.dnd.ca/links/wars/index.html
A clickable map and linked data base, from the Information Resource Centre of the Canadian Forces College, provides weblinks to numerous sites detailing every current major international conflict.

http://www.etown.edu/vl/
A rich and extensive set of links from this WWW Virtual Library: International Affairs Resources includes numerous sites for each region as well as links to key international topics as varied as international organizations, environmental issues, world religions, media resources, health, and human rights.

http://iisd1.iisd.ca/
The website of the International Institute for Sustainable Development offers information and essays on this topic, ranging from policy statements and economic data to book-length studies.

Credits

Photos, cartoons, and maps are reprinted with the permission of the following:

Index

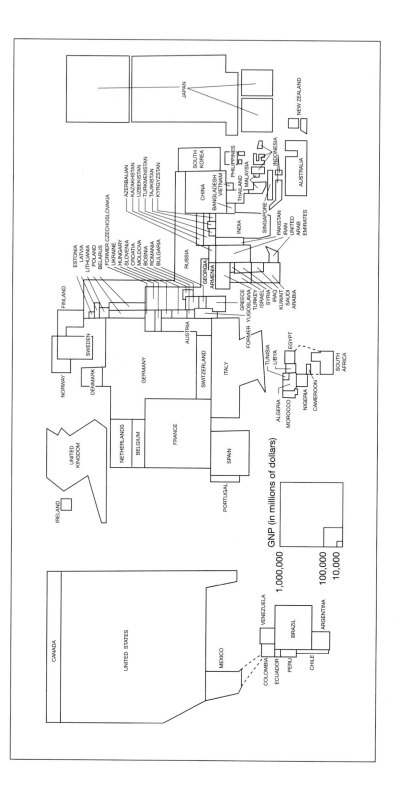

GNP (in millions of dollars)